KING ALFRE[
WIN[IN THE FAMILY

gripping account in which antiquity rests easily beside the present ...
Historians and the general public alike will find it fascinating reading.
There is simply nothing quite like it in print' *Boston Sunday Globe*

'[A] profound and entertaining book' D. J. Taylor, *Mail on Sunday*

'The ties Ball traces between his forebears and their slaves are never
more distressing than in their representations of the intimacy of so much
of slavery's cruelty, never more moving than when some glimmer of
humanity emerges amid the system's brutality'
The New York Times Book Review

'A humane, often moving interweaving of the history of the ante-
Bellum South with poignant encounters with fifth and sixth generation
descendants of the Ball slaves ... He is not rash enough to offer a
prescription for reconciliation ... but he is brave enough to take a
significant step down that path' Colin Cardwell, *Scotland on Sunday*

'Remarkable ... a thorough and important piece of research'
Philippa Gregory, *The Times*

'The author has understood something that most African-Americans
know intuitively: that history and the past are not irrelevant, and they
govern the present' Caryl Phillips, *Financial Times*

ABOUT THE AUTHOR

ABOUT THE AUTHOR

Edward Ball, journalist and seventh-generation grandson of Elias Ball, was born in Savannah, Georgia, raised in the South, and educated at Brown University in the North. A former columnist for the *Village Voice* in New York, he lives near Charleston, South Carolina. *Slaves in the Family* is his first book. It won the 1998 National Book Award for Non-fiction.

SLAVES IN THE FAMILY

Edward Ball

PENGUIN BOOKS

PENGUIN BOOKS

Published by the Penguin Group
Penguin Books Ltd, 27 Wrights Lane, London W8 5TZ, England
Penguin Putnam Inc., 375 Hudson Street, New York, New York 10014, USA
Penguin Books Australia Ltd, Ringwood, Victoria, Australia
Penguin Books Canada Ltd, 10 Alcorn Avenue, Toronto, Ontario, Canada M4V 3B2
Penguin Books (NZ) Ltd, Private Bag 102902, NSMC, Auckland, New Zealand

Penguin Books Ltd, Registered Offices: Harmondsworth, Middlesex, England

First published in the USA by Farrar Strauss & Giroux 1998
Published by Viking 1998
Published in Penguin Books 1999
1 3 5 7 9 10 8 6 4 2

Set in Monotype Bembo
Printed in England by Clays Ltd, St Ives plc

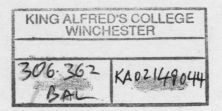

CONTENTS

SLAVES IN THE FAMILY

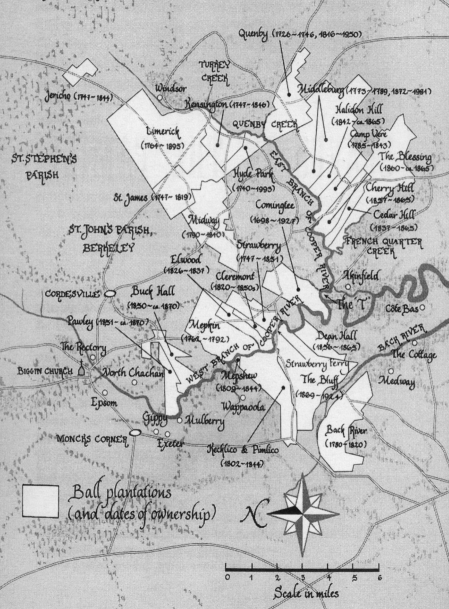

ST. JAMES' PARISH, SANTEE

Quenby (1726~1746, 1816~1850)

TURKEY CREEK

Windsor

Jericho (1747~1844)

Kensington (1747~1846)

QUENBY CREEK

Middleburg (1773~1789, 1872~1981)

Halidon Hill (1842~ca.1865)

Camp Vere (1785~1843)

The Blessing (1860~ca.1865)

ST. STEPHEN'S PARISH

Limerick (1764~1895)

St. James (1747~1819)

Hyde Park (1940~1995)

Cherry Hill (1837~1865)

Cedar Hill (1837~1865)

ST. JOHN'S PARISH, BERKELEY

Midway (1790~1810)

Cominglee (1698~1927)

FRENCH QUARTER CREEK

Strawberry (1747~1851)

Elwood (1826~1837)

Cleremont (1820~1850s)

Akinfield

The "T"

Côte Bas

CORDESVILLE

Buck Hall (1850~ca.1870)

Pawley (1851~ca.1870?)

Mepkin (1768~1792)

Dean Hall (1836~1865)

BACK RIVER

The Cottage

The Rectory

BIGGIN CHURCH

North Chachan

WEST BRANCH OF COOPER RIVER

Mepshew (1809~1844)

Strawberry Ferry

The Bluff (1889~1924)

Medway

Epsom

Wappaoola

Gippy Mulberry

MONCKS CORNER

Exeter

Kechlico & Pimlico (1802~1844)

Back River (1780~1820)

Ball plantations (and dates of ownership)

N

0 1 2 3 4 5 6

Scale in miles

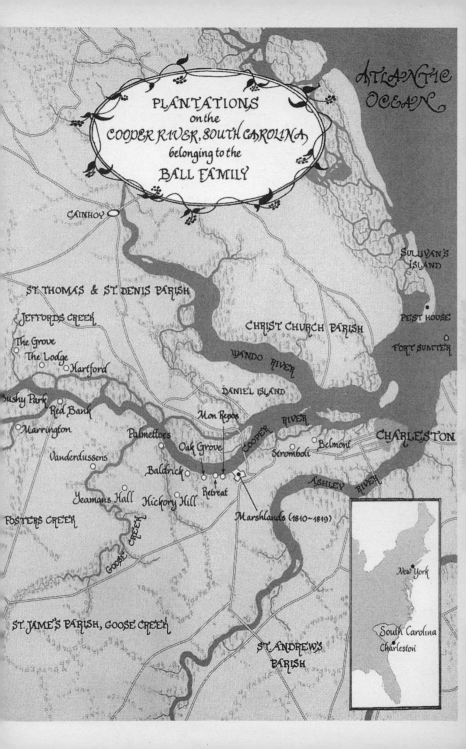

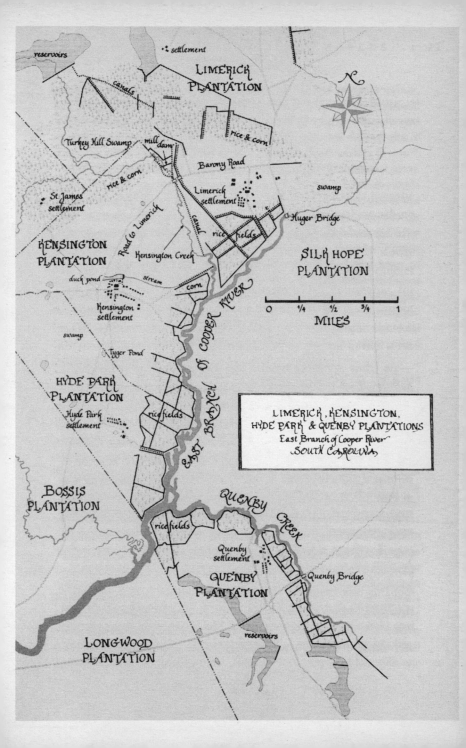

reservoirs

settlement

LIMERICK
PLANTATION

canals

rice & corn

N

Turkey Hill Swamp   mill dam

rice & corn

Barony Road

swamp

Limerick
settlement

St. James
settlement

Road to Limerick

canal

Huger Bridge

KENSINGTON
PLANTATION

Kensington Creek

rice fields

SILK HOPE
PLANTATION

duck pond

stream

corn

0   ¼   ½   ¾   1
MILES

Kensington
settlement

swamp

Tyger Pond

HYDE PARK
PLANTATION

rice fields

LIMERICK, KENSINGTON,
HYDE PARK & QUENBY PLANTATIONS
East Branch of Cooper River
SOUTH CAROLINA

Hyde Park
settlement

EAST BRANCH OF COOPER RIVER

BOSSIS
PLANTATION

QUENBY   CREEK

rice fields

Quenby
settlement

Quenby Bridge

QUENBY
PLANTATION

LONGWOOD
PLANTATION

reservoirs

1

⊱╼◈╾⊰

PLANTATION MEMORIES

My father had a little joke that made light of our legacy as a family
that had once owned slaves.

"There are five things we don't talk about in the Ball family,"
he would say. "Religion, sex, death, money, and the Negroes."

"What does that leave to talk about?" my mother asked once.

"That's another of the family secrets," Dad said, smiling.

My father, Theodore Porter Ball, came from the venerable city of
Charleston, South Carolina, the son of an old plantation clan. The Ball
family's plantations were among the oldest and longest standing in the
American South, and there were more than twenty of them along the
Cooper River, north of Charleston. Between 1698 and 1865, the 167
years the family was in the slave business, close to four thousand black
people were born into slavery to the Balls or bought by them. The crop
they raised was rice, whose color and standard gave it the name Carolina
Gold. After the Civil War, some of the Ball places stayed in business as
sharecrop farms with paid black labor until about 1900, when the rice
market finally failed in the face of competition from Louisiana and Asia.

When I was twelve, Dad died and was buried near Charleston.
Sometime during his last year, he brought together my brother, Theodore
Jr., and me to give each of us a copy of the published history of the

family. The book had a wordy title, *Recollections of the Ball Family of South Carolina and the Comingtee Plantation*. A distant cousin, long dead, had written the manuscript, and the book was printed in 1909 on rag paper, with a tan binding and green cloth boards. On the spine the words BALL FAMILY were embossed. The pages smelled like wet leaves.

"One day you'll want to know about all this," Dad said, waving his hand vaguely, his lips pursed. "Your ancestors." The tone of the old joke was replaced by some nervousness.

I know my father was proud of his heritage but at the same time, I suspect, had questions about it. The story of his slave-owning family, part of the weave of his childhood, was a mystery he could only partly decipher. With the gift of the book, Dad seemed to be saying that the plantations were a piece of unfinished business. In that moment, the story of the Ball clan was locked in the depths of my mind, to be pried loose one day.

When I was a child, Dad used to tell stories about our ancestors, the rice planters. I got a personal glimpse of the American Revolution, because the Balls had played a role in it—some of us fought for the British, some for independence. The Civil War seemed more real since Dad's grandfather and three great-uncles fought for the Confederacy. From time to time in his stories, Dad mentioned the people our family used to own. They were usually just "the slaves," sometimes "the Ball slaves," a puff of black smoke on the wrinkled horizon of the past. Dad evidently didn't know much about them, and I imagine he didn't want to know.

"Did I ever tell you about Wambaw Elias Ball?" he might say. "His plantation was on Wambaw Creek. He had about a hundred and fifty slaves, and he was a mean fella."

My father had a voice honed by cigarettes, an antique Charleston accent, and I liked to hear him use the old names.

"Wambaw Elias was a Tory," Dad began. "I mean, he picked the wrong side in the Revolution." When the Revolutionary War reached the South, Wambaw Elias, instead of joining the American rebels, went to the British commander in Charleston, Lord Cornwallis, who gave him a company of men and the rank of colonel. Wambaw Elias fought the patriots and burned their houses until such time as the British lost and his victims called for revenge. The Americans went for Wambaw Elias's human property, dragging off some fifty slaves from Wambaw plantation, while other black workers managed to escape into the woods. Wambaw Elias knew he had no future in the United States and decided to cash in his assets. Eventually he captured the slaves who had run away, sold them, then took his family to England, where he lived for another thirty-eight years, regretting to the last that he had been forced to give up the life of a slave owner.

In the Ball family, the tale of Wambaw Elias and his slaves passed as a children's story.

In my childhood, our family lived in various small towns and cities in the South. Dad was an Episcopal priest, so the houses we lived in belonged to the church, and my parents owned a single car. Throughout my spartan, God-fearing upbringing, I sensed we were different from other people. It wasn't merely that Dad was a clergyman, though certainly that set us apart; but "our people" had once controlled a slave dynasty.

The first piece of paper I remember my father presenting to me regarding the family was an obituary from the *Charleston News and Courier*. A long strip of yellowed newsprint, the clipping carried the headline "Isaac Ball, 88, Confederate, Dies." Isaac Ball was Dad's grandfather. He was born in 1844 on Limerick plantation, one of the many Ball tracts, and died in 1933 in Charleston. Dad used to call him Isaac the Confederate to distinguish him from the seven other Isaacs in the family tree, and because on April 28, 1862, one week after his eighteenth birthday, Isaac joined the South Carolina Militia, First Regiment, Artillery, and went to fight in the War Between the States. (The War Between the States is what the Civil War has been called in the South.) When Isaac was born, Limerick plantation, thirty miles north of Charleston, was the largest of the Ball plantations, measuring 4,564 acres. In the years before Isaac's birth, some three hundred people lived in slavery there. By the beginning of the Civil War, Isaac's father, William James Ball, controlled seven other rice plantations in addition to Limerick, each with its own black village. His Ball cousins and in-laws owned more land and people.

I have several photographs of Isaac, my great-grandfather. He was tall, lean, carefully dressed, and had thin brown hair that he lost as he aged. Isaac wore a mustache and a tuft of hair below his lower lip throughout life; the hair is dark in photographs from the Civil War era and white in later pictures. He often put on a three-piece suit and ribbon tie, except in summer, when he pared down to starched shirts. Among Isaac's pleasures was playing the violin. He was known to play Bach and, I believe, now and then a Virginia reel. In his later years, Isaac wrote poetry, though he never published it, perhaps because in his society the desire to publish was thought to be vain, a bid for attention. I have a few of his manuscripts. The verses consist of love lyrics to his wife, meditations on old things—one about a country church, another about rusting Confederate guns—and elegies about the Civil War, whose outcome caused him much sadness.

Dad grew up in the house where Isaac spent his last twenty years, and he had strong memories of the old man. Toward the end of his life, Isaac was nearly blind from glaucoma. As Isaac was losing his sight, Dad said, he used to shave with his eyes closed, explaining that he was rehearsing the necessity of having to shave blind. In his seventies and eighties, with pinhole vision, Isaac continued to get around town and took regular walks with a cane. Near the house where he lived, at the tip of a peninsula that forms the oldest part of Charleston, there is a delicate little park called White Point Gardens. The park contains a grove of oaks with overhanging moss and an octagonal bandstand, and is framed on two sides by the waters of Charleston harbor. Isaac would feel his way to the park and find the eastern edge of the green, where a tall seawall, known as the High Battery, stands against the tides. From this place it is possible to see, far out in the water, Fort Sumter, the old defense bulwark built on an island at the entrance to the harbor. On the morning of April 12, 1861, rebel batteries around Charleston opened fire on Federal troops stationed at the fort, loudly opening the Civil War. Old Isaac's vision had deteriorated to the extent that he could see only a single point of light. Standing on the High Battery, he would raise his cane to his shoulder like a rifle, and, aiming the stick at Fort Sumter, pretend to fire shots at the Yankees, vindicating the lost war of his youth, which robbed him of his patrimony.

My mother, Janet Rowley, born in New Orleans, also had a plantation heritage. Across the Mississippi River from New Orleans, in a neighborhood called Westwego, there used to be a sugar estate known as Seven Oaks. The sugar fields, workers, and mansion at Seven Oaks (built in 1840) were the property of one of my mother's maternal ancestors, Michael Zehringer. Zehringer's grandfather had come to Louisiana in 1720 from Franconia, a section of Bavaria; later the family changed the spelling of its name to Zeringue, the better to glide through the French-speaking caste of Louisiana slave owners. A granddaughter of the master of Seven Oaks, Marie Constance Zeringue, married a man named Yves Caesar LeCorgne. Marie and Yves had a great-granddaughter, Edna LeCorgne, my mother's mother, whom I loved.

A yellowing photograph of the Seven Oaks mansion used to hang in the hall of our house. The picture showed a whale of a building in Greek Revival style; six two-story columns lined each of the four facades, making twenty-four Doric columns all the way around. By the time of the photograph, the plantation had long passed out of the family and stood abandoned and decrepit.

In the family of my mother's father, the Rowleys, were more slave owners. (Rowley is my middle name.) In 1834, Charles N. Rowley, my mother's great-grandfather, married a Louisiana heiress, Jane Kemp Girault, who gave him control of her 2,200-acre cotton plantation, Marengo, and seventy-six slaves. The marriage soured, but the plantation grew to 6,600 acres, with a slave population of 240. Charles Rowley later went into the military, became a commissioned officer, and when the Civil War began rose to the rank of brigadier general, commanding the Sixth Brigade of the Louisiana Militia. Charles could not bear the defeat of the Confederacy; after the war, he fled the country for Brazil, leaving behind his wife and six children to join a faction of exiled Confederates. Brazil was a sugar-producing nation where slavery would not be abolished until 1888. Maybe Charles believed that if he had remained in the United States he would have been persecuted for his role in the war, or perhaps he simply could not let go of the lifestyle of slave master. In South America, Charles Rowley evidently once again acquired human property before he died in July 1869, at age sixty-three, in the province of Rio de Janeiro.

Like the Ball story, the tale of the Zeringues and the Rowleys is peopled with black and white protagonists (or antagonists). Although someday I may look into my Louisiana family, this story follows my father's clan, and the lives of the thousands they enslaved.

Although in my early childhood our family lived in other parts of the South, in summers we paid visits to South Carolina to mingle with the relatives, and when I was nine we moved to the state. Soon Dad took my brother, Theodore Jr., and me to see the old rice plantation district the Balls once knew as their neighborhood. The three of us drove north out of Charleston on a two-lane blacktop toward the upper streams of the Cooper River, where rice grew for more than two hundred years. Thick grass swallowed the edge of the asphalt, cicadas screeched in the branches, and a skyline of pine trees scored the horizon. I remember the suffocating heat that seemed to radiate up from the ground rather than descend from the sun and the air that felt like a wet cloth on the lungs. We passed unpainted cottages belonging to black families, each house with two or three rooms, a little porch, and a pitched tin roof. On one porch sat a thin old man wearing a blue workshirt.

"There's George," said Dad, pulling the four-door to a stop.

Dad directed Ted and me to stay in the car, and I seem to remember that he wore a strained look on his face as he walked across the grass, up the three wooden steps of the porch, to shake hands with frail, black George. I thought I saw him gesturing, pointing over George's head to some mile-away place. In a moment, George and my father disappeared into the cottage. Until that day, on every occasion when my parents bumped into friends, they had introduced us, but this time Dad had left off his manners. For half an hour my brother and I sat simmering on the hot vinyl seats of the car, swatting mosquitoes. Eventually Dad emerged from the house and made his good-byes. After this encounter, the rest of the day's tour, to an old church and down some dirt lanes, felt strange. On the way back to Charleston, Dad stayed quiet about George. We retraced our route past the empty tracts where the Balls used to rule and the flora grew in reverse, thinning and clearing. I never found out anything more about George (not even his last name), or about the mysterious thing that changed the expression on Dad's face.

I went to college and settled in New York, where I began writing for newspapers and magazines. Years passed, and occasionally I visited Charleston. From time to time, the "Ball book" came down off the shelf, and when it did the plantations shadowed my dreams. The Balls lived side by side with black families for six generations, but the story, as I knew it, was divided in two. On one side stood the ancestors, vivid, serene, proud; on the other their slaves, anonymous, taboo, half human. I knew a lot about the Balls, but I never knew much about the slaves, even though on the plantations black people far outnumbered white. What were their names? How did they live? Who were their loved ones? When did they leave the plantations, and where had their descendants gone? Could their families be found? But once the book went back in the bookcase, the dreams faded.

In the mail one year came an invitation to a Ball family reunion in South Carolina. The purpose of the event, as announced by its septuagenarian organizers, was to convey the plantation story to the younger generations. Everyone, however far away, was invited home to commune with the ancestors and bathe themselves in lore. Although the Ball lands had been sold when the rice business dwindled after the end of slavery, and the fortune was long gone, documents, pictures, and above all stories remained. My memories of childhood were beginning to be released, and the invitation threw open a door in my mind. I brought out a photograph of Isaac the Confederate, Dad's grandfather, and the faceless crowd of slaves gathered once again before my eyes.

Despite my having left the South, the plantation past was etched in my unconscious. The prospect of the family reunion pushed me, finally, to come to terms with it. To contemplate slavery—which for most Americans is a mysterious, distant event—was a bit like doing psychoanalysis on myself. Did the plantations form part of my identity? By outward measure, no. The wealth created by the slave system was destroyed, and the latter-day Balls had no inheritance from it. Some of the family had manners, others none; some had money and status, some neither. But inwardly the plantations lived on. In childhood, I remember feeling an intangible sense of worth that might be linked to the old days. Part of the feeling came from the normal encouragements of parents who wanted their children to rise. An equal part came from an awareness that long ago our family had lived like lords, and that the world could still be divided into the pedigreed and the rootless.

The invitation to the family reunion sat on my desk, beckoning. No one among the Balls talked about how slavery had helped us, but whether we acknowledged it or not, the powers of our ancestors were still in hand. Although our social franchise had shrunk, it had never-theless survived. If we did not inherit money, or land, we received a great fund of cultural capital, including prestige, a chance at education, self-esteem, a sense of place, mobility, even (in some cases) a flair for giving orders. And it was not only "us," the families of former slave owners, who carried the baggage of the plantations. By skewing things so violently in the past, we had made sure that our cultural riches would benefit all white Americans.

The subject of the plantations stirred conflicting emotions. I felt proud (how rare the stories!) and sentimental (how touching the cast of family characters!). At the same time, the slave business was a crime that had not fully been acknowledged. It would be a mistake to say that I felt guilt for the past. A person cannot be culpable for the acts of others, long dead, that he or she could not have influenced. Rather than responsible, I felt accountable for what had happened, called on to try to explain it. I also felt shame about the broken society that had washed up when the tide of slavery receded.

I decided I would make an effort, however inadequate and personal, to face the plantations, to reckon with them rather than ignore their realities or make excuses for them. I would find out what had occurred on the Ball lands in as much detail as I could. America was beginning to work through the tragic parts of its history, and the Ball name, once admired in a small corner of the country, seemed likely to become a casualty of that process, painted with infamy. Paradoxically, by describ-ing as honestly as possible what the family had done, I might clear some space around our name, and around us.

When finally I chose to look into the slave past, I felt a remarkable calm, and the rest of the path seemed clear. To complete the legacy, I would try to find descendants of the slaves. The plantation heritage was not "ours," like a piece of family property, and not "theirs," belonging to black families, but a shared history. The progeny of slaves and the progeny of slave owners are forever linked. We have been in each oth-er's lives. We have been in each other's dreams. We have been in each other's beds. As I prepared to go back to South Carolina, I thought we should meet, share our recollections, feelings, and dreams, and make the story whole.

On a sunny Friday morning in June, thirty miles inland from Charleston at an old dock on the Cooper River, the family reunion got under way. Some 150 relatives from around the state and scattered parts of the country climbed aboard a chartered boat for a tour of the river where the Ball plantations once stood and where their remnants still moldered on the banks. Many wore shorts and T-shirts in the Carolina heat, though a few women turned out in heels and jewelry. The youngest was less than a year, the eldest eighty-eight. Reeds brushed against the hull of the double-deck boat and greetings and laughter echoed over the water as each Ball walked the gangplank and made a little jump onto the deck. My brother, Ted, and his wife, Pam Taylor, came from Louisiana.

The engine turned over and we took our seats. In a moment the skipper rounded a bend in the river and we came in sight of the oldest Ball place, Comingtee plantation. It was here that the founder of the family, the first Elias Ball, came from England to live in the year 1698. (The name Elias Ball would be used for many future sons, including Wambaw Elias, the Tory who moved back to England two generations later.) The ruined brick hulk of the rice mill at Comingtee stood within plain sight. Sticking out of the mud near the riverbank were pieces of rotting wood shaped like the headboards of beds— the sluices that once controlled the flow of water onto the rice fields.

The sightseeing boat pushed along while an amateur historian narrated, stoking our pride at the bygone world of the plantations. The size of the Ball lands once ranged from small three-hundred-acre tracts, worked by thirty or forty field hands, to giant estates of three or four thousand acres, with hundreds of slaves. Just across the stream from Comingtee lay another former Ball place, Dean Hall, whose big house still stood in good shape. Some of the South's plantations were now used as second homes by wealthy families, but many had been swept away. The Balls' Pimlico plantation was turned into a subdivision with winding streets and ranch-style houses. A few miles up the river lay two old Ball tracts, Kensington and Hyde Park, whose buildings were mostly gone. Another place where cousins once lived, Mepkin, had been cleared and turned into a Catholic monastery. A forestry company had bought much of the family land and planted pine trees. We peered out over the water and murmured at our broken heritage.

In the slave days the rice fields lay at the edge of the river. Each

plot was surrounded by a "rice bank," an earthen levee several feet
high and perhaps two hundred yards long on four sides of the field. The
remnants of rice banks, eroded by the current, lay submerged in the
water, presenting obstacles for boats, and a hull with a draft of more
than a couple of feet could easily run aground. As the double-decker
headed for another bend, it lurched and teetered on one of the rice
banks. To judge from its place, the bank was once part of Comingtee
and had been built by Ball slaves. The pilot tried to dislodge his vessel,
stuck in the muck where the slaves had worked, but the helpless engine
made hoarse guttural sounds. Half an hour passed, then an hour.

"We're spending more time in the rice fields than our ancestors ever
did!" one cousin joked.

The decision came to abandon ship, and several speedboats pulled
alongside to help. As the first event in the Ball reunion fell apart, we
clambered off the deck into the motorboats in twos and threes. The
rescue operation ferried us away from the rice fields, back to firm land.

I moved from New York back to Charleston to carry out the search. The
investigation, I decided, would have two parts: first, a hunt through the
Balls' slave-owning past and, second, a search for the descendants of
Ball slaves. This double search—at a distance of many generations and
through the mists of segregation and distrust—seemed daunting to say
the least.

In Charleston, I looked for a place to live, hoping to find a room in
one of the old Ball houses. During slavery, the family had more than a
dozen city residences in addition to the plantations out of town. In the
early 1800s, the townhouse of Elias Ball, founder of the family, had
been sold away and was later knocked down. In 1838, three houses
burned in a fire. Most of the rest were wiped aside in waves of demo-
lition that began in the 1900s. But a handful of the old Ball houses
remained. There was a wooden one near the northwest corner of Ashley
and Bull streets that belonged to a family member in the 1850s, as well
as a three-story brick house on the northwest corner of East Bay Street
and Stoll's Alley, occupied in the 1830s by an heiress named Ann Ball.

A cousin who worked in a bank offered to help me find a place to
live. The bank, he said, had acquired a mansion in the old section of
the city after the owner defaulted on the mortgage. It was run-down and

neglected, but I could use the house until someone bought it. Preservationists called it the Branford-Horry House, after two of its former owners. It stood in a row of mansions on Meeting Street, the main avenue through the historic core of Charleston, on the northwest corner where Meeting intersects Tradd Street. Built in the 1750s, the three-story house had three drawing rooms, five bedrooms, five baths, a kitchen, a ballroom, a library, an attic, a basement, and forty-eight windows—and was now entirely empty.

My new Charleston home had no resemblance to my former New York apartment. Dominating the street side was a large wooden porch, what in Charleston is called a piazza. It emerged from second-floor height and hung out over the sidewalk, where five columns stood against the curb to hold the thing in the air. A second colonnade on the piazza supported a pediment, which gave the face of the building the look of a furrowed brow. The house was roughly square, the brick walls two feet thick, covered with beige stucco that was cracked and chipping away. Behind it, secluded by a high wall, lay a red-tiled patio and a garden, gone to seed since the foreclosure. The front door opened into a wide central hallway, on either side of which were large folding doors that gave into drawing rooms. The rooms were moldering, the air thick and bacterial. Puffs of ancient dirt breathed from crevices between the floorboards, and everywhere was peeling paint and water-stained plaster. Down the main hall lay the best-kept room, the library. Its walls and mantelpiece, made from thick cypress, glowed like an old page. A staircase rose from the hall, with a loud squeak in the seventh step. The ballroom on the second floor was lined with more cypress, broken up here and there by fluted pilasters topped with Corinthian capitals. Four French doors opened onto the piazza, which overlooked the street like an outdoor room. Elsewhere were two bedrooms, another drawing room, bathrooms, and, on the top floor, three more bedrooms, baths, a laundry. Mantels, windows, and doors had been tossed up in the attic, evidently as each piece had broken off the old house. I moved in with a bed, bookshelf, and two tables, which became the only furniture in the building.

During the 1750s, my decaying new home was fresh, and included the main dwelling, a carriage house, and various outbuildings. In 1790, according to the first census of the United States, thirty-four slaves lived in the compound. The workforce, whose names the census enumerator did not record, belonged to a family of eight whites in the mansion. It was the largest number of slaves living at any address in the city.

Slave owners rarely became artists. Despite their leisure, they did not paint pictures or perform music apart from recitals at home. They wrote, but only for a few readers. Rather than make art, slave owners collected things. They assembled people, land, and facts about both.

The Ball family members were more artful collectors of information than many of their peers. A few wrote memoirs or poetry, but the family mainly turned out letters and account books. The letters chronicled their lives, while the accounts detailed the rice business and the family's human property. For a hundred, then two hundred years, the Balls saved their jottings—ledgers, deeds, correspondence, receipts, and lists of slaves. First there were stacks of papers, then boxes and finally trunks. Each generation assumed care of the hoard and in old age conveyed the documents to their children.

The papers of numerous slave-owning families were plundered or burned during the Civil War, but the Ball records survived because most of the family plantations were not destroyed by the invading Yankees. At the start of the 1900s, the family began to deposit the lode in archives around the South, until nearly all of them came to rest in public hands. Historians call them the "Ball Family Papers," more than ten thousand pages housed in four libraries. The earliest page is an inventory of property from the year 1631. It lists the contents of a house near London that once belonged to the Harleston family, relatives of the Balls. The last letters date from three hundred years later in America, after the rice fields were put to rest.

For me to understand the plantation story and find the descendants of the slaves, the written record would have to provide the map. Oral tradition suffers from scarcity and omission. Among the Ball family members, who overflow with legend, memory became selective over time. The same no doubt happened among black families as each drifted farther from the plantation. Though the paper record had gaps, it answered the need for detail better than hearsay could.

Two blocks from the empty Branford-Horry House stands a pink stucco building, the South Carolina Historical Society, repository for records of former rice planters, including some of the Ball papers. Every morning, I walked to the cobblestone block of the library to read the family records, housed in climate-controlled rooms like specimens of an extinct bird.

At the beginning were two questions: Who were the Ball family? And who were the Ball slaves?

In the old days, a Ball household began simply enough, with a wedding. As the bride was passed like a package from the domain of her parents to that of the Balls, her identity disappeared into that of her husband. The new Mrs. Ball might own land or slaves (the two did not always come together), and a village of people could be her dowry. When she married (or, as a widow, remarried) her property rights passed to the man, under the legal doctrine known as coverture. The rule of coverture meant that in the eyes of the law a couple would appear as a single person, the husband, whose identity substituted for that of his wife. While keeping a hand on the transfer of property, traditional patriarchal marriage was also a way to manage sex, making sure neither the family name nor belongings would stray. The culture demanded sexual loyalty from wives more than from husbands. With all this, the Ball men owned most of the people, controlled most of the land, and left behind most of the records.

The mistress of each plantation did not have full command over the slave farm but became a co-master with her husband, using power as she was able. Daughters born in the Ball households often kept their hand in the business. Some signed a prenuptial agreement that preserved their property rights when they left to marry, and they affected the families they joined. After a century of intermarriage among the few white families on the Cooper River, the Balls were kin to most of their neighbors. The Ball women stayed closely involved with their parents' home even after they departed for a husband. Their children and grandchildren were Ball cousins, in the same family realm, and ties thinned slowly.

A workable definition of the Ball family for the purposes of my investigation soon appeared: they were men and women born with the name, women who took the name Ball with marriage, and one generation of the offspring of Ball daughters who had acquired another surname.

The Ball slaves were easier to define. Simply, Ball slaves were people owned by members of the Ball family whose lives could be traced in the surviving files.

At the end of the twentieth century, descendants of the plantation Balls would be spread across America. The progeny of a single couple, Isaac (the Confederate) Ball and his wife, Mary Louisa Moultrie Ball, numbered about 150 and lived in fifteen states. They were construction workers, realtors, schoolteachers, lawyers, secretaries, homemakers, professors, physicians, students, and librarians. There were also one chemist, a priest, a banker, and a fashion model.

How many people might be descended from Ball slaves? When the Civil War ended in 1865, the family held many plantations, all of them on the Cooper River: The Blessing, Buck Hall, Cedar Hill, Cherry Hill, Comingtee, Dean Hall, Halidon Hill, Hyde Park, Limerick, Pawley, and Quenby. According to the records that survived (not all did), at least 842 people were freed from these tracts. Others were freed from three Ball places—Kensington, Pimlico, and St. James—that were sold out of the family some years before fighting with the North began. These may seem like big numbers, but they are a tiny current in the sea: nearly four million black Americans were affected by the Emancipation Proclamation.

After freedom, the former Ball slaves made a distinct community. Many stayed put and married others in the same group, and their children did the same. Fifty years later, more married outside their old circle, half migrated to the North, and in other ways they came apart as a discrete society. Using an equation that made allowances for rates of marriage within the community, for average numbers of children, long-term migration out of the South, and the increase in life span, it was finally possible to calculate the progeny of freed Ball workers. By a conservative estimate, in the year 2000 there would be at least seventy-five thousand living descendants of former Ball slaves in the United States, and by a slightly generous guess, even more—nearly one hundred thousand.

Old papers are beautiful things. Coarse, mottled parchment containing business records sometimes has the look of white skin. The pages are veiny, with age spots, the black ink coursing down them like hair. In some places, the ink is as dark as the day it was unbottled, and the paper as blotchy as an English cheek. I read through the Ball papers, beginning with the story of the first Elias Ball, who died in 1751, at seventy-five; his will filled four pages with script. The paper was pierced here and there by holes, signatures of bookworms. A rip had been mended on the second page, and there, in the splotch of a dried glue stain, a thumbprint appeared.

The deeds were the most beguiling. They came with maps, or "plats," that showed the layout of a plantation and the location of its buildings. One plat had a red border, faded like a child's watercolor, while some pages had brown splatter marks, perhaps from ancient splashes of tea. Other papers had curled up from dryness or changes in chemistry. In the old days, each deed was folded into an envelope shape, tied shut with a strip of parchment, and sealed with red wax. The wax was crusty, with black streaks where the burning candle had dripped carbon into the seal.

I read the papers slowly, lingering on the chatty letters, smiling at the quirks of the garrulous Balls, savoring their loopy signatures. Then I found the slave lists.

There were bundles of them, in thick sheaves, each sheaf containing a stack. When a rice planter handed out shoes, he wrote down the names of who got them. To pay taxes, he made an inventory of his human property. If he bought fabric so people could make clothes, he noted how many yards were given to each person. When a woman gave birth, the date and name of the child appeared. And when Mr. Ball died, his executor appraised everyone before title passed to the heir. I began to count the names on some of the bigger lists, up to a few hundred, then lost track.

These documents chronicled only some of the dealings between black and white Americans over the span of centuries. The larger dynamic might be captured in an image borrowed from tales of maritime disasters. Occasionally after a shipwreck, two people among the dead wash ashore, locked in an embrace. At the inquest, coroners puzzle over the drowned bodies that clutched each other to the end. Finally, the investigators conclude that the drowning pair must have died simultaneously, because each was unable to release the grip of the other.

Shut in the vaults of the historical society's pink stucco building, I read as much as I could absorb. One family at a time, the stories surfaced, and in glimpses and parts I began to piece together what happened.

>-+◦>-◦-◦◦+-◦<

2

MASTERS FROM ENGLAND

Elias Ball, my great-great-great-great-great-great-grandfather, was born in 1676 in a tiny hamlet in western England called Stokein-teignhead. His life shows how one family entered the slave business in the birth hours of America. It is a tale composed equally of chance, choice, and blood.

The village of Stokeinteignhead stands in southern Devonshire, about two miles from the English Channel. Although I cannot fix his birthdate, Elias was baptized there on October 13, in the Anglican church. An older spelling, Stoke-in-Teignhead, helps to describe the place: the stoke, or settlement, on Teignhead, a rise of some hills along the River Teign, whose mouth opens into the Channel.

When I was a teenager, I traveled to Stokeinteignhead to stay for a week in the old man's hometown. I hitchhiked west from London to the hills of Devon, where the buildings grew few and the pasture large. Elias's village seemed not to have changed much since his childhood —a few stone houses with thatched roofs, most built in the 1600s, on a twisting road between fenced fields. About twenty miles away stood a narrow thatched farmhouse with an ancient stone gate. The stone, which looked like a Druid megalith, had a name chiseled into it: Balls. The farmhouse of the Balls. It wasn't Elias's home (too distant from his village), but likely it had been the house of a cousin. I've seen photographs of the interior of this Ball house, probably very like the one where Elias would have lived. It had low beamed ceilings and a great fireplace for cooking.

The green and brown fields of Teignhead made a lovely place to begin, but life in rural Devon in the 1600s must have been severe. Most people were peasants without land, under the heel of noblemen. Some men worked as mates on ships out of nearby towns such as Torquay, three miles south of Teignhead on the Channel coast at Tor Bay. The more fortunate were yeoman farmers who owned a few acres, which gave them a degree of freedom from the big landlords.

Elias's immediate kin were poor tradespeople and peasants. His parents, William and Mary Ball, evidently worked as tenant farmers, since William Ball's will shows that he owned no acreage and left few belongings to his children. Elias's older brother, William Jr., pulled himself up a step when, as a young man, he got an apprenticeship to become a tailor. Some of Elias's kin in surrounding villages were better off. One of his uncles, Charles Ball, left money to his children, as well as to what his will called "the poor of the Parish." The Devon Balls parceled out what bits they could to their sons and parceled out their daughters to Devon farmers.

Various other Ball families lived in England. In one branch—related or not, I don't know—there was once a man whose lasting fame probably reached the ears of young Elias: John Ball, the "mad priest of Kent." In the 1360s, John Ball, a clergyman in the city of York, defied the Church and went south to take up the cause of the peasants in Kent. Ball preached the goal of a classless society and communal property, and denounced the lords, for which reckless talk he was excommunicated and imprisoned, around 1366. As quoted in a biography drafted by his accusers, John Ball attacked the elite, saying, "Matters goeth not well to pass in England nor shall do till everything be common and that there be no villeins [serfs] nor gentlemen but that we may be all united together and that the lords be no greater masters than we." Released from jail, he again drew a following, preaching that all people were created equal and calling for the murder of the lords, the lawyers, and the justices, in order to level the class system. In 1381, John Ball emerged at the head of a mass peasant movement that raised a following of two hundred thousand, and marched on London. He was captured in

Coventry in July of that year. Imprisoned again, this time he was delivered to harsh justice. At St. Albans, outside of London, in the presence of King Richard II, the "mad" Ball was hanged, drawn, and quartered, and the four pieces of his corpse were later sent to four different cities in England.

Although no evidence links John Ball to Elias's family, he could have been ancient kin. In any case, his crusade against caste is relevant. When Elias was a child, his own family may have had the feeling of lost promise and things stolen. In the mid-1600s, some of the Devon Balls had been well-off people of high esteem, but something happened before Elias was born: the family got on the wrong side of history and squandered its privilege.

There is an old genealogy, made by one of the American Balls, which states that Elias's grandfather was a man called Robert Ball, a vicar in the Church of England. Robert Ball was born in 1600 not far from Stokeinteignhead and educated at Balliol College, Oxford. He married a wealthy woman named Mary Huchenson, from Exeter, the governing seat of Devon, and acquired some land. At twenty-four, the rich graduate received his parish assignment at a congregation in the port of Torquay, St. Mary's Church. In Robert Ball's England, a clergyman's godliness was not ruled out by his money.

Robert Ball's good fortune swam along for nearly twenty years, but everything changed as England drifted into civil war. In 1642, a rebellious Parliament fielded armies that marched against King Charles I and his loyal peers. A faction of the uprising, the New Model Army, led by the austere Oliver Cromwell, won the lead. Cromwell's army focused the energy of the vociferous Puritans, who hated the Church of England with its pompous bishops and dressed-up style of worship. As a clergyman in the state-run church, Robert Ball was a hired hand of both the king and the bishops. He was an obvious and detestable enemy.

When the New Model Army came through Devon, the Reverend Robert Ball climbed into his pulpit at St. Mary's and told his congregation to remain loyal to King Charles. For this, the vicar was captured and jailed. After paying bail for his freedom (perhaps from his wife's purse), Robert Ball took his family and fled. A year or so after the incident the fighting subsided, with Charles I pushed out of England onto the Isle of Wight. During the stalemate, Robert Ball returned home to find his house looted, his property confiscated, and St. Mary's in the hands of the Puritans. The war resumed in 1648, and Cromwell's army was victorious. King Charles was beheaded, and Cromwell took his place as chief of state. Robert Ball was ruined. The vicar spent his middle years fending off Cromwell's lieutenants, who demanded money from him, and trying to get back his wife's fortune. In the late 1650s, he regained control of St. Mary's. The Ball family, however, seem to have been broken by the events of the English Civil War.

Elias Ball's father, William, inherited nothing and acquired little. William Ball grew up and moved to the village of Stokeinteignhead, an hour's walk from Torquay. There he married a poor woman named Mary. The couple had four children, of whom Elias was the last.

During Elias's boyhood royal clashes came home a second time. After Cromwell's death, Charles II, son of the beheaded king, was restored to the throne. Many in the new regime wanted to take vengeance against the Puritans on behalf of the Church of England. But the new King Charles leaned toward Catholicism and ignored the Anglican Church, causing murmuring among the lords, who began to worry seriously when, upon Charles's death in 1685, the throne passed to his brother, James II, an avowed Catholic. King James looked to the Vatican and promoted the papacy, a turn of events that raised a panic in the old Protestant faction. In 1688, a cabal of English aristocrats invited William, Prince of Orange, to come to England from across the Channel in order to seize the throne from James.

Elias was twelve. To begin what would be called the Glorious Revolution, William of Orange landed in November with his army at Tor Bay, a half-hour gallop from the Ball home. The invaders would have swept past Stokeinteignhead on their way to Exeter and London, meaning that once again armed masses drove through the Ball homeland. As ardent supporters of the royal family, the Balls may have had to flee a second time. King James certainly fled, to France, and the quieter reign of William and Mary began.

It is not difficult to imagine how Elias's family, penniless on a little piece of land, might tell and retell stories about the luxury in which some of their relatives once lived. In this setting, the story of how Ball family money was cheated away would get a special hearing. The injustice seemed to link the little clan to great events. Wrongs could be traced in a line, from the lowly villages on the River Teign all the way up to the king. The Puritans, a mob of fanatics, had killed the head of state, who had ruled by divine right. And look at us now.

I suspect that the Ball family's experience of the English Civil War might have forced some of them to the most conservative side of the politics of their day. And, just perhaps, it might have left children like Elias with an appetite to wrest back what had been stolen from them.

In 1692, when Elias was sixteen, William Ball died. According to an inventory of his property, he didn't leave much: "twelve sheep, ten lambs . . . one old mare & coalt . . . one brass pan & kettle . . . one bed . . . [and] corn in the ground." Because Elias was William and Mary Ball's last child, by the code of primogeniture, in which rights pass to male children beginning with the first, he would have had no claim even to this paltry inheritance.

The village of Stokeinteignhead stood near ports that handled the growing ship traffic to America. In 1620, the *Mayflower* had sailed from the Devon town of Plymouth to Massachussetts, carrying a small band of Pilgrims. Since then, Tor Bay and its inland villages had given up thousands of sons and daughters as seamen or adventurers in the growing overseas empire. As they wrote home to report on their doings, and when the discouraged came back to England for good, stories of the colonies filled up regional lore.

As a boy, Elias heard about at least one colonial wayfarer, a man called John Coming (the name was variously spelled Cumming and Comyns), a half brother of Elias's father, an interesting uncle who went to America.

Uncle John had grown up in Devon and had become a sailor. In 1669 he signed on as first mate to the *Carolina*, a ship commissioned by investors to make the first permanent English settlement on the southeastern coast of North America. Unlike earlier attempts, the expedition succeeded. John Coming had married Affra Harleston, one of the few women aboard his ship, and returned to sea. He rose to the rank of captain and made round-trip voyages carrying people and cargo between England and the new colony, Carolina.

I imagine that Elias Ball met his uncle on the sailor's return trips to Devon, when Captain Coming passed through to see his kin. John and Affra had no children, and the childless captain may well have paid attention to his half brother's family. Whether in this way or some other, the idea dawned in John Coming's mind that there would be an inheritance overseas for one of his Ball nephews, should that nephew come to America to claim it. After much to-and-fro, John Coming ended his sailing days around 1682, then stayed in South Carolina, as the colony was known by then. (The other part, North Carolina, was largely untouched by the English, and would remain so for many years.)

The estate where John Coming lived was known as Coming's T. It stood on a river where two tributaries came together in the shape of the letter *T*. The tract was not a farm on the model of a tiny Devon holding of five or ten acres. Coming's T was grand, some 740 acres. It had another aspect, something unique to America that no English farmer, not even a lord, could claim: Coming's T was peopled by captive workers, African and Native American slaves.

John Coming and Affra Harleston were pioneers who gambled their lives and won. Their wager opened a path for their nephew, young Elias Ball. It began back in August 1669, somewhere near Dover, England, when John Coming boarded the frigate *Carolina*, bound for America. A long and light flagship, the *Carolina* had two sister vessels, the *Port Royal* and the *Albemarle*. The flotilla sailed from the Downs, some shoals off the Dover coast, then proceeded to Ireland to look for more passengers. From his Irish berth, Joseph West, captain of the mission, wrote to his employers, a group of investors known as the Lords Proprietors. West informed them that fewer Irish adventurers than he had predicted had come to the docks to board.

The muted interest of the Irish in the scheme came as no surprise, because the three ships arrived from England, which had lately done atrocious things in Ireland. During the second part of the English Civil War, in 1648, Oliver Cromwell's army had invaded Ireland and made prisoners of thousands. To punish his enemies for siding with King Charles, Cromwell devised a plan to deport the Irish captives to work in America. By this time, owners of English sugar farms on the island of Barbados were demanding workers—black, white, red, anybody. The Irish royalists were sent off to slavery in the tropics. Although over twenty years had passed, no one could say whether Joseph West's flotilla might be a trick to kidnap more victims.

At least one person on the docks, the young Affra Harleston, probably in her early twenties, paid no attention to the warnings that greeted the arrival of the ships. She had been born into a wealthy English family that had moved to Ireland some years before to escape the constant wars. Although she had been raised in Ireland and had received a fine education there, as demonstrated by several poetic letters that she wrote, later handed down among the Balls, she was evidently eager to abandon it. When the *Carolina* made port, Affra decided to go aboard, becoming one of seventeen women among ninety-two passengers.

The little fleet sailed from Kinsale, on the southern coast near the town of Cork, in mid-September 1669. Some weeks later the ships arrived in Barbados to pick up supplies and still more adventurers. By this time Barbados was peopled with tens of thousands of Africans, who outnumbered their English owners by a large majority. Although no clear evidence remains, some of the people who (unwillingly) joined the *Carolina*'s mission in Barbados may have been black slaves.

After a winter spent laid up in the Caribbean, the pioneers headed for North America in the spring. In late March 1670, the *Carolina* arrived at a marshy shore on the southeast coast of the mainland, and the two sister ships arrived a few days later. Some Native Americans (I prefer to call them simply Native people) greeted the strangers. The English-speakers must have been careful with their hosts, because the leader, or *cassique*, of the Natives, a tribe known as the Kiawah, took an interest. The cassique led the *Carolina* north to a handsome bay formed by two rivers. This new landing place lay about 250 miles north of St. Augustine, Florida, where the Spanish, hated colonial rivals of Britain, sat grimly in their forts. The English settled just inland from the ocean on a marshy riverbend.

First mate John Coming probably disembarked in the company of Affra Harleston. The couple had come to an arrangement during the long journey from Ireland. They seem to have expected they were in America to stay, because they were married at sea, or soon after they arrived.

The land the invaders called Carolina consisted of a flat, wet plain that unrolled from the beach and continued inland a distance of about forty miles. West of the wetlands lay a dry piedmont, with rolling hills and pine forest, and beyond that, three hundred miles from the shore, the mountain range of Appalachia. The Kiawah, who met the ships, were among two dozen small Native tribes or clans living on the coastal plain.

Others included the Edisto, Etiwan, Kusso, and Sewee, whose settlements, taken together, counted several thousand people. Farther inland lived the Catawba, and down the coast, in the direction of Florida, the Yamasee. The strongest people in the region, the Cherokee, lived farthest from the ocean. Cherokee villages stood in the foothills and mountains, but with their war-making might and constant trade down to Kiawah country, the Cherokee dominated everything in their path.

A visitor to Carolina in its first years described the coastal Natives as having "a deep Chestnut Colour." He reported that people wore clothing made from the skins of bear or deer, that the men had little or no hair on their chins, and that both men and women painted their faces "with different Figures of red." Their look was "well limb'd and featured" and they wore "their Hair black and streight, tied various ways, sometimes oyl'd and painted, [and] stuck through with Feathers." There were many competing clans, but this eyewitness description gives some idea of the people who would soon be asked to hand over their land.

Most of the coastal Natives lived in small villages and planted corn, or maize, and moved from time to time to take up new fields. The custom of seasonal drifting put them at a disadvantage against the invaders. It allowed the English to tell themselves they were not encroaching on other people's territory, because a nomadic people could not be said to own any land. The population of the Native villages was sparse, perhaps fifty to a hundred in each settlement, in part because the women practiced abortion. An ethnographer traveling in the 1700s noted that the Catawba relied on "frequent abortions of the young unmarried women . . . by medicinal simples . . . in which fatal science they are very expert."

The women tended the maize, while the men fished and hunted, using blowguns as well as bows and arrows. A typical meal of the Etiwan, who lived near the whites, would have been a venison stew with corn meal, or rabbit dressed with a sauce made from hickory nuts. For drink, the Kiawah and other clans made a tea from the cassena bush, a low shrub on the coast.

Within three months of landing, the whites revealed their long-range plans. By the end of the first summer, the immigrants, still living on ships anchored in the river, began to import African slaves. The black people were brought one or two at a time from older English colonies such as Virginia and Barbados. Within the year, the colony consisted of some two hundred whites and fifty enslaved blacks. With the black workers at their command, whites put to work a surveying instrument, seventeen and a half feet in length, known as "the rod." They built a village with regular streets and wooden farmhouses. Fields of corn, planted with seed borrowed from the Natives, lay at the edge of town. John and Affra Coming evidently had a house built in the new village, and settled in.

When the English arrived, they carried with them a social contract, the Fundamental Constitutions, written in London by the philosopher John Locke. At the time, Locke worked for Lord Ashley Cooper, one of the Lords Proprietors, investors in the Carolina colony. The Fundamental Constitutions consisted of 120 provisions, among which were careful terms for the establishment of slavery.

By the time of the founding of Carolina, the English colonies in America had evolved a three-tiered system of labor: enslaved people (Natives and Africans), indentured servants (usually poor English or Irish whites), and free citizens (Puritans and loyal Church of England flock). The Fundamental Constitutions, intended as a guide to the settlement of Carolina, discouraged the enslavement of Natives. From the experience of Virginia and Massachusetts, colonized half a century earlier, Locke knew that Native people would retaliate if the English tried to sell them. Rather than say as much outright, however, Locke framed the issue of slavery in religious terms. "[S]ince the Natives of the place who will be concerned in our plantation are utterly Strangers to Christianity," he wrote, "[their] Idolatry Ignorance or mistake gives us noe right to expell [them] or use [them] ill."

By contrast, the Fundamental Constitutions called for the subjugation of Africans, styled "Negroes." Locke evidently understood that an African's black brothers and sisters, back home, would have no means of reprisal against American captors. The religious scruples vanished, and Provision 110 read simply, "Every Freeman of Carolina, shall have absolute power and authority over Negro Slaves, of what opinion or Religion soever."

Slavery, a kidnap-and-sale system aimed against foreign people for the purpose of forced work, was not an English invention. Neither were the restrictions on personal movement, or the inheritance between generations of the status of slave. By the time the Carolina colony was founded, all of this was already thousands of years old. Slavery had thrived among the Jews; among black Africans, Greeks, Romans, and ancient Germans; and throughout the Holy Roman Empire, especially around the Mediterranean. The word "slave" itself derives from "Slav"; the Slavs were long victims of European slavery, captured from the eastern Adriatic and trade routes along the Black Sea. In central Europe, slavery began to fail toward the end of the eighth century A.D. and fell extinct by the middle of the fourteenth. It was revived after 1492, at the start of the age of American empire, when Spanish and Portuguese ships began to carry Africans across the Atlantic. Southern Europeans turned to Africa in part because the supply of Slavs had been cut by the fall of Constantinople to the Turks in 1453. In 1508, an early shipload of blacks arrived at Hispaniola, in the Caribbean. By 1540, King Charles V of Spain tried to halt the practice, decreeing the end of African slavery and freedom for blacks in Spanish dominions. The decree failed, African slavery returned, and the English soon copied the Spanish example. In a first expedition, in 1556, Sir John Hawkins sailed from London to some landing point on the West African coast, and sent eighty men on shore to trap people. Villagers fought back, seven whites were killed, and the poachers took just ten captives. Sailing farther south, Hawkins tried again, succeeded in filling his ship, and headed for the Caribbean. Eventually Europeans found an easier way of procuring workers, namely, encouraging black clans to fight one another and to sell their prisoners of war.

With his theories of representative government, John Locke would later become the philosopher of the American Revolution. He also proved to be a good theorist of slavery, writing what is perhaps the most apt definition of human property. For Locke, slavery was not merely a labor system, that is, a way of building a foreign colony. He described it instead as a permanent state of war. Any person who "attempts to get another Man into his Absolute Power, does thereby put himself into a State of War with him," Locke wrote after he left the employment of Lord Ashley Cooper and could speak freely.

John and Affra Coming, and other South Carolinians, did not invent the state of war that would push them to the top of their society. But what the English-speaking whites carried out in South Carolina—and throughout America—did have distinction. Through their attack on Africans, which brought millions to the New World, the English would become the most efficient slave makers in history.

Despite the ban on abuse of the Natives, within eighteen months the Carolinians enslaved local people alongside Africans. In August 1671, an immigrant from Ireland killed a Native man—from what clan, the records do not say—probably in an argument over bartered goods. Previously the colonists had been careful not to hurt their neighbors, who outnumbered them, but this murder shifted the ethnic winds. No evidence of reprisal for the death appears in the official account, and the whites seem to have taken the unpunished crime as permission to capture Native people. One month after the killing, settlers attacked the Kusso, to the southwest. The colonists believed the Kusso had been conspiring with the Spanish in Florida to plan an attack on the English. In addition to their conniving, real or imagined, the Kusso had been taking corn from fields planted by settlers. Angry farmers complained to the governing committee, known as the Grand Council, which called for penalties. Stating that "the Kussoe and other Southern Indians . . . doe dayly persist and increase in their insolencyes," the Council declared "an open Warr," beginning with the taking hostage of two Kusso who had the misfortune of being among the whites. In later years, John Coming, the goodly Ball uncle, would be a member of this same Grand Council and vote on similar policies.

The "Warr," which lasted a few days, was the first Carolina slave raid. Afterward the settlers debated what to do with their prisoners. The Grand Council decided that "every Company which went out upon that expedition shall secure and maintain the Indians they have taken till they can transport the said Indians." To "transport" meant to deport, or export, the prisoners to faraway slave buyers. Such transactions would speed up the removal of Natives from the land.

The slave raids picked up quickly after the first one. Hundreds of people were captured by white "Indian traders," who also sold deerskins. The majority of Native slaves were women and children, because the men, being adept hunters, proved better at escaping capture. A particular method of abduction evolved. The raiders would wait until the men of a village were away on a hunt and then fall on the people left behind. As the slave trade developed, the whites began to talk about building a wall around their settlement, an odd notion for a few farm-houses and one or two muddy streets. No retaliation ever came, however, because the English carried guns, the Natives, blowguns.

Most of the captives were sold to slave buyers in the other English colonies—Barbados, Jamaica, Massachusetts, and New York. In time, white Indian traders began to employ Native people to do their slaving for them. By distributing guns to some clans and not others, the colonists used rivalries between villages to get captives. The Carolinians goaded skirmishes and offered rifles to Natives for delivering people. Soon there appeared a steady flow of humans alongside the trade of pelts and rum. Eventually the whites, no longer fearing reprisal, kept Native workers for themselves and compelled them to labor rather than shipping them out.

Africans, meanwhile, came steadily into port. The black traffic was controlled from England. In 1672, the London-based Royal African Company secured from King Charles II a monopoly on the black slave trade into the British colonies. The company sent most of its ships to a long stretch of the West African coast between the mouth of the Gambia River and the eastern edge of the Gulf of Guinea. From depots, so-called slave factories, the ships brought their cargo to Barbados, Jamaica, the Bahamas, and other Caribbean islands. Until the end of the 1600s, nearly all of the blacks the Carolina whites enslaved were bought from Barbados.

John and Affra Coming probably were not involved in the slave raids, but Coming was almost certainly a slave trader of sorts, transporting people in and out of the colony. Soon after the first landing in Carolina, he gained the captain's berth in a ship called the *Edisto*, and afterward another vessel, the *Blessing*. As one of the settlement's chief mariners, Coming earned his living by shuttling cargo between Carolina and other English territories. Throughout the 1670s, when he was almost constantly at sea, it is likely that beneath his decks, Elias Ball's uncle carried Native people out of Carolina to Barbados, and Africans from Barbados back to the mainland.

John Coming was a man of simple beginnings, but Affra Harleston came from a landed family in Essex County, England. The Harleston farm was a place called Mollands, in South Ockendon, twenty miles east of the center of London and two miles north of the River Thames. It included a twelve-room house and evidently much land. An inventory of the contents of the dwelling, made in 1631 and handed down in the Ball family, describes the Harlestons' pewter plates, damask napkins, brass skillets, and featherbeds. These things did not signify noble status, to be sure, but they placed the family in the propertied class.

As with the Balls, the English Civil War turned the Harlestons' world upside down. In the 1640s, having shown loyalty to King Charles I, some of the family moved to Ireland to escape the tide of Cromwell. They had estates near Dublin, where Affra's mother, Elizabeth Harleston, controlled seven hundred acres. Affra was probably born in Ireland about 1645 and raised among English expatriates, who were accustomed to having Irish servants care for their children.

When Affra and John set up house in America, they had ambitions to build an estate, and began to look for workers. The couple turned first to other whites. In 1671, John Coming sailed the *Carolina* back to Britain and returned with five men and one woman—indentured servants who had contracted their labor for several years. Their names were John Chambers, Rachel Franck, George Gantlett, Samuel Lucas, Michael Lovering, and Philip O'Neil. At least some were Irish.

According to the Fundamental Constitutions, a white settler had a right to 150 acres for each laborer he or she brought to Carolina—white or black, free, indentured, or enslaved. For his first group of contract workers, John Coming got a piece of paper promising him nine hundred acres.

The six workers probably moved to the Comings' tract within the English settlement. Within a few months, however, there was an uprising in the household. In June 1672, while her husband was at sea, Affra Coming brought charges against John Chambers, Philip O'Neil, and one other worker, complaining to the court of "their disobedience to her in refusing to observe her lawful commands." A record of the hearing shows that the servants had been working for less than a year when they protested they were being badly fed by their employers. Philip O'Neil showed his opinion of Affra by "threatening to overset the Boate wherein she was" and by taking his food from her hands and throwing it to some dogs. O'Neil also threatened to run away and join the Natives. In her complaint, Affra sought to punish O'Neil for his "divers . . . gross abuses." When the decision came down, the servants were put in their place and the court ordered O'Neil tied to a tree for "one and twenty lashes upon his naked back."

For the next several years, John Coming continued to bring workers from Britain, although no further records show how they fared under the iron rule of Affra Coming.

About 1680, the settlement moved to a drier spot, the peninsula formed by the two rivers that came together in the harbor, a location more easily reached by ships. The immigrants had given their community a name, Charlestown. (A century later, at the end of the American Revolution, the city would be incorporated as Charleston. By using the briefer spelling, I will avoid the appearance of a scene change in midstory.)

About this time John Coming gave up the sea and, with Affra, turned in some warrants for land. The couple had already claimed about two hundred acres on the peninsula of Charleston and one three-quarter-acre lot in the new town. Because the whites distributed house lots in numerical order, John and Affra's town property appears in the deeds as lot 49. It measured 88 by 381 feet on what would later become the northwest and northeast corners of East Bay and Pinckney streets. The third and largest piece of land the couple claimed, in February 1678, lay about twenty-five miles inland from the coast, at the joining of two branches of a river known to the Natives as the Etiwan, after the people who lived on it. To the English, it became the Cooper River, after Lord Ashley Cooper, John Locke's paymaster. This was the river whose fork gave the name to the estate known as Coming's T.

The Cooper River flowed down from Coming's T along twists and turns into Charleston harbor, a water distance of about fifty miles. Though nearly twice as far as by land, traveling by water was faster, because no roads yet existed. The river was a tidal stream whose level rose five feet or more with each high tide on the coast. The brackish backflow came close to the T but went no farther, meaning that above Coming's T, the river ran fresh.

Coming's T was a big swath of forest (pine trees, oak, magnolia) mingled with thick swamps (cedar and gum trees). A stretch of marsh separated the firm land from the clear stream of the river. At high tide, the water covered the marsh, retreating at ebb to expose the mudflats and roots of abundant cypress trees. I suspect John and Affra were struck by the fecundity of the swamps, the draperies of moss, the tree canopies, and the abundance of game. There were alligators and rattlesnakes, bobcats, and an occasional bear—but there was also easy food for the table, including deer, duck, and possum. Close to the river, the soil felt like heavy loam in the hand, what the colonists called black mould.

Each new English plot had the rough shape of a rectangle or triangle, with one wavy border running along the riverbank and straight sides forming inland property lines. The estates asserted themselves neatly on plats but were invisible on the ground. Neither roads nor fences marked the boundaries, and written descriptions of land grants sound like directions for a walk through the woods. One plat described the border of a tract at the edge of Coming's T as "live oak, hickory, pine, dead pine."

When the English came, the Natives made room for them. One group of Etiwan numbered about fifty people who moved up and down the river that once had their name. For a time there was an Etiwan village across the stream from Coming's T, at a place called Hagan. Two Native trading posts covered the river, the nearest at a bluff known as Mepkin, three miles from the T. The Santee and others apparently passed through Affra and John's land to get there. More traffic moved a few miles to the west, on the other side of the western branch of the river, on the main path inland from Charleston. Natives, in various languages, named this route the Broad Path or Broad Way. The English called it the Cherokee Trail. The road began at the ocean and continued four hundred miles west and north to Cherokee towns in the mountains, then farther, beyond the Appalachian range to the Mississippi River.

John and Affra probably bought their first slaves about 1680. The term of indenture for their white workers had ended, and Coming had stopped his return trips to Britain. In the most likely scenario the couple simply went to the wharf in Charleston, where John had friends in the business, and bought two or three Africans.

One of the first tasks required by the new slave owners would have been to build a house at the T. The slaves may have cut the pine and hoisted the beams under John's direction. Eventually a simple wooden cottage stood in the shadow of two oaks. According to one member of the Ball family who saw the building before the Civil War and later wrote about it, the house survived for nearly two hundred years, until about 1866.

At the start there were no houses for the slaves. Archaeology in the area suggests that Africans and Natives built various shelters, such as huts with thatched roofs or lean-tos propped on saplings. Others slept under large shelters with four posts (but no walls) and a roof of leaves. Workers may have lived this way, half outdoors, for years before they built more permanent dwellings.

At least some of the Africans put up houses with earthen walls. Beneath the heavy soil of the Cooper River tracts lay a foundation of gummy clay. The clay, easily dug out, was mingled with thin sticks called wattle and piled in layers of ooze into the shape of a cottage. The walls were then cooked with fire to a hardness near that of brick. Topped with a thatched roof, the resulting one- or two-room house resembled some huts in coastal West Africa. Centuries later, this type of building would still be known among black Carolinians as a "ground house." In the hot climate, a ground house was more comfortable than a wooden cabin. Cooled by the night air, the clay held indoor temperatures down during the day.

If the majority of Native slaves were women, most of the black slaves were men. The Royal African Company kidnapped mainly males, whom their buyers wanted for the heaviest work. The Native women may have lived closer to, or even in, the white household with John and Affra, who made them cook, sew, and clean. As for the men, it is possible that master and mistress worked side by side with them, especially in the first years. John and Affra wanted to make the land conform to the English idea of a farm, and the work of clearing and marking out the property could not be done if the whites merely sat by. All may have dug drainage trenches and cut trees, fields, and paths.

Because of the scarcity of papers from the 1600s, I can only guess at the kind of force John and Affra used with their first slaves. But Affra Coming had petitioned a court to flog her Irish servant, Philip O'Neil, and John Coming, having made his way in the hard society of seagoers, was himself no stranger to brutality. Sea captains often practiced gruesome punishments on sailors, such as keelhauling, that is, dragging a man at the end of a rope beneath the hull of a ship. In the records of the colonial government are many descriptions of savage violence aimed at slaves. But about the exercise of power on Coming's T—the individual punishments, the coaxings, or the defiance—there is no evidence.

After twenty-five years of marriage, John and Affra remained childless. Two years after arriving in America, the couple took in a four-year-old named Peter Argent, the son of a neighbor. By the terms of a contract, the boy would remain with his guardians until age twenty-one. For unclear reasons, however, the colonial government took the boy away and gave him to other adoptive parents, and afterward John and Affra did not take in another child.

John Coming died November 1, 1695. In his will he left Coming's T and what he called his "Chattles" to Affra. "Chattel slavery," as opposed to "freehold slavery," was an English spin on the old system. A freehold slave was a worker, bound to a piece of land, who could not be transferred or sold away from the estate. The master of a freehold slave claimed possession of the individual's labor, not his or her person. Freehold slaves included those in bondage to the Spanish in South America and in some parts of Africa.

The English developed a different and more thorough form of bondage. A chattel slave was the equivalent of movable property and could be sold away like a horse. Also, the children of chattel slaves automatically assumed the slave identity of their mother, not always the case among freehold workers. In 1696, the year after John Coming's death, the colonial legislature in South Carolina passed a law asserting the new chattel status for "All Negroes, Mollatoes, and Indians which at any time heretofore have been bought and Sold." With that, for all purposes, the system was complete. There would be a hereditary caste of workers, presumably forever.

Following her husband's death, Affra Coming wrote home to her family in Ireland suggesting that she felt terribly alone, despite being surrounded by many people. "I am desirous to give you an account of my sad state of widowhood," Affra wrote to her sister in Dublin in 1696. "I am as one that is forlorn; having no relations to comfort me, nor friends to assist me in this sorrowful condition. By all that I can perceive at present, I appear as a sheep in the midst of wolves; but God I hope will be my good shepherd & preserve me as he hath done in many great dangers."

It may have been that Affra felt vulnerable, as a woman with property, around manipulative men who wanted her riches. A more likely interpretation is that she, "a sheep in the midst of wolves," feared the Africans and Natives whom she and her husband had held for fifteen years and who now surrounded her.

According to Affra's letters, John Coming wanted to leave part of his estate to one of his Ball nephews in England, and believed Elias's older brother, William, was the right one for the inheritance. Half would be his, and half would go to a nephew of Affra, a young man named John Harleston, who lived in Ireland. "His desire," Affra wrote her sister, meaning the wish of her husband, was to give Coming's T "to my nephew John Harleston and my nephew William Ball." Affra considered moving back to Britain from America but added, "I should be loath to leave it for their sakes till one of them come," that is, until an heir sailed over to take control.

Affra apparently stayed in touch with the Ball family in Devon, reminding them of what awaited in South Carolina. By this time, however, William Ball had passed the age of thirty and had long since become a tailor. He must have measured the prospect of a future in which he would have to change vocations—from making waistcoats for gentlemen to becoming a slave owner in America—and decided against it. And so the option fell to Elias.

It is a ripe touch that the Ball family's benefactor was called Affra, a name with an interesting etymology. The Phoenicians once called those who lived in North Africa "Afirs," apparently the Semitic word for wanderer. Romans borrowed the word from the Phoenicians, modified it to "Afer" (plural "Afri"), and the place where the Afers lived became "Africa." In the Old Testament, Ephah and Epher are descendants of Abraham and Keturah, Abraham's concubine, and the sons of Midian, Keturah's son. There was also the figure of Apherra, a servant of Solomon, whose descendants returned from exile in Babylon. It seems the name Affra, representative of North African people, was occasionally picked from the Bible by the English as a name for a daughter, such as the future slave owner Affra Coming.

The nature of Coming's T as a slave farm was no secret to Affra's English relatives. But what did Elias Ball, a simple young man in the provinces, actually know about American slavery? Apparently little. The Romans brought slavery to Britain with their invasion in 43 A.D., but human property had faded with the Middle Ages, replaced by the villein system, a form of serfdom. Probably the most Elias would have known was that the business was lucrative, from stories that filtered back to England of fortunes made in the colonies. Slavery was a kind of turbulence on the other side of the Atlantic that made money for those who could stomach it.

Affra Coming seems to have died in early 1699. Her will, dated 28 December 1698, contained her husband's wishes:

> I Affra Coming of yᵉ County of Berkly in South Carolina Widd° & relict of John Coming late of yᵉ Same County genᵗ decd. being Sick of Body but of a Sound & disposing memory . . . Give & bequeath all my Lands, Tenemᵗˢ Woods & Pastures wᶜʰ I now have . . . & every of their apurtenances unto John Harleston of Dublin in yᵉ Kingdom of Ireland genᵗ my Nephew . . . & to Elias Ball Son of William Ball half Brother of yᵉ abovesᵈ John Coming my most beloved husband, to have & to hold . . . in Joint-Tenancy & to their respective heirs . . . for ever.

Almost as an afterthought, Affra concluded:

> I Give unto yᵉ sᵈ John Harleston & Elias Ball all my Negroes & Indian Servᵗˢ Cattle Furniture, goods, Debts & chattels to be equally divided between them. . . . Signed Sealed & Published —Affra Coming

With Affra's death, the title of master settled on the young Elias Ball.

When Elias Ball sailed into the harbor at Charleston, in 1698, he was just twenty-two. He had traveled thirty-five hundred miles from England, a journey of perhaps six weeks, to claim his inheritance. As his ship edged into port, it would have been obliged to move slowly, because sandbars and oyster shoals lined the channel. From the deck, Elias would have seen a lush coastline, with reedy marshes edging the waterfront and green grass rising waist-high out of soft gray mud. Beyond the marshes stood the firm soil, and on it a curtain of trees and thicket so dense that light could hardly open it. One species of tree in particular would have been foreign to Elias's eyes, the palmetto, which grows only in semitropical latitudes. The palmetto has a tan trunk, naked of branches until the top, where long leaves emerge in the shape of open fans.

The harbor at Charleston was shaped by the confluence of the Ashley and the Cooper rivers. Flowing south, the streams formed a peninsula and met at a place called Oyster Point, a jutting piece of land colored white with shells. The Kiawah had long opened shellfish here, and there were still discarded mounds of shells. Around the eastern edge of the point ran the Cooper, around the west, the Ashley.

Charleston stood on the east side of the peninsula, a line of buildings about a half mile from start to finish, facing the Cooper River. The mud of the marshes kept ships from docking, except at a single pier built out from the town. A dirt road ran along the shore, but only four or five streets cut inland. Even to an English peasant, it would have seemed barely coherent enough to call a village, much less "Charlestown," namesake of King Charles II. The buildings were simple clapboard things with pitched roofs, though a few brick structures aimed for a more permanent standard of architecture. There were probably some houses in a state of ruin, and others charred black. That February an earthquake had struck, and the same month, a fire had burned a third of the town, including most of its best buildings. An aura of precariousness must have permeated everything.

Elias had probably never met an African, and certainly not a Native American. I suspect what he saw when he stepped onto the dock filled him with wonder and fear. Nearly every other person would have been black. The population of the colony, including the inland farms, numbered about 3,800 free whites and 3,000 slaves, most of them black. In 1698, South Carolina was already the slave center of North America, and its high proportion of captive workers was greater than that of any other colony on the mainland. It wasn't the blackness of the dock workers alone that would have caught the immigrant's attention. In the late 1600s, some slaves in Charleston had two letters—*DY*—burned into their flesh. The inscription was the mark of King James II, known before his accession to the throne as the Duke of York. As a principal in the Royal African Company, the Duke controlled most of the traffic of Africans sold into South Carolina, and every person was branded with his title.

Coming's T was nearly twenty years old. By this time the name had been worn down through repetition to the poetic "Comingstee." Within a generation it would smooth out to become simply "Comingtee."

Though Comingtee stood north of Charleston, no carriage roads reached Elias's new home, and by English standards the land outside town was virtually empty. Only a few dozen Natives lived in the vicinity of Comingtee, and within a radius of ten miles there lived no more than 250 slaves, free colonists, and indentured servants. Even in this general emptiness, Comingtee was considered one of the busiest estates. An Englishman writing about the colonies around this time observed that the "most noted plantations" along the Cooper River were Comingtee and a place called Silk Hope, owned by an older man, Nathaniel Johnson, who would later be governor of South Carolina.

Although there is nothing to prove it, Affra Coming was probably still alive to greet her nephew. But she died within a few months, leaving him alone with the new Ball slaves. In all likelihood, Elias moved into the house under the oaks, where Affra and John had once lived.

It must have been a chaotic, brutal time. One of the main battles, though certainly not the bloodiest, was the struggle merely to communicate. Of the Africans on Comingtee, some had lived in America for several years and spoke an English patois as well as their own language, such as Wolof or Fula. The Native slaves, too, spoke more than one language. Elias was the real stranger on the land, a prisoner of his West Country English.

Although many of his peers were illiterate, Elias had received a rudimentary education; he could read and write, but he was no poet. His spelling was improvised, as was the custom of the day. In an account book that he would later keep, there is an entry that reads, "23 January—Day that I sent my fouor Cheldren to Mr. Faur." His penmanship, which fills that old book, was scrawled to the point of hard-won. Somewhere along the way, however, he had learned double-entry bookkeeping. He was scrupulous with debts and had a grip on figures. To judge from the papers he left, one of his favorite things was to keep an eye on his property.

I imagine that during long nights at the edge of the swamp, Elias Ball brooded about the wager he had made with his life. The twenty-two-year-old farm boy seized his future: he would be a little autocrat in a corner of an unknown world.

3

THE WELL OF TRADITION

On a summer afternoon in Charleston, in the kind of heat that slows a person's walk, I went to visit a distant cousin, Elias Ball Bull. Elias was in his sixties and, by my count, the sixteenth male in the family christened with the name Elias since Elias Ball, founder of the family in America, died in 1751. My cousin's mother, Julia Ball, was a first cousin of my grandfather, Nathaniel Ball. She had married a scion of another old Carolina family, Francis Bull, giving her son his percussive two last names.

Cousin Elias had worked as a historic-preservation planner for the government in Berkeley County, the district where the Ball plantations once stood. I wanted to go over the family story with him, in hopes of finding a clue to the mystery of the descendants of the Ball slaves.

Elias lived alone in a two-story apartment house in the suburbs, in a compound of ten or twelve identical buildings put up in the 1970s. His situation reminded me that the offspring of the slave-owning families, fleeing the sinking ship of the rice plantations, did not necessarily land on high shores. He came to the door in a customary position, seated in a black aluminum wheelchair. Elias suffered a long-term disability and was able to walk with crutches, but around the house he preferred the chair. After decades of making accommodations in the walking world, Elias fused his incapacity with his identity. His upper body consisted of a pair of powerful arms on a great barrel chest, beneath which the dangling legs seemed too small. A paunch rode up over his belt to fill his shirt.

Cousin Elias had lived alone most of his life. His apartment consisted of four small rooms with low ceilings, hollow walls, and plywood doors. In one or two corners stood a piece of old furniture handed down from an ancestor. The humble setting did not flatter the antiques. Still, Elias was a superior caretaker of information. Bookshelves lined the walls, filing cabinets jammed closets, and in his study papers spilled out of their drawers.

For many years Elias had studied South Carolina history; he did not have a teaching career but published articles in small journals. When a railroad spur was planned to traverse Limerick plantation, an old Ball place, he got a commission from the government to write a historical survey. He was keenly interested in such subjects as the first (failed) attempt to colonize the Carolinas, made in the 1560s by France.

In the family of his father, the Bulls, Cousin Elias claimed another old Carolina clan, though in the eyes of some history buffs a suspicious cloud hung over that group. In the late 1700s, when South Carolina was still a British colony, one of Elias's paternal ancestors, William Bull, rose to become governor, a position he held on and off for nine years. When the American Revolution stirred, Bull had the misfortune of being in office. He tried to fight the uprising but went down with the English and eventually moved back to London. Ever since, a traitorous mist had enveloped the Bull kinspeople left in America.

Cousin Elias and I started by going over the contours of the Ball story, beginning in 1698 with Elias Ball's arrival on Comingtee plantation.

"We always called him Red Cap because of that little red cap he wore to hide his bald head," said Elias. "The Balls are noted for being bald-headed." He let out a guttural laugh, and his belly shook. The laugh, a deep, hoarse caw with rough edges around a baritone middle, filled the room.

Among his American descendants, Elias Ball is known affectionately as "Red Cap." The nickname came from a piece of clothing that he donned when he had enough money to commission his portrait, in the 1740s, when he was nearly seventy. In the portrait, Elias is old and rich, his belly large from abundant dinners. He wears a white scarf, dark vest, and collarless jacket, and his face, heavy with jowls, carries an expression of supreme confidence. On his large head is his signature red velvet hat, evidently covering the baldness of his later years.

"I've got some of the same genes myself," said Elias, touching his brow. I liked his irreverence; he did not seem to venerate the old emblems of family pride.

Elias Bull was not bald, however, but had thick, short hair, the hairline merely pulled back an inch from the brow. His hair was gray around the temples and still dark on top. The face beneath his broad forehead contained exaggerated features. Elias had large bushy eyebrows, and deep, sensitive, watery eyes that contained hidden reaches and thoughts. His heavy bags sagged down, drooping on their way to a pair of great jowls, the skin finally landing on the banks of a huge jaw. Elias's jaw and mouth dominated his face. It was a wide, capacious mouth, with thin lips, and the mouth was made more grand by the voice that emerged from it.

"You've heard the joke about the plantation folk?" Elias asked. "What do Charlestonians and the Chinese have in common?" His eyes glinted. "Both grow rice and worship their ancestors!"

Elias had a deep and cavernous voice, with a floor of gravel. His accent had a strong upcountry pitch, because his father and grandfather had been cotton farmers in a town called Stateburg, far inland from the port city of Charleston. Upcountry, the plantation crop was cotton, while toward the coast, with its tidal rivers, the old staple had been rice. Among white people, the upcountry accent differed from the coastal and Charleston brogue. Inland, the vowels seemed to emerge from the nose. Downstate, they shifted to the front of the mouth. The locale of Elias's childhood was imprinted in his voice. Yankees would call it a drawl, but in local terms it was simply more cotton than rice.

Our talk of Red Cap turned to the Ball family coat of arms.

"Red Cap was not entitled to that coat of arms," said Elias, referring to a family emblem we both knew well. He grew serious. "The English code is that the coat holds to the oldest son."

I nodded at Elias, sharing this apparent secret. When I was a child, in addition to baseball gloves and favorite jackets, I held on to two copies of the family crest, printed on old paper in black, red, and gold. The Ball coat of arms consisted of a shield, like that used in medieval jousting, topped with an eyeless metal helmet. On the shield, suspended against a field of red, appeared three black balls, each with a tongue of flame on the top. The red field was cut in two by a gray chevron, an inverted *V*. Underneath came the inscription "Ball family of Devonshire."

The emblem had a mysterious aura. It seemed to represent some long-ago and unknowable deed, probably soaked in blood, that involved swords and the clank of armored boots on the floor of a castle. As a child, I was lifted by the knowledge that this deed had something to do with me. I took it for granted that the Ball coat of arms and its train of glory, or murder, or castle building, had somehow been carried over to America and conferred on our mayonnaise-eating family. Cousin Elias told me that this was not so.

"The coat holds to the oldest son," Elias repeated. We both knew that Red Cap, the Ball immigrant to America, was a last son. That meant that the use of the family arms by the American clan presented, at best, something of a fraud. Elias and I nodded our heads up and down gravely.

"Here is the standard British heraldry." Elias drew back in his wheelchair, brought his hand to his face, and pointed a finger at the air.

"Let's say there were four sons," he began. "The first is entitled to the coat of arms—as is. Okay. The next son usually goes into the army or navy. Well, he gets a half-moon. All right. The next son is either military or clergy, and he receives a star. And the fourth son would get, for his coat of arms, a martlet. A martlet is a little bird, which, according to myth, has to be on the wing, because it has no feet. In other words, the fourth son inherited nothing."

In addition to the existence of the coat of arms, there was the matter of its imagery—black balls on a red field. The balls were an embarrassment, because they seemed to represent our peculiar name.

"Those cannonballs are not because of the name," said Elias, straightening the crooked past. "No, the Ball family coat of arms has three flambeaux. They are like cannonballs, only they have a tongue of fire coming out of them. What those things were, you use a catapult to throw them into the enemy's sails in order to set them on fire. The flambeaux represented military attack, from seafaring people, which is what you would expect from the Balls of Devonshire, on the English

Channel. And the gray chevron in the middle, the chevron means hospitality."

Our conversation moved back to the plantation story. Red Cap died in 1751, leaving behind many descendants and more than a hundred slaves. By that time the importation of Africans into South Carolina had begun to peak. Charleston was the most populous city in the British colonies south of Philadelphia, with a large black majority.

"Charleston was the South," said Elias. "There wasn't any other South. It dominated Georgia. North Carolina was nothing—never was anything. Virginia had no real towns, just little villages. The South was here, Charleston."

As we talked, I felt that Elias shared my interest in the lives of the slaves. He knew the family story had little to do with the coat of arms —that the Ball rice farms were no resorts but large and efficient work camps.

"Life on the plantations," I said, bringing the subject into the room.

"All right," said Elias.

"About how many slaves worked on each place?"

"That question cannot be answered," said Elias. "It depends on the size of your rice fields. A large part of them didn't work. They were too old and were supported, or they were too young and didn't work. So really you are only using about a third of the labor force. If you have one hundred slaves, only thirty of them worked. The others were supported, and those people were never sold. The plantation owners had to support them. If they didn't, they were through. The burden was accepted as part of life."

I admired Elias, because he spoke easily of the old days, but I wondered about his figures. One-third of the slave population at work seemed low. Older people were not sold, perhaps—they had no economic value; no one would buy them—but children usually carried water or food by the time they could run, and were sent to the fields by age twelve.

"Rice planting, they say, was easier for 'em than cotton," Elias continued. "Because the slaves had their task—generally one or two acres to be tilled in a day. After they were through with that, then they could take their gun out and go hunting. A lot of them had guns. People say, 'Oh, slaves with guns, how terrible!' They get all wound up over this business. But on the plantation, a lot of the slaves had guns."

This was the first I heard of guns in the hands of slaves. Were the plantations a more trusting place than some legends would have them?

"There were no slave uprisings!" Elias barked. "When the Civil War broke out, the white men went off to fight. There were no uprisings then! Life went on!"

Elias laughed his baritone laugh and waved his hand, dismissing the idea that there was discontent among the slaves. He exaggerated, yet he raised a real question. How did slavery continue for so long, nearly 250 years in English-speaking America? Why were there so few slave revolts? His implication was clear: the Ball slaves resigned themselves to their predicament.

"I knew a black woman who got a pension because her father fought beside his master in the Civil War," said Elias, wrapping up his case.

Of all the Ball family, Elias seemed to be the most curious, and passionate, about life before the Civil War. His grandfather had fought for the Confederacy, and I had the feeling that Elias had one foot planted in those days, even though they had ended long before his birth.

"How did the Balls treat their slaves?" I asked.

"Apparently very well," came the answer. "They were quite fond of them. There is the story that after the Balls left Comingtee plantation, some of them went back up to visit. The slaves turned out—I mean the former slaves—and said, 'Oh, the maussas is back!' They greeted the Balls with open arms! They gave them eggs and I don't know what all. It was very affectionate."

The "maussas" were the master and his family.

"The boredom was the biggest thing that hit them," said Elias, meaning the Ball family. "People don't realize, with the plantations, that they are so far apart, if somebody came to visit, they had to stay for at least two weeks. How lonely it was! They might not see another white person for six months. And nobody they could associate with, nobody. You did not associate with your overseer, and definitely not with your slaves."

Elias lifted his large chin, then tilted it back down.

"But kids were kids," he picked up. "The white children, the only people they could play with were the black children. Your son of the white owner usually had a friend that was raised with him, a black friend, and they were inseparable."

"It was lonely for the white people?" I asked.

"The slaves weren't the people who got lonely, because they had each other," said Elias. "The poor white people were the ones who were lonely there."

"They had it hard," I said.

"Yeah," answered Elias.

"You see, the overseer was not your equal," he continued. "He was a hireling. In most of America, you don't have the caste and class system. But you still have it here." Elias waved in the direction of the window. "And there are certain people you just don't associate with," he went on. "You definitely don't associate with any blacks. If you did, you've had it. You don't go to their homes and they sure as blazes don't come to yours, unless they are maids."

"What about the tradition of masters sleeping with their women slaves?" I asked.

"If the neighbors found out about it, he's had it," said Elias, without blinking. "It also undermined his authority. The same thing you find today. If a man is sleeping with his secretary, guess who runs the office? He'd best move on, and quick. I don't know of any Ball folklore about the men sleeping with their slaves. There is no record of what they did, because they didn't keep records of that. The Balls were pretty stodgy."

Elias's full laugh, from the belly, filled the room.

It was true, there were no records. But there was oral tradition. Families of color had stories of the white ancestor, or ancestors. Sometimes they knew who it was, sometimes not. If I was lucky, I might be able to find one such family. Surely there was, somewhere, a black clan with a bloodline that led to a Ball bedroom.

"If I went up to the area where the plantations once stood," I said, "I would probably find people living there, black people, descended from slaves who worked on the plantations."

"The settlement is called—I can't remember the name of the little settlement—it's on Hardscrabble Road or one of them," said Elias.

I concentrated on his face, chin and jowls, as Elias's mind rolled back over time. He seemed to be looking for a single fact among a thousand others.

"It's still there, the Ball Negroes still live there. I was there a long time ago," he said. "It has nice little houses scattered here and there and yonder."

Elias said that near Comingtee plantation was the village settled by

former Ball slaves. For a minute, he could not remember the name of
the place, then suddenly it came to him.

"The village where the Ball Negroes lived in, it's called Sawmill!"
he shouted. "I think it's on Hardscrabble Road. You go there and ask
them where is Sawmill, they can tell you."

A simple clue, and obvious, but only Elias, with his appetite for the
story, knew it. After the Civil War, some of the freedpeople picked up,
carried their belongings off the plantation, resettled together, and built
a community. I decided I would look for the village of Sawmill.

Family memory flows more completely through women. It is the women
who learn much of the lore and who convey it to the young. Men forget
the past in all its fleshiness and select which parts best fit into their
lives.

Dorothy Dame Gibbs was marinated in Ball family lore. On Thanks-
giving Day 1932, she married John E. Gibbs, whose mother was Anne
Simons Ball. From her mother-in-law, "Miss Annie" Ball, and from the
rest of the Balls, Dorothy soaked up the past. Anne Ball's father, John
Coming Ball, once owned much land and many slaves up and down the
Cooper River. By the 1930s, when Dorothy appeared, two places were
left, Hyde Park and Middleburg. The old plantation society was nearly
extinct, but breathing loud death rattles.

Dorothy rose into the air in front of me, first slowly, then with increasing speed. The seat of her upholstered chair levitated, lifting her
up and pushing her forward.

"This is my launch pad," she chuckled, ascending toward the ceiling. In a moment she stood on her feet, stooping forward in what was
nearly a bent-over position. Dorothy, nearly ninety, leaned because her
spine could no longer straighten.

Despite her years and her stoop, Dorothy still had a grip on life.
Beneath her white hair, she had a pair of bright, tolerant, amused eyes
that looked at me expectantly, as though she hoped I might drop a
devious remark. The motorized elevator chair helped Dorothy to get up
and down. The upholstered seat stood aloft in the air where she had
left it, like a hand waving. She went into the kitchen, produced an
elegant cup and saucer, and presented me with a cup of coffee. Then

she made her way back to her chair. She eased her behind onto the cushion and allowed the device to lower her slowly into the chair.

"Sometimes my chair frightens people," she said, her eyes laughing.

We sat in the corner of a small living room in her apartment at a retirement home. The apartment's rooms overflowed with furniture and pictures, photo albums and memorabilia, distilled from a large house in Charleston where Dorothy had lived for some sixty-five years. At one end of the living room, a window looked out onto a patio and lawn. White- and blue-haired women moved silently across the grass.

Dorothy reminded me how we were related.

"Your great-grandfather, Isaac Ball, was a cousin of Maria Louisa Gibbs, who was the mother of John Coming Ball, the father of Anne Simons Ball, my mother-in-law," Dorothy said.

It was the familiar haiku of Charleston genealogy. Dorothy traced the gnarled pattern of marriage and begetting in a single adept sentence. Dorothy's white hair fell just under her ears, and her blue-patterned dress ended below the knee. The lines on her face were deep and welcoming, and her mouth hung slightly ajar, ready to laugh at the right remark.

"John Coming Ball was the owner of Middleburg," Dorothy began, referring to her husband's forebear. "He was an orphan   his father died in 1852, when the boy was about four, leaving a widow and the one child. So he had some patrimony, some money."

The story started like others I knew. An inheritance of a plantation and slaves that went to a four-year-old.

"He was a minor during the War Between the States, he was sixteen or something," Dorothy continued. "He could have enlisted, but he was the only son of a widowed mother, so he was not allowed to go. He had executors or trustees taking care of his money. Well, he came through the war with some money. After it was over, John Coming Ball took this and bought Middleburg. By that time, he was twenty-four. Then he bought all the plantations on one side of the Cooper River all the way down to Cainhoy. That was The Blessing, Cedar Hill, and Halidon Hill. In some ways, his money was a disadvantage, because nobody else had it, and some people resented it. A lot of people plain didn't like him."

Dorothy giggled. She gave me a collaborating look. I knew something about John Coming Ball, reputed to be sour and purse-proud. He was said to have preferred a one-horse rig, with a gleaming white buggy, and to carry a riding crop. From up in the buggy chair, he could easily talk over the heads of the sharecroppers who walked alongside.

"Middleburg was actually always in the family, by different names —first by the Simons family, then the Lucas family, and finally the Balls. Most of the rice planters up the Cooper River were intermarried and first cousins ad infinitum. There were Balls, Porchers, Stoneys, Heywards, Hugers, and Bryans, and they were all related."

Dorothy sat perfectly still. She did not have many hand gestures, apparently because all of her energies went into her eyes and mouth. She began to tell me more about John Coming Ball, how he lost a house because it was paid for with Confederate money, and how he once gave plantations to his two daughters as Christmas presents. I liked this kind of storytelling, but I wanted to get over to the black side of the business.

"There was a man," I began, "whom I found in the plantation records, named Scipio." The Roman name Scipio appeared often among Ball slaves. It was first given to male children by their owners, later adopted by black parents.

"Yes, I knew a Scipio at Middleburg," Dorothy came back. "The Scipio I knew was grown when I came along. Maybe your Scipio was him."

I was struck by the turn of conversation. Dorothy was the rare white who knew stories about individual colored people.

"They would give Latin names to these people," she continued. "Most of the white people's education revolved around the classics, Latin and Greek. The Latin words were familiar, and those were the names they would give these people, because they ran out of names like James, and John, and Isaac. All of the classical names. Catullus . . . Julius . . . Caesar . . . Caesar was very common."

Dorothy described plantation life as well as she might have outlined her mother's face. Scipio was a slave whom I had seen in the records of Comingtee plantation, the Ball homestead, and now Dorothy told me about a Scipio she had known when she was a young woman. As I absorbed this fact, another unusual reality broke in my mind. In her youth, Dorothy would have known people who had been former Ball slaves.

"There's a story about Scipio," Dorothy continued. "Sometimes visitors from the North came to see the Balls, and they would be very critical of the situation, of slavery. Well, when that happened, the Ball master is said to have called one of the little Negro boys up to the house, Scipio. Mr. Ball would say to the visitor from New England, 'No, we treat them well, and we even educate them.'

"Mr. Ball would call up Scipio, and make him recite—I think it was Horace—in Latin," Dorothy said. "Just as a joke. Of course, Scipio didn't have the slightest idea what he was saying. Maybe he was reciting *Carpe Diem*, I don't know. So the little boy would recite *Carpe Diem* word for word, much to the astonishment of the person from New England, who would say, 'I didn't know you did that.' " Dorothy giggled, and her eyes darted. She had told the story many times, and it still made her laugh.

"Scipio would learn Horace by rote?" I asked.

"Yes, he didn't have any more idea of what he was talking about than I would know if I had recited Sanskrit," she said. "Of course, they really didn't get any education. It was a joke to Mr. Ball."

I smiled and shook my head from side to side, did my best to put a brightness in my eyes to match her own.

"One thing that bothers me is the way Northerners are so critical of the South—of its customs and manners and speech, and everything else," she continued. "Mostly they think a lot of misconceptions about us. They think we're lazy, we're slow, and we're unfair to the Negroes. On the contrary, we lean over backwards where the Negroes are concerned. I never had a hundred dollars in my life that some Negro didn't get in jail and I had to get him out. And yet the Northerners love us so. They think we are interesting and charming. The Southern girls are belles of the ball when they go North."

Dorothy had been something of a belle in her youth, though she took an unusual path for her generation. Dorothy Dame attended the College of Charleston, from which she graduated in 1926. Soon she got a job as a junior reporter, writing for the *Charleston News and Courier*.

"I was the first woman reporter the newspaper ever had," she said. "I covered culture—like arts and museums, and schools and education. I also covered some sports, like basketball. We went to work at noon, and stayed until the paper went to bed at midnight or one o'clock in the morning."

That Dorothy was a reporter in the 1920s, and wrote about basketball, set her slightly apart from other Charleston ladies. And her instinct for getting the story had spilled over to the plantation past.

"There was quite a difference in the Negroes who were imported as slaves," Dorothy told me. "There was a country from which slaves were brought where the people were physically attractive, and they had no body odor. And they were more intelligent. And they were selected as house servants. I don't know—is it Angola? I've forgotten.

"The servants that my mother had were from that group of people," she continued. "They were very intelligent, and, as I said, they had no body odor, which was very peculiar. These people were fairly light-skinned, not with a mixture of white blood, but naturally light. I knew that the buyers of Africans, in the eighteenth century, preferred some cultures of origin over others. I did not know that these preferences lived on in my own lifetime."

The phone rang, and Dorothy answered it. In a moment she put it down and returned to the subject.

"The other group," she continued, "they were real coal-black, and usually bullet-headed. They were round-headed, and hard-headed, too. They had tremendous, big strong bodies that suited them for work in the field. There is a Negro who comes to see me, who is six foot two, and weighs about three hundred pounds. He is like that, a great big ham of a man. I swear he could put a hundred-pound sack of rice on each shoulder and dance. And he's got hands that would cover my two. Anyhow, the ones who worked in the field had a terrible, strong, pungent body odor. You could hardly stay in the room with them."

Dorothy seemed to have a sensual memory of the plantations, everything clear, right down to racial categories. In a moment, her eyes became a little distant.

"Of course, it can work in reverse," she said. "I never realized that until I went to Japan. I was in public here and there, and I noticed that the Japanese would move away from us. I think they found that we had a body odor that was offensive to them."

In Dorothy's telling, white folks and black were like two tribes, living side by side. Or rather, there was one tribe on our side and several different ones on the other.

"During slavery, it was a community of interest," Dorothy continued. "One couldn't get along without the other. The Negroes couldn't live without the support of the white people. The white people couldn't live without the labor of the Negroes."

"As though there were two hands, left and right, and one could not work without the other," I said.

"The Negroes considered themselves part of the community," Dorothy answered. "They considered the Balls their family. They would have been insulted to be told their interests were not those of the Ball family."

It was lunchtime. I intended to leave, but Dorothy asked me to eat with her. After a moment with the motorized chair, we made our way to the dining room of the retirement home.

The room resembled a large bistro, with starched tablecloths and uniformed waitresses. There were about seventy-five tables, surrounded by dark wooden chairs with green-and-white-striped upholstery. We sat down, then ordered lunch from a black waitress.

"Just like white people, slaves could be very different," said Dorothy. "Some were very responsible, and some were no more responsible than birds in a tree. Some were born not very bright. A Negro woman might be a seamstress if she was smart and of the tribe that was suitable for housework. Then there would be a woman who would be a specialist in certain kinds of cooking. There were nurses, with some women skilled in medical things. Over all of them was the mistress, Mrs. Ball. The mistress usually had to know how to do everything—how to weave in the days that they wove, to sew, and be able to teach the young ones the same. She knew the right way to take care of furniture, and silver, and brass."

Dorothy's mother-in-law, Miss Annie Ball, was evidently just such a woman.

"The women worked hard, the white women," Dorothy continued. "Sometimes they would be in bed, and they would check the names of the slaves off, counting them out the window as they were going to the field. Mrs. Ball was still lying in bed. Then she would get up, and she would go to her work."

"How did the Ball family treat their slaves?" I asked.

"I think most of the slave owners were responsible, good people," she answered. "There were horrible things that happened, but I think they are more the exception than the rule. In our family that I know of, I think the slaves were well treated, well cared for. I think the Balls would have been very upset if there were any beatings of Negroes on their plantations."

This may have been what Dorothy had been told, but numerous records in the Ball family papers showed otherwise. When a Ball master was away, his overseer often wrote him letters to report on life at the farm. One overseer at Comingtee plantation in the 1830s, Thomas Finklea, did not hesitate to let Mr. Ball know when he whipped a worker, or had him "flogd," as he put it. Other records showed payments the Balls made to the Charleston Work House. The Work House, a brick prison that once stood at the edge of town, on the southwest corner of Magazine and Logan streets, was a city-owned building where a civil servant administered floggings for a fee. The Work House was used by slave owners who wished to punish their workers when in Charleston. The contract beatings ensured that the master did not dirty his trousers with blood. Like most of their friends, the Balls took advantage of the service and left notes to that effect in their account books. But Dorothy had no way of knowing this.

"I know that time and time again the Balls refused to separate families," she continued. "The only time they would want to sell Negroes, slaves, was when there was a death in the family and the estate would have to be settled in some way. But according to wills and according to stories I've heard, they were always very careful, even at a loss to themselves, to keep families together, and not to take children away. That was simply the disposition of the clan, the Ball clan."

In the archives of the State of South Carolina, in the city of Columbia, there were receipts for slave purchases made by the Balls, but there were also receipts for slaves sold by the family. These were fewer in number than the purchases, but they existed nevertheless, showing that people were in fact sold away from home, one at a time. It did not happen often, not every week or even every year, but it happened.

"My impression is that a good deal of consideration was given to the personal needs of the slaves as people," Dorothy said. "That was because the Balls were all fairly kindly people. Maybe they were ideal, or maybe I just heard the good things, I don't know. That's perfectly possible, you know. You know, families very seldom admit wrongdoing."

The room was full of people eating lunch. All of us who were seated had skin more or less the color of old paper. A salad came and was placed in front of me by a black hand.

SLAVES IN THE FAMILY · 57

I asked Dorothy whether she knew anything about the names people took.

"That's interesting," she replied, unblinking. "Often, Negroes, their biological father would give their name to his child. But they lived like animals, you know. Very seldom did a man and woman live together, even as common-law husband and wife. They were actually like tomcats. And so the names become confused. They changed names in a very confusing way."

"Why did they change their names so much?"

"Why do Negroes do anything?" Dorothy asked. "That's a different culture, and you're doing very well if you can learn what their culture is. You can't explain it all."

"I don't think black folks have a hard time understanding white people," I said.

"I don't think they do, so much," said Dorothy. "Somehow or other they are privy to almost all that white people do. White people have no secrets from Negro servants. Negroes have a lot of secrets from us. One reason the names get so confused is really—more consideration is given to breeding farm animals than to Negroes. They live and cohabit with anybody that suits them."

"Are you talking about two hundred years ago?" I asked.

"I'm talking about any time, right on down now to today," Dorothy answered.

"On the subject of tomcats," I said, "how common was it for slave owners to go to bed with their slaves?"

"Well, there were mulattoes, and quadroons. You don't use those words anymore, because most people don't know what they mean," Dorothy said. "In places like New Orleans, there used to be arrangements for young men to find a companion, a mulatto or quadroon woman. That was the French invention. The English would not do that. Whatever the English did, they would not organize it. Undoubtedly the miscegenation happened sometimes. It happened less in South Carolina than it did in Virginia. In Virginia, the Negroes are well adulterated."

"Thomas Jefferson was said by some to have had a long relationship with Sally Hemings, a woman to whom he had title on his plantation, Monticello," I said.

"Yes, that was because Jefferson's wife made him promise not to marry again," said Dorothy, rolling with the subject. "I don't know why she did, because she was a widow when she married him. She tied him up with a promise not to marry again after she died, which she did. And he took this concubine as a result. That was a fact."

"Did the Ball slaves sleep with their masters?" I asked.

"I never heard anything of that. And I don't think anybody else has even thought about it. There was a close intimacy in the households between whites and blacks, but very little cohabitation."

I did not believe I would hear many reports from the white side about whether Ball men slept with their slaves, so I let the subject drop.

"The fight against segregation in schools, I don't know if it was right or not," Dorothy continued. "I think the white children have to remain separate socially from Negroes. Otherwise you end up in marriages, sooner or later. Theoretically they should not be separated, but practically sometimes it worked better."

"What is wrong with intermarriage?" I asked.

"I don't know that I can even answer that. To me it is so repugnant—so awful—that I just can't accept it. Perhaps my views are Anglo-Saxon, I don't know. The French have always ignored the color line, always intermarried."

Dorothy went on, "Do you know the term 'brass ankle'? It's not a word you mention in polite society. Just like the word 'nigger'—nobody uses that anymore. I haven't heard that word in fifty years. A brass ankle was a mixed-blood person—Indian, Negro, and white. Three different people. They lived in the country, and had ankles that shined because of the mixture."

"I think we have two opposing myths," I said. "One is the myth of the gentle master. The other is the story of the rivers of blood that flowed from slavery. Where is the truth?"

"I don't know that you will ever find out," said Dorothy. "I think slavery was morally wrong. It always has been. It was wrong in Bible times, but it existed. The people who profited most from them were the slave traders. They persecuted them, and profited by them, and took no responsibility for them. They didn't care how many dead bodies they threw overboard on the voyage here. Slavery was accepted all over the world, from Bible times on. In the Bible, they speak of slavery as an ordinary thing. Wasn't it Benjamin who was sold into slavery in Egypt, and rescued by his brother Joseph? Throughout the Old Testament it was accepted, and nobody thought of it as being wrong or troublesome. People in the United States were probably the first group to consider the morality of slavery."

In Dorothy's view, the Americans had much to be proud of. The first stirrings of the antislavery movement occurred about the time of the American Revolution. A little earlier in England, however, a few writers and barristers raised a protest against the slave trade that was run out of the cities of Liverpool and Bristol.

"Slavery ended because there was a change in the religious idea, all over the world," continued Dorothy. "You simply cannot convince a Yankee that the Civil War was not fought over slavery. It was fought over states' rights. See, the Russians had slaves up until the time of the Great War, in 1914. But all over the world there was a change of attitude—just as there has been a change of attitude toward women and children. When I was a child, women and children were like chattels. Up until the time I was a child, a woman owned no property. She couldn't control herself."

The idea that all women were once like the black population on the plantations fit nicely into Dorothy's conversation, like a minor chord inserted briefly into a major-key concerto.

The dining room was beginning to empty out. Waitresses cleared the tables, and elderly people moved slowly out of the room.

"Where do you think the former slaves went?" I asked.

"Well, it was a terrible and irresponsible thing to free slaves without providing for them," said Dorothy. "When freedom came, the white people realized that it was not an open door to success and happiness and safety. White people knew that there was going to be pandemonium, and it was. The Negroes were taken advantage of by unscrupulous strangers, and they were taken advantage of by each other. They were terribly dishonest and cruel to each other. To this day they are not accustomed to taking care of themselves.

"After the Civil War, I think many of them stayed, or kept up with the Ball family," she went on. "Then many of them began heading north along the East Coast. They would drop off at Washington, or Philadelphia. Some of them got as far as New York."

Perhaps in Dorothy's youth, the children of the Ball slaves remained in touch with the Balls, but no longer. I had asked around the family, and no such people could be found. There were no "faithful mammies" whose families went back to the days before freedom and who continued to work for the Balls.

I mentioned that I was looking for some of the families of the descendants.

"I think that's great," Dorothy replied. "They may say they were not well treated. All I know is that they were well treated. You may get the word that they were not. I would be surprised, because I don't think it's been characteristic of the whole Ball clan to act with anything less than kindness to other people."

Despite her familiarity with the old days, Dorothy had no special clues to where the families of the former slaves might be found.

I thanked her for lunch. Later, as we said good-bye, her eyes got a thoughtful look. She paused to give me one final opinion.

"It's strange," Dorothy mused. "In the old days, there was no feeling of restraint or embarrassment when Negroes and whites were together. Now if you attend a Negro wedding or funeral, even if you are invited, you feel a little uneasy. You don't know whether people are really welcoming you or not."

In hopes of sharing the task of finding the descendants of the slaves, I talked with other older relatives. Ten or fifteen kin had reached their late seventies or eighties. They were the keepers of family lore, and the Ball name was one of their prized possessions.

Among the cadre of elders was a cousin whom I will call Fitzpatrick Ball. Fitz, in his late seventies, had been first cousin to my father. Fitz's father and my father's father were brothers. To me, Fitz was a first cousin once removed.

Cousin Fitz was trim, vigorous, and charming, and wore his advancing age lightly. He had a ruddy face and a good shock of white hair. Unlike the majority of the family, Fitz had a portion of Scotch-Irish ancestry, which, some said, played a role in his personality. Many of the Balls had a phlegmatic temperament, but Cousin Fitz was alert and quick of speech. He had a jocular style of conversation, and knew the family lore intimately.

During the Second World War, Cousin Fitz had been in the service, as had my father. Fitz was fond of telling me a story about Dad from the war. In the middle of the war, Fitz and Dad found themselves together on furlough in San Francisco, far from the palmetto trees and old streets of their upbringing in Charleston. Dad, who was a bit older, had been in California for a while and had the use of a car, a good luxury for a soldier. He also possessed a booklet full of fuel ration coupons, a precious necessity. San Francisco was overrun with enlisted men, said Fitz. It was also packed with barrooms, and women who made their living from the soldiers. The details were always blurred, but Fitz wanted me to know that night after long night, Dad and he caroused the port town. After the war Cousin Fitz attended medical school and became a physician in Charleston, with a long career.

One day I called Fitz to ask for a particular piece of help. I was not prepared for his reaction.

"I don't want to have anything to do with this!" he yelled into the phone. "That was a brutal period, the time of slavery, yes," he said, breathing hard. "But there's nothing that anybody—not you or me or anyone else—can do about it!"

"If the past was, as you say, brutal, isn't it better to talk about it than to remain silent?" I answered.

"What you are doing can only cause trouble!" he came back. "This will court anger, and it will divide people!"

I had always admired Cousin Fitz. He was a doctor with a record of helping people, and I had no desire to contradict him.

"I think the way you are going about this thing is provocative," he continued. "It will produce dissension, or worse. You know, in my lifetime, there have been race riots!"

For Cousin Fitz, the trouble was not the legacy of the plantation. He thought the subject of slavery no longer had any importance, and it was even out of our power to make sense of it. The problem we had to worry about, Fitz believed, was the pathology of other people on the subject of race.

I said mildly, "There are people in the family who support what I'm doing, younger people."

"Just what I thought!" Cousin Fitz exploded. "That it would be the younger generations who think this thing is positive. That's just what I was afraid of!"

Somewhere along the way, Fritz had heard that I was interested in the subject of white-black sex. This was the last thing he could tolerate, and suddenly it leaped to his mind.

"This business," he said, sputtering, "this suggestion of some sort of copulation between the slave owners and the slaves—that's provocative! You'll lose control of it!"

Fitz exhausted himself, and fell silent. I made no effort to speak, because I felt he would hear no defense.

"I'm sorry," he said quietly. "I don't want anything to do with it."

Earlier, I had spoken with younger relatives and tested their feelings. One cousin in her thirties, who lived in Buffalo, New York, offered strong encouragement. Another cousin, a realtor in Charleston with whom I had spent time when we were growing up, also urged me to continue. A third cousin had gone to work as a schoolteacher in an all-black school. She took me aside and told me not to stop for any reason.

Within the Ball family, the plantation stories functioned like a giant self-portrait. I was making a new painting that might change the look of the past. I talked to close and distant cousins, old and young, at churches, dinners, and picnics. In general, the oldest generation worried that I wanted to alter the family story; it was plain in their eyes. People in middle age seemed ambivalent, at times curious and at other times apparently fearful. Many of the young adults offered support, secretly or out loud.

There was also a difference of opinion between the sexes. The women in the family seemed considerably less nervous about my inquiry than the men. This included both women born with the Ball name and those who took it on with marriage.

After I talked with Fitz, I contacted another older cousin, a retired gentleman with a melodious name. I will coarsen it a bit and call him Bennett. Cousin Bennett Ball was a businessman in his eighties, with horn-rimmed glasses and a gentle voice. He had attended Harvard Business School, but that was long ago, and he betrayed no evidence of having acquired Northern manners.

"I just don't want to get involved," he said quietly. "I knew your father when we were growing up. I had such good family relations with him and your grandfather. I just want to keep it that way."

There was a strange tone in Bennett's voice that I could not immediately name. His speech had the sound of resignation. Instead of expressing anger, Bennett reacted as though he had seen something large bearing down on him, inevitably, at a good speed. He only wanted to step aside.

"You're going about this thing differently from the way that I would," he said, simply. "And it doesn't mean I dislike you. It doesn't mean I'm not happy to have you as my cousin. I just don't understand why you're doing it the way you're doing it. I just don't want to get involved. You're a good cousin and I want it to stay that way."

I felt chagrined, as though I had mistakenly taken something from him. Bennett and I talked for a moment about Isaac Ball, my great-grandfather and Bennett's grandfather, who had fought in the Civil War. We traded a few details about Isaac's life. I laughed at a memory, Bennett laughed, and the pressure eased. Then his tone changed. Bennett was no longer laughing, and he was no longer resigned.

"My father didn't own slaves!" he snapped. "And my grandfather didn't own slaves. To do this is to condemn your ancestors! You're going to dig up my grandfather and hang him!"

4

BRIGHT MA

It was September, and overcast in Harlem. The clouds had the tin coating the city of New York gives the sky, and the summer heat had not yet been cleared from the air, which seemed to lie stagnant in the alleys, between the buildings. An aroma of grit rose from the surface of Malcolm X Boulevard, and in the thin light and old heat, the street smelled sharply.

On a visit to New York from my borrowed house in Charleston, I attended a meeting of a black genealogy group. The Afro-American Historical and Genealogical Society was founded in the 1970s by people who sought to uncover as much as they could of their family history. The group in New York had dealings with similar associations elsewhere—Chicago, Philadelphia, Washington, and some smaller towns. A rendezvous took place every month at a public library in Harlem.

I arrived on a Saturday morning at a squat brick building on a corner of Malcolm X Boulevard and found the meeting on the second floor. The room measured some twenty by thirty feet, and was low ceilinged, with fluorescent lights between suspended fiberglass panels. A brown table whose veneer felt like hard vinyl filled the center of the room. Lavender carpet covered the floor, and at one end of the space stood an old filing cabinet.

Around the table sat twenty women and five men, ages thirty to sixty-five. From earlier visits, I recognized everyone in the room except one woman, who sat next to me. I had joined the group in hopes of finding clues that might lead me to the descendants of Ball slaves. Although most of us had both European and African ancestors, I was the only member of the organization who did not live under the sign "black."

Dance music drifted into the room from a radio on the street, and a gentleman in oxford shoes and khaki trousers stood up to close the window. The meeting began as it always did, with introductions, as each of us stated our name and the nature of our genealogical research. I reminded the gathering that I was attempting to locate families who had come from the Ball plantations in South Carolina, that I was a descendant of the owners of those plantations, and that I hoped to find out what became of a few of the families formerly enslaved by my ancestors. Polite nods bobbed throughout the room, acknowledgment of the familiar. The one dissent came from the woman I did not recognize, who began to shake her head from side to side.

She sat on my left, at arm's length. She wore a beige jacket and skirt, gold-rimmed glasses, and had close-cropped natural hair, with touches of gray. Her skin was brown, her facial features smooth, her expression calm; with some uncertainty, I put her age at about forty-five. Staring at the purple carpet, the woman listened and continued to shake her head, left to right. Finally she spoke.

She said that she was on the way to see her grandchildren and had not intended to come to the genealogy meeting, but that some things were foreordained. She looked around the room, caught the gaze of others, but did not turn to me. The woman added that she was researching her family, who were from Moncks Corner, in Berkeley County, South Carolina. A gesture without a look came in my direction. She couldn't believe the coincidence, she said, but had to believe it.

In the end the woman preferred privacy, so I will call her Denise Collins—a name other than her own.

Denise Collins said that her mother used to talk about the Ball family, and that her great-grandmother, Katie Heyward, was in slavery on a Ball plantation.

All stayed quiet. It was as though we wanted to hold on to the moment, the recognition. Soon there was an exhalation of sighs, followed by a ripple of murmurs. I turned to look at Denise Collins and was greeted with her profile, because she continued to avoid my gaze.

When Denise Collins finally looked at me, I saw her as though through a frame and she glowed with an intense clarity. We stared at each other for an instant, mutterings and gestures around us.

We got up and went into the hall. It was cream-colored, featureless, and had an unpleasant echo. Denise Collins held out her hand, which trembled visibly. She looked at me with a light in her eyes, bewildered, her expression equal parts anguish and hope. I would like to have opened my arms to her. I would like to have spoken kind words, but I could not bring myself to say them.

As we stood in the dim hall, I realized that I had no credibiity with this outwardly gentle stranger. In her eyes, I might be no different from the person who had forced her mother's grandmother, Katie Heyward, into the fields. The evidence of my name was against me. I stammered a few words, but as I stood with Denise Collins, I knew that if I was to reach out to her family, and share something with them, I would have to earn the privilege of their copany.

A few days later the sun took only a small corner of the naked blue sky. It was an uncomfortably clear light. New York, on a fine day, can seem grotesque. On that blue afternoon, I visited Denise Collins and her family.

We met at Denise's apartment in Harlem. The building was a four-story brownstone in a row of identical houses put up in the late 1800s. Each building measured exactly twenty-five feet in width. When they were built, the brownstones housed single families, but they had long ago been broken into apartments, one or two per floor.

Denise Collins, quiet and watchful, met me at the door and led me inside. She was out of her business suit, and in pants and a shirt. I gave her flowers.

We entered her apartment at the top of a flight of stairs. The door opened into a living room with windows onto the backyard of the building. There was a small kitchen in the middle of the apartment, and two bedrooms down a short hallway in the front, facing the street. We sat in the living room, which was lightless, a typical New York apartment on a blazing day. There were two low sofas, a coffee table, plants by the window, and a fireplace. Two large boxes sat against the wall, one containing a new television, the other a new microwave oven.

Denise Collins looked in the direction of the appliances, said that she worked hard for a living, then she smiled for the first time.

I looked in the kitchen and saw a sign that she might smile again, because Denise had cooked a large dinner for my visit. The dishes were distributed in piles on the countertops—ham, macaroni, greens, potato salad, and a pie.

Denise Collins said that she had two grown daughters. As she arranged our table setting, Denise's movements were small and precise, her voice quiet. She either carried a load of worry or was unsure how to talk to me. Three children, ages four to eight, appeared from a bedroom. They were her grandchildren, Denise said. They were in for the afternoon while their mother, Denise's daughter, did errands. The children introduced themselves, disappeared, and soon I heard television in the next room.

The doorbell rang and Denise's cousins came into the apartment. They were siblings in their thirties and forties whom I will call Daniel and Carl Jenkins, using two more substitute names. Carl Jenkins, a stout man in a gray workshirt, had sensitive lines on his face and careful speech. Daniel Jenkins, a bit younger, had a sinewy frame and a bright, friendly manner. The brothers shared the same mahogany skin.

After introductions, we traded briefs on our lives. The cousins were raised in Queens, across the East River from Manhattan, and lived in New York suburbs. Denise was the only one who preferred Harlem. All three had jobs with the city or state, and all fit into the hardworking middle class. Denise worked for the New York Department of Transportation, in a computer training division. Daniel investigated insurance fraud in government medical programs. Carl worked for an agency that housed homeless people. Of all of us, Carl saw the most extreme New York. He spent his nights patrolling one of the largest homeless shelters in the country, at Bellevue Hospital on Manhattan's East Side, where nearly a thousand men came to the door every sundown.

There was little small talk. Carl led the conversation by naming the places in Africa from which people had been extracted. He pointed out that some slave ships on the way to South Carolina stopped in the Caribbean to sell people to the sugar plantations of the islands. Daniel wondered aloud whether the cotton slavery of Alabama and Mississippi had been worse than the rice slavery of South Carolina and Georgia. It probably had been more gruesome, I replied. The cotton planters went into business by buying people from the older slave states of Virginia and the Carolinas, then marching them in long coffles toward the Mississippi River and to virgin land.

Denise Collins sat quietly, listening to us measure the merits and demerits of different slaveries. Then she looked at me and emerged from her silence. Black history had been stolen, she said. Black culture had been robbed.

Denise Collins appeared to me to be a woman of beautiful sadness. Her eyes were windows of sorrow. When she spoke, I finally understood the nature of her quiet manner.

"They tried to steal it," I said, "but they didn't succeed. Listen to American music. Blues, jazz, and what they turned into. The only art forms the United States has given the world are black."

Denise answered that no, black history had been taken and destroyed, and that as a result black people were lost.

In a moment, Denise brought out a little booklet that resembled a corporate report. It ran to thirty pages, bore a date from the previous summer, and showed a title on the cover: "Heyward Family Reunion." A drawing of a tree appeared in the booklet, with the names of people, Denise's relatives, written in the branches. I opened to the first page and read paragraph one of the Heyward family story: "Our history began many years ago in a rural community near Moncks Corner, South Carolina. A slave named Binah, living on a Ball plantation, gave birth to a daughter, Katie, who was known lovingly as 'Bright Ma.' "

Denise said that after freedom Katie had become Katie Heyward, her mother's grandmother.

Daniel put in that the family was actually from a village called Cordesville, and that most of their dead were buried in a cemetery next to a Cordesville church. I knew the church, and the graveyard, because the village of Cordesville was a settlement near the oldest Ball plantation, Comingtee.

"A lot of people moved off the plantations to build a village," I said. "There was a sawmill where the young men worked." Denise replied that her mother had told her about the mill.

The sound of the television burst from the front of the apartment.

Denise's grandchildren wandered into the living room, trailing shouts. She quieted them, and sent them back.

Denise pointed out that the family did not know which plantation Katie came from, and Daniel and Carl nodded in agreement. The Heyward family history consisted of oral tradition. It was credible—I had little reason to doubt it—but there was no paper trail. Where did our stories cross?

From my bag I brought out a pile of photocopies, plantation records, and distributed them around the room. The records included a roster of slaves on Comingtee plantation and a two-hundred-page ledger documenting several other pieces of land. Each of us took a stack of records and began poring over it, looking for Katie and her mother, Binah.

The room fell silent as we scanned the names. Half an hour later, we had nothing—several women called Binah and one or two named Katie, but no link between them.

Then, from her own materials, Denise pulled out a copy of a page from the federal census of 1900, taken in the district that contained the village of Cordesville, South Carolina. (She had done her own rummaging in archives.) The census showed Katie Heyward and her son, Denise's grandfather. I took down the information. It was a lead I hoped might take me back to the plantation the Heywards called home.

Denise then gave me the name of an elderly cousin, her grandfather's niece, Katie Roper. Katie Roper was in her eighties, she said, and lived in South Carolina. She had been named after Katie Heyward, or Bright Ma. When she was a child, Denise added, Katie Roper knew Bright Ma. Maybe from somewhere in her memory, the old lady could tell a story about Bright Ma that would provide the missing link.

I returned to South Carolina, went to the archives, and dug through the Ball family papers. Soon I found the ancestors of Denise Collins. They appeared on birth lists of slaves and in correspondence between the Balls, some of which mentioned slaves in the lineage of Bright Ma. The family's link to the Balls spanned three generations and three different plantations.

The Heyward family story began on Limerick plantation. In March 1764 Elias Ball Jr., son of Red Cap, bought a tract known as Limerick, named after the hometown in Ireland of the land's first white tenant. The plantation had been operating since 1710. At 4,564 acres, it would become the largest piece of land in the Ball realm and, eventually, home to the greatest number of slaves on any of the family places. Limerick stood at the headwaters of the eastern branch of the Cooper River, about a day's trip by flatboat from the port at Charleston. After the Revolutionary War, Limerick came into the hands of Elias Ball III. A grandson of Red Cap, Elias III was born in 1752 and died in 1810. In his last years, Elias III fought swelling in his legs from gout. Elias III acquired a nickname that distinguished him in the family story I had heard from my father: Old Mas' 'Lias (Old Master Elias). The Balls borrowed this way of talking about a distinguished ancestor from the local black dialect, Gullah. Old Mas' 'Lias never married, trudged slowly with his swollen legs, and owned large numbers of people. So he was, in fact, an old master.

Sometime after the Revolution, a slave named Tenah appears in the Limerick records. In some cases it is possible to identify the ethnicity of African captives from the single name that survives on lists of slaves. "Tenah" (if pronounced Teh-nay) would be the English spelling for a girl's name common among the Mende in West Africa. The Mende lived in a region that would later encompass the nations of Guinea and Sierra Leone. The Revolutionary War disrupted things on Limerick, not least the paperwork, so I cannot say whether Tenah, or her parents, might have been the first to come from Africa. But it is quite possible that Tenah's culture of origin was among this clan; circumstantial evidence supports this conjecture. South Carolina slave owners bought many people enslaved in the region of Sierra Leone because of the captives' familiarity with rice and irrigation. More convincingly, Elias Ball III had an uncle, Henry Laurens, in the slave-trading business in Charleston. Laurens often received ships from a depot in the Sierra Leone River known as Bunce Island, where captives were held before being deported. In Charleston, Laurens did business with the Ball family, his in-laws, and Elias III would have bought people from his uncle's firm.

Based on the year Tenah began to have children at Limerick, I put the year of her birth at about 1780. Tenah had a brother at Limerick, a bit older, named Plenty, and their children evidently grew up side by side. An ordinary path would have taken them to work in the rice fields by age twelve or thirteen. To judge from their later lives, however, Tenah and Plenty seem to have come from a family of craftspeople. Blacksmiths, carpenters, seamstresses, and other trained workers lived somewhat apart from the majority of the field hands, who worked in gangs in the muddy rice plots.

By the first years of the 1800s, Tenah was in her early twenties and living with another Limerick slave, Adonis. Tenah and Adonis had one child, Scipio, their first of a long marriage; thirty years later, the couple still appeared on plantation lists together. Next door in the slave village lived Tenah's brother, Plenty. By this time, 1805, Plenty was a carpenter, a job that gave him high status among both blacks and whites.

Tenah's and Plenty's families were vigorous and valuable—at least, Old Mas' 'Lias saw them that way. In 1810, a month before he died, Elias III settled the division of his property. The owner of Limerick deeded his plantation and almost all of his human property to his nephew, a twenty-five-year-old bachelor, Isaac Ball. Elias III then singled out the families of Tenah and Plenty for a particular fate: they would go to Isaac's brother, John Ball Jr.

John Ball Jr. already owned Comingtee plantation. Perhaps the gift of a pair of slave families was simply a toss of the dying man's spoils, so that Isaac's brother would not feel left out. But whatever the reason, Elias III inserted the following little paragraph in his will, which altered the lives of nine people:

> I . . . give to my said nephew John Ball, the younger, for ever, my pew in the middle aisle of St. Philip's Church, Charleston, and two families of Negroes, to whit, Plenty (a carpenter), his wife Chloe & their three children, Nancy, Little Plenty & Cato, and Adonis & his wife Tenah with their two children, Scipio & August, & all the future issue & increase of the females.

Because Comingtee was a few miles downstream from Limerick, Tenah, Adonis, Plenty, Chloe, and their children packed, said good-bye to their village, and moved. At that time, Comingtee was home to more than one hundred black people, a family of overseers, and the family of John Ball Jr. At twenty-eight, John Jr. lived in the mansion with his three children, all under age six, and his twenty-six-year-old wife, Elizabeth, pregnant with another child.

Tenah's husband, Adonis, became an animal minder in the barnyard at Comingtee, where his specialty seems to have been pigeons. From time to time, Adonis would be asked to send some of his birds to Charleston, where they would be cooked and eaten in the Ball town-house when John Jr. was in town.

On September 8, 1815, Tenah and Adonis had another child, Binah. The common practice of parents in slavery, when they were able to control the names of their children, was to call newborns after one of the grandparents. In this case, "Binah" may well have been the name of Tenah's African mother. Like the name Tenah, Binah (if pronounced Beh-nay) can be read as the English rendering of a girl's name commonly used among people from the inland of Guinea and Sierra Leone.

On Comingtee in the 1820s, Tenah and Adonis were relatively priv-ileged people on the dirt slave street. Not many had the choice to use West African names, or to keep animals rather than work in the fields. Fortunate though they were, Tenah and Adonis sometimes felt the whip. On one occasion, in October 1827, Thomas Finklea, the overseer at Comingtee, noticed that two sheep were missing from the plantation herd. Making a search of the slave settlement, Finklea found suet in the house of a field hand named Daniel, and the bones of a sheep in the garden behind the cabin belonging to Tenah and Adonis.

"i think old Adonis assisted in the butcherry," Finklea wrote to John Ball Jr. in one of the weekly reports he sent when the master was away in Charleston. "i have had all flogd that live in that house whitch is Adonis Tenah & Linda & have had Daniel in limbo since munday morning & have him flogd morning & night to make him tell hue as-sisted in the butchery   it apears that he will not tell."

Tenah and Adonis were whipped for (allegedly) taking a bit of meat to add to their gruel of corn and greens. Daniel was beaten twice a day for a good stretch, but held his silence.

Another description from the period and place may help to convey what happened to Denise Collins's ancestors. In the early 1800s in Charleston, a white woman, Angelina Grimké, who was raised in a slave-owning family that kept a large upcountry plantation, decided that she could no longer put up with the violence that her family relied on for their comfort, and therefore left South Carolina permanently for the North. Grimké published essays about her youth, and in one, she de-scribed the wounds left by a flogging: "[T]he treatment of plantation slaves cannot be fully known, except by the poor sufferers themselves.

. . . One poor girl . . . showed me the deep gashes on her back—I might have laid my whole finger in them—large pieces of flesh had actually been cut out by the torturing lash."

There is a bitter joke, from some anonymous survivor of slavery, that makes light of the cruel absurdity of the slave's situation. One day, a slave stole a ham from the plantation storehouse and put it on his family's dinner table. Soon the slave was called to account for his master's stock of cured hams. When confronted with the evidence—a ham bone found in the trash pile—the slave made a great show of denying that he had stolen anything. The logic the thief offered could not be argued with. "We belong to the master," he said, "and the ham belongs to the master. I was just rearranging the property."

By 1830, two decades after they arrived at Comingtee, Tenah's children were grown, and had moved out of her cabin. Plenty was a widower, having lost his wife, Chloe. Chloe's daughter Nancy had grown up and gone to work at another plantation, leaving her father with one grown son, Cato, at home. In a few years, the old carpenter himself, Plenty, disappears from the plantation books. He may have been either sold or swept away in one of the periodic epidemics that decimated the slave street.

Tenah's family had their share of sickness and work injuries. Adonis hurt his arm in the mid-1820s, and the injury lingered for some time, while in letters from the overseer Tenah is sometimes described as falling ill. On one occasion, in August 1833, Tenah was recuperating from some illness at the plantation infirmary, or "sick house." That same week, workmen were replacing the porch of the sick house, which had rotted. A black carpenter named Bristol sawed and hammered for days outside Tenah's room. The noise probably did little to help her bed rest, and the return to work was only slightly less attractive than the pounding of tools in her ears.

John Ball Jr. died in June 1834. I cannot say what affection, if any, Tenah's family felt for him. It is almost certain they feared his death, because the demise of a slave owner meant that his human property might be sold. When John Jr.'s will was read, the terms came down that the executors should sell much of the estate if they deemed it "necessary or advisable," and shortly most of his belongings, including his people, were auctioned.

The day of the estate sale, Tenah, Adonis, and Binah stepped up on the auction block. Standing below them in the pit full of bidders was John Jr.'s widow, his second wife, Ann Ball.

A painting of Ann Ball from about 1825 shows a composed woman with a determined gleam in her eyes. Although her husband's will called for the estate to be dispersed, Ann had another plan. Her male kin among the Balls advised her against it, but Ann wanted to buy back as much of the estate as possible and run the plantation business herself. For this reason, when Tenah and Adonis looked down from the auctioneer's platform, they may actually have been pleased to see Mistress Ball, because the widow might buy them back and bring them "home," a more preferable alternative than being snatched away to pick cotton in Alabama or Mississippi. On a list of people purchased by Ann Ball that day, the first names that appear are "Adonis, Tenah, [and] Binah." The family was bought with two other people for $1,525. Before the day was done, Ann bought 210 children, men, women, who were about to be separated, blood from blood, and shipped out.

Ann Ball managed the plantation for several years. Adonis finally died; then Ann Ball herself died in June 1840. That year Tenah's daughter Binah gave birth to the child named Katie, who would come to be known as Bright Ma.

With the death of Mistress Ball, random happenings in the big house once again posed a threat to the colored people. The children of Ann Ball included a daughter, Ann, and a son, Keating. Keating, twenty-two, had studied medicine, but with his mother's death the dutiful heir abandoned a doctor's career. He inherited Comingtee—with Tenah, Binah, and Katie—and moved into the old house. Keating's sister Ann married a physician, Dr. Elias Horry Deas. It was the usual generational shift, only before long there came an evident quarrel between the heirs.

There is evidence that Keating Ball saw his sister and her husband, known as Horry, socially because he kept a diary in which he noted their dinners together and reciprocal house visits. Horry Deas practiced medicine in Charleston but apparently liked the world of rice planters from which his wife came, and angled to join the slave-owning class. During the dinners with Keating, the three may have talked about the rice business. It also seems possible that they argued about who should get the Comingtee slaves, because suddenly Keating's daybook shows that he stopped having dinner with his sister and brother-in-law.

On March 20, 1841, Horry and Ann Deas filed suit against Keating, as well as a Ball cousin and the executor of the disputed estate, seeking redistribution of the Ball inheritance. Most of the property in question consisted of people on Comingtee. The result of the lawsuit was a writ of partition issued by the court, which divided the slaves of the deceased Ann Ball. Ownership of Tenah, her daughter Binah, and the infant Katie fell to Horry and Ann Deas.

After the lawsuit, Horry's new possessions stayed at Comingtee while he continued to practice medicine. Perhaps Keating shared with Horry some of the profits made by the people who now belonged to the doctor. Nine years passed, during which Keating made amends with Ann. Horry Deas finally grew tired of medicine and bought a plantation on the Cooper River, called Buck Hall, intending to staff it with Comingtee workers. The day arrived when Horry came to collect the people his wife had won in court.

At the end of the growing season, in the winter of 1850, Keating summoned his workers onto the lawn of Comingtee to announce the news that their village would be split in two. He noted the event with a terse entry in his diary: "24 January 1850 . . . This day completes my 32nd year. Today gave notice to the Negroes as to who belonged to Dr. Deas . . . A general gloom seemed to pervade the negroes at the idea of parting with each other."

Lined up that day to hear their owner's little speech were Tenah, Binah, and Katie. Tenah was about seventy, Binah thirty-five, her daughter Katie ten. The paperwork does not show whether Binah's husband was included in the deal. It is likely that he was not and that Binah was forced to abandon the father of her daughter at Comingtee.

Having been moved once from Limerick plantation, in 1810, Tenah's family was now moved from Comingtee to Buck Hall, the last station of their journey.

The records of Buck Hall, a 635-acre plantation, have not survived, but the slave population probably numbered about seventy-five. It appears that Tenah died soon after the family's move. In time, Binah found a second husband, named John. Katie grew up and took a husband named Zachariah. At Buck Hall, Binah and Katie, who came from a family once in the artisan class of the plantation, lost their status. They were apparently put to work as field hands, who waded in the mud of the rice fields in gangs. With their new positions came a new master, Horry Deas. There is evidence that Dr. Deas, a first-time slave owner, was detested by the field hands. Some years later his own daughter would write of her father, timidly, "He could not get along with" the black people.

Ann Ball Deas, now the mistress of Buck Hall, died in 1859 at age forty-four, leaving Horry Deas a widower. In December of the following year, a meeting of would-be revolutionaries in Charleston drafted a document known as the "Ordinance of Secession," which announced the withdrawal of South Carolina from the United States. The rebels got what they wanted, a Confederate States of America, but the Southern nation lasted just four years. An end to the trek, of sorts, finally came for the family.

In January 1865, Federal troops under the command of General William Tecumseh Sherman swept through Georgia and paused in Savannah, where they contemplated whether or not to destroy Charleston, ninety miles away. Horry Deas, the widower, trembled alone at the Buck Hall mansion, his daughter having fled for the town of Greenville to escape the almost-certain attack. The village of black workers bided their time. The Federal forces headed for the capital at Columbia instead, leaving Charleston to surrender to the siege fleet that rode in the harbor. A few days later, Yankees meandering inland from Charleston arrived on the lawn at Buck Hall. When they came, Binah and John, standing with Katie and Zachariah, were able to see firsthand the destruction of the old world.

In the first week of March a raiding party of Federal soldiers came to Buck Hall and headed for the slave street. They appear to have landed from a gunboat, the *Potomaska*, captained by a Navy man called F. M. Montell. According to a letter written by Horry Deas, the Yankees recruited newly freed slaves to their side and soon, with the column of freedpeople, made their way to the big house. The detested doctor waited there, powerless to stop them. The raiders stripped the house of furniture, curtains, and silver, carried some of the loot to the cabins, and loaded other pieces onto a boat sent in the direction of Charleston. When the house was bare, the former slaves burned it to the ground. Next the raiders torched the barns, stables, and other work buildings. (They left their own houses, the old slave cabins, standing.) The freedpeople's rage finally expired on the little grain that had kept them captive, as they burned what remained of the rice crop from the previous year.

"[N]ot a solitary chair, table, or pillow left," wrote Horry Deas to his daughter. "I have saved a few blankets [and] a mattress. . . . The serv^ts about the house have taken themselves off and are wandering about the city."

And with that, Binah and Katie expressed their appreciation for the care so long extended to their family by the Balls.

The blue of the sky in South Carolina seemed paler than that of New York. In the strong Southern light, the sky washed its pigments until they faded like old cotton. Under that distant and gentle sky, I paid a visit to the granddaughter of Katie, or Bright Ma, one of the last slaves at Buck Hall.

Denise Collins's cousin Katie Roper lived near Charleston in a simple brick house, with two of her children and two of her grandchildren. "We're very proud of her," Denise Collins had said, in Harlem, as she wrote down Mrs. Roper's address on a piece of paper.

I had driven into a modest subdivision, built in the 1960s, with streets lined by identical brick houses. Each one-story rectangle occupied about a third of an acre in the shadow of tall pines. Katie Roper greeted me in her living room. She wore a dark pleated skirt, cut to the knee, and a cotton shirt. A thin woman, she stood five and a half feet tall and had strength in her grip, but I saw that her eyes seemed clouded. As we shook hands, Mrs. Roper was aware that I was peering into her eyes. She explained that she suffered from glaucoma and cataracts, and that she was blind in her right eye, with little sight in her left.

"But it don't bother me none," she said with a subtle smile, releasing my hand.

Katie Roper had an oval face and rich lips, which came to a slight, pleasing smile. The line of her chin sloped delicately, and I could see that in her youth she had been a beautiful woman. She wore a gray wig, short and straight, combed up and back in the style of a good matron. Katie Roper brought her chin down and looked up at me demurely from under her eyebrows. The smile came again, decorous and subtle, and she used her face sweetly, luring my attention.

Mrs. Roper knew who I was, because she knew the names of the slave owners. Aside from the Balls, there were the Cordes family, the Harlestons, the Irvings, the Lucases, the Stoneys, and on and on.

"I was always taught that my father was Cordes, and my grandmother was Ball," said Katie Roper. She meant that her kin had come from a Cordes plantation on one side and a Ball place on the other.

Katie Roper's potent voice betrayed her decorous expression and small frame. Its vibrations pierced the room, humming like a transformer, and was echoed in her strong movements. Though she was thin, she moved quickly, striding around and tossing out her hands. While Mrs. Roper's face resembled that of an elderly debutante, her strong body belonged to the women the debutantes called "help."

Katie Roper's two daughters, Charlotte Dunn and Delores Singletary, both in their forties, showed immediate kindness. Effusive, with a voice like a horn, Charlotte had inherited some of her mother's bluntness. Delores took her mother's demure side, all subtlety and withdrawal in her face. Delores's son Michael, a tall and handsome seventeen-year-old, stood by, gently quiet, a masculine example of the family's reserve.

Whereas Katie Roper had a birdlike frame, both of her daughters were solid women. I learned why when I looked into the kitchen. Spread out on the countertops were a pile of fried chicken, fried potatoes, vegetables, rice, dessert, and sweet drinks. As I eyed the food, a rustle of laughter ran around the room. Charlotte gave her sister an elbow in the ribs.

Throwing down her forearms, Katie Roper took her place on the sofa. The laughter died down, and we opened the family story.

After the Civil War, black people were able to use family names for the first time. At Buck Hall, Binah and John took Rivers as their surname. Katie and Zachariah became Mr. and Mrs. Heyward. It's not clear when Katie Heyward earned her nickname, Bright Ma.

"The furthest back I've been able to uncover," I said, "your ancestors were living on a place called Limerick plantation, at the head of the eastern branch of the Cooper River, north of Charleston, soon after the American Revolution." I took some papers from my bag and said, "This is a list of people living on Limerick. On it are Tenah and Adonis, the most distant forebears I could identify."

I looked up to solemn stares and flat, grim mouths.

I described what I knew of the lives of Tenah and Adonis at Limerick. Then I went over the family's move to Comingtee plantation after the death of their owner, Old Mas' 'Lias.

"I can't make excuses for it," I said. "That's what happened. The family was just given away."

I came to the name Binah. The family's oral tradition, which I had first heard in New York, mentioned Binah. But the tradition had no word about her life, and did not say where she might have lived.

"This page is a record of people born on Comingtee plantation," I said, holding a photocopy. "Binah was born there on September 8, 1815."

"Oh, Lord," said Delores.

There was an intake of breath in the room.

"Oh, Lord," echoed Charlotte. "We didn't know what—we didn't know where—or the age." Charlotte's hornlike voice pierced the air. "All we had was a name."

I told the tale of the family's next and last move, to Buck Hall. I brought out a labor contract from 1866 that listed Binah, who used her new name, Binah Rivers. And it listed Binah's daughter, Katie, with her new surname, Heyward. Binah and Katie were illiterate—it was against the law for slaves to read and write—so in place of signatures, the women each had marked the contract with an X.

We passed the pages around, and Katie Roper spoke up for the first time.

"Didn't have the education to write," she said. "It's been back a long time." Her voice was slow and deliberate. "Buck Hall," she said. "My grandmother, Katie Heyward, used to talk about it."

All eyes turned to Mrs. Roper. Everyone in the room, except me, had heard her talk about the past. Mrs. Roper's kin gave way once again so the stories could get air.

"My grandmother was very small," she began, "a cheerful little lady. She was very active. She moved!" Mrs. Roper fingered the air. "It was a good thing she liked to move, because if she didn't, probably I'd never remembered her."

Mrs. Roper's voice and body commanded the room. She shook her head, and I thought I could see the woman she was describing in front of me.

"We called her Bright Ma," Mrs. Roper said. "She was an ex-slave."

"Was she fair-complected?" Charlotte asked her mother, although she had heard about Bright Ma many times.

"No, she wasn't," said Mrs. Roper. "We just called her Bright Ma as a nickname. Sometimes she would take me for walks. One day, she said she was going fishing. I asked my mother can I go. So I went with her, cane fishin' pole on her shoulder. When we got down there, Bright Ma showed me on the riverbank, by the water. She said, 'I want to show you what happened to me when I was a girl.' And she said, 'You know, the maussa then wanted to whip me.' "

Mrs. Roper studied me with her unblinking eyes.

"So she wanted to show me how she ducked this whippin'," she went on. "And to save the whipping of her 'hind, she walked this riverbank. 'Boss man there walking down the riverbank,' she said. They thought they had penned her up. One man went this way, one went the other way."

Katie Heyward was born in 1840 on Comingtee, and moved to Buck Hall in 1850. The event she had described to her granddaughter might have taken place in the 1850s. It had been seventy years since the fishing trip with Bright Ma, but Katie Roper was still excited by the memory. Her voice got louder.

"Well, she tied her dress around her waist, and put the line pole down and bucket with the bait. I said, 'Bright Ma, where you going?' She just mashed the weeds down, and she pitched overboard! She ducked in the water, and swam. I got excited, and started crying. And I screamed murder! I said, 'Oh Lord, the 'gators going to eat her!' That's what was in my mind. She swam around and came back ashore. I said, 'Bright Ma, why you do that?' She said, 'Don't cry, I'm all right.' "

I knew the riverbank. It was muddy and lined with marsh grass, with a clear landing where boats went in. If Katie Roper was ten at the time, her grandmother would have been eighty when she dived into the river.

"We went back home, then she said, 'I showed Gal how I had to save a whippin'.' My nickname they used to call me at that time was 'Gal.' I said, 'Bright Ma, you wasn't afraid of the water?' She said, 'No, because I was going to get a hard drive.' "

"Who was going to beat her?" I asked.

"She didn't say," answered Mrs. Roper. "She might have said more, but she went in the water, and that take everything I remembered away."

Mrs. Roper's story slowed.

"After that, I got sick," she said. "I had hot fever. But I was too scared to tell my mother how I got it. I said, 'Bright Ma, you mean they would whip you?' It made me feel very bad, that she had to run to keep somebody off. And from that day to this, I don't like water. It turned me off, seeing her in the water. My daddy was a fisherman, but after that, he never got me in his boat to go fishing."

Katie Roper's story of how she came to fear water stayed with me, a memory broadcast through the decades. For the Heyward clan, the story of Bright Ma worked like the oral tradition in the Ball family, in which the dead fed the dreams of the living. Later, when I met more of the Heywards, it seemed that everyone knew about Bright Ma. She was their indissoluble bond.

I asked whether the other old people from Mrs. Roper's youth talked about what happened to them.

"No," replied Mrs. Roper. "The older parents come up under such strain, with slavery, until they didn't tell the children things they should have told them. They didn't talk about it. I don't think they wanted the children to really know."

Mrs. Roper was describing the silence of survivors, after whose lives the memories of slavery were few.

"If I know something happened to me that was very bad, I wouldn't tell my grandchildren, because it doesn't make them feel good," she went on. "So I feel sure that they didn't tell their children."

Former slaves often did not tell the worst of it to young people, who never felt the lash, which means that an end to the lore began soon after freedom.

"But see, my grandmother was something," Mrs. Roper said, staying with her memory. "Bright Ma got up in the morning early, and walked in the trees. She was like a prophesier. She would sing, and testify, and there wasn't nobody around."

I pictured a small, strong old woman, who marched though the pinewood near the riverbank, preaching to the trees.

"The children laughed at her," Mrs. Roper kept up. "I've seen it. But some of the things she said was true. One thing she said, she told me there would come a time when sons wouldn't know their fathers, and fathers wouldn't know their sons. That's here today! She said a time would come when daughters wouldn't know their mothers, and mothers wouldn't know their daughters!

"Another thing she said," Mrs. Roper said with a hard face. "A day would come when a man's life wouldn't be valued even like a bird's! A time when man will think more of animals than of human life!"

"Because people are cruel," I said.

"They're cruel," Mrs. Roper replied.

Katie Roper was born Katie Simmons, in January 1912, about a mile from Buck Hall, where her grandmother had been in slavery. The girl would have a life that blended the old days with the new. Katie's mother was Charlotte Heyward, the second of Bright Ma's five children, and her father Wesley Simmons, from a few miles away. Katie grew up in a four-room house, with two brothers and one sister. Later, her grandmother, Bright Ma, would move into the crowded home. The house was made of wood, whitewashed, not painted, with a porch on two sides and a tin roof. There was a fireplace where the cooking was done, a well outside for water, and an outhouse. No paved roads could be found ten miles in any direction, and the nearest neighbors lived a quarter of a mile away.

"The interior was wallpapered," said Mrs. Roper. "My parents couldn't afford wallpaper, so we used the newspaper, and the funny papers. We got a lot of kick out of looking at the funny papers on the wall, or any book paper on there."

Her parents had a piece of land, she said, and planted cotton.

"I planted plenty of cotton, and I also picked cotton," said Mrs. Roper. "Sometimes one of the worms sting you. They got some big, hairy worms, green. They're fire. They don't bite you, but the hair is what stings you. I'd get a little piece of fennel and rub it in."

Her father, Wesley Simmons, was also a fisherman, who set traps for the carp that ran in the Cooper River. Mrs. Roper described her father as a tall, thin man who went to his cotton fields in the morning and rowed out to his fish traps in the afternoon. When the cotton was in, Wesley Simmons took it to a nearby "gin house," where a cotton gin pulled the seeds from the boll. At the end, the cotton was baled and sold to the white "factors," or buyers, for whatever price could be had.

"My father always said that long ago, they had two packages to give away," Katie Roper began. "When they called to get the packages, the white man went in and come out with his package. He opened it. He got the pen and pencil. Then the black man went in for his package. He come out, opened it. He got the shovel and the hoe." Mrs. Roper smiled a little, flat smile.

"It's true," I said.

"It's true till it ain't funny," she replied.

When she was a girl, Katie Simmons went to the local one-room schoolhouse, "a little shack there" for black children. It was open only a few months of the year. White school officials knew, and sometimes hoped, that children would be in the fields with their parents. Attendance was not required, but Katie Simmons finished the fifth grade.

One day, in 1921, Katie came home to find that her father's mother, her grandmother Eleanor Simmons, had died.

"For some reason, her house caught fire with her, and she burned up in the house. That was in January," said Mrs. Roper. "In March, you turn your ground over for planting. So we went in the fields, and we children used to go around the ground and pick up little bones, and say, 'We found Grandma's bones!' "

Mrs. Roper laughed, showing her teeth. Then she tilted her chin down and looked up demurely beneath her eyebrows, a little embarrassed.

No doctors visited the black folk in the country, because nobody had fee money. For medicine, the country people turned to the woods.

"They would go out there and dig the herbs. They used to get something called snake root," said Mrs. Roper. She paused, and peered at me with a smile. "You wouldn't know nothing about it. Anyway, they would put moonshine on it, and give the children that for fever. And 'life everlasting.' That was good for fever and cold. Now, if they catch you with life everlasting, they'll lock you up! They'll say you got marijuana."

"Life everlasting would make you sweat," Mrs. Roper's daughter Charlotte put in. "And it got the fever out. Then people started smoking it." Charlotte shrugged, and raised her eyebrows.

"Another thing," said Mrs. Roper. "Today, if you scratch your leg, you got to go to get a tetanus shot. The older people, you know what tetanus shot they get? They go to the house and see where that spider web comin' down, and twist it on a stick and get it, and push it into that cut, and put turpentine on it. Then they put a penny on it. That's the old country remedy."

When Katie Simmons was eighteen, her mother died, which meant she had to go to Charleston, move in with an uncle, and look for work.

"My first job was minding babies, looking after the kids for a family. They were Greeks. I also washed, and I cleaned their house. You know what my salary was? A dollar and a quarter a week."

Mrs. Roper looked to the floor, trying to retrieve events, or perhaps trying to shake off their memory.

"After a year, I got a job at Roper Hospital," she said, naming a local place that, by coincidence, carried the name of Katie Simmons's future husband. "That was a slave job."

"Did you call it a slave job when you did it?" I asked. Mrs. Roper had a slightly fierce expression, and for the first time a bitter sound came with her hard, strong voice.

"What else would you call it?" she said. "I talk plain. I cleaned and waxed the floors, twelve hours a day. You had to get up on the ladder and wash the walls down to the ground. For the floor, on your knees, you put the wax down with the cheesecloth, smear it down. These knees were as black as your pants." Mrs. Roper grabbed her knees. She rocked in her chair and brought up an arm.

"The woman over me, her name was Mae Huzzie—and she was a hussy. She would go in her room, lay down in her bed and sleep, come back. Then she would go tippin' around to see if you loaf. That's what she called it, 'loaf.' You see, back in those days, you ain't nothin' but a trash!"

Mrs. Roper fell quiet, and the anger fled her face. Then she spoke up, milder than before, and resigned. "It's past. It's gone by. But I would just like to tell some of them a piece of my mind, and let them know how I feel."

Katie Simmons met Ned Roper, her husband-to-be, at an outdoor dance in 1934. Ned Roper came from a family that had some land near Charleston. They courted for three years, married, and took a two-room apartment. It was the Depression, and Ned Roper got a job in road construction for the Works Progress Administration. Mrs. Roper's husband was also an unrivaled cook, and when World War II began Ned

Roper joined the Navy and became a chef. He worked on troop ships in the Pacific, cooking for hundreds of men.

"He went to Shanghai, all those places," Mrs. Roper remembered. "He said the food that they didn't want on the ship, they was gonna put it in the garbage. He said some of the poor people in China, they swam on the side of the ship, and he dropped it over the edge so they could get it."

Back home, Katie Roper gave up washing floors and became a midwife.

"I had my delivery bag, a little briefcase," she said, the slight smile returning. "I had my silver nitrate. The silver nitrate you put in the baby's eye when they come into the world, because they might contract something from the birth canal. I had my gauze for the umbilical cord after you cut it and tape it down. If you look in the vagina, you can tell the reactions. If it's a breach, the first thing the baby does is move the bowels."

She birthed hundreds of children, all of them under the unwritten law of race separation.

"All my babies were black babies I delivered," she said. "If a white mother had wanted a black midwife, they had plenty of opportunity to get it, but they didn't want it."

Ned Roper came home from the war, and the couple moved back to the country, to his parents' farm near Charleston. They gave up cooking and midwifery to become farmers, working sunup to sundown, planting sweet potatoes, butter beans, corn, green beans. At first they used a horse, but that was too hard, so the couple got their own tractor.

"If you have good credit, you can get anything," said Mrs. Roper.

After eleven years of marriage, Katie Roper began to have children. There were five, beginning with Charlotte in 1948. The growing family put up a vegetable stand on the road in front of their house, "just a big table with a shed over the top," and sold produce. Eventually they got contracts to sell to grocery stores, and later they trucked to supermarkets. The children grew, married, worked.

"My husband died on a tractor," Mrs. Roper said. "A massive heart attack, on September 18, 1978, between three o'clock and three-thirty. He went in the fields, and I went into the barn. I looked up and saw him on the tractor, but he was slumped over. I called his name, and he didn't answer."

Mrs. Roper moved in with her daughters, Charlotte and Delores. The women gave Katie Roper grandchildren, and the family moved into a new cycle.

When Mrs. Roper finished, I looked at her teenage grandson, Michael, sitting quietly on the sofa. Michael wore a short Afro and horn-rimmed glasses. He was handsome and friendly. When I asked, he said that he was applying to colleges and had plans to become an engineer. Then he fell silent again, polite, waiting, watchful.

The Heyward clan, descendants of Bright Ma—at least, those who knew about each other—numbered more than 150. The Ball family of whom I was aware amounted to about the same. Bright Ma's progeny lived in nine states. By one count, there was one household in Connecticut, one in Florida, and one in Maryland. There were also two households in Massachusetts, two in New Jersey, seventeen in New York, two in North Carolina, twenty-six in South Carolina, and two in Virginia.

In the weeks and months after I first spoke with Katie Roper, I visited Heyward families in three states. I drove miles to have dinners and make small talk and large with various kin. After several trips, I returned to Charleston, and to the tall pines of Mrs. Roper's yard. I sat with the elderly lady and her daughters, as we had sat before. We knew each other better, and fell into plain talk.

"How do the white people feel about what you're doing?" Mrs. Roper said.

I replied that some liked it, some did not.

"You don't have to tell me. I know how the world's made up," she said. "But remember the Twenty-seventh Psalm. 'Who do I fear? Of who am I afraid? When my enemies came for me, they stumbled and fell!' "

We sat outdoors this time, and there was a cool wind. Mrs. Roper wore a blue cardigan sweater and pants. As we went over the past, we talked about the worst things, and tried to make sense of them. The story that haunted us was the sickly memory of the beating of Tenah and Adonis, the two most distant Heyward ancestors, for killing a sheep. We dwelled on the details—how the overseer had whipped the couple,

who were in their fifties, and how their neighbor, Daniel, had refused
to say who had made off with the sheep.

"Yes, it was rough," said Mrs. Roper. "But then, what could you
do?"

"It was worse than rough," I said.

"They ate the meat because they were hungry," said Charlotte, Mrs.
Roper's daughter with the booming voice. "Why should you beat someone because they are hungry?"

"You didn't need to go that severe," said Mrs. Roper, nodding.

"Just hearing that was upsetting to me," said Charlotte. "I can understand now why Bright Ma jumped in the water."

Delores, Mrs. Roper's quiet daughter, spoke up. "There were a lot
of African Americans who decided that this was not the life for them,
and that they would rather die," she said. "You can become so overwhelmed that you feel hopeless. You lose all faith, and the next thing
to do is just give up."

Charlotte said her feelings about her family had changed.

"When I saw the document with the *X*, with Bright Ma's signature,
I felt I had brushed up against something," she said. Charlotte made a
wave motion with her body, bumping the chair. "I felt I'd hit the past.
It was not a chilling feeling. It was more a feeling of awe, a kind of
presence. Praise the Lord. Let it be. Amen."

5

▶━◀━○━▶━◀

A FAMILY BUSINESS

Before I reached my teens, our family lived in a house on the beach at Sullivan's Island, a narrow sandbar near the mouth of Charleston harbor. The island took its English name from a sea captain who lived out among the dunes in the late 1600s. Sullivan's Island was a quiet oceanside village, with neither a traffic light nor even a restaurant. Year-round residents like ourselves lived in creaky cottages on the ocean, or along the handful of streets off the water. The loudest sound during the day came from the crashing waves, and at night from the frogs that sang in the gullies. My family's small, five-room house among the dunes had a screened porch facing the Atlantic. In the morning, I used to watch the shrimp boats chug into the waves. Their diesel engines made a gargling sound, and the waves shook the webs of tackle and nets hanging over their decks.

On old maps, Sullivan's Island looks like a skinny check mark on the Atlantic coast. A bit of sand begins inside the shelter of the port, dribbles down a few hundred yards, then turns up and northeast, continuing narrowly for about two miles. Between the island and the mainland lies a distance of less than a mile. The island has changed a bit in shape since the time of Elias "Red Cap" Ball, the immigrant from England and first rice planter in the family. But in his lifetime, as later, most of the landside channel was filled by a muddy marsh, with the exception of a quiet inlet known as the Cove. Ships once docked in the Cove, where they were sheltered from the ocean.

In 1707, the legislature of South Carolina passed a law that called for the construction of a brick building on the Cove. The structure had dimensions of sixteen by thirty feet and was known as the *lazaretto*, or alternatively, the "pest house." The term "lazaretto" comes from Italian and means leper's house or plague hospital, a place where the diseased poor, especially foreigners, could be forced to stay. "Pest house" arose in the spare imagination of the English colonists. The pest house was to provide a quarantine place where pestilence from the sea—diseases found among ship passengers—might be allowed to run its course.

According to law, all ships carrying slaves were required to make a first landing on Sullivan's Island and deposit their human cargo at the pest house. Here, the Africans would wait for at least ten days, and up to three weeks, until they had been glanced at by a health inspector. If the new Americans were still alive at the end of the quarantine, they would be released to their captors and sold at auction in Charleston, five miles away.

During the youth of Red Cap, the city of Charleston became the Jerusalem of American slavery, its capital and center of faith. In the time of the heaviest traffic from Africa to North America, South Carolina was the most likely point of entry for ships. A reliable estimate has it that between the years 1700 and 1775, more than forty percent of the Africans arriving in the mainland colonies of Britain came through Charleston. Most first touched land on Sullivan's Island. The dead were thrown overboard. Those who had survived the Middle Passage—the second leg of the triangular travel for British ships, which sailed from England to West Africa, Africa to America, and finally back to England—stayed under guard in the pest house. People who died during the quarantine were evidently buried in mass graves.

"There are few Ships that come here from Africa but, have had many of the Cargoes thrown overboard," wrote Alexander Garden, the port physician of Charleston who met slave galleys at Sullivan's Island for many years. "Some [have lost] one-fourth, some one-third, some lost half; and I have seen some that have lost two-thirds of their slaves. I have often gone to visit those Vessels on their first Arrival, in order to make a report of their State of health to the Governor and Council, but

I have never yet been on board one, that did not smell most offensive and noisome, what for Filth, putrid Air, and putrid Dysenteries . . . it is a wonder any escape with Life."

One summer after Elias Ball's plantations were up and running, corpses began to wash ashore. A ship captain had evidently waited until making port to discard bodies from the hold of his vessel. Thrown overboard, the children and men and women rolled face down onto the land, to decay in the June heat. The governor of the colony complained in the *South Carolina Gazette* "that a large number of dead negroes, whose bodies have been thrown into the river, are drove upon the marsh opposite to Charles Town, and the noisome smell [is] arising from their putrefaction." The governor offered a reward of £100 to any person who would identify the culprit. He was to be punished not for his crime against life but because the corpses posed a health hazard to the white citizens.

The pest house was taken down at the end of the 1700s, but it stands firm in my mind. My childhood idyll has dropped its mask, and I sometimes shovel the graves in my sleep. The ships left from sandy coasts in Africa and aimed for my fragrant beach. Two coasts, like two cupped hands, one on each side of the ocean. The dead washed ashore, and their dark hair made curls in the water. Death was a master who came from England.

In a pamphlet published in London at the beginning of the 1700s, a writer describing South Carolina told English immigrants about the workers they could buy for their land. For 1,000 to 1,500 acres, the author recommended "15 negro men [and] 15 Indian women" for field work, in addition to three Native women to cook, and three black women to milk cows, mind hogs, and do washing. In 1698, when Elias Ball arrived in South Carolina from Devon, there were perhaps twenty Africans and Native people living in slavery on the 740-acre Comingtee farm. No business records of the place survive from before the year 1720, so I cannot tell the names of these first people.

Among the early slaves, the Native women washed, made clothes, cooked, minded the hogs, and did much of the planting and tilling. The mainly black men were occupied in cutting trees from the forest and

ELIAS "RED CAP" BALL

Elias Ball (1676–1751), son of peasant parents in Stokeinteignhead, Devonshire, England, was twenty-two when he inherited one-half of a 740-acre farm in the colony of South Carolina, with a village of about twenty Native American and black slaves. Elias came to America in 1698 to claim his legacy. Some forty-five years later, he commissioned this portrait of himself wearing a red velvet hat, for which his descendants gave him the nickname "Red Cap." Elias died in 1751, leaving five white children who survived into adulthood (as well as, it appears, two children by his housekeeper, a slave named Dolly).

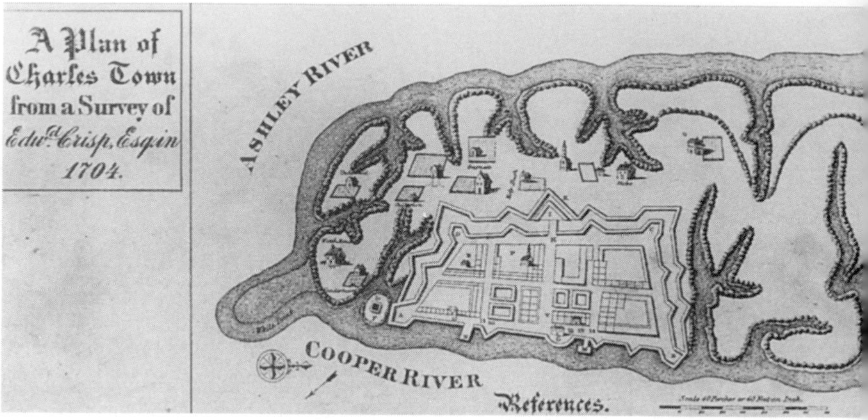
A Plan of Charles Town from a Survey of Edwd. Crisp, Esq. in 1704.
ASHLEY RIVER
COOPER RIVER
References.

About the time Red Cap arrived in America, Charles Town (later Charleston), settled by English colonists in 1670, was a fortress amid fields and bog.

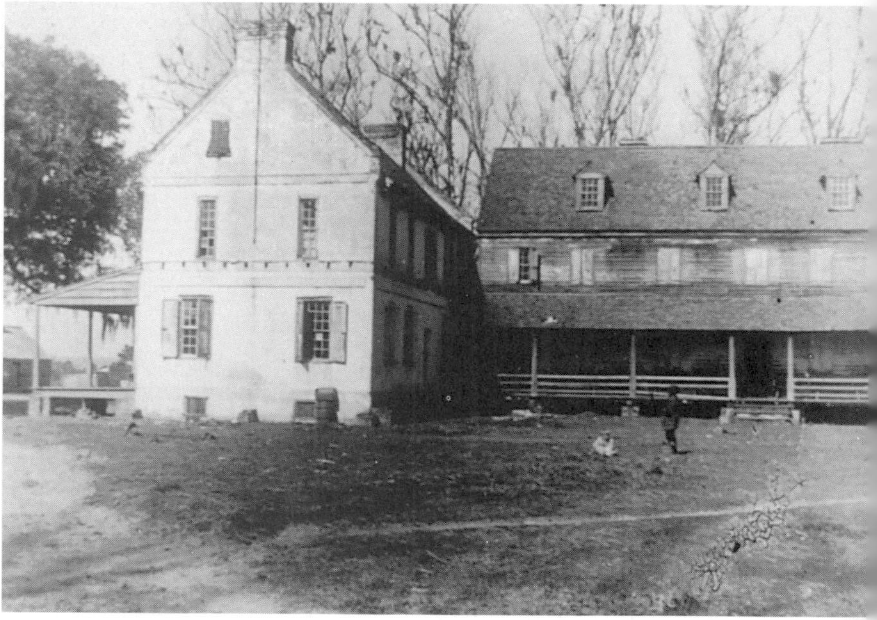

Red Cap's inheritance, a farm twenty-five miles north of Charleston called Coming's T (for his uncle, John Coming, who preceded him to South Carolina), would become Comingtee plantation. It had an L-shaped albatross for its main house, the brick part of which was built in the 1730s when Elias wanted a new home. Views from the front door extended past slave cabins and barns to the Cooper River, five hundred yards distant. A long, narrow wooden addition came after the Revolutionary War; the photograph dates from about 1895.

To irrigate the rice fields that became the economic motor of [Com]ingtee, Red Cap ordered slaves [to da]m a creek and create a reserve, [o]r artificial lake, at the center of the plantation where, though [surr]ounded by swamp, it resembled the rim of an alpine forest.

[In] 1739, when an artist first depicted its waterfront, Charleston, population 6,300, was a noisy port at the fringe of the [Brit]ish Empire. At sixty-three, Red Cap handed Comingtee to his sons and retired to Charleston to live as a rich squire. [Red] Cap's house faced the water just outside the frame of this painting, to the right of the steeple of St. Philip's Church.

BROUGHT to the WORK-HOUSE

Cato. a run-away negro man, who speaks bad English, belongs to Mr. Gideon at George-Town.
A run-away negro fellow, belonging to Mr. Leffene.
And another run-away, belonging to Mr. Elias Ball.

[In] March 1751, a few months before his death at seventy-five, Red Cap probably saw this newspaper advertisement [int]ended for his eyes. It had been placed in the South Carolina Gazette *by the warden of the Work House, the jail and [whip]ping center for slaves in Charleston where recaptured workers were brought by runaway-hunters hoping for a reward.*

EARLY LEGACIES

Elias Ball Jr. (1709–86) expanded the Ball holdings in land and captive workers, moving away from his birthplace, Comingtee plantation, to his own tract, Kensington. By the second generation of the family business, Native American slaves were replaced entirely with Africans and American-born blacks. In his will "Second Elias" Ball told his heirs to do one of two things with their profits: either lend money at interest or "buy Young Slaves."

The typical master's dwelling, or "big house," on a rice plantation—such as this one built at Kensington in 1747 f Second Elias—was comparatively modest, a wooden box with a porch. Its simplicity suited the early role of slave-own families, who were more like bosses of work camps in the wilderness than gentry on manicured estates. A century late after cotton had overshadowed rice as a crop and slavery had spread to Alabama and Mississippi, the more familiar G Revival mansions finally appeared—their columns and boastful bulk replacing the subdued Carolina style.

A ruined slave cabin at Kensington, about 1975. In the 1700s, the first houses for workers were probably built from wet clay that was then cooked hard by fire; the roofs were made from thatch.

Second Elias Ball took out many advertisements for people who escaped from Kensington, including this notice, which appeared in the South Carolina Gazette *on October 20, 1766. (The ads nearly always pictured a man on the run, with a spear.) It ist a dragnet for "Three New Negro Fellows" (that is, Africans), whom Second Elias had named Primus, Caesar, and Boson (Boatswain) before they fled. Primus, who had "a large scar on one of his shoulders," may have already escaped once and taken a whipping for it.*

R UN AWAY from my plantation, in *St. Stephen's* parish, in *August* last. Three New Negro Fellows, named PRIMUS, CÆSAR, and BOSON; had on when they went away, negro cloth jackets and breeches, took their blankets and axes with them, can speak little English.—Primus is a pretty tall fellow, and has a large scar on one of his shoulders.—Cæsar is a stout well-made fellow, a little yellowish, but not so tall as Primus.—Boson is a short black fellow, with a very full beard.——Whoever delivers the said Negroes, or either of them, to me at my plantation at Santee, or St. John's, or in Charles-Town, to Mr. Thomas Lind, shall receive Five Pounds currency reward, ELIAS BALL.

The only grave marker to survive in the slave cemetery at Kensington is the headstone of "Old Peter," born (his owner estimated) about 1726, died 1816.

THE BALLS' REVOLUTI

*Henry Laurens (1724–92) was
married in 1750 to Eleanor Ball,
nineteen-year-old daughter of Red
Cap. In partnership with his broth
in-law George Austin (husband of
Ann Ball, another of Red Cap's
daughters), Laurens built the larg
slave-trading firm in the British
colonies, Austin & Laurens. The
company brought some seventy-eig
hundred Africans to Charleston in
single decade, 1751–61, earning
two owners £156,000 in commissi
enough to make them and their w
four of the richest people in Ameri
During the American Revolution,
Laurens entered politics; he becam
president of the Second Continent
Congress in 1778 and, while saili
to Holland to negotiate a loan for
rebels, was captured at sea by the
British and imprisoned in the Tou
of London for the duration of the*

*Ann Ball (1701–65), first child of the family born in
America, was also the first of the Ball women to marry
(around 1737) a slave trader (George Austin).*

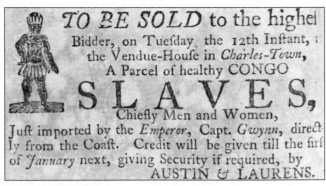

The firm of Austin & Laurens placed many newspaper advertisements for its auctions. This one announces a sale of people taken from near the mouth of the Congo river, to be held in Charleston on May 12, 1752.

TO BE SOLD to the highest Bidder, on Tuesday the 12th Instant, at the Vendue-House in *Charles-Town*, A Parcel of healthy CONGO **SLAVES**, Chiefly Men and Women, Just imported by the *Emperor*, Capt. *Gwynn*, directly from the Coast. Credit will be given till the first of *January* next, giving Security if required, by AUSTIN & LAURENS.

Near the end of the Revolutionary War, Henry Laurens was released from prison in London and went to Paris to join his colleagues from the Continental Congress who would negotiate the terms of peace. In 1782, John Adams (left), John Jay, Benjamin Franklin, Henry Laurens, and Franklin's grandson William Temple Franklin posed for a portrait, "American Commissioners of the Preliminary Peace Negotiations with Great Britain," begun but never finished by Benjamin West. The Founding Fathers' record on slavery was mixed. Future President John Adams never owned slaves and once wrote Thomas Jefferson, "Slavery in this Country I have seen hanging over it like a black cloud." John Jay owned at least two people, Benoit and Abby; Abby accompanied Jay to Paris and ran away during their stay there, only to be retrieved and jailed by the French police, put on her trail by Benjamin Franklin, who had influence with his hosts. Jay experienced a shift in conscience and became founding president of the Society for Promoting the Manumission of Slaves in New York. Benjamin Franklin kept house slaves for more than thirty years, the last dying in 1781. His newspapers accepted advertisements for slave auctions as well as ads for runaways, and he may have sold slaves himself in small numbers—all of this before becoming, in his eighties, president of the Pennsylvania Society for Promoting the Abolition of Slavery. Henry Laurens's Charleston firm sold tens of thousands of people, some of them to his in-laws, the Ball family. William Temple Franklin, the illegitimate son of Benjamin Franklin's illegitimate son William, accompanied his grandfather to Paris as a secretary; he probably owned slaves. On the blank right-hand side of the painting, never sketched in, was a place for the British representative at the peace talks, Henry Laurens's business partner in London, Richard Oswald. Oswald owned slave ships that delivered human cargo to Charleston and was proprietor of Bunce Island, a prison on the west coast of Africa for black captives bound for America.

TRANQUIL-HILL

The Seat of M^rs. ANN WARING

Another Ann Ball (1753–1826), a granddaughter of Red Cap and niece of Ann Ball Austin, moved in 1774 with her husband, Richard Waring, to Tranquil Hill plantation on the Ashley River, which was depicted in this watercolor from about 1800 with two slave cabins, a shed without walls, and a winnowing house (on stilts, with a pert cupola). During Revolution, the British swept through South Carolina and a nineteen-year-old slave named Boston escaped from Tranqu Hill to the royal side. Boston became Boston King, made his way to New York and then to Nova Scotia, and eventually went to West Africa to become part of a new colony of free blacks: Freetown, Sierra Leone. In 1798 Boston King publish one of the earliest "slave narratives," a short autobiography in which he fondly recalled his family at Tranquil Hill but said little about his mistress and master.

On March 16, 1792, Boston King, thirty-two, arrived in the harbor Sierra Leone with his wife, Violet, in a British flotilla that carried twe hundred other escaped American slaves; a painter recorded the sce

AN AGING DYNASTY

John Ball (1760–1817), son of Second Elias and Lydia Ball, fought on the American side in the Revolution, settled at Kensington plantation, married twice, fathered sixteen children, and became the richest of the Ball rice planters. In his will he decreed that most of his belongings be sold; they were, in an auction in 1819 that brought $227,191 for, among other things, 367 people, about half of John Ball's inventory.

...ia Caroline Swinton (1786–1847), daughter of a planting ...mily on Edisto Island, South Carolina, became the second ...e of John Ball in 1805, when John was forty-four and she ...en. The sons of John's first wife came to lament Caroline's ... spending and the feckless ways of her young children; she ...ully acquired a nickname in the family: "Buzzard Wing."

...otes in their account books show that John Ball and his kin were customers of the Work House, a city-run institution for ...e imprisonment and torture of Charleston's slaves. Put up in the 1730s and later rebuilt to resemble a medieval citadel, the ...ork House employed civil servants who whipped black people (in soundproof rooms that muffled screams) at the request of ...their owners or of the police, at twenty-five cents per flogging. Angelina Grimké Weld, born into a plantation family in ...arleston and later an abolitionist who lived in the North, wrote that after people were beaten here, "so exceedingly offensive ...s been the putrid flesh of their lacerated backs, for days after the infliction, that they would be kept out of the house—the ...mell arising from their wounds being so horrible to be endured. They were . . . not in a condition to be seen by visitors."

John Ball Jr. (1782–1834) attended Harvard College (class of 1802) and while in school was warned by his father not to listen to the "liberal principles" (chiefly the idea of abolition) prevalent in New England which were "against the interest of the southern states, tending to the ruin of your own family & fortune." John Jr. returned to South Carolina and by 1824 ruled (with his brother Isaac) over an agrarian industry with 1,290 slaves. In 1832 he became a leader in the first wave of rebellion in the South when the states' rights movement defied taxes imposed by Washington and began to threaten secession from the Union. John Jr. posed for this miniature by Charles Fraser, a painter of palm-sized portraits.

Ann Simons Ball (1776–1840), the second wife of John Jr., was near equal to her husband in plantation management and evidently had a military style, which left her with a family nickname "Captain Nancy." This painting by Samuel F. B. Morse from about 1825 shows Ann's steely only somewhat softened by lace. On one occasion when Jr. was out of town, Ann wrote her husband to report that had personally whipped the laundress, Betty, for not cleaning the bath towels properly.

CHARLESTON.

FRIDAY MORNING, JULY 19, 1822.

The Court of Magistrates and Freeholders, convened for the trial of sundry persons of color, charged with an attempt to raise an Insurrection in the State, have unanimously found the following GUILTY, and passed upon them the Sentence of Death, be carried into execution on Friday Morning, the 2 inst. on the Lines, between six and nine o'clock in morning :—

JULIUS, the Slave of Thomas Forrest.
TOM,   do. of Mrs. Russell.
JOE,   do. of Mr. Jore.
MINGO,   do. of William Harth, Jun.
SMART,   do. of Robert Anderson.
PARIS,   do. of Mrs. Ball.
POLYDORE,   do. of Mrs. Faber.
ROBERT, ⎫
JOHN, and ⎬   do. of John Robertson.
ADAM, ⎭
LOT,   do. of Mr. Forrester.
LEWIS,   do. of Mr. Cromwell.
JACK,   do. of Mrs. Purcell.
SANDY,   do. of Mr. Schnell.
JACK,   do. of Mr. Glen.
PHARO,   do. of Mrs. Thompson.

The Court still continues assiduously engaged the trial of others apprehended for the above cri

In summer of 1822, a planned slave revolt in Charleston known as the Denmark Vesey Conspiracy ended in dozens of trials and thirty-five hangings. Among those condemned was "Paris . . . the slave of Mrs. Ball" (in the nineteenth-century English of the Charleston Courier, "do." abbreviated the word "ditto").

Unlike other men in the family, many of whom wore hats or wigs to cover their creeping baldness, Isaac Ball (1785–1825, brother of John Ball Jr.) combed his hair forward and grew bushy sideburns to distract attention from his naked head. He died of malaria at age forty, leaving behind a thirty-one-year-old wife, Eliza, and several children.

Eliza Poyas Ball (1794–1867), wife of Isaac Ball and mistress of Limerick plantation, did not conceive a child in the first seven years of marriage; as a result, she and Isaac adopted their nephew, James Poyas, a boy of about six who was (as both she and her husband were) a descendant of Red Cap.

4,564 acres, Isaac and Eliza Ball's Limerick plantation was the largest of the family lands. By 1925, about the time this photograph was taken, the main house at Limerick (fifteen rooms, sixty-nine hundred square feet, built from black cypress from the nearby swamps) was two hundred years old and slipping into unpainted neglect. The building stood at the end of an allée of oaks, losing a fight for space against an encroaching thicket.

James Poyas (1806–50), a great-grandson of Red Cap and the adopted son of his uncle and aunt, Isaac and Eliza Ball, grew up at Limerick plantation, never married, and appears to have had a liaison with a Limerick field hand named Diana, with whom he had a child named Frederick, in 1841.

Frederick Poyas, right, born 1841, was the son of Diana, a slave on Limerick, and (in all likelihood) James Poyas, whose name he took after the Civil War. According to family tradition among his descendants, as kin to the Balls the mulatto Frederick bought fifty-seven acres of land from his white family; on this land he raised his own children and, about 1885, was pictured in this charcoal drawing, with his wife, Caroline, and son, George. Descendants of Frederick Poyas live in Ohio, Pennsylvania, and South Carolina.

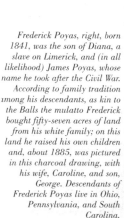

In 1810, Isaac and Eliza Ball bought four lots in Charleston and joined them into a single parcel of 177 by 200 feet. In the back of the lot they built a small village of stables and slave dwellings, and in front a three-story brick mansion of some ten thousand square feet, with walls teemingly decorated in Federal-period woodwork. A staff of eighteen black people ran the house and lived in the compound behind. The house, photographed in decline, was demolished about 1920.

Florence Poyas (1872–1952), second daughter of Frederick and Caroline Poyas, photographed about 1895, is said by her black descendants to have gotten a job as a cook for an out-of-state family with the help of the Balls. On the payroll of her Northern employers, she traveled each year from South Carolina to New York in the company of her husband, Joseph Wilson.

Leon Smalls, fourth-generation descendant of Frederick Poyas and a member of the Masonic Order, Prince Hall Lodge, Philadelphia; photographed in 1990.

Carolyn Smalls, sister of Leon Smalls, with James Goodson, her future husband, on their first date; Philadelphia, 1972.

Fredie Mae Smalls (standing at right), a great-granddaughter of Frederick Poyas, and her husband, Postal Smalls, at their fiftieth wedding anniversary party, in 1990, amid some of their great-grandchildren.

Michael Goodson (smiling), son of James and Carolyn Smalls Goodson, 1978.

Carolyn Smalls Goodson and the author, Charleston, 1997.

extracting wood by-products such as tar and pitch. Elias's land had roughly one square mile of pine and other trees. Black sawyers cut the trunks, split the logs, and then floated the wood downriver to Charleston for export. Logs and rails from the Cooper River farms went to Bermuda, which had a large shipbuilding industry, and to Barbados, already deforested by clear-cutting. On the Barbadian sugar farms, wood from South Carolina fueled fires that boiled the sugar cane. The slaves' labor brought revenue for their owner and prepared land for future planting.

In the early 1700s, the making of naval stores took as much time as timbering. Naval stores included tar, pitch, resins, and turpentine, all made from processing trees. Captains used these goods to seal vessels against leaks and to otherwise maintain their ships. The Comingtee account books show hundreds of barrels of tar and pitch sold for a continuous profit. Elias also kept stocks of cattle. The first South Carolina whites had imported cattle from Virginia in the late 1600s, and the animals multiplied in the semitropical climate. The dismembered livestock gave up beef, tallow, and hides, and the farmers of South Carolina exported thousands of barrels of beef and pork annually, mainly to the British Caribbean.

To feed themselves and their owners, the workers at Comingtee grew corn, peas, and sweet potatoes. (Initially both whites and blacks acquired these shared staple tastes from the Natives.) "Guinea corn," first brought to the colony on ships from African coasts, supplemented the maize, or "Indian corn."

In his solitude, Elias Ball may have marveled at the fully formed world to which he held title. Barely out of his teens, and raised in a faraway country with its own economy, he could hardly have known how to make, raise, extract, and produce all the local goods and foods. I imagine that during the first years after his immigration, Elias had only a vague idea how to manage his copious inheritance, and that he was forced to put himself under the apprenticeship of his slaves.

About 1699, Elias was joined by John Harleston, co-inheritor of the estate, who arrived from Ireland with his sister, Elizabeth. John and Elizabeth Harleston were probably in their early twenties, like Elias. As with her aunt Affra Harleston, who had joined John Coming on the *Carolina*, it is unclear why Elizabeth chose to come to South Carolina. She may have read the older woman's letters to Dublin, been intrigued, and sought to follow in Affra's path. It seems more likely, however, that Elizabeth came as a bride-to-be in an arranged union with Elias, because the two were married soon after she reached Charleston.

Elias, Elizabeth, and John may have worked side by side with their human property in some tasks—cutting trees, making soap and clothing, preparing food. Life for everyone on Comingtee was fueled by a similar grueling routine. But in time, the white immigrants could remind themselves of the purpose of the system and shift the burden of work to other shoulders.

One group of Elias's neighbors on the Cooper River, the Anabaptists, did not take part in the arrangements growing up all around them. In December 1696, thirty families of Anabaptists arrived from Maine. They settled at a place called Biggin Swamp, six miles up the Cooper River from Comingtee, where they acquired eight hundred acres. The "dissenters," who protested the ways of the Anglican Church, began to build their community, refused to buy slaves, and relied on their own labor. No Anabaptist writings survive to cast light on this rare self-reliance, but the reasons for it are not difficult to imagine. Their renunciation of the slave business set the New Englanders apart from other white Carolinians—so far apart, evidently, that after ten years the settlement failed. The dissenters could not build a settlement based on free labor in the midst of a captive society. In 1708, shunned by their peers, the Anabaptists began to sell off their land, and within a few years they left. With that, the single local pocket of antislavery disappeared.

Soon after Elias arrived, an unwanted harvest came in from the fields, when in September 1700 word spread of an imminent uprising of Native slaves. It was reaping season, a time when the workload doubled and the white grip on life tightened. According to an official account, a slave owner came down the river to Charleston, trembling with fear, to spread the news that two Native slaves were planning a revolt. The report had come from one of his own workers, who had disclosed the plot. An alarm was raised and many settlements evacuated, the white planters hurrying to Charleston to batten down. But fear followed them, and "yᵉ people in town thought themselves as little safe as those in yᵉ Country," according to the record. In all likelihood John Harleston and Elias and Elizabeth Ball were among those who fled; at the time Elizabeth was pregnant with the first Ball heir. The two Natives accused of plotting the revolt were captured and jailed. "Yᵉ people are now easie again," the account concluded, "& wee have Ordered yᵉ 2 Slaves yᵉ first proposers of this warr to be Transported." In the end, the rebellious Natives were shipped away to the sugar fields of the Caribbean.

Fear of a Native uprising seems to have subsided, for not long afterward, seeking to make life more comfortable, the Balls expanded operations. In 1702, Elias bought 150 acres from his neighbor, the owner of the tract known as Silk Hope, and in the next two years added another 700 acres. Most of the land sold for the token sum of one shilling per hundred acres. John Harleston does not appear on the land records. The purchases pushed the Ball land north and east of Comingtee, away from the river landing.

To cultivate new land required more people, and although no receipts survive from these transactions, I suspect that Elias bought workers along with the acreage. At the beginning of the 1700s, the Royal African Company, headquartered in London, sold people for between £20 and £30 per adult. The company once had held a monopoly on the human traffic to the English colonies, but by the beginning of the century private traders also worked the business. These local entrepreneurs sold higher, up to £35 per person.

Elias would probably not have hired white servants, who had gone out of favor with landlords. Indentured servants averaged £3 per year for their labor, amounting to £30 in expenses for ten years. Unlike the Puritans, their immigrant cohorts in New England, South Carolina whites were not seekers after God. They were seekers after wealth, and with Africans selling at £25, it made sense to buy them.

When he finally bought, Elias probably would have picked Africans. Starting in the late 1600s, there was a tariff on the import of African-born slaves to South Carolina, a tax that led landowners to purchase most of their black workers from Barbados and other British islands, where many had actually been born. In 1703, however, the colonial legislature dropped the tax, and afterward nearly all new black workers came directly from the West African shore. Elias may also have bought people from a Native clan such as the Catawba or Etiwan. Compared to blacks, Native Americans were a bargain. In a pamphlet from 1712, the price of a young Native woman was quoted as low as £18. Native workers could also be purchased with animal skins rather than cash. In a court case about this time in Charleston, a Native adult slave was appraised at 160 skins, while a child was recorded sold for 60 skins.

The hides usually came from deer, but beaver and other skins could be substituted. The equivalence of pelts and people would have been the idea of the white "Indian traders," who had plenty of both on hand.

In 1705, only five hundred whites and blacks lived in St. John's Parish, the church district that included Comingtee (later called St. John's Berkeley, when the county called Berkeley was divided from the county of Charleston). It was a tiny population, but already four out of ten were slaves. Evidently this was not enough. Next door to Comingtee, on a tract named Strawberry, lived landlord James Child, Elias's friend. Early on, Child and Elias had become partners in a venture to put a ferry on the Cooper River, the Strawberry Ferry, which landed conveniently near the edge of Elias's land on Child's property. In 1706, Child devised a new plan, this one to bring more workers to his and Elias's neighborhood by going into the domestic slave trade. That summer he persuaded a band of Cherokee warriors to attack a nearby village and bring the captives to him, in exchange for a share of the profits. The scheme went off and the Cherokees returned with 160 prisoners, a large human harvest. Child then traveled downriver to Charleston, where he put some of the Natives up for sale.

No hard evidence survives that would show whether Elias Ball actually participated in the slave raid, though he would certainly have known about it. Still, in a Ball family memoir written in 1786 by Elias's grandson John, there is a telling description of Elias's braggadocio. "My grandfather . . . was bold and resolute," the grandson wrote after Elias's death. "He had frequently commanded scouting parties after Indians."

In their first fifteen years of marriage, Elias and Elizabeth Ball had five children who lived past infancy. Ann was born in 1701, and Eleanor in 1707; a son named Elias came in 1709, and another daughter, Elizabeth, followed in 1711. Their last child was born in 1714 and named after Elias's uncle, the first owner of the Comingtee farm, John Coming. With all the children around, John Harleston, who had been living with the Balls, apparently decided to get out of the way. In 1708, he married a woman named Elizabeth Willis and moved to the opposite end of Comingtee, about a mile east of the first settlement. There must have been a fishing hole there, because the couple called their place Fish Pond.

In middle life, Elias found himself at the center of a war with Native people. Government records from the period are filled with accounts of assaults, rapes, and murders committed by whites against Native clans. The attacks seemed endless, and no appeals by Native chiefs to the colonial authorities could stop the slave trade. After decades of living at the mercy of the colonists, Natives in the Carolinas decided to put up a last fight. In spring of 1715, fifteen Native nations formed an alliance, with the aim of pushing the whites out of North America and into the sea. The allies included the Alabama, Apalache, Catawba, Choctaw, Coweta, Creek, Edisto, Etiwan, Santee, Sara, Savannah, Tallapoosa, Waccamaw, and Yamasee peoples. When the whites raised a militia to defend the colony, Elias, thirty-nine, signed on as a captain.

Elias received command of a company on the eastern branch of the Cooper River, "his" river. The wording of his officer's commission shows that whites believed they were about to be engulfed by a general colored uprising that might bring Natives into collusion with blacks. The owner of Comingtee was told to "take into your charge the said patrole and as you shall see occasion both by day and night to patrole from plantation to plantation and in case you meet with any opposition from Indians or Negroes or any of the King's enemies you shall kill, destroy and take prisoners all such opposers and enemies as aforesaid." That summer Captain Ball evidently went on a search-and-destroy campaign, killing any Natives or black slaves who got in his way.

While Elias released streams of blood in defense of his life and property, a tiny number of English-speakers saw the war as a kind of justice visited on the whites. Gideon Johnston, vicar of St. Philip's, the Anglican congregation in Charleston, believed the catastrophe was divine punishment for the slave owners. "[A]ll we can doe is, to lament in Secret those Sins, which have brought this Judgement upon us," Johnston wrote to his church superiors in London. "[O]ur Military Men are so bent upon Revenge, and so desirous to enrich themselves, by making all the Indians Slaves that fall into their hands, but such as they kill . . . that it is in vain to represent to them the Cruelty and injustice of Such a procedure."

Six months later, when the fury of the so-called Yamasee War ended, the Natives were defeated and forced into a diaspora. The Creek nation migrated west toward the French colony of Louisiana. Other people, including the Apalache and Savannah, were decimated and dispersed. Only a few hundred Edisto and Etiwan, dependent for their survival on the deerskin trade with whites, stayed within reach of Charleston. The war marked the beginning of the march of English-speaking people from the Southern colonies across the continent; afterward, white settlements were no longer confined to a narrow strip along the coast.

With the red people out of reach, the enslavement of Natives quickly diminished until it became an oddity next to black slavery. In the colonial government in Charleston, a Commission on Indian Affairs that once dealt with the Natives was dismantled. In one of its last acts, in 1716, the commission issued a decree intended to prevent further uprisings. Henceforth, it stated, white Carolinians were "not to buy any [Native] male slaves above the age of 14 years," because captive children would be less apt to fight back than adults.

After the war, Elias acquired still more land—in deals whose terms show the tracts were spoils awarded Captain Ball for service in the campaign. In September 1716, a few months after the last skirmishes, he picked up eight hundred acres in a bargain brokered by the governor, Robert Daniel. Three years later, he bought another twelve hundred acres, most of it through then-governor Robert Johnson. Now the land Elias once co-owned with John Harleston made up only a small part of his estate, as the Ball family holdings measured some twenty-seven hundred acres. Comingtee stretched about a mile along the banks of the Cooper River, and ran deep inland. Across the water and upriver three miles was a new Ball place, Dockum, whose name came from the Native people who fled from it. Another tract, called Cypress Grove, lay to the northeast in neighboring Craven County. Still others that Elias took up were so new to white hands that they had no English name.

The population of Africans and American-born blacks on the Balls' new real estate grew as well. In 1720, there were 1,439 slaves throughout St. John's Parish—almost ten times as many as fifteen years earlier—of whom Elias owned perhaps 40. Seventy-five percent of the people in St. John's, the Ball district, were black. This ratio—three forced workers for each free person—was much higher than that in Virginia, the original English home of American slavery.

At the end of August 1720, Elizabeth Ball fell ill with malaria. The disease, a strain known as falciparum, was carried in the bite of the anopheles mosquito, which thrived in the swamps. In a letter, her brother wrote that Elizabeth "was taken with a Malignant Fever, and was very delirious," then died. Eleven months later, in July 1721, Elias remarried. He was forty-five, but his new wife, Mary Delamare, was about twenty, the same age as his daughter Ann. Ruler of a huge realm, with a new wife half his age, Elias was no longer a bewildered immigrant but a landlord and planter, the patriarch of Ball family lore. His land, too, also took on a new identity. With its village of people and stream of exports, Comingtee was not a farm but the first Ball plantation.

Settling in with Mary, Elias began to straighten out his accounts. After twenty years, he and John Harleston formally divided the property they had inherited together. Elias got Comingtee, as well as a piece of the townhouse property in Charleston known as lot 49, while John got several hundred acres next to the growing city. Elias bought a new account book, a two-hundred-page ledger, in which to record the pulse of the business, including the names of the black people whose lives mingled with his own. Elias and his oldest son would keep the ledger for the next fifty-eight years. The book survived, one day to yield some of its secrets.

The first person in slavery to the Balls who can be identified by name was a woman called Bella. On November 10, 1720, Elias made a note that "Bella had of me 3 yards of negero cloth." It was a Thursday.

"Negro cloth" was a coarse blend of wool and cotton that slaves were given for garments, a fabric manufactured in Europe and distributed by American slave owners. Whites did not wear Negro cloth, whose name and texture separated servers from served. The fabric sometimes took another, more poetic name, "oznaburgs," from Osnabrück, a town in northern Germany known for its textiles. The rough blue or sometimes white cloth was the standard uniform on the Ball plantations from the earliest colonial days until well into the 1800s.

To judge from the small size of her allotment of cloth, Bella must have been young, perhaps ten years old. In the practice taking shape, adults received five or more yards of oznaburgs per year, children about three yards. Bella reappears in the account book several times, always in the context of taking her basic needs for survival—usually cloth but

also blankets and occasionally a pair of shoes. According to the slave
lists, Bella lived for at least another thirty-three years. No record of her
birth or death, and no record of children, if she had them, has survived.
We know her only as a person trying to clothe herself.

The first record of the Ball family's purchase of people reads as
follows:

1721
Bought
Fatima
Hampshire
Plymouth

The woman (or perhaps girl) and two men (or boys) were bought apparently after they spent two weeks at the pest house on Sullivan's
Island. The year 1721 was a slow one for the slave traffic. In twelve
months, only 165 black captives were imported to Charleston. The previous year, more than six hundred slaves had arrived, while a decade
later, thousands would be brought in each year.

Two of Elias's new slaves were given names of places in England,
the county of Hampshire and the city of Plymouth, near Elias's home
in Devon. The captives probably spoke languages that their owner did
not understand; nevertheless, the two men would have to answer to
place-names that Elias knew from his youth. A beguiling name, Fatima,
appears on this list. The historical Fatima, the favorite daughter of Mo-
hammed, died in the year 632 A.D., probably in her twenties, and memory of her life held long power over Muslims. Islam made converts in
sub-Saharan Africa, some of whom were brought to America. Could the
Fatima of Comingtee have been a Muslim who had somehow held on to
her birth name?

Perhaps a different Fatima rattled around in Elias's imagination, the
tragic Fatima of French folklore. Fatima was the unfortunate seventh
wife of the Chevalier Raoul, the noble tyrant known more commonly as
Bluebeard. According to the well-known French fable, soon after her
marriage Fatima found the bodies of Bluebeard's six previous wives in
a locked room of the Chevalier's castle. As punishment for prying loose
his secret, Bluebeard dispatched his seventh wife to join the others.

The disaster of being captured and dragged across the Atlantic had not broken Fatima's will to live. In 1725, four years after her purchase, Fatima had a baby girl, Pino. During the 1700s, slave women at Comingtee gave birth to their first children at the average age of nineteen. Fatima was therefore perhaps fifteen when she was bought. A few years after Pino, Fatima had a son, Giley. Only once in a while did Elias and the other Balls write down the names of the fathers of slave children. Nevertheless, there is evidence that the father of Fatima's two may have been a field worker named Sam.

What can be said about Fatima's life? All the memorial to her that is possible can be put in the form of a slender biography:

Fatima: Born about 1706 in West Africa. Enslaved 1721. Traveled by ship to Charleston, in the English colony of South Carolina. Bought by Elias Ball, plantation owner. Taken to Comingtee, the Ball place on the Cooper River. Worked in the fields there. Took a mate, perhaps named Sam. Gave birth to a daughter, Pino, in 1725; and on April 23, 1742, a son named Giley, who died as a child. Watched her firstborn grow up to be a slave. Died on the plantation. Was laid in a cemetery far from home.

In December 1722, for the first time, Elias noted that he had sold someone. He did not name the woman or man, but the buyer was a neighbor called William Rhett. In 1717, Rhett had built a house in Charleston five minutes by foot from Elias's own townhouse. The two may have made a handshake deal while standing in the street. Elias thought nothing of the transaction. On a page where he wrote down Rhett's debts to him, he scrawled that Rhett had delivered a quantity of rice worth £80 "Due In part for a Negro."

The person sold to William Rhett was one of many people handed from owner to owner in friendly bargains. Planters along the Cooper River bought and sold workers among themselves and bartered for them as they did for animals. Sometimes plantation owners sold people they felt they could not control, and sometimes they sold people who didn't work as hard as demanded. From time to time, masters sold people merely because they didn't like them.

This sort of traffic, so casual as to be off the tax books, irritated the colonial authorities. In an attempt to collect revenue from it, in 1723 the colonial legislature passed a bill setting up an outdoor market to be held a mile from Comingtee, in a little village near the dock of the Strawberry Ferry. At the market, one Saturday each month, buyers and sellers were required to collect taxes on "every horse, mare, gelding, calf, or slave" sold. I imagine Elias bought and sold people here on an occasional weekend walk.

One more first bears retelling, the first recorded episode of people who tried to flee. On September 4, 1731, Elias wrote the following: "Memorandum . . . Taken with the runaway Negroes a shirt & shift and a jacket and britches." On this occasion it was not quite harvest season, but crops stood high in the fields and preparations for bringing them in had begun. Facing an autumn of round-the-clock work, at least two people had made a break. To judge from the clothing they took, which likely belonged to their owner, the runaways were men. In general, field hands dressed in rough-cut trousers and pull-on shirts. By stealing Elias's clothes, a runaway might be able to convince a marshal that he was a trusted servant who had merely been sent on an errand. Without knowing their names, it is difficult to say more about the runaways. They were probably not the first to have gotten free, if only for a short while, and they would not be the last.

The story of Elias's runaways may have ended with a memorable scene. The South Carolina law concerning the treatment of runaway slaves dated from 1690. It had been revised in 1712 and in future years would periodically come up for rewriting by the legislature. In Elias's day, according to the statute, the punishment for a first attempt to flee slavery was whipping. For the second offense, the runaway was to be branded on the right cheek with the letter *R*. For a third offense, one ear was cut off. A fourth offense brought the removal of the other ear for women, and another brand; for men, the law called for castration.

With his second wife, Mary, Elias started another family. Despite his peasant background and the distance of South Carolina from England, Elias worked hard to surround his children with elite forms of European culture. The Ball youths went to school in a nearby village where the teachers were Huguenots, French Protestants whose worldliness surpassed that of the English immigrants. To give his home an air of gentility, Elias hired a music teacher to come to the plantation and give lessons. In the 1730s young Sarah Ball took instruction on what the family called "the viol." This was the viola da gamba, a popular six-stringed instrument that anticipated the cello. A few years earlier Johann Sebastian Bach had composed "Three Sonatas for Viola da Gamba and Clavier," better known as the Gamba Sonatas, and an up-to-date music instructor may have known the work. After Sarah had been playing for a while, Elias himself got interested and made a note of "cash paid for My Learning Musick—£10."

The music lessons made a strange scene at the Ball house. Every week or two, a studious teacher rode along a muddy road up to Comingtee, sheet music and instruments sticking out of a saddlebag. Perhaps several Africans, returning from the fields, greeted the white visitor. Then, with the sounds of crickets in the grass and alligators thrashing in the ditches, the Ball family gathered in the living room to learn the fine points of a fugue. Two of the children, Sarah and her half-brother John Coming, also took dance lessons, training that prepared them for social events in Charleston. At quadrilles performed in the townhouses of the landed class, the children of the plantation owners were expected to meet appropriate mates.

Smoothing his image, at some point Elias trained himself to develop a taste for wine. According to his records, for many years Elias bought gallons of rum, which he gave to friends, used to pay bills, and no doubt drank himself. But there was a new drink, Madeira, making its way around well-off households. Madeira came from the island of the same name off the northwest coast of Africa. The imported drink was the colony's first real taste of wine, and accounts show the sudden appearance of it on Comingtee. With a glass of the reddish brown liquor in hand, Elias made a polished old soldier.

At the end of the 1720s, Elias reported to the government that his property consisted of 4,328 acres and forty-three slaves. The hand that picked up the viol and poured a glass of wine was less comfortable carrying a bludgeon to patrol his vast estates, and Elias started to bring in white assistants to help supervise. The first he hired was a man named Andrew Songster, who, he noted, "came to my house to live." Songster was paid in goods, mostly rum, in addition to cash. When Songster left, he was replaced by another man, John Netman. By hiring plantation helpers, Elias separated himself from daily farm business and freed his time for more leisure.

By the early 1730s, Elias and Mary Ball had four children living with them in the old wooden cottage that had served as the master's house for half a century. Elias decided to build larger quarters, and sometime before 1736 the Ball family moved into a new, two-story brick house. The building was probably put up by slaves under the direction of white foremen. Its brown bricks, each shaped and baked, would also have been made by black hands. The house was a simple symmetrical building, with two rooms on the first floor and two on the second, plus a garret. The front door stood in the middle of the west facade, with no columns and no pediment, three steps up from the soggy ground. It had no porch and no architectural ornament. The new house may have been spartan, but it was big, brick, and dry. It would survive for more than two hundred years before it fell to ruin in the 1960s.

With the construction of the house, Comingtee took its final form. The master's dwelling, or "big house," faced west, toward the Cooper River, whose waters could be seen five hundred yards away. The slave village, or plantation street, lay behind and east of the big house. In later years it consisted of a group of wooden cabins in a row and nearby workshops for the carpenters, blacksmiths, leatherworkers, and other craftspeople. There was a barnyard with stables, a poultry house, a brick oven, a smokehouse, and the hutches of a beekeeper.

Off in the woods, between the big house and the dock, lay a well-tended clearing, about an acre in size, secluded among some white oak trees and ringed by a little eddy that drained into the river. Here was the graveyard where the slaves were buried.

There is a story, which has the smell of legend but which I nevertheless like, concerning the beginning of rice cultivation on the plantations. In the late 1600s, it goes, a ship sailing from Madagascar, the island off the southeast coast of Africa, happened into Charleston. Somewhere beneath the boards of his deck the ship's captain carried half a bushel of rice. On a whim, several plantation owners decided to try the new crop. Truth or fable, early plantings of rice in South Carolina began about 1695. Five years later the colony shipped thirty tons a year to the Caribbean islands, and three hundred tons to England. By 1708, rice had become South Carolina's largest export.

Elias had sold timber and beef in his first years, but now everything changed. Rice would become the manna of the Balls and the bane of thousands of blacks. The little cereal would bring the plantation owners a life of comfort for six generations.

Rice was not a rich person's food, but it had two attractions: it filled the belly and did not spoil. In Europe, the grain bought by poor people for the family table was also used to feed armies and gangs of workers. The cultivation of rice was, at least initially, something Elias and his peers knew nothing about. In parts of West Africa, however, rice was an old staple, grown along the Gambia River, for instance, and in Sierra Leone. It wasn't long before planters recognized that some of the Africans they owned possessed a knowledge that could earn them profits. The strain of rice grown by the Carolina slaves, refined through years of experiment, became known as Carolina Gold.

Before long, Carolina Gold was the engine of the regional economy, dominating every aspect of daily life, black and white. The first rice fields lay in the swamps interspersed with the forest, just off the riverbank. Here, men and women cleared acres among the tupelo gum trees and bald cypress trunks. In March the field hands planted the provision crops—corn and sweet potatoes—in fields set aside to feed the plantation. Then they turned to rice. The slaves prepared the ground beginning about April 1. Because the wet soil swallowed both horses and plows, animal power could not be used, and the hand-held hoe became the rule. The hoe was a wooden stick the length of an arm, with an iron blade at one end. The work began with weeding, every inch of the field pulled cleaned by fingers or turned by the blade of the hoe. Next came the digging of long furrows, about eighteen inches apart, until the slaves had turned out several hundred empty, striped acres. In New England, a modest-sized field might be prepared by four horses and two drivers with plows. On Comingtee, with the handwork, the same field took twenty people.

In the parts of Africa where rice predominated, women took the job of seeding the ground, and the same arrangement survived in America. In late April gangs of women walked through the fields, spreading, or "broadcasting," the rice in the furrows.

Rice is a thirsty plant that requires irrigation. To comply, Elias Ball commanded that a little stream which emerged in the middle of Comingtee be dammed. One year, teams of male slaves hauled enough earth into the path of the creek to create a water reserve, a lake six feet deep and several hundred yards across. The men next dug ditches from the edge of the reserve to the fields, until Comingtee resembled an arterial system. The rice fields were like living tissues, fed and drained by veins of water that led back to a great heart, the reserve, which swelled silently in the middle of the property.

In late spring the workers brought the first flow of water from the reserve to the fields. To flood the young shoots of rice, slaves opened a wooden lock or dike; to drain, they cut the flow. In summer the afternoon arrived with a baking heat. The crop was doused and drained at periodic intervals, and teams of workers returned frequently to the fields to weed. The flooding meant that slaves spent much of the year up to their knees in mud.

By early September, the mature rice plants unrolled toward the horizon at shoulder height. Harvest began when the workers cut the reedy crop with sickles, pieces of iron two feet long and shaped like half-moons. The stalks were then laid out to dry. After a day or two in the sun, the rice was bound into bundles and brought to the barnyard. Field hands carried great stacks on their heads to oxcarts or piled them on barges that wandered the inland creeks.

The growing season made up the shorter part of the work cycle, the longer and more tedious phase coming next at the barnyard. First came threshing, or flailing. A flail was a piece of leather about three feet long, like a strop, attached to an equal length of wood. Field hands laid the rice on the ground and flailed or whipped it to separate the grain from the stalk. Next, the husks were removed. A rice grain has an outer husk and an inner cuticle, and both had to be sheared off. In the mid-1700s, workers used hand-operated mills, built from wood slabs two feet across. The slabs pressed and revolved against each other, and there were cuts or corrugations that ran from the middle to the edge, through which the rice grain moved as the pressure of the rotation pulled off the husk. The inside cuticle, harder to remove, had to be pounded away from the grain. Coming at the end of the season, in November and December, the pounding was the most onerous work of the year. The equipment consisted of a large hollowed-out mortar about waist-high, and a pestle a yard long. The workers put scoops of rice into the mortar and pounded with the pestle until the grain emerged naked from its shell. It was a jolting, sweaty, repetitive job. When the contents were clean, the mortar was emptied and another load dumped in. For two months, a constant sound of *thrup, thrup, thrup* came from the rice barns. A field hand might pound seven mortars, or about fifty pounds of rice, in one day. The pounding sometimes broke the rice, which made it unsalable. These half-grains, categorized as "Negro rice," were collected from the ground around the barn to become part of the workers' food. Plantation owners and their overseers kept a punishing eye on the barnyard to make sure people broke as little rice as possible.

Finally came the cleaning of the crop. Field hands used a basket called a fanner, woven from tall grass. Fanners were flat disks about two and a half feet in diameter, with a raised lip around the edge, made with a beautiful spiral weave that went from the center to the edges. Workers brought the basketmaking tradition from West Africa, along with the method of cleaning rice. A field hand in the barnyard put about a pound of rice with its chaff in the basket, then tossed it up and down in a breeze. The chaff flew away, leaving the heavier grain.

In colonial days, an acre of rice produced between twenty and forty bushels, each bushel at sixty-five pounds. An individual was thought by his or her owner to be capable of handling about four acres. An average yield amounted to four and a half barrels of rice per worker, and with a barrel at five hundred pounds, a single person meant more than a ton of rice.

In Elias's time, the crop went from Charleston to England, where it was taxed and reshipped to continental Europe. Early buyers of Comingtee rice included Portugal, Spain, and Gibraltar, as well as England and Ireland, but the largest buyers were in the northern ports. In the 1730s, three-quarters of the rice exported from the hot Cooper River went to kitchens in Bremen, Denmark, Hamburg, Holland, and Sweden. Carolina Gold soon gained an international reputation, drawing higher prices than other rice and becoming the premium grade in Europe. Rice from South Carolina could be recognized at a glance as buyers looked into the two sacks displayed by any seller in London. In the first bag was the seed, with its gold-sheathed kernel, and in the second, the finished grain, which gleamed the whitest white.

In the early 1730s, a young black woman named Dolly came to work in the Comingtee big house. Elias's second wife had three children at the time, and Dolly probably helped with the young ones, cleaned house, and cooked. A little homage to Dolly appears in the published Ball memoir. "Perhaps the name that stands out above the others is 'Dolly,' " wrote one of the Ball women at the beginning of the twentieth century.

"We know little about her, but enough to show that she was well thought of in the family. Perhaps she had 'minded' the children, and been a faithful nurse in illness. The ministrations of such humble friends of the family—they were surely no less—have soothed many a bed of suffering; and in death their hands have tenderly performed the last offices."

It seems strange that the name of a slave would evoke sentimental memories in the family of her owners some 150 years after her death. Just as strange is the aside "We know little about her," which seems to contradict the familiarity of the memory.

Dolly was born in 1712, though I cannot say where and I can only fix the year of her birth from a note about her death that states her age. Dolly was evidently more than a good housekeeper. In his will, dictated in 1750, Elias devoted considerable thought to Dolly, whom he called his "Molattoe Wench." As used then, the word "mulatto" described children of black mothers and white fathers. (In Elias's day, the children of one Native and one black parent were called "mustees" by whites.) Since the colonial legislature had already passed a law forbidding sex between white women and enslaved blacks, the white mother of a daughter of color would have been subject to prosecution. Therefore, in all likelihood, Dolly's father was white, her mother black.

It is undeniable that white men on the plantations forced and persuaded black women to have sex with them, and evidence of white-black sex appears in official records from the earliest days. In one case, from 1692, a woman named Jane LaSalle filed a petition with the Grand Council, the highest authority in Charleston. The petition involved her husband, who had left her for a black woman, probably one of the white couple's slaves. The abandoned wife appealed for help, and the Grand Council ordered the husband to return to his spouse, or else pay her a sum of money. The public nature of the case and matter-of-fact way in which it was disposed give reason to believe that interracial sex was a common part of Elias's world.

Because the earliest Ball plantation records date from 1720, and Dolly was born in 1712, it is difficult to say who her parents were. I don't believe her father was Elias Ball. I suspect, from much circumstantial evidence, he bought her as a child and later grew fond of her. During her youth Dolly seems to have gotten unusual attention. At age sixteen, according to plantation accounts, Dolly fell ill and Elias quickly summoned a doctor to the plantation to treat her. The following year, he again called a doctor for Dolly and paid a high fee for the cure. It almost never occurred, on the remote plantations, that a slave was singled out for individual medical care. Physicians were scarce, and doctors had to be enticed with large sums of money to make trips to the country, since they could easily find patients in Charleston. But thanks to Elias, Dolly received house calls, the only black person on Comingtee to warrant such attention.

The pattern of care continued throughout Dolly's young life. On one occasion Elias had special shoes made for her. Beginning in the colonial days, plantation owners hired shoemakers to sew one kind of footwear for themselves and their families and another kind, called Negro shoes, for slaves. Once, Elias hired a shoemaker from the nearby settlement of Goose Creek to sew shoes for his son, and, in the same order, to make similar high-priced footwear for Dolly. There is no evidence that other slaves ever received such treatment.

Dolly was about twenty when she went to work in the Ball house. After a year or two there, she began to have children. Her son Cupid was born in April 1735. Because the slave owners often left out the name of the father in records of slave births, I cannot say who Cupid's father was. In all likelihood he was another slave on Comingtee, because Cupid went on to become a field hand, lived his entire life on Ball plantations, and died sometime after 1784.

In the 1730s, Elias and Mary were also having children. Mary gave birth to her last, a son, in 1734; he died as an infant. There is no record of Mary's death, but soon after the birth of her final child, Mary herself passed away and Elias buried her sometime around 1735, ending a marriage of fifteen years. Upon Mary's death, Elias was left with three daughters to look after—Mary, Eleanor, and Sarah—ages two to thirteen. In 1736, he turned sixty. When Elias married Mary Delamare, he had made clear his preference for younger women. Now Dolly, twenty-four, was on hand.

Mary's death seems to have made possible a liaison between Elias and Dolly. On September 16, 1740, Dolly gave birth to her second child, who was given the name Edward. Among the slaves on Comingtee, none carried English forenames. What's more, when Edward grew up, records show that the Ball family paid him respect. Edward was given his freedom and lived among the Balls, who handled his business affairs. When he died, at eighty, his will and other papers went into the Ball family collection. According to probate records, Edward was a mulatto, described in his estate papers as "a free yellow man." If Edward had been able to take the name of the man whom I believe was his father, he would have been called Edward Ball.

A few years later, while still working in the big house, Dolly had another child who received an English name, Catherine. Like her brother Edward, Catherine would also later gain freedom, evidently granted to her by the Balls. The two siblings, Catherine and Edward, were the only people owned by Elias who would ever be freed from slavery.

Around the time Dolly began to have her mulatto children, sex between whites and blacks was a topic of sharp discussion in the local newspaper. The frequency of the editorials suggests that Elias and Dolly's relationship had plenty of precedent. In July 1736, one writer for the *South Carolina Gazette* pleaded with "Certain young Men" of Charleston to hide their relationships with colored women. He called on them to "frequent less with their black Lovers the open Lots and the . . . House on the Green between old Church street and King street." If they did not keep their heads down, he added, other whites might step in "to coole their Courage and to expose them." The writer ended his cranky editorial with an appeal to white men to stay away from women slaves, if only in solidarity with other whites. White women, he maintained, were "full as capable for Service either night or day as any Africain Ladies whatsoever."

When he sat down to write his will, Elias kept young Dolly high in his mind. After declaring that his property would pass to his white children, he added this unusual clause: "I give & Bequeath the Molattoe Wench called Dolly to such of my children as she shall within three months next after my Decease make her Election for her master or mistress." Elias wanted Dolly to be able to decide her fate after he was gone: she was to choose which among Elias's white children would give her a home. It was an incomplete gesture—Dolly could select only her next master or mistress, not freedom—but in this way Elias acknowledged her humanity. The telltale clue is the phrase "within three months next after my Decease." Dolly would have a period of mourning to collect herself before deciding her next step, a graceful interval of grief.

If Dolly and Elias kept up a relationship for several years, was it rape? Or could they have cared for each other? Mockery and danger would have faced the couple on both sides. Not only would Elias have felt ostracized by some whites, but Dolly may have angered some of the other slaves at Comingtee by sleeping with the master. As for the sex itself, could Elias and Dolly both have felt desire? Or did Dolly trade sex (willingly or not) for more lenient treatment? Despite the pitiful circumstances of their attachment, could these two have, somehow, loved each other?

I imagine several of these things may simultaneously have been true.

6

>─⬧─○─⬧─<

WRITTEN IN THE BLOOD

I had reason to believe that I was related to a black family in Pennsylvania, though I could not be sure where the family had once been enslaved, on which plantation owned by the Balls; neither did I know who among the Ball slave owners might have been their ancestor. As I drove to our first rendezvous in Philadelphia, I wondered how it could be settled whether we actually shared some blood.

It was February, and there had been a snowstorm in the Northeast. The roads were plowed and scattered with rock salt, which flew up from the wheels and pelted the car, making a noise like rattling fingernails. A chalky mud covered the windshield, and the snowy banks of the Delaware River looked like fields of cotton.

I had received a letter from a woman named Carolyn Smalls Goodson, inviting me to visit. Carolyn Goodson's family tradition held that some of her ancestors were enslaved by the Balls. Since she was a child, she had heard that her great-great-great-grandmother was bought by the Ball family off a slave ship. In America, she was told, this African forebear had become the mother of a man named Frederick Poyas. The father of Frederick Poyas, tradition said, was one of the Ball men.

"I feel a very strong connection to you," Carolyn Goodson wrote. "Our lives have touched, and we are no strangers to each other. . . . I hope that you will be able to help me as I am willing to help you. There are so many unanswered questions, so many things about the past I want to understand."

I made my way through the muck and slapping slush, through a large, hilly park in northwest Philadelphia, to a well-kept neighborhood of stone and brick. The settlement of Philadelphia had been cleared on the shores of the Delaware in 1682, by the followers of William Penn, a thirty-eight-year-old aristocrat who had gotten a grant of land in the colonies in exchange for money the British Crown owed his dead father. Penn and his adventurers were Quakers, from a small group of religious dissidents in England. Although at the outset the Quakers owned people, in time they recanted and became the loudest voices in America for the end of forced labor. In March 1780, in the middle of the Revolution, Pennsylvania became one of the first states to pass an abolition law, promising freedom to the children of enslaved blacks. In the 1920s, and again after World War II, black people migrated out of the South to Pennsylvania and factory jobs.

Carolyn Goodson's family had a two-story home on a block of brick-and-stone row houses. The neighborhood had been built in the 1940s for working people, and each house had a little lawn in front and a single-car garage in back, facing an alley. Though the street looked empty in the snow, the sidewalks had been shoveled and the driveways cleared, signs of civic responsibility.

Carolyn Goodson's face was radiant as she opened the door. She embraced me, and told me to use her first name. Carolyn was in her midforties, but looked ten years younger in trousers and a long-sleeved white satin blouse buttoned to the neck. Her brown hair fell in long braids around her shoulders, and her skin was the color of cherry wood. The roseate tint of her hands and face glowed against the whiteness of her shirt. Next to her red-brown skin, Carolyn's eyes were her most pronounced feature—clear, loving, vulnerable.

The house felt roomy, with three bedrooms upstairs, living and dining rooms, kitchen and basement. In the living room were black chairs and a sofa; in the dining room, a large table and sideboard with china; and in the kitchen, new cabinetry and a bright linoleum floor. There wasn't a particle of dust in the house.

Carolyn had been married for many years, but had lately divorced. She introduced me to her sons, Michael, in college, and Randall, in high school and a basketball player. Carolyn's sister, Beatrice McGirth, the oldest of eight siblings, had also come to talk. She was in her fifties and had a no-nonsense air, though she went by the nickname Bea. While Bea McGirth was raising her children, her husband had died, and she now lived alone in Philadelphia.

Michael Goodson was handsome and soft-spoken, with respectful manners and an unblinking clear gaze like his mother's. He knew that I had been visiting black families.

"I have one question, Mr. Ball," Michael said, soon after we met. In the pause, I wondered whether it would be about common blood. "What's it like to go everywhere and be surrounded only by black people?"

"Maybe it's like being black and going through life surrounded by white people," I answered.

After dinner, Carolyn, Bea, and I sat under a light around the dining-room table.

"I graduated from high school in 1968," said Carolyn, "and came to Philadelphia immediately. I was seventeen, turning eighteen that summer."

At the time, she was Carolyn Smalls.

"My first job was at a hat factory. I helped to make hats, and steam them," Carolyn said. "I was only hired for a short period, then they laid everybody off. After that, I started working at Sears. I got the job at Sears over the Christmas holiday. What we did, it was a packing department that if you ordered clothing through a catalogue, the clothing would come to us, and we would pack it. It was a hard, demanding job. Every fifteen minutes you would have to drop ten customers' orders— box them, tape them up, and tie them with strings. After Christmas, I had made plans to go home, and everybody else was laid off, but they kept me on."

Carolyn's eyes were loving. The whiteness around the brown iris glowed, and her eyelids hung softly. There was something accepting and tolerant about her eyes that lingered even after she looked away.

"Did you send money home?" I asked. She had grown up in the country, in South Carolina, in a cottage with no electricity.

"Yes, because of the conditions at home, it was so poor," she said.

"We were all somewhat ashamed of the house we came up in. It had only one bedroom, and a wood stove. Our walls were wallpapered with magazines. My parents couldn't afford to buy wallpaper. That was a game for us—we would lie in bed and tell the next brother or sister to find this particular word. A few people around had electricity, like our next-door neighbor. We always looked at them as if they had a little money. We would beg our neighbor to let us come watch their TV."

I asked what the family did for light, and to keep food fresh.

"We had an old icebox that they would get ice by the pound, and lamp light, oil or kerosene," Carolyn said. "When I turned eleven, my parents took the money they had on a ten-year policy and put electricity in the house. That was 1961. We didn't have bathrooms, even after we got electricity, just outdoor toilets."

Carolyn's eyes met mine, and her face continued to glow. It occurred to me that as a child she had seen the end of the segregation laws in the early 1960s, and I asked for a story. She looked at the table, and a hazy scene seemed to gather in her memory.

"I remember that grandmother took me from South Carolina to New York, to visit my aunt Beatrice," Carolyn said. "When we boarded the train in Charleston, I looked up and saw that we were in one car, and white people were in another. In fact, we had to pass through the white car to get to the black car. It was summer, and the temperature was different in the white car. It was cooler. I seem to remember also that the white car was more plush. Of course, all the porters were black, and well-dressed, and one of them must have led us to the black car. It was perfectly strange."

Carolyn said she was living with her brother in Philadelphia, and dating men, when she got a job at Thomas Jefferson Hospital, as a clerk in a nurse's unit.

"My first decent job."

She moved out of her brother's house and into an apartment in 1972. Then Carolyn Smalls met James Goodson.

"I got married," said Carolyn, "but I didn't do it in the order you should have done it. My son Michael was born in July, and James and I got married the next June. He was a bus driver for the Transit Authority. We separated two years ago. Seems like a long time." The memory of the divorce cast a brief shadow on Carolyn's open face.

"I was at Jefferson fifteen years when I requested to look at my personnel file," she remembered. "It was on microfilm, and going through it, I read the notes on my first job interview. It said I was 'a dull person with possibilities of being sharpened.' Looking back, I think I was a dull person. Coming to Philadelphia, I had to learn how to speak all over again. Even though we studied English in school, we didn't speak it."

"You spoke country English," I said.

"Back home, our English teacher would say about the way we talked, 'This is going to hurt you later on.' But everybody else spoke the same way."

I asked Carolyn how she spoke.

"It was a broken dialect," she told me. "Instead of saying 'this,' I would say 'dis' and 'dat.' It wasn't important to use the past tense. 'I break that glass.' Not 'I have been,' but 'I been.' And, 'gimme dis.' If somebody insulted you, it was 'I frauded you.' Everything was quick and easy—just get it out, no need to concentrate."

Gullah, the black English of coastal South Carolina and Georgia, is thickest on the sea islands, a necklace of sandy islands from Charleston to Savannah, though it was also spoken in old inland rice lands like those on the Cooper River. The dialect, which came from a mingling of English with West African grammar, helped shape a national black English in the post-Civil War period.

"I hear country English, or Gullah, as a beautiful thing, not as bad English," I said.

Carolyn smiled, as though surprised, then gave her own assessment of white English. "Yes, and I find white people have what I call a 'drool.' It takes them forever to say one thing. They just drool things out."

This gave us both a laugh, and Carolyn grinned, a powerful smile, like a flare in the room. Carolyn had a large set of teeth, and when she smiled, peeling back her lips and screwing up her nose, she got them all into the open.

Carolyn's sister, Bea McGirth, wore a lavender jacket and matching pants, and her hair was treated with straightener. Raised in the same two-room house as Carolyn, Bea Smalls moved out and married her husband, Barry McGirth, in the early 1960s. She had two daughters, Carrie and Willa. Barry McGirth died in 1977, and Bea went to work.

"He left me no money," Bea said. "As a matter of fact, an insurance policy didn't even pay his funeral, so I had to pay it at fifty dollars a month."

Ten years later, the children raised, she moved alone to Philadelphia. I asked what launched her journey North.

"Money. I was in debt to the top of my head. My baby daughter was in college, and I had borrowed and mortgaged everything for her education. I moved to Philadelphia with fifty dollars cash."

In Philadelphia, Bea got a job in a nursing home, and later in a hospital. When we met, she had worked for many years as a supervisor in the hospital's dietary department.

As we went over the lives and loves of the two sisters, one story hung in the air between us. All of us knew it, and wondered how to make sense of the tale. Suddenly Bea McGirth's eyes leveled, and in her matter-of-fact way she began to talk about our presumed common blood.

"I lived with my grandmother, Carrie Nesbitt, when I was in my teens," she said, "starting in 1959. She was my mother's mother. We used to sit up late at night and make quilts, and while we sewed, I used to ask her a lot of questions concerning the family." As they quilted, Bea said, Carrie Nesbitt used to talk about her own grandparents, Frederick and Caroline Poyas, whose name was pronounced "pious."

"She said that Caroline Poyas was strict, and part Indian," Bea remembered. "She didn't know what tribe. My grandmother said that she kept her hair long. She either just pinned it up, and it was long and straight, or she just wore it down. And Frederick Poyas—my grandmother said that his father was white."

"Did she ever say who that might have been?" I asked.

"No, but from what my grandmother said about the Balls, they must have been—their masters must have been the Balls," Bea came back. It sounded like an answer to a slightly different question, until Bea finished the thought. "The Balls had allowed Frederick Poyas to buy a piece of property from them, and my grandmother seemed to think that he might have been the son of one of them."

Bea had a polite way of putting it: about Frederick Poyas, Carrie Nesbitt "seemed to think that he might have been" the son of a Ball slave owner.

"Did your grandmother tell this to you as a matter of fact," I asked, "or as a terrible fact?"

"Just in conversation," said Bea.

"In my generation," Carolyn put in, "there were babies born from white men in relationships with black women. It was no secret in the community who these children belonged to. I'm sure there were problems with the wives of the white men to see these mixed kids walking around."

Later I learned that Carrie Nesbitt, the quiltmaker and source of the story, was born in 1893, within arm's reach of the Civil War. For income, she worked as a midwife and, as a person who delivered babies, was not likely to be fazed by talk of white-black sex.

Bea and Carolyn said that the two-room, lamp-lit house where they grew up stood on the same piece of land that their great-great-grand-father, Frederick Poyas, had bought from the Ball family. When the sisters were children, there was a framed portrait on the wall depicting Frederick Poyas and his Native wife, Caroline. The picture, drawn in graphite, showed three people posed outdoors in front of a shed—two men in dark, skinny jackets and a woman wearing a full-length skirt and high-necked blouse. Carolyn and Bea described the picture, and I had seen a reproduction of it. Along with Frederick and Caroline Poyas it showed George Poyas, one of their sons. To judge from the detail of expression, the faces had been drawn from a photograph, which had since been lost, while their bodies belonged to no one in particular, sketched like cutouts. In the picture Frederick Poyas had light skin, thin lips, and parted hair. His gaze was focused, beneath straight eyebrows, and he had a rather grim, flat mouth. He could easily have been a mulatto. Later Bea told me that when Frederick and Caroline Poyas died, they were buried not on their own piece of land but at Halidon Hill, a tract on the east branch of the Cooper River formerly owned by the Balls.

When Bea and Carolyn were girls in the 1950s, they lived near Middleburg plantation, one of the last places held by the Balls. At the time Middleburg was the property of Marie Ball Dingle, a woman in her sixties who had inherited it from her father. Marie was married to an artist named Edward von Siebold Dingle, although for some reason Edward Dingle was known in the family as "Peter." Peter Dingle made paintings of birds, and trapped and stuffed various species around the plantation the better to arrange the ornithological specimens in his studio. I imagine Peter and Marie were an odd couple in the eyes of neighboring blacks, the more so because they spent almost all of their time at home. In any case, Bea remembered going fishing on Middleburg. Every time, she and her family went to the big house to ask permission.

"Marie Ball lived on the plantation, and it was always a question in the back of my mind," said Bea. "She was hostile to some people, and she couldn't see very well. But when my mother and I came to the door to go fishing, she would say, 'Who's that out there?' 'It's Fredie Mae,' my mother would say. 'Oh, okay,' she would say. It was like, 'It's okay if you come.' It was always okay for us to go fishing, and it was always a question in the back of my mind—why?"

"Because there was a connection?" I said.

"Marie probably had been told that there is a relationship there, and that we were family," Bea said.

Bea sifted her memories and laid them out straight, like a math teacher demonstrating an equation. There was no written proof, but there were many stories, and I was beginning to feel the preponderance of the evidence.

Frederick and Caroline Poyas had a daughter named Florence. "Aunt Florence was kind, humble," Bea said. "I knew her—she died in 1952, when she was about eighty years old. It appears that my grandmother said that the Balls loved her." Bea's polite phrasing came back—"It appears." "They said that if Caroline and Frederick would allow them, they would take her and educate her."

"My mom said that she studied cooking," Carolyn added.

"Aunt Florence started traveling with a Yankee family, and cooking for them," Bea went on. "They were seasonal people, the Yankees, who came down to hunt, and would go back North. When Florence got married, her husband traveled with her." It was rare that black country people got work with travel, and such a cook's job would have been a prize.

"A reason why the Balls might have done that, help her to get a decent job, is because she was kin," I said.

"She was part of the family," Bea answered. She smiled for the first time since she began her story.

"Marie Ball was married to a German guy, Dingle, who was very quiet," she went on. Bea seemed to be picturing Peter Dingle and Marie Ball in her mind. "She ran the house. He didn't have nothing to say.

They would come to see Florence, driving very slow. Marie would be sitting up there, her hair in a bun. Her husband drove so slow, I don't know how he didn't get a ticket!"

I looked at Carolyn, and she broke open her many-toothed smile. We all smiled a moment, then fell serious.

"Anyway, they would come to see Florence," Bea went ahead. "After Florence passed, I remember Marie and her husband came to give their condolence."

There was a silence in the room, and I thought I heard the humming of the refrigerator. I felt a pack of emotions and was not sure which to single out and hold.

"Part of the touching fact of our getting to know each other," I said, grasping for words, "is the possibility that you and I are distantly related."

Carolyn nodded, and so did Bea. There was a feeling of roominess around the table, as though we had walked into a clearing from the woods. We talked some more, until eventually Carolyn picked the right emotion, and laid it out.

"The only thing that can cure what's happened," she said, "is for us to administer love."

Carolyn and Bea did not know the name of the white man who fathered Frederick Poyas. I might have accepted their oral tradition that he was a Ball, but this would not be enough to satisfy a skeptic.

Frederick Poyas had left a drawing of himself, but his descendants did not know when he was born. In the federal census for the year 1880, Poyas and his family of five children, living near the Balls' Limerick plantation, are described as mulatto, the only family designated by that term for miles around. The census enumerator took down the age of Frederick Poyas as forty. The number might have come from Frederick himself or perhaps from a neighbor's guess, which meant his birthdate fell around, but not necessarily in, 1840.

I looked in the Ball slave lists for the birth of a child named Frederick. In records for Limerick plantation, the largest Ball place, one appeared, born to a field hand named Diana on June 25, 1841. Mulatto children were often given names that distinguished them from the larger slave population, and Frederick was such a name. Checking other slave lists, I found this was the only Frederick on any of the Ball places for some twenty-five years.

Mulattoes often were fathered by the so-called young master, the unmarried heir to a plantation. In the year of Frederick's birth at Limerick, there was indeed a young man around the place, my great-great-grandfather, William James Ball, born in October 1821 to Isaac and Eliza Ball. When William was only four, his father died of malaria; William grew up with his mother, possessed of large estates managed by executors. When the child Frederick was conceived at Limerick, about November 1840, William would have been nineteen. Fourteen months later, in February 1842, William married Julia Cart, a seventeen-year-old girl from a Charleston family.

From the circumstantial evidence, it seemed likely that William Ball might have fathered Frederick. William was on the plantation at the time, in power, and about to marry.

I looked further for clues. Frederick's mother was named Diana. His descendants described Diana as the African "bought by the Balls from a slave ship." Unfortunately, I could not determine Diana's ancestry, nor much else about her life. She may or may not have been born in West Africa. However, records show that when Frederick was born, Diana already had a two-year-old daughter, Harriet. After Frederick, she had another daughter, Lizzie, in 1842. The father or fathers of the children were not named by the young William Ball, who by this time was keeping the slave lists. But one thing leaped out from the pages: in 1849, William decided to send Diana and eight-year-old Frederick away from Limerick to Cedar Hill plantation, a tract about eight miles down the Cooper River, where some seventy-six slaves lived and worked. Diana's child Lizzie had died; Lizzie's sister, ten-year-old Harriet, was not sent to Cedar Hill. According to William's ledger, Harriet stayed at Limerick, where she was apparently taken in by a black woman named Eve.

For the next few years, Diana and Frederick stayed together on Cedar Hill. Diana appears for the last time on slave lists in 1856, after which she apparently died. Frederick continued to live at Cedar Hill until at least 1860. That year William wrote down Frederick's name for the last time, and struck a line through it. The line did not mean he was dead (which William would have noted with a date) but that he might have been either sold or moved to another plantation. A year later, the Civil War began and William stopped keeping his slave lists.

The pieces fit crudely together into a pattern familiar around the South: a young master fathers a child with a black woman, gets married to a white woman, and eventually sends his mulatto son and the mother away from home.

The story seemed persuasive but in fact I had no thread that would link the child Frederick with the mulatto Frederick Poyas. Suddenly, one appeared. As it happened, there was another young master raised at Limerick about this time, William's first cousin, James Poyas. James Poyas was born in 1806 at Windsor plantation, to Windsor's owners, Henry and Elizabeth Poyas. When he was about seven, James was given up for adoption to his uncle and aunt, Isaac and Eliza Ball, a mile away at Limerick. Eliza Ball had been born Eliza Poyas, at Windsor. Isaac Ball and Eliza Poyas were married in 1811, but for several years had no children. Eliza turned to her brother, Henry Poyas, who agreed to surrender his son James so that the couple might have a boy to raise. Little James Poyas moved to Limerick around 1813. Even when Isaac and Eliza Ball (without explanation) began to have their own children five years later, James, by this time twelve years old, stayed on in the house. James Poyas grew up alongside his young cousin William, but never married. He became a rice planter and slave owner on the Cooper River, like the rest of the Balls, and died in 1850 at age forty-four.

In addition to being an adopted son, James Poyas was a blood member of the Ball family. Because of the frequent intermarriage of the plantation families, both James and his adoptive parents were all, in one way or another, descendants of Elias "Red Cap" Ball. James's biological father, Henry Poyas (1787–1824), was a son of a Catherine Smith (1768–1836), of Old Goose Creek plantation, herself a daughter of Elizabeth Ball (1746–87), who was, finally, a granddaughter of Red Cap.

Having learned about James Poyas, I now suspected that he, and not William Ball, was the father of Frederick. Three pieces of evidence pointed to this conclusion—two of them circumstantial, one physical. First, in the year of Frederick's birth, James was thirty-five, unmarried, and living near Limerick. Second, at the end of the Civil War, when young Frederick became free and able to choose a surname, he took the name Poyas. The third piece of evidence was the most convincing. Shortly before his death, James Poyas had his portrait taken using the new photographic process, the daguerreotype. In the picture, James, wearing a jacket and tie, has a focused gaze beneath distinctive eyebrows and shows a rather grim, flat mouth. It was a simple matter to compare this image with the drawing of Frederick Poyas in the hands of his descendants. Frederick's portrait was probably made during his forties, about the same age at which James had his picture taken. There is an unmistakable resemblance. The "mulatto farmer" of the census has the same flat mouth, eyebrows, and cheekbones as his putative father.

By the standards of his caste, James Poyas had a conventional life. At age nineteen he was involved in an auction of some black people whom his aunt evidently wished to be rid of. The same year, 1825, he inherited money from Isaac Ball, the late owner of Limerick. Using the capital, James bought Cedar Hill plantation, a 996-acre place a few miles from home. Twenty-five years later, on January 1, 1850, James signed a deal to sell Cedar Hill to his cousin and adoptive brother, William Ball. James was on his deathbed, and William wanted to expand his own business. Four days later, James died.

Frederick Poyas was freed from the ownership of William Ball in 1865, at age twenty-three. His story continues in his family's oral tradition. Frederick married Caroline, from a Native family in the area, and started a family. The couple had eight children, beginning with Frederick Jr. at the end of the Civil War and ending with George, fifteen years later. Soon, Frederick Sr. bought fifty-seven acres of land from the Ball family, at a price of fifty cents an acre, and moved with his family there. Rebecca Poyas, the second child, was born in 1866. Rebecca grew up and married James Nesbitt, and they had a daughter named Carrie in 1893. Carrie married Frank Ladson, and they had a daughter, Fredie Mae, in 1924. In 1941, at age fifteen, Fredie Mae married Postal Smalls. The Poyas homestead was handed down to Fredie Mae and Postal Smalls. Fredie Mae Smalls had eight children, two of whom would grow up to be Carolyn Goodson and Bea McGirth, of Philadelphia. The descendants of Frederick Poyas who remain in touch with one another number about fifty people, in Florida, Maryland, Ohio, Pennsylvania, South Carolina, and beyond.

On a Sunday afternoon in February, I visited Leon Smalls, another descendant of Frederick Poyas and, more distantly, Elias "Red Cap" Ball. Like his sister Carolyn, Mr. Smalls lived in an attached brick two-story on a street of nearly identical houses in Philadelphia. It was good family quarters in a hardworking neighborhood.

Leon Smalls greeted me at the door with the corners of his mouth turned down. He was a strong man in his fifties, with short hair, a broad, implacable face, and brown, unlined skin. He wore a button shirt, dark workman's trousers, and sneakers. Mr. Smalls took in a long breath, and exhaled it slowly through his teeth. In marked contrast to Carolyn, Leon Smalls seemed to have a closely watched anger.

"I don't know what this is all about," he said with a hard handshake, disdaining either me or the idea I had asked to visit. I could feel his anger as I walked into the house.

A collection of potted plants stood in the foyer, brought in against the cold. The living room had furniture with plastic covers, and a big television. We settled at the dinner table, and Leon Smalls propped his head on an index finger and thumb. He refused to look at me, preferring the tabletop. Carolyn Goodson sat, circumspect, on a nearby sofa. Mr. Smalls's wife, Phoebe Ann Smalls, a slender, gentle woman, brought me a drink and settled nervously near her husband. Mr. Smalls and I sat within reach, and I could sense him seething, as though he could hardly stand to be in the room. When I described again what I was doing— visiting black families whose ancestors were enslaved to my family— his simmering increased.

Leon Smalls was born in 1942 and, like his sisters, raised on the old homestead of Frederick Poyas. After he finished high school, in 1961 Mr. Smalls became the first of his siblings to move to Philadelphia. I asked him why Pennsylvania, and not some other place.

"I had an uncle here. I could find somewhere to stay until I could get on my feet," he answered, in a blunt baritone voice. "I got a big job—$1.09 an hour. I could make $100 a week, but that means working a hundred hours a week." Mr. Smalls seemed to spit out his story, his voice wet with sarcasm.

"It was a linen company called Apex, since went bankrupt. I sorted linen. Everything come bagged up—the napkins go one place, table-cloths another place, uniforms another place." He pursed his lips, and a ripple of contempt rolled across his face.

"I came North because, as a young African American in the South during those days, if you weren't lucky enough to get a job hanging sheetrock, there was nothing to do!" Mr. Smalls kept his eyes fixed on the tabletop. "I worked for Apex about a year. From there I went into automobile body and fender. I worked there until I got my first break. I painted a guy's car, and he liked the job. He offered me a job, and I told him I was not going to go back to work in an automobile garage. He says, 'Can you drive a truck?' I says, 'Yes.' He said, 'Come see me on Saturday and I'll put you to work.' I did such, and I've been driving a truck ever since."

Leon Smalls looked at me for the first time.

Soon he married his wife, Phoebe Ann. After a stint in the military, he began to drive rigs for the Ford Motor Company.

"In 1970, I feel like if I'm going to be on the street, driving a truck, I might as well do something and make some money out of it," Mr. Smalls went on, unblinking. "I went back to school and got my degree to drive a tractor-trailer. I started hauling automobiles for Ford Motor Company July 6, 1970. I'm still there."

"You haul tractor-trailers with ten cars?" I said. I hoped that by sticking to concrete things, we might communicate.

"My equipment is built for twelve small ones," he answered.

"Where do you drive them?"

"From Maine to Florida—all over the Northeast and Southeast."

"I imagine you're well-placed in the union."

"Yeah, I'm as far as I can go. I'm a member of International Broth-erhood of Teamsters, 312, out of the town of Chester."

"You must have a position of influence," I said.

"Yeah, I'm union rep."

Describing his job, Mr. Smalls released himself a bit. There were about ninety union members in his truck terminal, he said, including seventy-four drivers, eleven mechanics, and three clerks. "I'm an ex-steward, but everyone comes to me as if I'm still the steward. It's hard to say, but I'm about the last say in my terminal. It's something that I've built and I would hate to see torn down."

On good wages, Leon and Phoebe Smalls had raised two children, Leonard and Methena. Leonard Smalls, in his twenties, was in the Army. "He's in Colorado now," said Phoebe Smalls, speaking softly. "Methena, she's out of school, and enrolled as a cosmetologist. She works at a beautician shop. She's a shampooer there."

I turned the conversation back to Mr. Smalls. "Did you take part in any of the protest movements of the 1960s?" I asked.

"No."

Leon Smalls leveled a vehement stare.

"Would you have liked to?"

"No. I had all the opportunity in the world to, but I didn't choose that route. I wasn't brought up that way, and I still don't believe that that is the answer." He spoke with a staccato diction, like a manual typewriter, loud and clattering. "You see, Martin Luther King, as much as he did, and there was progress made, but the man gave his life, and I still don't see us much further than before his time. Many people benefited by him, in a sense more Caucasian than blacks. He don't get that credit. You go into the Appalachian Mountains of Pennsylvania, those people were living like pigs up there until equal rights came about. And in order to distribute a piece of pie to us, they had to get their fair share. Yeah, they love him up there. But you come into the major cities, the first thing out of a Caucasian's mouth is 'Who the hell is Martin Luther King? He's just a nigger that got killed, that's all.' No, I didn't get into the protest, because protesting made me bitterer than I am."

When I began looking at the plantations, and speaking with descendants of Ball slaves, I thought that I might meet with a certain amount of rage. I presumed it would be directed at me. In fact, I had been surprised at how little rage I had found—that is, among black people.

"You are conscious of your bitterness," I said.

"Very much so, that's my personality."

"When did you become an embittered person?" I felt a twinge of admiration for Mr. Smalls, who both felt bitter and watched himself feeling it.

"I can remember my first day that I realized that I had a problem," he said. "I was about sixteen years old. I was working for a guy in Mount Pleasant, South Carolina, and we used to take peaches around the state and sell them by the bushel. We went to a place where we needed gas in the truck, and they had a big sign on the pumps, 'No Negroes or niggers allowed inside.' I could buy their gasoline, but I couldn't go inside. I had a problem with that. Things like that lay fresh in my mind."

Mr. Smalls snapped a new gaze in my direction.

"And if you would check the bloodline of some of these so-called righteous fellows that put those signs up, they had as much 'Negroes or niggers' in them that I have in me!"

Leon Smalls's face trembled a bit. Staring at me, he took in a deep breath through his nostrils and let it pass into the room.

"We today think that things have changed," Mr. Smalls went on. "No. Behind our back we are criticized the same identical way. I work with a group of people who, the only difference is they leave their sheet at home. But they still have them in their closets."

"Teamsters?" I said. He was referring to the hoods and sheets of the Ku Klux Klan, though neither of us let those words pass our lips.

"Yeah, they call themselves 'brother.' Yeah, we are all union brothers. Such is not the case. It hurts them to their heart to know that a black man is putting food on the table."

Behind me I heard a rustling on the sofa, although I could not see Carolyn Goodson, the source of the noise.

"See, a white man is sneaky," said Mr. Smalls. "He is the type who will throw the brick and hide his hands. You have to be attentive to what he say and do."

"You would or would not characterize yourself as a racist?" I asked.

"By no means do I consider myself a racist," he answered, "nor would I want anybody to consider me an Uncle Tom."

It was time to come around to the facts. "I'm not shying from things, Mr. Smalls," I began. "I'm trying to learn the whole story. Frederick Poyas, your great-great-grandfather, it seems that his father was a member of the Ball family."

"Yes, I'm very aware of that," said Mr. Smalls, exhaling. "That is something that we knew and could not discuss. We know that going to school we were called 'red' and 'cracker.' " Mr. Smalls's skin was darker than that of his sister Carolyn, but it may have darkened with age.

"For us growing up," Carolyn put in, "we were lighter than the average people around us. Not only the skin, but the texture of our hair.

They would say, 'You got white people's hair.' There was always fighting about it." I looked at Carolyn's skin, with its rose tint.

"We fought many days because we were lighter," she went on. "It was very painful. The kids of our generation would always say, 'Who's your mother and father?' I remember them even saying that the mattress on our bed was from a white man. My mother talks about it, the family history, more now, but she didn't talk about it all when we were small. The reason for that is that not everyone is so open and able to accept what happened over a hundred years ago."

Leon Smalls peered at me. "These are some of the things," he said, "I'm quite sure that your great-grandfather, or whatever, if he was alive, he would get very angry about. But interbreeding was something that happened in those days. These guys rode around and walked around on their horses as if they were kings during the daylight hours, and at night, they did their share of slipping around in the slave quarters, and their wives knew it as well as anyone else. That will make them turn over in their graves about their bastard children, about who they weren't man enough to come forward and say, 'That is my child.' Why do you think we are so messed up in colors? Think about it. We all come here one color. We couldn't interbreed ourselves."

"Isn't it better to talk about it than not to talk about it?" I said.

"It's better to talk about it," came the answer. "And as I was saying, many Caucasian Americans have traces of Negro blood in them, too. So the same way how the slave master was slipping around in the houses at night, his mistress was also slipping around in the big house during the day. It happened."

"What do you feel about the idea that you and I are distantly related?" I asked.

"It doesn't faze me, because it's something that I had no control over," Mr. Smalls said. "I'm not going to jump off a bridge because it happened. It don't bother me one way or the other, and my life goes on. I just don't want it to end up similar to *Imitation of Life*."

"You're referring to the movie?" I said.

"Yeah."

Imitation of Life, directed by Douglas Sirk, a German immigrant not especially known for his treatment of race, came out of Hollywood in 1959. It was a big-budget melodrama, shot in the pinks and blues and greens of late-1950s Technicolor, the story of a colored girl who tries to pass for white. In the plot, a white stage actress named Lora Meredith (played by Lana Turner) hires a live-in black housekeeper, Annie Johnson (Juanita Moore). Annie Johnson has a daughter, Sarah Jane, whose pale skin evidently comes from a white father, long absent. Sarah Jane (played by Susan Kohner) grows up and tries to pass. She leaves home and cuts off contact with her mother. Annie Johnson grieves as her daughter disappears into white life, never to return. Eventually Sarah Jane's mother dies of apparent sadness. At the funeral Sarah Jane reappears for the first time since leaving home, throws herself on the casket, and apologizes to her dead mother for having abandoned her.

"The sad part of the movie," Leon Smalls remembered, "is the part about the Negro mother losing her child, the fact that she wants to be white. Things of that kind have been happening since the beginning of time. It's saddening for an African American to see someone as trying to portray themselves as something that they are not, but it's been going on forever."

Leon Smalls bit down on his words, which escaped his mouth as though they were trying to flee.

"Until you walk in my shoe you don't understand what makes us tick and what makes us feel the way we feel," he said. "The racial situation, it's worse today than it were then, when I was young. As an eighteen-year-old African American male, you are fast becoming an endangered species, simply because the opportunity of employment is just not there for you. The world will tell you, 'There are plenty of jobs out there.' But what they are going to do for you is give you wages you can't buy clothing with. If you look around, you can walk into any establishment that is paying a decent wage, and you'll find the racial balance almost nine to one Caucasian. So that tells you there. And you walk into a place that is six-to-one African American, you walk out because you know they are not paying anything."

It occurred to me that Leon Smalls was not a person filled with rage, after all. His dominant emotion, perhaps, was pessimism. Pessimism is more corrosive than anger, and more complete. Anger settles in a clenched jaw, while pessimism fills the body to the fingertips.

"Do you have a ray of hope in your heart for the future?" I asked.

"No, I really don't see anything great coming to my people within my time," he replied, his baritone firm. "We have to have hope, without it we are doomed. But then they say, hope ends in frustration."

I admired Leon Smalls. From the well of his despair, he had brought up an accommodation of his own design. His bitterness protected him, while he left open the dim prospect of a different life.

Mr. Smalls talked about his children, his work, and his pleasures. He told me that he kept a vegetable garden, on some land owned by a friend a half-hour drive from his house. During the warm months he spent every Saturday alone with his vegetables—corn, okra, string beans, cucumbers, sweet potatoes, mustard greens, and tomatoes. They were Southern vegetables for the most part, which he grew in the short Northern season in defiance of the climate.

As I made to leave, I thanked Mr. Smalls.

"Yeah, well," he answered.

"I know your heart is heavy," I said. "One reason I wanted to see you was to take a step, to make a gesture, and hold out my hand."

"No problem," said Mr. Smalls. "Someone has to break the ice. I gotta give you credit, you were man enough to do it."

Michael Goodson sat at the dining-room table in his mother's house in Philadelphia. Michael was twenty-one, handsome, polite, tall, and mild-mannered. His eyes, like those of his mother, were clear and white. But while Carolyn Goodson's eyes were vulnerable, Michael's eyes showed determination. When he directed his eyes, it was as though Michael held out two white lights, unblinking, focused, adamant.

Born in Philadelphia, Michael was a student at Temple University, where he studied biology and anthropology. He had attended an all-black Catholic school, St. Raymond, then transferred to Martin Luther King Jr. High School, a large, all-black public school. Michael graduated first among a class of five hundred students before enrolling at Temple. In college, he was a cadet in the Reserve Officers' Training Corps (ROTC), which helped pay tuition, and he had plans to go to graduate school.

Michael was the one who had asked what it was like for me to be surrounded by black people, so I returned the question by inquiring about his dealings on the white side of the color line.

"I first had to deal with white people when I was about thirteen," he said. "Before that, I had no white friends. I guess I saw white people from a distance, or as teachers in school." There was something matter-of-fact about Michael's manner that reminded me of his aunt, Bea McGirth; and for that matter, his uncle, Leon Smalls. "When I was thirteen, I got involved with the Civil Air Patrol, an auxiliary of the U.S. Air Force. The Civil Air Patrol teaches search-and-rescue techniques, like what to do in the event of a plane crash. And also some things about aeronautic technology."

With his direct manner, Michael Goodson seemed self-possessed and as free of stress about blackness and whiteness as a person might be. "I've never had a problem with white people, and never have been thought to have a problem," he said.

"You and your mother have reached some accommodation with racial identity that is rare," I said. "You seem to have drained yourself of anguish."

"I guess," he came back. "My friends these days, I guess you would call them 'multicultural'—they're black, white, Asian, Latino."

Later Michael and I talked more by phone. In one conversation, we wheeled between subjects, finally settling on South Carolina, our shared ancestral home. He loved the South, he told me. "In the South," said Michael, "the white people are more hospitable. White people speak to you who don't know you."

Michael recalled trips he had taken to the South to visit family. One of the great places of escape, he said, was a certain fishing hole near his grandparents' land.

"My cousin, Steven Smalls, and I, with my other cousins, went fishing constantly," said Michael. "There is a swamp behind my grandmother's house in South Carolina that is plentiful with fish. Every time we went down there, we came back with bundles. We didn't have a string to hold them on, so Steven and I used branches to thread them through the gills."

Michael Goodson told his fishing stories with softness and regret in his voice, and less assertiveness than usual.

"To keep the mosquitoes away, Steven and I hung cloth dipped in oil all around us, and burned it for the smoke. Later we would go hunting for squirrels, with a twenty-two rifle. Steven and I had an inseparable bond," he said.

Michael was in mourning for his cousin Steven, who was shot to death November 26, 1994, at the age of twenty. Steven lived in Charleston but "grew up in the country," according to Michael. After high school, Steven got a job with a computer repair shop, because, Michael said, he liked to take things apart, to see how they worked.

"Steven sometimes came to Philadelphia," Michael remembered. "One Christmas he visited, and we spent a lot of time talking about the future, like what our sons and daughters would call each other when we grew up, what kind of houses we were going to have, and how we were always going to go fishing and hunting together. Steven was so easygoing, I don't see how anyone could not like him. If people didn't like him, it was because of the fact that everybody else liked him."

The week he was killed, Steven Smalls had gotten a job in the city of Greenville, in upstate South Carolina, at an engineering plant. He had found his first apartment and was packing to make the move from Charleston.

"In my dorm room, I keep a photograph of the two of us together," Michael told me. "In the picture, we are dressed up for a wedding anniversary party. Steven's wearing a gold jacket and matching pants, and I'm wearing a blue suit with a white shirt."

By the family's account, on Friday, November 25, 1994, Steven drove from Charleston to James Island, a suburb of the city. A keen deer hunter, and good with a rifle, he planned to stay with a friend for the night and go hunting later in the weekend. That night Steven went with friends to a bar, the Lake House Club, in a section of James Island known as Mosquito Beach. Around midnight, an argument suddenly erupted inside the club. The bartender did not want a fight on his watch and so turned everyone involved in the commotion out into the parking lot. As the crowd stood on the pavement outside, the ruckus softened. A few moments later, however, one of the men who had come out of the bar approached Steven Smalls from behind and called out his name. Before he turned around, he was shot five times. He died in the parking lot.

The funeral service took place at the Azalea Drive Church of Christ, in Charleston. Michael Goodson drove down from Philadelphia with many other family members. Newspaper and television reporters had covered the killing, and hundreds of acquaintances of the family came to the service. Michael was one of the pallbearers.

"A lot of my family believe the first bullet killed him," Michael told me. In the cemetery, the Smalls and Goodson families stood over the grave, and the lid of the coffin was raised. "He looked so much at peace.

When somebody gets killed, the grimace they had normally stays on the face, due to rigor mortis. But my cousin looked like he was resting."

There was an evenness in Michael's voice, and an absence of rage, as though the anger he might have felt about the crime had been siphoned off.

"I miss him every day. We had a bond that a lot of people in their lifetime don't find. I could always talk to him, and he had an answer for everything. The answer was so simple, but so right."

I asked Michael about his cousin's killer, and he told me that three people had been charged—one with the murder, and two as accomplices who helped him get away.

"In any way justice can be served, let it happen," he said. "If they convict them, all right. But what they do to them doesn't matter, because it's not going to bring my cousin back. I don't wish that these people have their lives taken because they took my cousin's life. I don't wish them any harm. There are times I wish I could be in the same cell with them. All the pain and anger I've felt, they would catch that rap. But I have to let things take their course."

I had never met Steven Smalls, another descendant of Frederick Poyas, and of the Balls, but I decided to try to pay my respects by attending the trial of his accused killer. On a Wednesday in late October, I arrived at Courtroom B of the General Sessions Court, Charleston County, South Carolina. The room had rectangular fluorescent lights in a dropped ceiling, brown steel doors, and a big kitchen-style clock on the wall. Nearby, a gold-colored seal, which looked like tin, represented the authority of the state. Some sixty people, most of them black, sat on courtroom benches that resembled church pews made from painted pine.

On one side of the middle aisle sat the family of the victim, on the other, the defendant. Michael Goodson's grandparents, Postal and Fredie Mae Smalls, sat with their kin, all of them motionless. I could see the family resemblance among them. The defendant's clan were more restless, young and old, wigged and braided, thin and heavy, all shifting and looking around. The judge was a thirty-five-year-old white man with dark hair, deep-set eyes, and a prominent chin. In the jury box sat eight whites and four blacks.

The defendant was twenty-three-year-old Tony Lewis McNeil, nicknamed T.J. McNeil's two co-defendants had already been tried and jailed on lesser counts. McNeil himself was small, about five feet, seven inches, and 140 pounds, and wore a blue blazer that did not seem to fit. His head was nearly shaved, and he sat with his shoulders slumped, facing the judge. From time to time he turned around to look at his family, and when he did I saw that McNeil's face appeared very young, and very scared. Throughout the trial, McNeil, who was black, sat between his two court-appointed lawyers, a man and a woman, both white.

Larry Deas, an accessory to the murder, had plea-bargained and had been brought in from jail to testify. Deas was twenty-five, dark black, with short untreated hair. He wore a white shirt and oversized khaki pants without a belt; as he took the stand, his pants sagged, showing his underwear. Sitting in the witness box, Deas rocked back and forth, and his mouth drooped open.

Early in the trial, the Charleston County Medical Examiner testified that an autopsy found five bullets in Smalls. He had been shot four times in the back, and once in the right side. He seemed to have been running when he was hit with the bullets.

"We keep guns," Larry Deas said about his friends, "because nowadays, it's not that we start no trouble, but when something happens you want to protect yourself. You know Mosquito Beach. Everybody out there got a gun."

Deas testified that he was leaving the Lake House Club when McNeil, or T.J., shot Steven Smalls. Then, Deas said, "I got into my truck, drove around and picked up T.J. When T.J. got into the car, he just turned to me and said, 'He dead.' " Deas said he and McNeil made a getaway and later buried T.J.'s gun, along with a shotgun they had, in a corn field.

The trial, which lasted five days, had a feeling of inevitability about it. McNeil had admitted to police that he had shot Steven Smalls, and eyewitnesses placed the gun in his hands. In court, McNeil invoked his Fifth Amendment right to silence and did not take the stand. The public defenders assigned to McNeil tried to make a case that he had shot Smalls in the back in an act of self-protection. A couple of witnesses testified that Steven Smalls had a gun, or that he was wearing a jacket with a bulge in it which might have been construed to be a gun. The night of the crime, however, no witnesses made such statements, and no gun was found on the body by police.

After two hours of deliberation, the jury found Tony McNeil guilty of murder and possession of a gun in the commission of a violent crime. He was sentenced by the young judge to life in prison for the murder, and five years on the gun count. Serving the sentences concurrently, McNeil would become eligible for parole after twenty years.

Before the verdict, there was a moment when I looked at the victim's grandparents, Postal and Fredie Mae Smalls. I had gotten to know Mr. and Mrs. Smalls, two loving people in their seventies, and felt much affection for them. Postal Smalls was a stout and jolly man, but the mood on our side of the courtroom was quiet, watchful. As members of the jury returned from their chambers and took their seats, Postal Smalls tipped his head back, and slowly closed his eyes.

Over a couple of years I spent much time with members of Frederick Poyas's family. During some of these visits, the radiating smile and limpid eyes of Carolyn Goodson fixed in my mind. Once Carolyn and I were on the way to have lunch, talking about the past. She reminded me that it was possible both to laugh and to weep about the old days.

"I have a friend," said Carolyn, "who gets all exasperated about it, and he makes me laugh. He says, 'I don't understand these white people! They forced us to come here . . . then they hate us!' "

I laughed, and Carolyn peeled back her lips and showed her teeth, but her laughter was a little sharper than my own. As we arrived at the restaurant, Carolyn put in another word.

"I don't know," she said. "Maybe you can tell me." I looked at her, and could not tell for a moment if Carolyn was about to laugh or to weep. "I mean, the plantations, who thought this thing up? Who said, 'Okay, we're going to go to this continent, take a bunch of people, chain them up, bring them over to this place, and make them work.' Who was standing around and said, 'Hey! That's a great idea!' "

I laughed and shook my head, but Carolyn was no longer laughing.

7

>―◦―◦―◦―◦―<

THE MAKING OF A DYNASTY

In 1736, a young African woman, perhaps sixteen, set foot on the dock at Comingtee plantation. She arrived alone, in all likelihood having been sold away from her parents. Elias Ball, who bought her in Charleston, named her Angola Amy.

When Amy reached Comingtee, there were other people on the place with names that told where they came from, like the field hands Mandingo Jack and Igbo Clarinda. "Mandingos" were what whites called the Mandinka clan, in the vicinity of the Gambia River, where Jack evidently grew up. Igbo Clarinda came from the delta of the Niger River, where the Igbo (or Ibo) people lived.

Angola Amy was part of a different group. During the 1730s, people whom slave buyers called Angolans began to stream to America, with thousands each year brought to South Carolina from the area around the mouth of the Congo River. In a twelve-month period between 1736 and 1737, 2,891 Angolans arrived alive at Charleston, including young Amy. They came on nine different ships: the *Berkeley*, the *Bonetta*, the *Garlington*, the *London*, the *Phoenix*, the *Scipio*, the *Shepherd*, and the *Speaker*, as well as one ship whose name was not published with the others in the Charleston newspaper.

A few years after she came to Comingtee, Amy took a mate, Windsor.

In time, she had seven children: Christmas, Easter, Judy, Surrey, Dinah, Sabina, and Cleopatra. Amy and Windsor worked for the Ball family for nearly fifty years, until their deaths around 1790, when, according to plantation lists, they were still a couple. Their descendants would continue working for the Balls for another five generations, and Amy's kin grew until her American relatives became the single largest clan of black people on the Ball rice tracts, her direct progeny numbering nearly 180 over the course of 150 years. In early 1865, Angola Amy's great-great-great-granddaughter, twenty-one-year-old Penny, would be freed from Comingtee, along with dozens more of Amy's descendants. Eventually, I would meet some of Penny's progeny, who by then carried the name Gadsden. Later, I will tell the story of one of these families, eighth- and ninth-generation descendants of Angola Amy.

For English slave dealers, the word "Angola" referred to an area on Africa's Atlantic coast, north and south of the Congo River, which cuts east to west across the belly of Africa, two thousand miles below the great bulge in the northwest of the continent. Portuguese adventurers built depots and set up a trade in slaves on the coast south of the Congo in the 1600s, calling the area around their forts Angola. The trading posts stood in a local district, the Mbundu kingdom, from which captives were deported to sugar plantations in Portugal's chief colony, Brazil. Wary of armed rivals, British slave ships avoided the shores of Angola. English captains traded instead with black slave sellers along a hundred-mile stretch that began at the mouth of the Congo and continued north. This area, the coast of Loango, included a port settlement, Cabinda. The Royal African Company, which brought slaves to Charleston, made the Loango coast its trading base, so much so that the company's records from the 1720s show that all of its ships going to central Africa during that time listed Cabinda as a destination.

By the time Amy was captured, whites had long before given up making raids themselves and instead operated forts on the coast known as "factories." These were heavily armed buying centers to which black slave-handlers delivered their merchandise in exchange for guns, rum, and fabric. The captives brought by the black middlemen to the factories had previously been held by chiefs and headmen farther interior, away from the coast. These chiefs rounded up victims in several ways—by staging raids on villages for the purpose of getting prisoners of war, by punishing people in debt through sale into slavery, and sometimes by selling members of their own tribe for personal profit. With this black involvement at the source of the capture business, slavery became a shared venture.

Forced labor was practiced in West Africa before the Europeans began to carry people off, but it was not plantation slavery like that in America. West African slavery consisted of the subjugation of whole villages by invading chiefdoms, which led to arrangements that resembled the vassal societies of feudal Europe. As it was in medieval England, the vanquished were required to make oaths of obedience to the conquerors, and to meet obligations; slaves were attached to a piece of land and made to work it, giving tribute to their lords in services and in crops but holding on to personal identity. By contrast, American slavery meant the denuding of individuals of all rights and property, one person at a time. In the Asante kingdom of southern Nigeria, for example, a slave could own property, testify in judicial processes, own a slave him- or herself, intermarry with the kin of the ruling family, and be an heir to his or her master—none of which rights were held by captive American blacks. When the Europeans arrived on the African coast, this patriarchal system became rapidly more harsh, and the pace and methods of slave capture were sharpened to suit white demand.

Angola Amy may have been a captive brought to shore from the interior, east of Loango, but people shipped out by the English also came from black slave suppliers to the south, that is, from Portuguese Angola. A trading network among the Vili tribe used a caravan system to smuggle people out of the Portuguese sphere and a hundred miles north, to British depots, which for some years offered higher prices than their rivals. Although I cannot say precisely where Angola Amy was born, or where she was captured, it is possible she left Africa after several days' march in a slave coffle from south of the Congo to the northern Loango coast, where she boarded a ship at Cabinda.

The English looked for people around the Congo River in part because captives from the region, compared with other Africans, could be bought with goods the British had in abundance. At the Gambia River, a week's sail up the coast, a slave might be got for trade goods, like knives and guns, amounting to £9 or £10 sterling. At Cabinda, by contrast, slaves were sold by black captors in exchange for mere cloth, an English specialty. The unit of currency was a length of fabric called a *peça*, or piece (also a *cabeça*, or head), based on the amount of material thought necessary to clothe one person, usually two yards, sometimes a bit more. Before 1750, the average price for a healthy worker at Cabinda ranged between fifteen and twenty pieces—a saving that the slave handlers may have passed on to South Carolina customers like the price-conscious Elias Ball.

Because their human cargo was relatively less expensive, the ships that plied the coast around Cabinda may have been larger and more miserable than the sloops sailing from elsewhere in Africa. In 1736, when Amy was hijacked, the number of people leaving Cabinda averaged 325 per ship, more than that of ships sailing from other ports.

Elias Ball was now a sixty-year-old rice planter, one of two hundred or so men who controlled large Carolina estates. He had bought Amy as a business decision, merely to increase his cache of workers. After thirty-eight years as a slave owner, Elias would seem incapable of thinking about Amy as a person, yet his business had recently turned slightly away from the worst cruelty of its early years. The threat of violence was no longer the only incentive used to get Africans to go along with the system; now, in some cases, money actually changed hands. About the time Amy arrived, Elias had begun to pay his slaves for a kind of extra work. For black families, an income, however small, was a way to snatch a bit of comfort. For Elias and other planters, a thin system of wages was a means of buying cooperation.

The unpaid workweek on the plantation lasted six days, including a half day on Saturday, with Sunday off. Away from the master's rice fields, however, some people raised goods that they sold to Elias. A Comingtee slave named Abraham raised fowls, and in 1728 earned the sum of £1 10s from Elias for eighteen birds. The same year, a field hand named Marcia raised some hogs, which Elias bought for several pounds. The number of such deals—money for work on the side—doubled and tripled in a few seasons. In January 1736, Elias distributed more than £50 among twenty-two people for food they grew on their own. The workers usually sold him small amounts of rice grown in tracts separate from the main fields. In the mid-1730s, Windsor, Angola Amy's partner, grew three bushels of rice, for which Elias paid £1 3s. A man called Carolina raised twenty-nine bushels, and a field hand named Devonshire, twelve. Abraham, the bird man, was the most entrepreneurial, one winter selling thirty-four bushels of rice, which earned £12 15s for his family.

To raise these extra crops, workers seem to have negotiated a set-aside of a piece of land, one extra plot going to each household. The plots were as small as a tenth of an acre per family, though some were larger, and lay behind or near each cabin. Later Elias evidently saw the backyard rice market as competition and therefore started paying field hands only for corn. Slaves also grew vegetables and kept chickens on "their" land, not to sell, but for their own use. One thing remained constant about the wages: Elias made sure people never saved enough money to purchase their own freedom. The practice of paying slaves seems to have lasted for two or three generations, until the American Revolution, after which it disappears in the Ball accounts.

Another innovation, the "task system," arose to regulate the amount of unpaid labor each person was forced to do. A task was a specific measure of work that could be completed in a day. The most typical task called for a field hand to hoe weeds from around rice plants on a given piece of land—specifically, one-quarter acre, or about 105 feet square. After the plot was finished, the worker had the rest of the day off. Tasks eventually covered all plantation operations, from caring for horses, to pounding rice, to making fences. For removing the husk from the rice grain, the daily quota was seven mortars of rice pounded in a day, and for fences, one hundred logs split into rails, each rail twelve feet.

The task system differed from the gang system on sugar plantations in the Caribbean. A slave gang on Barbados worked all day under a white overseer, while in Carolina workers went into the fields at sunrise under the command of a black "driver." Eight or nine hours later, a worker might finish the task. The task system gave slaves more control, as well as time to work on their own plots for spending money.

Elias Ball's records show that many hands bought personal property with wages picked up on the side. A trade developed in caps, handkerchiefs, smoking pipes, blankets, and knives. Most who grew extra food for money, and thereby acquired little luxuries, seem to have been men, although women may have had goods other than corn to sell, perhaps yarn made from fleece or clothing sewn on off-time. The most inventive person in the subsidiary economy, however, was a woman named Hannah.

Hannah was a field hand, apparently without a partner, who grew neither corn nor rice, but tobacco. In the 1720s one of Elias's daughters, Elizabeth Ball, married Richard Shubrick, a ship captain. After that, Shubrick and Elias sometimes sold people to each other—one of whom was Hannah. Elias first called her Hannah Shubrick to signal that he had gotten her from his son-in-law, and later Captain Hannah, I suspect either because Shubrick had been a sailor or because Hannah was personally commanding. After a few years working tasks in the rice fields, Captain Hannah planted her own set-aside, choosing tobacco as the crop. In 1740 she collected £2 15s for the leafy plant, more than several of her neighbors earned from corn. It is possible that Captain Hannah brought her tobacco-growing skills with her from Africa. Tobacco was common in parts of West Africa, and at least some black Carolinians may have carried the skill with them when hijacked to America. Perhaps Captain Hannah knew of the tobacco markets in Virginia, several hundred miles north, and realized she could always get a price for her harvest. Or maybe Hannah herself smoked tobacco.

Red Cap was old and rich, had lived a long time in the swamps, and wanted to get out of the daily business of rice planting. In the late 1730s he sealed his decision: he would move to Charleston. In preparation, he began to hand over his estate to his sons, Elias Jr. and John Coming Ball. As a gesture, the father gave his namesake a thousand acres so the young man could try his hand as a plantation patriarch. The tract, known as St. James, stood farther up the Cooper River, north of the old Comingtee homestead. That same year Elias also bought ten new slaves, perhaps to give to his younger son. Next he hired a new overseer, Charles Pemberton, and began to turn over responsibility for Comingtee to him. The new overseer took wages in kind—tobacco, sugar, and a gallon of rum a week. In May 1738, Elias had Pemberton take up residence in the original wooden dwelling house on the plantation. Pemberton worked with a slave called Quaco to repair the old building before moving in. Finally, in February 1739, Red Cap retired from rice planting and moved to his house in Charleston.

After he was in town just six months, a violent black uprising exploded. A small band of Angolans began a desperate bid for freedom that became the largest, bloodiest slave revolt in the British colonies of North America.

The rebellion started on a Sunday, the single day off for slaves and the day almost all free people left their townhouses and plantations to attend church services. The Christian sabbath became the moment in the routine of society when slave owners felt the most vulnerable. Chances of a "servile revolt," everyone knew, were highest when white people gathered to give thanks for the blessings of supremacy that God had bestowed. On September 9, 1739, the much-feared Sunday uprising came twenty miles southwest of Charleston, along the banks of the Stono River, in St. Paul's Parish. The Stono River ran parallel to the coast for a few miles before cutting inland and, like the Cooper, was home to a dozen or more rice plantations. On the banks of a western tributary of the Stono, an hour or two before dawn a group of blacks led by a slave named Jemmy left their houses. They broke into a general store, over-powered and decapitated two white men guarding it, and made off with guns and powder. They left the men's heads on the steps.

A number of slaves had already made their way from Charleston to St. Augustine, the Spanish outpost in Florida a little more than two hundred miles away. So many had run south, in fact, that escaped slaves filled a black village north of St. Augustine, at a place called Fort Mose. Jemmy's band marauded through the Stono district, evidently heading toward Florida. As they marched, the rebels burned houses and killed every white person in their path. By midmorning, the insurgents num-bered about fifty and were marching with drums and a banner when they were spied from a distance by the lieutenant governor of the colony, William Bull. Bull rode off for help and got word of the rebellion to Charleston, where alarms went out to the white population. Some years later, one of Elias's grandsons, John Ball, would write down the story of how his grandfather once found himself in a fort inside the city "in time of an alarm"; I suspect this was during the Stono events. Although he had been a militia captain in a war against Native people twenty-five years earlier, this time Elias hid. According to his grandson, how-ever, he still had some taste for the fight. While behind the barricades and awaiting the all-clear, Elias "offered to turn out and take a wrestle" with one of the other old men in the fort.

Back on the Stono, William Bull converged on the uprising with a mounted army of whites. The rebels had swelled to between sixty and a hundred slaves, and had stopped in a field near the Edisto River, several miles from their starting place. When the militia arrived, they turned their guns on the rebels. Some blacks fired first (according to white accounts), while others fled into the brush, and many were caught and killed. A few slipped away and returned to the plantations from which they had escaped. Later found out, some in this group were decapitated and their heads placed on mileposts along the Stono River road.

Memories of the Stono Uprising reverberated among whites for generations, and the rebellion no doubt also survived in lore passed down among slaves. It would later emerge that most of the rebels came from the Angola region. A new slave law soon tightened the grip of tyranny: "An Act for the Better Ordering and Governing of Negroes . . ." was passed by the legislature in May 1740. Added to a group of "black codes" already on the books, the so-called Negro Act of 1740 became the main law governing black life for the next eighty years.

The Negro Act ordered a system of passes for slaves who left the company of their owners. People discovered away from their plantation home could be seized and whipped, and those resisting arrest might be killed. The law stated what clothing slaves were permitted to wear ("negro cloth . . . blue linen, check linen . . . callicoes, checked cottons, or Scots plaids"). It prohibited blacks from carrying guns, except when hunting for food for a master. And it reasserted the principle of white rule, such that any slave "who shall raise or attempt to raise an insurrection in this province" would face death.

Not having been affected by the Stono Uprising, Elias applied himself to leisure. In the forty years since he had come to America, Charleston had grown into a commercial center as active as Philadelphia or New York. A gridiron of streets extended half a mile across the marshes of the peninsula, and new trenches for runoff and sewage kept things relatively clean. There was a market square with shops and taverns in the middle of town, at the corner of Meeting and Broad streets, as well as gardens and public squares. The city had plenty of diversions for whites—social clubs like the South Carolina Society, where men played cards and talked business, taverns with cockfights, and a horse track on the outskirts of town. But the most appealing new entertainment for both men and women was a new theater on Dock Street, near the wharfs. White townspeople flocked to the stage to see local troupes put on popular plays imported from England.

Charleston was only the fourth largest but easily the blackest American city. The population of South Carolina stood near sixty thousand, of whom over thirty-nine thousand were black. About twelve thousand people lived in Charleston, more than half of them in slavery.

Elias's townhouse stood near the Cooper River, overlooking the wharfs, on the corner of what would later become Pinckney and East Bay streets. To the east of the house lay the river and to the south, a little creek. Elias did not necessarily make housing provisions for his domestic slaves. The majority of black people in Charleston lived behind the houses of their owner, in the backyard, in huts or even under the stars. Perhaps Elias followed the lead of some of his neighbors and put up a small, secure building at the back of his lot. Although they were not yet common, a few such buildings had appeared around town. These slave dwellings, called dependencies, were sturdier and more comfortable than the cabins of the plantation.

As I mentioned earlier, Dolly, Elias's house slave and the presumptive mother of two of his children, seems to have lived with the old man throughout the 1740s. There are notes in Elias's accounts about Dolly traveling from Comingtee to be with him in the city. I cannot say in what manner she lived, but she does not seem to have been an idle mistress. She probably cared for Elias's white children in addition to her own.

Like a benevolent patriarch, Elias distributed favors to his children and grandchildren. The treats often took the form of people whom Elias thought he didn't need and whom he sold to his kin at discounted rates. In one such deal in 1741, Elias sold two men—"Alexander & Othello, alias Quaco," according to the deed—to George Austin, one of his sons-in-law. Quaco was apparently the carpenter who had repaired the old house at Comingtee three years earlier. The men came with instructions that they be given to George Austin Jr., Elias's four-year-old grandson.

When he was not making provisions for family, Elias occupied himself with luxuries. One of the perquisites of wealth was the rare ability to produce an image of oneself. To make his gift to posterity, Elias turned to a painter named Jeremiah Theus. An English-born portrait artist, Theus showed good timing, arriving in Charleston from London in 1740, before other painters had yet come to the colony. Theus set up shop on the market square at the corner of Meeting and Broad streets, put a sign in his window, and waited for business. Soon a procession of moneyed citizens made its way to his studio—society ladies, rice planters, slave traders, politicians.

Jeremiah Theus seems to have developed a working method suited both to the high demand and to the climate of his new hometown. The painter's clients naturally wanted to be pictured in their best finery, but for many months of the year the heat of Charleston made long sittings in heavy clothes unpleasant. Theus made things easier by painting, in advance, a series of torsos on canvases. Some were fat, some thin, some squat, some long—but every body, though headless, wore dignified clothes. When someone came for a commission, Theus would show him or her his collection of torsos. The client would choose one, then sit for an abbreviated pose as Theus painted a head on the prefabricated trunk.

One day in the early 1740s, Elias Ball presented himself to Theus for a portrait. He chose a picture of a heavyset body wearing a dark jacket and white scarf, a clothing style that Theus seems to have used several times. In fact, when finished, Elias's portrait, from the neck down, closely resembled that of another Theus subject, planter Gabriel Manigault. The two portraits show the men wearing identical clothes, with Elias's body about thirty pounds heavier than that of the slender Manigault.

Elias's finished portrait shows a face, heavy with jowls, that carries an expression of supreme confidence. What satisfaction Elias felt may have come from his having beaten the odds against death. He had lived most of his nearly seventy years in the British colony of South Carolina, where the majority of people made their way to the grave not long past youth. Something more, however, seems present in his blue eyes. When Elias sat for the painter, he was seated, as well, on top of an agricultural empire. Like a Roman noble, he owned vast lands and numerous slaves. In a few years the human and real estate would pass to his children, but for the time being it was his alone. In the painting, Elias wears the red velvet cap that would be responsible for his family nickname.

Elias must have been pleased with Theus's work, because before long he commissioned a portrait of his daughter Eleanor. Unfortunately, the artist was less gifted at painting women than men. When Theus painted Eleanor Ball, a girl of about twelve, he attached her face to a torso with full breasts. On top of the shimmering bodice (cut low, with a lace fringe around the bosom), he placed a head whose mouth resembled a large *V*. To finish, he painted a pair of globular, close-set eyes, not unlike those of a frog.

Jeremiah Theus stayed in business for nearly thirty-five years, during which he seems to have remained the only painter in town. Elias and his kin liked, or tolerated, what Theus did for them, for eventually they commissioned him to make nearly a dozen paintings of themselves.

After the Stono Uprising some families decided to get out of the rice business. Here and there, slave owners cashed in their estates and returned to England, driving down the cost of land. With their lives potentially at stake, Elias's sons might have considered another path than the one cleared for them by their father. But the Ball heirs pushed forward and expanded the family empire.

Elias Jr. had just turned thirty. (In family lore he would be called Second Elias to distinguish him from more than a dozen other Eliases in the clan.) John Coming Ball, the younger son, was twenty-five. Second Elias and John Coming seemed to have viewed events like the Stono Uprising as a business risk; they merely hoped something similar wouldn't happen again, or to them. John Coming Ball acted first in the growth plan. In March 1740, six months after the rebellion, he bought a tract about six miles up the east branch of the Cooper River from Comingtee. A neighbor, Richard Gough, let it go at a good discount. The young heir had evidently read about a beautiful park in London on land once owned by Edward Hyde, Earl of Clarendon, for he called his new stake Hyde Park.

The six-hundred-acre parcel was vacant, and John Coming set about settling it. The early records of Hyde Park were destroyed in a fire around the time of the American Revolution; therefore, it is difficult to say much about the black people who lived there in the first years. After buying the land, however, John Coming took a large loan from his father, used, I imagine, to purchase several dozen people. To make the plantation into a working rice farm, the slaves would have begun the arduous work of clearing and laying out fields. The process took one or two years, as at least 150 acres were flattened and cut into smaller tracts. Irrigation trenches had to be dug around each field, and tons of earth shoveled out and carted off. Outbuildings were raised, including a barn and houses on a slave street.

While this was being done, John Coming called for his own house. One of Red Cap's hands, a builder named Amos, seems to have been instrumental in the construction. Amos lived first on Comingtee in the 1730s, when he sold his corn crop to Elias, taking clothing and money as payment. After that he became a traveling carpenter. By 1741 he was no longer confined to the plantation but began to work on the Ball family's various houses. With another carpenter, Salisbury, Amos ranged around the rice country doing repair work. There was a time when, according to Second Elias, "Salisbury & Amos went to town to work for my father," probably to repair the townhouse, and another when "Salisbury and Amos shingled [the] Coming Tee House in 5 days."

Records show that Amos went to work at Hyde Park sometime after its purchase. The house turned out to be bigger than the one at Comingtee, but equally plain, a boxy, two-story wooden building with a long covered porch and a pitched roof. Amos was likely the carpenter who laid the beams, raised the roof, and hung the window sashes. In any case, the house was finished by fall 1743, standing near a creek that flowed into the main stream of the river, with cabins for field hands nearby. That October, according to one record book, Amos left Hyde Park for other jobs.

While the Hyde Park house was going up, John Coming married Catherine Gendron, daughter of a family of French Huguenots. The couple moved to the new plantation about the time the last rice bank was being leveled.

His work for John Coming done, Amos returned to an itinerant life, doing construction here and there as the Balls demanded. In March 1745, he went to work for one of Red Cap's daughters, Ann Ball, and her husband George Austin. The couple had a plantation on the Ashepoo River, southwest of the Ball tracts a day and a half on horseback. Amos may have been sold to Ann and George, just as Red Cap had earlier sold the couple Alexander and Quaco. After going to Ashepoo, Amos disappears from the extant records of the family.

Second Elias, the other heir, already had in hand a thousand acres, the St. James tract, but when his brother moved to Hyde Park, he stayed on at Comingtee alone. According to Ball family lore, the bond between

John Coming and his brother was sentimental and strong, and Second Elias felt abandoned by John Coming's move. "There ever subsisted the utmost harmony and brotherly affection between them," one of their sons wrote forty years later. At one point, Second Elias bought a surprise gift of a hat for his brother, who had a small head. The man sent to procure the hat reported back in a letter, "I searched the whole stores in town but could not get one hat small enough [for less than] 40 shillings. . . . I did not let [the shopkeeper] know who it was for."

Second Elias, yet unmarried, felt increasingly isolated and apparently grew disconsolate. Red Cap seems to have been aware of his son's discouragement, because at one point the old man bought a parrot and sent it up the river to the lonely bachelor. Apparently, however, the talking bird was not enough to console him. Second Elias preoccupied himself with a garden to distract his attention, one winter noting that he had "finished ye garden here at Comingstee."

Soon, however, Second Elias's loneliness ended. Family tradition has it that during his twenties the young heir had fallen in love with a woman from nearby Strawberry plantation, Lydia Child. Lydia was the granddaughter of James Child, the well-known slave catcher in the area who once made captives out of 160 Natives. After Lydia Child married a man named George Chicken, Second Elias had resigned himself to bachelorhood. (It could not have helped that Lydia had to be addressed in the street as "Mrs. Chicken.") In 1745, however, George Chicken conveniently died, and two years later Second Elias and Lydia were married. He was thirty-eight, Lydia in her twenties, and the mother of a little girl, Catherine Chicken.

In February of that year, 1747, the same family that had sold Hyde Park to John Coming sold another piece of land to Second Elias, for £3,400. The empty 670-acre tract bordered the south side of Hyde Park, and Second Elias wondered what to call the place. Apparently having read about the grounds that adjoined Hyde Park in London—Kensington Gardens, which had abundant green meadows and a playful building, the Orangery—Second Elias called his plantation Kensington.

The clearing and building, house planning and barn raising began anew. Amid the activity, Second Elias arranged for the building of a dwelling that would, like the plantation itself, imitate his brother's tastes. A tall, airy box with a veranda, the house at Kensington stood in a grove of outspreading oaks.

When Lydia and Second Elias moved to Kensington, they arrived with perhaps seventy-five slaves. About half the families came from Comingtee, including Angola Amy and her children. By this time, three of Angola Amy's children had been born—a boy, Christmas (born one year on that day), four; a girl, Easter (born during Holy Week), two; and another girl, Judy, one. When she moved to Kensington, Amy was forced to leave the father of her children, Windsor, who stayed behind on Comingtee. So it developed that Amy and Windsor had what would be known as an "abroad marriage," that is, a marriage spanning two plantations, an arrangement that became common among slave families.

There are no descriptions of black wedding ceremonies in the Ball papers, no references to "jumping the broom" or other rituals that may have taken place on the slave street. One reason could be that for the first hundred years most of the Ball slaves were not Christians, and their masters did not care to write down, or perhaps even understand, black family arrangements. Polygamy, a custom brought on the slave ships, survived in the rice district for at least a generation or two; it faded with time and when blacks began to see it as sinful. The most likely reason that domestic partnerships between blacks often went unrecorded by the Balls is that slave marriages were not taken seriously by whites. In the eyes of the law, marriage between black partners had no legal force, because masters reserved the right to separate couples for the purpose of sale; to acknowledge unions would make this impossible. But the long togetherness of Angola Amy and Windsor proves that unions did take place, with and without wedding ritual. After most of the slave population was Christianized, which occurred in the early 1800s, plantation churches were built near the cabins and wedding ceremonies were performed by black preachers. Those days at Kensington, however, were a long way off.

With her marriage to Second Elias, Lydia Chicken brought property inherited from her dead husband, including Strawberry plantation. She also brought the people on Strawberry, among them a young couple, Radcliffe and Amy, and a girl named Jenny Buller. Jenny Buller, about ten years old, had the rare privilege of having two names. An exception to the name rule—single names only for slaves—occurred when the number of people on a plantation grew too large, causing repetition. Jenny Buller evidently carried a surname because Second Elias already owned a field hand named Jenny, a few years older. The story behind the name Buller has died with the lore of an earlier time, but at Kensington young Jenny would become a conspicuous figure. One of the Balls, writing in the twentieth century, had much to say about her:

> [T]he name of "Jenny Buller" is frequently met with in the plantation records of the second Elias Ball, and sometimes in Lydia Child's little memorandum-book. In the note-book it is stated that she was sent to a physician "to be cured of a sore leg," and came back. The result of this doctoring does not appear to have been a "cure," for she ultimately lost the leg and hobbled around on a wooden stump: "doing as much work as a man." . . . The family, as a general rule, were proud and high-tempered . . . and many of them were prominent about the plantation and in the household.

With the building of Hyde Park and Kensington, the transfer of authority from Red Cap to his sons came to an end. The Ball family stood at the center of a little world consisting of five plantations— Comingtee, Hyde Park, Kensington, St. James, and Strawberry. The Cooper River was the Balls' river, or so everyone might have thought.

In the summer of 1748, word of another slave uprising was whispered down the stream, and a bloody revolt almost exploded on the lawn of Second Elias's new home, Kensington. A hundred-page report commissioned by the royal governor after the incident tells the story of the alleged conspiracy.

The events began a short distance downstream from the Ball lands, on Back River, a tributary that entered the Cooper, where a family called Akin owned a plantation. The master of the place, James Akin, was well known to the Balls, since Red Cap had once leased him a woman named Cornelia for six months. Akin's brother Thomas owned a second plantation closer to Kensington and Hyde Park, near the headwaters of the east branch of the Cooper River, at a place called Irishtown. On the Akin place at Back River, known as Akinfield, there lived a slave named Agrippa, a boatman.

One day in June 1748, Agrippa and several other men set off in a boat on an errand to Charleston. Their owner, James Akin, gave them passes and sent them to bring back some oyster shells to make lime. A few miles downriver, Agrippa and the other men stopped at the plantation of one Colonel Alexander Vanderdussen, on Goose Creek. An immigrant from Holland, Vanderdussen had the reputation of being a violent master. On the boat dock, Agrippa fell into conversation with three of Vanderdussen's slaves—his black driver Pompey, Pompey's wife, and another man called Billy. According to the official account, the men began to talk about the chances for a black uprising on the river. Everyone recalled the Stono events eight years before; then the black rebels had been slaughtered, but what was to prevent the revolt from succeeding this time? The rebellion would begin on the plantations, move to Charleston, climax in the killing of white people and burning of the city, and end with the escape of the rebels by boat to Florida. Agrippa and his would-be cabal finished their conversation by discussing where they could comandeer the right ships for the getaway.

The men completed their errand and decided to meet again. A few weeks later, Agrippa went by boat with Joe, another man from Akinfield, up the east branch of the Cooper. They ostensibly went to visit Joe's brother Ammon, who lived on the other Akin place at Irishtown. Between Akinfield and Irishtown lay the main Ball tracts—Comingtee, Kensington, Hyde Park.

When Joe and Agrippa rowed upriver, they stopped at Fish Pond, the plantation owned by the Harleston family, cousins of Second Elias, where they had words with the black driver, Thom Paine. It's clear that Thom Paine was well known to the Balls, because Second Elias used to summon him to take rum and food over to the Harleston family. (The Thomas Paine who was the pamphleteer and author of the democratic manifesto *Common Sense*, and is famous for his role in the American Revolution, would not arrive from England to the colonies until 1774, so the slave Thom Paine seems to have gotten his name from some other source.) Thom Paine got into the boat, and the men shoved off for the Ball place, Kensington.

Second Elias would not have been surprised when Thom Paine, Joe, and Agrippa pulled their boat up to his dock; it would have appeared to be business as usual. The young men were met at river's edge by Second Elias's man Pompey. Pompey was about twenty, and a recent arrival from Comingtee. Another man, Tom, also appeared at the riverbank. This Tom (in the governor's account) was actually "Tom White" to the Balls. Bought and brought to Comingtee in 1731, when he was nine, Tom White was an Angolan. At the time of these events, he was twenty-six years old and married to a woman named Julatta, who had three children. At the edge of Kensington, the rebels seemed to be meeting a second time to make plans.

Joe fixed the canoe, and Pompey stepped aboard. In their conversation, Joe told Pompey and Tom White about a rendezvous planned for that night upriver, at Irishtown. Pompey told Joe that he couldn't come, but said he would tell some other people at Kensington, and they might show up. Tom White agreed to go. The men made their goodbyes, and Joe shoved off.

It was Saturday night, the only night when black people did not have to worry about work call the following day. The meeting went off as planned at the Akin place in Irishtown. Tom White was there and, while Pompey stayed away as he said he would, several other Ball slaves showed up. Among them was a man named Carolina, a young fisherman immediately recognizable by a scar on his arm. Violet, a field hand in her twenties, also stopped by. It is impossible to say exactly what happened at Irishtown that night. When the Ball workers were later interrogated, they claimed to have played music and danced through the early morning. But whatever happened, a fierce act of repression soon killed the memory of it. After the Saturday rendezvous, Joe, who had first rowed up to Kensington, was accused of having burned a barn. Perhaps the arson came as the initial act of the rebellion, or perhaps Joe could no longer contain his rage. Joe may even have been framed. In any case, the plantation patrol, a nighttime posse of armed whites who rode through the rice district, arrested him. He was tried in Charleston by the court that dealt with charges against slaves, and executed. If a plot had been imagined by the Ball workers, Joe's death put an end to their dreaming.

When rumors started to circulate, the governor, James Glen, appointed a committee of prominent slave owners to investigate. The committee summoned witnesses, and a slave named Robin, from Akinfield plantation, was brought down to Charleston to testify. Robin implicated Thom Paine of Fish Pond, as well as a slave named George, on the Akin land. Then she fingered the four slaves belonging to Second Elias—Tom White, Pompey, Violet, and Carolina.

The four from Kensington were brought down to Charleston and locked up in the Work House, the prison for slaves. Tom White, the Angolan, was interrogated first. Both whites and blacks would have remembered that the plotters of the Stono Uprising came from the same region as Tom, so perhaps he was chosen because of his homeland. By this time the Ball slaves must have realized that they faced the penalty of death. None of the Stono rebels had gotten away alive, and the Negro Act of 1740 called for executions. Tom White decided to talk his way out.

In his testimony, summarized by his white questioners, Tom admitted that on the Saturday in question he had seen Joe and had spoken to him. Tom further admitted that he had gone to the Akin place at Irishtown that night but, he went on, the meeting was a house party. There were "a good many Negroes" there, Tom said, and no whites. Someone had brought a banjo, and the blacks "ate and drank, played and laughed," and the dancing went on all night. Trying to throw his questioners off the trail, Tom finished by admitting that he knew the Harlestons' Thom Paine, also in jail, but that Thom Paine never showed up at Irishtown.

The investigation continued for weeks, with a stream of witnesses called before the committee. James Akin testified that from time to time runaway slaves hid out on his plantation. He remembered one slave named Limerick, who he said had fled from the Balls. Limerick, said Akin, "was afterwards shot and killed" by a plantation patrol. (No record of Limerick appears in the Ball papers from this period, and I found no mention of his murder beyond this passing reference.) The investigators filed Akin's testimony and continued their probe.

Dozens of slaves testified, as did several whites. The witnesses brought to the examining room gave incompatible stories, and some simply stonewalled. The conflicting tales bewildered the esteemed citizens of the governor's panel, who soon decided they were getting nowhere. The problem was the slender evidence—a single dead slave, Joe (or perhaps two, counting Limerick), and a welter of rumors. For the blacks the problem was that conspiracy to revolt meant a guaranteed death penalty, perhaps by torture. The suspects had no choice but to deny everything.

Months after the alleged events, in January 1749 Thomas Akin, owner of the Irishtown plantation, came forward in a huff. He had had enough of the confusion, as well as of insinuation that his business harbored violent resisters. Akin testified that in his opinion, the Ball slaves were telling the truth: there had been no plot, and there was nothing to the affair. Furthermore, Akin (making the strangest charge yet) said that the dastardly rumor of the plot was merely a piece of trouble contrived by a few gossiping slave women. Akin claimed to know four quarrelsome women on whom the whole matter could be blamed. They belonged to his brother, James Akin, and could be found on Akinfield plantation.

Weary of the whole business and anxious to find culprits, even innocent women, the rattled investigators fixed on the rumor explanation. James Akin summoned a woman he owned named Kate, whom he described as a notorious gossip. Then Akin fingered the other three, his slaves Robin, Sue, and Susannah. The panel quickly agreed that the alleged plot must have been a false rumor concocted by Akin's four suspects. In their final report to Governor Glen, the committee had reassuring words. Nothing, in fact, had been planned, and no slave had even discussed rebellion. Four cantankerous women had merely stirred up the panic in their desire to make trouble.

Kate, Robin, Sue, and Susannah did not get the chance to testify or to defend themselves. Scapegoats to white confusion and fear, they were sold and deported, probably to one of the Caribbean islands. The Ball slaves Carolina, Tom White, Pompey, and Violet were released from the Work House and returned home. Governor James Glen called together the owners of the many suspects to brief them on the case. The announcements took place on an afternoon in February 1749. At the meeting, Second Elias, perhaps grateful, listened carefully to the report of the politician whose job it was to protect him from harm.

Red Cap must have known he was nearing his end, but at age seventy-three he believed he had one last task. The job concerned his daughter Eleanor, the only living child from his second marriage. One of the high desires of a rice planter was to see his daughters married to good husbands. In the eyes of her father, a decent man for Eleanor would be a person with station and money. If love came in addition to these things, so much the better.

Eleanor had grown up considerably since Jeremiah Theus had painted her portrait, and soon after she turned nineteen, she was engaged to an auspicious young man, the twenty-six-year-old merchant Henry Laurens. Red Cap clearly regarded Laurens as a good match, though not necessarily because of his family background. The son of Huguenot parents, Laurens had a father who had been no more than a successful saddlemaker. Although not rich by plantation standards, the ambitious parents had nevertheless found a way to send their son to London to be "finished." In England, Laurens served as an apprentice at an import-export firm that did business with the British colonies. Back in Charleston, he cut a figure as a young cosmopolite.

Laurens had known Eleanor since she was a girl, but he had delayed asking her to marry until she reached a suitable age, and until he had established himself. The profession Laurens chose was certainly profitable—it would allow him immediately to support a family in high style and showed every sign of future growth; if well-handled, it could make a fortune for the leatherworker's son in a few short years. In short, putting his rare international contacts to use, Laurens became a slave trader.

Slave dealing was a business in which the Ball family already had good connections. Red Cap's daughter Ann's second husband, George Austin, who owned the plantation on the Ashepoo River, also sold people off the ships that arrived from Africa into Charleston. Even so, Austin was a dilettante compared to some others in the business.

When Henry Laurens returned from London, he persuaded Austin to let him come into the slave business as a junior partner. By the late 1740s, the firm was called Austin & Laurens. Soon Laurens's indefatigable work habits, his British friends (who owned slave ships), and his sharp sales technique (he knew the merchandise better than most) made him the dominant partner. About the time Eleanor Ball said yes to her fiancé, Laurens was showing signs of being the most aggressive slave dealer in the city.

The wedding took place at Comingtee in late June of 1750. For some years, none of the Balls had lived in the Comingtee house, and the ceremony and party filled it up perfectly. Most of the white neighbors, along with a contingent of Charleston guests, came to celebrate. To host the event, Red Cap traveled from Charleston to Comingtee one final time.

What Elias regarded as a good marriage turned out to be a prize match. The family-run firm of Austin & Laurens took over the Charleston slave-selling trade. Before he turned thirty-five, Eleanor Ball's husband would become the largest slave trader in the British colonies and one of the richest men in North America. Later, I will give an account of Austin & Laurens's business, and of some of the people, including children, the firm sold.

With his last daughter married off and his sons established on plantations, Elias must have thought his time had come. Two months after Eleanor's wedding, he drew up his will. In the document, dated August 31, 1750, Red Cap stated his claim: "I, Elias Ball of Charles Town in the province of South Carolina, Gentleman . . ." Elias had indeed become what in colonial America passed for a "gentleman." His estate included a house in a provincial capital, Charleston, and thousands of acres of land north of the city. It also included 116 people.

Red Cap's slaves, with their progeny, ensured that the next generation of Balls—and the next, and the next, and the next, and the next —would never dirty a hand. Elias personified a new kind of American, a slave-owning landlord who emulated the European elite. Using his money, he had tried to equip himself with the manners and belongings of ladies and gentlemen. Many would-be gentlemen like him, however, came from people of modest means, and the English gentry and nobility were not quick to forget this. Long after the American planters had assumed the airs of a musty aristocracy, with portraits and genealogies and pounds of silver plate, their European mentors continued to regard them as something like well-dressed bandits.

In the last week of September 1751, Elias died at age seventy-five. There is no record of the cause of his death, but the end came in the fall, which often meant fever. Red Cap may finally have succumbed to the malaria of the marshes that carried away so many whites. In a posthumous inventory, the colonial government itemized his possessions. He owned slaves (valued at £19,010), land, houses, livestock, furniture, and silver—but only a single book, a Bible. By his own account, Elias had led a charmed existence, one actually bathed in the light of the Lord. In his will, Elias referred to his fortune as "such worldly Estate wherewith it has Pleased God to bless me." He had ingested as much land and as many people as could be swallowed into a single life. As a businessman and a father, he had latched on to what was there to be taken, defended it when it was threatened, and handed it on to his children.

8

SAWMILL

In my search for the descendants of the Ball slaves, one memorable clue had come from my cousin Elias Ball Bull. Elias was the amateur historian who had spent years crisscrossing the rice district in his work as a preservation consultant, documenting the surviving buildings. After the Civil War, he had said, some of the freed workers moved out of their cabins on the Ball plantations to build a village of their own, called Sawmill. "I think it's on Hardscrabble Road," cousin Elias told me. If Sawmill still existed, a few of the original families might still live there.

Sawmill did not appear on any maps, and the Ball land once spread over a dozen miles. To begin the search, I drove out of Charleston along a two-lane highway that cut like a gray tendon through evergreen woods, and came to a pineland village called Cordesville. Cordesville used to be one of the dry places to which white families retreated, with house slaves, to escape the malaria that crept through the wet rice land in summer. The oldest Ball tract, Comingtee, lay a few miles south.

A white wooden shack with a porch and tin roof stood hard by a railroad crossing beneath a painted sign: COUNTRY STORE, CORDESVILLE, S.C. The store was once a railroad stop where black sharecroppers bought food, hardware, cloth. It looked shuttered, but a television murmured behind the door. Inside, a large musty room was weakly lit by two fluorescent bulbs. The store had waned with the town. The shelves were empty, and the main item for sale appeared to be the junk food in plastic bags that hung on racks. Two black women sat at a table, watching a game show.

"Do you know how to get to Sawmill from here?" I asked. "There's only about ten houses there."

"Sawmill Road?" said one.

"Have you heard of something called Hardscrabble Road?" I came back.

"Hardscrabble?" said the woman. "There's Hard Pinch Road up a little bit."

"Hard Bench?" I asked.

"Hard *Pinch*." She gave directions.

It was winter, and the damp of the nearby swamps intensified the cold. A canopy of low clouds looked like silver-and-white gloves traced in the sky. I came to a road lined by modest brick houses and older wooden cottages, unpainted for half a century. Here and there, trailers stood on cinderblocks, fighting for space with the surrounding thicket. The buildings were overwhelmed by too much land. The cottages were some of the houses where black families moved after leaving the plantations. Some headed to New York, or Washington, D.C., but a good many stayed.

A young black man with a sharp expression stalked over. "Don't you park here!" he sneered, then spat.

At the next house, dogs leaped and barked in the dirt yard. A television inside was turned up loud enough that the laugh track echoed in the woods. I knocked, but no answer came. A gentle-looking teenager stood by the road, eyeing me curiously. I told him I was looking for families who had been around for a long time.

"How long has your family lived here?" I asked. An invasive hello, the question of a bill collector.

"I wouldn't know," he said, "but my aunt does." The lanky black student walked to a trailer where two women sat in the window, silhouetted against the lighted room. He pushed open the door and spoke, and the silhouettes began to flail their arms.

"I told you, don't you bring nobody in this yard!" came the shouting across the dirt. "Who is he?! Get him outta here!" The gentle teen came back to me, shook my hand, shrugged his shoulders.

As I went from house to house, night approached and the clouds above the tree line burned with an orange glow. A few people wanted to talk, but none could, or would, tell their family story. Two or three times, a door slammed in my face.

I came back to Cordesville the next day and soon found the village once called Sawmill. The name had disappeared on the lips of all but a few old people, but the settlement remained, a few modest houses, each with three or four acres, on a single road that curved through the trees. It had no stop signs and no stores. The foundations of the old sawmill lay off in the pines, and a church stood in the middle of things. At the church, the minister's wife answered the door, a welcoming woman with a pleasing face and a brass pin on her dress that read I LOVE JESUS.

"We haven't been here that long," said the woman, "but the man over there has." She gestured across the road.

The man across the way led me to another man, a bit older, who led me to still another, who said, "I know who you want to talk to. There's a woman who lives on the river road. She's old, and has a good memory, and she knows everything about this place. Her name is Georgie Richardson."

Georgianna Gadsden Richardson lived on a dirt road about five miles from what used to be Comingtee plantation. Her house, a little blue cottage, stood in a clearing framed by the woods. On one side of the house was a trailer, on the other another cottage in a state of collapse. The older cottage tilted to the left, was missing a wall, and had a rusting refrigerator inside. I later learned that this had been Mrs. Richardson's first house, destroyed by Hurricane Hugo in 1989. It was a cool day, and a teenager was playing basketball in the middle of the clearing— Mrs. Richardson's youngest relative on the scene, Marcill.

The blue cottage, built to replace the old, had four rooms and a linoleum floor. Mrs. Richardson sat in an armchair in a tiny front room, a walker at her side, looking every month of her eighty-something years. She wore a checkered cotton dress and square glasses over clouded eyes, while the right side of her face appeared sunken in—from an operation, she said—and her mouth showed only a few teeth. The hair on her head had turned white and was falling out, though a hat covered the remainder. Her fingers were crooked and her palm a little rough.

"Mr. Ball!" Mrs. Richardson almost shouted. "You must be the greaty of the greaty!" She laughed a sandpaper laugh. She meant that I would have to be one of the youngest in the Ball family. "The grand-chirren of the grand-chirren!" she said.

It had been some time since Mrs. Richardson had spoken to a person named Ball, but she knew the legacy.

"All my people from Com'ntee," she began. She pronounced the name "Common-T," the local black sounding of the word. "My grand-mother, great-grandmother, aunt, uncle, all of them from Com'ntee. They leave Com'ntee when that man bought it and drove 'em away from there. That's why they come to Sawmill." Mrs. Richardson was loud and friendly, and spoke a strong Gullah.

Comingtee, the first Ball plantation, beginning in 1698, was also, two centuries later, one of the last. After the Civil War it carried on as a sharecrop farm. Many of the former slaves stayed for fifty years, living in the same cabins they had long occupied, working the same fields. In time, the rice crop dwindled to a third, then a tenth, of its old measure. Sometimes the Balls leased the plantation to entrepreneurs who wanted to try the rice business; later they ran it themselves, until it failed. By the mid-1890s, the main dwelling had fallen into disrepair and the black families coaxed subsistence from small plots. The heirs to the property could no longer afford it. In 1901, Alwyn Ball Jr., a cousin raised in New York who had made money without the benefit of slavery, bought the land and restored the main house. In 1918 the family of Alwyn Ball formed the Comingtee Corporation, with hopes of selling lumber cut from the woods. There was a sawmill a few miles away that hired black men, and trees from Comingtee began to feed it, but the forestry busi-ness didn't last. In March 1927, after 229 years as Ball family property, Comingtee was sold to a U.S. senator from New Jersey, Joseph Freling-huysen. The politician used the main house as a vacation home, the woods for hunting. In 1949 the land was sold to the West Virginia Pulp and Paper Company, which wanted the pine forests for cardboard and paper, and the duck blinds and deer stands as outdoor leisure to en-tertain clients. The big house was abandoned, the old slave cabins pulled down. By the time I found Sawmill, the same dirt roads crossed Comingtee, but only two buildings from the slave days remained, both in ruins.

"The greaty of the greaty!" Mrs. Richardson laughed again. "The children born on the plantation, the black children, they used to call them 'the Ball children,' because the Balls had that place. When somebody had a baby on the plantation, they would say, 'Who had the Ball?' My daddy's a Cordes, from Mepkin plantation, and my ma's people is Ball, from Com'ntee, so I got all kind of blood."

I asked Mrs. Richardson how many black people lived at Comingtee when she was a child.

"A good bit."

"Fifty?"

"More than that," she answered. "All of my people lived there. They used to work in the Com'ntee big house. Titty Mack, my aunt, she was there. And somebody else used to be cook. I wash dishes, and they do the cooking."

Mrs. Richardson's memories came from the 1920s, when the old slave street was still standing.

"It ain't no street, it was dirt and sand," Mrs. Richardson corrected me. "It was behind the big house. You leave the big house from the back, and go a little ways. Lemme see, Sam was at the head. You pass his house, and get to Elijah house. Then Dye house. There was Elijah, Dye, and Bristol." Mrs. Richardson looked at the floor. "I can't remember all of them, but plenty of them people stayed. I think there was five house on the street. The house was made of board. They ain't have no porch, just a tree you sit under when you get hot. There was two families in the house, in two rooms, and a brick chimney in the middle. In the front of the house, there was a field where everybody get their own piece to plant."

In the 1800s, someone had taken a photograph of some of the Comingtee cabins. It showed a row of skinny wooden houses, each built for two families, just as Mrs. Richardson described, five to ten people a room. There were more in the woods.

I brought out a list of names from the first census made after the Civil War, in 1870, in hopes that Mrs. Richardson would recognize some of them, people who would have been old when she was a child, but her face fell.

"I can't read," she said, brushing the page.

Mrs. Richardson's eyes looked away, and she was silent. She closed her mouth and her smile went flat. I had embarrassed her.

"Mrs. Richardson," I said, "what my family did to your family, long ago, was a crime. One reason I came is to try to answer for that crime."

"Thank you for coming," she replied. She made a fist. "Some people keep their hand boxed up. I don't box 'em up." Opening her fist, she said, "See, I keep an open hand." Regaining her pride, she continued, "They tell me, 'Miss Georgie, don't mind you can't read, because you got good experience, you got memory.' "

Mrs. Richardson's mood lightened. "I was christened in Com'ntee church. Plenty people still went to that church when I was a girl. We used to walk from Sawmill to go to Com'ntee, bare feet and carry our shoes, going to church. They had a high choir, up overhead." She pointed at the walls of her living room, to a choir loft in her mind. "Before you got to the church, you would start to hear 'em singing through the woods. And their feet . . . *dum-ta-da-dum, ta-da-dum, ta-da-dum*. We get there, take the brush, wipe off your feet, put on your shoes, and go inside."

We talked for a while about church, and I told Mrs. Richardson that the previous Sunday I had not gone.

"The Devil put a hat on your head and shoes on your feet and a glass in your eye!" she said, scolding. "Devil's a strong man!"

I asked about the settling of Sawmill, the village that appeared in the shadow of Comingtee.

"Everybody built they own house," she said. "When they left Com'ntee, they got slab wood from the sawmill, and build they house in the moonlight. Some built a pole house, some board. My daddy had a house of board, but it ain't had but one room." A board house was an airtight cabin made from planks. A pole house was a log cabin whose gaps were filled with clay and straw.

"They cut the pole, build the house, and put the straw in there and put the clay between 'em," Mrs. Richardson went on. "They build the chimney with clay. You cut off the end of the pine sapling, cut down the sapling, and peel 'em down. You stack 'em there, and put the clay between there. But oh Lord, if it rains, you have to keep a fire all night, so it don't fall."

"Why didn't they use brick?" I asked.

"They ain't had none!"

None of the houses with clay chimneys survived, but there were photographs. The clay looked soft, with the ends of sticks poking out.

"If it rained, then the chimney ran down the chute with the water," I said.

"That's right! My daddy kept the fire all night when it rained, so it wouldn't fall," she finished. "Mostly this time of the year, you could smell the wood burning. That green oak smells so good. Oak's the one that holds the heat. The pine makes the ashes, but that oak burns all night. Throw it on that fire, you got a heater."

Mrs. Richardson laughed. Her voice was rising, and she was getting excited. She paused, let her tongue out a bit from her mouth, laying it on her lips, then pointed a finger at the window.

"The windows, you made 'em out of board, and put 'em in, on hinge. Glass windows was for people who rich! For make a bed, you take a crocus sack, a big sack you get feed in." (A crocus sack was a big burlap bag that held animal feed, or potatoes.) "You finish the feed, and you get the sack. To make a mattress, you had four sack on the bottom, four on the top. You get a big needle and thread 'em together to make the mattress. Then you go in the woods and you rake pine straw, put it in the mattress, and stuff 'em down, pack it down, then sew 'em up. For a pillow, you take some old clothes you don't want, wash 'em clean, put 'em in a sack. You sleep good."

Mrs. Richardson smiled and laughed a raspy laugh. She was rocking back and forth. Suddenly she stopped, and her face tightened.

"Oh, what them old-time people been through!" she shouted. "Hard times! Hard slavery! But it's going to be all right. When Gabriel blow the trumpet, then the dead in Christ got to rise!"

In the weeks and months that followed I saw more of Georgie Richardson and her family. On my first return visit, I noticed that the wreck of a house next to her cottage had been pulled down and carted away. Mrs. Richardson's husband, Robert, had long been dead, but she had more kin who lived in the trailer that stood a few yards from the blue cottage—Barbara Jean Richardson, her husband Leroy, and Barbara Jean's three children. Barbara Jean was a stout woman in her late thirties who went to work at 5:00 A.M. as a cleaner for the local power company, and finished the day at 1:30 in the afternoon. Her husband worked for the Department of Roads and Bridges in Berkeley County, cleaning out ditches and hauling dirt and sand to construction sites. Barbara Jean called Mrs. Richardson "Mother," and the elderly woman had raised her, but she was actually Mrs. Richardson's grandniece, born to a nephew. Barbara Jean's three children were Marcill, Steven, and Shanice. Marcill, the basketball player in the dirt yard, was finishing high school, Steven a bit younger, and Shanice not yet ten. In addition to Barbara Jean and her clan, Mrs. Richardson had family not only all around South Carolina but in Georgia, New Jersey, North Carolina, and farther.

Plantation records showed that Mrs. Richardson was the great-great-grandniece of one of the prominent figures on Comingtee, Maum Mary Ann, the last mammy of the slave days. In the family memoir, there is a description of Maum Mary Ann written by Anne Deas, whose mother, Ann Ball, had grown up on Comingtee: " 'Maum Mary Ann' was the housekeeper at Comingtee. [She] had the keys of storeroom and pantry, 'gave out' the meals, made the bread, and supervised the house generally." She had "clean white palms and a cheerful face," according to Anne Deas, who added, "I never saw her without a large white apron and a bright-colored 'head-handkerchief.' "

Maum Mary Ann became Mary Ann Royal after the Civil War. She died just one year after freedom, in the spring of 1866, at eighty. Her last owner, Keating Ball, wrote a eulogy for her in one of his account books:

Mother Mary Ann Royal, a faithful servant true Christian, who died on 31st March and surrendered her spirit to her Creator, in peace, charity and goodwill to all the world, including her former Owners, to whose family she always returned, with marked gratitude all kindness ever received, and They and their descendants always received her as one of the Family and a sincere Friend, even when a slave and after her being declared Free under the War Act.

There is a photograph of Maum Mary Ann in her last days. The picture shows a shrunken, heavily aged woman seated in a wooden chair. She has one eye fixed on the camera, and her other, a walleye, turned away from it. The old woman seems as though she is merely tolerating the presence of the photographer. And she looks exhausted.

Maum Mary Ann's husband was known as Captain Daniel, the pilot of the Comingtee schooner that went to and from Charleston carrying cargo and white people. Though this was a privileged job, sometimes Daniel ran up against plantation rule. One fall, in 1833, Daniel evidently drove the boat up into the marshes. He was whipped for it, and his crew members were beaten with switches. The overseer at Comingtee, Thomas Finklea, wrote his boss, John Ball, to tell the story. "Daniel let the sloop [run a]ground," Finklea said, adding that another boatman, Jack, did not take as many loads of rice as he had been ordered. "i had them both flogd & stade at the ferry until the sloop got under way," Finklea went on. "I had the bote men switched and [Daniel] thought hard of it."

Maum Mary Ann's brother, Surrey, had five children who survived to adulthood and who took the surname Pinckney after freedom. (According to Keating Ball, Surrey died in 1862, at ninety.) One of Surrey's children, Celia, born in March 1833, married a Comingtee field hand named Stephen, who used the name Green after the Civil War. Georgie Richardson was a great-grandchild of Celia and Stephen Green.

Captain Daniel Royal, Maum Mary Ann's husband, held the job of schooner pilot until the last decade of slavery. The assignment ran in families, so Captain Daniel's nephew and namesake, Daniel Pinckney, born in 1840, took over the job from his uncle.

"I heard about Dan Pinckney," said Georgie Richardson, who came along just about the time the boat pilot died. "He used to go to Charleston in his towboat to bring food. Them Pinckneys left some children, too." She named the children, and placed their families within a few miles of us.

I asked Mrs. Richardson about her own life. She was born Georgianna Gadsden on May 3, 1910, in Sawmill, to Thomas Gadsden, of Mepkin plantation, and Celia Gadsden, of Comingtee. Her mother, born Celia Blake, was sometimes called Diane. Her father was a field hand in the last years of rice planting.

"My daddy said he used to go to the rice field at five in the morning, and they would hoot for one another," said Mrs. Richardson. "Hoot, because you don't know who all is going, so they would hoot to let 'em know they on the way. And they would hoot back to let 'em know they heard. They go down there to Mepkin, and down to Comingtee. I have a reaper in the house now that my daddy used to cut rice with."

Georgie Gadsden was feeble as a girl. "I was the sickliest child. They told me I was the sickliest they ever had, and they had my box already made," she said, laughing.

The box was readied for the wrong person. When she was five, Georgie witnessed the death of her mother, Celia Gadsden, in childbirth, an event that became her earliest memory.

"The day my mother died," said Mrs. Richardson, "I was a child, and we went in the woods to pick those little blue huckleberries. I had my little pan. I picked the pan full, so I went back in the room, and Da was in the bed." "Da" was Georgie's mother. "And my aunt was there, my daddy's sister, Titty. So I went back in the room where Da was, and they didn't see me. They had the door shut, and I opened the door, and they had Da covered with a sheet over her face. I didn't know she was dead. I pulled the sheet and I saw the blood on her face, so I went to wipe the blood from her face, and Titty came running in the room. She said, 'Come on out of there!' And I said, 'I wanted to give Da some huckleberries! Look at her bleeding!' And Titty pulled me, and I had to pull from her to get to Da. And they had the little baby wrapped up in a blanket. Titty said, 'Ah, Lord, these children see a hard time when they mother is gone.'

"Pa went to get some boards to make her box," Mrs. Richardson went on. "They got the pine, and a man came with his saw and his nail and things, and he made a box that evening before the sun went down. Pa got moss, and put the moss in the box, and I saw Titty take a sheet and tear the sheet. I was a child! I wondered what did they tear that sheet for? They put it all around the box on the moss. They washed her off. People used to put turpentine on the body then, to keep it from smell. Then they must have put clothes on her, and took her and put her inside the box. Pa hitched up the wagon. He had an old mule, named Minnie. Some other men was there with him, and the four of 'em lift up the box and put it in the wagon and went to Com'ntee that evening. They put her underneath the tree, a big oak tree, for the night. And they buried her the next day. I wasn't there when they funeralized the body. I was small, they left me home." Mrs. Richardson slowed her story and looked to the wall. "Ashes to ashes and dust to dust."

The baby boy born from Celia Gadsden's death was given to a relative to be raised, but he died in childhood.

"The baby boy, my aunt raised him," said Mrs. Richardson. "They called him B-Boy. And you know what caused him death? He ate the green peach off the tree and that caused him malaria. He must have been around about seven."

Celia Gadsden and B-Boy weren't the only ones to die within reach. Georgie had two sisters, Belle and Sing, who died young.

"How did they mark the graves?" I asked.

"They didn't put a tombstone like they do now," she answered. "They would cut stakes, cedar stakes, then peel 'em. Cedar don't rot right off, you know. One stake for the foot and one for the head. The head was bigger. Then they put flowers on the grave."

Only one other child of Georgie Gadsden's generation survived, her brother Daniel, called Bubba, two years younger than she.

After her mother died, Georgie Gadsden went to work for the family.

"I went to school for a little while and stopped," she said, "must have been in the third grade. When I went to school, my aunt came and took me out. She carried me home to dig bait, to go fishing. Pa and them caught the fish, and when they came back from fishing, I had to clean 'em."

When she turned ten, Georgie Gadsden came under the rule of a new woman. "My father married a mean woman, named Martha," Mrs. Richardson said. "My stepmother made me wash all the clothes, overalls, everything. I used to have a big pot to scald the clothes, and you put your clothes in the big pot, and stick your stick in it, and put in lye and Gold Dust—you know the Gold Dust with the little black children on the red box? I put four buckets of water on the quilt until that quilt drained, until the water turned light and all that dirty water came out. And if I hang that quilt on the line and it ain't clean, my stepmother would take it and throw it on the ground and make me wash it again. I used to wring the overalls. I twisted it, and then I rinsed it with three waters, until the last water was clean. Then I cooked flour starch by mixing the flour up. You get a pan, put water in it and dip that thing in it, then wring it and hang it up. And you iron it with a steam iron. To clean the floor, I used the bucket and mop, and brick dust. We used to beat the brick until you get dust, then spread it on the floor. You get on your knee, and scrub it with a big crocus rag."

There wasn't much food, and drinking water came straight from the Cooper River.

"Daddy used to get the river water in a bucket, and it was salty water sometimes. He shake it so the dirt would settle." Mrs. Richardson let her tongue out of her mouth, and put it on her lower lip. "These children today, they ain't want this for eat, ain't want that for eat. *Shoo!* I was glad for get it! 'Cause I didn't had it! One apple a week, cut in half between the two of us—Bubba get half, I get half. Mr. Ball, for eat, we had a spoon of grits on this side of the plate, a spoon of rice on that side! Sometimes Pa kill a chicken out the yard. Pa get the breast and the leg. Bubba got the foot, and I got the head."

"What about the woods?" I asked.

"My Pa used to hunt a lot," came the answer, "for coon, possum, and polecat. He would skin 'em for eat. But something caused me to stop eating possum. One day, Pa carried a dog to hunt. And somebody out in the woods was dead, and they didn't bury 'em deep enough. The dog bark and bark, and trace the possum. When he got 'em, the possum been dug in the grave and eat the man."

Mrs. Richardson looked at me with her clouded eyes. "I come up in the rough time!" she said. "Man, these children today, they rich!"

When Georgie Gadsden was a teenager, she had a baby, whom she named Celia Ann, after her mother. "My own child, I didn't raise that," she said. "My brother Dan raised her. My brother said I couldn't carry that girl, because a man could throw it in my face." She gave up Celia Ann, she said, so that the man she married wouldn't use the baby against her. Celia Ann eventually settled in New York, married, had a long working life as a seamstress, moved to Pennsylvania, and retired in New Jersey.

When Georgie Gadsden was in her teens, a relative went to work in the house at Comingtee, and Georgie occasionally went with her to do the wash. She worked off and on there and at a neighboring plantation, Rice Hope, until she was married, in 1930, to Robert Richardson. By this time, rich families from the North had bought up many of the plantations, using the old houses as second homes and the land as deer- and duck-hunting grounds.

"After I married, I moved to Glebe plantation," Mrs. Richardson said, naming a place six miles from Comingtee. "We fished on Glebe, then sometimes we go to hoe the bank. When the Yankee people come down to shoot duck, you had to hoe the bank, and cut grass so they could walk to the duck blind. My husband carry the Yankees out in the boat, and put them in the blind. Sometimes he hoed the path for your foot, so there weren't no snakes. Snakes were bad then, you know. I know a man who die from a rattlesnake. He was puttin' up his shovel, where he hide it, and a rattlesnake hit him on the arm. Killed him right there. At Glebe, we lived in a house with another family. There was two big rooms—one family on this side, one on that side. The room was big enough I could put two beds, a trunk, and a dresser."

Robert and Georgie Richardson next moved to the little piece of land where I met Mrs. Richardson and family. "My husband piece up the house. He had to get board off the river, and patch 'em up," she said, pointing at the window. The house was the one damaged by Hurricane Hugo and finally pulled down. "It ain't had but two room."

Soon Robert Richardson got a job in Charleston, thirty miles away. The United States had entered World War II, and the Navy shipyard, a big employer, put out a call for men. Mr. Richardson cleaned the pipes used in ship repair and lived away from home.

"Did you have a job?" I asked.

Mrs. Richardson's expression went flat. She thought for a moment, looked down, murmured something. It was a stupid question. The idea of employment didn't fit country life, with its daywork, chicken coops, and corn fields.

"I had a job one time," she said finally, "doing laundry at Mepkin plantation. And I did laundry at Rice Hope, when Miss Luce used to be there."

When she married Henry Luce, who founded *Time* magazine in 1923, Clare Boothe Brokaw became Clare Boothe Luce—"Miss Luce." Henry and Clare Boothe Luce bought Mepkin plantation, the homestead of Eleanor Ball and her husband, Henry Laurens, in the 1760s, three miles from Comingtee. The Luces made Mepkin their second home, traveling to South Carolina from New York for weeklong stays. At some point, the Luces decided to build a house at Mepkin, designed by architect Edward Durrell Stone in a Modernist style. The result was the only piece of white, rectangular, flat-roofed architecture on the old rice banks of the Cooper River. Evidently, while the house was under construction, the Luces spent part of their time at Rice Hope, next door to Comingtee. At Rice Hope, Georgie Richardson did their laundry.

"Miss Luce come from up North," said Mrs. Richardson. "They used to come shoot duck, and muddy up them jackets. When I came, Miss Luce give me them things for wash, and they ain't had no electric machine. I did it by hand, on a washboard. She would come back, give me ten dollars, or something. Sometimes during the week, Miss Luce and her family have us come around the back of the house. There was a porch where they sat on. They used to like to hear colored people sing."

"What did you sing?" I asked.

" 'Old Time Religion,' songs like that."

A sawmill that went up near Comingtee gave other jobs. "A lot of people used to work at that sawmill. My brother Dan used to work there, and all them—Frank Fayall, Mackie Bennett," Mrs. Richardson remembered. "They didn't pay much, but you got money."

Barbara Jean came into the room.

"Mother, how is Mr. Ball treating you?"

Barbara Jean, in her late thirties, was friendly, loud, and solid. By this time I had gotten to know her a bit.

"All right," said Mrs. Richardson, scratching a laugh.

Barbara Jean came in with Shanice, who was tall for her age, and beautiful, with big eyes. She wore an orange tank top and little shorts, and she sat in Mrs. Richardson's lap. I knew that Barbara Jean wasn't Mrs. Richardson's daughter, and asked about her parents.

"My father, Rias Richardson, was her sister-in-law's son," said Barbara Jean, pointing at Mrs. Richardson. "The sister-in-law didn't want my father, so she and her husband raised my father from a three-months baby. When he growed up, my father became a young man in the military, and had me by my mother. My mother didn't want me, wanted to give me away. So she, Mrs. Richardson, took me in as a three-months baby, just like my father, and raised me." She pointed again. "That makes her my mother," said Barbara Jean, looking at her great-aunt, Georgie Richardson.

"My birth mother never had another child but me," Barbara Jean went on. "She died when I was five, in a car accident, so I never had a chance to know her. When I found out who my natural parents were, I was twelve years old. I went to spend a Christmas with my father. This man came knocking to the door. I said, 'I don't know you!' He had a hard time convincing me he was my uncle, my birth mother's brother. Then we got to know each other. When we went to see my grandmother, she thought I was my uncle's girlfriend. He said, 'No, this is your grand-daughter.' Nobody in the family knew me.

"I grew up with two names," Barbara Jean said. "My birth mother named me Doreen Smith. But I grew up with the name Barbara Jean Richardson, and wanted to keep that. When I was eighteen, I legally changed it on my birth certificate. My natural father, Rias Richardson, he lives in Charleston. He's a longshoreman who works at the Port Authority. It's a good-paying job. What he would make in two days, it would take me two weeks to make it. With him, I have three sisters and two brothers, and there is a bunch of other ones. One I just found out about a couple of weeks ago. It felt good because she was older than me. I go and see them sometimes. I would like us to be close-knit, but it's not that way. Because of all that happened, that's why I try to tell my children who their parents are, so when they grow up and go out, they won't say, 'Momma didn't tell me this, Momma didn't tell me that.' "

Barbara Jean's three children came by two different husbands. When she left her second husband, Barbara said, he had a fit of jealous rage. One day she went to the grocery store and came home to find that her trailer had been burned to the ground. Barbara Jean signed up for public assistance.

"I went on the welfare system for a while, but didn't like that," she remembered. "I said to myself, I had to get a job. Finally I got one, at the power company. Then I bought the trailer where I live now."

I looked at Barbara Jean's beautiful child Shanice.

"Do you work around the house, like your grandmother used to?" I asked.

"I help her do the dishes," said Shanice, "and mop up the floor, and clean the house." She rolled her tongue around her lips, in the style of Mrs. Richardson.

"Have you been to Charleston?" I put in. Shanice shook her head.

"Don't shake your head," said Mrs. Richardson. "Cows shake heads."

Shanice wrapped her arms around herself. Then she unlaced them, and cracked her knuckles.

The old slave cemetery at Comingtee had been off-limits to black people since the 1930s, when it fell behind the lines of new owners. The cabins came down, paths disappeared, and, with no one keeping them, graves vanished in the thicket. Georgie Richardson's mother was buried on Comingtee, and her sisters and brother also ended up there, but Mrs. Richardson had not been to the cemetery since she was a young woman. It was too late for her to go, she said, because she could no longer navigate the brush. With Mrs. Richardson in mind, I looked for the graveyard in the woods.

There were other slave cemeteries on the old Ball lands. The one at Kensington plantation had a stone marker that still stood, placed there by one man's owner. "To the memory of Old Peter," it read, "who died 10th Jany 1816 about 90 years of age faithful & honest thro' life   Born & died in the family of Ball's."

It was cool and bright the day I went to Comingtee to hunt for the graves, accompanied by a search partner, Stanley Richmond. Mr. Richmond, in his early sixties, stood about six feet, had a full head of hair with no gray, and the body of a man half his age. He had worked thirty-one years for the forestry company that owned Comingtee and knew the place like anyone. Mr. Richmond was married to a woman whose family descended from Comingtee slaves. "That's what her granduncle told me," he said. "All of them had to move to Sawmill." I looked in the records, and his wife's forebears indeed appeared there.

Stanley Richmond's skin was deep black, with the gleam of graphite, and his hands were rough from a life of handling tools and brush. He had an oval face, with heavy jowls, a flat nose, and full lips. His smile showed one gold tooth in the middle of a full row of white, while from behind the teeth came a deep voice, like the blast of a tuba. When he shouted into the woods, the leaves seemed to shake. The day we went to the plantation, Mr. Richmond wore a plaid shirt, green camouflage pants, a cap and boots, and thick eyeglasses.

The Comingtee land had been corporate property for some decades. Westvaco Corporation (the old West Virginia Pulp and Paper Company) used it to court customers, whom they flew to South Carolina to hunt and fish. Mr. Richmond and I raised dust on the narrow road as we drove onto the estate, and the acrid smell of the dirt mixed with the slender odor of pine needles. The road passed between walls of forest, along the edge of swamps, and through more woods. Although he had not been to the slave cemetery for twenty years, said Mr. Richmond, he thought he could find it. I was skeptical. The barns and slave houses, carpenters' shops and stables, smokehouses and kitchens, were all gone, and many of the old fields had grown up with trees. Even some of the paths between the white and black settlements on the place, trampled down for two hundred years, had disappeared.

"There was like a ditch around the cemetery," said Mr. Richmond, getting out of the car on a skinny dirt road. "Water come in there, and during that time, you could only get across when the tide is low. When the tide is up, the cemetery is an island. Some of the older people, who is dead and gone, they said that's the only way you can bury people there, was when the tide is down, then you can go across." Mr. Richmond's baritone voice echoed like a broadcast between the trees. The woodpeckers stopped their knocking, and the mockingbirds fell silent.

The hunt was made harder by the effects of a storm. In September 1989, when Hurricane Hugo came through Charleston and swept past the Cooper River district, great pines broke off in midtrunk and heavy brush was rearranged like balls of dust. The worst damage came from the river, when the tide surged and washed a five-foot wave over the cemeteries. As the water receded, it scraped away topsoil and, presumably, wooden grave markers.

Mr. Richmond had been to the site several times after someone showed it to him, but my only clue to the location of the graveyard came from the Ball memoir:

> The negro cemetery—in plantation parlance, the Buryin' Groun'—is a grove of tall white-oaks and hickories, half-way between the house and the river. . . . Shade and silence reign there, and under the carpet of fallen leaves lie generation upon generation of a simple people, who were, in the main and according to their lights, faithful and attached to their masters.

If Mr. Richmond pointed out a place near the one described in the Ball memoir, I could be sure it was the right one. I brought a photocopy of an eighteenth-century plat of the property, which showed that the oldest road, the path from the main house to the river, had never changed. As we walked in the white dust, suddenly Mr. Richmond stopped and pointed into the brush. On the treeline were the tops of the white oaks.

"Them wood markers probably done rotted out," said Mr. Richmond, "because there was some rotted out when I been here last. They wasn't nothing written on it. They just had 'em at the head of the people. At the foot they put these little things with the name, and the year you born and the year you die. But them things so light, they been washed out."

We tramped into the woods along the remains of a path. Fallen pines blocked the way, and brambles pulled at our clothes. There were clumps of palm fronds at waist height that looked like big green hands.

"I recognize this thing," said Mr. Richmond, grabbing a big frond. "These were near the graves. We used to come right by these things to go to the graves."

We came to a muddy channel, crossed it, and walked onto higher ground. An area of half an acre appeared a little clearer than the rest of the forest floor. Mr. Richmond stopped and fell silent. His voice, for the first time, was quiet.

"This is it," he said. "You see right here, it's a grave." He traced a sunken place the length of a body on the ground with his foot. "It's sunken in the ground, it's the width of a grave, and it's the length. Once that box get rotted, the earth been on the top goes down. And here too." He stepped on another sag in the leaves.

Mr. Richmond said in passing that he used to have a job with an undertaker in a nearby town. He dug graves, drove a hearse, and spent a lot of afternoons in cemeteries.

"This is our place," he said finally.

Around the ground were other sunken shapes, where a coffin beneath had rotted and the earth collapsed like a lung. I looked down and realized I was standing on a grave, and wondered if it was that of Georgie Richardson's mother, or her ancestor, Maum Mary Ann. There were no stones, and no wooden markers.

"The tide from Hugo came up real high," said Mr. Richmond. "They washed the markers away. Them markers likely at the bottom of the river."

...

A short distance from Comingtee stood the St. James Reformed Episcopal Church, a white cinderblock building framed by pine trees. Most of the parishioners came from Sawmill, and Mrs. Richardson's family belonged to the congregation, which traced its history to the slave church on the plantation. One Sunday I went to St. James with Georgie Richardson and her family.

It was raining, and a gray cloud canopy darkened the church door. The damp seemed to silence the neighborhood, the grumble of tires on asphalt making the only sound. Mrs. Richardson wore a dress and hat; Barbara Jean put on a white robe to sing in the choir, and Barbara Jean's children turned out in their best clothes.

The sanctuary of St. James contained twenty plywood pews, painted brown. Three fluorescent lights hung from the ceiling, veneer paneling covered the walls, and in place of a crucifix was a cloth mural, a reproduction of an Italian Renaissance painting of the Last Supper, in red, blue, and gold polyester. According to the minister, the congregation numbered thirty-two. The turnout included fifteen in the pews, plus a choir of ten. As Mrs. Richardson introduced me, I recognized family names from Comingtee—Simmons, Wilson, Fayall, and others. Mrs. Richardson and I took our place in the second pew, and the first hymn came up. There were no instruments, just voices, clapping, and a tambourine.

Episcopalianism, brought from England by the colonists, was the religion of the masters. After the Civil War, most black people joined Baptist or Methodist churches, rejecting the prayers of the slave-owning class. St. James, however, stayed with the old liturgy. The minister was a tall man with a big jaw and a clear, booming voice. As he read the order of worship, I recognized prayers from the days of King George III, redolent with the "thees" and "thous" of the old Book of Common Prayer.

I held the prayer book in front of Mrs. Richardson so she could follow. She looked away, and ten minutes later I remembered she did not read.

The story of St. James was the story of Sawmill. In the 1840s, there was a couple on Comingtee, Binah and Brawley. Brawley was the hogminder, Binah a field hand, and the two lived in a cabin on a rise known as Indian Spring Hill. Brawley was a plantation preacher who gave sermons and gathered a following until about 1850, when he and his wife built a little clapboard church. Binah and Brawley became leaders on the slave street, Brawley preaching in the field hands' church for many years. After the Civil War, the question arose of what to do, right away at least, with freedom. Some held that everyone should stay on the plantation and work as sharecroppers, while others wanted to leave. Brawley preached in favor of staying; listening, most of the Comingtee people signed the sharecrop contract. At another Ball place, Limerick, most everyone left.

A few years into Reconstruction, Brawley died. His congregation kept going and built another church, bigger than the first, a rectangle with a vaulted ceiling and a steep roof. The building was made from pine and contained not a single nail, all joints being held together with pegs. The church pooled resources and bought a bell, which they placed in a little belfry above the front door. Mrs. Richardson would one day be baptized in this church. When the black people had to leave Comingtee, they decided to move the church to Sawmill. A new site was selected, the windows battened down, the bell removed. The building was hoisted onto wheels, rolled to a little clearing at the edge of Sawmill, set down, and consecrated as St. James Reformed Episcopal Church.

"A good bit didn't know how to write in those days," said Mrs. Richardson. "But they had church. Preach out of the Bible, and had a good time, too! Someone would come to church and read to people, and they would memorize it. I can't read the Bible, but when I go to church, I take the Word."

The original peg-and-board building served until Hurricane Hugo took it down. The congregation selected another site a short distance away, and put up the new cinderblock building. Someone retrieved the bell from the rubble of the old church. It was brought to the new building and placed in a corner, as a shrine.

After services I went into a back room to see the bell. It was cast iron, twelve inches across at the mouth, and painted silver. When I rapped it, it made a high, pleasing sound.

In 1736 the girl who would be called Angola Amy was brought from the vicinity of the Congo River in Africa to Charleston, South Carolina, where she was bought by Elias "Red Cap" Ball and taken to Comingtee. The papers showed that Georgie Richardson, in addition to coming from Maum Mary Ann, was the great-great-great-great-great-granddaughter of Angola Amy. Amy's daughter Easter, born in 1746 at Comingtee, grew up and gave birth, in 1778, to Judy, who had a daughter named Dorcas, born 1805, who had Celia in 1833, who had Dorcas in 1854, who had another Celia in 1875, who gave birth to a girl called Georgianna, in 1910, who grew up to be Georgie Richardson.

With this revelation, Mrs. Richardson and her family joined a rare group of black Americans. Few people could state the name and place of origin of an African forebear. But Angola Amy, captured and sold as a girl, had left a long paper trail. Soon after I learned of her distant African ancestry, but before I had a chance to tell her the story, Georgie Richardson died, at eighty-seven, of heart failure. I attended her funeral, held at a church near Sawmill, Holy Comforter Reformed Episcopal, sister church to her own St. James.

The church had standing room only when the service began on an old hymn, "Nearer My God to Thee." In front of the plain room, lying on a gurney with wheels, was Mrs. Richardson's white coffin. It stood closed, and its silver handles gleamed. Mrs. Richardson was a church-going woman, and out of respect, five pastors had come to conduct her funeral. Each clergyman gave a eulogy, followed by a hymn. The alternation of homilies with singing took time; the service lasted two and a half hours.

Barbara Jean, her husband Leroy, and the three children sat in the front pew. Mrs. Richardson's daughter, Celia Ann, had come down from New Jersey. The grieving of Georgie's family sometimes grew loud, and when that happened, a woman would appear from the back of the church with a paper fan, which she waved over the mourners to cool their tears.

When the service ended, the coffin was opened and placed in the doorway of the church, so that mourners could file past and say good-bye to the deceased. On the way out, I looked at Mrs. Richardson for the last time. Her face was heavily powdered, her mouth wired flat, and she wore a gray wig. A half hour later, at the gravesite, I stood under a green tent in the crowd of black mourners. Two gravediggers lowered the coffin into the ground, and covered it with a concrete slab.

9

><+><+>○<+><+><

BLOODLINES

With the death of the founding patriarch, Red Cap, in 1751, the Ball family business centered on three plantations, or work camps, near Charleston—Comingtee, Hyde Park, and Kensington—each with seventy-five to a hundred slaves. The little American business Red Cap took on in 1698 had grown to a scale far beyond what he had envisaged.

To convey a legacy of any kind from one generation to the next was a rare feat in colonial America. Evidence shows that most of the other white families the Balls knew from the early years had died out or moved away. In the 1720s more than 150 family names appeared in the registers of St. John's Parish, the church precinct the family called home. Fifty years later, only five of the original surnames would remain: Ball, Broughton, Cordes, Harleston, and Ravenel. The Balls had become part of a tiny hereditary cadre.

Red Cap had fathered twelve white children by two wives, the last when he was nearly sixty, a boy who died in infancy. Of the four who survived into the late 1700s, two had inherited most of the patrimony. John Coming Ball, thirty-six at his father's death, lived at Hyde Park with his wife, Catherine, and several children. Next door, at Kensington, forty-one-year-old "Second Elias" Ball lived with his wife, Lydia, and their children. None of the family lived at Comingtee, which had become purely a rice farm, run by overseers. Of the two sisters who shared the Ball legacy, Ann, who was fifty when her father died, had two children, lived in Charleston, and was married to the slave trader George Austin. Ann's sister, twenty-year-old Eleanor, had married Henry Laurens, Austin's partner in the import-export firm of Austin & Laurens, which sold some rice and tools, but mainly human beings. John Coming was the richest of the four siblings, the new young patriarch. In addition to Hyde Park, he owned a sixteen-hundred-acre tract, Cypress Grove; a parcel called Three Mile Head; and much other land. His holdings in 1751 amounted to 14,459 acres and 216 people.

There were three measurable parts to the success of a plantation family: land, money, slaves. About this time, the landowning elite added a fourth: blood. The mystical properties of blood—their own and that of their workers—were included in the language with which the Balls described their world.

Blood could be seen at work in horses. In the 1750s horse tracks were cleared in the village of Childsbury, next to Comingtee, and Moncks Corner, a few miles northwest; and later the Strawberry Jockey Club opened on land adjacent to Second Elias's Strawberry plantation. Horse racing became a main social occasion for whites outside the city of Charleston, and the Balls would have attended many races. To be sure, they had an appetite for the chase, but more fascinating was the element of blood. Racehorses were said to be blooded, and thoroughbred racing meant the competition of animals subjected to controlled breeding. A certain "Red Doe stock," horses descended from a fast mare called Red Doe, became famed along the Cooper River, and most planters clamored to own a few. At Kensington, Second Elias Ball kept a notebook about his stables, in which he recorded the birth and parentage of his horse teams. "Charlotte foaled a bay horse colt got by a woods horse," he wrote. "Sylvia foaled a black mare colt with a small star got by Shim." The stable book confirmed the ancestry of each horse, and traced the path of its blood.

A horse was a piece of animate property, not unlike other breathing possessions. One day, Second Elias made a note that he had traded one blooded thing for another. "I made a [deal] with Mr. Philip Sandford," he wrote. "I gave him one young Negro man . . . for two horses, one . . . a bay horse that was old."

Blood coursed through the family business, until the bloodline of black people became almost as important to Second Elias and John Coming Ball as their own English blood. Just as they saw themselves as part of a lineage—English parents, rice planters—the brothers began to see blacks as products of bloodlines. The notion of blood meant that for a long time the Balls thought of Africans in terms of their tribe and birthplace. One year Second Elias wrote down the birthplace of thirty-five of his male slaves at Comingtee plantation. "Gambia" he put down for some, "Angola" for others. The categories were rough, but real. Other men he described as "country-born," meaning born in South Carolina. For Second Elias, country-born blacks may have been less desirable, because their blood had been diluted after a generation in America.

Second Elias's brother-in-law Henry Laurens understood blood better than anyone. As an importer of people, the husband of Eleanor Ball was in the business of bloodlines and throughout his life paid attention to the cultural origins of the Africans he sold. Eleanor's spouse came to consider himself something of a connoisseur of black clans and blood. He gave instructions to his ship captains, the men who dealt on West African coasts, and insisted that they bring home the right kinds of people.

"The Slaves from the River Gambia are preferr'd to all others with us save the Gold Coast," Laurens wrote to one captain in 1756. "Gambias" included people from the Gambia River and the latter-day nations of Gambia and Senegal. The Gold Coast was what eventually became the Republic of Ghana, where gold as well as people was traded. "Gold Coast or Gambias are best," Laurens wrote to another man. "Next To Them The Windward Coast are prefer'd to Angolas." The Windward Coast was a west-to-east stretch of shore from Cape Mount to the port of Assini—what would eventually become the nations of Liberia and Ivory Coast. Angola lay twenty-three hundred miles to the south, around the mouth of the Congo River.

Long before the idea of race came along, the Balls paid attention to a hierarchy of black people based on clan and tribal origin. Henry Laurens told ship captains to write down what he called the "Species" of slaves on their cargo lists, since different tribes (as everyone knew) had different traits. The idea took hold that the blood of people determined who they were and what they were capable of doing. The English were born to rule, the "Gambias" to till rice.

Black blood could be good or bad. If Second Elias liked "Gambias" (his lists have many), the people he tried to avoid buying were "Ebos" (that is, Igbo). The Igbo lived in the area known as the Bight of Biafra, centered in the delta of the Niger River, and brought low prices on the market. It was not because they were unable to do heavy work, or even because they were less familiar with rice agriculture than people from the Gambia, where rice was a staple. Igbo were thought by planters to be morose—so melancholy, whites thought, that they had a reputation for suicide, which made them a risky investment. They were, in fact, statistically prone to hurl themselves into the Atlantic, killing themselves before their captors had a chance to sell them. Henry Laurens once wrote a letter complaining about suicide in the ranks of Igbo; another time he instructed one of his contacts that Igbo captives, should the ship be forced to buy any, should be between the ages of fifteen and twenty. According to Laurens, young Igbo people were "not accustom'ed to destroy themselves" as much as the adults. Laurens evidently found out otherwise, because he later revised the age limit downward, to fourteen. The Igbo affinity with suicide became so well known that a boat landing in the vicinity of Beaufort, down the Atlantic coast from Charleston, acquired the name Igbo Landing. Numerous people plunged in the waters there after they glimpsed the welcome they were about to receive on the American shore. Whether their deaths came from melancholy in the blood or intelligence is unclear.

Ideas about blood grew more elaborate, until slave buyers like Second Elias believed each African clan to have deep-rooted traits. In the second generation of the Ball business, planters who bought large numbers of Africans developed the following beliefs:

- Mandinka people, from the Gambia region, were good-looking and gentle of manner, but could not be trusted.
- Coromantees, from the Gold Coast, were strong, courageous, and stern, but bore grudges.
- Popo people, from the region around the port of Whydah, east of the mouth of the Volta River, were the most reliable slaves that could be found. They were accustomed to hard work, had an even temper, and were both dextrous and obedient.
- Slaves from the region the traders called Sierra Leone, which reached from the Casamance River in the north to Sherbro Island, three hundred miles south, were regarded as good all-

around "rice Negroes," because they had grown rice for centuries.

• Angolans, from north and south of the Congo River, were
thought to be less vigorous than Popos, but mechanically
minded and attractive, although apt to run away—and sometimes to stage uprisings.

In 1762, Henry and Eleanor Laurens bought Mepkin plantation,
three miles north along the Cooper River from Eleanor's birthplace,
Comingtee. In becoming a landowner, Laurens finally joined blooded
plantation society. Peopling Mepkin with workers was no difficult matter, and Henry and Eleanor divided their time between Mepkin and
their house in Charleston. Laurens knew little of rice agriculture and
relied on advice from his brothers-in-law in the Ball family. What Laurens did understand was classification. The ship captains who reported
to him often brought back unusual plants, roots, and seeds from overseas, which Laurens, in gardens he kept in town, used to develop his
interest in botany. He placed the specimens just near his house, where
his slaves tended them. Laurens was said to favor a particular species,
the Chinese tallow tree, *Stillingia sebifera*, which has heart-shaped
leaves and a little waxy berry that grows in clusters. Perhaps Laurens
himself got down on his knees from time to time, weeded the ground
around his foreign saplings, and then labeled them.

Second Elias Ball came from English blood, on both his mother's and
father's side. In paintings that survive, the middle-aged rice planter has
a distracted air, his chin disappears under heavy jowls, and he appears
portly and bald. Second Elias had three sons, whose patrimony he had
to worry about. Fortunately for him, as his boys grew into adulthood,
rice sales soared and the family man collected a windfall.

In the 1750s, Britain went to war with France over the American
territories and the issue of which monarchy would dominate the eastern
half of the continent. In the so-called French and Indian War, dozens
of Native clans fought on the side of the French in an effort to break
up English rule. The battles unfolded in the northern colonies, far from
the Ball tracts, but the war brought a boom to the rice business. Rice,
as a grain, was seen as versatile, durable, and filling. With its regiments

roaming the hinterland, the British crown bought up the crops of the Carolina rice planters. The price of rice nearly doubled in the last years of the 1750s, handing the Balls a lucrative reward.

Looking after his own, Second Elias chose this moment to expand the business. In March 1764 he bought Limerick plantation, intending the place as an inheritance for his sons, who were still young enough to play on the lawn. John Coming Ball's place, Hyde Park, bordered Limerick, the better for family togetherness. At first Limerick came empty, since the workers evidently moved with their owner before the sale. Though there were no people, the seller, Daniel Huger, was not above pawning a few items with the house. Among other things, Second Elias picked up a mahogany dressing table, two wine decanters, a bed, a set of china, and ninety-five pigs. Now there were three Ball plantations in a row on the same side of the Cooper River—Limerick, Hyde Park, and Kensington—a solid block of fifty-eight hundred acres.

In addition to the new land, the profits from the rice boom also went into education, as Second Elias and his generation hired tutors and governesses, and sent their boys to local academies run by European teachers. The Ball sons studied mathematics and rhetoric (for the sake of business), while the girls went to finishing schools or a domestic arts academy where, under the guidance of well-dressed matrons, they learned to do needlework, to speak French, and to dance. Although they paid attention to literacy, the Balls were not interested in serious study. Some sons of plantation owners went to England to be educated, but not the Ball boys. Literature did not arouse the family, except as an adornment to table conversation, and the art of painting they regarded as the work of craftsmen. In fact, Second Elias appears to have been suspicious of people who thought too much, though in this he was not alone. In 1748, the Charleston Library Society, the first public book collection, was established in the colony. The initial subscribers amounted to seventeen people.

The Balls and their friends took strongest interest in fine things you could put your hands on. To judge from his letters, Second Elias was a mild-mannered, even shy, man, but he seemed to know what he liked. One of the main interests of the Balls was to have just the right decor for their houses, for which Second Elias turned to an English carver named Thomas Elfe. Born in London in 1719, Elfe moved to Virginia and finally made his home in Charleston, where, between 1747 and his death in 1775, he carved furniture for the slave-owning rich. Elfe worked in mahogany, the favored material for china cabinets and chests of drawers. He used raw wood from forests in the Caribbean, which in contrast to the muddled brown of some mahogany had a luminous, golden hue. In one year, Second Elias had Elfe make him a mahogany bed, an armchair and a footstool, two mahogany dining tables, a dozen dining chairs with scroll backs, and what he called a slab table, apparently with a marble top.

In addition to collecting furniture, the Balls commissioned paintings of themselves, calling again on the portrait artist Jeremiah Theus, as Red Cap had done. Second Elias commissioned Theus to paint him twice, the first time about 1760, when the master of Kensington was fifty. In the second, later portrait, he wears a white wig with little curls over the ears, and a silvery blue jacket over his large stomach. Around the same time, Second Elias had Theus paint his sons, Elias III and Isaac, who emerged from the process looking like two child dandies. In his painting, Elias III, about twelve, wears a royal blue waistcoat, satin vest, and ruffled shirt; his blond hair has been set with curlers, and he holds a small leatherbound book. Little Isaac looks about the same, only in place of the book he has a red-headed bird perched on his left hand.

The children's pictures must have gone over well, because many other family members soon headed for the artist's studio. From Hyde Park, Ann Ball, daughter of John Coming and Catherine Ball, came to sit for her portrait. She was eighteen, and on the eve of her marriage to Richard Waring, of neighboring Dorchester County. Ann's portrait shows the teenage bride-to-be in a velvet jacket, white satin waistcoat, and a string of pearls.

On top of pictures, good furniture, carriages, silver, and china, the Balls liked their clothes. The girls went to Charleston to be fitted for dresses. On one occasion, a daughter of John Coming Ball, Eleanor, took herself to a clothier named Jacob Tobias. Tobias was one of the city's population of Sephardic Jews, immigrants who went into businesses like shopkeeping and dry goods rather than plantations and slaves. According to the receipt, Tobias fitted Miss Ball with a brown dress and "whalebone corset," and finished it with a mantua, a loose-fitting silk gown. The Ball women did not necessarily spend more than the men on finery; in fact, the conspicuous peacock of the family was Second Elias's youngest son, John Ball. Born in 1760 on Kensington, by his teens John Ball had accumulated an extensive wardrobe. He first got a slave seamstress to make ruffled shirts for him, and by the time he was fifteen his armoires were so full that the young master felt obliged to keep a notebook about what he owned. For each item, John wrote down when the piece was laundered by his female valet, Diana.

Diana was about forty when she began to care for John's things. She had a son, Devonshire, and a daughter, Nanna, whose own clothing evidently did with less of their mother's care. John's laundry went to Diana every week. A fairly typical load, jotted down by the boy, consisted of ten shirts, eight pairs of socks, five pairs of stockings, four jackets, four handkerchiefs, and two pairs of breeches. These were the everyday things. A little finer, and apparently washed less often, were two pairs of white breeches, two polka-dot jackets, two purple "persian jackets," and six pairs of "mosquito boots," high shoes against the country mud. Diana no doubt handled them all gently. Once, John made an inventory of the best rack in his wardrobe, writing down that he owned three coats (one blue, one brown, one gray), a pair of polka-dot velvet pants, no fewer than twelve pairs of black velvet breeches, and twelve pairs of silk stockings.

Young John's father wrote him letters complaining that all he thought about was his looks, and the boy did play the vain prince. By later standards, however, the youth seems to have neglected one thing that can make a dandy appealing: according to his notes, John put on a fresh shirt at least every morning, and clean pants every second or third day, but sent only one pair of underwear to Diana to be washed each week.

With spotty written evidence, the daily lives of the slaves flash up only in glimpses during the second generation of the Ball places. There were hundreds of people whose biographies boil down to just a few episodes. But single memories are better than none.

Indiana was a field hand on Comingtee, the daughter of Igbo Clarinda. In 1762, Clarinda believed she would become a grandparent when Indiana became pregnant with her first child. The mother-to-be was twenty-two, and she had even picked out a name for the child, Carter —but the infant was stillborn. Second Elias noted the births of slaves, usually with a date and the name of the mother, but of Indiana's son, he made a little joke. "March 10," he wrote, "Carter, Indiana's son was born dead as a D'nail." No one else needed to know the wisecrack, certainly not Carter's mother. Indiana herself did not reach an old age, dying a few years later at thirty-four.

Death came often and unexpectedly. It struck hard in the life of one mother, whose boy, Friday, lived only ten years, until 1773, when Second Elias noted that he had "died of fits." The numbers could hardly be worse: about half the black children born on the Ball tracts died before the age of fifteen. The most frequent cause of death seems to have been infection, but sometimes death came by accident. In 1770, a Gambian named London and his companion, Dinah, had a daughter, Pretty. Dinah, nicknamed Dye, was the daughter of the field hands Angola Amy and Windsor, who by then had many years behind them. On February 23, 1771, in her third month of life, Pretty burned to death. It was winter, and few if any of the slave houses had chimneys, the only source of warmth being an open fire kept in the middle of the room. Pretty probably was placed too near the fire on a cold day. The family may well have thought they were vexed, because some years later Amy, Pretty's sister, was killed by lightning.

Another cause of death was violence. Probably one of the most talked-about events on the slave streets of this period was a murder that took place in 1766 at a plantation twenty miles north of Comingtee, called Wambaw. Henry Laurens and one of his Ball in-laws shared title to the forty-three-hundred-acre tract, known by the Native name for a creek that ran through the property.

It began with a ménage that involved two sisters and one man. A slave named Chloe, living at Wambaw, took up with a field hand called Matthias, who lived at John Coming Ball's Hyde Park. In time, Chloe's sister Isabel also began sleeping with Matthias, evidently without Chloe's knowledge. On a Saturday in April, Isabel went up from Hyde Park to Wambaw, likely traveling long hours at night by foot. When Isabel finally arrived, she gave Chloe some sort of drink, perhaps as a gift. The potion contained a poison, and Chloe died the next day.

Henry Laurens described what happened in a letter to one of the Balls. "Wambaw, 2d May," he began. "Dear Sir, Upon my coming to this place I was inform'd of the sudden death of Chloe. . . . It seems Isabel had droped some threatenings towards Chloe which [the overseer] will further relate to you."

No record of a trial survives. In one likely outcome, John Coming Ball, owner of the murderess, would have been forced to pay his in-law for damage to property, the loss of a field hand. The criminal herself would have faced worse—for the murder, of course, but more harshly for how she carried it out. Whites feared the knowledge of poison among blacks, because it could easily be turned on masters by their cooks. Eventually, the South Carolina legislature passed a law that prohibited black people from teaching the deadly art. "[I]n case any slave," the law dictated, "shall teach or instruct another slave in the knowledge of any poisonous root, plant, herb, or other poison whatsoever, he or she shall suffer death as a felon." Isabel may well have faced execution.

Shortly after he came into his inheritance, Second Elias placed the following advertisement in the *South Carolina Gazette*:

> Run away from my plantation . . . a middle sized negro man, named Carolina, has the mark of a large wound on one of his arms . . . and is well known in and about Charles Town, where he was for some years a fisherman. Whoever takes up and delivers him to Austin and Laurens in Charles Town, or to me at my plantation . . . shall have Five Pounds reward . . . Elias Ball.

Carolina and his companion, a woman named Patra, had an eleven-year-old son, Truman. To judge from the number of advertisements the Balls placed in newspapers, Carolina was only one of many slaves who tried to escape, often walking off in the night. To flee the plantation was a treacherous business, and had been since the start of the colony, long before 1690, when treatments for runaways were encoded in South Carolina law. A chronicle of sorts of the people who tried to escape captivity, and what happened to them, can be put together merely by reading contemporary newspapers.

Carolina, the fisherman who took off, was a veteran in defiance. In 1749 he had been jailed and questioned for conspiring with other slaves on the Cooper River to rise up against the rice planters, and he was lucky to get away with his life. When he ran from Second Elias, however, Carolina did not get far; a year after his escape, plantation records show him back on the farm.

Carolina may have gotten "the mark of a large wound on one of his arms" while plying his fishing trade, but more likely it came from a beating laid on by Second Elias or one of his overseers. Lashings with the cat-o'-nine-tails, beatings with sticks, and burnings of flesh all left tracks that Second Elias and his peers advertised as "distinguishing marks." Carolina was not the only slave of Second Elias who had been beaten enough to leave scars. In October 1766, Mr. Ball placed this ad: "Run Away from my plantation . . . Three New Negro Fellows named Primus, Caesar, and Boson [Boatswain]. . . . Primus is a pretty tall fellow, and has a large scar on one of his shoulders."

The *Gazette* gave the Balls a place to cast the net after the escape of their workers. Advertisements for runaways usually appeared with a picture, an image of a black man running, carrying a spear. More people tried to escape in South Carolina than anywhere else in colonial America, twice as many as fled in the two other major slave provinces, Virginia and Maryland. It may have been that bondage in South Carolina was simply more violent than that farther north. Based on the number of ads, more women tried to flee the rice plantations than the more northern tobacco farms—one of four of the total. But finally, neither sex nor geography could predict who would make off; evidently the childhood memories of those who escaped had more to do with their behavior. More than six out of ten runaways from the Balls and their peers had been born in Africa.

One February, Second Elias ran the following announcement in the local paper:

Run away . . . two young Negro fellows, one this country born, named Tom, a middling tall fellow, has one of his toes cut off; the other is a fellow of the Guiney [Guinea] country, something shorter than Tom, of a black complexion, named Jemmy . . . a reward of ten pounds for Tom, and five pounds for Jemmy, on delivery of them.

Like Carolina, Tom with the missing toe was evidently from a rebellious family. Young Tom's mother was a field hand named Julatta, and his father was Tom White, the Angolan arrested in the alleged uprising scheme of 1748. By custom, Tom Jr. would have gone in the rice fields when he turned twelve, so that when he escaped, at age twenty-six, he had likely been working thirteen years. After he took off, young Tom disappears from plantation records. He may have either died or, unlike the majority who fled, gotten away for good.

Runaways often fled, were brought back and punished, then left again. In Second Elias's day, some slave owners may have continued to advocate castration—the penalty for repeated escape that dated from the pioneer days—though few masters actually admitted to the practice by writing it down. In a more common punishment, ears and toes were severed (though not hands, required for work). Young Tom's missing toe, mentioned in the paper, may have indicated a previous escape attempt.

The thought that Second Elias Ball practiced amputation on his workers is supported by other evidence from the days of his father. One year, when Red Cap was still alive, the *South Carolina Gazette* ran an ad stating that a slave named Booba had just been captured and waited in jail in Charleston. He "says he belongs to Mr. Ball," the paper said, meaning Red Cap. After listing the man's clothes, the *Gazette* ended its description this way: "Two Toes upon each Foot seem as if they were cut off."

The slave child named Edward—presumably the son of Red Cap and his "Molattoe Wench" Dolly—presented a problem. To start, he was of the wrong blood, but he also had the misfortune of being born at the wrong time, after the Stono Uprising of 1739. Prior to the Stono rebellion, many brown and yellow children gained freedom in quiet acts of liberation, or manumission, carried out by their owners. The slave uprising changed things. The so-called Negro Act of 1740 took away from plantation owners the right to grant freedom to slaves. Afterward, a planter who wished to free one of his children would have to petition the colonial legislature in a cumbersome process that risked exposing his sexual life to public ridicule.

Edward was born too late and therefore couldn't easily be freed. When the child turned one, Red Cap deeded the infant to another of his many progeny, his one-year-old grandson Richard Shubrick. The child of Elizabeth Ball and Captain Richard Shubrick, little Richard lived with his parents at Quenby plantation, a few miles up the river from Comingtee. The idea seemed to be that Edward and Richard would grow up together. An arrangement like this was common, the colored child playing the part of the white child's personal servant and companion. (Edward would also be out of the way.)

Baby Edward did not immediately leave his mother's side, however, and a wait of sorts commenced, until eventually death intervened to spoil the plan. In 1746, when Edward was five, Elizabeth Shubrick died. Soon her widowed husband moved to England, taking Richard Jr. with him. Edward never had the chance to join his new owner, and he and his mother Dolly stayed at Comingtee. When the Shubricks moved to England, Edward entered a legal limbo. He became the property of an absent slave owner and was thus neither free nor slave. In February 1748, a few months after the child turned seven, Elias put in place another plan. Edward, his mother, and his siblings (his half brother, Cupid, and his sister, Catherine) went by themselves to live at St. James, the tract owned by Second Elias about a mile from Kensington.

Dolly was thirty-six, Red Cap seventy-two. Maybe Red Cap had grown tired of her, or perhaps he was tired of the mutterings of his Charleston neighbors about a house full of mulattoes. A likely explanation for the change is that none of the Balls actually lived at St. James; Elias's white children would no longer have to see their aging father's dark companion or their own dark kin.

Sometime after Red Cap's death, Edward gained his freedom. Although no papers survive that would show the date or the method of his emancipation, later in life Edward would be described as free in court papers. I suspect that the second generation of Balls, owning up to their father's child, simply began to treat Edward as an ex-slave, if not as a brother. Relationships like this were rare, but kept up over time they gained the force of law.

Edward acquired the nickname Ned, or sometimes Neddy. At age twenty-three, he came back to the Ball neighborhood to live, and seems to have moved onto Kensington plantation, owned by Second Elias. In the cold of November one winter, one record book notes that Neddy borrowed a blanket from the main house. He must have been penniless to have asked for bed covering normally earmarked for field hands, but he also must have had special privilege to get it from the master's dwelling house, where other nonwhites could not easily enter.

At Kensington, Edward pulled himself up from poverty, beginning as a leatherworker. Throughout his twenties and thirties, Edward tanned hides and sold what he made from animal skins. His clients included the Balls and their neighbors, the Harleston family, while his main income came from manufacturing "Negro shoes," the cheap footwear distributed each year on the plantation. With a large population on most places, a shoemaker with connections could keep busy, and records show that Edward sold hundreds of pairs to planters on the Cooper River. It was not the best of jobs, because the mark of a shoemaker was his smell. Leatherworkers tore skin from the backs of carrion to get raw material, and in one process that Edward may have used, cured hides in vats of urine. The smells could not be washed off. People downwind knew he was coming each time Edward emerged from his shop.

As a "free person of color," Edward was legally entitled to take a surname. Probably from his work, Edward became Edward Tanner.

For a second income, Edward Tanner worked for the Balls as a hostler, or horse-minder. Accounts show that he kept a stable and provided stud services for his presumptive kin. Second Elias went often to Edward Tanner to buy riding and carriage horses or to hire a stud to impregnate one of his mares.

As a businessman with a leather shop and stable, Edward Tanner would seem to have succeeded in his world. He was one of a tiny number of his special class, free people of color. In 1760, South Carolina counted a population of ninety thousand—some fifty-five thousand blacks and thirty-five thousand whites. In 1768, about the time Tanner got under way as a shoemaker, tax records show that there were only 159 free nonwhites in all the province. Tanner did well, but he was very much alone, and the place of mulattoes could be tenuous. They often lived in isolation from both whites and from the black majority, accepted by neither.

Edward Tanner's life included more liberty than that of other colored people, but he was no stranger to sadness. His sister Catherine (or Kate), about whom few details survive except her name, also gained freedom from the Balls, after which she moved north of Charleston, along the coast, to St. George's Parish. Kate may have given support to the isolated Tanner, but in 1768, when she was about twenty, Kate died. That September, the Court of Ordinary summoned her brother to the city of Charleston to administer her estate.

In her last appearances in the plantation records, Edward Tanner's mother, Dolly, is listed as living at St. James with her son Cupid and

a man called John. John may have been Dolly's partner after Red Cap
sent her away. Once her free son had gotten on his feet in business,
Dolly evidently fell sick, and Second Elias noted simply that "Old Dolly
died ye 5 Dec 1774, age 62." She was still a slave, still clothed and
housed by the Balls. Manumission might come to the children of slave
owners, but it was still rare for a mistress.

According to a conservative estimate, during the centuries of the slave
trade, nearly 9.5 million people were carried from Africa to European
colonies in the Western Hemisphere. Of these, a little under 450,000
went to the territory that would later become the United States. The
majority set foot in North America in the 1700s, and a large portion of
them entered through Charleston: between 1701 and 1775, forty-six
percent of the black people entering the British mainland colonies came
by way of South Carolina. Another large influx arrived in Charleston in
the first decade of the 1800s, in a great rush before the African slave
trade was outlawed in 1808.

The numbers of the South Carolina traffic are important in the legacy
of the United States. Perhaps four out of ten black people in the United
States have African ancestors who first arrived on this continent at the
Charleston coast. That figure, forty percent, recalls another point of entry
for Americans: Ellis Island in the harbor at New York. The same number of all Americans, four out of ten, descend from people who arrived
at Ellis Island during the great wave of European immigration, between
1890 and 1925.

During a single generation, from 1735 to 1775, 1,108 slave ships
arrived with their cargoes in Charleston harbor. During this time, the
peak of slave shipping, two Ball in-laws became the largest slave
dealers in North America. In the ten years between 1751 and 1761,
George Austin and Henry Laurens brought sixty-one slave galleys to
the Charleston wharfs—the largest number of any slave importer in the
city, and the heaviest volume in the territory of the future United States.

Austin and Laurens did not write down the African names of people
aboard their ships; they were simply "Negroes" until sold. Nevertheless,
it is possible to estimate the numbers of people imported. In the first
decade after his marriage to Eleanor Ball, Henry Laurens paid import
taxes on behalf of his firm amounting to £68,010. Based on an average

duty of £10 per adult slave, this amounted to sixty-eight hundred adults (an adult in the tax law being anyone above age ten). Children, who were untaxed, came to another thousand at the minimum. Therefore, in a single decade, Austin & Laurens sold a total of some seventy-eight hundred people.

Slave traders worked on commission, ten percent of the sale price. In the decade of the 1750s, the cost of a black child in Charleston hovered around £100. A strong young man would bring up to £300, a woman slightly less than that. The average sale price for men, women, and children, estimated on the low side, stood near £200 per person. On a volume of seventy-eight hundred people, Austin and Laurens would have had revenues of £156,000, enough to make them and their wives, in only ten years, four of the richest people in America. It is impossible to state an equivalent sum in dollars, because the Balls lived in an agrarian world in which the relative cost of food, clothing, and shelter stood in entirely different proportion to that within industrial society. But in the 1770s, when plantation land was selling at about £1 per acre, a two-thousand-acre tract was thought to be sufficient to support ten whites and a hundred black workers. In other words, the ten-year income of Austin & Laurens would have been enough to purchase seventy-eight plantations, on which 8,580 people might live indefinitely.

By the mid-1750s, George Austin had largely withdrawn from Charleston to his plantation southwest of town, Ashepoo, and Henry Laurens ran the business. Laurens wrote the Balls, keeping them up-to-date on how well he was making out. In a letter to his brother-in-law John Coming Ball, Laurens boasted, "Our people [customers] bought slaves with great spirit all the last summer & even 'till the month of October they gave so high as £330 for some very prime Gambia men." Elsewhere he reported, "We have two . . . Vessells now in port, [but unfortunately] between them they have not more than 240 Slaves, which are but a trifle to the number wanted."

To keep in touch with customers, Laurens ran ads for his merchandise in the *South Carolina Gazette*. Headlines read "Just Imported," or "Negroes," while the ad named the African birthplace of the new Americans. The announcements were usually accompanied by a picture of a black figure wearing a skirt made of palm fronds, sporting a grass headdress.

Though they dominated the market, George Austin and Henry Lau-

rens weren't the only Ball kin in the business. In 1764, another of Red
Cap's daughters, Elizabeth Ball, married Henry Smith, scion of a family
that also sold people. Smith's brother was a partner of Miles Brewton,
in the firm Brewton & Smith, which occasionally rivaled Austin & Laurens in number of Africans imported. In the year following Elizabeth
Ball's marriage into the Smith family, Brewton & Smith docked fourteen
slave galleys. At a low estimate of 200 per ship, that meant nearly 250
people per month.

So large were the numbers, and so small the feeling of the slave
dealers, that a term came into use: "refuse Negro." A refuse Negro was
a person who either was unhealthy, did not listen to commands, or was
simply bad tempered. Planters wanted to avoid buying refuse, by which
they meant "human trash." Laurens explained to a customer: "Several
small parcels of Negroes have been imported here from the West India
Islands and the best of them have sold pretty well but there is generally
a mixture of refuse Negroes among such."

With slave traders in the family, it was an easy matter for Second
Elias and his brother to get people. Records show that after the marriage
of Eleanor Ball to Henry Laurens, Austin & Laurens became a main
supplier of slaves for the family, since, like any clan, the Balls bought
from their own. In June 1756, Second Elias opened the *South Carolina
Gazette* and read the following ad:

> Just imported in the *Hare*, Capt. Caleb Godfrey, directly from
> Sierra Leon, a Cargo of Likely and Healthy Slaves, To be sold
> upon easy Terms, on Tuesday the 29th Instant [day of] June, by
> Austin & Laurens.

Sierra Leone lies on the west coast of Africa about five hundred
miles south of the mouth of the Gambia River. It was given its name
by Portuguese explorers in the sixteenth century, but by Laurens's day,
the British had taken the trade away from the Portuguese. At the trading
depot, a short river emptied into the Atlantic where a peninsula thrust
into the ocean. Along the coast and going a hundred miles inland lived
the Limba, Kono, Mende, Susu, Temne, and Vai tribes, among others.

Henry Laurens's ships traded from a prison near the mouth of the
Sierra Leone River, on an oval rock called Bunce Island. About a third
of a mile long, Bunce Island stands in the current of the river several

miles upstream from the Atlantic. It was leased from local chieftains by a business associate of Laurens's in London, Richard Oswald. On the northwest end of the island stood a fortified manor, ringed with cannons, where the English slave handlers lived, and where they received the captains of the galleys. Behind the manor was a walled yard where captives were held, chained together in circles, until their numbers grew large enough to fill the belly of a ship.

In early 1756, after spending from a few days to several weeks at Bunce Island, one group of 170 prisoners was herded into the hold of the *Hare*, which weighed anchor for Charleston.

Henry Laurens was a formal man with a sharp temper and a judgmental eye with his merchandise. When the *Hare* was still at sea, he wrote several letters to friends complaining that he was already swamped with business, and saying that he would prefer that the ship go to another port. "The place is quite clog'd with slaves that God knows what we shall do with them," he told one man. When the *Hare* reached Charleston, only about 110 people on it were still alive. "[R]eally they are a wretched cargo," Laurens wrote a friend. "They are a most scabby flock, all of them full of the Crocheraws"—meaning the yaws, a contagious skin disease. Nevertheless, Laurens placed his advertisement for this group of "Healthy Slaves."

Second Elias took himself down to the docks and his brother-in-law's office. The *Hare* evidently brought a good supply of children, and Second Elias picked out six of them. Although most plantation owners bought on credit, Laurens noted in his account book that Mr. Ball paid in cash. Second Elias made a note about the deal in his own records: "I bought 4 boys and 2 girls—their ages near as I can judge Sancho = 9 years old, Peter = 7, Brutus = 7, Harry = 6, Belinda = 10, Priscilla = 10, for £600."

In the height of a mean summer, the children were taken to Comingtee plantation. Their parents had been left either on the dock in Charleston or in their villages back home.

After the sale, Laurens reported that some buyers had been angry, and had believed the *Hare* was full of refuse Negroes. "Besides many . . . meager ones there was several that were quite grey with Age," he said. Still, to keep up good business relations, Laurens wrote his supplier in London, fifty-one-year-old Richard Oswald, who actually controlled the ship, thanking him for sending the business to Austin &

Laurens, and apologizing that the firm did not get more money for the Bunce Island cargo.

Second Elias, the gentle and portly father, seemed to prefer buying children. A few years after the purchase of these young ones, he made this note: "[I] Bought 13 Gambias Young Negroes . . . 11 boys and 2 girls for £200 a piece which is £2600 & stake them to be about 12 years of age or there abouts."

Austin & Laurens was dissolved in 1762, after which Henry Laurens spent less time on the docks and more time with his wife, Eleanor Ball. Taking on a new partner named George Appleby, Laurens would continue to sell people, although fewer than before. In a few years, following the death of his wife, Ann Ball, George Austin would move back to England, taking his fortune with him and ending the era of the great Ball slave business.

The six children from Sierra Leone would have six different fates, each typical in its way. Belinda appears nowhere in the records after her purchase; she either died or was immediately resold. Harry grew up to be a field hand and seems to have lived alone until death. Brutus worked until at least 1784, when he disappears from the records—dead or sold around age thirty-five. Peter grew up to be the man Second Elias called Mandingo Peter. Peter found a partner named Monemia and had children by her. By 1777, Mandingo Peter had moved, evidently with his family, from Comingtee to Kensington, where he disappears from slave lists in 1816, apparently dead around sixty-seven. Sancho worked as a field hand on Comingtee, where he found a partner in a woman named Affie, with whom he had at least three children—Sancho, Saby, and Belinda; the family was moved to Kensington sometime before the American Revolution. In 1780, during the Revolutionary War, Sancho was one of at least fifty-one people who ran away from Kensington, seeking freedom with the British Army. He was later returned to the plantation. In February 1819, at seventy-two, Sancho was separated from his wife and children, who were sold off Kensington in an auction, bought by a man named T. Scriven. Sancho presumably was too old to interest Scriven, and may well have watched as his family was taken from him. He finally died Christmas Day 1833, at eighty-six.

Priscilla must have been a strong girl, because she lifted herself up and carried on. Within ten years, Priscilla had found a partner, Jeffrey, and made a family. By 1770, when she was twenty-four, she had three children; later she had many grandchildren.

Throughout the 167 years the Ball family owned slaves, and among the approximately four thousand people born or bought into slavery to the Balls, Priscilla and her five companions from Sierra Leone are among the few people about whom it can be determined, based on written evidence, precisely where they came from in Africa.

Priscilla's descendants would continue to live on Ball plantations until Emancipation in early 1865. That year, Priscilla's great-great-grandson, Henry, would be freed from William Ball's Limerick plantation. One day, I would meet some of Priscilla's descendants.

10

>-‹•›-‹•›-○-‹•›-‹•›-<

"YOURS, OBEDIENTLY"

There was a death in the family, and in the mail came a letter of condolence:

Feb. 20, 1926
Mr. Isaac Ball
King Street
Charleston, S.C.

Dear Mas' Isaac,
Mrs. Richardson up here told me that your wife has pass away. I'm sorry, tho she don't know me. I consider all Balls are connected with my old Master. I have them to respect. There are no white people that I can regard more than I do the Balls. My Father told me that Mrs. Julia [Ball] named me, and that I was christind by Bishop Howe in Mistress arms. Well Mas Isaac I am up here, in Sumter Co., hoping to make sometime up here, but there are no people like those on the Coast, our white people. Our old Masters and their children. My father's people were never free and they were never slaves, so far as the word slave may mean. I can remembered that my old Masters gave my

Grandmother her Freedom and a servant to wait on her. . . .
Hope you are well I am teaching and preaching up here. . . .
                              Yours, P. Henry Martin. Box 38, Pinewood, S.C.

Isaac Ball—my father's grandfather, and the Ball Dad called Isaac the Confederate—was eighty-one when he received this note of sympathy from a former slave. Born in the 1840s on Limerick plantation, Isaac grew up surrounded by hundreds of black people. After fighting in the Civil War, he came home and married a young woman from a neighboring plantation, Mary Louisa Moultrie, with whom he had twelve children. In February 1926, after fifty-six years of marriage, Mary Louisa died. One of Isaac's daughters had to read the letter to her father, who was blind from glaucoma.

Dear Mas' Isaac . . . My father's people were never free and they were never slaves, so far as the word slave may mean.

The words may have touched something in the old man and eased his grief. Isaac saved the letter, which became part of the family archive. Generations later, when I encountered P. Henry Martin's letter, none of the Balls knew any longer who he was, and no one could say where his kin might be living. With the help of a friend, I got on the phone to families named Martin in South Carolina and soon found the grandson of P. Henry Martin.

Thomas Martin was a retired teacher and assistant principal. The first time we spoke, Mr. Martin told me he had been trying to find out more about his grandfather. P. Henry Martin had died in November 1933, when Thomas was only a few months old. But before his death, the elder Martin had written out a family tree, beginning with his own generation. Thomas Martin had been looking at the document, he said, and wondering about the past.

Thomas Martin lived in a prosperous black neighborhood in Charleston, on a street lined with homes from the early 1900s. Many had porches, several had columns, and a few had a picket fence around the property line. Mr. Martin lived in the handsomest building on the block, a large white two-story house, with four tall columns holding up a distinctive pediment.

The grandson of P. Henry Martin was in his sixties, and carried himself with reserve. His face was long and serious, showing few laugh lines. He had a high brow, pronounced jowls, gray hair at the temples, and eyes that seemed melancholy. Mr. Martin wore a sweater pulled over a long-sleeved shirt, and dark trousers.

I entered the big house through a living room with a fireplace. Various diplomas rested on the mantelpiece, advertising the degrees in higher education achieved by members of the family. In the dining room was a large table with king-sized chairs, and a fish tank with bright tropical fish. A vinyl easy chair squeaked as I lowered myself into it.

Thomas Martin did not know that his ancestors came from a Ball plantation. He was soft-spoken, and I responded in kind, with careful words about the subject. I handed him the letter written by his grandfather, and he read it through to the end. Mr. Martin put down the letter, and repeated the words that caught my attention.

" 'My father's people were never free and they were never slaves,' " he said. "That's a very poignant sentence."

Mr. Martin had a phlegmatic delivery that reminded me of a personality trait among some in my own family. He seemed taciturn and, as he read his grandfather's words about slavery, sounded almost neutral. Perhaps he wanted to be polite, because we didn't know each other, but the words surprised both of us.

"My grandfather seems to have been a person who possessed a lot of gratitude," said Mr. Martin, coming around to the idea. "Maybe they, his family, weren't treated as the average slave."

Mr. Martin said that his grandfather had been a minister and schoolteacher. He lived for a time in Charleston, then in a country town a day or more by horse from the city. For income, he worked as a carpenter and bricklayer. As an ex-slave, he had an incomplete education; nevertheless, it was far better than that of the majority of former field hands. P. Henry Martin devoted himself to teaching and providing for the destitute children who walked off the plantations after the Civil War. Though Mr. Martin knew all this, he said he knew little about his grandfather's early life.

"You know, my father said that *his* father used to say, 'If you are ever in trouble, go see one of the Balls in their Broad Street office.' " The distant memory came back on Mr. Martin's long face. "My father never said why—or that there was a connection to the Ball plantations."

There was a rising in his voice that said we had struck something, like a boat against a submerged tree, and we nodded at each other. The Martin family had this trace of lore about the slave days, half hidden, half in the open.

In a moment, Mr. Martin disappeared and came back with an old photograph. It showed a black family consisting of nine people, handsomely dressed, posed in a photography studio. The family sat on wicker furniture against a backdrop that resembled a Victorian parlor. The portrait had been taken around 1900, when an urbane English style crept into the lives of upwardly mobile Americans. The boys wore knickers and jackets with little ascots at the neck, and one girl had a dark dress with long sleeves and ruffles at the shoulder.

"This is a picture of the entire family up to a certain time," said Mr. Martin. "My grandfather, my grandmother, Anna Cruz, their children."

The two parents, P. Henry Martin and his wife, Anna Cruz, appeared to be in their forties. Anna Cruz had a broad face and straight hair gathered in a bun. Mr. Martin said that he had heard she had Native ancestry. There was a circle around her head, and numbers written on each person in the photograph. Long ago, someone had made the markings, but Mr. Martin didn't know who.

"My grandfather wrote a tablet with information about each of his children," said Mr. Martin, bringing out a little booklet. The booklet ran to fourteen pages and contained the names and birthdays of the minister's children, their first words, and other firsts. "Maybe the numbers on the photograph were his private code."

Mr. Martin pointed at a boy in the picture, about thirteen years of age, wearing breeches and a coat with wide lapels. "My father," he said.

From the photograph, it was obvious that P. Henry Martin had done well after the end of slavery. He wore wide-rimmed eyeglasses, a starched shirt, and a satisfied expression. His seven children were carefully attired. He had a trim mustache, and laid his eyes firmly on the camera. Mr. Martin put back the picture and eased into his chair.

"I think if my grandfather were here now, he probably would be murdered," he said suddenly.

"Why?" I asked.

"If he were to tell the average black youngster about his association with the Ball family, they would resent it so much. They would be so angry, because of his kind feelings towards the white people, that they would do something to him."

I uncovered more about the life of P. Henry Martin. He was born simply Henry on October 6, 1855, at Limerick plantation. Henry's father does not appear in the plantation records, but according to slave lists his mother's name was Dinah. Near the end of his life, P. Henry Martin would write several letters to the Balls, his former owners, and in one he would remind them that his grandfather was a man named Peter Robards. Although his letter does not say so, I suspect Robards was white. Martin would point out in his correspondence that the Ball family "gave my Grandmother her Freedom and a servant to wait on her." Freedom for Henry's grandmother may have been a late reward for years of hard work—or it may have been that she was the mistress of Mr. Robards, a person known to the master's family. In any case, Dinah's infant was baptized in the arms of Julia Cart Ball. Julia, Isaac Ball's mother, was thirty-one at the time. Inside the master's house, she held the child as an Episcopal clergyman poured water on his brow.

The closeness of the baby Henry to the Ball family probably meant that his parents worked in the plantation mansion as house servants. If Henry's grandfather was white, his parents may well have been light-skinned, and many house slaves came from families with both white and black forebears. The child's intimacy with the master's family seems to have become a theme of his life.

When Henry was nine, the old world came to an end. On Sunday, February 26, 1865, a band of soldiers in blue uniforms arrived on the lawn at Limerick. The Federal troops told the slaves they were free— a fact they knew the moment they saw the cavalry, whose arrival they had been expecting. Some of the freedpeople, with some soldiers, emptied the food storerooms, then searched the mansion. Henry later remembered that while the raid was going on, he found himself walking around, going from building to building. At one point, he happened on the cooper's shop, where he saw several old men praying. When he asked the elderly slaves why, Henry was told that they were pleading with the Lord not to let the Yankees burn the plantation buildings, as they had been known to do.

After the war Henry took part of his grandfather's name, Peter, and added the surname Martin. Sometimes, for good measure, he would sign with his grandfather's surname, as well: Peter Henry Robards Martin. P. Henry Martin seems to have spent his teens getting a rudimentary education. In 1866, the occupying Yankees opened the first school for blacks in the area, the Nazareth Church School, in the town of Pinopolis, a few miles from Limerick. The Bureau of Refugees, Freedpeople, and Abandoned Lands—the Freedmen's Bureau—was disdained by local whites for doing this. According to a report in the agency's files, at the National Archives in Washington, D.C., most landlords in the Cooper River area did not favor the education of black people, though a number of middle-class whites, evidently in Charleston, did. The one-room school closed in March 1868, and another school opened in the neighboring town of Moncks Corner, where there was apparently less hostility. A white woman named Mary von Hagen did the teaching. It is likely that P. Henry Martin, then thirteen, got his first taste of written language at one or both of these schoolhouses. He later lived in Pinopolis, location of the first school, where he taught black children, reliving the scene of his own early classroom awakening.

Young P. Henry Martin developed a close relationship with Isaac Ball, one of four brothers who lived at Limerick. When Martin was twenty, Isaac was in his early thirties, and running another plantation as a sharecrop landlord. Martin may have worked for Isaac doing carpentry. Their friendship seems to have been real, because later Martin would credit Isaac, saying, "he set me right in the church."

About 1880, when he was twenty-five, Martin married Anna Cruz and the two moved to Charleston. In the city, Martin became involved with the founding of a black church, on Smith Street. With a religious conversion helped along by his moderate book-learning, he gave sermons at the new church as a deacon, while continuing to earn an income from carpentry and construction.

Isaac Ball traveled a similar route to Martin, back and forth between Charleston and the countryside. Isaac's sharecrop farm was an old plantation called The Bluff, which stood on the west branch of the Cooper River across the stream from Comingtee, and had been inherited by his wife; he also did business in the city. It is likely that Isaac gave Martin referrals for work and helped him in other ways. In letters that Martin later wrote to the Balls, the ex-slave asked his former owners for donations of clothing and books to be used at black-run schools. The requests were perfunctory, as though he was used to making them, and the Balls evidently complied.

P. Henry Martin and Anna Cruz had ten children, three of whom died young. Their second child, Peter Henry Jr., born in 1886, grew up to become a roofer. Peter Jr.'s son, Thomas Martin, would become an educator and assistant principal of a public high school in Charleston. The roofer and the educator each broke off a piece of the ex-slave's skills.

After the children were raised, Henry Sr. moved inland to the little town of Pinewood. At some point, he built a church and, when it was finished, started a school inside for the children of the parishioners. Martin lived in other country towns and in each place seems to have devoted himself to the education of black children.

When he grew old, Henry Martin renewed his acquaintance with the Balls, who had enslaved him and also helped him. In the 1920s, when Martin was in town, he visited Isaac, blind and in his late seventies. Martin was given the gentle reception extended to family retainers. It's not clear how often Martin and Isaac saw each other when they were old men, but it was at least several times. After one such visit, in 1932, Martin wrote to thank his hosts:

> I arrived home safe, we are all well. It was a deal of pleasure for me to find you all. When I got home and spoke of seeing my old and young mistresses, the young negroes laughed, but I told them as long as there are Balls that I will have mistresses and masters. I remembered when the Yankees came to Limerick and wants to burned master dwelling house. . . . And they asked the people what they want out of the house. They said master [William James Ball, Isaac's father] was good and kind to them and they would take nothing out of master's house. When Christmas came that year master called up all the people and told them because they was so good not to take anything from him as other people had done down the river, master give them an ox name Mulberry for their Christmas. . . . I can remember many things of old Limerick [like] some of master's animals names. [He had] two bird dogs, Bounce & Bill. Mas Frederick Gibbs [William Ball's brother-in-law] had a dog at

*Windsor named Riot. Master told me once that he wants me to
remember that there are no better people than my father's
people . . .*

> *I am your obed't
> Henry*

On March 26, 1933, Isaac died, and the news traveled the same day
to Martin. By this time, he had moved back to Pinopolis. The day after
his former master's death, he wrote a letter of condolence addressed to
one of Isaac's children, Julia Ficken:

*Pinopolis, S.C.
March 27, 1933*

*Mrs. Henry H. Ficken
35 Meeting St.
Charleston, S.C.*

*My dear madam,
The sadness of the passing away of Mas Isaac came as a blow
to me. He's the last of my oldest masters. Mas Isaac has done a
deal for me. Bishop Thomas said in his council Mas Isaac had
spoken very well of me. [He] set me right in the church. I was
to have seen him last year but was unable. He promised me
some books and other things but he has gone to his long home.
Writing you I can't keep my eyes dry. Mas Isaac and Mas Elias
treated me as one who belongs to the family. His mother named
me. The last word my father told me was on his death bed, he
said when I need advice always go to a Ball. We will bow from
above.*

> *Your obedient Henry*

After the burial, Julia Ficken went up to Pinopolis with some friends
to visit Martin and thank him for his letter. Martin wasn't home, so Julia
left him a note. Martin was touched, and replied:

> *My dear mistress . . .*
> *My father's people was loved by the Balls. . . . I was picked*
> *and cared for by Mas Willie, Mas Isaac, Mas John, and Mas*
> *Elias [four Ball brothers at Limerick]. Master Isaac was the*
> *most fine in the bunch. If he was alive and doing business I*
> *would be under him now. I told the world, as long as there are*
> *Balls I will have mistresses and masters.*
>
> *P. H. Martin*

P. Henry Martin died later that year, in November, eight months after the death of his former master.

Not all ex-slaves experienced the same world after freedom. Where many ex–field hands struggled, former house slaves sometimes found themselves in a stronger economic position. Their old masters helped them to get loans and housing, they got better educations, they got their photographs taken, and some simply earned more money. As a member of a family who had lived among the Balls, P. Henry Martin seems to have done better than many freedpeople. But his improved station in life seems to have been bought with subservience. He addressed his white helpers as "Master" and signed his letters "obediently."

Victor Martin, the third child of P. Henry Martin and Anna Cruz, was born in 1889. One of Victor Martin's daughters, Mrs. Carutha Williams, was still living. I visited her to talk about what happened to the Martin family in later years.

Carutha Williams was in her seventies, gentle and soft-spoken, with a reserve that resembled that of her cousin, Thomas Martin. Like Thomas Martin, Mrs. Williams had a large house, having landed comfortably in widowhood. Mrs. Williams had a sweet face, a genuine smile, and a careful handshake. Nearly blind, she stretched out her hand waiting for my grasp. She moved slowly around her living room, which she knew from before her sight failed, guided me to the dining-room table, and sat down. With soft, polite cadences, Mrs. Williams finished the story of P. Henry Martin, as far as she knew it.

"His oldest child, Henrietta, died as a young woman, of tuberculosis," she began.

Although she couldn't see it, Mrs. Williams held in her hand the photograph of the Martin family in their late-Victorian costumes. She had had it reproduced and distributed throughout the family. Mrs. Williams had memorized the positions of the children in the picture, and counted them off as she spoke.

"There was another daughter, Rosa, born about 1898." Rosa married a man named Johnson and had children in Maryland and New York, said Mrs. Williams. "There were twins, a girl named Mattie and her brother, Morris." Mattie married and moved away in the 1920s, then fell out of contact with the Martins. "Morris disappeared from the family entirely," said Mrs. Williams. "He joined the service at the time of World War I, and sent postcards back from time to time. Every year someone would get one, generally from the New Jersey, New York area." Then the cards stopped coming.

Mrs. Williams spoke neutrally, and it seemed her evenness disguised a melancholy mood. In her stories, I saw the large, prosperous Martin family drift away from each other. The plantation legacy was never a simple story of recovery and perseverance.

Victor Martin, the third child and Mrs. Williams's father, grew up and moved with his wife to Bryn Mawr, Pennsylvania, to take a job at the women's college of the same name as the town.

"We moved to Pennsylvania," Mrs. Williams remembered of her childhood. "Each building of the college had its own dining room and pantry, with maids, butlers, and bellhops. My father was a pantry man, where he made the salads. My mother, in another dormitory, was a waitress. The students were girls from rich families from around the country. My mother always talked about the movie actress Katharine Hepburn, because she was a student when my mother worked there. She knew Katharine Hepburn, and served her in her dormitory. The girls at Bryn Mawr were mostly generous. They were very free, and happy people." Mrs. Williams paused, then said flatly, "As long as you took care of them."

Anna Cruz died in the early 1900s. Her widower was remarried, to a woman named Ida Royal.

"My grandfather had an eleventh child by his second marriage," said Mrs. Williams. "A man we called B.B., for Barnabas Blyden. He had a family, too."

After Mrs. Williams went through all the children, she came back in her stories to Charleston. P. Henry Martin Jr. married Jennie Singleton, a woman in good circumstances. With the marriage came a good piece of property in Charleston. This consisted of a lot and buildings at 18 Norman Street—a two-story house in the front, and a cottage in back—property that became the Martin homestead in the city. The house seemed to represent the continuing good fortune of the Martin clan. It was the first house built on its block after the lane was cleared and given its name. It was the first house in the neighborhood that had running water, and the first with a telephone. (The number in the 1920s consisted of a mere four digits, 8383.) The house had the first complete bathroom in the neighborhood, with a tub, toilet, and basin, at a time when almost all black families had outhouses.

Mrs. Williams, born Carutha Martin, lived briefly at the family homestead. When she was a teenager, Carutha Martin carried forward the success of the family, becoming one of a small number of black women who were able to attend college.

"I went to South Carolina State College," she said, naming the historically black school. "I was lucky. I graduated in May 1944. My first job was in Alabama, as a secretary on the campus of Tuskegee Institute."

After two years in Alabama, Carutha Martin came back to Charleston, was married, and settled in the city. She smiled sweetly as she talked about her husband, Clarence Williams, who died in 1981. In her early married life, Mrs. Williams worked in a black high school in the city, the Avery Normal Institute. It was the second of her jobs with a black-run school.

"Was there a change in racial climate that you can remember in the early 1950s?" I asked.

"In the 1940s, I was young, and it didn't matter," Mrs. Williams said. "Or it mattered, but we just had hope. We didn't have a clear picture of anything happening. But when court decisions started being made, then breakthrough came."

Mrs. Williams referred to local cases involving integration at the workplace. Many of the lawsuits emerged from the courtroom of J. Waties Waring, a white federal judge in Charleston who, in the late 1940s, made a series of rulings that favored black civil rights.

"That was when the government said that some black people should work in offices in the shipyard," Mrs. Williams remembered.

The Navy shipyard, a little upriver from Charleston harbor, was one of the largest employers in the region. As workplace segregation began to loosen, Mrs. Williams, a well-educated, mild-mannered woman, found herself on the front line of change.

"All the black people who worked in the shipyard until that time were caretakers, or clean-up people, and some mechanics," she said. "With the legal breakthrough, there came a struggle, because white people were not interested in seeing black people move in. In 1954, I took the tests for a job at the shipyard, and was hired as a secretary. The room I worked in had one hundred and twenty people in it."

"How many black folks worked in that room?" I asked.

"I did," came the answer.

"Can you remember what it felt like the first time you walked into that room?"

"I was scared to death," said Mrs. Williams. "I was an aggressive person to a point, but had never had to face that type of aggression before. I had one man in my area—I worked as a typist for ten men— one man refused to talk to me. He refused to let me come near his desk. He got a small table and put it behind his desk and told me, 'Hey, when you have something for me, put it on there.' One day, my boss had a lot of papers for a booklet to be put together. It had about a hundred pages. He had a long table, and we set up the pages together. And a man across the room yelled out, real loud to us, so that everyone could hear, 'Hey, Langley, you sure have stooped low!' It was rough."

"You persevered," I said.

"I needed a job," she said flatly. "It got better as more came in, and the others decided we weren't going anywhere, so we might as well get along."

Mrs. Williams tried to end her story about white behavior on a more flattering note.

"When I retired, in 1984," she said, "the office was just like what a group of people working together should be. We came a long way."

"I would never sign a letter 'obediently,' " said Thomas Martin. He held one of his grandfather's letters in hand. "It would have to be someone I admire or someone like a parent." He put the letter aside.

"My father was a roofer," he began. "He always encouraged me to go to school, because he didn't want me to do that work. Still, in summers I worked as his helper."

Mr. Martin confided that he was a poor roofer. "I was afraid of heights," he said, a little embarrassed. "I climbed the ladder one day, up to the third floor. I looked down, and gripped the ladder and couldn't turn loose. My father had to come get me."

Mr. Martin said that his father worked for a construction company, H. A. DeCosta Co., run by a black man, Herbert DeCosta. At the time, Nathaniel Ball, my grandfather, was also in the construction business. His firm, N. I. Ball & Son, found itself in frequent competition with the DeCosta company. Their workmen were acquainted with one another—and Grandfather Nat would likely have known Mr. Martin's father.

"Daddy wasn't a religious person, despite his father being a minister," Mr. Martin continued. "But one year, Daddy was convinced by one of the men at the DeCosta company to join St. Mark's Church."

St. Mark's Episcopal Church, founded in 1865, was one of the churches of Charleston's African American elite. Most of its parishioners had light skin, because many of them were descended from slaves who had white fathers. The families of such people were often given their freedom before the Civil War and eventually made up a separate social caste in Charleston. In the slave days, some attended white churches, but after Emancipation—partly from choice, partly because the white churches no longer wanted them—the mulatto elite founded a new church, St. Mark's.

"Most of the people who go to St. Mark's are light-skinned Negroes," Mr. Martin went on. "After a time, my father stopped going to St. Mark's. I asked why, and he said that church was not for him. He said, 'Your comb has to go straight through your hair, and I don't have that kind of hair.' He felt ostracized, and he never went to church again."

The roofer P. Henry Martin Jr. died April 19, 1957.

"There is a legend in our family about his death," said Mr. Martin. "When Daddy became ill, I was sent for. He told me that he was dying, and that he would die on my birthday. I was born on Good Friday, and he died on Good Friday 1957."

Mr. Martin was born April 14, 1933, and christened Thomas P. Martin.

"I had a visit from a cousin in Chicago recently, and she said, 'Now you look like your father, Uncle Tom.' Everyone called my father Uncle Tom.

"I went to school at Immaculate Conception, on Coming Street, from kindergarten through twelfth grade. It was black, then. In the late 1960s, it became integrated." Mr. Martin said, in an aside, that he himself was Catholic.

"I attended Tuskegee Institute—which is now Tuskegee University—with the help of the United Negro College Fund. I graduated in 1955 with a bachelor's degree in education. I did some graduate work at Temple University, in Philadelphia. And I got my master's degree in education from South Carolina State.

"While in high school, I met my future wife. Her maiden name was Rosalind Duncan."

Later, I met Rosalind Martin. Her quietness matched that of her husband. When I asked her what she did, Mrs. Martin told me that she sang in the church choir and taught Bible classes. Mrs. Martin had just had a birthday, and there were gifts lying around the living room. The most visible was a sweatshirt with a logo from the local military college, the Citadel. Mrs. Martin explained that her daughter's boyfriend was enrolled there.

"My first job was as a teacher at Burke High School, in Charleston," Mr. Martin said. "I worked on the dramatic guild and on the school paper there. I moved from there to the guidance office, then to assistant principal. I was there for thirty-something years before I retired. Burke High School is all I know."

Mr. Martin told me that he had two children, a son who was lately in the Navy, and a daughter, Thomalind, who was getting a degree in speech pathology at one of the state schools.

At that moment Thomalind came into the room. She was a gentle and pretty young woman with self-effacing manners. In her shyness, she seemed to share the reserve of much of the family. Thomalind said that when she finishes her master's degree, she might work at a clinic. Or she might, like her father and great-grandfather, teach.

Although P. Henry Martin was born on Limerick plantation, his grandson Thomas Martin had never heard about it, let alone seen it. When I proposed that we visit Limerick, Mr. Martin agreed that it was a home-coming he wanted to make.

The remains of Limerick stand at the headwaters of the east branch of the Cooper River, north of Charleston. Its history goes back well before the Balls bought it. In April 1709 a man named Michael Mahon took possession of the tract. According to the deed, Mahon, who was from Ireland, got that part "now Call'd or Known by ye Name of ye Midle Setlement or Lymerick Plantation containing three thousand five hundred acres of Land," apparently named after the city of Mahon's birth. Mahon owned people who worked on the land for him, but after four years he sold the land (and perhaps the people) to Daniel Huger, a French Huguenot, and emigrated to Barbados. In about 1720 Huger built a large wooden house at Limerick; the building would stand for some 225 years and eventually become the home to generations of the Ball clan. Huger acquired more land and slaves, and made Limerick into a rice plantation. With his death in 1754, the patrimony passed to his oldest son, Daniel. Ten years later, in March 1764, Daniel Huger Jr. sold Limerick to Elias Ball, oldest son of the first Ball immigrant to South Carolina.

At Limerick's peak production, in the early 1800s, there were ten rice fields lining the river, and 283 people who worked them. Twenty-three buildings stood on the property, including slave quarters, barns, chicken houses, stables, and the Ball mansion.

After the Civil War, Limerick continued in business as a sharecrop farm with about thirty workers. The rice hands could not be made to work as they had in the past, and the white people reaped shrinking profits. In 1890, William Ball, the proprietor of Limerick, sold a piece of the land to a phosphate mining company. William James died in 1891, and in 1895, his kin lost the rest when a creditor called in a loan.

In the early 1900s, Limerick was sold many more times. One by one, buildings deteriorated and were pulled down. By the 1940s, the slave cabins that stood between the main dwelling and the rice fields were gone. The big house itself was a ramshackle pile, though still home to several families. In 1945 the mansion was completely consumed by fire. Ball family tradition has it that one of the tenants, after being told to move out, set the blaze. Thirty-three years later, in 1978, bulldozers tore up the remains of the foundation of the house to make way for a railroad spur. The track, laid over the site of the old house, belonged to the East Cooper and Berkeley Railroad and was meant to serve a plant owned by the Amoco Chemical Corporation, a few miles away on the Cooper River.

On a rainy day in June, Mr. Martin and I drove up to Limerick. Late in the afternoon, the weather cleared, and a hot sun raked across the pines and swamps. The only sign of the former plantation was an allée of live oaks that marched in a line from the two-lane public road toward the site of the old mansion. At the end, where the big house once stood, a railroad track crossed the path.

The allée of oaks was said to have been requested by Julia Cart Ball, who moved to Limerick in 1842 after her marriage to its owner, William Ball. A team of men would have been called away from the rice fields to do Julia's bidding. It was Julia Ball who, some years later, named Thomas Martin's grandfather and held him in her arms as he was christened.

Mr. Martin was quiet and watchful as we strolled beneath the oaks. Until this moment he had shown few emotions about the past. On the subject of slavery, he seemed to prefer a respectful, almost intellectual detachment.

"This is hallowed ground," Mr. Martin said suddenly. "I feel like I'm walking in the footsteps of Jesus."

A pale orange light came from the west and threw long shadows of the tree trunks across the path. In the distance were the low silhouettes of two brick houses, built in the 1980s by the latter-day owners of the plantation.

"Some of my friends would resent this, our being here together," said Mr. Martin, looking around carefully. "Some of my in-laws, in fact, resent it."

For the first time, Mr. Martin allowed himself to ruminate. "The letters you showed me from my grandfather to your great-grandfather—I don't recognize his treatment during slavery as, say, the kind of slavery that television would have shown. There is nothing about his having been beaten. I have to wonder what kind of people the Ball family were."

I agreed that the letters seemed to contradict the usual stories about the plantation system.

"I know very little about slavery," he said, "because we weren't taught very much about slavery, about our ancestors. The only thing we were able to do was imagine."

We approached the railroad tracks, crossed them, and walked past the two brick houses toward a pond. An empty lawn to the right was all that was left of the old slave street. On it once stood twelve cabins, each housing up to twenty people.

"When I was in my twenties, I had a different impression about slavery," Mr. Martin continued. "I was not forgiving. I was unable to do what I wanted, and I blamed it on slavery, or rather, on white people. My philosophy has changed since I was a young man. Terrible things happened to our ancestors, but we've got to make something of ourselves."

I asked Mr. Martin whether he thought there was anger among black people.

"Yes. How many people would do what we are doing now? The first thing they would ask is, 'How much am I going to get out of it?' I don't think that we will ever get anywhere, blacks and whites, until we're able to sit down together."

The pond was round and still. The oak allée once made a grand avenue in front of the mansion, while behind it the pond gave a pleasing view from the back porch. Algae like green smoke now choked half the lagoon, and a cluster of lily pads filled up the middle part, with long shoots rising from the water into the air. A rowboat was tied at the edge of the pond. We climbed into it and paddled out into the water lilies.

The Ball papers contain the record of the girl named Priscilla who was brought from Sierra Leone to Charleston in 1756. The descendants of Priscilla could be identified in the slave lists, and among them, it turned out, was P. Henry Martin. One afternoon early in March, I went to visit the Martin family to bring the news about their African forebear.

Carutha Williams, the clerk in the Navy Yard integration case, was there, as were her cousin Thomas Martin and Mr. Martin's wife, Rosalind. The Martins' daughter Thomalind also showed up, along with Mr. Martin's sister, Rosina Martin. Rosina, about sixty, wore pants and a button shirt, and had her brother's quiet nature. We sat in the living room, among the family's diplomas and tropical fish.

"Sometimes it's possible to put together family trees for people in slavery," I said, "and what I have is an ancestry for the Martin family that goes back to a girl named Priscilla, who came to Charleston in the year 1756, from the Sierra Leone River, in West Africa." I brought out a family tree mapping the lineage. "I don't have any evidence of her African name, only the name Priscilla. After she arrived, on a ship called the *Hare*, she was sold, on June 30, 1756, to a man called Elias Ball II, who brought her to Comingtee plantation, where she established a family that continued to live in slavery to the Balls for a hundred and ten years. Seven generations after Priscilla comes you, Mr. Martin. She was a child when she was taken, ten years old—the records of Elias Ball say as much."

There was silence, and the Martins looked at one another, trying to decide how to react. The first one to speak was Mr. Martin's sister, Rosina.

"Why would they sell children?"

More exchanges of glances around the room.

"Yes, why would they sell children?" I repeated, because I did not have an answer. It wasn't clear whether Rosina referred to the white slave-handlers, like Henry Laurens, or black slave-sellers, who had put Priscilla on the market in Sierra Leone.

Matter-of-factly, Carutha Williams said, "Girls, because they could soon procreate, and boys, because they could work."

"It was an evil business," I added, "but the thinking was that young people would live longer."

The Martins knew how rare it was for Americans to be able to identify African forebears. "Very few people can do this," said Mr. Martin.

The Martins stayed quiet another minute about the news, studying each other and the family tree.

"We have a Priscilla living now," said Mrs. Williams, "who is P. H. Martin's great-granddaughter." Rosina read off a few names of her ancestors in slavery, comparing them to living family members.

"On the west coast of Africa, there were a number of prisons where people were held before the ships arrived," I went on. "The place where Priscilla was jailed in Sierra Leone is called Bunce Island. On that place, in the Sierra Leone River, there are the remains of the prison from which Priscilla was taken and where she had her last glimpse of her homeland."

"The prison is still there today?" asked Mr. Martin.

"The ruins," I answered.

"It blows your mind," Carutha Williams said mildly.

I told the Martins I intended to go to West Africa to visit Bunce Island, because the Balls evidently took a number of people from there.

Mrs. Williams said, "Well, I'm old now, but if I was younger, I would go with you to Africa."

Thinking about Priscilla, the Martin family began to smile at one another in a bewildered way. Suddenly there was a wave of laughter around the room, and everyone was talking at once. It was the first time I had heard Thomas Martin laugh since we met.

11

❧━━━◦━━━❧

A HOUSE DIVIDED

It was called the War for America in Great Britain, although in the Southern colonies it might well have been called the War with the Slaves. The American Revolution came to the doors of the plantations, and when it drifted off, perhaps one in three black people were gone with it—most to the Caribbean, some to Canada. The Balls tried to hold on to their human property and, to do so, took sides with both armies. Cousin fought cousin, brother fought brother, and the Ball slaves faced a stark choice, whether to hunker down in their cabins or flee to the British Army as it passed through the country. Many took their chances with King George III, and some got free in the bargain; but more stayed home, unable to leave their children, or afraid of the outcome if caught trying to escape.

During the fight for the United States, seven years in the making, sometimes a black hero stood up against heavy odds. One man, Boston King, fled from his home on the Balls' Tranquil Hill, made his way to Nova Scotia, and eventually boarded a ship bound for Africa, returning in the end to the coast from which his father had come. The records of Tranquil Hill have not survived, though I imagine Boston King was not the only person to flee. But he was absolutely unique in another respect: as far as I can determine, he was the only person among the thousands of Ball slaves who ever published the story of his life. The story of Boston King—the Ball slave who reversed the black diaspora—is the tale of a true rebel.

At the beginning of the Revolutionary War, the Ball family was spread out on seven plantations in the "low country," the watery flatland of South Carolina that hugs the ocean, and the clan had entered its third generation in America. Second Elias Ball, master of Kensington, turned sixty-seven in 1776, an age that made him family patriarch. (Elias's richer, younger brother, John Coming Ball of Hyde Park, was already dead.) But power moved away from Second Elias and down toward the young, who numbered about ten adults and lived here and there across thirty miles. In the northwest corner of the Ball domain, Tranquil Hill was the home of Second Elias's niece Ann Ball Waring. In the direction of Charleston, to the south, lay Old Goose Creek, sometimes called Yeamans Hall, home of another niece, Elizabeth Ball Smith. In the middle stood worn family ground—Comingtee, Hyde Park, Kensington, and Limerick—while to the northeast lay Wambaw plantation, property of one of Second Elias's nephews. The Ball holdings amounted to thousands of acres and perhaps five hundred black people.

In numbers, the white presence in North America was slight. English colonists covered the East Coast, but their property lines reached only a few hundred miles inland. To the west lay Native people, vast land, and the thin settlements of the French and Spanish. At the northern limit of English habitation stood Massachusetts, New Hampshire, and Nova Scotia, the last a peninsula taken from France. Georgia and north Florida formed the southern border, Florida having been recently won from Spain. In 1750, one out of five people in British North America was a black slave, or three hundred thousand in a population of 1.5 million. Forced labor was the law of the realm, but there was already a "slave line" dividing the colonies. New England property holders owned fewer acres and smaller numbers of people than their counterparts in the South, to the extent that by the 1760s nine out of ten blacks lived in the five Southern colonies—Maryland, Virginia, North Carolina, South Carolina, and Georgia. Of these, South Carolina was the bulwark of plantation slavery. There, in 1770, six out of ten people—more than

75,000 in a population of nearly 125,000—were working in the rice fields.

After the French and Indian War, which ended by treaty in 1763, taxes fell on the colonies to support the British armies that remained in their midst. The Stamp Act of 1765 was supplanted by the Townshend Duties of 1767, which stirred a protest movement to ban imports to America. In between, the Declaratory Act of 1766, in which Parliament asserted sovereignty over the colonies "in all cases whatsoever," angered American merchants. The Balls paid little mind, because taxes on paper, paint, and manufactured goods did not affect plantation grandees, whose black people made most everything consumed. And, since the family fortune came from rice exports to England, it would be unwise to risk upsetting the client whose business paid for one's luxuries. It was probably against the better judgment of the Balls that in September 1774, delegates from around the colonies came together in Philadelphia as the Continental Congress and, defying the Crown's taxation and policing measures, voted to ban most trade with Great Britain. When five South Carolina delegates threatened to walk out unless an exception to the embargo was made for rice exports, the grain was removed from the list of banned goods, and the Balls narrowly missed economic ruin.

The first member of the family to take an interest in the rebellion was the oldest son of Second Elias of Kensington, Elias Ball III, the one who—in his dotage thirty years later, ridden with gout—would be known as Old Mas' 'Lias. In 1775 he was still young (just twenty-three) and so it would be better here to call him Third Elias. A few months after the Continental Congress, a Carolina version, the Provincial Congress, was called in Charleston. Stepping forward to prevent more risks to the business, Third Elias ran for and won a seat.

In spring of 1775 the rebellion became linked in the minds of Southern whites with a threat to slavery. On May 3, a letter arrived in Charleston from a man named Arthur Lee, a Virginian then visiting London who was known to have antitax, or rebel, sympathies. Lee reported he had heard that King George's ministers had been meeting about how to put down the resistance. The British government, Lee said, was discussing a new tactic, namely, to offer freedom to blacks who deserted their rebel owners and joined the king's troops, which were bivouacked in the cities. In other words, if war came the British would call on the rice workers to revolt. News of the letter's contents spread throughout the city. Five days later, on May 8, word came from Massachusetts that fighting had actually broken out. A pair of bloody battles between rebels and a British company had erupted three weeks earlier in the towns of Concord and Lexington. The rumors intensified in Charleston when, on May 29, the *South Carolina Gazette* published the text of a second letter, also from an American in London, also on the subject of black revolt. According to the latest hearsay, King George now planned to arm American slaves against their masters. "[S]eventy-eight thousand guns and bayonets," wrote the anonymous correspondent, were soon "to be sent to America, to put into the hands of N*****s." (The newspaper printed asterisks instead of the word "Negroes" so that black couriers would not be alerted by a word they were likely to know.) This latest report implied direct British backing of an uprising. For whites, what had started as a tax quarrel was now an issue of how to protect their own lives.

A few weeks after the warning about the "N*****s," Third Elias decided the time had come to join a militia; he signed up with Job Marion's Company, one of several private armies mobilizing in the crisis. "I have entered into a Volunteer Company," he wrote to his brother John. "I am much in want of a gun to have a Bayonet fixed as my old piece is too short. I beg you will let me have yours . . . til we have better times [and] then I shall give you one equally as good."

Other news from London told Third Elias that the old arrangements with workers were not necessarily permanent ones. In 1765, an American slave named James Somerset had gone to London with his owner, Charles Stewart. Stewart then left England without Somerset but later returned to London and tried to reclaim his property. The black man went to court to protest that he was now free and, in February 1772, the presiding justice, Lord Mansfield, agreed, ruling that as soon as a slave set foot on English soil, he or she became free. News of the case echoed through American drawing rooms—the first repudiation of forced work by the mother country and, in effect, the beginning of an antislavery cause that would eventually work its way across England and travel to America.

As whites armed themselves for the struggle, blacks did their own planning. In early 1775, the *South Carolina Gazette* reported an indictment against a white citizen for allowing his house to be used as a meeting place for black discussion. The citizen, Peter Hinds, was accused of bringing "Negro Preachers" into his living room, "where they deliver doctrines to large Numbers of Negroes, dangerous to and subversive of the Peace, Safety, and Tranquility of this Province." The debates included the idea that the fight with London might mean emancipation.

White fear grew when news arrived that the governor of Virginia, John Murray, Earl of Dunmore, had actually issued a freedom proclamation. Murray decreed that slaves who left their masters for the royal side would be set free, and it was reported that three hundred blacks had formed a regiment under Dunmore's command, with special uniforms that bore the inscription "Liberty to Slaves."

When a new royal governor of South Carolina, Lord William Campbell, arrived in Charleston in mid-June 1775, he entered a city churning with white fear and black discontent. Campbell wrote to his superiors in England that "it was . . . reported and universally believed that to effect [a slave insurrection] . . . 14,000 stands of arms were actually on board the *Scorpion*, the sloop of war I came out in." The governor was astonished at the level of white alarm. "Words . . . cannot express the flame that this occasioned amongst all ranks and degrees; the cruelty and savage barbarity of the scheme was the conversation of all companies."

The rebel Carolina militias came under a committee, the Council of Safety, which directed them to harass Campbell and drill for war. Henry Laurens, the wealthy slave trader and Ball in-law, served as chair, and the Council of Safety quickly drafted a plan to defend the colony in the event of British attack. If the fight arrived by sea, Laurens argued, there would have to be an evacuation from plantations within twenty miles of the water. "All the negroes . . . should be removed upon the approach of the enemy . . . by which all communication will be cut off between the enemy in the town, and the negroes in the country."

The administration of Governor Campbell could not contain the rebellion, and after three months Campbell realized he had no chance of holding power. In mid-September 1775, the governor moved with his entourage aboard the *Tamar*, a British sloop riding in the harbor. The *Tamar* and two warships then anchored themselves next to Sullivan's

Island, where Africans were quarantined around the pest house. Campbell's little flotilla, five miles from the city, made the last enclave of the
king's authority in Charleston. Third Elias's brother, fifteen-year-old
John Ball, noted these events in a letter: "I dare say you know it very
well there has been the dickens to pay about our Governor [Campbell]
who is now found out to be an old Traitor. . . . [Last week] he went
down on board the man of war."

When Campbell's ships anchored, black people, having heard of
Lord Dunmore's promise in Virginia, began to escape the plantations
and head for Sullivan's Island. They took over the pest house, evidently
recruiting what slaves were there, and tried to get aboard the ships. By
December 1775, about five hundred black fugitives (including some,
perhaps, from Ball plantations) had camped on the island, building a
village of huts in the woods. Governor Campbell, trying to wait it out,
let everyone stay. In the eyes of the American rebels, the British were
now conspiring with the slaves.

In late November Third Elias, the militiaman, wrote to his brother:
"We are making all warlike preparations to ingage with the men of war
wenever tha [they] think proper. . . . There is a twenty-four pounder
[cannon] fixing up at the end of Mr. Laurens' wharf. . . . [We may] go
down & attack the men of war."

The first fight of the Revolutionary War in the South Carolina low
country was an attack by white rebels on the campsite of unarmed
blacks. As chairman of the Council of Safety, Henry Laurens ordered
the assault. "Sir," he wrote to Colonel William Moultrie, "[Y]ou are
hereby ordered to detach two hundred men . . . to Sullivan's Island,
there to seize and apprehend a number of negroes. . . . The pest house
to be burned and every kind of livestock to be driven off or destroyed."

On December 19, a party of fifty-four soldiers, perhaps including
Third Elias Ball, made its way to Sullivan's Island. The raiders disguised themselves as Native people, wearing feathers and face paint,
evidently because they didn't want to be identified by Governor Campbell's troops. The costumed whites killed several runaway slaves and
burned their houses. Although most of the refugees had escaped into
the woods, Henry Laurens gloated over what he called the raid's success, saying that "it will serve to humble our Negroes in general &
perhaps to mortify his Lordship [Governor Campbell] not a little." A

few days later, Campbell cut moorings and sailed for England, his three ships carrying an unknown number of escaped slaves.

Six months later, in June 1776, a flotilla of nine British warships under the command of Sir Peter Parker arrived off Charleston to retake the city. To control Sullivan's Island was to control the narrow channel giving access to the port, and thus to dominate the city itself. By this time, rebels had buttressed and occupied a fort on the island near the old pest house. On June 28, in the battle of Fort Sullivan, Parker's frigates tried to bombard their way past the fort and into the harbor. The 435 defenders fought back under the command of Colonel William Moultrie, who had led the earlier attack on the black fugitives. Failing to get past the island, Parker called off the siege. Ten days later the flotilla withdrew and sailed for New York. Royal authority collapsed, and the war left town for the next four years.

A first draft of the Declaration of Independence, debated in the Philadelphia Congress in June 1776, denounced the slave business. A committee of five delegates led by Thomas Jefferson presented a document that singled out King George III as the author of an incomprehensible crime. "[The King] has waged cruel war against human nature itself," read the draft, "violating its most sacred rights of life and liberty in the persons of a distant people who never offended him, captivating and carrying them into slavery in another hemisphere, or to incur miserable death in their transportation thither."

This passage did not sit well with South Carolina's delegates to the convention. After delegate Edward Rutledge lobbied to delete it, the sentence was cut from the final document, to Jefferson's long-standing disappointment. Still, the paradox of establishing the democratic ideal alongside a national system of forced labor began to dawn on American whites. The New England colonies, along with Pennsylvania and Delaware, outlawed the slave trade, and in April 1776 the Continental Congress banned the import of Africans to any of the thirteen colonies. They did so partly out of enlightened conscience, and partly to keep more collaborators away from the king's troops.

Most of the Ball kin had no desire to change a society that placed them at the top, but there was at least one member of the family who believed the end of slavery was a goal of the rebellion. John Laurens, born in 1754, was the first son of Eleanor Ball and Henry Laurens. After his mother died in 1770, the sixteen-year-old was sent by his father to school in Europe. While his Ball cousins learned their lessons from tutors and in simple provincial classrooms, John went to London and Switzerland. As a student abroad, he seems to have come in contact with progressive political thought—Enlightenment notions of the social contract, individual liberty, and natural rights. Although I cannot say that John, in Switzerland, met François Voltaire, who lived near Geneva, or Jean-Jacques Rousseau, who was Swiss-born, I suspect he may have read their works or at least encountered their followers. Whatever the source, John Laurens returned to America from Europe in April 1777 possessed of a remarkably broad mind.

At twenty-three, John was handsome, articulate, cosmopolitan. By this time, fighting had spread through the Northeast, and John's father, Henry, had become a national figure. Using the influence of the Laurens name, the pupil secured a position as an aide-de-camp with General George Washington. The fact that the young man's mother was named Ball, and so was Washington's, did not hinder his search for employment, either. (George Washington's mother, born in Virginia, was a woman named Mary Ball, although the Virginia Ball family came from a different part of England than the South Carolina clan.) John Laurens began traveling with the revolutionary command. By late 1777, he felt comfortable enough with Washington, who was commander of the Continental Army, to propose to him a new phase in the war. Philadelphia had fallen and France had not yet entered the fight on the side of the Americans. The future looked doubtful. John's idea was to raise a black rebel regiment in South Carolina. As he described it to Washington, black men who enlisted would receive their freedom after a tour of duty. In February 1778, while at the bleak winter camp in Valley Forge, Pennsylvania, John Laurens wrote a letter to his father on the subject. Henry Laurens was elected president of the Continental Congress that year, and his influence over the affairs of the United States was great. Between them, father and son might change the outcome of the war.

"A well chosen body of 5000 black men," John Laurens wrote, "properly officer'd, to act as light troops, in addition to our present establishment, might give us decisive success in the next campaign." As implicit criticism of his father, the slave trader, John added, "I have long deplored the wretched state of these men, and considered in their history, the bloody wars excited in Africa, to furnish America with slaves—the groans of despairing multitudes, toiling for the luxuries of merciless tyrants."

These were strange views for a young man of privilege, and the elder Laurens wrote to his son, wondering about the reaction of General Washington to the scheme. John Laurens wrote back, "You ask, what is the general's opinion, upon this subject? He is convinced, that the numerous tribes of blacks in the southern parts of the continent, offer a resource to us that should not be neglected. With respect to my particular plan, he only objects to it, with the arguments of pity for a man who would be less rich than he might be." In other words, Washington wanted to use blacks in the war but balked at giving freedom to black soldiers because their owners would never accept a deal that would rob them of property. Henry Laurens, his mind crowded with the politics of getting rich landowners to risk everything in rebellion, rejected his son's plan. "There is not a Man in America of your opinion," he wrote back. The dismissive father advised John to return to South Carolina and forget about his "Negro scheme." He concluded, "You will have many advantages . . . in raising a Regiment of White Men."

John Laurens left Valley Forge, returned to Charleston, and presented his "Negro scheme" to South Carolina's Provincial Congress. The representatives, like John's cousin Third Elias, were appalled, and many seem to have worried that the gallant and worldly soldier might be able to pull it off. Frightened, the delegates debated a measure to surrender Charleston to the British and take South Carolina out of the war in the event black troops were actually allowed to serve.

Returning to the front, John Laurens fought in various battles and was named a colonel. He traveled to France, raised money from the courtiers of Versailles for the Continental Army, came back to South Carolina, and got himself elected to the local assembly. Cloaked with his new status as an officer and diplomat, Colonel Laurens again brought the issue before the Carolina legislature, but this time he was shouted down. He wrote to George Washington to describe what had happened: "[I was] drowned out by the howlings of a triple-headed monster, in which prejudice, avarice and pusillanimity were united."

Three months after his last attempt to enlist black soldiers, John Laurens was killed in a skirmish with British troops on the Combahee

River in South Carolina. It was August 1782; the war was almost over. He was twenty-seven.

Another defiant thinker, the slave who would become known as Boston King, was born in 1760 on White Hall plantation, twenty-eight miles northwest of Charleston. White Hall was a 526-acre tract whose main house stood on a bluff not far from the narrow stream of the Ashley River. The names of Boston's parents have not survived, but during his last years, Boston described them in his memoir. His father was born in Africa, although the son does not say where, and after his capture became the black driver of the work crews at White Hall, with much influence over the fields. Boston's mother was a nurse and seamstress who looked after the sick in the plantation infirmary and made clothes for field hands.

In the 1760s a girl named Ann Ball, the youngest child of John Coming Ball and his wife Catherine Gendron, was growing up on Hyde Park plantation, twenty miles from White Hall. Within a few years, Ann's life would cross that of Boston, when she became one of his owners. In 1771, Ann turned eighteen and married Richard Waring, a twenty-three-year-old scion of a well-established rice family on the Ashley River. In the words of one memoirist, Richard Waring was "a gentleman of liberal education, benevolent heart, engaging deportment, and friendly disposition," while Ann made "a courteous and cheerful companion." The ceremony took place at Ann's home. Two years after the wedding, when Boston was thirteen, the owner of White Hall sold his property to the young Mr. and Mrs. Waring. The couple took possession of the land and people in early 1774, and, making the purchase their own, renamed the place Tranquil Hill, evidently for the bluff on which the house stood. With the former Ann Ball in the big house, Boston became a Ball slave.

Under the new ownership, sixteen-year-old Boston was made an apprentice in Charleston, an assignment that gave him a sharp taste of discipline. "After being in the shop about two years," he wrote about this period, "I had the charge of my master's tools, which being very good, were often used by the men, if I happened to be out of the way. When this was the case, or any of them were lost, or misplaced, my master beat me severely, striking me upon the head." Boston remembered that once some nails were missing from the shop. "For this offence I was beat and tortured most cruelly, and was laid up three weeks before I was able to do any work."

Ann Waring's Tranquil Hill was soon embroiled in the Revolution. In late 1775 the Council of Safety ordered the nearby village of Dorchester fortified against British attack. The defenses came early, but they would eventually be used in May 1778, when General William Moultrie, the former colonel from Sullivan's Island, made camp with troops near Tranquil Hill. Boston, eighteen, would have known about the proclamation of Lord Dunmore, which offered freedom to blacks who joined the British cause, but at this point Boston was working on a plantation twelve miles distant. He may have begun to contemplate how to get his freedom, but the king's army was nowhere in sight.

In spring of 1779, after a long absence, England brought the war back to the Southern provinces, with royal troops and columns of German mercenaries. A British force captured Savannah, below South Carolina on the Atlantic coast, and the invaders then fought their way to a point outside Charleston. General Moultrie returned to camp near Tranquil Hill on his way to face the threat. In June, Henry Clinton, commander in chief of the British forces, issued a decree that escaped blacks would be permitted to follow the movements of the king's troops. If the English came within reach, slaves could join them and expect to be fed and protected.

Boston evidently decided that his moment had come, and the nineteen-year-old stole away from Tranquil Hill, leaving his parents behind. "I determined to go into Charles-Town, and throw myself into the hands of the English," he wrote. "They received me readily, and I began to feel the happiness of liberty, of which I knew nothing before."

Boston attached himself to a British officer, a Captain Grey, staying with Grey for some months, working as he could for the British victory. In February 1780, Commander Henry Clinton and a large force besieged Charleston, and the British cavalry took the village of Dorchester, near Tranquil Hill. Battles were being fought around Charleston, and Boston put himself in danger to help the cause. By this time, he had finished his service with Captain Grey and begun to travel with another officer, a Colonel Small, whom he remembered with some disappointment in his memoir:

I entered into the service of [Colonel Small], the commanding officer. . . . [O]ur situation was very precarious . . . for the Americans had 1600 men, not far off; whereas our whole number amounted only to 250. . . . Our commander at length determined to send me with a letter [to get reinforcements], promising me great rewards, if I was successful in the business. . . . [I] set off on foot about 3 o'clock in the afternoon; I expected every moment to fall in with the enemy, whom I well knew would shew me no mercy. . . . I came to Mum's [Moncks] Corner tavern. I knocked at the door, but they blew out the candle. . . . [That night, Boston finished his reconnaissance and delivered the letter.] Next morning, Colonel Small gave me three shillings, and many fine promises, which were all that I ever received for this service from him.

Charleston fell on May 12, 1780, and the Union Jack was once again raised over the city. With the British in control, Boston must have felt that his daring had paid off and he would certainly be free.

A few months later, Boston's former master, Richard Waring of Tranquil Hill, died at thirty-three. Waring, and his widow, the former Miss Ball, probably never found out what happened to the escaped worker. A few years after the Revolution, an amateur artist made a watercolor for Ann Waring, depicting Tranquil Hill. The plantation scene shows a two-story house on a bluff, flanked by several ramshackle slave cabins and a winnowing house, a work building where crops were gathered. Underneath the image, the artist placed a caption: "Tranquil-Hill, The seat of Mrs. Ann Waring, near Dorchester." No slaves appear in the picture.

The Ball family in general did not believe in democracy. They were pragmatists who wanted to keep their land, slaves, and social position. Four years after the Declaration of Independence, however, the fall of Charleston did cause some rift in the family. While most now took the safe course and sided with the British, a few backed the cause of the new nation.

Again in command of Charleston, British authorities called for an occupation force to be made from local recruits. Third Elias was one of the first to sign up. Having served in a rebel company and as a delegate to the insurgent assembly, Third Elias now switched sides and styled himself a Loyalist. Elias's cousin, twenty-two-year-old John Coming Ball of Hyde Park, also threw himself at the feet of the Crown. In July the two cousins became junior officers in a new British unit, and the call went out for a suitable commander. For this job, which would require a certain ruthlessness, a third member of the family stepped forward, "Wambaw" Elias Ball.

Wambaw Elias was thirty-six and had much of the fierceness of his grandfather, Red Cap. Raised on Hyde Park, Wambaw Elias lived at Wambaw plantation, on the Santee River north of Limerick, with his wife, Catherine Gaillard, and their five children; he was a brother of Ann Waring of Tranquil Hill. When Wambaw Elias joined the royal militia, he approached the British commander, General Charles Lord Cornwallis, who gave him twenty-six men and made him a colonel, a high rank that matched the passion of Wambaw Elias's support for the distant king. Wambaw Elias was a half brother of John Coming Ball, one of his lieutenants, and a cousin of Third Elias, another of his officers.

Despite the family's Loyalist, or Tory, sympathies, at least two relatives stayed with the rebel underdogs. It can be difficult to follow the lives of white women on the plantations, since their letters were less often saved and they appear less frequently in public documents, but records show that one of the patriot stalwarts was Elizabeth Ball Smith, of Old Goose Creek plantation. Elizabeth's husband, Henry Smith, died shortly after the fall of Charleston, but that year and the next the widow allowed Continental Army troops and rebel militia to take supplies from her storehouses. The other supporter of the rebellion was John Ball of Kensington. In 1779, emerging from his youth as a dandy who loved clothes, John signed up with a militia, Daniel Horry's Light Dragoons, a company of fifty to a hundred men. Dragoons were mounted infantry, and John's unit was one of ten in the Second Regiment of Provincials under General William Moultrie. Though only nineteen and with no military experience, when he enlisted, John was received in the manner accorded a young man of privilege, and named second lieutenant.

As a junior officer, John had the opportunity to keep up his stylish appearance. The obligatory uniform for his rank, as described in one muster roll, included "a blue cloth coatee, faced and cuffed with scarlet cloth, and lined with scarlet. White buttons; and white waistcoat and breeches . . . [plus] a cap and black feather." For dress parade, officers were required to wear powdered wigs.

John Ball was one of the youngest men in his regiment, but perhaps the richest, and the duty of feeding the roaming troops fell to him. The company sometimes stopped in at Kensington plantation or another of the Ball places, and John had food sent out to the field. Hundreds of rebels ate beef and pork from the Ball commissary and rice from the barn, until finally, in his account book, John complained that his entire stock of two hundred barrels of rice, or fifty tons, had been eaten up by troops. Military life was not as rough as it might have been, because a number of black people traveled with John's unit as servants—so many that in a copy of his company's orderly book, he mentions the barracks for the white soldiers and refers to the "Negroes apartment" nearby. The closeness of black and white on the front can be seen in one letter John wrote home, in which he describes a military maneuver, then mentions Hammond, a valet from Kensington. But even though his every need was met by a personal servant, John seems to have had little patience for the war, and not much feeling for the cause. In a letter from Drayton Hall, a plantation where he rested a few days, he noted:

> [O]ne night at 10 O'Clock [we] sett off with Count Polaski [Kazimierz Pulaski, a Polish nobleman fighting for the Americans who was later killed at Savannah] . . . whose camp was then at Bacons bridge. . . . [W]e took a terrible route towards Ashley ferry & then retreated back again without ever seeing an Enemy. . . . I assure you I have seen hard duty enough & . . . I never lik'd the regiment but now I hate to be in it & the least thing that offend's me now will make me quit. . . . Hammond came up with my Portmanteau but very few cloaths was in it & not having an oportunity of having any wash'd up this way so you must needs that I am in a very dirty condition.

Sometimes John traveled with London, a thirty-six-year-old Gambian. London was the husband of Dinah, one of the daughters of Angola Amy and Windsor. "London is up here with me and all my things," John wrote home from the Stono River, south of Charleston. "We are encamp'd with Polaski's Cavalry about 2 miles in the rear of our army as I am told." The scene of a Gambian and a young plantation dandy stalking the wilderness on the hunt for German mercenaries under the pay of King George III stands as one of the less well-known episodes of the Revolution.

In January 1780, John paused in his maneuvers to marry his first cousin, eighteen-year-old Jane Ball. The couple had practically grown up together, John on Kensington plantation, Jane a mile away on Hyde Park. At the time of the wedding, Jane was living at Tranquil Hill with her sister, Ann Ball Waring. Family relations were becoming increasingly complex. Jane was a sister of Wambaw Elias, the Tory colonel, while John, the bridegroom, remained a rebel (even if less than ardent). The ceremony took place at Tranquil Hill, from which Boston had escaped. On top of all this, the uncle of the newlyweds, Henry Laurens, had been taken prisoner. Laurens, fifty-six, was sent by the Continental Congress to Holland to negotiate a loan for the United States. He was captured at sea, brought to England, and jailed in the Tower of London. At the Laurens home, Mepkin plantation on the Cooper River, the British took further revenge, burning his house to the ground.

In late spring 1780, General Cornwallis sent a flotilla up the Cooper River to take its main crossing point at Strawberry Ferry. On the east bank of the crossing stood Strawberry plantation, property of the young Tory Third Elias, and the warships, riding at anchor, could be seen in plain view from Comingtee. Cornwallis himself and a company of soldiers took up residence eight miles to the northeast, at Silk Hope, near the headwaters of the eastern branch of the river, half an hour from Limerick and Kensington. The force of the Crown now gripped the southern and northern boundaries of the main Ball lands.

When the British settled in, a black exodus from the Ball places began. It started with one or two people, who were followed by a few more, until a human stream flowed from the fields. John Ball, home at Kensington on furlough, wrote down the names of the fugitives. "May 7—Toby gone to the [British] camp, & Hyde Park Abraham," he noted. Every day, someone else decided to take a chance. "May 9th—Phoebe & her daughter Chloe . . . 10th—Charlotte, Bessy & her children, Roebuck, January, & Betty . . . 11th—Yamma . . . 12th—Patra & daughter Julia . . . 13th—Flora & child Adonis . . ." The runaways, not including children, ranged in age from twenty-three up to fifty-seven, and the typical means of escape was by boat, at night. One morning John realized that fifteen people had disappeared in twenty-four hours. "Pino went in my flat [boat]," he noted on June 1, "and carried with him his wife Nancy, Little Nancy, Polly, Dick, Jewel, Little Pino, Nanny and child Nelly, Peter, Eleanor, Isabel, Joney, Brutus, Charlotte." The next day a field hand named Humphrey followed.

Sometimes people were captured on their way to British lines. John noted that "Charlotte was brought home & stayed a week," before she left again. Among those who fled and did not return was Hammond, the valet who had brought John's portmanteau to the battlefield. Eventually at least fifty-one people, or about one-third of the plantation, fled from Kensington and stayed away for good.

The lure of freedom must have been great, but there were reasons not to leave as well. Some stayed because of their children, since it was difficult for parents to flee toward the unknown with babies in their arms. Others may have stayed because the British, after all, had organized the slave trade, which made their promise of freedom dubious. A few people fled but then came back voluntarily, evidently skeptical that their lives would improve with English bosses.

Just as John Ball's notes show there was a mass escape from Kensington, signs suggest a similar flight took place from all the Ball places. During the war the British published an occupation newspaper in Charleston, the *Royal Gazette*, which ran lists of fugitives and named their owners, including people belonging to the Balls. After the war, in a petition to the South Carolina Assembly, a group of landlords in St. John's Parish complained that fully half of the adult black men they owned had gone to the British side and not come back. According to one estimate, made by a rice planter at the end of the war, throughout South Carolina, some twelve thousand black people fled their homes in hopes of getting free.

While black workers escaped, white rebels did their best to harass the British. The most famous of the militia leaders was a gangly backwoodsman named Francis Marion. Marion, a fifty-year-old Huguenot, practiced an early form of guerrilla warfare that earned him the nickname "the Swamp Fox." The Swamp Fox would appear without warning out of the forests at the head of a few men, strike at bewildered redcoats, then vanish like a shout. Marion was well known to the Balls from a wily trick he played during one of these run-ins. At the town of Kingstree on August 27, 1780, Marion's raiders pounced on the company led by Colonel Wambaw Elias Ball and his two kin, Third Elias and John Coming Ball. Colonel Ball took the worst of it, with sixty men killed or wounded to Marion's thirty. Ball family tradition has it that at this battle, Marion took prisoner not Wambaw Elias himself but, as a practical joke, his horse, leaving the colonel to walk. For the rest of the war, the story goes, Marion could be found on the back of a black mare he called Ball.

During this time Lord Cornwallis's headquarters at Silk Hope lay a few miles upstream from Kensington. Cornwallis was a middle-aged nobleman, Second Elias, Kensington's owner, a seventy-one-year-old widower, one of the rich old men in the neighborhood whom Cornwallis thought it appropriate to visit. The presence of the Swamp Fox in the area, however, made these visits somewhat tense. Should Cornwallis have been taken prisoner by Marion while on a social call to Mr. Ball, it would have been a great setback to the British cause. Apparently the general was afraid of being caught inside the Kensington house, surrounded by an ambush, so the visits he made followed a careful etiquette. Cornwallis positioned his guard and entourage near the house, and the general himself never actually entered the doorway. Instead, Second Elias and his guest talked on the porch, within clear sight of the approach road and the Swamp Fox's preferred terrain, the thicket.

The decisive battles in the Ball neighborhood took place during one week in the summer of 1781. On July 15, at Strawberry Ferry, British forces came ashore from their frigates and marched to a chapel, Biggin Church, a few miles north on the river road. As the troops disappeared up the path, a rebel detachment fell on the contingent left behind, took fifty prisoners, and burned four of the ships anchored in the river. Evidently the loss encouraged the British to mount a revenge march. At Biggin Church the dispatch from the ships met the Royal Nineteenth Regiment to make a combined force of six or seven hundred. The following night, their commander, a Colonel Coates, gave the order to set fire to the church. As the building burned, at about three o'clock on the morning of July 17, the column of men fell in and headed east, toward the Ball places.

Colonel Coates and his men moved from plantation to plantation on a search-and-destroy march. Approaching the Hyde Park gate, they met no opposition. As they passed on to Kensington, nothing stopped them. At Limerick no rebels appeared. Although records do not exist to confirm it, I suspect that a crowd of black people emerged from each gate, met the column, and fell in behind, because the red-jacketed infantrymen would have been seen as liberators.

Beyond Limerick and around a corner lay Quenby plantation, on the east side of the east branch of the Cooper River. Elizabeth Ball, one of Red Cap's daughters, had been mistress of the place, although the day the British made their march, Quenby and the people on it were owned by Elizabeth's son, Richard Shubrick, making it a Ball plantation once removed.

Coates's regiment reached Quenby Creek, a stream that empties into the Cooper; a wooden bridge across the creek gave the only access to Charleston by road on that side of the river. With some five hundred men, perhaps including black fugitives, in his column, Coates crossed the bridge and waited for his rear guard. The British loosened the planks of the bridge in order to dismantle it. Suddenly a large American cavalry arrived on the scene, the Swamp Fox among them. Coates's group fell back and headed for the Quenby settlement.

The so-called Battle of Quenby Bridge began in the afternoon. When the Americans charged on their horses, the bridge, its boards in disarray, fell to pieces. Stopped short, they went upstream, rounded the head of the creek, and came back down to meet Coates for the fight. By this time, three o'clock in the afternoon, Coates's detachment had taken cover in the Quenby slave houses and the Americans held positions around the two-story main dwelling house. None of the accounts say what the owners of Quenby, or the slaves, were doing at this time; but all those who had not fled for their lives had to make a decision and take sides. On the slave street stood some twelve cabins made of clay. When the seven hundred patriots led by Francis Marion and General Thomas Sumter attacked, they were easily repelled. The clay walls absorbed the American musket fire, giving safe haven to the British. Marion later wrote that Coates's men had been "posted in houses with Clay Walls which was very Difficult to penetrate without a field piece," meaning that nothing would have done damage but a cannonball. The firefight continued for three hours, the British inflicting most of the casualties. Marion and Sumter withdrew at dusk, with sixty killed or wounded, to the British count of six dead, thirty-eight wounded. The dead from both sides were buried along the road leading up to Quenby bridge.

The Americans lost the fight but won back control of the countryside. Strawberry and Silk Hope plantations went back to their owners, and the British retreated to Charleston, never to come up the river again. When the occupation ended, the Ball plantations were wrecked—storehouses empty, buildings damaged, rice fields gone to seed. And everywhere the slave streets looked abandoned.

The fugitive workers would be known as black Loyalists, because they remained loyal to the king's cause. Most worked for the British Army as laborers or laundresses, messengers or stablehands, though some attached themselves to officers, whom they served as valets and cooks. Others were kidnapped by soldiers who treated them as loot from the war, eventually to be sold. A lucky few—among them Boston, from Tranquil Hill—managed to get completely free of all masters. Boston had taken the surname "King," maybe in deference to King George III, who had guaranteed his freedom.

When Cornwallis finally gave up, the general marched his army north toward the final battles of the war, at Yorktown, Virginia, and perhaps one or two thousand black fugitives went with him. Boston King found another way out, boarding a warship bound for New York. In the memoir he later published, King recalls his flight from South Carolina with unemotional calm: "I went to Charles-Town, and entered on board a man of war. [W]e were going to Chesepeak-bay . . . stayed in the bay two days, and then sailed for New-York, where I went on shore."

The *Memoirs of the Life of Boston King*, a twenty-page autobiography printed in Britain in 1798, represents one of the earliest pieces of writing in English composed by an ex-slave. Years later, when the abolition movement gained momentum, hundreds of life histories would be printed under the names of people who escaped. The story of Boston King predates all but a few of them. In his memoir, King says little about his education but mentions that his father used to read to his family. "He worked in the field till about three in the afternoon, and then went into the woods and read till sunset," King wrote. It was a rare thing that a slave could read and write, but by whatever means, Boston's father had become literate. It is likely he taught his son something of what he knew.

Boston King wrote his memoir near the end of his life, and there is little in his tale about the Ball family. As a fugitive, he was careful not to say much about his former owners, since the rest of his people were left behind on the plantation and could be dealt with harshly by an angry reader. Rather than dwell on his childhood, King focused on scenes from his long journey out of captivity.

"[In New York] I went into the jail to see a lad whom I was acquainted with," he wrote. "When I saw him, his feet were fastened in the stocks, and at night both his hands. This was a terrifying sight to me, as I expected to meet with the same kind of treatment, if taken in the act of attempting to regain my liberty." Plantation owners clamored for the return of their property, some coming to New York from far down South to make a search. The Continental Army helped masters recapture people from behind British lines, and King remembered these kidnappings, which could take place without warning:

> [W]e saw our old masters coming from Virginia, North-carolina, and other parts, and seizing upon their slaves in the streets of New-York, or even dragging them out of their beds. Many of the slaves had very cruel masters, so that the thoughts of returning home with them embittered life to us. For some days we lost our appetite for food, and sleep departed from our eyes.

For several months King found himself again taken captive, this time by whites in Brunswick, New Jersey. Then he escaped once more. Held by rebel forces, Brunswick lay against the Raritan River, while the British camp stood several miles away, on Staten Island. King wrote:

> I . . . observed, that when it was low water the people waded across the river; tho' at the same time I saw there were guards posted at the place to prevent the escape of prisoners and slaves. . . . [At the end of a Sunday, his captors in bed, King made his way to the bank.] [A]bout one o'clock in the morning I went down to the riverside, and found the guards were either asleep or in the tavern. I instantly entered into the river, but when I

was a little distance from the opposite shore, I heard the sentinels disputing among themselves: One said, 'I am sure I saw a
man cross the river.' Another replied, 'There is no such thing.'
It seems they were afraid to fire at me, or make an alarm, lest
they should be punished for their negligence. . . . I traveled till
about five in the morning. . . . [King hid himself the following
day, and the next night, stole a boat.] I proceeded forward, thro'
bushes and marshes, near the road, for fear of being discovered.
When I came to the river, opposite Staten Island, I found a boat;
and altho' it was very near a whale-boat, yet I ventured into it,
and cutting the rope, got safe over. The [British] commanding
officer, when informed of my case, gave me a passport, and I
proceeded to New-York.

When the United States claimed victory over the British in the South,
the Ball Loyalists were called to account for having sided with the
enemy. In early 1782, Wambaw Elias, his family, and at least two other
Ball Tories huddled in Charleston with the defeated British. Word came
that Wambaw plantation and its people were to be seized by the Americans in an act of vigilante justice. On February 24, in a last desperate
act, Wambaw Elias took off into the country with a detachment of British
cavalry, aiming to capture the people on the Wambaw slave street and
carry them to Charleston. Arriving at the plantation, the company tried
to corral the unarmed blacks, and the embittered colonel managed to
kidnap some workers, but most escaped into the woods.

Wambaw Elias knew the British cause was lost and he would soon
have to leave South Carolina. The raid having failed, Elias settled on
another plan to force his slaves to follow him out of the country. He
sent instructions to an overseer still at Wambaw to withhold food from
the black people, but the overseer evidently refused the order and continued to distribute provisions. In a letter, Wambaw Elias complained
about the white man's defiance: "[R]ice and corn [were] supplyd my
Negroes contrary to my positive order. I directed they should not be
supplyd in order that I might get them down [to Charleston], but my
order was not regarded." Colonel Ball believed that by starving people
he could make them obey.

The slaves at Wambaw were next attacked by the Americans. A

company of rebel militia went to the plantation and seized several dozen workers, but the majority once again fled into the forest. The soldiers took the unlucky captives down the Santee River to Georgetown, on the coast north of Charleston. There, on June 22, 1782, fifty-two former Wambaw workers, consisting of nine families, were separated from each other and sold. The American patriots took home £1,553 for their work.

The sale left a final group of perhaps a hundred still on the plantation. These families, who had twice evaded capture, were finally sold by their owner, Wambaw Elias, to his cousin and fellow Tory, Third Elias. Evidently with the help of British soldiers, Colonel Ball grabbed the final group and hauled them to Comingtee. Third Elias of Kensington signed promissory notes for £8,000 and took possession of the black village. With this deal Wambaw Elias had the guaranty of money, and he and his wife, Catherine, and their children fled with the British after they surrendered Charleston. The other Ball Loyalists, who had acted less fiercely for the king, stayed behind.

In mid-December 1782, a flotilla assembled in Charleston harbor for the final evacuation. In addition to Colonel Ball and family, between 5,500 and 6,000 black Loyalists climbed aboard. Some were runaways hoping to get their freedom; others were captives of British officers, new masters; still more belonged to fleeing whites, who had no intention of freeing them. As fugitive blacks, they had no papers and no defenses, and their destiny would not be sweet. Most who left seem to have gone to Florida, which was soon to be given to Spain, and to the Crown's colony of Jamaica. Between 1775 and 1787, the black population of Jamaica rose by sixty thousand, a good number coming from the United States. In the Caribbean, a few Carolinians lived out their lives in freedom, and some stayed under the rule of new bosses, as servants. Many, however, were put back into the labor market, seized by traders who sold them to plantations around the islands.

Not surprisingly, Wambaw Elias and family did better. After a period in Florida, they made their way to England. Wambaw Elias was the first member of the Ball clan to go back to Britain since Red Cap had arrived in America in 1698, but by this time three generations had passed, and Red Cap's American descendants had lost all ties. Wambaw Elias arrived in the mother country as a stranger. He did not make much of an effort to renew family connections. Perhaps he was unsure of himself, or he might have worried that the Devon Balls, who had never tasted American wealth such as his, would be beneath him. He wrote simply, "I enquired when passing through Devonshire about people of our Name & was told their was several familys in good sircumstanceis."

In England, Wambaw Elias seems to have missed wielding the power of an American master. "The servants [here] are a very troublesome sett of people," he wrote to his Loyalist cousin in Charleston. But Colonel Ball was relieved to find that a royal commission had been established to compensate Loyalist Americans for their lost estates. Elias filed a claim for Wambaw, asking for £23,573 from the Crown and locating witnesses among other Carolinians who might support his story about what he was once worth. As he waited for his hearing, Elias wrote frequent letters to his cousin in America, always asking about the £8,000 due for the last Wambaw slaves. Finally, the hearing was called, and among other witnesses a man named Francis Peyre proved to be a good talker. Peyre corroborated the colonel's claim but added in passing that "Mr Ball was always ashamed to possess below 2 and 300 Negroes." Whatever his shame, Wambaw Elias was given £12,700 sterling from the British Treasury, and a lifetime pension. The colonel and his family would live well on this bounty, and on the money they finally got from America for the Wambaw people.

Moving to the outskirts of Bristol, Wambaw Elias set himself up as a rice sales agent, or factor. He sold Carolina rice on the British market, for a commission, and exported tools and manufactured goods to America. His clients were the handful of Southern planters he had managed to keep as friends. Colonel Ball's children married into English high gentry families, and for decades he wrote a stream of vituperative letters to relatives in South Carolina, criticizing their new nation. Wambaw Elias never returned to America, and died thirty-eight years later, in 1822.

On December 31, 1781, Henry Laurens was released from the Tower of London in exchange for Lord Cornwallis, who had surrendered in October and was captive in the United States. In 1782, Laurens went to Paris, where he met the American delegation that negotiated the preliminary terms of the peace. In France, Laurens joined his old colleagues from the Continental Congress—John Adams, John Jay, Benjamin Franklin, and Franklin's son, William Temple Franklin—and, after some haggling, the treaty was signed. (The formal Treaty of Paris was signed September 3, 1783.) An American-born painter, forty-five-year-old Benjamin West, depicted a meeting of the preliminary negotiations. The painting shows the Americans around a table, with Laurens standing behind Benjamin Franklin, a copy of the terms unrolled in front of them. It is a curious work, the left half of the canvas full of the Americans, the right side nearly blank. West abandoned the painting midway through (and, though he lived another thirty-five years, he never went back to it). He earned a rich living from British patrons, most of whom no doubt scorned the new republic, and evidently there was some grousing about this painting that celebrated the revolutionaries. On the right of the canvas, West had planned room for the figure of Richard Oswald, Henry Laurens's onetime business partner in London, who had helped to get Laurens out of the Tower and who represented the British in the Paris talks. Oswald, a slave trader born in Scotland, held leases on Bunce Island, in the Sierra Leone River in West Africa, the prison from which Laurens, in Charleston, extracted many workers, some of whom he sold to his Ball in-laws. West depicted Laurens, himself fresh from prison, as patchy and ghostlike.

Back in Charleston, Laurens's nephew Third Elias Ball prepared for the worst. He had switched sides in the middle of the war, from rebel to Loyalist, and now the victors looked for revenge. The South Carolina legislature passed a resolution that Comingtee plantation would be confiscated as punishment against the Ball family. A few months later Third Elias sought and won a reversal of the judgment on the defense that he had started out the fight with the Americans. The reprieve angered Charleston whites. Third Elias wrote to a relative:

> [P]eople in my situation . . . we are in general lookd on as black sheep. . . . I was told by a man I was slitely acquainted with that there was upwards of 600 men in the town was determind we should not remain in the State above ten days & that hand-bills was published by them in consequence of those determinations. I felt very quare [queer] on this information. . . . I wish my concerns would permit my going to England.

In the end, Third Elias was not lynched. The threat of revenge faded, and although he longed for safety in the mother country, Third Elias established himself at Limerick plantation. His brother, John Ball, the rebel, settled down with his wife, Jane, on Kensington. The two siblings got over their political differences and began to work together once again.

A slave list made the year after the war names only 123 workers belonging to the brothers, though before the Revolution there would have been twice that number. John and Third Elias had lost much. Because so many had fled, the Ball slaves were now young, mostly in their teens, or old, some of them no doubt wishing they had taken their chances with the British. A letter written by Third Elias gives a sense of the situation after the war: "[S]ettling my plantations almost anew, [I am] plagued almost out of my life with the negroes not knowing how to work or an unwillingness in them and running away."

In the summer of 1783, in New York, British ships loaded with soldiers and black Loyalists prepared for the last evacuations from America. At least three fugitives who had fled the Balls in South Carolina, and made their way eight hundred miles north, readied to leave. Because American masters considered the escaped workers to be stolen property, before the ships were allowed to sail, the United States demanded a list of the runaways in hopes of later getting reparations from Parliament. Among the names on the list is that of Frank Symons. Symons, forty-five, was described by an American inspector as "formerly slave to Edward Simmons [of] Charleston S°Car°." Edward was the husband of Lydia Ball Simons, who had grown up at Kensington, and the couple lived in the townhouse Lydia inherited from Second Elias Ball. Frank Symons had apparently made his escape from the Ball house, then traveled up the East Coast, where he boarded the British frigate, the *William & Mary*. Another person making a getaway was twenty-year-old Polly Shubrick, who had escaped from Thomas Shubrick, a nephew of Elizabeth Ball. Polly Shubrick, only fifteen when she left Charleston, boarded the *Providence*.

On July 31, at a dock in New York, the fugitive Boston King boarded the *Abondance*, in the company of 132 others. When King walked onto the gangplank, he was checked off by an inspector, who took down this description: "Boston King, 23, stout fellow, formerly the property of Rich. Waring of Charleston, South Carolina . . . left him 4 years ago." Aboard ship, Boston King was accompanied by his wife of three years, Violet King, an escaped slave from Wilmington, North Carolina, whom he had met in New York.

"[S]hips were fitted out, and furnished with every necessary for conveying us to Nova Scotia," wrote King years later.

The fate of Boston King, his wife, and the other New York fugitives would be somewhat better than that of the Charleston runaways who found themselves recaptured in the Caribbean. Nova Scotia was then a British province that did not join the new republic and that Britain had chosen as a place to relocate black Americans. On this cold peninsula lived a group of Native people known as the Mi'kmaq. Ten thousand French peasants, whose families dated from the time when Nova Scotia was a colony of France, had been exiled in 1755, and their houses stood empty.

The black fugitives, arriving in Nova Scotia in the summer, congregated in the settlements of Birchtown, Preston, and Tracadie. Boston and Violet King, and the other Loyalists, met a cold reception from local whites, but eventually King found work as a carpenter and, later, a fisherman. The couple lived in the black village at Shelburne, then moved to Birchtown. At some point in his journey, Boston King experienced a religious conversion and became a Christian. Perhaps his rare good fortune had ignited his faith, which grew so strong that in Nova Scotia he began to preach.

"In the year 1785, I began to exhort both in families and prayer-meetings, and the Lord graciously afforded me his assisting presence," King wrote.

King became a Methodist minister, founded a church whose congregation consisted of escaped blacks, and became a leader among the black Loyalists. Although he had survived a harrowing escape and had to struggle to make his way in a strange land, he believed his situation to be far better than that of some. "I found my mind drawn out to commiserate my poor brethren in Africa," he wrote. "As I had not the least prospect at that time of ever seeing Africa, I contented myself with pitying and praying for the poor benighted inhabitants of that country which gave birth to my forefathers."

The white inhabitants of Nova Scotia did not welcome the influx of black Americans, and as the years passed, the lives of the immigrants worsened. Land that was promised to them never materialized, and the black villages were subjected to attacks. For their part, many workers raised on large, fecund plantations could not adjust to the small plots and cold soils of the north. In 1792, nine years after the evacuation to Nova Scotia, the British government called for another resettlement plan that would bring some twelve hundred people to a new colony, in Africa.

The destination of this new exodus would be a port where the king had influence, a peninsula on the western bulge of the continent, at Sierra Leone. Though Sierra Leone was a major slave center, home to Bunce Island, the British organizers of the colony included several abolitionists who hoped to stamp out the human market with the settlement of free blacks. Boston and Violet King, who were more comfortable than most in Nova Scotia and under no obligation to leave, signed on to the scheme. "Their intention being, as far as possible in their power, to put a stop to the abominable slave-trade," King wrote, "I resolved to embrace the opportunity of visiting that country."

A flotilla was outfitted to set sail, and at age thirty-two, accompanied by Violet and many from his congregation, Boston King walked onto yet another gangplank. On March 6, 1792, he and the other colonists arrived on the western shore of Africa, once again to begin a new life. Boston King became one of the first citizens of a society founded by ex-slaves, a founding father, so to speak. The colonists called their settlement Freetown.

Some years after he arrived in Africa, Boston King sat down to write the story of his unusual life. He had seen much and had become something of a weary man from all of it. "It is by no means an agreeable task to write an account of my life," King began. Thinking back to his old masters, Ann Ball and Richard Waring, King offered a stark assessment: "In the former part of my life I suffered greatly from the cruelty and injustice of the Whites, which induced me to look upon them, in general, as our enemies."

12

>-+<>-0-<+-<

THE WIDTH OF THE REALM

There is a joke in my family about the way we used to marry each other: Each time a Ball baby was born on the plantation, his or her parents would hold the infant up to the light. If they could see through the child, the next person in line to marry was told to pick someone from farther away.

Marriage between cousins was common in the planter families—rather, it was expected. To choose a mate from inside the cousinhood seemed right, because a wedding within the clan kept intact estates and black villages that would otherwise be divided by fresh blood. Since other colonial families did the same, the fund of suitable mates never grew much. Anthropologists call it endogamy—the prohibition of marriage outside the group, in this case the caste of slave owners. The Anglican Church, citing the book of Leviticus, banned sex between close kin. Nearly all the rice families, including the Balls, were careful Episcopalians, but they did not mind trespassing the old Mosaic law. So they married each other, as an aunt of mine used to say, "until they all grew tails."

The habit ended when the plantations died. My father told me that when he was a young man, he dated one of his first cousins. The two went to dances, tea parties, events at the local college—and they might have married had they not been cousins. When my father met my mother, Janet Rowley, it was in her hometown, New Orleans, some seven hundred miles from Charleston and the watery Ball blood. His choice to marry someone "from off," as it was called, was part of a new family trend, one that developed in the twentieth century and saved us from genetic backwash.

The third generation of the Balls came into its role after the American Revolution. Earlier, I described how John Ball, in the middle of the war, married his first cousin, Jane Ball, daughter of John's uncle, John Coming Ball. Jane was a delicate-looking woman from Hyde Park, the plantation next to John's own, Kensington. She seems to have been devout and dutiful, to judge from her letters, which dwell on the subject of God and her happiness as a mother. Jane's health gave her trouble throughout life, however. Sometime in her thirties, she developed an uncontrolled swelling in one hand. The hand grew so large, and so painful, that Jane was obliged to keep it on a pillow whenever she sat at a table. "[M]y hand has prevented me any social intercourse with my Neighbors," she wrote a relative, "being [that I am] confined to the House." Jane's husband, a practical man, thought the solution would be for Jane to give up a few fingers. "Your mother has been very poorly with those unfortunate fingers of hers [which] have continually increased in size," John told one of his sons. "I am sure there is one cure & that is, to get them cut off . . . but she can't bear to hear of it & I am afraid will never stand the amputating knife."

John Ball, the former dandy, was a gourmand with an appetite for large living. In a painting he commissioned about 1800, he appears with grape-red cheeks and intelligent eyes, a full head of red-brown hair, and a satisfied smirk. I can only guess at his weight. Once, while vacationing in Newport, Rhode Island, John wrote a relative, "I was too fat before [and] coming here will, & does increase it, which encumbers me vastly. . . . I believe if I once get to Kensington again it will be difficult to move me." By 1790 John and Jane Ball, approaching thirty, had five sons.

Third Elias, John's older brother, lived at Limerick, a half-hour walk from Kensington. The only image of Third Elias—or Old Mas' 'Lias—dates from his childhood, when a portrait of him was made dressed as a little lord, with a glamorous coat, haughty posture, and blond curls. Although Third Elias never married, I believe he had a companion in a slave woman named Nancy. At his death, possessed of hundreds of people, Third Elias gave freedom to this single woman: "[Nancy] shall be permitted . . . to reside in the House she at Present Occupies, with the use of her Garden, & be supported on the Plantation with Provisions, during her life, and . . . on the first day of March in every Year, so long as she shall live, [my nephew] shall pay her, in good & lawful Money, the sum of one hundred dollars." Manumission accompanied by money was a rare thing. A pension almost never came as a simple gesture of kindness but rather was the sign of a special relationship. Every subsequent spring, the nephew noted in his ledger that he had dutifully paid Nancy's income, proving that the Balls took her seriously, and that exceptions to the rules of cousin-marriage might be tolerated.

On August 8, 1786, when Second Elias Ball had died at Kensington at age seventy-six, his will had left two plantations to his eldest son, Third Elias, two to his younger, John, and a house in Charleston to his daughter, Lydia. In the will, the old man had advised his heirs to do one of two things with their money, either to lend it out at interest or to "buy Young Slaves."

A few days after the funeral, twenty-six-year-old John Ball sat down to write a memoir of his kindred, a little ode to his own blood. He titled the eight-page manuscript "A Short History of the Family of the Balls." In the handwritten text, John recounted the story of Red Cap's immigration to America, described each of Red Cap's children and grandchildren, and added a mandate to his descendants to write their own memoirs "for the satisfaction of posterity." John's little bit of literature was a sign of the high role that the family saw to be theirs. "I hope one of my sons will put this work into better language," he wrote, "and continue the genealogy, with an injunction for its continuation from generation to generation."

With their father's death, John and Third Elias divided "their people." The Revolutionary War had depopulated the rice fields, and the number of slaves at Kensington stood at 123. The brothers' aunt, Judith Ball, had died recently on Hyde Park, leaving thirty-eight people, who went to the hands of her children. On each of some five other plantations, between fifty and a hundred people lived as the property of Ball cousins and kin. On January 22, 1787, John and Third Elias summoned the remaining Kensington workers. The brothers evidently mustered the village into a line, then walked along the row, studying the black bodies, assigning each person a value, the better to make a division. When the process was finished, Third Elias marched off to Limerick with sixty-two people, valued at £2,790, and John ordered the remaining sixty-one back to their cabins.

In 1790, the first census of the United States recorded a national population of 3,929,214. Of these, 697,624 were black slaves, or about one in six people. Among the more than ninety-six thousand households in the new country that included slaves, nearly eighty thousand were in the South.

With their conspicuous wealth, even if depleted, the Balls saw themselves in the mainstream of the nation's history; but things had changed in the North. At the dawn of the United States, the English writer Samuel Johnson wisecracked about the Americans, "How is it that we hear the loudest yells for liberty among the drivers of Negroes?" After the Declaration of Independence, the country began to answer. In 1785, the New York Manumission Society was formed—and John Jay, a signer of the peace treaty with Britain, was appointed its president. Whereas in South Carolina slaves confiscated from people who had opposed the Revolution were sold, in New York individuals in the same category were now freed. Schools for black children opened in Philadelphia and New Jersey. In Pennsylvania, a group calling itself the Abolition Society began agitating for the end of the whole system, and similar associations soon took shape in Delaware and Rhode Island. By 1790, each of the New England states had passed laws that gradually or immediately abolished human property. That year, Boston became the first city in the United States with no slaves at all.

To the Ball family and friends, it appeared that a menace was gathering above the Mason-Dixon line, the border that separated Maryland from Pennsylvania. Instead of stonewalling, however, the family first responded to these changes and life began to get a little easier down home. To judge from his correspondence, John Ball heard the message of humanity and even philosophized about the different political climate. Writing to one of his sons, John offered a new theory of the work system, one that combined compassion with exploitation and emphasized the duty of the master toward his people:

[I]f revolutionary principles do not prevail to the destruction of southern property, you may enjoy the good things of this world

& relieve many of your distress'd brethren. —feed the poor &
clothe the naked—but always have in mind that our first charitable attentions are due to our slaves—cause the sick to be well
nursed and attended—the young, aged, and decrepid to be
clothed & fed with the same care as the most useful—the well
to be treated with mildness humanity and justice—consider their
situation and strive to make the bitter portion of slavery as comfortable as the local situation of your native state will admit.

In the wake of the Declaration of Independence, the Balls took comfort in a new explanation of their world. The plantations had a harsh
beginning, yes, but things had moderated; and in the place of grasping
violence there had developed a society based on a wise paternalism. To
be a slave owner now, after the war, was to be something like a strict
father, demanding with one hand, rewarding with the other.

In this period, letters between people in the big houses speak more
noticeably about the workers' health, and show a new degree of concern.
"I hope Hagar and all the sick are getting better," Jane Ball wrote in
one of many notes. "I am sorry to hear there is so much sickness [at
the house] in Hasell Street. It must have been a complete hospital in
our yard." It wasn't only talk. At the beginning of the nation, the Balls
turned some of their profits toward better medical care on the slave
street. In the past, rice planters used to double as physicians. "[M]y
father in his day had been very expert with the Lancet," John Ball told
a relative. Plantation medicine once consisted largely of bleeding, the
practice of cutting the flesh with a blade, or lancet, usually at the affected part of the body. Now, however, trained doctors brought a trunkful
of cures. Previously, a single epidemic of smallpox might carry a whole
village to the grave, but now the Balls took care to protect their slaves
against infectious disease. For example, Alexander Garden, a physician
employed by John Ball, used the new smallpox vaccine to inoculate
numerous people on Kensington—charging a high price.

The family had hired doctors before, but never under contract. Back
River was a plantation owned by John's twenty-seven-year-old cousin,
John Coming Ball, a war veteran on the British side. John Coming had
a reputation in the family for fecklessness, but after the truce he acquired Back River, a twelve-hundred-acre tract with about eighty people, and, belying his poor fame, opened an account with a physician in

the county, Samuel McCormick. For the next several years, McCormick made regular visits to Back River, and left bills that show the changes in medicine.

In February 1785, field hands Pompey and Binah evidently picked up some bacteria that opened sores and inflamed their skin. McCormick gave them each an "antipsoric ointment" to calm their itching. Binah's condition went away, but Pompey's lingered. On a return call, McCormick's answer was an "ointment lint dressing." Three weeks later one sore needed further attention, and McCormick applied more dressing, but Pompey's wound still did not heal. The doctor came back a fourth time and applied "ceraic ointment," a stiff dressing made of beeswax dissolved in alcohol and mixed with lard. After that Pompey's skin seems to have healed, or else the patient got tired of McCormick's constant handling. Intestinal worms were a common ailment, especially among the young, many of whom died from them. To one girl, McCormick gave "3 anthelmintic powders," hoping to kill the parasites. When a field hand named Marcus fell ill, perhaps with a flu, the doctor thought some strong purges would bring him back. One day, in two rapid swipes, he gave Marcus "a vomit" followed by "aperient salts" that emptied his bowels. The diarrheic purge seems to have been one of the doctor's favored prescriptions, handed out dozens of times.

In addition to such violent treatments, which spread as much pain as repair, the Ball slaves had alternative medicines—cures brought from West Africa and mingled with Native American medicine. At one point, John Ball wrote a friend for advice about dysentery, which could quickly kill a person with its bloody diarrhea and dehydration. A bit later, he received the answer that a cure might be found in his own backyard. "[T]he plant [I] mentioned is the Binnay, which is cultivated in almost every plantation in [South Carolina] by our Negroes for their own use," the friend wrote. "They commonly pound the seed and parch it, and when thus prepared its taste is exactly like our parched ground nuts; they also use it frequently to make soup." The Balls were probably aware of the non-chemical medicine and previously had avoided it; now, from time to time, they began to turn to black doctors themselves. On one occasion white physicians apparently did not know what to do after a field hand was struck by a poisonous snake. John later noted in his account book that he personally "paid Mrs. Motte's black man Jack for curing a fellow of a snake bite."

There is evidence that among the black doctors who did business on the Ball plantations, some may have had an actual role as priests. One trail of religion would seem to go back to the powerful Yoruba culture of the coasts around the Niger delta or, alternatively, to the vicinity of the Congo River. At three Ball places—Limerick, Mepkin, and Pimlico—archeological digs on the slave streets have brought up small clay pots that healers may well have used to prepare medicines. The Bakongo people live in a region near the old slave ports of Angola, from which tens of thousands came to South Carolina. Bakongo culture dominated the African coast at the time the Balls bought most of their workers. In Bakongo practice, almighty God, *Nzambi*, has a power that can be influenced through medicine. Priests or mediums make sacred medicines called *minkisi*, concoctions of plants, in clay pots about the size of half a cantaloupe.

In the 1790s, John Ball paid Robin, a free person of color, as a plantation doctor. Robin's first patient seems to have been a woman named Hagar. In 1795, John had leased Hagar from a neighbor, and during her tour of duty, Hagar slept with a Ball slave who was carrying a sexual disease. Hagar's owner, Joseph Willingham, asked Mr. Ball to hire Robin for a cure that white medicine could not provide. John later wrote Willingham to report that he had done so: "I am to pay Robin 30 [shillings] for curing Hagar of the venereal disease (by your desire)." Robin must have done something right, because records show that he stayed on around Kensington for another twenty-five years. During that time Robin saved money from his work, which he deposited with John Ball, who kept a careful account of it.

The plantation system held on after the Revolution, despite its weakened state. John, the rebel, and Third Elias, the Tory, had put aside their differences in order to rebuild the family dynasty. At first, some of the Balls teetered on the verge of bankruptcy, and Third Elias wrote a cousin several times with the complaint that he couldn't pay his debts. It appeared that the old ways might be forced to evolve—perhaps in the direction of free labor—but a change in farming methods intervened to help reinforce the previous arrangements.

Earlier, I described how, in the time of Red Cap, most rice was grown in fields carved out of the inland swamps, and black workers irrigated the crop from reserves of water created by dammed streams. Some plantation owners worried that these fields had been exhausted. Meanwhile, miles of untouched marshes lined the channels of the Cooper River. Each day at high tide, the backflow from the sea swelled the river and flooded the marsh; at ebb the water dropped, exposing the mudflats. After the war, planters looked on the mud at the edge of their property and saw it as potential cropland.

Throughout the 1780s and 1790s, the Balls and other planters directed their slaves to move the rice fields from the swamps down to the banks of the stream, creating fields that made use of the tides. The process had begun in some places before the war, but now it proceeded apace. To reclaim the marsh as arable land required earthworks. First, the workers constructed levees, or rice banks, around rectangular plots laid out in the mudflat. A rice bank stood about six feet high and had one or more openings so that tidewater could be admitted to the field. The flow was controlled by a large wooden sluice, or trunk, which resembled a guillotine with the dimensions of a barn door. When opened at high tide, the trunk allowed the tide to flood the field. With the trunk closed, the water stayed on the crop. Opened again at ebb, the trunk drained the plot and the field dried hard.

It may have been that this method, tidal rice farming, was brought to America by West Africans, who showed the technique to the Carolina landlords. A drawing made by an English traveler in Sierra Leone in the year 1794 shows rectangular rice fields surrounded by banks, with a portal for water to pour in and out. Tidal agriculture would not have been taught to Africans by whites, because the traffic of culture between Africa and America moved in a single direction. Before tidewater farming, each field had to be weeded by hand with a hoe. By watering the plots and trapping the flood, workers now suffocated some of the weeds in a bath known as the "long water," while the rice plants standing above the flow survived. Tidal farming saved weeks of stooped-over hoeing during the season, and fewer workers were needed to cope with more land.

Third Elias had more people than his brother. He had bought about a hundred workers in a deal with his Tory cousin Wambaw Elias, before the cousin fled for his life and for England. These workers transformed Limerick. A map of the property from 1786 shows 95 acres of rice fields in production, while a second map from a decade later shows 135 acres of fields, nearly half again as much. Third Elias, who also owned Comingtee, was complimented by his kin for converting the land. "Your present plan on improving and cultivating your tide lands at the T, I approve of much," a cousin wrote to him. "You might remember I strongly recommended it to you."

The work of making the new fields fell heavily on the remaining Ball workers, because merely to build the rice banks was a vast project. First, the workers cleared the marsh of trees and brush. Then, men, and probably women as well, dug canals and cleared ditches on the edge of the fields. Next, they moved hundreds of tons of earth by oxcart and shaped the miles of banks by hand. Finally, carpenters constructed dozens of the big rice trunks required for irrigation. By 1800, the combined rice banks on the plantations along the east branch of the Cooper River measured some fifty-five miles and contained more than six million cubic feet of earth. The building went on for years, and by the time of the ratification of the Constitution, the rice boom had returned. Rice exports from Charleston grew by half, from 14,500 tons in 1784 to 23,400 tons in 1789.

Third Elias rewarded the people who brought him back to solvency with a shower of extra clothing. In summer of 1787, he distributed great quantities of new blankets and cloth, as well as "6 dozen checked handkerchiefs." Then he rewarded himself, buying new workers with his windfall profits. In one deal Third Elias added twenty-six tenants to the Limerick cabins, including a young couple named Charles and Peggy, five families with children, and a single man, Cudjo. A couple of years later, he bought again, though this time he carped about the price. "Negroes bought the 30th of March . . . at Ben Steed's sale," Third Elias wrote, "Thom & Molly, Aspath & Dido, Cuffy & Amy, Dublin & Bella—for the enormous sum of . . . £1365." The African slave trade to the United States had been temporarily halted by the Constitutional Convention in 1787, as white Americans felt their first doubts about it. A few years later, it would be opened again before a final ban in 1808. Elias's new people probably came either from Virginia or from less successful rice planters going out of business.

The new workers made a difference, but the population of Ball slaves would have grown even without them. From the account books, it is possible to reconstruct the growth of families. The clans of Angola Amy and Priscilla—to name just two women born in West Africa and bought by the Balls in the 1700s—made up large kin groups on the family lands. Amy and Priscilla now presided over their descendants as aging matriarchs. By the end of the 1700s, the women's children and grandchildren gave birth to several babies a year, yielding dozens of workers to the rice fields and kitchens.

Although evidence is sketchy, it appears that after profits returned, new cabins now went up along the slave streets. Among the family papers is a two-page formula "for making a tar floor," dated July 1794 and signed by Third Elias and John. The recipe describes how the "hands" are to make a hard, dry floor that can be swept and washed clean. Along with the floor formula, the brothers also wrote down a recipe for making whitewash. The thick exterior paint, concocted of boiled hides and lime, would become the standard coat for the houses of field hands, according to a family member who later saw and described the slave cabins. In 1792, a rice planter advertised in the *South Carolina Gazette* for someone who could build new cabins on his land, implying that other planters were doing so at this time. The ad describes a two-room house whose style would be typical on many of the Ball tracts: "A negro house, twenty Feet long and ten Feet wide, with Posts in the Ground, six Feet Story, a Division in the Middle, a Door to each Tenement, and a good Pad-lock to each Door." And not least, throughout this period John Ball employed a team of carpenters consisting of seven men—Bristol, Daniel, Julius, Marcus, Peter, Pompey, and Strephon. According to their owner's notes, the men were busy all the time. Under the influence of the new paternal ideal, it stands to reason John would have had them build new housing.

The Balls took back their lifestyle as rice barons. On one tax return, John noted that he owned no fewer than ten carriages. In his own tax filing for 1790, Third Elias, the thirty-nine-year-old bachelor, noted that he owned three plantations—Strawberry, Comingtee, and Limerick— consisting of 8,528 acres and 246 people. The fief made him the second largest slaveholder in St. John's Parish. The largest was his uncle, Henry Laurens, with 298 people. A few places back on the list, with 188 hands, was brother John.

In May 1787, delegates came together in Philadelphia for the Constitutional Convention, where they debated a new form of government that would replace the Articles of Confederation. The subject of slavery shadowed the chambers. Arguing about population counts for the purpose of taxes based on density, Southern delegates claimed that slaves were not chiefly people but property, like livestock, and therefore should not be counted. When the issue was the apportionment of seats in the new House of Representatives, however, Southerners fought to put black workers in the category of human beings, because doing so gave the landlords more influence. Northern delegates ridiculed the double standard, but the Southern landlords would not move. As a compromise, the Constitution of the United States would include the "three-fifths rule": in matters of both taxes and representation, an enslaved black would be counted as sixty percent of a white person. Two years later, when the First Congress was seated, slavery appeared first on the agenda. When antislavery groups petitioned the legislature, the skittish new lawmakers coughed up another compromise. This time they issued a report that recommended Congress take up the subject—but only in twenty years, after everyone had cooled off.

The Balls heard the message of democracy, and it frightened them. Although the subject was smothered by Congress, it flared more strongly abroad. Wambaw Elias Ball, the Tory in England, began to send reports to his American kin on the terrible success of the French Revolution, which had erupted across the English Channel. Wambaw Elias dismissed the idea of equal rights and made it clear that he, for one, had "so harty a detestation of the French Leveling principles." After Louis XVI was removed and the Constituent Assembly in Paris produced the Declaration of the Rights of Man, the expatriate Ball worried about what might happen next. "I hope those French dogs will be thoroughly humbled," he wrote. "Not content with destroying themselves, [they] wish to ruin all the nations around them."

The message from France was the collapse of the caste system and the redistribution of wealth, and soon the news came home to Charleston. In 1791, in the French colony of Saint Domingue, on the island of Hispaniola, whites were killed and hundreds of plantations burned in a rebellion of sugar slaves and free mulattoes led by François Toussaint L'Ouverture. Before long, some ten thousand white refugees sailed for the United States. A good number arrived—pockets empty, and terrified—in Charleston, where they became living examples of what democracy could mean.

On their farms, the Balls kept a worried lookout for people who might try to act out the lesson of Saint Domingue, which would eventually become the black nation of Haiti. Since colonial days, the rice planters had organized "slave patrols," ten or fifteen men who prowled the dirt roads at night, weapons drawn. The patrols interrogated black people, looked for runaways, and tormented the bold. A revolving system of assignments placed the Ball men on these dragnets every few weeks. In typical orders for the year 1792, John Ball received the following notice: "You are appointed Commander of the Patrol to ride at least once a Fortnight and more often as is necessary . . . from Hugers Bridge [at Limerick] to Comingtee inclusive." The commission listed fifteen men to police the neighborhood, including John, Third Elias, two cousins named Harleston, and several overseers.

John and Third Elias patrolled the east branch of the Cooper River, but on the west branch different companies held sway. One spring John received word from his overseer at a west branch plantation that two Ball slaves had been attacked by the patrol. According to the overseer, R. Matthews, it was a Sunday and the two men, Guy and Peter, were out on their own errands when the patrol stopped them and asked their business. Guy and Peter "had no passes," said Matthews, "however . . . in addition to beating the two men severely about the head and body, one of them was tied up and sorely whipped."

From the family's point of view, the disruptions in the business seemed always to be someone else's fault, coming from rebellious field hands or from France, never from the basic order in the rice fields. Increasingly, threats also came from the North. Slavery was ending in the Northern states, and that must have been both frightening and intriguing. The trouble was that the North, in addition to taking the reckless step of outlawing human property, was the better educated and more populous section of the country—and since the war had taken the lead in the national economy. Where South Carolina had no formal higher education, New England had genuine colleges. (A modest school had been incorporated in Charleston in 1785, and a slave trader named Benjamin Smith, brother-in-law of Elizabeth Ball, left £1,000 to endow it; but nobody took the result seriously.)

John Ball had traveled to Philadelphia before the Revolution, and perhaps he wanted to see the North again, the better to understand it. Or perhaps, with his sons growing up, he wanted to look into their schooling. For these and other reasons, in 1796 John suggested to Jane a trip up the East Coast.

In the early summer, the family readied itself for a five-month journey. The entourage consisted of John, Jane, their fourteen-year-old son John Jr., an unmarried cousin named Polly Smith, a footman called Adonis, and Binah, a domestic slave. (Though they shared the same names, this Adonis and Binah came from different families than the Adonis and Binah who would become forebears of Katie Heyward, or "Bright Ma," and whose story I've already told.) Binah, forty-one, and Adonis, probably in his late twenties, were Kensington's "show people." Adonis had been John Ball's valet for a decade, minding his wardrobe and handling his calls for food and drink. Both Binah and her children had served in the big house for years. According to a pocket-sized travelogue, John sent spending money ahead to New York—"$1500," he wrote, in the new currency of the dollar rather than the old English pound—and on June 11, 1796, the party of six went to a Charleston wharf to board the sloop *Romeo*.

Nine days later, the *Romeo* sailed through the narrows at the entrance of New York harbor. That evening, the Ball party checked into a boardinghouse near the foot of Manhattan run by a Mrs. Best, and the following day John bought a city directory and a map. New York, population thirty-five thousand, was already the largest city in the country, and the nation's commercial capital. With slavery on the wane, a Southern traveling party made a conspicuous sight on the street. There is evidence that the Balls, Adonis, and Binah were quite aware they had arrived in a new world, one in which the differences between server and served were supposed to appear less brutal. John's travelogue contains no personal observations, but much can be seen in the receipts from his expense record. One of the first things John did was to purchase new clothes for Adonis and Binah. Adonis got a pair of breeches and stockings, and later John hired a cobbler to produce a pair of shoes for Binah, who was accustomed to wearing "Negro shoes" if any. The two servants were in this way outfitted in a finery they never put on at home.

The matter of appearance settled, the Carolinians began to look around. On the first day in town, John noted that he gave Binah $1 and instructions to come back with six glasses of ice cream. With four whites and two blacks in the party, presumably everyone got a dish. Then, breaking more protocol, John arranged to give Adonis and Binah a spending allowance. The weekly sum was small, but the sight of a Southern slave spending money in New York made good diplomacy. On several nights, the Balls "went to the plays." At the same time, according to his notes, Adonis and Binah saw the circus at Rickets Amphitheatre. The Balls shopped and took carriage tours. One day John bought himself four pairs of ribbed silk stockings and a pound of hair powder for his wig. Jane Ball treated herself to her own silk stockings and three bottles of perfume.

After ten days of carousing, the Balls brought the New York leg of their journey to an end. They made their last big purchases, John a gold watch and chain (for a crisp $148) and Jane a closetful of clothes. The travelers settled with Mrs. Best—paying $84 for the rooms, and $117 for a memorable amount of liquor—and boarded a ship bound for Rhode Island.

Newport, Rhode Island, was a resort for rich families from Boston and New York, as well as increasing numbers of slave-owning Southerners. The Bostonians came with Irish servants, the Southerners with black. In New York the Ball entourage might have disappeared in the crowd, but in the small circle of Newport society, the pressure to put on a show was heavy indeed. The day after they arrived, John gave Adonis $4 to buy himself a hat and told him to distribute tips among any servants with whom the Balls might come in contact. A few days later the performance took another turn when John bought Adonis a new pair of boots. Adonis and Binah were likely aware of the theatrical nature of their master's doings, and knew they were to play well-born, well-treated slaves. In Newport the family went yachting, played cards, and did more shopping. John noted that while he and Jane went to a play, Adonis spent $1.50 "for riding out."

John Jr., the only child on the trip, was a meek boy in his teens. His father seems to have been thinking about where to send him for his education. Newport, where the family passed the summer months, lay within reach of Boston, the nation's intellectual center. At the end of the heat, on September 6, the Ball party set out for Boston to enjoy itself further, and perhaps to look at a school. Arriving the following afternoon, the family checked into a boardinghouse known as Mrs. Hatch's, on Federal Street. Two days later, John noted that he had paid a toll to cross the Charles River into Cambridge, home of Harvard College. John made no notes about this excursion, but two years later John Jr. would return to Cambridge as a Harvard freshman.

Back in Boston, John bought some cigars and books; then the Carolinians returned to Newport. The trip was nearly done. Before leaving for home, however, there was one important matter: as they packed to leave Rhode Island, John bought twelve kegs of pickled lobsters. When the travelers set sail for Charleston, the heavy, sloshing barrels were rolled aboard ship with them. By the first week of November, the lobsters and the Balls reached Kensington.

The trip to the North began a series of tours that the Balls would take up the East Coast in the company of black servants. Each time, a handful of house slaves had the privilege of seeing a world away from the work camps down South. On one of these junkets, in 1806, John's son Isaac traveled to Washington, D.C., accompanied by a free black man named Nat Ball. Nat Ball had been manumitted from Back River plantation and had taken the family name. When Isaac and Nat Ball visited Washington, the occupant of the President's mansion was a Virginian named Thomas Jefferson. "[We went] from Georgetown to Washington . . . to visit the President's house, with which I was much pleased," Isaac wrote home one day from the capital. "We met the President riding on horseback when we were on the way to the house, but as the visit was intended to the house and not the man, we proceeded."

John Ball Jr., the first child of John and Jane, had a reputation as being timid. In a portrait made when he was an adult, John Jr. does in fact look withdrawn. Third Elias gave the opinion that his nephew was intelligent but awkward. For a while, John Jr.'s parents thought to send him to university in London, in hopes of shaking him into adulthood, but weighing their son's personality, and mindful of American pride, they reconsidered.

Harvard College opened its doors in 1636, sixteen years after the Pilgrims dropped anchor at Plymouth. Letters of recommendation from John Jr.'s teachers did the trick, along with good money. Harvard sent word that in addition to references, a deposit of two hundred ounces of silver would be required. The family complied, and the boy was accepted. John Sr. once complained that "my education was too much neglected by my fond Father," and to judge from the letters he wrote his son, the father tried vicariously to improve on his schooling through the young man's own. "[Y]ou must be sensible that from your rank and fortune you might make a respectable figure in life," John Sr. wrote to his son. "Harvard College is certainly the most reputable within the U[nited] States & upon this ground I chose it for compleating your Education. . . . I prefer'd your being educated in America upon patriotic principles."

In July 1798, sixteen-year-old John Jr. sailed alone to Massachusetts and made his way to the campus. It consisted of four small buildings surrounded by some fields. There was a steepled church nearby, and a pasture where farmers grazed livestock. The student rented a room through an acquaintance his parents knew from Newport, and settled in.

John Jr. was one of sixty-seven young men in the entering class. His father wanted him to jump ahead, and thought money might help. "I see by one of the [school] rules that you might have enter'd higher in the College by paying so much for it," the elder John wrote. "Would it not have been better to do so?" John Jr. declined and set himself to the usual course of Latin, logic, mathematics, natural science, and philosophy. In addition to book learning, John Sr. was determined that the student keep up with other young scions. "Pray does any of the students at Harvard live in a higher or better stile than yourself?" the father asked. "[A]re there any respectable young gentlemen who keeps a servant & horse, or horses, do let me know."

The worried father also feared the pleasures that tempted rich young men away from home, especially sex and drinking. "Remember my son that I advise you as your friend & father to avoid evil company," came the warning. "Drinking, gaming & the company of lewd women are the vices most destructive to young men, the two former are even worse than the latter. . . . When all combines, destruction is the inevitable consequence. Shame & disgrace afflict parents and relatives, and death is wish'd for by all to cover the infamy of the family."

Jane Ball seemed oblivious that her son might seek out prostitutes, and instead wondered whether he would fall in love. "Let me know," she wrote, "if your heart is still your own. I hope it will be invulnerable yet for a while to the shafts of that little blind deity [Cupid] who spares neither sex nor age." Jane asked whether women in New England were better-looking than Southern ladies. "Do you find the fair sex of the north outrival ours in beauty? Their climate gives them the advantage in complexions but for softness, delicacy, & expression of features we are able to stand the comparison."

Talk of sex among the Balls, as among polite society in general, was always an occasion for euphemism. But there was one young man, John's fourth son, William, whose candor was greater than that of his kin. In fall of 1805, eighteen-year-old William James Ball went to Edinburgh, Scotland, to study medicine. In contrast to his brother, the quiet Harvard boy, William was chatty and sarcastic. On one occasion, he wrote his brother about a trip he planned to make to a brothel outside town, and claimed he wasn't looking forward to the experience:

> [I]t is now cucumber times with me. I am to set out in a day or two with a few others to make an excursion on foot into the highlands, whence it is very probable I shall return a very expert performer on the *fiddle*, which species of *music* I don't think I shall be extravagantly fond of.

After the trip, he wrote again, joking that he had not had sex, after all: "Of my excursion . . . I did not become a fiddler although I was somewhat afraid of it one night from the nature of the Inn."

Sex must have been on William's mind, because about the same time, the student wrote another of his brothers with a curious suggestion. "Dear Isaac," he advised, responding to a melancholy note from home, "You ought now to get a plaything [who will] amuse you at a leisure hour when setting by the fireside of an evening." William's coy advice may or may not have been his way of saying that twenty-year-old Isaac might consider having sex with one of the black women at Kensington.

The vulnerability of his sons to lust or to love was only one of John Sr.'s fears. The greatest menace, he thought, came from the new politics. Evidently the family's trip North had shown Mr. Ball that a dangerous liberalism stalked places like Massachusetts. Objectionable ideas about the South were gaining favor among some Northern whites, and what was at stake in his sons' education was no less than the safety of the family fortune. In one letter, the worried father wrote the Harvard student with a stark picture of the consequences of emancipation, and told him to close his ears to the radical talk of abolition:

> By being at such an University, you have the best chance in the United States for Education, & Boston & its vicinity may properly be class'd among the most polite & hospitable people in our States. As it is [however] you are in danger of imbibing principles in the Eastern states that will be against the interest of the southern states, tending to the ruin of your own family & fortune—however liberal those ideas may appear, the carrying of them into practice would be attended with the most direful effects. Carry in your mind that whenever a general emancipation takes place in S° Carolina & Georgia, you are a ruined man and all your family connexions made beggars.

In the summer of 1802, John Jr. finished his studies and returned to South Carolina. The dreaded liberal education had had no deranging effect. Within two years, the young man did what was expected of him—he married one of his first cousins and took possession of Comingtee, with more than a hundred slaves.

The Ball plantations made a closed world, pleasant at the top, hard at the bottom, resistant to change. It wasn't merely the two brothers; the women in the family would also not be moved. John's sister, Lydia Ball Bryan, had outlived her husband and inherited the land and people at Camp Vere plantation. John's half sister, Catherine Simons, lived as a widow next door to Camp Vere, at Middleburg. A few miles west on the other the branch of the river, his cousin, Eleanor Ball Simons, was mistress of Lewisfield; and twenty miles away, on the Ashley River, another cousin, the widowed Ann Ball Waring, lived on Tranquil Hill. Between them, the four women oversaw perhaps four hundred people, and miles of rice.

When the war between Napoleon and the rest of Europe drove up the price of rice, John Ball Sr. and Third Elias used the money to expand operations. Third Elias hired Jonathan Lucas, a neighbor who had developed a design for a mill that could grind the husks off rice using water power. Lucas built one of his machines at Limerick, relieving the Ball slaves somewhat of the tedious process of cleaning tons of rice by hand. Also at the start of the 1800s, Third Elias, although he already owned three places, bought two more, adding seven hundred acres on the west bank of the Cooper River. The tracts were called Pimlico and Kecklico—the name of the first from a neighborhood in London, the second from a Native language. John, meanwhile, bought a place called Midway, at the midpoint of the public road between the two forks of the Cooper River. A few years later, for $20,000, he bought an eleven-hundred-acre tract known as Belle Isle, on an island near the city of Georgetown; six months after that, the purchase of a smaller plot close to Charleston called Marshlands brought his portfolio to seven plantations.

In 1794, Eli Whitney patented the cotton gin, which allowed workers to tease out the seed from the cotton fiber, saving hours of handwork. At the same time, industrialization in England brought about factories that could produce great quantities of fabric from the raw cotton. "King Cotton" would soon transform the economy of the South, draining influence away from the rice planters and bringing a great increase in the demand for field hands. The international human trade was temporarily suspended in 1787, but the cotton farmers now brayed for new workers. Congress had postponed action on slavery until 1807, and white Southerners worried that the Washington government might outlaw "live cargoes" altogether after the deadline. On December 17, 1803, the South Carolina traffic in Africans was resumed. No other Southern state reopened the trade. In the next four years, more than thirty-nine thousand people would be imported to America through the city, the heaviest traffic the port had ever seen.

For the first time since before the Revolution, Africans flooded onto the Ball lands. John began to add workers one month after the ban was lifted, when he noted that he bought "six new Negroes . . . Moses, Aaron, Nathan, Ishamel, Israel, and Esau." "New" meant newly captured. Later he added twenty-two people in a single day, two-thirds of them men, one-third boys: "11 May 1804, bought of Wm. Boyd, 15 new negro men at $315 [each] . . . [totaling] $4725" and "7 new negro boys at $280 . . . $1960." John then went back to the wharfs to buy women, "7 new Negro wenches . . . Rosina, Juno, Judy, Tenah, Pallas, Bobbet, Molly."

At Pimlico, one of the new tracts, Third Elias began to write the simple word "African" next to names on the slave lists. Although Third

Elias's father, or his uncle Henry Laurens, might have jotted down the port or tribe from which a person came, by this time the Balls either did not know or did not care. In any case, the numbers were too big to bother with details. In 1805, Third Elias filed a property tax return with the state of South Carolina in which he claimed to own five hundred people, more than double the count he reported fifteen years earlier. (The real figure may well have been higher, since taxpayers regularly undercounted in order to pay less.) At Limerick, there were so many people in the slave cabins that Old Mas' 'Lias seems to have reverted to the earlier practice of taking away from some mothers the freedom to name their own children (perhaps because, without surnames, there was the likelihood of duplication), since some names on the rolls were not likely to have been coined by mothers. Limerick had a man called Dolphin and man called Bengal. One person—of what sex it is impossible to say—was known as Jew.

The more people there were, the less was said about them. With twelve plantations between them, the brothers had little contact with field hands, and family papers reflect the distance. Whereas previously the Balls made notes about individuals, after about 1800 they merely kept lists. Spending more time in Charleston, the family relied on overseers to manage the business, distribute food, and punish. As the number of people grows, too, it becomes more difficult to see into their lives; but occasionally a single event in the plantation records gives a sense of what happened to the "new Negroes," orphaned from family and cut off from home. One incident, involving four black girls and two white, says much about the Ball realm.

"Your dear mother has been extremely ill," John wrote to his son in 1804, "with a similar (but more violent) pain in her side like that she had at Hyde Park just before you left." In a letter, Jane compared her own life to a "declining sun which is now past its meridian." A bit later, John reported that Jane's "lungs were much affected." She died in early October. Nine months later, John married Martha Caroline Swinton, a young woman from another rice family whom everyone called by her middle name. John was forty-four, and Caroline nineteen, younger than two of John's sons. From a miniature painting, it appears that she was very feminine, with a limpid beauty. Caroline was also quite fertile, because a little less than nine months after the marriage, she gave birth to twin girls, Martha and Caroline. The father was beside himself and in his excitement looked around for the right gift of love and celebration. Soon it dawned on him—he would give twins to the twins.

Calling the family around, John presented each of the infants with a pair of child slaves. The children came from Pimlico, Third Elias's place, where John was pleased to find "two twins for my daughters." One set of the twins was American-born, the other recently imported. To baby Caroline, he gave an American girl named Sally and a girl called Korah, an "African" in his notes. To baby Martha, he gave Sally's sister Dye and Korah's sister Beda. The American-born girls were daughters of a Ball slave named Beck, while the African twins, each perhaps ten years old, had been in America no more than a year. Out in the fields, newly arrived workers stood a chance of meeting others from home. Instead, Korah and Beda found themselves submerged in white life. Taken from their own parents, the children were dropped into the home of the Balls, pieces of loot in a memorable prank.

Along with the black children, John gave his baby girls silver mugs engraved with their initials, and a pair of silver spoons. Finally, he turned to their mother to offer her her just reward. Caroline Ball was a person who would become well known in the family for her fashion sense. Soon after she got up from her birthing bed, Caroline went to her clothier, and, on her husband's account, bought twelve pairs of shoes.

In 1807, pushed by abolitionists, the British Parliament tried to outlaw the international trade in Africans. The Crown believed it could enforce a ban by outfitting a fleet to patrol the West African coast. Slave galleys captured at sea were brought back to the shore and their cargoes of people let go, often at the home port of the British fleet, in Freetown, Sierra Leone. The same year the U.S. Congress voted to ban indefinitely the import of Africans to the United States, effective January 1, 1808. By this time the population of black slaves in the country approached one million. The ban, decreed from both Washington and London, slowed but did not end the traffic into Charleston. Dealers kept business alive, though at a lower threshold. On January 4, 1808, three days after the American ban took effect, the *Charleston Courier* openly advertised the sale of 300 "prime windward coast slaves," 100 "prime young congo slaves," and 240 Angolans. After that the trade turned into smuggling, and the Balls stopped writing down their purchases.

Third Elias died in 1810. An obituary in the *Charleston Times* offered the opinion, discreetly worded, that the master of Limerick was a dull-minded procrastinator: "Mr. Ball was more remarkable for strength than brilliancy of understanding; for accuracy than acuteness of perception. He was more discriminating than ready . . . more disposed to receive than to communicate ideas." The newspaper concluded that despite his slowness, "The most conspicuous trait in Mr. Ball's character, however, was benevolence. . . . It was seen . . . whether he who cried to him for help was a stranger or a friend, a white man or a son of Africa."

Third Elias's nephew Isaac, who had bumped into Thomas Jefferson, got Limerick and its 283 people. Isaac, twenty-five, took his inheritance and approached a suitable bride—his cousin, Eliza Catharine Poyas. They were married within a year and, with their new wealth, decided to build a mansion in Charleston. With slave carpenters and masons, a great house in the South cost much less than a comparable house in the North. Isaac and Eliza bought four lots next to one another and combined them into one, at the northeast corner of what would become East Bay and Vernon streets. While Isaac noted that the bricks for the house cost $699, five black men working for a week dug the foundation for just $10, paid to their owner. The young couple found woodworkers to carve elaborate interior paneling in the new Federal style. They paid sculptors for busts of two recent national heroes, Benjamin Franklin and George Washington, and placed the art on the parlor mantelpiece. When the house was finished in 1813, Isaac and Eliza had one of the grandest residences in the city. Census records show that when the couple lived in the mansion with two children, eighteen black servants lived with them, replying to their demands for comfort and keeping the building in operation.

"I have got a sore leg," John Sr. wrote to his son in 1816. "I believe there must be something hereditary in the Ball family about bad legs. My father was many years before his death afflicted with a humour in his legs. . . . I have perhaps lived too high." Before John Ball died in

1817 at age fifty-seven, he possessed seven plantations and 695 people. The inventory of his property ran to twenty-four sheets, half the pages devoted to names. An occasional note here and there described their physical problems ("one leg," "invalid") or mental state ("crazy"). For someone who had once lectured his son about "our first charitable attentions," John left strange instructions. His will called for the sale of all the land and most of the people.

The auction house of William Payne & Son handled the business, and the sale began Monday morning, February 8, 1819. For two days the auditorium thronged with merchandise and buyers, as one family after another stepped up onto the block—367 people all told. The two new young patriarchs, John Jr. and his brother Isaac, picked up many of the spoils. John Jr. bought the Kensington and Midway lands; Isaac bought Hyde Park. Consulting with each other, the brothers decided to purchase some of their father's workforce. John Jr. bought back sixty-six people, for $39,285. Isaac bought sixty, at $37,791. These families were returned to their homes, having escaped an unknown fate.

The main tenet of white paternalism was simple enough: that black families should not be separated for money. This time, however, the Balls heard the rustle of cash, and caused a small diaspora. From Marshlands plantation, thirty-nine people were sold to fourteen different buyers. From Belle Isle, thirty-one people went to eight buyers. From White Hall, twenty-three went to nine buyers, and so on. By the end of the sale, forty people had been sold in lots of two or three, and an additional fifty had gone on the block alone. These last were torn completely from wives, husbands, children, parents.

Some of the buyers, no doubt, worked for the new cotton planters. Rice had been good business for more than a century, but cotton land was opening in the West, as Native people were being driven out. Mississippi had become a state in 1817, followed by Alabama in 1819. It was not unusual in this period to see long columns of black people tramping in chains through the wilderness, on a forced march from South Carolina to the new cotton plantations. The Ball auction was nicely timed to meet the demand.

When William Payne tallied the proceeds, John Jr. and Isaac must have been pleased at the yield of $227,191. Again, although it is impossible to make a comparison to later dollar values, in this period the Balls paid their overseers—the foremen of large enterprises, something

like plant managers—an average of $1600 per year, money enough to
support a large family and have savings left over. The auction drew
nearly 380 times this sum. The dead man's beautiful widow, Caroline,
probably felt relief that she and her young children would have no
anxiety about money.

Sometime before the Civil War, a white traveler in South Carolina
overheard black workers singing in a barnyard, and wrote down the
words of the song:

> *Johnny, come down the hollow,*
> > *Oh hollow.*
> *The nigger-trader got me,*
> > *Oh hollow.*
> *The speculator bought me,*
> > *Oh hollow.*
> *I'm sold for silver dollars,*
> > *Oh hollow.*
> *Boys, go catch the pony,*
> > *Oh hollow.*
> *Bring him round the corner,*
> > *Oh hollow.*
> *I'm goin' way to Georgia,*
> > *Oh hollow.*
> *Boys, good-bye forever,*
> > *Oh hollow.*

There is no way of knowing how the remaining Ball slaves consoled one
another and recovered from the breakup of their world. But it appears
that within three years, at least some were prepared to reply to what
had happened. In June 1822, a black ship carpenter named Peter was
arrested in Charleston on a rumor and accused of taking part in a conspiracy to overthrow white rule. Peter Poyas belonged to a brother of
Eliza Ball, Isaac's wife. The prisoner's home plantation, Windsor, stood
just north of Limerick, Isaac and Eliza's country home. As it happens,
Windsor was also the place where Mrs. Ball was born. Presumably Isaac
and Eliza would have seen Peter around, but the accused had since
come some distance from Windsor. He lived in Charleston, had his own

shop on the Charleston wharfs, and had taught himself to read and write.

Peter was interrogated by the Intendant of Charleston, James Hamilton, head of the city's guard and patrols. The prisoner proved composed under questioning and nonchalant in his denials, actually managing to reassure the nervous police. Peter was let go, and a black informant was instructed to spy on him.

Meanwhile, a slave already in detention, William, announced that there was in fact a plan for an uprising, due to go off Sunday night, June 16, at midnight. The authorities dismissed the new rumor. But on Friday, June 14, a slave owner came into the Intendant's office in a panic. The man had not known about the investigation but had just heard from one of his own workers about the conspiracy. It was set to go off in two days, he said, on Sunday.

Patrols cut the roads into and out of town, and the city fell under the grip of an occupation. The guardhouses were fortified, and four companies of militia paraded the streets throughout Sunday night, brandishing their guns. Monday morning arrived without incident. The weekend had been "an occasion involving such deep interest and distressing anxiety," according to a report, especially "among the female part of our community."

A Court of Magistrates and Freeholders convened to investigate and make arrests. The list of conspirators grew as new names were extracted from each prisoner seized. Peter was arrested a second time, his name on the lips of half a dozen suspects.

As the dragnet widened, a young slave named Paris, identified by the court as belonging to a Mrs. Ball, was implicated. This time the trail of subversion led right to the family hearth. Paris seems to have been the property of Ann Simons Ball, mistress of Comingtee and the wife of John Jr. After John Jr. lost his first wife, he had married Ann Simons, an independent woman whose letters show that she held strong opinions about obedience among workers. A slave named Paris was born at Comingtee on January 16, 1805, to a field hand called Hagar. If this was the same person, he must have been sent during his childhood to work at one of the Ball houses in Charleston. Court papers say that "Paris Ball" was hired out in the city to William's Wharf, probably as a stevedore. The wharf job put him not far from the carpentry shop of Peter, the lead prisoner.

The investigators titled their report "An account of the late intended

QUENBY PLANTATION

Jane Ball (1823–1905), daughter of Isaac and Eliza Ball, posed about 1841 for the brothers and artists James and Robert Bogle, one of whom painted faces and hands, the other drapery and decor. Jane played the harp, which followed her into a brief marriage to John G. Shoolbred (who died in 1842 six months after the wedding, before their only son was born) and through a fifty-seven-year widowhood, including a period during the Civil War when the harp and Jane both traveled to the state capital at Columbia, where it was supposed they would be safe from the marauding march of the Federal army led by General William Tecumseh Sherman.

At her father's death in 1825, when she was two, Jane Ball inherited Quenby plantation and its population of so[m]
one hundred people. The Balls kept the land for another 125 years, selling Quenby in 1950
to the Whitener Lumber Company for $60,427.

During the Revolutionary War, on July 17, 1781, Quenby was the scene of a battle between a British regiment
numbering five hundred and a force of seven hundred American rebels. The British took cover in the clay slave hou[se]
which absorbed much of the American musket fire; the rebels lost and the dead from both sides were buried besi[de]
the road leading past the Quenby gate.

Nat Watson (about 1845–1922), left, known to the Balls as "Daddy Nat," his wife Binah, standing, and family, on the steps of the unpainted main house at Quenby, about 1905.

...Watson continued to work as a house servant for his ...r owner, Jane Ball Shoolbred, and after Jane's death ...r nieces, until shortly before his death in 1922, ...enty-seven.

Binah, a former slave at Quenby and wife of the plantation valet Nat Watson, sometime after the Civil War.

MIDDLEBURG

When Catherine Chicken—daughter of Lydia Chicken Ball and stepdaughter of her husband, Second Elias Ball—mov to Middleburg plantation after she married its owner, Benjamin Simons, a few years before the American Revolution Middleburg was already one of the oldest houses in South Carolina, the first part of it having been put up in 1699. I 1789, when Benjamin Simons died, the plantation passed to the couple's three daughters; but in 1872, another famil member, John Coming Ball, bought it back. The photograph dates from the 1890s.

Ball family lore reports that Maum Sue—who after the Civil War was the "mammy" at Middleburg, on whose steps she sits—was once a slave belonging to a free Negro. At emancipation she went to work as a cook in the pay of twenty-four-year-old John Coming Ball, who had become a sharecrop landlord.

Each plantation had a lockup for disobedient workers—at Quer it was known as "Mudlong's closet." At Middleburg about 1962 Louise J. DuBose, a reporter for The State newspaper of Colum and Edward Dingle, husband of the plantation's owner, Marie I visited the slave jail at Middleburg, which consisted of two tiny rooms, each about three by six feet, with barred windows overhe

In the old style of rice farming, at the end of the growing season field hands pounded the raw grain to remove its husk, using a waist-high, hollowed-out mortar and a pestle a yard long; a scoop of rice went into the mortar and was beaten until the contents emerged naked white. The big rice mill at Middleburg, built about 1794, stripped the husk off the grain and thereby eased one demand on black muscle power.

Elias Ball III (1752–1810), grandson of Red Cap, was about thirteen when his portrait was painted. In his later years he fought swelling in his legs from gout (he trudged rather than walked). He never married, and he lived at Limerick plantation as virtually the single white person among 250 blacks—two traits that gave him the family nickname "Old Mas' 'Lias."

Except for this nineteenth-century photograph, there is little record of the life of Pino, who lived on Cedar Hill plantatic the property of William James Ball, where he built this house for himself (and, evidently, his white cat). The chimney w made of clay, with a ladder at the ready for repairs during rainstorms.

Fortune Ford, a worker on Comingtee plantation in the 1890s; he was probably the son of Fortune, a field hand on Comingtee in his twenties at the end of slavery.

A worker at Comingtee whe name has vani but who was g a saintly coror someone who scratched the emulsion off th negative.

...e harvest of rice at Comingtee, with the swinging scythe.

...e barn at Comingtee with a two-horse rig and driver, in the 1800s.

Hannah, Comingtee, 1800s.

*Children were the water- and food-carriers on the farm, and these four gir[ls]
drawing a bucket from the crane well at Comingtee, would have done a
similar errand several times per day.*

WAR

Charleston in an engraving from 1851, seen from the southern tip of the city's peninsula, looking north over the seawalls of the Battery and the trees of White Point Gardens. At the right flows the Cooper River, at the far left the Ashley.

… Cart Ball (1824–58), wife of William Ball and mistress … merick plantation in the decades before the Civil War, … early 1850s in what appears to be a portrait of a dress. … died two years before South Carolina's secession from … nion; when the war came, her four sons put on the … derate uniform.

William James Ball (1821–91), patriarch of the Ball family at the time of the Civil War, was of the first generation to shun portrait painters in favor of photography; this daguerreotype dates from about 1852. In contrast to his uncle, John Ball Jr., an active secessionist, William showed little interest in the rebellion against the North, believing that war would jeopardize his control of eight plantations and some 620 blacks.

During the Civil War the bombardment of Charleston by Federal guns was a notable news event, reported in a Dece 1863 issue of the Illustrated London News, *which published engravings along with its coverage.*

Nat (or "Daddy Nat," left accompanied the four Bal brothers from Limerick an cousin John Shoolbred Jr. Quenby plantation as a pe servant during their tours in muddy Confederate car Although the Ball boys we lowly privates, Nat gather firewood, carried their bu and cleaned their clothes.

After the fall of Charleston to the Federals on February 17, 1865, the first troops to occupy the city were black units. Harper's Weekly *published an engraving captioned* "The Fifty-fifth Massachusetts Colored Regiment Singing John Brown's March in the Streets of Charleston."

c Ball (1844–1933), second son of William Julia Ball, enlisted in the Confederate army an artilleryman the week of his eighteenth thday and was assigned to help keep off a ral invasion, manning guns at the mouth of rleston harbor. At war's end, retreating with federate troops through North Carolina, he d his brothers surrendered to the detested eral William T. Sherman. Isaac posed four s after the truce, on the eve of his wedding.

Isaac Ball and his wife, Mary Louisa Ball (1846–1926), about 1920, after fifty years of marriage, standing in front of the main house at The Bluff plantation; Mary Louisa inherited The Bluff from her father, and she and Isaac ran it as a sharecrop farm after the Civil War. By this time blind from glaucoma, Isaac lived in Charleston but made weekend visits to The Bluff, where he held the rapt attention of his grandchildren, including my father, with stories of the old days before emancipation.

THE EBB

*Limerick plantation remained in the [hands]
of the Balls until the 1890s, by whic[h time]
the family could no longer afford to [keep]
the house, though they held to the lu[xury]
of a buggy and driver. Fifty years la[ter, in]
October 1945, a disgruntled tenant f[armer]
evidently set a fire that destroyed the
225-year-old wooden mansion.*

*Varying numbers of black families stayed on the land
after freedom, working as sharecroppers in the same
fields where they had been enslaved—including
this family at Comingtee plantation . . .*

. . . and this family at C[

Robert Nelson Jr., son of "Robtie," the last slave butler at Limerick, posed with his wife, Nannie, about 1900.

In the late 1800s, Sarah (whose last name is gone from family memory) fished in the flooded rice fields at Quenby, a shirt tied around her head against the sun, and just out of reach of a curious pig.

Crossing the Cooper River on the Strawberry Ferry, about 1900.

After the Civil War, most of the Balls continued their practice of moving off the plantations during summer to escape malaria, and resettling (with house servants) in the neighboring village of Cordesville. There they attended services at this gingerbread chapel, the Episcopal Church of the Holy Innocents, large enough to hold the thirty or so whites who made their summer home in the pines, but not their black retainers.

Some of the Ball ladies and a male companion on an excursion to the bea at the Isle of Palms, near Charleston, about 1910.

About 1920 Maum Agnes (seated, blind) and her family—Bella, left, Isaiah, and a visitor, far right—were among the last black sharecroppers at Brickyard, a section of Quenby plantation.

In 1925 Lydia C. Ball, raised at Lim plantation, founded the Plantation M Singers, a group of ten white women Charleston who performed black spiri dressing for their concerts as slaves (apparently putting on blackface). Lyc costumed for a performance, saved a her mementos a complimentary revie concert from the Charleston News an Courier, *which observed that the "dic attire, attitudes, expressions, and the of the singers were typical of that rap disappearing, respectful, superstitious indolent, but ever faithful and good- race, the 'old fashioned' plantation r*

ANGOLA AMY AND THE GADSDEN FAMILY

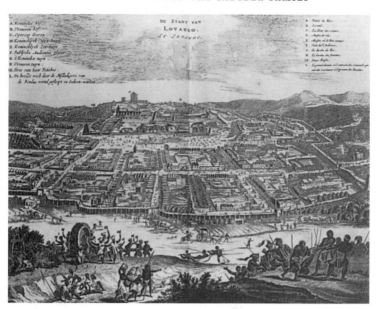

A young woman whom Red Cap bought in 1736 and named Angola Amy may have come from this place. English slave dealers bought people from an area they called Angola, chiefly the kingdom of Loango on the West African coast just north of the Congo River. An engraving made by a Dutch artist in the 1600s depicted Loango's rather grand walled capital.

he family of Angola Amy (born about 1720, ed about 1790) became the single largest clan black people on the Ball rice plantations. Mary nn Royal ("Maum Mary Ann," born 1786), the st mammy at Comingtee plantation before the ivil War, photographed here, married into Amy's mily.

The "slave street" at Comingtee plantation; the Cooper River flows in the distance, seen through a tunnel of Spanish moss (Tillandsia usneoides, which produces delicate green flowers between April and June). Angola Amy's descendants lived in these railroad car–like houses, each with two rooms—one family per room, and a brick chimney with two fireplaces at its base, one hearth facing each room.

Georgianna Gadsden Richardson (1910–97), center, a great-grandniece of Mary Ann Royal and a direct descendant of Angola Amy, in a Polaroid photograph taken in Charleston, about 1968. Mrs. Richardson stands with her husband, Robert Richardson, and their nieces and nephews.

The Gadsden-Brown family of Cordesville, South Carolina, 1997. Georgianna Gadsden Richardson (seated in the middle) and, left to right, Barbara Jean Brown, Leroy Brown, and Barbara Jean's children, Shanice, Marcill, and Steven.

insurrection among a portion of the blacks of this city." They concluded that the scheme, headed off at the last moment, was supposed to have had three phases or military strokes. From James Island, across Charleston harbor, a party of rebels had planned to land at the southern tip of the city, where they would make an effort to capture the main arsenal and guardhouse. Meanwhile, another party was to have seized the guardhouse at the north end, on the narrow pass out of town known as the Neck. A third assault was to take place at the rice mill owned by Governor Thomas Bennett, on the banks of the Cooper River.

The "father of the plot," in the words of the court, was a man named Denmark Vesey. Vesey was a free black carpenter in his fifties. According to testimony at his trial, for four years Vesey had planned the uprising, with Peter as his first lieutenant. The two men, witnesses said, had taken their inspiration from the 1791 revolt led by Toussaint L'Ouverture in Saint Domingue. Vesey was a Christian, even something of an evangelist, whose favored passages in the Bible concerned the enslavement of the Jews. He was known to tell the story, over and again, of how the Israelites were delivered from four hundred years of captivity and made their way out of Egypt. Witnesses said that Vesey would often cite one verse, Exodus 21:16, to stress how black hardship might be brought to an end: "[A]nd he that stealeth a man, and selleth him . . . shall surely be put to death."

The trials began June 19 and continued for a month. Peter was the fourth tried. According to the court, Peter "possessed the largest share of the confidence of Denmark Vesey" and was "the most efficient of all the ringleaders." Many witnesses named Peter as the recruiter who had brought them into the conspiracy. In the course of testimony, it emerged that Peter had written letters to Saint Domingue, seeking help for the uprising from the black government there. The court, impressed, called him a man of "boldness and sagacity." Peter was apparently also military-minded, his job in the scheme having been to lead the assault on the main guardhouse. After a two-day hearing, the court found that Peter had made "great efforts to induce others to join in the insurrection" and sentenced him to hang. According to court papers, while in jail awaiting death, Peter told his comrades to keep faith. "Do not open your lips!" Peter was overheard saying. "Die silent, as you shall see me do!" Denmark Vesey, "in whose bosom the nefarious scheme was first engendered," came to trial June 27, and was sentenced to die with Peter.

Vesey also refused to talk. Although the court papers bulge with testimony, they contain nothing from Vesey or Peter themselves. The two men were hanged, along with five others, on the second of July.

There are three pieces of evidence that show how the Balls felt about these events. While they wrote much to one another, the letters from the summer of the conspiracy have strangely disappeared from the family papers. Of the few that survive, none mentions the arrests or trials. This odd omission is made more peculiar by the fact that family correspondence resumes in the fall, after the case was closed. Either the Balls regarded the conspiracy as unimportant, which is unlikely, or what letters they wrote to one another about it have gone missing. Nevertheless, one measure that the family was overtaken with fear can be found in a religious diary kept by twenty-eight-year-old Eliza Ball, who had grown up at Windsor plantation, as did one of the ringleaders, Peter Poyas. "O heavenly Father," wrote Eliza, composing a prayer about the uprising. "[H]ow great has been thy mercy to us, in a public way in protecting and saving us & our city from fire & murder which threatened us . . . from a class of people among us, continue this thy mercy O God in still protecting us from such an evil. . . . Change their hearts O Lord that they may never meditate such evil things, but may live in peace, contentment as thou willed."

A letter from a distant relative points to more distress. "May the Almighty protect you . . . from their devilish machinations," wrote John Moultrie, an in-law in England, to Isaac Ball. "[I]n these times of emancipation freedom and liberality, you gentlemen freeholders in the Southern States will be in constant apprehensions [of] insurrection and murdering of the Whites."

A third piece of evidence comes from oral tradition. A cousin told me the story that when she was a child in the 1950s she sat with her grandfather and mine, Nathaniel Ball, as he was telling plantation tales. Grandfather Nat described how on the night of the expected uprising the Balls armed themselves with guns in their houses; bonfires were set around the district, and the family stayed awake till dawn, trembling at every noise. Grandfather Nat would have said more, but he was interrupted by his daughter, who stopped the story so as to prevent the old man from frightening his grandchildren.

When a new round of trials began, Paris Ball went before the court on July 16. Beyond a birthdate, the Ball records are silent about Paris.

He pled not guilty to the charge of "attempting to raise an insurrection among the Blacks against the Whites." The testimony of Monday Gell, an Igbo who ran a harness-making shop, was crucial to Paris's fate. Monday Gell had plotted with Peter and Vesey, then turned state's evidence. When he took the stand, the harness-maker said that Paris was in league, too.

"[He] frequently came to me to know how the thing was going on," Gell testified. "The week after Peter was taken up," Paris "came to me and said, 'Your name is called—be on your guard.'" Gell depicted Paris as a footsoldier who had surrendered eagerly to the plot. When another defendant giving evidence for the state, a black man named Perrault, took the stand, he confessed and also implicated Paris. "I knew that he [Paris] knew of the business," Perrault said. "I saw him at Monday's [harness shop] and heard him speaking of it. He was as much in it as I am."

Either Paris Ball himself refused to testify or his words were ignored by the court. On Friday, July 19, he was sentenced to death.

With the second of their people slated to die, the Balls were probably frightened out of their wits, and feeling betrayed. The family was convinced that it treated workers with the watchfulness of parents. I have often heard this characterization of relations between the family and the slaves myself, from one or another relative. There was some proof of this assertion, to be sure, in the span of the business. By 1822 the Balls had been in the plantation trade 125 years. If their people were badly handled, no amount of force could have kept them down so long. So why would Peter and Paris, raised in the contented clan of Ball slaves, want to kill those who looked after them?

One night after reading about Paris Ball, I returned to my temporary home in Charleston, the Branford-Horry House on Meeting Street. In the court papers, I had seen mention of a conspirator who once lived at the same address. The plotter's name was John, a coachman who belonged to rice planter Elias Horry, owner of the house at the time. According to witnesses at his trial, John had a piece of personal property, a sword, and in the weeks before the uprising often talked about what he planned to do with it. John said that when the signal went out, he intended to run upstairs in the mansion and kill his master and family in their beds.

"I'm ready whenever the blacks break out," John boasted to one witness, who later turned against him. The coachman was arrested, tried, hanged.

That night, I returned to house where John had once lived, went upstairs, and closed and locked the door.

The investigation and trials of 1822 continued for eight weeks. Thirty-five were hanged, and fifty-two acquitted. In the end, the family seems to have extended forgiveness, at least to Paris. On July 24, 1822, two days before Paris was to hang, the Balls filed a petition with the governor, asking that he be deported rather than killed. Peter was a ringleader, everyone knew, but Paris was a follower. Governor Bennett agreed, and commuted the young man's sentence to "banishment beyond the limits of the United States."

Three months later, on Saturday, October 26, the *Carolina Gazette* ran a small notice about several slaves, including Paris, who had been pardoned from death. They were aboard a cargo vessel in the harbor, the newspaper reported. The governor had set a deadline for Paris Ball and his comrades: "seven days for the vessels in which they have been shipped to leave the port."

13

>─+─◊─+─<

A PAINTER'S LEGACY

One day at the end of winter the telephone rang and a voice said, "This is Edwina Harleston Whitlock." The voice wavered with age but had a beautiful diction, every syllable crisp. "I understand you have been trying to research your blood relations of color."

It was a gentle sentence that did not reveal its motive. I had received unpleasant phone calls and letters from white people who had strong views about protecting "our race," and I suspected this was the beginning of a similar communication. My suspicion did not relax when I heard the name "Harleston," a family associated with the Balls from the time Elias "Red Cap" Ball married Elizabeth Harleston in South Carolina, around 1700, and continuing straight down.

"I've been talking to descendants of people whom the Balls enslaved," I said. "Some of them might be also descendants of the Balls."

I could not say, from her voice, whether Edwina Harleston Whitlock would describe herself as white or black. (The old middle category, mulatto, was no longer operative.) Whatever her appearance, she had a memorable way of speaking, and she began to unroll a story over the phone. Edwina Whitlock listed her forebears, who, as it happened, were also some of my forebears; and as she spoke, her dialect had the rhythm of a dance, with poised stops and starts, and coy bursts of laughter.

Finally, the voice arrived at the name of a couple that seemed significant.

"My great-grandparents were Kate Wilson and William Harleston," said Edwina Whitlock.

I knew William Harleston as one of the Ball cousins from the mid-1800s, but I did not know Kate Wilson. "Was Kate Wilson a person of color?" I asked.

"Yes, of course," the voice said. "In every sense of the word, William Harleston, the rice planter, and Kate Wilson, his slave, were man and wife. They had eight children, one of whom was my grandfather. I am one of their descendants."

Edwina Harleston Whitlock made her home in Atlanta, having moved to Georgia after retirement to be near her daughters. She was in her seventies, and had been widowed for many years. Mrs. Whitlock lived in a prosperous neighborhood, in a house with a lawn under the shadow of some pine trees. It was a bright day, and the brick of her house seemed grainy in the full, rounded light of the Southern afternoon. Mrs. Whitlock opened the door and stretched out her hand, but my first gaze fell behind her, because she stood at the entrance to what looked like a portrait gallery. For a moment I ignored her outstretched hand as I peered at the walls lined with paintings. Even in the dimness, I could see the pictures, many of them portraits, with some landscapes in between.

Edwina Whitlock wore black trousers, a white long-sleeved shirt, black hoop earrings, and light pink lipstick. Her face described a smooth oval, and her eyebrows were very fine. Mrs. Whitlock's skin was the color of brown paper, or the color of sepia from an old photograph, and her hair was white. Her eyes glinted, and she had a slight smirk.

"It's a great pleasure," said Mrs. Whitlock, with a pause, "to meet a long-lost cousin."

Edwina Whitlock's daughter, Mae Whitlock Gentry, was also on hand. In her late thirties and slender, she was an editor at the *Atlanta Journal-Constitution*, and had much of her mother's face and eyes. She was divorced, she later said, with two daughters, Alison and Sylvia.

Mae Gentry, her mother, and I sat around the kitchen table, and went through the family story.

"The lineage begins with John Harleston, who immigrated in 1699," said Mrs. Whitlock, "with his sister, Elizabeth Harleston."

"Elizabeth Harleston married Elias Ball, founder of the American Ball family," I said.

"Yes," answered Mrs. Whitlock.

"That means that our earliest connection is through the parents of Elizabeth and John Harleston," I finished.

"So you really are cousins," said Mae Gentry, a little surprised. "I suspected as much."

"So are you," Mrs. Whitlock corrected her daughter, then giggled.

Our common forebears were white people, it appeared, whereas Mae Gentry and Mrs. Whitlock "lived black." I fell silent, waiting for the story of how the two sides crossed.

"The son of John Harleston," Mrs. Whitlock went on, "was John Harleston the second, and that John's son was William Harleston the first. William the first had five children, including William Harleston the second. William the second was the common-law husband of Kate Wilson."

Mrs. Whitlock's voice meandered hauntingly, beginning a sentence in a low register, wavering on a phrase, then shooting up an octave, finally drifting down to a satisfying cadence, like a cello performing a partita. As Mrs. Whitlock spoke, the rests and measures seemed to appear in the air.

"Who was Kate Wilson?" I asked.

"Kate Wilson was my father's grandmother," Mrs. Whitlock answered. "She was born in 1820, we think in Barbados. William Harleston built a house for Kate in Charleston, at 28 Laurel Street, now called Ashe Street. When he died, in 1874, William Harleston stipulated in his will that his property was to be equally divided between his white relatives and, as he put it, 'my colored woman Kate, formerly my slave.' Kate lived in that house until she died, in 1886."

"Pretty much it was a marriage," Mae put in, "because William Harleston never had a white wife. He had one other child that we know of by another black woman, Sibby, or Hattie. So he wasn't completely faithful to Kate."

"Was it common for white planters to sleep with their slave women?" I asked.

"How many people in Charleston do you know who look like us?" Edwina Whitlock replied, an eyebrow raised.

"Some," I said truthfully.

"Yeah, it was common," Mae Gentry came back. "We don't believe it was common for planters to leave their property to these women. In fact, this is the only case I have heard of."

Mrs. Whitlock's face showed undiluted pride. These events had determined the pattern of her life, and she embraced them.

"Kate and William had eight children," Mrs. Whitlock said, "including my grandfather, Edwin G. Harleston, who was born in 1852. One of his sons was my father, Robert Harleston, and another was my Uncle Teddy Harleston, or Edwin A. Harleston, who raised me." The cast of characters filled up, and I momentarily lost the thread. I asked about Uncle Teddy. "The painter, who did those pictures in the living room," Mrs. Whitlock answered. Our families were apparently connected, but the Harlestons had something the Ball family could not boast, a serious painter.

"Now, who was Mary Louisa Moultrie, I mean, to you?" said Mrs. Whitlock. The surprises came more quickly, as Mrs. Whitlock dropped a familiar name.

"Mary Louisa Moultrie was my father's grandmother," I replied. "She died in 1926."

"My grandfather, Edwin G. Harleston, was married to a woman named Louisa Moultrie," Mrs. Whitlock said with a smirk.

The Balls and the sepia-toned Harlestons moved another step closer together. Louisa Moultrie, I assumed, had been a woman with skin not unlike that of Edwina Whitlock, whose life, somehow, must have touched that of my great-grandmother. She was not "my" Mary Louisa, but the same name had been given to both a white and a mulatto child.

I asked what had happened to Kate Wilson. Mrs. Whitlock explained that her story did not end well. Kate Wilson inherited money and a house from her slave-owning husband, William Harleston, but after his death, she was humiliated by his jealous relatives. It seems William Harleston's sister, Hannah, had a son named Benjamin Huger, who, under ordinary circumstances, would have been Kate Wilson's nephew.

"According to my Uncle Teddy," said Mrs. Whitlock, "Benjamin Huger went to Kate's house, and there he persuaded her to sign all of her property, except the house, over to him." For the first time Mrs. Whitlock's face fell slightly. "Maybe Kate was ignorant, I don't know," she said.

"Probably she was," said Mae Gentry.

"That's the story of the South, state after state," Mae's mother finished.

Kate Wilson was buried in Charleston, in a cemetery where mulatto families bought plots. Her gravestone made no mention of her white husband.

"Mae, when did your mother start talking to you about this family business?" I asked.

"Ever since I can remember, I heard the stories," she said, rolling her eyes. Mrs. Whitlock giggled, and her eyes gleamed.

"My baby son," Mrs. Whitlock remembered, "one day he said, 'I'm sick and tired of hearing about all these dead people! I've got a Harleston problem of my own!' "

Mrs. Whitlock laughed tenderly. Kate Wilson had lost everything, a white cousin was sitting in her kitchen, and it was all very amusing.

There was a real if distant blood link between us by way of Red Cap's wife, Elizabeth Harleston, and his brother-in-law John Harleston. I suspected there might also be a link through Mrs. Whitlock's great-grandmother, Kate Wilson. In the paperwork a plausible connection soon appeared.

Mary Louisa Moultrie, my father's paternal grandmother, was born in 1846 on The Bluff, a 1,203-acre rice plantation on the western bank of the Cooper River. Her father, Dr. William Moultrie, a physician turned slave owner, was co-owner of The Bluff in partnership with members of the (white) Harleston family, the clan of his first wife, Hannah Harleston. Mary Louisa grew up on The Bluff and eventually inherited a stake in the land. In 1869, she married Isaac Ball, a twenty-five-year-old war veteran as well as my father's eventual grandfather, the one my father referred to as Isaac the Confederate. Isaac and Mary Louisa settled at The Bluff and had twelve children, one of whom was my grandfather, Nathaniel Ball.

In the 1920s, Mary Louisa Ball wrote down her memories of childhood on The Bluff. In the memoir, a few typewritten pages, Mary Louisa refers to her father as "the old gentleman" and describes the dinners that the slaves of the family would serve. "Uncle John and Uncle William Harleston, two old bachelors who lived across the river at Elwood, always came every evening to take supper," she wrote, "and then after spending the evening with the old gentleman, would be rowed home again to their bachelors' abode."

"Uncle William Harleston" was the "bachelor" with the black common-law wife, Kate Wilson. At the time, about 1850, he lived at Elwood plantation, a 605-acre tract across the river and two miles upstream from The Bluff. An unmarried man with a slave mistress was not a person who moved easily in white society. Yet he was family, so Uncle William was invited to dinner (though without his black lover) and his indiscretion overlooked.

As it turned out, a few years before these memorable dinners, the two Harleston brothers had bought their home from the Ball family— along with, it appears, a slave named Kate. It may well have been this Kate, formerly owned by the Balls, who would become the matriarch of the mulatto Harleston clan.

Kate's road to common-law marriage took a meandering route. Among the many Ball men in the rice business, there was a playboy youth, Alwyn Ball. In 1826, Alwyn, eighteen and newly married, inherited some money from the estate of his father, John Ball Sr. Alwyn used the cash to buy Elwood plantation in a foreclosure sale from the sheriff of Charleston, and moved onto the land. Three years later, Alwyn took possession of eighty-two people, valued at $18,601, who lived at another Ball tract, Pimlico, in a division of more of his father's property. These workers moved to Elwood, and on the list of their names there appears that of Katey, a girl valued at $300. Alwyn's Katey, or Kate, was the only person of that name who came to live at the plantation.

Six years passed, and in July 1835 Alwyn Ball died of malaria, at age twenty-eight. The executors of his estate sold Elwood and its people to a partnership consisting of Dr. William Moultrie and John Harleston. William Moultrie remained over at his home on The Bluff, but John Harleston decided to move to Elwood, together with his brother William Harleston, the two of them being unmarried. William Harleston was thirty-four when he arrived, and Kate, resident on the land, perhaps fifteen. Through these twists and turns, typical of the time, I gathered that the Balls had been the means of introduction between Kate Wilson and her future husband.

The story told in the family of Kate's descendants is that she moved eventually to the house in Charleston that William built for her and did not live with him on the rice farm. Kate would have had plenty of company among other black mistresses of white men in the city. Records show that of the thirty-two hundred free black people in Charleston, women outnumbered men almost two to one.

William stayed for a time at Elwood but later moved to a plantation called The Hut, not far from the Balls' Comingtee. At the time, Comingtee was the home of another bachelor, Keating Ball, who kept a diary. In his little daybook, Keating once made a note about his neighbor (and cousin) William Harleston. Keating was struck by the way William acted with his slaves. William, wrote Keating, was an unusual member of white society in that he could occasionally be found in the company of his workers, actually lending a hand. A diary entry that Keating made in January 1849 describes some road repairs being done by a team of William's laborers, and by William himself: "[T]he hands in the roads [came] from Fish Pond and Hut plantations. In the road work I found Mr. William Harleston of the Hut plantation an able assistant and to him the credit is due of any good work done."

No photograph of Kate has survived, and it is difficult to say from what place she took the name Wilson. When William Harleston died in 1874, his eight mulatto children took his name.

"There is a published genealogy of the Harleston family," I said, "which states that William Harleston was unmarried."

"I know," said Edwina Whitlock with an amused air. "I published an essay somewhere that says that writer didn't do a good job of researching, because there were plenty of black Harlestons around, and everybody knew them. My aunt used to say that the postmen at that time were black, and anything that came to Charleston addressed to Harleston, they brought the things to us. We knew all their business— I mean, all y'all's business."

Mrs. Whitlock raised her eyebrows, giggled, and put her tongue on her upper lip. The past seemed lighter than it might have been. Then her manner suddenly went flat.

"There's an expression to refer to children," she said without smiling, "who are called 'step-asides.' That means that the white father does
not acknowledge his black children. He has them, and he 'steps aside.'
You never heard that expression?"

Edwina Harleston Whitlock was born Gussie Louise Harleston, September 28, 1916, on the third floor of a large house on Calhoun Street in
Charleston. On the first floor was the Harleston Funeral Home, a prosperous business owned by her grandfather, one of the sons of Kate
Wilson and William Harleston. The funeral home benefited the entire
family and gave the mulatto Harlestons a high standard of living, with
chauffeurs drawn from the ranks of hearse drivers, and servants. The
burial trade—"They called the business 'the firm,'" said Edwina
Whitlock—was one of the few ventures in which it was possible for a
black family to earn considerable sums of money, because white mor-
ticians would not handle the corpses of black people. On the second
floor of the building was a rented hall, and on the third, two family
apartments. One of these apartments was the home of Robert Harleston
and his wife, Marie Forrest Harleston, parents of Edwina Whitlock.

When Gussie, or Edwina, was two, it was discovered that her parents
had contracted tuberculosis. The disease later killed her mother, and
her father remained ill for many years. In the crisis, the child was given
to her uncle and aunt to be raised.

Gussie's new guardians were her father's brother, Edwin A. "Teddy"
Harleston, and her mother's sister, Elise Forrest, themselves married.
Uncle Teddy and Aunt Elise lived comfortably on the firm, but they
worked hard at their preferred vocation: art. Elise Harleston was a photographer, and Edwin Harleston was a painter who had trained at the
Boston Museum of Fine Arts and the Chicago Art Institute. As a young
woman with a close attachment to her adoptive father, Edwin, Gussie
would one day legally change her name to Edwina, to give honor to him.

In the 1920s, Uncle Teddy and Aunt Elise were perhaps the most
prominent couple in Charleston in the politics and culture of black life.
In 1916, Edwin Harleston became one of the founders of the South
Carolina chapter of the National Association for the Advancement of
Colored People, and served as its first president. By 1919 the NAACP
chapter had eight hundred members, and Harleston launched its first

major action, a march on the state capitol to protest the exclusion of black teachers from jobs in Charleston's black public schools. On January 18, 1919, with Edwin Harleston at the front of the column, black protesters from around South Carolina arrived at the capitol to present the state legislature with a petition, signed by 4,734 heads of households, criticizing the teaching ban. The legislature responded by removing the ban from the education code.

As a child, Edwina Harleston witnessed meetings of the NAACP in the Harleston home above the firm on Calhoun Street.

"Du Bois was our greatest intellectual since the Civil War," Mrs. Whitlock stated, sitting at her kitchen table. W. E. B. Du Bois was born in 1868 in Great Barrington, Massachusetts, and educated at Fisk University, Harvard, and the University of Berlin. His book *The Souls of Black Folk*, published in 1903, was the founding manifesto of black identity in the twentieth century. When Edwin Harleston ran the Charleston chapter of the NAACP, Du Bois was editor of the association's magazine, *The Crisis*, which had a circulation of more than fifty thousand. At the end of his life, Du Bois would renounce his U.S. citizenship and move to Ghana, despairing of any answer to the race stalemate in America. Du Bois, said Mrs. Whitlock, came to Charleston from time to time on NAACP business, and socialized with the Harlestons.

"I guess I was eight when I remember Du Bois came," Mrs. Whitlock recalled, looking at the table. "They used to have meetings at our house. There was a long hallway, and a door going to the studio, which was huge, with thirty or thirty-five people in it. I was always kind of bad, I was curious. I saw these people walking down the hall going to the studio, and got down on my hands and knees, looking at 'em. And they were talking, and I saw Du Bois looking around to see who was looking at him. Then he pulled his crotch up, and adjusted it." Mrs. Whitlock giggled, and her eyes glinted. "He must have felt my presence, the way he was looking around. That's my recollection of the great man." Mrs. Whitlock laughed, and the specter of the saintly Du Bois fled the room.

Edwina Whitlock was the child of a privileged mulatto family. When she was a girl, she said, she did not feel the struggle of working black people.

"My grandfather owned a lot of tenements where people rented," she said. "We would be going to collect the rents, and he would say to me, 'You talk to these people! They're putting bread in your mouth. Don't think you are any better than they are!' So I would go skippin' along, and the tenants would say, 'Oh, here come Mr. Harleston and his grand.' "

Edwin and Elise Harleston raised their adopted girl until Edwin Harleston's death in 1931, when his niece was fourteen. Edwina Harleston went on to attend the Avery Normal Institute, a high school for children of the city's elite class of light-skinned African Americans, and then Talladega College, a private black school established in 1867 in Alabama, graduating in 1939. From there she went to graduate school in journalism at Northwestern University, in Evanston, Illinois.

Edwina Harleston began a career in journalism at the *Baltimore Afro-American* and later returned to Illinois to work for the *Chicago Defender*, both newspapers produced by black staff for black readers. She met her future husband, Henry Whitlock, whose family owned the Gary, Indiana, *American*, a weekly black paper in Whitlock's home state. They married in 1945, bought the newspaper from Henry Whitlock's father, and ran it for fifteen years. Edwina Whitlock wrote a weekly column.

"My husband was the only person who could sit at a linotype machine and write an editorial," Mrs. Whitlock remembered, a little proud. "I used to write a column called 'First Person Singular,' and I would send it to him. He would change it, and it would come back to me to proofread. I would change it again and send it back to him." Mrs. Whitlock gave a twinkling glance. "And that's when the Coke bottles started flying. He was pretty good at ducking."

I asked what she wrote about.

"Things that the white papers ignored that were going on in the black community," she replied.

When Henry Whitlock died in 1960, Edwina Whitlock sold the *American* and moved with her four children to Los Angeles. The family lived in California until her retirement. When the children were grown, Mrs. Whitlock returned to Charleston, her childhood home, after an absence of fifty years. She lived in South Carolina for twelve years. Finally, at age seventy-five, she moved to Atlanta, to be near two of her children.

...

Paintings done by Edwin Harleston hung in Mrs. Whitlock's living room. Half of them were portraits, half landscapes. At Uncle Teddy's death, Mrs. Whitlock had inherited some of his work, and in her older years spent much time getting his name around museums and into art history texts. A walk around the living room showed much about the Harlestons and the history of the black South.

"That's Teddy Harleston, a self-portrait, and that's his wife, Elise," said Mrs. Whitlock, in front of two paintings. Mrs. Whitlock's daughter, Mae Gentry, joined our private gallery tour.

Elise Harleston was painted by her husband in the year of their marriage, 1920, when she was twenty-eight. The painting combined Baroque chiaroscuro with realist character study. Elise's figure appeared to be lighted from above, with her body disappearing in dark shadow. She had an oval face and full cheeks, and her husband had given her remarkable deep eyes.

Next to her painting was one of the artist's self-portraits. Edwin Harleston had painted himself with chiseled features and close-cropped hair, against a blood-red background. Like his wife, he was lighted from above, although there was even more contrast, with deep, dark passages. The light whitened his forehead and nose, while the lower half of his face was thrown into black, as though he had been made of two colors.

"Did you see Congressman Miller?" asked Mrs. Whitlock, pointing at another picture.

"He was the last of the black Reconstruction congressmen," said Mae Gentry. She meant last in the sense that he was the final black congressman elected after the Civil War in the years before white people took back control of Southern politics. The painting showed a use of light and shade similar to the first two.

"This is of Aaron Douglas," said Mrs. Whitlock, moving to the next.

The painting showed a handsome man in a blue shirt, with a painter's palette and brush in hand, looking straight at the viewer. Behind him was a glimpse of a mural, as though he had just stepped away from it. Mrs. Whitlock explained that Edwin Harleston's last major work, in 1930, was a collaboration with Aaron Douglas, another African American painter. Together the two made a series of murals at Fisk University, in Nashville.

"The murals show a history of the black man from ancient times, going back to ancient Egypt," said Mae.

...

The story of Edwin Harleston, painter, grandson of the slave Kate Wilson, had been published by Mrs. Whitlock in an essay she wrote for a museum catalogue to accompany a show of his work.

Edwin A. Harleston was born in Charleston on March 14, 1882, one of eight children of Louisa Moultrie Harleston and "Captain" Edwin Gaillard Harleston. Captain Harleston was so named because he once operated a schooner on the Atlantic seaboard. Louisa Moultrie Harleston had been born free during slavery and, to judge from her name, may well have been a mulatto from The Bluff plantation, home of Mary Louisa Moultrie Ball.

When Edwin Harleston was a boy, one of his aunts, Hannah Harleston Mickey, owned a funeral home, once run by her husband. Aunt Hannah invited Edwin's father, Captain Harleston, to run the business. The captain agreed, ran the company for many years, then set up his own firm, the Harleston Funeral Home.

As a pupil at Simonton Public School in Charleston, Edwin Harleston made sketches, to which he devoted much care. At the time the teachers were white, and not likely to conceive of a future in art for their black charges. According to Mrs. Whitlock, one day Edwin brought to school a drawing he had made of a horse, and showed it to a teacher. Eyeing the page, the woman observed, "That's nice, Edwin. Maybe you'll grow up to become a hostler." To Edwin's parents, the idea that their well-heeled child was being patronized by a white teacher, and compared to a stable boy, was like a dose of acid. When Edwin told his mother about what had happened, she pulled him out of the Simonton School.

In 1896 Edwin enrolled at the Avery Normal Institute, where his graduating class numbered six students. Edwin went on to Atlanta University, a black institution where, among the faculty, W. E. B. Du Bois had a job as a humanities professor. In Atlanta, Edwin studied a quasi-classical European curriculum, played football, and sang in a quartet. In time, the ambitiousness of the Charleston mulatto could be heard in the nickname that other students gave him—Teddyseus.

The year Edwin went to college, Du Bois was writing *The Souls of Black Folk*. Harleston the student and Du Bois the teacher became friends.

In 1904 Edwin Harleston applied to Harvard University, from which Du Bois had graduated, and was accepted in the fine arts department. At the time, according to Mrs. Whitlock, Harvard admitted black men with bachelor's degrees but required them to enter the university as third-year undergraduates. Rejecting this second-class policy, Harleston opted to enroll at the School of the Boston Museum of Fine Arts instead. When he arrived in Massachusetts in fall of 1905, he found he was the only black student in the program.

To earn money, Harleston worked as waiter at one of the Harvard student clubs. In the self-portrait that Edwina Whitlock showed me in her living room, Harleston wears a bright white shirt and black bow tie—the uniform of a waiter.

After graduation, Harleston stayed in Boston until 1913. In Charleston, his father had built a new funeral home, and he insisted that Edwin come home to work in it. Obediently, the painter enrolled in a three-month course at the Renouard School of Embalming, in New York, then moved home to Charleston and entered the funeral business.

Within a few years, Edwin was a prominent businessman and president of the local NAACP. He detested being an undertaker and worked in off-hours to develop his painting career. The trouble was that no economic place whatsoever existed for black artists in the South during the early 1900s. Charleston black society was small, and never flush enough to support a painter who might document it. Many of Harleston's portrait commissions came from out-of-state rich blacks, and from whites.

After Edwin married Elise Forrest, a Charleston-born schoolteacher whom he had been seeing for seven years, the couple decided to attempt an artistic partnership and open a studio, in which he would paint and she would be a photographer. Before they married, Elise Harleston left teaching and was sent on Edwin's money to study photography in New York, at the E. Brunel School of Photography. She finished training at Tuskegee Institute, in Alabama, and returned to Charleston for the wedding. The Harleston Studio opened in 1922, and the collaboration worked for a time. Elise would photograph her husband's subjects when they came for a sitting, and later Edwin would finish the paintings, using Elise's photographs as a guide.

In the early 1900s, French Impressionism and its derivatives enjoyed a vogue in America, long years after they had been superseded in Europe. The "new" painting dwelled on gardens and flower paths, which meant that artists had to do on-site outdoor painting from life. Edwin wanted a teaching job in art that had become available in Washington, D.C., but in the period's stylistic changes he was told he could not be hired unless he painted landscapes. Edwin had trained in the academic tradition of the Beaux-Arts, with its emphasis on portraiture and realism. To extend his range, and perhaps to get away from the funeral business, in 1924, at forty-two, Edwin enrolled in the School of the Chicago Art Institute, where he stayed for two summer sessions. When he returned to South Carolina, Edwin knew he would have trouble with his painting, especially turning out the floral scenes that had become so popular. The South had a unique problem he had not faced in Illinois, namely, segregation, which kept him from visiting public parks and gardens.

Magnolia Gardens, a languid preserve of lily ponds and flower beds on the Ashley River near Charleston, was one of South Carolina's most beautiful parks. The only blacks (or mulattoes) permitted on its grounds were the black workers who kept the gardens. Edwin wrote to park officials asking permission to enter the gardens in order to paint. When, as expected, he was refused, Edwin, in pursuit of the Impressionist materials of the late Claude Monet, decided to go undercover. At Magnolia Gardens, there was a group of latticed wooden bridges that arched over meandering streams, decorative follies that, as it happened, were built and maintained by one of Edwin's cousins. Disguising himself as a workman on one of his cousin's maintenance crews, Edwin managed to get onto the grounds, carrying a satchel with some carpenter's tools, as well as a camera. In several visits, the painter secretly photographed the dogwoods and tulips, rose walks, and lilies. Back in his studio, working from the pictures, he made more than a dozen paintings.

In 1926 the Charleston Museum was asked by the mayor, Thomas P. Stoney, to put on a retrospective of Edwin Harleston's work. By then he was known to whites as "Charleston's colored artist." Anxious to please the mayor, museum director Laura M. Bragg consented to the unprecedented plan for a show of paintings by a Negro. When approached, Edwin agreed and began to crate his paintings for the move across town to the museum. According to Edwina Whitlock, Edwin was thrilled that at last recognition had arrived. But political maneuvering occurred, and three weeks later a letter arrived from Bragg explaining that the trustees of the museum had met and vetoed the idea of the show. "The exhibit would hurt and not help you at the present time," she wrote.

Edwin Harleston's last major work was the collaboration with painter Aaron Douglas on a series of murals at Fisk University in Nashville, in 1930. The ambition of Aaron Douglas, who brought Edwin on the job, was to chronicle black history from before enslavement in Africa to the American present. Edwin moved to Nashville to execute the project in the Fisk library reading rooms. As he worked with Douglas, from time to time Edwin wrote home to describe the murals to Elise.

"The figures in both rooms are conventional—after the the Egyptian manner—and deal with the general history, economics, and culture of the race," he told Elise. "The whole thing will fit very nicely with the architecture of the building, which is Gothic, the adaptation being from far back in African architecture as exemplified in the 'set back' treatment of towers, as in old Timbuctoo."

In October 1930, the painter wrote Elise: "We are done! Finished!! Completed!!! 670 linear feet of mural decorations of a unique type done by Us, of Us and for Us."

The Douglas-Harleston murals, depicting a black saga that begins before contact with whites, represent an early achievement of Afrocentric American art.

A few months later, in May 1931, Captain Harleston, the painter's father, fell ill with pneumonia in Charleston. As the old man lay dying, Edwin bent over and kissed him on the lips. Ten days later, Edwin Harleston himself was dead of pneumonia, at forty-nine.

Two years after his death, the painter got the show he was denied in life, when some of his work was exhibited at the National Gallery of Art, in Washington.

"All of them," said Mrs. Whitlock, wrapping up her story, "all the Harlestons, right on through, we are writers, artists, musicians. There is a whole lot of talent. I have a first cousin who is a music arranger. One of the Harlestons was president of City College in New York. There is a General Harleston, in the Pentagon." Even as Mrs. Whitlock boasted of her family's high standards, it did not sound like vanity.

Another descendant of Kate Wilson and William Harleston, and one of the various Harleston progeny involved in the arts, worked in the music business, and could be found living in Los Angeles. Ray Maith Fleming was born in Charleston and raised as one of the heirs to the family funeral business. As a youth, however, Ray Fleming had left his heritage behind. In California, and now somewhere in his fifties, Fleming worked as a music producer, with an inventory of pop credits behind him.

It was a mild, cloudless afternoon in Los Angeles when I first visited Ray Fleming. His apartment building resembled countless others in southern California—low, beige, rectangular, with balconies and sliding glass doors—conforming to the local genre of sunbelt Modernism. The building stood inside a block-long compound surrounded along the sidewalks by a high iron fence. Security gates controlled access, and tenants who entered the compound looked around before punching in their numbered codes.

Ray Fleming came down to one of the iron gates, and we made our way past two swimming pools surrounded by patio furniture. He wore a red polo shirt, khaki pants, and loafers, stood medium height, and was handsome. The Pacific sun against the poolside patio created an incandescent field of light that seemed to whiten my skin, while Ray Fleming's color was tawny brown, like maple syrup.

As we arrived in his apartment, a vivacious woman wearing sandals and a housedress entered the room. She had straight brown hair cut in a bob, a bright manner, and was white. Ray Fleming introduced me to his wife, Tina De Fazio. Tina brought soft drinks, left the room, and a boy of about four rushed over and jumped on Ray Fleming's lap. The child had curly hair and skin the color of blond wood.

"Say hello to your cousin, Giovanni," said Ray, flashing his eyes and laughing. The child looked at me with wide eyes before he went off to join his mother.

Ray Fleming had a fine baritone voice, and his gaze was direct. He had the aura of a person who was not afraid to talk about anything.

"You're married to a white woman," I said.

"I'm married to the right woman," Ray answered. "She happens to be white. She was born in Italy, but raised in Canada. I met her in New York City twenty-five years ago, and we never parted. It gets better every day, because she has expanded me as a person."

"What do you think about fact that you and I are distant cousins?" I asked.

"I always knew you were there," he came back. "I just didn't know you. It was like a missing link, but you always knew what the components were."

"The connection is distant," I said.

"But it's real," Ray replied. "And not only that, it's a journey."

Ray Fleming's grandmother, Katherine Harleston, was a sister of the painter Edwin. Ray was a great-great-grandson of Kate Wilson, and Giovanni the next generation down.

"We knew we weren't complete Africans," Ray began. "I knew the Harlestons were from England. I've known that for a very long time. You just know that there were English in your background, among other things. That was a matter of fact. I love all of me, that's how I think of it. I love all of me."

Ray Fleming spoke emphatically but did not gesticulate. He merely raised a finger now and then, or at the most shifted his shoulders when he finished a thought. Like his cousin, Edwina Whitlock, Ray Fleming used his voice to hypnotic effect, spinning out his sentences in a flourish.

"I don't love black people any more than I love white people, or people I haven't met," Ray said. "Because love is open and universal. I don't even love my kids more than I love other people's kids. I have more responsibility for them, but it has nothing to do with my overall love."

Ray Fleming had left home in his youth, and now spoke in a way that would be unfamiliar in parts of the South. It was as though he had invented a second person, and added him to the Southerner with the deep black-and-white history.

The apartment had an L-shaped carpeted living room, an open kitchen, and two bedrooms down a hallway. The most noticeable piece of decor hung on the wall—four gold records, trophies from Ray Fleming's years in the music business, markers of the distance he had come from home. I asked Ray to tell me his story, and he unrolled it smoothly, as though used to talking about himself.

"I was born on Calhoun Street, Charleston, South Carolina," he began. "My father was a bachelor, and my mother died when I was two years old."

"The Harleston funeral home was on Calhoun Street," I remembered, "with the apartments above."

"The Fleming family owned it by that time," Ray said, speaking of the family of his grandfather. "Or it was a Harleston-Fleming partnership. The Flemings were from St. Augustine, Florida, and all the black professionals in the South knew each other. One of the Flemings married a Harleston woman, and that's how they got into the business.

"My father moved in the mulatto world. He was mulatto, a very handsome guy, with a mustache. All the women loved him. He was a bachelor, he had a building, and he had money. He was rich, simple as that. My grandmother used to say, 'They were well-to-do.' "

Ray laughed and rocked forward, but he pursed his mouth. It was a restrained laugh, as though he was unsure how to feel about his connection to an old black elite.

"The mulattoes had more money than darker-skinned people," I said.

"They had more money and more education," Ray said. "The Harlestons were like that. A lot of the moneyed blacks adhered to a societal standard in everything they did, from their dress to their food. They could afford it, and they knew the best of everything."

"Did they shun darker-skinned people?"

"No! My father did not shun. All of his girlfriends were dark-skinned!" Ray laughed. "I wasn't dark, but I wasn't mulatto. I was in-between. I was welcome on both sides. But a funny thing I noticed about a lot of mulattoes around Charleston is that the women didn't always marry. It's as though the women, if they couldn't find a matching mulatto, couldn't have a family. A lot of the darker black men were afraid of them. They didn't think they could rate, so they didn't approach them."

As a child, Ray lived for a time in the house with the funeral home. "We had five-course meals," he said. "Edwin Harleston's paintings were on the walls." Downstairs, the mortuary business never stopped. "The clients were the mulattoes, and I would be in there during the embalming sometimes. But the motto of the funeral home was, 'No one is denied services because of financial condition.' The Harlestons were always altruistic people. They always had, so they always gave."

I could see a handsome youth in Ray Fleming's aging face. But

Ray's physique was strong, his wit intact, and he moved gracefully through a story.

"It was a charmed life," he went on. "For instance, the city pool was right behind our house, on George Street. I used to stand in the backyard as a kid, and all the whites would be swimming, and I'm looking right through my gate at their fun. I had a friend named Tony Haynes, who was light-complexioned and could pass for white. He used to say, 'Man, I'm not going all the way over to that colored pool.' He would say, 'I'll meet you all later'—and he would go jump in the white pool!"

This time Ray let go a laugh that opened all the way, then he put on a conspiratorial look.

"He could have been put in jail, or a reformatory," Ray said. "They would have said, 'He's got plenty of nerve! He's an uppity nigger! The next thing you know, he'll be with one of our daughters!' We were just playing a trick on the white man." Ray shifted his shoulders. "We knew white people weren't doing anything different than we were. We were just doing it in a different place."

From time to time as a young man, Ray also got into trouble over the rules of the skin game.

"The mulatto women were very fair," he remembered. "I had instances where the police stopped me because they thought I was with a white woman. I will never forget, I was walking on Rutledge Avenue with Ella Sanders. The Sanders family were very fair. It was dusk, and the police pulled over. They made me come over and identify myself. 'What are you doing with her?' the cop said. 'We go to school together,' I said. 'Oh, you mean . . .' he said. 'Yeah, that's what I mean—she's black.'

"You see, the police were all white," Ray remembered. "The funniest thing, when the first blacks came in as cops, they picked men who were nasty to black people. The black cops wanted to prove they weren't lenient, and they got to be hated by black people. We used to say, 'Bring back the white folks, this Negro's beating me to death!' "

Ray Fleming made the whole race business seem comical, almost foolish. It was easy to laugh with him.

"Everybody has their story, but the stories are really the same story," he went on. "Put some color in it, it's no different. White people came from Europe, they had nothing. They fought and survived. An 'indentured servant'—that's just a pretty name for a slave. At any time you could be bought, sold, whipped, raped, no matter what your color. The Irish have the same story. They came over in boats, in what they called the 'coffin cabin.' So many of them would die on the way over here. They would write back to Ireland, telling people not to come because the plantation owner was working them to death."

"The Irish had it as bad as the blacks?" I asked.

"Had it worse in some ways," Ray answered, "because the blacks were worth something. The Irish owed money, but the blacks were paid for, so they were more protected."

Giovanni came back into the room and sat on his father's lap. Ray resumed his own story.

"I knew I wanted to choose my own course, that they couldn't hold me down there, in the South," he said. "I told my old man, 'I'm not going to be an undertaker! I don't want to go to the Cincinnati School of Embalming!' So nobody took over the funeral home. When my father died, that was the demise of the family funeral business. I moved to New York, about 1957."

In New York as a young man, Ray said, he took to Greenwich Village. It was the beginning of the white counterculture of the period, and instead of living entirely in Harlem, Ray crossed back and forth between the white and black worlds. In downtown Manhattan he hung out in coffee shops, met women, attended poetry readings.

"Jews taught me a lot," Ray remembered of the time. "They were very open. I remember one guy who called himself Yogi. His real name was Harold Zimmerman. He wore an earring, and this was the late fifties! He brought me copies of Nietzsche. He loved to talk about Cervantes, and even St. Augustine." In addition to hanging out in Village cafés, Ray kept up a second nightlife along 125th Street in Harlem, at the Apollo Theatre and other temples of rhythm and blues.

"In the Village, a Jewish friend of mine, named Harvey, said, 'Man you need a job. You're getting thin. These girls ain't going to take you in forever. Get a job.' I said, 'Harvey, I'm not used to doing work.' 'Be a salesman,' Harvey said. So I started working at a record store, in midtown Manhattan. When I was a teenager, I played the trumpet, and the saxophone. It's what led me into the music field. The record store was on Forty-second Street between Seventh and Eighth avenues, and it was run by Syrian Jews. I used to be able to memorize thousands of records. People would come in, tell me a lyric, or hum the tune, and I could name the song. It made me valuable, and after a while I became the music buyer. I was late to work five years in a row, but it didn't matter. 'Leave him alone,' my boss used to say. 'We need him.' The Twist was big in those days, so I wrote a song, 'The Whole World's Doing the Twist.' The owners of the store paid to produce the record, and we played it in the store, and around town. That gave me a taste for the business.

"I started making friends and falling in with music people. I met a guy from Texas, Jimmy Jones, who had recorded a number one pop record, called 'Handy Man,' in 1960. Jones said, 'You're a good music writer.' After a while he introduced me to his producer, and I got signed on Screen Gems Music, on retainer, to write songs. I was in my mid-twenties."

Along the way, the songwriter started using a stage name, Beau Ray, that reminded people of his good looks.

"Then I got interested in jazz. I hung out at Birdland, on Broadway and Fifty-second Street. I stopped going to the Apollo and listening to the R&B groups, and I was in the jazz clubs every night. After a while I began to produce records of my own, black acts. Every time I produced something, I would sell it, get money, and do more."

Beau Ray Fleming signed on a jazz singer, a crooner named John Lucien, and with him cut an album for one of the big music houses, RCA. "They called him the new Nat King Cole," said Ray. "Then I did a record with a guy called Milt Matthews, blues rock, also with RCA." Beau Ray made his way through the next decade, producing here and there until the 1970s, when he picked up on the dance scene and began turning out disco music.

"One of my acts was called Mandrill," Ray remembered. "They were seven guys, Panamanian, Cuban, Puerto Rican, and Jewish. They had a top-ten record called 'Fence Walk.' Another disco act I had was called GQ, which I produced for Arista Records. I had a group called Sun, which we produced with Capitol. And there was Zulema, who was a girl who did a kind of symphonic soul—with strings, horns, percussion. Her big record was 'Wanna Be Where You Are.'"

In the 1970s, Ray's company was known as Royal Gentlemen Productions, with offices at 12 West Fifty-sixth Street.

"We had a whole floor," said Ray. "I had three personal assistants. I was living large."

We got up from the sofa and went to the hallway where the four gold discs hung on the wall in frames. There was a 1973 album by the group Mandrill, a 1978 record by Sun, titled "Sunburn," a 1979 compilation of dance songs, "A Night at Studio 54," and a 1979 single by the group GQ, "Disco Nights."

In the 1980s, Ray's business came apart. A sadness came over him as he told this part of his story, and his monologue broke up into a few stray facts. Ray's face fell for the first time as he groped for an explanation.

"You get caught up in your own charisma," he said, looking down. "I did too much celebration, and not enough work."

When the money stopped flowing, Ray's wife, Tina, started working, and the two moved from New York to Los Angeles. When we met, Ray Fleming was trying to get back into the business, putting himself in touch with people he had known years earlier, and finding new talent.

"I've got one record of jungle music and techno that sold big in Europe, and I've got a female black crooner," he said.

Ray pulled out a new compact disc, his first recording in several years. It would be coming out soon. On the back of the package there appeared a few liner notes, and at the bottom of the label an acknowledgment that read, "Thanks to the Fleming family, to the Harleston family, and thanks to the people and my friends in Charleston, South Carolina."

Ray shifted his shoulders. "Never mind the record business. Charleston is in my blood. I'm going to be buried there."

It was a cool, rainy afternoon in Charleston when Edwina Whitlock took me to visit the grave of her great-grandmother, Kate Wilson. The descendants of Kate Wilson were spread from coast to coast. Edwina Whitlock had lived away from Charleston much of her life and did not get back often, but she had come from Atlanta for the weekend.

"Your hair is changed," she said when we met. "It's more curly. Are you trying to be black?" Edwina laughed familiarly.

On that gray day Edwina Whitlock looked typically stylish, in a black overcoat with a flared lapel, and trousers. She carried an unusual carved cane, with naked figures on it, which completed her image of handsome eccentricity. We went out to lunch before the rain began to fall; then, with umbrellas high, we headed for the cemetery.

We arrived in a small patch of three or four acres at the northern edge of Charleston, the graveyard of the Unity and Friendship Society, a social club of light-skinned blacks founded in the 1840s. The cemetery contained many families of elite people of color, most of them descended from mulattoes who got free before the end of slavery. In a single place, the gray of the light on the green plain of grass was interrupted by a fresh grave smothered in bright flowers. As we walked between rows of neat family plots, Edwina pointed with her cane at the headstones.

"Now, here is Dr. McFall," she said, aiming. "He was a real civil rights person. And he supported Uncle Teddy. What I mean is he bought Uncle Teddy's paintings." A bit farther, "These are the DeCostas." The DeCostas were an old Charleston family of Sephardic Jews who at some point crossed over; most who now carried the name were prosperous blacks. "This woman's husband was a doctor and a very dear friend of Uncle Teddy's. They used to go hunting together."

Edwina Whitlock pushed on between the graves. "You could write a history of Charleston blacks just walking through this yard," she said. In front of a big granite headstone, she pointed. "Oh, here is the Mickey family—Hannah Harleston Mickey. Hannah was one of Kate Wilson's children with William Harleston. She married a man named Mickey, and had five children. One of them, Ellen, the youngest, she shot a man. You see, Ellen was in love with the man's wife, and wanted to do him in." Edwina Whitlock cocked her head and giggled.

"Ellen was in love with the wife?" I asked.

"Yes. I don't know if she killed the husband. This might have been about 1925."

"She was a lesbian, and she was jealous that this man was married to her lover?" I clarified.

"That's it," said Edwina. "Uncle Teddy, in one of his letters, writes to his wife that, 'We had to spirit Ellen out of town.' You know, we have a lot of scandals in the family, and some of them don't come out until later."

Edwina shrugged and walked ahead. "Now, where's Kate?" she said. "Oh, there."

We came to the handsome granite marker inscribed with several names. The first read, "Kate Wilson Harleston, November 17, 1886." The name William Harleston did not appear on the stone. Edwina looked down, squinted between the raindrops, and teetered on the soft ground.

"You see, sometimes the white man gives his bastards his name, but makes no provision for them at all," she said. "Those are the step-aside children. But one thing about William Harleston, he bought a house for Kate, and I know he left it to her. He did that, so I think I can forgive him."

14

►·◄►·◦·◄►·◄

THE CURSE OF BUZZARD WING

There is a legend in the Ball family; some call it the curse of Buzzard Wing. "Buzzard Wing" was the posthumous nickname attached to Martha Caroline Swinton Ball, the coddled, beautiful second wife of the richest of the rice planters, John Ball. Caroline, as she was also known, was the young mother whose infant twins each received a pair of child slaves. It is said that Buzzard Wing put a curse on the descendants of John's thrifty and devout first wife, Jane Ball—that is, a curse on the rest of us.

Caroline was born on Edisto Island, south of Charleston, and raised in the tiny white world of that fundamentally black place. A miniature painting of her in her twenties depicts her as comely and complacent, with sly eyes and ringlet curls dripping around her forehead. In 1805, at nineteen, Caroline married John Ball, forty-four, and soon gained a reputation among her stepchildren (who were slightly older than she) for frivolous spending and wild fertility. The stacks of receipts that survive show that Caroline's world turned on an axis of shopping. In a modest excursion, a trip to the clothier in 1813, she came home with a feathered hat, beaver gloves, a fur stole, a bottle of pink dye, "a Moroccan dressing case," some silver tassels, a broach, and "two ounces of spangles." Caroline's large wardrobe evidently needed care, because one year she bought a man who could work on it—George ("a tailor," in the bill of sale, "and lame in the hip"). She probably spent large sums on maternity wear. In twelve years of marriage to John Ball, Caroline gave birth to eleven children, including one born after her husband's death, which occurred when she was thirty-one.

A cousin of mine remembered the lament about Buzzard Wing uttered by his great-grandmother, Mary Gibbs Ball. Mary lived through the Civil War and watched the family fortune vanish. "Greatie used to say," my cousin reported, "that when all the slaves had gone, and she was plowing the field by herself, she would lift her eyes to the sky and shake her fist at old Buzzard Wing." Greatie evidently thought the Balls had ended badly—between the Confederate defeat and the loss of the slaves—because of a single successful gold digger.

With the death of John Ball in 1817, John Ball Jr. and Isaac, thirty-five and thirty-two, respectively, took charge of the family. Their three full brothers were dead, but John Jr. and Isaac had a brood of half siblings to provide for—Caroline's nine surviving children, all under age twelve. Money was not a problem. In 1821, John Jr. noted that he had invested $167,537 in stock for Caroline's children, an enormous sum. Labor was also available. In 1824, Isaac Ball owned 571 people on six plantations, while John Jr. personally owned 542 and managed another 173 people belonging to his half brothers and half sisters.

The problem in the family was the young widow, Caroline, and her grasping ways. Shortly after her husband's death, Caroline sued the Balls, evidently for a larger portion of the inheritance (the will divided an amount equally among the widow and her children, meaning Caroline got one-tenth). Next, she married a rice planter named Augustus Taveau, known for his gambling and dissipation. In a letter to John Jr.—who controlled the estate of his father and therefore any money going to Caroline—Buzzard Wing announced her wedding to Taveau, then asked for money, enclosing a doctor's bill. The doctor had prescribed port wine for a recent illness, she said, and, "being short of cash," she had bought the liquor on credit. Regarding the "medicine," Caroline asked John to pay. "If you do not come" to the wedding, she wrote, "you could send the check enclosed by Bob [a messenger], who is coming on Monday."

Caroline had five more children with Taveau, bringing her output to sixteen babies in a little more than twenty years. Shortly after the marriage, Caroline and Taveau, out of money, sued the Balls for mismanagement of the trust fund set up to support Caroline's children by John Ball. Two years passed and Caroline sued again (the third lawsuit), claiming that John Jr. was not sending her enough to raise the young ones in proper style.

John Jr. and Isaac lived much of the time with their families in Charleston—John on Hasell Street, Isaac in his mansion on East Bay and Vernon streets. Buzzard Wing's children lived with her and Taveau. By the 1820s the Ball world was no longer the old country idyll of meadows, three-day parties, and friends seen at church. The family lived a city lifestyle fueled by plantation earnings. With thirteen hundred workers between them, the two brothers were captains of an agrarian industry. The work camps themselves were left to be run by overseers, while John Jr. and Isaac focused on money. Previously the Balls had bought new lands and new people with their profits; now they speculated in stocks. John Jr.'s account books, with their meticulous and constant churning of investments, would make for an auditor's case study.

Far from the master's authority, and white society, the Ball slaves carved out separate lives. Field hands, especially, saw few whites—the overseer's family and a few hired extras—and on visits the Balls were not likely to recognize many of them. This lack of contact gave black people more freedom, but it also brought more insecurity. With so many hands, it was easy for John Jr. and Isaac to treat "their people" like pieces of equipment. Throughout the 1820s, accounts show that black villages were often broken up by the renting out of single workers, or whole families, who were told on short notice to pack up and move out for six months or a year. The fees that resulted went into John Jr.'s revenue books, next to the interest payments and dividends.

After John Sr.'s death, relations between Buzzard Wing and the children of his first wife, Jane, became testy. John Jr. sent Caroline an inventory to make sure she knew that everything in her house, down to "2 ironing tables . . . and 4 toilet covers," would be counted as part of her inheritance. As executor of the estate, John Jr. made Caroline sign receipts for money he sent her to buy clothes for her children. In reply, she sent him nuisance bills, including one from her pharmacist for castor oil and "4 tablespoons Spanish flies," an aphrodisiac.

John Jr. and Isaac worried that Caroline's ways might be passed to her children, which could tarnish the family name. Among Caroline's children were three brothers close in age—Alwyn Ball, Hugh Swinton Ball, and Elias Octavus Ball. Alwyn's portrait, a miniature, depicts him as rather sweet. But a painting of Hugh Swinton (who went by Swinton) shows a somewhat jaded, dark-haired swain. Elias Octavus got his unusual name by being the eighth person in the family to carry the name of the patriarch. When their father died, all three were younger than ten. In their teens, they became restless. John Jr., himself a dutiful father of seven, complained in a letter about the added responsibility he had looking out for the young men, especially because they had begun to show signs of greed. The brothers, he wrote, had "the same thirst for money" he saw in Caroline, and John worried that the boys might become rakes. "My only hope [rests] upon their being far removed from the influence of their mother," he told a friend.

Taking things in hand, John Jr. and Isaac decided to send their half brothers to military school. In 1823, Alwyn, sixteen, Swinton, fifteen, and Elias O., fourteen, were packed off to Patridge's Military Academy, in Norwich, Vermont. Once they arrived, Isaac wrote the students to reassure them amid their loneliness and to insist that this was surely the right path. The boys should apply themselves and become good soldiers, Isaac said, because inevitably more black revolts would have to be put down.

"[R]ecollect for what purpose you have been sent to Capt P[art-ridge]'s Academy," Isaac wrote, raising an imaginary index finger. "That we will stand in need of military men before many years will have rolled over our heads I feel confident, for the abolition societies of Europe and of some of our own northern brethren appear very anxious to set our slaves in commotion."

The teens, who were accustomed to light tutoring and heavy spending, seem to have been put off by the spartan living conditions and endless drills. They rebelled, and began to plague the schoolmaster, Captain Alden Partridge, with demands for cash. When Patridge refused them money, they stopped going to classes. Sensing that their half brother John would not bail them out, Swinton wrote to Isaac instead, complaining that the military school reminded him of the plantations— only now he stood on the wrong side of the deal:

It is almost as bad as slavery here for we cannot go out of the village without being called to account and we have to attend four roll calls a day and are not allowed to leave the quarters after 2 o'clock. I am likewise in debt and I will be obliged to sell my watch to pay if I don't get money from home. We were obliged to sell some clothes to get money. . . . [Captain Partridge] has not given us a cent since we have been here nor have we received a cent from home which I think is a very hard case as it is our own money.

Before Partridge had the chance to kick them out, Alwyn and Elias O. picked up and left, using money from the sale of their clothes to pay the trip to Charleston. (Swinton reconsidered, and decided to stay on.)

A little desperate, John Jr. next tried sending Alwyn and Elias O. to boarding school in England. In June 1824 he placed them in the hands of his rice agent in Liverpool, Thomas Crowder. John enclosed a draft for £300 and a nervous note to the effect that he simply did not know how much money Crowder would have to spend on the boys.

In Liverpool things with the two dropouts worsened. Thomas Crowder soon found himself fending off the brothers' demands for cash, and their new schoolmaster, the Reverend James Balfour, wrote to John Jr. with upsetting reports. Balfour complained that the boys were "independent," refused to learn Latin, and were "backward." Alwyn and Elias O. did not make friends, Balfour added, because merely being around students their own age reminded them of how little they knew. John Jr. wrote letters imploring his half brothers to straighten out, and sent embarrassed excuses to their guardian. "In fact, sir, my brothers are sons of a second marriage," John explained to Crowder, "and unfortunate [to have] a mother, who thinks much more of the external acquirements than of those qualifications which give respectability and usefulness to a community; and this will account to you in some measure why my brothers are so backward."

After six months in England, Alwyn and Elias O. dropped out, to the relief of the schoolmaster. Crowder wrote to John Jr. that he tried to get them a private tutor to carry on their education. After actually meeting the brothers, however, no tutor would take the job. Finally, Crowder found a recent graduate of Cambridge who agreed to teach the two at home, for £100. Alwyn and Elias O. were sent to live with the young man's mother.

The lessons had just begun when Alwyn went to Crowder and announced that the money John Jr. had sent to pay for his education was really his and that he wanted it. When Crowder refused, the brothers stopped seeing their tutor and began stealing away at night. Crowder reported that they quickly got into bad company, carousing with what he called "strolling players," hard-drinking minstrels. Alwyn and Elias O. demanded money to travel around England, evidently with the minstrels, but Crowder again refused. Frustrated, the boys decided they would just go home. In a last letter, Crowder said that Alwyn and Elias O. had appeared at his door and handed him invoices for debts they had run up, which came to more than half the annual salary of their teacher. The tutor demanded to be paid in full for the year, because he had turned down other offers to instruct the wild Ball boys. Politely, Crowder told John Jr. that he was fed up. "It is clear that nothing but an unlimited credit would satisfy them," he wrote, and that "a desire to improve themselves is not in their intuition. . . . I should be very unwilling to take upon myself the responsibility which an idle life led in this country by them would entail upon me."

Alwyn and Elias O. sailed for Charleston in February 1825. John Jr. added up the money he had spent on his brothers' English lark— $2,674 for seven months—and charged it against their future inheritance.

Despite having twelve plantations and a capacity to spoil children, the Ball family were members of an increasingly obsolete class. Since 1670 and the founding of South Carolina, Charleston had been the reigning city in the South. Rice had built the regional economy and had driven the capture of countless Africans. But in the early 1800s, money and influence began to ebb from the hands of old rice landlords like the Balls. Rice lost its role as a symbol of Southern life, and King Cotton took its place.

I've pointed out how the decline of the rice barons began with Eli Whitney's cotton gin. Cotton had long been grown in South Carolina, but only on the islands between Charleston and Savannah, where the "long-staple" variety of the plant did well, staple being the fiber or wool in the boll. This premium strain would not grow in the rolling piedmont of the upstate, where only "short-staple" cotton, with its coarser, shorter fiber, thrived. Short-staple cotton required never-ending handwork to clean, because its fibers clung to the seed more firmly than those of the long-staple variety, so the more common plant did not catch on—that is, until the invention of the cotton gin. Eli Whitney's cotton gin, with its revolving cylinder lined by teeth, pulled the seed from the raw fiber, and made the piedmont cotton profitable.

The second strike against rice came in the form of a long ditch, the Santee Canal. The Santee River, whose tributaries drain half the state, reaches deep inland in a curving path toward the middle of South Carolina. Compared to the Santee, the Ashley and Cooper, two rice rivers that end in Charleston harbor, are little streams. Rice planters could drift their crop down to the city on the Ashley and Cooper, but because the Santee emptied into the Atlantic in the wrong place, so to speak (to the north of Charleston), cotton growers in the middle of the state had a harder time delivering their harvest. In 1800, the state government opened the Santee Canal, which, by linking the Santee and Cooper rivers, allowed upstate cotton planters to float their yields directly to Charleston. Within a few years, the canal brought millions of pounds of cotton down the Cooper, past the Ball lands, to ships waiting in the harbor. In 1830, a typical year, 720 cotton barges made their way through the canal to the sea, carrying a harvest of seventy thousand bales, each bale five hundred pounds. The Santee Canal helped feed the new textile mills of England and the American Northeast, and sped the shift from rice to cotton.

"Cotton is king" became the motto of state boosters. Ambitious white men, born low but looking for wealth, turned to the plant. As cotton drained influence from the rice landlords it handed power to new families, who had no stake in the paternalism that the Balls told themselves should govern dealings with black workers. With their ancient lands and dissipated sons, the Balls must have seemed past their time, a weak elite ready to be pushed aside.

After conquering South Carolina, cotton spread west to Alabama, Mississippi, and Louisiana—an expansion made possible by the removal of the Native people. The Creek tribe had lived in Georgia and points west since the early 1700s. After 1810, the Creeks were forced out and, with the Cherokees, marched on the infamous Trail of Tears to the Southwest. The cotton kingdom absorbed their land, and a stream of black workers sent in from South Carolina and Virginia drove the boom. Between 1830 and 1860, the tobacco planters of Virginia (another antique class) sold out of that state some three hundred thousand black people, who were walked in coffles as far as Arkansas. New Orleans arose as the South's premier city, and Charleston fell behind. To many white Southerners, Charleston soon became like its rice planters— quaint, out-of-date.

The Ball boys were not the only ones who kept their hands in the purse; Caroline's daughters also lived in order to spend. Eleven-year-old Lucilla Ball, in one trip to the clothing store (probably with her mother, who saved the receipt), bought some "Grecian bootees, silk shoes, [and] moroccan slippers." Later, she picked up a "long shell comb, feather fan, kid shoes, [and] seal-skin shoes." About the same time Lucilla was buying her pile of footwear, which she would outgrow in a few months, her younger sister Lydia picked out "an ivory-handled whip." At $3, the whip cost more than the weekly wage of a cook.

By the time Alwyn and Elias O. failed out of English boarding school, Swinton, the third brother, had dropped out of Partridge's Academy and returned to Charleston. His uncle Isaac was in the city when he came home. "Swinton arrived here the beginning of November," Isaac wrote, "but what he means to do with himself I can't say." Before the month was out, the seventeen-year-old launched a buying spree, picking up closetfuls of clothes and sending the bills up the family chain. His wardrobe arranged, Swinton next bought a horse on which to parade himself around town. The weary John Jr. paid up, but when the young man asked for a roll of cash, John refused. Swinton wrote him an airy note, "But money I will have when I want it."

Alwyn and Elias Octavus returned from England in spring of 1825. Not to be outfestooned by Swinton, fifteen-year-old Elias O. went to his clothier and bought a blue velvet coat, a pair of white satin pants, several silk handkerchiefs, and a black velvet vest. Although the three Ball brothers now lived just a few blocks from John Jr., they dealt with their money source by messenger, evidently afraid to ask him in person. Elias O. wrote John Jr. to request that he now be given a valet. It was only fair, Elias O. said, because his brother Alwyn had two personal slaves. Elias O. asked for "a boy from Pimlico on the same conditions which Alwyn has Joshua and Katy. If you comply with my request I shall choose a boy named Toby, as he is the only one calculated to serve as a waiting man." John Jr. relented, and poor Toby was brought down from the plantation to follow the young playboy around.

By the terms of their trust fund, Buzzard Wing's sons would come into their inheritance when they turned twenty-one or when they were married, whichever came first. The battle over spending money continued until the idea dawned among the brothers to marry. In 1825, Alwyn, still seventeen, was engaged to Esther McClellan, teenage daughter of a planting family north of Charleston. When Alwyn reached eighteen, they were married, and John Jr. was forced to begin liquidating the brothers' investments to turn over a portion to the newlyweds. (Alwyn wasted no time with the new money: soon after the marriage, he bought nine people from a Charleston doctor, perhaps to staff his house.) Elias O. waited a bit longer, marrying at twenty to rice heiress Amelia Waring. Swinton, however, followed brother Alwyn's example, proposing at seventeen to one Anna Channing, child of a Boston family whom he had apparently met on vacation in Newport, Rhode Island. The wedding took place in New York City in March 1827 (Swinton was eighteen years, six months), attended by a handful of witnesses. A few days later, the groom wrote to his brother John Jr., in Charleston. Now that he was married, Swinton wanted to know, exactly how much would he be receiving?

There may be something to the curse of Buzzard Wing. With the appearance of Caroline Ball, a kind of obliviousness becomes a family trait, and at the same time the destiny of the clan begins to be visible. In the decades just before the Civil War, the Balls were in some ways more detached from black life than they had been during 130 years in the plantation business.

I previously introduced Ann Simons Ball, the second wife of John Jr., who helped her husband run the family lands. Ann's portrait, painted by Samuel F. B. Morse, shows a handsome woman of nearly fifty, flashing a severe expression. The painting seems apt, because Ann

approached plantation management like a soldier, giving lie to the view
that only men had the stomach for the violence of the business. For her
military style, Ann acquired the family nickname Captain Nancy.

Captain Nancy's letters to her husband are full of advice on how to
handle field hands, with admonitions that he was not being strict
enough. In a typical note, Ann told John Jr. to discipline the workers
who seem to have been resisting orders at Midway plantation. "I really
regret extremely the vast trouble you have with your Midway gang of
Negroes," she wrote. "Let me entreat you my dear John . . . if possible
put a stop to this. . . . Don't you think you had better break up that
whole set, dispersing them among your other negroes, and form a new
gang?" (Years later, when John Jr. died, Captain Nancy was advised by
the men in the family to sell everything. Instead, she bought back 215
people from the estate auction—including Tenah, Adonis, and Binah,
ancestors of the family I met in New York and South Carolina—for
$79,855, and took over the business.)

Ann Ball, who was six years older than her husband, seemed to
evolve a partnership with John Jr. in which she set a steely tone. One
day she personally whipped the laundress, Betty, for not properly cleaning the bath towels. After the incident, Captain Nancy sat down calmly
and wrote her husband to explain:

> [Y]ou will not only be surprised, but provoked at the strange
> conduct of Betty in your absence. . . . She had brought in some
> towels so badly washed that I gave them to be done over. They
> were brought to me a second time too badly done to be put up
> —and accompanied by an impertinent manner. I was in my
> chamber & not saying much but taking down the little whip in
> our dressing room whipped her across her shoulders two or three
> times. Her astonishment almost made me laugh. . . . I immedi-
> ately wrote a note & made Peter take her to the workhouse,
> requesting that she be kept in solitary confinement until you
> called for her. She walked out of the yard with a most haughty
> air. . . . If agreeable to you, I will not think of returning her to
> the field, but keep her [in Charleston] & make her wash.

At Ann's command, Betty was taken to the Charleston Work House.
Members of the Ball family, and most of their friends, were customers

of the Work House. Account books show occasional payments the Balls made to the warden in charge for whippings or jail terms. A single whipping was priced at twenty-five cents; jail time ran higher. One year, John Jr. paid $65.25 for accumulated fees. The building, put up in the 1730s on the edge of town, not only served as a prison where disobedient blacks could be jailed, but the yard next to it doubled as a marketplace for people undergoing a second or third sale. The Work House also was one place in town used for the execution of blacks accused of crimes. In 1769, on its grounds, a slave called Liverpool, and his wife, Dolly, charged with poisoning a white baby, were burned alive.

There is no evidence of what precisely happened to Betty within the walls of the Work House, but Ann Ball knew that she had sent the laundress to be tortured. A short time after Captain Nancy used "the little whip in our dressing room" on Betty, a German nobleman, Karl Bernhard, Duke of Saxe-Weimar, visited the Work House and described what he saw:

> In it there were about forty individuals of both sexes. In the basement, there is an apparatus upon which the negroes, by order of the police, or at the request of their masters, are flogged. The latter can have nineteen lashes inflicted on them according to the existing law. The machine consists of a sort of crane, on which a cord with two nooses runs over pullies; the nooses are made fast to the hands of the slave and drawn up, while the feet are bound tight to a plank. The body is stretched out as much as possible, and thus the miserable creature receives the exact number of lashes as counted off!

The attendants at the Work House, the Duke noted, were black, on the theory that discipline could produce more suffering when it came from the hands of other blacks.

If Betty did not feel the lash, then she might have been subjected to a more ingenious torment, the treadmill:

> A tread-mill has been erected in a back building. . . . [T]wo treadwheels [are] in operation. Each employs twelve prisoners. . . . Six tread at once upon each wheel, while six rest upon a bench placed behind the wheel. Every half minute the left hand

man steps off the treadwheel, while the five others move to the
left to fill up the vacant place; at the same time the right hand
man sitting on the bench, steps on the wheel, and begins his
movement. . . . Thus, even three minutes sitting, allows the un-
happy being no repose. The signal for changing is given by a
small bell attached to the wheel. The prisoners are compelled
to labour eight hours a day in this manner. Order is preserved
by a person, who, armed with a cow-hide, stands by the wheel.

The inmates of the Work House, the visitor pointed out, were said to
"entertain a strong fear of the tread-mills, and regard flogging as the
lighter evil!"

By the time of Betty's punishment, attitudes among Northern whites had
begun to shift on the subject of human property. As I mentioned earlier,
whites in the North, after the American Revolution, seemed to lose their
taste for keeping blacks captive, and most states passed laws that allowed for gradual emancipation. As slavery moved Southwest, Northern
politicians now worried about the nature of a larger America and the
balance of national power. The so-called Missouri Compromise of 1820,
which slowed the spread of forced labor, was the first sign of a standoff
of cultures that would culminate in the Civil War.

The Northwest Ordinance, an agreement on frontier policy, brought
Ohio, Indiana, and Illinois into the United States as "free-soil" states,
with a ban on unfree labor. Louisiana, Mississippi, and Alabama, meanwhile, joined the country as slave areas. When Missouri was proposed
as a slave state in 1819, Northern lawmakers objected—partly on principle and partly because the opposing cultures, South and North, were
balanced in Congress. The Missouri Compromise brought Missouri in
as a slave state and set up Maine as free. Then, foreshadowing a dead-
lock, Congress drew a geographical line across the huge Louisiana Purchase, at latitude 36° 30', north of which slavery was not to cross.

In 1824, the Ohio Resolutions emerged from the legislature in that
state, calling for the end of unfree labor and proposing emancipation at
the age of twenty-one for any slave born after the enactment of the bill.
Northern states backed the plan; Southern newspapers mocked it. South
Carolina lawmakers asked their governor to send a resolution to Ohio

stating that "the people of this state will adhere to a system, descended to them from their ancestors, and now inseparably connected with their social and political existence."

Many of the Balls, even while observing these threats to their society, remained nonchalant. One of John Jr.'s sons, in New York for a bit of fun, wrote home that he had gone to a show at a theater run by free blacks. The eighteen-year-old joked that during the program, all he could think about was how the black performers would be better off down South, on a plantation, bent over with a hoe. "The Black Gentry of New York have opened a theatre and tell fine stories about their brethren at the South in the cotton and rice fields," young Mr. Ball wrote. "I wish that some of them were in Carolina [where] they would learn to play on the Hoeboy, which would be a useful accompaniment."

In 1826 a series of mysterious nighttime fires swept through Charleston. Although three blacks were eventually convicted of multiple arson, the fires continued after the accused were jailed, striking the fear of general black subversion into white hearts. A year later, on July 4, the Manumission Act took effect in New York, freeing the last ten thousand slaves in that state. As the challenges came more swiftly, John Moultrie, a relative of the Ball family in England, wrote Isaac Ball to report on the British situation. Things were bleak in London, Moultrie said, because there was a move in Parliament to wipe out slavery altogether in the Caribbean sugar colonies. At the head of the campaign was a persuasive agitator named William Wilberforce.

"I must inform [you] that there will be dreadful work in the W. Indies, in consequence of that old fool Mr. Wilberforce's infatuation," Moultrie wrote to Isaac, "and before any steps can be taken to prevent it there will be a massacre of all the white population. . . . [U]nder the mark of humanity and benevolence [Wilberforce is] hatching much mischief, and ultimately doing the Negroes no benefit who are much happier and better taken care of in their present situation than they will be when emancipated."

Though the Balls were slow to react, other white Carolinians jumped at the slightest touch. In 1826 a congress of Spanish-American nations was called in Panama, and President John Quincy Adams suggested the United States send a delegate. Southern congressmen opposed, pointing out that the conference would be attended by representatives from Haiti, the free black state founded on a slave revolt, and stating that any U.S.

presence would appear to condone uprisings. The especially touchy Robert Y. Hayne, senator from South Carolina, explained in a Capitol speech: "The question of slavery must be considered entirely as a domestic question. . . . To touch it at all is to violate our most sacred rights—to put in jeopardy our dearest interests—the peace of our country—the safety of our families, our altars, and our firesides." If the federal government in any way tried to interfere, Hayne finished, "we will consider ourselves as driven from the Union."

John Jr. and Isaac eventually realized that the winds were changing. In 1825, as Isaac Ball, forty, lay dying of malaria, he called for a clerk to draw up his will. When he dictated his last wishes, he inserted a worried remark about the future of the business: "I consider the tenure by which certain species of property is held in this state may become very uncertain." If emancipation was imminent, Isaac made clear, then all of his people should be sold before it happened, so his children would not lose their inheritance.

When the subject of emancipation took the national stage, however, it first wore the costume of a debate over taxes. The elite of the South remained tied to the agrarian economy, while in the North the rich had moved into manufacturing and trade. In 1828, Congress passed a protectionist tax to shield new Northern commerce: duties of thirty to fifty percent on all imported goods. With their farm economies, Southern whites took no benefit from the tax, which they saw as a hardship directed personally at them. The tariff pitted one regional system against the other, forced labor against free. Southern newspapers called it the "Tariff of Abominations"; South Carolina went into rebellion, and the Balls went along.

John C. Calhoun, son of a middling Carolina family who had married a rice heiress, had been Secretary of War under President James Monroe, and Vice President under John Quincy Adams. When the tax passed, Calhoun was Vice President under Andrew Jackson. In an essay denouncing the bill, Calhoun devised a theory of "nullification," by which states had the hypothetical right to cancel laws made in Washington. The national government, Calhoun said, was a union made of individual state powers, or sovereignties. Since only joint power of the states could change the text of the Constitution, each state must also give consent to a change in its political condition, such as vulnerability to tariffs. The Constitution gave federal courts high jurisdiction in U.S. law, but final say over national laws was a right reserved to the states. Nullification meant that a state reserved the authority to reject Washington's decree on the basis of states' rights.

When Calhoun in this manner gave them a reason, the Balls came out of their silence and became tax resisters. The family had long stayed away from public life, but in 1830 John Jr. broke tradition and went into politics, joining the states' rights cause. Calhoun's scheme launched a political movement and a party. As a big slave owner, John Jr. was just the sort of person nullification was meant to defend, so he went on the ballot for the South Carolina legislature. But the Balls were not known as vigorous speakers or crowd pleasers, and in the October election John lost. Staying with the movement, however, he did some maneuvering and six months later got himself appointed a vice president of the States Rights Party.

By the logic of states' rights, the grab of power by the federal government, in the form of taxation, might open the way to the control of slavery from Washington. Sometimes this view was expressed outright; sometimes it stayed tacit. The States Rights Party called on South Carolina to "interpose her state sovereignty," in the words of Calhoun, and refuse to let customs officials collect the money. In July 1832, Congress raised the stakes by passing another tax, and John Jr. used the occasion to run on the States Rights ticket for the Charleston City Council, this time winning for his home ward. A bit later, when the South Carolina legislature called for a special congress on the tariffs, to be held in the capital at Columbia, John Jr. was chosen as a delegate.

The so-called Nullification Convention met and solemnly "nullified" the 1828 and 1832 tariffs. President Andrew Jackson threatened a military siege of Charleston, and the hero of the movement, Calhoun, resigned the Vice Presidency. Governor Robert Hayne persuaded South Carolina lawmakers to fund a state militia in the event Washington invaded, and upwards of twenty-five thousand men volunteered for the hypothetical ranks of a "secession army." Other Southern states sent resolutions denouncing South Carolina and ridiculing nullification. Yet the secession army caused Washington to lose its nerve. In March 1833, Congress passed the Compromise Tariff, which shrank the tax rates, and when Calhoun supported the compromise, the states' rights movement was able to claim victory. Two weeks later John Jr. and the other nullifiers met again and reversed their earlier acts. The party backed down, and the crisis was defused.

Soon after the climax, a report arrived on John Jr.'s desk from the overseer at Comingtee plantation, which would have freshened his memory with regard to the reasons behind nullification. Thomas Finklea, the dutiful Ball manager, wrote his boss to say that he had just had a field hand named Morris shot for trying to escape.

Thomas Finklea ran Comingtee and another Ball place for some ten years. In about half his letters to his employers, he describes beatings he gave to disobedient workers. In July 1833, when Captain Nancy and John Jr. were in Charleston, Finklea reported that four escaped men had been sighted near Comingtee. He had called up the slave patrol, consisting of white neighbors, but to no avail. A few days later he heard that the men had been spotted again "near Mrs. Laurens' gate." One of them, Morris, had been at large for four months. This time, after calling out the patrol, he said, "I wished eatch to be well armed as those runaways I understood had bayonets & one or two guns." Finklea was accompanied on the hunt by Scipio, an obedient Ball slave, as well as Ned, a house man who belonged to Benjamin Read, owner of neighboring Rice Hope. Ned carried a gun, as did the white men. The orders of the hunting party were to hail the runaways three times, then, if the prey would not surrender, to shoot. The men prowled until Scipio spied Morris in a pasture. Evidently when Morris was called to stop, he refused, causing Scipio to move in and Morris to reply by brandishing a sword. Finklea reported, "Ned shot the fellow as I had ordered for the runnaway wold not stand but resisted & tried to kill Sipio with a sword." Morris's gunshot wound stopped his running but didn't kill him. He survived, recovered, and was put back to work.

After decades of fitful protest, the abolition movement was beginning to get on its feet in the North. In 1831 in Boston, William Lloyd Garrison, a twenty-six-year-old journalist, founded the *Liberator*, a newspaper devoted to bringing an end to human property. The State of Georgia announced a reward of $5,000 for Garrison's arrest, on a charge of sedition. Not all Northern whites, or even many, cared for Garrison; in 1835 a Boston mob grabbed him and pulled him through the streets at the end of a rope. But Garrison stuck with his paper and continued to hector whatever audiences would listen. Meantime, in the West, Theodore Dwight Weld lectured the antislavery cause on the same circuits traveled by revivalist preachers. Weld was married to Angelina Grimké, who, with her older sister Sarah, was one of two prodigal daughters of Judge John F. Grimké, chief justice of the South Carolina Supreme Court. As I've already described, in the 1820s Angelina (along with Sarah) left her slave-owning family and moved North, where she spent much of the rest of her life publicizing the brutalities of her family and former friends. Theodore Weld would eventually publish a book, called *American Slavery As It Is*, which included Angelina's bloody stories about Charleston. In December 1833, William Garrison, Theodore Weld, and a handful of others formed the American Anti-Slavery Society. A few years later Frederick Douglass escaped slavery in Maryland and joined the cause. Then, in 1843, Sojourner Truth, emancipated in New York, left the state to crisscross the country on an abolition crusade. Two years later Douglass published his popular autobiography, while Truth became a magnetic draw on lecture tours.

Abolition got under way at the same time as nullification, and the moral badgering heard in the North was probably received with jeers and backslapping in the meetings of John Jr.'s States Rights Party. Eight months after the first issue of Garrison's *Liberator*, Nat Turner, a slave in Virginia, staged an uprising with seventy comrades, in which almost sixty whites were murdered. To Southern whites, the *Liberator* seemed to lead directly to Nat Turner. Reacting to the abolitionist press, Southern writers coined their own new genre, the pro-slavery essay. One Charleston pamphlet, "Refutation of the Calumnies Circulated Against . . . Southern . . . Slavery," by Edmund Holland, pointed out that forced labor was sanctioned by the Bible and that it was simply necessary to agriculture, since without blacks the Southern economy would collapse. Another Charlestonian, Edward Brown, in "Notes on the Origin and Necessity of Slavery," explained that "slavery has ever been the stepladder by which civilized countries have passed from barbarism to civilization" and concluded by saying, "universal equality [is] but another name for barbarism."

The Balls did their part in the defense, turning out pro-slavery writings of a more lyrical sort. One of the Ball cousins, Catharine Gendron Poyas, celebrated the happy world of the plantations in a series of sentimental poems. Catharine, known in the family as Cousin Kate, was the daughter of Henry Poyas, whose sister, Eliza Poyas Ball, was the widow of Isaac Ball of Limerick. Cousin Kate did not marry, and it was said she was melancholy due to various broken loves. In any case she had time on her hands, which she spent writing at Limerick on long visits to her aunt Eliza Ball. Kate eventually published two volumes of verse, in which the most memorable poems are the ones about slavery. She referred to blacks as "the sable train" and used the biblical designation "the sons of Canaan." (The Canaanites were said by pro-slavery writers to be the dark clan of Africans descended from Noah's son, Ham, whom Noah had condemned to servitude.) One poem, which Cousin Kate wrote during Christmas with the Balls and called "Limerick; or Country Life in South-Carolina," contained the following verses:

> 'Tis christmas—and the sable train rejoice:
> Now in their humble cottages the voice
> Of song and mirth is heard; and three full days,
> They may amuse themselves their several ways.
>
> . . .
>
> The greater number stay at home and dance,
> And gayly, too, as any sons of France,
> From morn to night, from night to break of day,
> Still do they dance the happy hours away.
>
> . . .
>
> Returning, one perchance may careless roam
> To where the negroes have their village home;
> Its cleanly rows, of cottages so neat;
> The hearty welcomes that your presence greet;
> The quiet calmness that pervades the spot,
> Show that the sons of Canaan dark, are not
> The poor depressed mortals they are thought,
> Tho' they say "master," and are sold and bought!

In 1834, South Carolina lawmakers passed a bill banning literacy among blacks. For teaching a black person how to read, whites would be jailed six months and fined $100, while free colored people, in addition to being fined, would get fifty lashes. The American Anti-Slavery Society responded with an avalanche of pamphlets, addressing several thousand to Charleston whites in July 1835. Seeing their contents, postmaster Alfred Huger confiscated the pamphlets, which were later burned by a mob. The Charleston City Council then passed an ordinance banning "inflammatory and seditious" writing of similar type. The following February, in Washington, Representative Henry Laurens Pinckney of South Carolina presented a bill that would prohibit Congress from considering petitions which challenged the legality of slavery. This "gag rule" prevailed, and the abolitionists were silenced.

The curse of Buzzard Wing seemed to come into full force around the time of these events. In June 1834, at age fifty-one, John Jr., the Ball family mainstay and supporter of the secessionist cause, died of malaria. Five weeks later, on August 1, the British Parliament emancipated more than seven hundred thousand slaves in nineteen colonies in the West Indies, compensating their former owners with £20,000,000 sterling. Carolina whites murmured gravely that the end was on them. The curse seemed to spread to Buzzard Wing's own children. In July 1835, Alwyn Ball, one of the playboy brothers, died at age twenty-eight, leaving behind five children. One of Alwyn's sisters, Caroline Olivia Ball, who married at seventeen, died at twenty-two, leaving two children. But it was the second of Caroline's profligate sons, Swinton Ball, who would face the most spectacular death.

After he married the New England heiress Anna Channing, Swinton and his wife had several children, but all died as infants. Anna and Swinton traveled constantly—to New York, Newport, Europe, and back—their lifestyle supported by Pimlico, a plantation they hardly ever visited. Occasionally Swinton would sell a few of the hundred or so workers from Pimlico, perhaps when he and Anna wanted cash. He sold three women in January 1834, and ten people in March 1837. Swinton and Anna often traveled by land, because "Anna dislikes the sea exceedingly," as Swinton wrote to a relative. In the early summer of 1838, when Swinton was thirty, he and Anna made an exception to their rule and boarded a steamship in New York, the *Pulaski*, bound for Charleston. En route, on the night of June 14, the boilers exploded and blew the ship to pieces. Swinton and Anna drowned.

Following the accident, a lawsuit arose, *Ferris Pell* v. *E. O. Ball*, in which the family of Anna Channing, who had brought money to the marriage, challenged the Balls for the dead couple's wealth. Swinton and Anna had each written a will leaving the majority of their property to the other, which meant that the issue of the case was a seemingly locked riddle—who had died first? If Swinton, then the Channings would inherit; if Anna, then the Balls. The Channing family produced a survivor of the shipwreck who claimed that in the water next to the sinking steamer, the voice of Anna could be heard calling out for Swinton, but there had been no reply. From this testimony, the court concluded that Swinton had died first. Not only Anna's property, but more than half of Swinton's, went to the Massachusetts family.

Pell v. *Ball* dragged on for years after a second issue arose, involving the Pimlico workers. Having won possession, the Channing family (from Boston, center of the abolition movement) wished to sell most of the slaves so that they could bring the money home to New England. The sale of individuals would raise more cash than the auction of intact families, and the Channings made clear this was their wish. Objecting, the Balls claimed that tradition and principle should prevent the black families from being split apart. The protest had the fragrance of spite, since the Balls themselves had auctioned off men and women one at a time. For whatever reason, however, the Southern court ruled against the Northerners, and in a decision handed down in March 1845, the judge "decreed . . . that the negro slaves [be] sold . . . in lots, according to families."

John Jr. had played a part in the first duel with the North, which ended in a stand-off. The last generation of the Balls to come of age in the slave period, that of John's children, retreated from city life and hid themselves from politics. The years leading up to the Civil War produced the most acid American quarrels since the Revolution, but they were fights to which the family seemed almost oblivious. Just as they had before 1776, the Balls waited until the last before committing themselves to the revolt, and even then they were reluctant rebels. Once the struggle began, however, ten sons in the Ball cousinhood would eventually put on the Confederate uniform.

When Isaac Ball, John Jr.'s brother, died of malaria in 1825, his will had granted the biggest plantation, Limerick, to his four-year-old son, William James. William's fortune rested in the hands of trustees while he grew up with his widowed mother, Eliza. William's uncle John had graduated from Harvard, but his father had skipped college, and William himself showed little interest in school. When his mother made him go to the state college in Columbia, the student argued with her. "I did not mean to say that a college education was useless in general," he wrote home, at seventeen. "I meant to say that I thought it of not much importance to me, as I still do say." William seems not to have finished school, and instead got married in 1842, at age twenty, to Julia Cart, a fragile seventeen-year-old.

The rest of his father Isaac's estate went to William's sister, Jane (Quenby plantation), his brother John (Hyde Park), and his uncle John Jr. (Jericho). Limerick, Hyde Park, and Quenby stood within a couple of miles of one another. Photographs of William Ball show that he grew to be a wiry man with angular cheeks, thin lips, and a beard. According to family tradition, he had a gracious speaking voice, which he often used to beguile the congregation in the Episcopal chapel near Limerick, where he read services when the priest was away on rounds. By the 1840s, William had become the dominant brother by default. When his sister Jane's husband died in 1842, he took over management of Quenby. Several years later brother John died, at twenty-seven, and Hyde Park became William's responsibility too.

As young masters, William and Julia Ball thus controlled three plantations and some 450 black people. Then, in the month they married, William acquired Halidon Hill, downstream from Limerick; and in 1850, from a cousin, he bought Cedar Hill, an 876-acre tract so narrow as to look like a pencil on a map. William and Julia made a handsome couple in their photographs, slim and well-dressed; the young wife concentrated on her children and social rounds, while her husband built up the business.

The slavery fight temporarily halted as America grew west. In 1845, Texas—a piece of Mexico colonized by Southerners, and briefly an independent nation—came into the union as a slave state. The following year, American armies invaded the rest of Mexico from the Texas platform to grab more land. The Mexican War ended in 1848, with Mexico giving up half its national domain; those lands eventually became Arizona, California, New Mexico, and more. Northern lawmakers saw the war as a bid by Southerners to extend slavery and seize control of Congress by force of numbers. Representative David Wilmot of Pennsylvania drafted the so-called Wilmot Proviso, which prohibited human property in any territory invaded by the army. Abraham Lincoln, a freshman representative from Illinois, denounced the war and supported the ban, but Wilmot failed to get the votes.

While the fight raged in Mexico and Washington, William Ball went about family routine, teaching himself to be an entrepreneur. Records show he experimented with his workforce, rotating people from one plantation to another depending on the season and his whim, until hundreds were moved around over a ten-year period. In addition, William involved himself in the marriage life of his workers, to the extent of choosing partners for them. Half a century later, a former Ball field hand, William Gaillard, said in an affidavit that he had been one of the ones Mr. Ball picked up and moved. Gaillard, by then an old man, told a hearing officer that "I was owned by William Ball. I was born on Limerick plantation but was sent to Cedar Hill before I was grown." In the same case, an army pension hearing, a former worker named Patty Moultrie testified that she was married to her husband, Stepney Moultrie, at William Ball's command. "I don't know my age, but I am over sixty," Patty Moultrie told a magistrate in 1903. "I was owned by Mr. Ball . . . was born and raised on Halidon Hill but was taken over to Cedar Hill before I was grown. About three years before the [Civil] war started I was given to Stepney by my master and we were married on Cedar Hill."

In April 1852, at another states' rights convention, South Carolina delegates voted to withdraw from the union, but they backed down when other Southern states balked. Ordinary Northerners could not make sense of the posturing of the Carolina radicals, and apparently neither could William. Ball family lore has it that William thought secession was a bad idea. The white South would risk its social system, he believed, and probably lose. In the North, while no whites (save perhaps a few around Garrison) wanted to go to war on behalf of black people, after twenty years the abolitionists had begun to pique the mass conscience. In 1852, Harriet Beecher Stowe, a daughter and sister of clergymen, published *Uncle Tom's Cabin*, the melodramatic novel that depicted slavery as a passion play with a cast of saintly blacks and sadistic whites. A typical scene of the book is an episode in which Eliza, an escaped slave, trudges from Kentucky toward freedom across the frozen Ohio River, in effect, walking on water. *Uncle Tom's Cabin* would eventually outsell every other book printed in nineteenth-century America, with the exception of the Bible. In 1854 the Republican Party was founded in the North—a movement staked on the idea that the Western territories should be settled by free workers rather than slaves—and one early convert was Abraham Lincoln, a former congressman looking for a way to renew his political career. Meanwhile, the Underground Railroad out of the South, which had brought thousands from the plantations to Northern cities, fell afoul of the new Fugitive Slave Law. Many more than just abolitionists denounced the statute, which required public officers in the Northeast and Midwest to help recapture escaped blacks and levied heavy fines and jail terms on those accused of aiding runaways to freedom.

To judge from their behavior, and from the chatty tone of their letters, William and his cousins seem to have been unconcerned with the clash between North and South. As it long had been, the family remained spread out across St. John's Parish. In addition to the six tracts he now controlled, William had a cousin at Comingtee and one at Buck Hall, and by marriage he was related to most of the rice families within twenty miles. The Balls focused alternately on easy living and how to make the biggest crop, and William threw himself into church work, becoming a leader of the vestry at the local chapel. For something more to do, William, his cousin Keating S. Ball, and several neighborhood men formed a business group they called the Strawberry Agricultural Society. At their meetings, the men discussed not politics, not secession, but the vagaries of corn, peas, and potatoes. Minutes from the monthly roundtables, with William's name on them, show that the twenty-five-member group wrote reports on different methods of curing bacon and appointed committees to study livestock and rice. The society left no list of assignments, only committee names, but William may have been among the members of the "committee on manures."

William and Julia's second son, Isaac Ball, my great-grandfather, was born at Limerick on April 21, 1844. Isaac never knew Buzzard Wing,

318 · Edward Ball

who died when he was an infant, but his generation, more than any other, would feel her malediction. He came of age on the battlefield, turning twenty-one the week his unit surrendered to the Yankees in North Carolina, and until his death he never forgot that his patrimony went the way of the capitulation at Appomattox Court House.

William and Julia did everything they could to insulate their children, and I suspect baby Isaac arrived to many welcomes, but the birth of the boy was rung in by a murder. Sometime in the spring of 1844, not far from the Limerick mansion, two Ball field hands, a mother and son, killed their work-gang leader. William kept no notes about what happened, but a newspaper reported that the criminals were Amelia and Sambo, of William's Halidon Hill, and the victim a man named Jingo, the plantation driver. Amelia (who was known to William as Melia) was about forty-four and the partner of a man called Pino; they had seven children, ages four to twenty-one. Sambo, Amelia's second son, was nineteen. Amelia's family had lived on Limerick before William shifted them off to Halidon Hill, a few miles downstream, where they came under the rule of the black foreman Jingo. It was two years later that Amelia and Sambo killed Jingo—for what reason, no evidence survives. They were swiftly taken away and tried before the Court of Magistrates and Freeholders, which judged Sambo the murderer and his mother an accessory; and the two were sentenced to be hanged near the scene of the crime. Sambo did hang, the first day of August, but his mother received a commuted sentence, to be sold out of state. In 1847, William sold Amelia for $400 to a Daniel Cook, a slave dealer who probably took her in the direction of Mississippi. Her six remaining children were thrown to the care of her partner Pino, on Halidon Hill. The name Amelia lingered on at the plantation, when one of her daughters later named a child after the murderess.

Isaac grew up at Limerick with the familiar comforts, including a private tutor and violin lessons. On trips to Charleston, as part of his education, he attended the theater. A letter he wrote when he was nine years old gives a glimpse of the boy's perceptions and a look at the way blackness figured in local costume. When Isaac was a child, he went to the popular minstrel shows—comedy revues in which white musicians, wearing blackface, imitated plantation blacks for a white audience. After seeing one such show in Charleston, Isaac wrote his mother to report:

I went to see the Campbell Minstrels. . . . [T]hey painted their mouths white and their faces black one had some bones rattling he could rattle them better than any one I ever saw two had banjos two had fiddles one had a harp and one had a tamborine the one tamborine when he was playing he made believe that he was vex[ed] and knocked it on his head he kicked it and boxed it and the one with the rattles rattled them as loud as he could and afterwards jumped very high and fell on the chair and played many songs and one said that one day while he was crossing a bridge something tript him down and he fell in the water and stuck as high as his eyes in mud he said that nobody was with him and there was no house within a half mile off and one asked him how did he get out . . . [and] he said that he ran to the house and got a shovel and dug himself out. . . . [After] the end of the first part & they came out again with the music and danced I never saw a black person dance the negro dance better and longer. . . . [G]ive my love to all your affectionate son Isaac Ball.

Isaac had no sisters, but he and his three brothers—William (Willie), John, and (yet another) Elias—studied, courted, hunted, and (not so profligate as the three sons of Buzzard Wing) planned to follow in the steps of their parents. All ended up fighting for the Confederacy.

William and Julia were content with the rhythm of country life, and anyway, the strong rice economy meant there was plenty to do. In early 1857, William bought Cherry Hill plantation, a tract with 1,039 acres plus 2,500 acres of pine forest. The following year, workers on Cedar Hill, the skinny tract, produced 11,097 bushels, amounting to 316,077 pounds of clean rice. Although no cosmopolitan investor like his uncle, John Jr., William did keep track of the business, opening, for example, a diary about sickness and death on the slave street. His death diary listed no names, just the ages of the dead and causes of demise: lockjaw (a baby, age nineteen days), convulsions (age two), drowning (a man, thirty-seven), pneumonia (fifty), consumption (fifty-eight), old age (eighty-five).

In 1857, William had reason to hope the secessionist movement would settle down or be appeased, so the Balls could hold on, because that year a favorable decision came down from the Supreme Court, in *Dred Scott* v. *Sanford*. Scott, a slave from St. Louis, Missouri, had sued for freedom after having passed through a free state, but his plea was rejected by Chief Justice Roger Taney of Maryland. Taney wrote that Scott had no standing to sue, because he was property, and, as was plain from the Constitution, the United States was a white nation in which black people could never be citizens. The Dred Scott decision gave confidence to the secessionists, and mystified blacks and whites in the North.

Julia Cart Ball, Isaac's mother, died in July 1858 after a long illness. In time, the widower William would remarry, at age forty-one, to a cousin, twenty-six-year-old Mary H. Gibbs. All of his papers from this period suggest that William went energetically about his business, and did little else. He schooled Isaac and his other sons in plantation management and, at least some of the time, thought about the needs of the black people. On one trip to town, William brought back fine gifts for several Limerick field hands. A notebook shows that a man named Brawley got a "pair of fancy pants"; Esau, "simple milled pants"; Aurelia, a black satin vest; Jeffrey, a pair of merino wool trousers; and Cuffie, a frock coat.

In October 1859, John Brown, a fifty-nine-year-old white abolitionist, armed with guns and followed by eighteen accomplices, seized Harper's Ferry on the upper Potomac River, hoping to spark a general slave uprising. Brown held his ground and issued a proclamation, but Colonel Robert E. Lee of Virginia put down the revolt, and Brown was hanged. The event threw fire on the white South's fears about abolitionists—but William Ball was not among those who seemed to notice. A few months after Harper's Ferry, an event that by most accounts stunned the country, William went ahead and bought still another place, The Blessing, a 631-acre tract next door to Cedar Hill. The deal, his last, brought to eight the number of plantations under his control.

In November 1860, Abraham Lincoln, a known opponent of slavery, won the presidency without carrying a single Southern state, and the secessionists seized the moment to provoke the final split. The election probably disappointed the Balls, but William did what was normal for him—ignored the outcry. Three days after the November 6 vote, a mass meeting and debate on secession was called in Charleston, and William stayed home. A week after the election, after more rallies and demonstrations, William's notes show that his mind was on buying little luxuries for his slaves. On Friday, November 14, William directed work on the harvest at Limerick, and made a note that a field hand called Molly wanted him to get her a piece of calico cloth in exchange for seven chickens she had sent to the Ball dinner table in Charleston. And, oh yes, he wrote, Leah had given him seventy-five cents to buy shoes for Caesar, her son.

South Carolina voters elected delegates to the final secession convention, but neither William nor any of his kin seemed to pay attention, let alone try to get on the ballot. The meeting opened December 17, 1860, in Columbia, but, amid rumors of smallpox, adjourned and reconvened in Charleston the following morning. For two days, 169 delegates debated the foregone conclusion and, on December 20, voted unanimously to secede.

"We the People of the State of South Carolina," read the so-called Ordinance of Secession, "[declare] the Constitution of the United States of America . . . repealed; and that the union now subsisting between South Carolina and other States, under the name of 'The United States of America,' is hereby dissolved."

15

THE SIEGE

At the moment of secession in 1860, the Ball world was a flourishing antique, five generations and 162 harvests old.

"Then came the war, 'the Confederate War,' " wrote William's second wife Mary Gibbs Ball, remembering events. "When the 'Ordinance of Secession' was signed & South Carolina left the Union, a free & independent state, what a thrill went through every son & daughter of the Palmetto State & as each Southern state came in, with what joy we looked forward to our Southern Confederacy."

The men in the family took little comfort in the coming of the great struggle, but the Ball women seemed to regard the end of the United States as a glorious feat. Swept up by their enthusiasm, young Ball sons enlisted as they came of age; but loath to give up their comforts, they brought personal servants with them to the battlefield. The Ball slaves, at least initially, were largely impassive. By this time, most workers lived in a necklace of pacified villages, robbed of the ability to resist. The rice harvests, in any case, continued on time until the end of the Civil War, with no black revolt and only the slightest evidence of sabotage. When the Yankees finally arrived, there was real exultation on the slave street, but emancipation brought a simple finale—no glory, merely two days of drunkenness, broken china, and confusion. Then the

Northerners were gone, leaving whites and blacks as they had found them, a gulf separating the races, with new rules on paper and nothing at all like them in practice.

At the start of the rebellion, William James Ball, thirty-nine and father of four, controlled eight plantations on the Cooper River, a checkerboard block of land six miles long and two wide; more than six hundred black workers were under his hand. William was a widower, his wife Julia having died in 1858. He fed a constellation of white dependents, including his four sons by Julia, his widowed sister Jane Shoolbred and widowed sister-in-law Maria L. Ball, the women's four children, and his sixty-six-year-old mother, Eliza. A few miles southwest of the main tract, Limerick, stood the home of William's bachelor cousin Keating S. Ball, Comingtee, and its village of some 160 blacks. On the west fork of the river lay Pawley and Buck Hall, properties of Dr. Horry Deas, who was the widower of Keating's sister, Ann Ball Deas; and Dean Hall, a thirty-one-hundred-acre tract belonging to Elias Nonus Ball (in continuing Latin wordplay, the ninth Elias), twenty-five-year-old son of the dissipated Elias Octavus. All told, by my best count, at least 842 black people lived on the family lands.

Rice remained profitable, but the Ball world had shrunk since the onslaught of cotton—from several parishes to one, and down from an earlier peak of thirteen hundred workers. Nationally, however, the slave system had quadrupled in two generations. According to the Bureau of the Census, in the summer before secession the population of the United States numbered 33,440,000, of whom some 3,950,000, or twelve percent, were in slavery (compared to one million in 1810). A little more than 375,000 heads of household in the United States owned people, a number that represented just under one-quarter of the white population in the South. Within that group, twelve percent owned more than twenty people, but this tiny minority—one of a hundred Americans—held half of the total number of black workers.

Despite leading the rebellion, the city of Charleston was far off the national stage. Charleston counted 40,500 residents, making it only the twenty-second largest city in the country, compared to its fourth-place standing at the start of the American Revolution. Most of the Balls had traveled north at some point in life, but in 1860 the upper United States did not look the same to a middle-aged rice planter who might have seen New York in his youth. The South had not industrialized, while the smokestacks of Massachusetts now produced more manufactured goods than all of the states of the future Confederacy combined. The nation had thirty-one thousand miles of rail, most of it above Virginia; there were three thousand steamboats on American rivers, but apart from the Mississippi River, they plied canals in states between Chicago and Boston. In addition to the South's conspicuous lag in technology, Southern whites who visited the North were sometimes embarrassed at the superior literacy of Yankees, a product of traditional neglect of books down home. Slaves were denied reading, but so were most Southern whites, only one-third of whose children were enrolled in school, compared to three-quarters of white children in the North.

Despite all of this, there is little evidence that the Balls personally envied the better schools, bigger cities, and booming middle class of the North. In fact, they loved their own society and seemed to regard Northerners as denizens of an excessive region—a place too fast, too crowded, too smart.

South Carolina broke off in December. Four days later, the secession convention in Charleston produced a document—"Declaration of the Immediate Causes Which Induce and Justify the Secession of South Carolina from the Federal Union"—that explained what it had done. The pronouncement said flatly that the state had left the union because of attacks from the North on the rights of slave owners:

> [A]n increasing hostility on the part of the non-slaveholding States to the Institution of Slavery, has led to a disregard of their obligations. . . . [T]he non-slaveholding States . . . have denounced as sinful the institution of Slavery; they have permitted the open establishment among them of societies, whose avowed object is to disturb the peace and to eloign the property of the citizens of other States. They have encouraged and assisted thousands of our slaves to leave their homes; and those who remain, have been incited by emissaries, books and pictures to servile insurrection. . . . [T]he public mind must rest in the belief that Slavery is in the course of ultimate extinction.

The rebellion may have begun thirty years earlier as a tax revolt, but in the words of the rebels, it ended as a war to defend the right to hold human property.

South Carolina was followed by Mississippi, Florida, Alabama, and Georgia. "If you get your papers you will see that Georgia has seceded," Eliza Ball wrote to her son William the third week of January 1861. Louisiana and Texas came next. On February 9, in Montgomery, Alabama, the new government of the South was chosen by delegates from the seven states in rebellion. Jefferson Davis, a former U.S. senator from Mississippi, was named provisional president of the Confederate States of America.

Drafted in a few days, the Constitution of the Confederacy copied the U.S. Constitution nearly verbatim, deleting parts that interfered with slavery and adding passages that strengthened it. "We, the people of the Confederate States . . . do ordain and establish this Constitution for the Confederate States of America," it began. A new passage, Article IV, section 3, read: "The Confederate States may . . . form States to be admitted into the Confederacy. In all such territory the institution of negro slavery . . . shall be recognized and protected." War was not necessarily inevitable, and negotiations to avert it were hastily arranged in Washington. But at his inauguration in Montgomery on February 18, Jefferson Davis raised the stakes, saying, "[W]e must prepare to meet the emergency and maintain, by the final arbitrament of the sword, the position which we have assumed among the nations of the earth."

William's four sons, all younger than eighteen, were too green for the service; but twenty-six-year-old Elias Nonus Ball of Dean Hall was not. Nonus, an unmarried grandson of Martha Caroline Ball (or Buzzard Wing), became the first family member to offer himself to the gathering army. Four days after President Davis's inaugural, Nonus wrote to Robert Barnwell Rhett, a former U.S. senator from South Carolina and one of the leaders of the breakaway movement. Rhett had drafted the secession ordinance that started the crisis in train and had been considered for the Confederate presidency, but lost out to Davis. Nonus used the excuse that he was friendly with Rhett's son, R. B. Rhett Jr., editor of the *Charleston Mercury*, the most strident secessionist newspaper in the South.

"I would respectfully ask you to use your influence in my behalf,"

Nonus wrote expectantly. "I desire a captaincy, and if that is impossible, a 1st Lieutenancy in the Cavalry. I wish to enter this arm of the service as I am acquainted with its drill manual, having served four years as a dragoon officer." Nonus meant that he had been a night rider in the slave patrol, his regular duty as a property owner. He also wrote to William Porcher Miles, former mayor of Charleston, former U.S. congressman, and a member of the Military Affairs Committee of the provisional Confederate Congress in Montgomery, with the same request that strings be pulled. "I have studied closely the different works on cavalry tactics," Nonus told Miles, as though reading about horses would get him the job. Nonus seems to have some of the fecklessness of his father, Elias Octavus, who, forty years earlier, dropped out of military academy in Vermont, quit school in England, and never finished his education. Nonus had been master of Dean Hall for just four years, and still had not paid for it, yet he told Miles, "[I]f I succeed in getting a commission, I intend making the Army my profession, as I am tired of planting."

Rhett and Miles did not respond, so Nonus finally wrote to the Confederate Secretary of War, LeRoy P. Walker: "I have only to say that all I have to offer to our Confederacy is a true heart, a sharp blade, and a hand that knows how to use it." Nothing worked, and eventually Nonus gave up. A year later, in March 1862, he enlisted in Rutledge's Regiment, a cavalry company, as a private.

A separate Southern government was already in place when, on March 4, 1861, Abraham Lincoln addressed the Confederacy from his own inaugural lectern in Washington: "In *your* hands, my dissatisfied fellow countrymen, and not in *mine*, is the momentous issue of civil war. The government will not assail *you*. You can have no conflict, without being yourselves the aggressors." In Charleston, Rhett's *Mercury* reviewed Lincoln's speech, saying, "A more lamentable display of feeble inability to grasp the circumstances of this momentous emergency, could scarcely have been exhibited."

"Well, I suppose the war will come," wrote Eliza Ball to a friend who lived upstate. "God has so far kept us from any attack, but it does not seem as if they will settle affairs amicably." In an afterthought she pointed out, "[T]he Ladies generally are very warlike."

In the five months after Lincoln's election, between November and March, rebels had seized nearly all federal depots south of Virginia—

custom houses, post offices, and army outposts. Fort Sumter, in the middle of Charleston harbor, was one of a handful of stations still in the hands of the national army. Symbolically, Sumter was the most important federal presence in the South, since Charleston had triggered the Confederacy. For several months, Carolina rebels and the federal garrison at the island fort stared at each other across the mile distance separating Sumter from shore. On April 8, President Lincoln informed South Carolina that he would attempt to re-provision the fort in order to keep it in Union hands. At 4:30 A.M. on April 12, as the supply ships approached the harbor, rebel gunners on nearby James Island opened fire on Sumter, and the war began.

The Balls were on their plantations, north of the city.

"I remember, I was staying with my sister at her plantation, Hyde Park, when the battle of Fort Sumter was going on," Mary Ball, William's second wife, wrote in her memoir. "The report of the guns from our batteries & the Fort were heard distinctly at our homes on Cooper River. The houses were jarred & windows shook. . . . I will never forget the feeling I had when we heard those guns, or the feeling of joy, thankfulness & triumph when we gained the victory."

After the bombardment ended and the Yankees surrendered, the *Charleston Courier* asked Cousin Kate, the Ball poet, for a verse to celebrate the start of the struggle, and she gave the newspaper a poem called "Greeting for Victory":

> [O]ur God hath blessed us, brothers,
> Blessed our valor, blessed our cause,
> In a way shall make the kingdoms
> Of the whole round world to pause,
> Deep reflecting; was there ever
> Such deliverance wrought on earth—
> So sublimely grand a pageant
> To announce a nation's birth?

William, according to letters, feared the worst, but Mary Ball put her heart into things:

[Later] our troopers were going to Virginia to fight, & we would go to see our brave soldiers go off on the train, we cheered

them until we were hoarse. Those soldiers I believe were the
bravest of the brave & I love to think of them. . . . I never will
forget the feeling we had seeing them go off at night, the stars
bright over head & the bands playing the inspiriting tunes of
"Dixie."

There is only circumstantial evidence for the way the Ball slaves took
the news of war. Work continued, but William's notes show that between
1860 and 1861, harvests on five of his plantations declined sharply,
falling a full third. The precipitous drop may have been due to poor
weather—or just perhaps, there was a work slowdown.

By the time of secession, most of the Ball workers were third- or
fourth-generation residents on the same pieces of land, members of
families that had largely adapted themselves to subservience. The last
attempted revolt against white power had occurred around the figure of
Denmark Vesey in 1822, prior to most living memory. Open defiance
had become infrequent; when resistance appeared at all, it took the
form of petty theft, broken tools, or the intentional misunderstanding of
instructions. As for individual acts of rebellion, the frequency of runaways had declined, even while the Underground Railroad had grown:
South Carolina was too far below Pennsylvania for any but the most
daring to try to flee North. With the exception of valets who traveled
with white families, few blacks had been out of state. Most knew nothing
of Africa, although residual medicines, conjures, and spirits survived to
animate everyday life. Nearly all Southern blacks were Christians, converted in the first half of the 1800s; each community had its own church
and black pastors, most of whom preached that a better home awaited
in the afterlife.

For many years, the Ball masters had called them "servants," the
word "slave" having been poisoned by abolitionists. As the family saw
it, a typical relationship between landlord and chattel was the one William had with John, a horse-handler he called "Ostler John." A few
years before the war, William eulogized John in one of his ledgers:
"Died on the 2d of January. Ostler John, a faithful, good servant, aged
about 65 years, much regretted by the family, and also by his fellow
servants, for many years he had entire charge of stables, garden &

numerous other trustworthy occupations in which he was active and faithful unto his death."

The day after Sumter, Lincoln's cabinet approved his first call for seventy-five thousand troops; later he would ask Congress for four hundred thousand additional soldiers, then more. The Federal armies began to take shape when five companies of infantry marched into Washington from Pennsylvania, followed by the Eighth Massachusetts and the Seventh New York.

South Carolina was organizing its own troops, but apart from Nonus none of the Ball men were interested. The men in William's generation stayed close to their homes, taking advantage of a provision passed by the Confederate Congress exempting large slave owners from active service. In mid-1861, Keating Ball of Comingtee, forty-two, seems to have felt the pique of conscience: he suddenly signed up with the First Regiment Artillery, a unit certain to go to battle; but his tour of duty lasted only fifty-two days. The time up, Keating resigned and joined a nominal home defense unit called the Etiwan Rangers. William followed Keating's example and laid low, signing up with a fire company. Neither would see action in the war.

Encouraged by the victory at Sumter, four states in the upper South—Arkansas, North Carolina, Tennessee, and Virginia—pulled out of the Union. Later, Kentucky and Missouri would be divided, each state with both a Confederate and a Union government. Prospects seemed good for the Confederacy, and white life remained unthreatened. William's sons stayed busy with school and finer entertainments. Six months after secession, Eliza wrote to a woman who had once been governess to William's sons: "You ask about the Boys Music, it is really fine performing, Willie on the Piano & Isaac the Violin, they play together, all the grand Opera Music, most difficult pieces, & can play at sight, excepting some intricate passages—it is not like Children practising, but fine orchestra playing."

With wealthy Virginia on board, the Confederate Congress voted to move the rebel capital from Montgomery to grander quarters in Richmond, Virginia, within striking distance of Washington. "Virginia don't deserve it," Eliza wrote bitterly about the shift of power from the deep

South to the mid-Atlantic. "[H]ad she not delayed so long to secede, we perhaps might not have had such a war, now it seems that Carolina and Virginia are to have the front of the Battle & . . . we may lose many a true heart & brave soldier."

President Lincoln ordered a blockade of Southern ports, and by the middle of May the U.S.S. *Niagara* patrolled the waters off Charleston. Union ships were sent to bottle up trade at New Orleans, Savannah, and Mobile, Alabama; the Southern economy began to choke. Fighting began sporadically with skirmishes in June at Big Bethel, Virginia, and Boonville, Missouri, and shelling of Confederate positions by U.S. gunboats on the Virginia shore. The first major clash exploded July 21 with the Battle of Bull Run, or Manassas, Virginia, between thirty-five thousand Confederates and thirty-seven thousand Union men; the day ended with a rout of the Union and 847 dead between the sides. In subsequent weeks, blood flowed again at Wilson's Creek, Missouri, and Cape Hatteras, North Carolina.

In the summer of 1861, hundreds of slaves, later followed by thousands, began to escape to the Union side, imitating their forebears during the Revolution, when blacks fled the rebel Americans toward freedom with the British. Union General Benjamin Butler, commander of Fort Monroe, Virginia, wrote Lincoln and his Secretary of War, Simon Cameron, to ask what he should do with what he called "contrabands," meaning the nine hundred escaped blacks suddenly with his army. Instructions came back to put them to work against the South. Soon the Federals had a growing corps of teamsters, scouts, and cooks—and later, former slaves who became black soldiers in blue uniform.

Most Northern whites had only vague enthusiasm for black freedom; for his part, Lincoln did not think straightforward liberation would work. In April, a month after he took office, the President had showed interest in a freedom-and-resettlement scheme that would send black Americans out of the country. Lincoln had made contact with the Chiriqui Improvement Company, a coal-mining concern in what would become the nation of Panama, about a plan for the deportation and colonization of freed blacks to Central America. A few months later, in Missouri, Major General John Charles Frémont, in a more humane gesture, took things into his own hands, writing an "emancipation proclamation" that declared free those workers who had fled rebel Southerners. When Lincoln heard of Frémont's unauthorized proclamation, he apparently still thought the answer to slavery was to empty the land of Negroes. The President knocked the general down, calling his decree "dictatorial" and saying, "[It] will alarm our Southern Union friends, and turn them against us."

Charleston had been ringed with batteries, forts, and earthworks, but fifty-five miles south lay the relatively unprotected coast at Port Royal, around the mouth of Broad River, which flowed to the sea past the long-staple cotton islands of St. Helena and Hilton Head. In early November 1861, a Union fleet of seventeen vessels under Flag Officer Samuel F. DuPont and twelve thousand troops under Brigadier General Thomas Sherman sailed from Virginia to stage an invasion. After a four-hour bombardment, Yankee armies occupied Port Royal and set up a huge camp, placing a blade in the side of the Confederacy and posing a menace to Charleston, a day's trip away. With the Yankees so near, Charleston rebels shored up fortifications. The Confederate government called for plantation owners to send blacks to do the work, and in December 1861, a month after the Port Royal invasion, William Ball complied, sending twenty-five men from Limerick, Halidon Hill, and Cedar Hill to dig trenches and strengthen Fort Moultrie, on Sullivan's Island.

As the blockade of the harbor wore on, everyday articles like sugar, coffee, and writing paper began to vanish. At the start of the war, George Alfred Trenholm, a former South Carolina state representative, was a principal of Fraser & Trenholm, a cotton shipper with a fleet of vessels; soon Trenholm became the most successful of several blockade runners in the city. ("We have given up long ago Tea & Coffee," William's sister Jane wrote a friend. "This paper I am writing on is sample paper given me by Mr. Foster, who picks up many things in this way by being with Trenholm.") Goods that Trenholm brought in—sometimes on his personal ironclad gunboat, the *Chicora*—sold for outrageous prices, and not everyone could afford the black market. The *Charleston Courier* helped by running an item about purifying sea salt, "to be used to cure bacon," since imports had been stopped. There had been no battles, apart from Sumter, but an economic war began to be fought at home by women, both white and black, who ran the plantation households and tried to find ways to keep up the old comforts. With cheap clothing from the New England mills no longer available, one of the Ball ladies made (or had her slaves make) hundreds of shirts and trousers; she then sold them to the Confederacy.

Around the country were few fights, and the huge armies remained slow to leave their camps. Lincoln despaired at the lack of progress. On February 16, 1862, the Federals saw a breakthrough on the Cumberland River, when Fort Donelson, Tennessee, a Confederate stronghold, fell to Union hands after a brief siege; an army of twelve thousand rebels surrendered. With that, Kentucky was gone to Federal domination, and Tennessee seemed vulnerable. Ten days later, Federal troops took Nashville.

The Limerick Balls seemed not to worry. Cousin Kate wrote a friend with the news that "William Ball made his boys come home & go to college [and] John Shoolbred [William's nephew] is to join the boys at college the first of March." From Charleston, Eliza wrote William with mild complaints about Confederate taxes and word of trouble at school with William's teenage son John.

Southern whites were enlisting, but evidently not quickly enough, because the Confederate Congress began to talk of a draft. "I am glad to see that the men are volunteering as it would be a great disgrace for Charlestonians, who have always done so much talking, to be drafted," wrote twenty-year-old William Jr. (Willie) to his grandmother Eliza. Eliza wrote Willie's father, who may have still been waffling, to remind him of the godliness of the war: "The Bishop addressed the Ladies association on Monday. He spoke of war as a necessary evil to purify a nation & bring out good feelings in people. . . . [H]e told us plainly . . . [t]he Enemy were strong & well prepared & we of this state particularly they would wish to crush."

In March 1862, eleven thousand Federals and fourteen thousand Confederates clashed in the Battle of Pea Ridge, Arkansas, yielding eighteen hundred killed or wounded. The rebels retreated, worsening their prospects and putting Missouri in danger of falling to the Union. A month later, a Confederate advance in the far Southwest was defeated near Santa Fe, New Mexico Territory. Then came the charnel house of Shiloh. On April 6 and 7, forty-two thousand men in Ulysses Grant's Army of the Tennessee and twenty thousand in the Army of the Ohio under Don Carlos Buell held their ground against forty thousand Confederates at Shiloh, Tennessee. The rebels eventually retreated when reinforcements failed to materialize. The South alone counted 1,723 killed, 959 missing, and 8,012 wounded. The same month, Union troops crept closer to Charleston, occupying Edisto Island thirty miles south.

In Richmond on April 16, President Davis signed a law that called for conscription and mandated three years' service for every white male between the ages of eighteen and thirty-five. Rather than be summoned, the Ball boys chose this moment to enlist. On April 28, twelve days after the draft law, Hugh Swinton Ball, twenty-five-year old son of Elias Octavus, namesake of the drowned Swinton Ball, and brother of Nonus; William's son Isaac, who had just turned eighteen; and Isaac's older brother Willie enlisted in Captain Edward Parker's Company, First Regiment, South Carolina Artillery. (The other Limerick brothers, John, sixteen, and Elias, thirteen, were still too young, but would later join the cause.) Although the three Ball boys were mustered as privates, Isaac evidently showed an organizational bent, because he would later be named secretary of his regiment. Drawing on his music lessons, Hugh Swinton auditioned and was made the regiment bugler. For most of the war, the young men would be artillery gunners, paid thirteen dollars a month.

The First Artillery Regiment was known as "Marion's Brigade" because its commander, Brigadier General Nathan G. Evans, had been born in Marion, South Carolina. Evans, a thin man with a beard shaped like the tail of a platypus, was nicknamed "Shanks" by his troops because of his skinny legs. Shanks's men, including Captain Parker's company, were assigned to the defense of Charleston and dispatched to positions around the city. The main bastions of the harbor consisted of Fort Johnson, on James Island at the southern lip of the port; Fort Moultrie, on Sullivan's Island facing the northeast channel; and Fort Sumter in between. Several more batteries stood on Morris Island, a strip of sand along the ocean next to James Island, the most important fortification there being Battery Wagner. Because the Federals were creeping north from Edisto, the Ball boys were sent immediately to James Island, where they joined some fourteen thousand other men hunkered against an expected Yankee invasion.

Their first weeks in gray uniform were full of fighting. A large force of Union troops had anchored in gunships offshore and set up campsites on John's Island, another muddy sea island separated from James Island by the thin Stono River. On May 23, 1862, Captain Parker's artillery, along with eight companies of infantry and two companies of cavalry, crossed the Stono and swarmed onto John's Island in order to drive the Yankees back to their boats. To the rebels' surprise, however, the island was empty of both Yankees and plantation owners, and peopled by slaves. Shanks Evans wished to prevent the blacks from fleeing to the Yankee side. In his report on the maneuver, he wrote, "[The] negroes were immediately ordered to be removed, and the troops had collected about 200 before I left. . . . I have directed them to be sent to workhouse to be fed and taken care of by the owners. I was compelled to issue rations to them till provisions could be secured."

The Federals next managed to land seven thousand troops on the southwest end of James Island with the intention of pushing through toward Charleston, about seven miles away. Three weeks after the John's Island incident, Union Brigadier General H. W. Benham attacked a rebel position on James Island known unambiguously as Secessionville. On June 16, the Yankees were turned back, with nine of their officers and 187 enlisted men killed or missing, and 459 wounded, compared with the Confederates' 60 killed or missing, and 144 wounded.

A week later, the Ball boys' company, stationed elsewhere on the island at Simmons' Bluff, watched as two Union gunboats approached, a side-wheel and a three-masted vessel. The ships opened fire on the camp, and the rebel artillerymen were ordered to move their pieces; but the road was too muddy and they could not get them into firing position. A party of Yankees landed, burned some tents at the camp, then withdrew.

The harrowing events that put the three Ball boys at risk seem finally to have frightened the older family members. From Charleston, Eliza wrote a friend upstate: "We have just returned from the country . . . & here find such numbers of families all on the move & every one asking you, when and where you are going?—that has quite astounded me, & I feel at a loss what to do. . . . Oh how sad and dreadful is this war—the general opinion is, that the whole seaboard will be taken by the enemy."

The Ball women made plans to move upstate and wrote Julia Obear, the former governess to William's sons, to ask if she could spare room in her house in the town of Winnsboro. The former employee was willing, but the problem was the excess of Ball slaves. Already by this time, William's sister Jane seems to have thought the whole predicament through, from invasion to emancipation and the aftermath. As she weighed the prospect of moving with her mother, Jane wrote Julia Obear:

> We could come to you [as refugees] easily if we knew what to do with all our Negroes, do you think we could find any places to hire any out or even to take them for their feed & clothes, I mean house servants—The plantation people I fear we will have to leave to take their chances. . . . [O]f course if Charleston is taken, our river will not be safe. If we leave now, we will not be able to see what can be done, but I would not like to stay *here* with the Yankees & Negroes who I think will be very insolent when freed. . . . [E]ven should we lose all our Negroes which is all the property I have, we expect to undergo hardships & trials if our Men have it, why should not we expect to have trials also? God sees that it is needful for us, or he would not permit it to come on us.

That same month, May, Lincoln moved a step closer to the thing that Jane feared when he signed a bill that abolished slavery in the District of Columbia.

Jane and her mother decided to rent a house in Columbia, a hundred ten miles inland, rather than Winnsboro, and moved there with William's two younger sons and several house slaves. The disappearance of his sister and mother and the absence of all of his sons left the widowed William at Limerick, alone in the midst of the black village. The war worried him more than anyone else in the family, and he seems to have sought his typical respite from politics: plantation work. William passed the days with what he knew, dutifully counting his stock, noting that he had 161 cows, calves, oxen, steers, yearlings, and bulls at Limerick alone. In his solitude, William suddenly took interest in one of his first cousins, Mary Huger Gibbs, at neighboring Windsor plantation. Mary had a long face, straight brown hair, and sad eyes. William evidently proposed in the fall of 1862, and, two days before Christmas, they were married. William was forty-one, and Mary twenty-six. The new Mrs. Ball evidently took William's mind off the war, because he wrote a stream of notes to his mother about his happiness. Eliza Ball, who no doubt knew Mary but was more concerned with her own hardships "marooning" in Columbia, was feebly sympathetic. "I am glad you are so pleased with your wife that you have to write [her] name so often in your letters," she told her son.

"I do order and declare that all persons held as slaves within said designated States, and parts of States, are, and henceforward shall be free." President Lincoln had come the rest of the distance toward unconditional freedom, and the Emancipation Proclamation was issued January 1, 1863. It was merely a piece of paper, but now the North as well as the South could point to the same reason for the fight.

News of emancipation had little effect in the Confederate camps near Charleston. William continued to send work teams from Limerick to James Island, where they dug fortifications for weeks or months. On one occasion, Willie wrote his father: "I saw Cupid yesterday, he says that the boys [black Limerick crew] . . . are anxious to get home again, and are continually asking when they will get off. If you could send down another squad . . . I think it would be worthwhile." Later he added, "The Yanks continue to hammer daily. . . . Our negroes don't like it much, as the shells come too near to please their tastes."

By this time, 1863, seventeen-year-old John Ball, Willie and Isaac's brother, joined the family contingent on James Island. John had the blessing of his grandmother, who told his father somewhat ominously, "John . . . longs to do his share in defence of his country & a S.C. [soldier] of the low country could not meet death in a more preferable place than in defence of our dear old city." In addition to John Ball, Jane's twenty-year-old son John Shoolbred signed up and soon arrived to join the rest of the Ball boys. In early 1842, William's sister Jane had married John G. Shoolbred, who died when Jane was six months pregnant, leaving a posthumous son at Quenby, John Shoolbred Jr. The boy was raised largely among his cousins on Limerick, who invariably called him by his surname. Shoolbred had a thyroid condition and grew to a weight of three hundred pounds, which made the simplest tasks difficult and caused him to rely heavily on his valet, Nat. Nat himself was born about 1845 and raised at Quenby, where he became known among the Balls as "Daddy Nat" for his reliable responses to their every need. According to family tradition, Shoolbred was so fat he could not get on his horse without Nat's help. As I have mentioned, many of the Confederate sons of planters were served by personal slaves. When Shoolbred enlisted in a Charleston defense company, he arranged to bring Nat with him, as was his privilege.

After Nat and Shoolbred arrived at camp, Nat became a constant companion and servant to the Ball cousins, minding their clothes, stoking their fires, and bringing packages the thirty-five-mile distance from home. "Nat has not arrived, but we expect him today, with the boxes, which I will return at the first opportunity," wrote Willie to his father. One Christmas in camp, according to Willie, the Ball soldiers "sat down to turkey and fried ham. I expect Nat could best tell how it was appreciated, as I don't think he got even a bone to pick."

On James Island, the Ball unit settled into camp life, playing a waiting game with the Yankees. Weeks of idleness often came to abrupt end in fierce artillery fights as Federal gunboats appeared in the water and staged landings on vulnerable beaches. On January 30, on the Stono River, Isaac and Willie's artillery unit, with infantry, took an eleven-gun Union boat, the *Isaac Smith*, capturing the vessel, its eleven officers, and 108 men. Sometimes the brothers wrote home to report on their doings. "I just received a letter from Willie," Eliza told William excitedly. "They had a brisk engagement on Friday with 2 gunboats & disabled one, which had to be burned. Fortunately none of them were hurt, though shot & shell were thick over them."

Although Isaac did not send descriptions of his work as a gunner, there is one surviving account that gives a sense of these shooting matches. Isaac's friend and comrade-in-arms D. E. Huger Smith kept a wartime diary, in which this passage appears:

John's Island, 1863
Isaac Ball was the Corporal or Gunner of the piece at which I was serving. He was sighting the gun for the next charge when a shell struck the trail between his legs and carried away the lock-chain. I was acting as No. 6 and had in my hands a shell which I was handing to No. 2. As he reached to take it a fragment of the lock-chain actually cut the skin of his throat for one or two inches. He staggered back exclaiming, "Great God, I am wounded." Then drawing the back of his hand across his throat,

he looked me wonderingly in the eye and said, "No I am not!"
Then taking the charge he placed it in the gun.

The Federals made continual attempts on Charleston. On April 7, 1863,
nine Union ironclads entered Charleston harbor and struck at Fort Sumter, the key to a seagoing invasion. The ships were pounded with twenty-
two hundred shells from Confederate guns, and got off only 154 shots
before being forced to withdraw. After the repulse of the ironclads came
a change of command in the Federal Department of the South, and a
new assault was quickly planned. Confederate defenses around Charleston had shrunk to fewer than six thousand men, as many were transferred to the interior; of these, three thousand were on James Island and
a few hundred on adjacent, thinly defended Morris Island. In June,
seeing this vulnerability, the Federals accumulated nearly eleven thousand men at the mouth of the Stono River in preparation for an assault
that would begin at the southern end of Morris Island and move to its
northern tip to overtake Battery Wagner, a Confederate fort from which
Sumter could be bombarded.

On July 10, the attack on Morris Island began; the Ball boys were
on nearby James Island with the majority of troops. The Federals swept
up the length of Morris Island and stopped at the face of Battery Wagner. Meanwhile, thirty-eight hundred more attackers convoyed up the
Stono River to strike at positions at James Island. The first assault on
Wagner, on July 11, ended in a Federal retreat. On July 18 came a
second assault as five gunboats shelled Wagner from 9 A.M. till dusk.
At 7:45 P.M., six hundred men in the Fifty-fourth Massachusetts, a black
unit, charged the fort, a suicidal mission that left 262 dead, along with
their commander. The bombardments and charges continued for days,
then weeks, until the approach to Battery Wagner was a carpet of
corpses and dead cavalry horses rotting in the summer heat.

"What dreadful battles have gone through on Morris Island," Eliza
wrote William. "God was with us, or such a force could never have been
repulsed & so many vessels at once sending their shot & shells." William was evidently again showing his despair for the war, because his
mother added, "Don't seem to give up entirely, before the servants particularly, as I have heard you say." A few days later she scolded her

son again: "Willie says . . . he had a letter from you lately & says you are the most despondent man he ever knew of in his life; that you write as if we were all to be destroyed. You should not write so desponding to our dear Boys, they are bearing all the trials and hardships of the war & exposed to all the dangers, they want encouragement."

The defense plan called for a rotation of men at Wagner every few days. Jane described the reason this way: "The Regiments there have to be constantly changing, the men get exhausted and cannot eat [the] only good well being spoiled with the rain washing the blood of the wounded into it, and the shells send up fragments of Yankees out of the sand all outside of the Fort, for they were not buried deep, so I don't wonder they have no appetite."

Soon it was the Ball boys' turn. Eliza wrote William, "Willie tells Jane that John and Isaac leave on the 5th [of August] for Battery Wagner to be there 3 or 4 days to man 2 howitzers. . . . He seems to regret being left behind & parted from his Brothers & says he could not fight alongside of braver or cooler Boys."

Later Willie had his own tour at Wagner, and told his father what he witnessed:

We left this island [James] last Friday week for Morris Island, and reached there about daylight on Saturday, our detachment remaining at Battery Gregg. On Monday we relieved the men at Wagner. . . . The Yankees kept advancing their parallels day and night, and on Tuesday their rifle pits were 25 yds from ours. Their next step was to take our pits, and on Tuesday evening about dusk, they made the assault, our boys met them bravely, and after an engagement of about an hour's duration, they retired. The artillery did not participate as the contending parties were too close to each other. . . . [O]n Wednesday . . . they opened a heavy fire with mortars, which was kept up without intermission until sunset, when it suddenly ceased, and the next minute they were into our pits. We opened on them with canister and shell, but it was then too dark to see what damage we did. . . . They did not remain quiet, but poured volley after volley of minié balls amongst us, killing one or two of the other companies, but doing no damage to any of us. I can't conceive how we escped, as our guns were struck frequently, and the sand flung over us by their balls. . . . On Monday they fired three shells at a 42 pds cannonade, the first struck the gun, splitting it, and wounding five of the six in the detachment. . . . In addition . . . their sharpshooters keep up a continual practice at any one who dares to raise his head over the ramparts.

After fifty-eight days of siege, Battery Wagner and Morris Island were evacuated by the Confederates. Now in control of Morris Island, the Federals installed an eight-inch Parrott rifle, nicknamed the "Swamp Angel," that could hurl two-hundred-pound shells as far as Charleston, seventy-nine hundred yards away. The Swamp Angel began firing on August 22, when it unleashed sixteen shots. The next day, it fired twenty, the last of which disabled the gun after only thirty-six shells. Other Federal artillery bombarded the city. One shell struck a wall of the Ball house on Vernon and East Bay streets, ending up in the basement. The house was empty at the time.

Increasingly desperate, Eliza wrote her son to encourage that he consider sacrificing the lives of slaves, who were, she believed, expendable: "The call for negro labour is continued & pressing. Have you sent any & cannot you arrange it? Jane is ready to spare some, as a duty to try & save our city & country. What would be the loss of them in comparison to our children & friends?"

Jane, still writing from Columbia, feared the imminent fall of her home city, and worried about her precious possessions:

I dread to think what a famine will be in the land if all our crops are destroyed in the low country. . . . The little meat that is packed up [at Quenby] had better be shared out to the people at once before the Yankees destroy it. . . . I hope [my] harp may someday arrive [in Columbia], but if destroyed in town, I will not break my heart as I never expected to have seen it last year again. The family portraits will be of little use to us if we have no home again in this world. . . . We must remember Job how much he had to bear. . . . My dear Brother, Our time of trial is at hand and I do not see what we are to do for our poor Negroes.

They will have to take to the Woods when the [Federal] Boats
go up the river. I hope we will be able to prevent the Yankees
landing in Charleston. I fully expect it to be in ruins.

Despite the crisis, the city survived the Federal onslaught for another
year. The number of Ball sons in gray uniform continued to grow. William's youngest, Elias, enlisted at sixteen in a company of "Stono
scouts," who did reconnaissance against the Federals. On John's Island
in July 1864, young John Ball was hit in the cheek by a bullet or a
piece of shrapnel; he recovered and kept the scar. Also that year, Shoolbred was struck in his achilles tendon by a minié ball, a wound that
put him out of the service and caused him to limp the rest of his life.
The worst loss came in late summer, when Isaac B. Gibbs, twenty-fouryear-old brother of Mary Ball, William's wartime bride, was killed in
Virginia.

Isaac B. Gibbs was born in 1840 to Mathurin Guerin Gibbs and
Maria Louisa Poyas, both from families who had intermarried with the
Balls. Isaac grew up with the Ball brothers and their cousin Shoolbred,
and joined "Hagood's Brigade," a regiment under General Johnson Hagood, whose fights took Isaac up and down the South. In August 1864,
Isaac was with his regiment south of Petersburg, Virginia, which had
been under siege as the last stand of the Confederates against Federals
who were trying to get at the capital, Richmond, a few miles away. An
army of seventeen thousand under General Ulysses Grant arrived from
the east to meet Petersburg's defenders under General Robert E. Lee,
twenty-five hundred men arrayed in fifty-five batteries around the city.
Grant swept from the east to the west, trying to outflank the Confederates, and along the way came to the tracks of the Weldon Railroad,
which ran from Richmond through Petersburg to states farther south.
Hagood's Brigade was called on to defend the rail.

On Sunday, August 21, 1864, the Federals started to tear up the
tracks, and Hagood made a stand. At 9:00 A.M., Confederate artillery
hit Union positions, after which Hagood advanced. The Federals answered with guns, and most rebels stopped their charge, with the exception of Isaac Gibbs's regiment, which continued. When seven
hundred men headed for the top of a hill near the rail, they faced a

three-sided fusillade from several thousand Federals. An hour later, five hundred lay dead or wounded; one was Isaac Gibbs.

A eulogy was published in the *Charleston Courier*: "I. B. Gibbs of Company B, 25th Regiment, after hours of intense agony, is supposed to have expired during the night. . . . He died in his 24th year leaving the odor of a good name and a life of sanctity."

Mary Ball remembered, "We heard of my brother Isaac's death from a comrade who had been a prisoner but was exchanged. He had spoken to Isaac when he lay dying on the field of battle, suffering fearfully."

At the place where Isaac died, there is an eight-foot granite obelisk, put there by relatives of the five hundred Confederates a generation after the Civil War. The empty field is quiet, despite a two-lane road passing along its edge, and the remains of a Federal fort stand within a hundred yards. The inscription on the monument reads: "Here a brigade . . . commanded by Brig. Gen. Johnson Hagood charged Warren's Federal Army Corps, 21st day of August 1864, taking into the fight 740 men, retiring with 273. No prouder fate than theirs who gave their lives to liberty."

"It is Christmas again," Willie wrote home from John's Island in 1864, after two and a half years in the same muddy tent. "This is decidedly the darkest day that the Confederacy has yet seen, and I fear that our turn to suffer and lose our homes is nigh at hand. . . . I trust we will be able to show a good fight for the old city. . . . Wishing you all a quiet, happy Christmas, and hoping that we will all meet in safety at home by the next."

By the end of 1864, Jane, her mother Eliza, and their house slaves had come home from Columbia to Limerick, evidently because the women wished to be present when the Yankees eventually arrived. The Federal assault that would finally succeed came in January 1865 from Georgia, in the form of General William T. Sherman's army. To coincide with Sherman's arrival in South Carolina, a Yankee assault from the sea was planned at Bull's Bay, about twenty-five miles north of Charleston. At Sewee Bay, just south of the expected landing, the Confederates put together a token defense consisting of 250 men from the Ball boys' unit, armed with only four artillery pieces.

On January 18, 1865, Willie wrote home:

The city is to be evacuated, and very soon. I have no "official" notice of it, but every indication proves that it is to be done. . . . I now regard our chances of success as more than doubtful, and unless Providence interferes in our behalf, I think that there is no hope for us, as our people are thoroughly "rotten." A great many people are moving to the city, intending to take the oath of allegiance. I can't advise you what to do, as the whole country may be overrun. I felt the other day [on furlough] that I was seeing the last of my dear old house, and it was a severe trial to me. I can't see why God has sent such trials upon us, but he must have some reason for it. . . . May he protect you all from the outrages of the enemy, for Christ's sake.

The Federal landing was set for February 12, but the action stalled until the 16th, by which time the evacuation of Charleston had been ordered. From Sewee Bay, Captain Edward Parker and the Ball boys withdrew upstate. The road of retreat led right through Limerick, and Parker's company stopped on the plantation for the night.

"We took as many in our house as we could, and some camped in the yard," Mary Ball remembered. "When they went, we felt truly desolate. I wept when they burnt Huger's bridge after going over it. . . . The last night they were with us at Limerick we tried to sing hymns together. It was Sunday. Some could not sing, but wept."

The last day of slavery came at Limerick on February 26. William Ball sat in the dining room, a Bible in front of him, reading aloud to his family and a few of "his people." The local clergyman had made himself scarce during the fight, so William read church services for gatherings at home. It was a Sunday, and everyone in the room, black and white, knew the end was upon them. Before long, a dispatch of "greasy Yankees," as William's son Isaac called them, would arrive in the allée of oaks outside the door.

The prayer group numbered perhaps ten. Seated around the table were William's mother Eliza, his sister Jane, and his wife Mary; rounding out the table was William and Mary's four-month-old daughter, Eliza. Behind the whites, in the corner and along the plastered wall, stood an elderly black woman, Maum Hetty, the plantation's black matriarch, who lived nearest the family and ranked first among Limerick's house slaves. Hetty had brought up William's four sons by his first wife, and raised her own children on the side. Next to Hetty, probably, stood Robert, or "Robtie," the butler as well as the Ball brothers' companion and valet. Robtie was said to be especially good with a story, and used to bewitch the boys for hours with tales of an old trickster, Brer Rabbit.

The Bible reading, from the book of Lamentations, was a mournful passage about the miserable fate of Jerusalem, condemned by God for its sins. "She that was great among the nations, and princess among the provinces," read William. "She weepeth sore in the night, and her tears are on her cheeks . . . for the Lord hath afflicted her for the multitude of her transgressions." According to Mary Ball, the white people in the room thought the Bible passage fit their predicament.

At the end of 1864, an army of sixty-five thousand under General William Tecumseh Sherman had marched from Atlanta to Savannah, pulling down buildings, tearing up railroads, and burning a giant swath. Sherman's army stayed in Savannah for six weeks, then headed for South Carolina. Everyone expected Charleston to be the next target, but the marauding Federals turned away from the city and burned the capital of Columbia instead. Charleston surrendered the same day, February 17, to gunboats in the harbor. A week after the victors arrived, they sent raiding parties to the plantations; as William was reading from the Bible, a cavalryman and his company suddenly rode up to the mansion. A man in a blue uniform dismounted, threw open the door, and demanded to talk to the black village.

The crowd came from the cabins behind the house. Among the group was Henry, a nine-year-old boy with a broad face and light skin. Years later, Henry (by then known as P. Henry Martin, whose family story I told earlier) would recall this day in a letter to Mary Ball. A young woman named Sylvia, one of the plantation seamstresses, also came down. Before the war, Sylvia's owners had bought their clothing from stores; but after the blockade of Charleston, Sylvia had been pressed into service, making William's shirts from coarse homespun. The gardener Daddy Ben, who kept the yard and flower beds around the big house, hobbled out as well. (When he was a boy, Ben had fallen from a horse and broken his leg. Plantation medicine was severe—someone called for an amputation and Ben got a wooden leg.) Then the rest came down, and the Yankee told the crowd they were free.

The Ball women at this time evidently worried about rape. Throughout the war, the Confederate press had stoked morale with charges that if the Southerners gave in, Yankees would "ravish the South," and with hints that freed black men would do the same. Mary Ball wrote that when the celebration began outside, she and her sister-in-law, Jane Ball Shoolbred, ran upstairs. Each woman put on two heavy dresses, loading themselves down in a way that would frustrate sexual attack. William had buried the family silver in a swamp near the house, but some of the more delicate jewelry could not stand the mud. Grabbing these last pieces, Mary and Jane put them in cloth bags and stowed the loot next to their bodies, under layers of petticoats.

The first soldiers appeared and caroused through the house. They did little damage, and the worry that the women might be forced to have sex with the enemy, or with field hands, vanished. Later Mary Ball remembered that some of the Yankees were actually gentle. ("We thought they were rather polite.") Mary and Jane took off their double dresses, which were too hot.

The family had heard that the raiders usually went straight to the liquor. A second cavalry company rode up to the main house, and two young men from this new group surprised everyone by asking for a pitcher of milk and molasses. Maum Hetty brought some out and gave it to them. When they had drunk it down, Mary remembered, the soldiers remarked that it was the best molasses they had ever tasted.

Before the day was out, a third Yankee company showed up on the lawn at Limerick. All of its soldiers were black, with the exception of their commander, a white colonel. Paying no attention to the mansion, the black Federals went straight to the barnyard, where they found the large bell that had been used to call the slaves to work. Saying little, they took the bell down from its mount and smashed it to pieces.

The commander of the black company, a Colonel James Beecher, came from a family of antislavery activists in the North. His half brother, the Reverend Henry Ward Beecher, was an abolitionist and pastor at Plymouth Congregational Church in Brooklyn; his half sister was Harriet Beecher Stowe. James Beecher himself was a former missionary who had lived several years in China. After he joined the Union Army in 1861, Beecher, then thirty-three, was appointed lieutenant colonel of the 141st New York Volunteers, and later was given the task of recruiting a black regiment, the First North Carolina Volunteers. Beecher opened a recruiting office in New Bern, North Carolina, raised the regiment, and served as both commander and chaplain. It was this unit, most if not all of whom were freed slaves, that invaded Limerick and destroyed the work bell. Without really trying, Colonel Beecher, standing at the head of the North Carolina Volunteers, advertised the righteousness that had overtaken the war after the Emancipation Proclamation of January 1863. The Balls must have felt that an ambassador from President Lincoln himself had come to call.

Night fell, and the black soldiers celebrated with the freedpeople on the old slave street. The white Yankees made camp in the yard in front of the main house, while Colonel Beecher sat in the dining room with other officers, talking to William and family. William seems to have entertained the colonel with a mixture of grace and disdain. Every so often, William would call out to Maum Hetty for table service, but each time, according to Mary Ball's memoir, Beecher refused to allow Hetty to serve him, even to bring a pitcher of water, saying that she was no longer a slave and could not be bossed. Another officer opened a bottle of wine looted from a neighboring plantation. Despite the hospitality, Beecher evidently felt a certain menace and declined to drink, saying the wine might be poisoned. William took offense at the suggestion that a Southern gentleman would poison a bottle of wine and, pouring a glass, drank it down. He offered the next one to Beecher, who took it, and the unlikely drinking partners toasted into the night.

While the Balls stayed shuttered indoors, the yard outside rocked with drunkenness and joy, and from the parlor Mary heard repeated calls to burn the house. No one dared light a match, however, because the colonel was inside. Eyeing the ruckus from the window, William invited Beecher to spend the night in the parlor and leave his soldiers to pitch tents on the grass. William's invitation may have been a gesture of friendliness—or just as likely, he wanted fire insurance. The looting began when one soldier pried open the food storage. Half the hams and bacon were given around, while other soldiers dug through the garden behind the house, looking for hidden treasure. Some of the freedpeople looted, some not, and it went on until the Yankees grew tired and the plantation went to sleep, a crowded military camp. More looting started the next morning when soldiers burst into the main house and began rifling for hiding places. Finding nothing, and frustrated by the absence of silver, they seized on a china cabinet. Some of the former slaves carried off pieces of porcelain, and the Yankees smashed the rest on the brick cellar floor. The storeroom was broken open again and this time, cleaned out.

A similar scene was repeated on all the Ball places, as each was raided by Yankee troops. The Balls feared the worst, but in the end the soldiers and freedpeople just snatched a few hams. The single exception came at Buck Hall plantation, formerly home to William's cousin, Ann Ball Deas, and since her death, to her husband, Horry Deas. The Buck Hall mansion, work buildings, and crop (but not the slave cabins) were burned to the ground by Federal soldiers and freed Ball slaves. Despite the slaughter of the war, no one, not even on Buck Hall, was hurt.

Twenty-four hours after reaching Limerick, the Federal troops readied to leave. The last group of soldiers pulled down the rail fence that ringed the plantation yard, then they were gone. William and Mary Ball felt bitter and humiliated. As the stragglers marched off behind the U.S. flag, Mary cringed. "It could never be my flag again," she wrote, "after being disgraced."

William's four sons made their way north with the remnants of the Army of Tennessee under General Joseph E. Johnston, heading for the last battles in North Carolina. General Johnston had been stripped of command by President Davis in July 1864 but was restored to rank February 25, 1865, just in time to lead the retreat from South Carolina. Isaac Ball, now a corporal, was assigned to "Rhett's Brigade" under Colonel Alfred Rhett, an infantry formed out of the First South Carolina Artillery after the evacuation of Charleston. Rhett's Brigade was placed at the rear during the retreat.

In early March, General Grant ordered General Sherman to move north out of South Carolina, and ordered another force, headed by Phillip Sheridan, down from northern Virginia to meet him. Sherman's army left Columbia in ashes and began to chase General Johnston. The Union plan was to converge the armies in North Carolina—squeezing Johnston (and the Ball boys) in between—then to move on to the Confederate capital at Richmond. To prepare for this pincer maneuver, Federals under General Jacob Cox were sent to New Bern, North Carolina, to capture the railroad there, in order to have a straight line to ship supplies from the coast to the middle of the state. In all, the Union troops numbered ninety thousand, against Johnston's 21,500.

With defeat in sight, Isaac began a diary as he retreated into North Carolina. He evidently thought he might be killed, and wanted to leave something for his family about the last weeks. The entries in the diary are terse, however, revealing his movements but few emotions. From time to time, Sherman caught up with Rhett's Brigade, the rear guard, and drew them into a fight. This happened at Cheraw, South Carolina; afterward, Isaac wrote merely, "[I was] Part of the battle." A few days later, he added: "March 3rd, Sharp skirmish in the village, Capt had his horse shot while defending the bridge. . . . Compelled to abandon our caissons [gun carriages] for want of horses."

In early March, the "Hampton Legion," a large group of cavalry and infantry commanded by General Wade Hampton, joined Johnston's retreat. Hampton's ranks consisted of sons of wealthy South Carolina families not unlike Hampton himself, a cotton planter. Isaac's unit marched for a week from Cheraw, retreating seventy-five miles through constant rain, until the Ball brothers came to Fayetteville, North Carolina. "Dried clothes," Isaac wrote on March 11. No sooner had they hung out their uniforms than Sherman also reached town, pushing them farther. Isaac wrote: "Hampton had a brush with the Yanks in the town, [and we] evacuated."

On March 8, in a last desperate act, the Confederate Senate in Richmond approved the mustering of blacks as soldiers, but the war would be over before the rebels could try to raise a black unit. Sherman, in Fayetteville, sent messengers to get troops under General Schofield to join him in a two-pronged attack on Johnston at the town of Goldsboro, fifty miles away, to the northeast. Sherman sent word he would move on March 15 toward Goldsboro after a feint at Raleigh, which lay due north. "Ordered to Raleigh to be re-equipped," wrote Isaac on March 12, and on March 15, "reached Raleigh."

Sherman headed for Raleigh, then swung toward Goldsboro, while Generals Cox and Schofield led troops inland from the coast. Johnston attempted to fight both advances, from his left and right, taking a stand at the town of Bentonville. Between March 19 and 21, the Confederates attacked Sherman's left wing, but the Yankees fought off three assaults, and Johnston was defeated. The battle was the last significant rebel effort to halt Sherman. On March 23, Sherman and Schofield united forces at Goldsboro. Johnston wanted to follow Sherman north, hoping to join General Robert E. Lee, but Lee was preparing to evacuate Petersburg in the face of General Grant. In a gamble Johnston put a few troops on the roads he thought Sherman would take toward the Confederate capital at Richmond.

Isaac and his brothers, still in Raleigh, missed all of these fights. On March 24 Isaac wrote, "ordered to Hillsboro."

Hillsborough, thirty miles northwest of Raleigh, was a town where Johnston hoped to fall back and wait for Lee, who was trying to join the fight in North Carolina. To Isaac, the zigzag retreat through the South may have seemed like the last act of the disaster—a struggle for principles in which he believed and, at the same time, a futile fight for his inheritance. The wait went on for days, because Lee was hemmed in in Virginia by a hundred thousand men under Sheridan. On April 3, Union troops occupied Richmond, and Lee broke west, pursued by Grant, who wanted to keep him from meeting Johnston. The Ball brothers waited in Hillsborough until April 5, when Isaac wrote, ominously, that he was "ordered to the front." The front was back in the direction of Goldsboro and Sherman.

On April 6 came the last major fight between Grant and Lee, with huge losses to Lee; and on April 9, Lee surrendered at Appomattox Court House, Virginia. The fighting continued, however, in North Carolina. Sherman moved toward Raleigh on April 10 to meet Johnston's return, with skirmishes along the way. Isaac wrote that on that day his unit camped outside the town of Smithfield, five miles from Sherman. On April 11, Sherman's troops entered Smithfield and learned the news of Lee's surrender; fighting still continued, as the Confederate government, fleeing Richmond, arrived in an entourage in North Carolina. The Ball brothers fell back with Johnston toward Raleigh, then beyond, retreating seventy-five miles. By this time, President Jefferson Davis and his cabinet had joined the retreat with Johnston and set up a temporary Confederate capital in the town of Greensboro, under Johnston's guard, in north-central North Carolina. The Ball boys camped outside town with the units that surrounded Davis and his last stand.

On April 14, Lincoln was assassinated in Washington. Johnston decided to negotiate with Sherman, and after a meeting near Durham on April 17, the two generals signed an armistice. The Ball boys waited for orders. A week later, the armistice was rejected by Lincoln's successor, President Andrew Johnson, because the agreement called for the Federals to recognize existing Southern state governments. Jefferson Davis told Johnston to keep fighting, and take his army south, but Johnston defied his president and returned to the negotiating table. This time, on April 26, the Confederates relented, and agreed to give up all weapons and public property. The following day came the surrender, and Isaac wrote: "guns turned over to the Quarter Master in Greensboro."

Six hundred twenty thousand Americans were killed in the Civil War. The Ball boys had participated in the last fighting east of the Mississippi. According to a history of their regiment, written by an officer in their unit, on the day of surrender, "the companies were skeleton companies." The retreat from Charleston had gone into the field with forty-five officers and 1,000 infantry, and ended with eleven officers and 125 men.

Isaac seems to have been aware of the new world he now occupied. An event he recorded in his journal shows that he got a taste of the new order, in which all had been turned upside down. When he and his brothers were running from the Yankees, and hoping not to be killed, one day, Isaac wrote, "Begged for the first time for a meal."

16

>-◆>-○-◆-◄

AFTERMATH

One summer my parents took my brother and me to the Lincoln Memorial, in Washington, D.C. I was five years old, thirsty, and not much interested in Abraham Lincoln; but I knew in some way that he was the most significant of the presidents, and his big statue marked a highlight of our pilgrimage from the South to the capital. The sun bounced sharply off the white Colorado yule marble of the fake Athenian temple, and in the blinding light, it was impossible to see past the columns through the great open door. Inside, our eyes adjusted to the dim and our ears to the voices that banged against the vaulted ceiling. My mother, who had a reverence for authority, quieted her two sons with hushing noises as we approached the rope cordon behind which Mr. Lincoln tucked his feet. Ignoring the statue, my father turned to read the words chiseled on the wall—the Second Inaugural Address, the address at Gettysburg—and to look at the murals, "Unification" on the north wall and "Emancipation" on the south, the latter with its image of the Angel of Truth freeing a slave and the allegorical figures of Justice and Immortality as witness. In his shorts and tropical shirt, Dad looked like the Everyman of summertime Washington, and not especially like a person who had heard Lincoln-hating stories as a young Charlestonian.

From my short perspective, the huge head of Lincoln, with its high brow and concave cheeks, and the fingers like marble cucumbers, appeared grotesque. But despite feeling a vague repulsion in the presence of the stone giant, I remember being fascinated by the statue's eyes. They were weary, cavernous eyes, focused on some distant scene— perhaps the future of America, or the tour buses releasing crowds on the lawn.

In spring of 1862, near Hilton Head Island, South Carolina, black Americans began to use surnames for the first time. Federal troops had occupied part of the state, and the whites had fled, prompting a Union commander, Major General Ormsby M. Mitchel, to tell former slaves they could now use two names. Three years later, after the final surrenders, freedpeople around the South followed suit.

The common view is that black people adopted the names of their former owners, but that was not the case at the Ball places. Although a handful of workers took the name Ball, most chose some other name. (In a few cases, slaves seem to have had concealed surnames, which emerged after freedom.) Oral tradition in the Ball family has it that the last masters asked former slaves not to take our name. The Balls, who held themselves above blacks, thought the appearance of black families called Ball would diminish their status. An equal worry seemed to be that masters feared that darker families named Ball might be taken as sons and daughters of whites. Some freedpeople, no doubt, wanted to take the name Ball. It could be recognized far from home and might help in such things as looking for a place to live or trying to get credit to buy land. But most people went out of their way to find other names.

In the end, one or two people on each plantation took the name Ball, while most black families on Ball lands made other choices, including Aiken, Anton, Ash, Bennett, Black, Broughton, Brown, Bryan, Campbell, Cigar (or Segar), Coaxum, Collins, Dart, Drayton, Easton, Ellington, Evans, Fayall, Ferguson, Fleming, Ford, Fork, Frost, Gadders (or Gethers), Gadsden, Gaillard (Gillard), Gainey, Gamble, Garrett, Garsing, Gibbes, Gilbert, Gillon, Graham, Green, Guinness, Hamilton, Harleston, Harris, Hasgill (Haskell), Heyward (Haywood), Horlbeck, Irving, Jenkins, Johnson (Johnston), Jones, Ladson (Ladsdon), Lance, Lash, Lawrence (Laurence), London, Lonesome, Lovely, Lucas, Martin, Matthews, Maxwell, McKnight, Middleton, Miles, Miller, Moultrie, Nelson, Nesbitt

(Nesbeth), Oliver, Owens, Parker, Pinckney, Poyas, Pritchard, Randolf (Randolph), Read, Richardson, Rivers, Roberson (Robertson), Robinson, Roper, Royal (Ryall), Scott, Seymour, Shepherd, Simmons, Simon, Singleton, Stewart, Thompson, Vandross (Vanderhorst), Wade, Waring, Warren, Washington, Watson, Waylan, White, Wigfall, Williams, Wilson, and Withers.

Sometimes people invented names or had them arrive by accident. I met one family called Fashion who told the story of a pair of brothers, their ancestors, who got freedom and didn't want the master's name. One day the brothers were talking about an alternative when they spied a box on the table on which was printed the word "Fashion"—and they took the suggestion.

From The Bluff plantation, property of Isaac and Mary Louisa Ball between 1869 and 1924, came the story of a woman named Marly One. In the early 1900s, a curious Ball, visiting The Bluff, asked Marly One about the source of her unusual name. Marly One replied that her grandfather was living on The Bluff at the end of the Civil War, when the Union troops came through, and that a short time later there came a man, working for the army, assigned to take down the names of the freed blacks.

Marly explained to Miss Ball, "And the man went up to my grandfather and said, 'What's your name?' My Granddaddy said, 'Jack.' And the man said, 'Jack what?' And Granddaddy said, 'Jack One.' " "Jack One" was the number one man called Jack on the Bluff.

Following the defeat of the Confederacy, the Ball family felt the slow retribution of financial decline. About a year after the fighting, William Ball, the last rice planter, sold four plantations—The Blessing, Cedar Hill, Cherry Hill, and Halidon Hill. Letters show that he wasn't liked by the blacks on them, and that the houses for whites had been looted. Mary Ball remembered that the contents of the mansion in town, which had been removed to the country during the bombardment of Charleston, had disappeared. "The lovely furniture from the house on East Bay Street was sent up to Cedar Hill and most of it was missed," she wrote. "The Yankees took it out of the house and gave it to the Negroes."

William Ball tried to set himself up as a sharecrop landlord, but with little success. The sharecrop system gave former slaves a livelihood when farmwork was the only black skill that would sell on the labor market. Many black families went back into business as hired hands with the same landlords that had owned them, on terms that prolonged the old arrangements, with the modification that violence against workers would not be tolerated. In the usual deal, workers received one-half of a season's rice crop, the balance going to the former master. William Ball found that few people wanted to work for him, although some of his cousins and sons did better at persuading people to return to the rice fields. Whereas William had some 620 workers before the Civil War, only 29 put their names on William's first labor contract at Limerick, in March 1866. Everyone else, apparently, wanted nothing to do with him.

The Ball mansion in Charleston had been hit by an artillery shell during the war, but later patched up. In 1866, the house was appraised at $10,000. The Balls could not pay for further repairs, and the building decayed. The appraisal fell quickly to $9,000, then lower. William and his extended family of eight moved out and began renting the house to cover taxes and insurance, letting the building to an Irish tenant at a mere $50 a month. In 1878, the appraisal dropped to $5,000, and rent slid to $33. Finally, in March 1879, William sold the house for $5,105 in railroad bonds. The building later became a dormitory for railroad workers before being demolished about 1920.

When the end came, the Ball family's scattered members were unsure how to support themselves, and some lost control of their lives. Alwyn Ball Jr., son of William's cousin Alwyn, moved to New York and became an alcoholic. "I went one and a half years ago to an asylum for intemperance," Alwyn wrote from the North in 1872, "spent one year and have been home six months and can truly say that with God's help I have been effectually cured of all desire for drink." After the fountain of cash from the rice fields was cut off, Alwyn needed money to support his family. He sold his silver to pay creditors, and, desperate, seized on the idea of a little retail business in New York, "a butter stand in the main market." Alwyn wrote William to ask for the money ($300) to buy the booth. If cousin Ball couldn't provide, Alwyn said, he would start selling the furniture.

By the mid-1870s, the Limerick fields were mostly fallow, and perhaps a hundred black people lived in the old slave shacks, squeezing life from the corn fields and hog pens. A tax return from 1876 appraised the property, with its 4,603 acres and twenty-five buildings, at $10,153. In the next ten years, William sold pieces of the land to stay afloat, and in 1890, after various smaller sales, got rid of a five-hundred-acre chunk to a phosphate company, which dug up the swamps for the mineral. About the same time new county lines were drawn, and the Balls' old district, St. John's Parish, fell within the borders of a new Berkeley County. (St. John's Parish became St. John's Berkeley Parish.) As the borders of the Ball world closed in, the family grew nostalgic for slavery. In 1891, three months before his death, William sent a sentimental letter to a relative, in which he made it known he would take it all back, if he could.

"I can yet read and write without glasses, but do use them at times," wrote William, who was sixty-nine. "I have hitherto had many, very many blessings to be thankful for through life, and if God has ,seen fit to visit me with cares and poverty in my old days, it must be for some wise purpose. . . . We had quite a pleasant home party during the Christmas holidays. . . . However, Xmas now-a-days can't compare to those of the good old days in slavery times, thanks to Mr. Lincoln and his co-adjutors."

William died in April 1891, leaving behind his second wife, Mary, their seven children, and four grown children by his first wife. Two years later, one of William's creditors called in a loan for $2,000 and, when a roomful of Ball heirs couldn't pay, sued for title to Limerick. The last of William's land, with the house, sold for $1,298. The Limerick mansion, built in 1720, quickly fell into decline. In the 1930s the interior was photographed; the building had become a boarding-house for tenant farmers, who decorated the walls with magazine covers and filled the parlors with rickety beds. In 1945 the house burned to the ground.

The final enclave gone, the Balls moved to Charleston to look for other means of support. William's son Isaac the Confederate had raised a family on The Bluff as a sharecrop landlord, but he gave up in the mid-1890s after a hurricane in 1893 destroyed much of what remained of the rice fields. My Grandfather Nat, Isaac's son, remembered the move to town, when he was thirteen. The family piled belongings onto a horse cart, he said, and rode the slow thirty miles to Charleston along rutted roads. Isaac managed to hold on to The Bluff, which consisted of 1,123 acres on the west branch of the Cooper River, until 1924, when it was sold.

By 1900 the Balls in Charleston slipped into professional jobs, and lower. One of the sons of William and Julia Cart Ball worked for the Tuxbury Lumber Company, while other family members went into the fertilizer business or sold insurance. A grandson from Limerick, William Moultrie Ball, became the city's Superintendent of Parks and Playgrounds. Another grandchild got an education better than that of his brothers and sisters and became headmaster of Montgomery Bell Academy, a private school in Nashville, Tennessee. The family gradually drifted and grew level with the rest of the white population, amid the poverty of the South. One grandson from Limerick, I. G. Ball, tried something that would have shamed his older kin—running a hardware store. Opened in the early 1900s, the Ball Supply Company, on King Street, sold caulk and screwdrivers until the late 1940s.

My grandfather, Nathaniel I. Ball, the fifth son of Isaac and Mary Louisa Ball, got a job with a fertilizer company and, when he was twenty-nine, married Susan Magdalene Porter, daughter and granddaughter of Episcopal clergymen. Later he started a small contracting business that did renovation work, using a backyard shed for an office. Eventually Grandfather Nat had four or five employees, black men who did plastering, painting, and roof repairs. My father, the contractor's second son, Theodore Porter Ball, attended the local College of Charleston, went to Virginia Theological Seminary, and became an Episcopal priest. At forty-two, he married my mother, Janet Rowley of New Orleans, daughter of a clerk who worked for a Louisiana utility company. I was born in Savannah, Georgia, where Dad ran a parish, St. Paul's Episcopal Church, and earned a clergyman's salary of a few hundred dollars a month. I went to college, at Brown University, in Providence, Rhode Island, on a scholarship and loans. There was no land, no inheritance, no slave money.

In 1880, the "colored" made up sixty percent of South Carolina's residents. During the twenty years between 1860 and 1880, the black population of Charleston rose by two-thirds as thousands of ex-slaves streamed to the city, looking for work. Some families stayed close to the

Balls, working as housekeepers, but most looked for a new identity. Around the South in general, blacks separated from whites, and whites pushed them away with neglect and violence. In 1896, the Supreme Court case *Plessy* v. *Ferguson* allowed segregation to become law, though by this time black and white veterans of the plantation had already set up parallel societies.

At the start of World War I, fifty years after emancipation, most families of former slaves had lost touch with the Balls, whose whereabouts they might have known but whose faces they did not. A black migration that had been trickling out of South Carolina before the war accelerated when black veterans returned from Europe, and thousands moved north to new lives. Between 1900 and 1940, the proportion of black citizens dropped by nearly thirty percent, as people left for Washington, Baltimore, Delaware, Philadelphia, New York, and Boston. In 1923, the white population of South Carolina outnumbered the black for the first time since the mass slave escapes of the American Revolution. White terror worked neatly with black striving to drive people away: the last of hundreds of lynchings in South Carolina occurred in 1947, for which thirty-one white defendants were acquitted. The migrants to the North built families there and lost connection with the South, until, by World War II, few of the Balls and few of the grandchildren of ex–Ball slaves knew where their opposite numbers might be found.

The oldest person I believe I've met was the son of a Ball slave. Because his family wanted privacy, I will call him Benjamin Nesbitt, an alias. Benjamin Nesbitt's father was born near the end of slavery on one of William Ball's plantations, while his wife's family came from a place that belonged to William's sister Jane. When we met, on a country lane lined with the houses of his children, Mr. Nesbitt was in his late nineties. As I arrived at his house, the clouds opened, and a rainstorm darkened the eaves and rattled the roof. Mr. Nesbitt was a small man, further shrunken by time, with a spread of short white hair and a face of fifty lines. He had little physical energy but was a vigorous talker. His wife, nearly the same age as he, sat nearby but said nothing, leaving her husband to hold forth.

"Me and my wife are way up in age—and no thinking about it—I can't do anything, she can't do anything," Mr. Nesbitt said, his voice a tray of gravel.

I asked how his family got off the plantation.

"That's way back yonder," he answered. "My grandmother raised her children off of corn, and, to my knowledge, hard labor. At that time, things were rougher. You had to stay on that farm from black to black. You go in the dark and you come in the dark. Working for the white man, when he gave you something you said, 'Thank you, sir,' and you go on about your business. In those days, when they said you had to get up and go, you had to get up and go."

Mrs. Nesbitt looked at her husband, expressionless, her mouth flat, and sighed. She seemed accustomed to the crisp monologue.

"My father move over here with his mother's people and then he bought a piece of land, fifteen acres," Mr. Nesbitt went on. "Do you know what land cost back then? Thirty cents an acre. Do you know what he started with? Five bushels of potatoes. The whole thing cost thirty-seven dollars."

"What is your earliest memory from childhood?" I asked.

"I could see my parents' house on the plantation. It was a little old pole house," he said. "They put the pole one on another, and then they put clay, because the pole can't lap down, you know? They put clay around the whole house, and then they took the clay and built a chimney. That was a rich man's house in the poor time."

It was a cool day in December, and the rain stopped drumming on the roof.

"I went to school a little while. Oh man, the school house looked like a dog house. It had benches built in it for you to sit on, and the teacher had a stool in the middle and the benches were all around it and he taught school. If you didn't pay attention, he would take a strap and cut your head off. The old man couldn't keep me in school because I had to mind the rest of the children. So I didn't know nothing about no school book no more than what I heard. I still can't read and write."

Across the room, Mrs. Nesbitt raised her head a little, but not much, catching her husband's eyes.

"I been married sixty-eight years," the old man continued. "All I know is we've been living a rough life. After I got married, I was working for fifty cents a day, and that was on Cedar Hill plantation. Didn't know anything about gas, electricity. One man put me down to fifty cents a day, said he didn't care whether I wore clothes or not. In 1930, people were working for fifty cents a day that had ten children! You go to the store, you could get a sack of grits for a dollar. If you're lucky, then meat—three and four cents a pound—but sometimes, no meat. Then that's all you had to eat, corn grits, with cow peas thrown in."

Mr. Nesbitt's eyes stared straight, looking back over the twentieth century.

"I'll tell you the truth, then we'll stop," he said. "When President Roosevelt came to office, I'll tell you what he started off with. He had a truck with a load of provisions on the outside of Quenby plantation —where there was a big schoolhouse, the white man's schoolhouse. Roosevelt fed the black people there for about four months. He stopped feeding the people, and then he put them on the job for ninety-two cents a day. The WPA gave out jobs digging ditches on the side of the road, just to raise wages so you could get something to eat. It went up to ninety-five cents, ninety-six, and it kept going up. It went up to ninety-eight cents a day, and they took two cents out of that for Social Security."

"Did you take one of those jobs?" I asked.

"I had to. In those days, we were living a dog's life. You couldn't get shoes, had to make dresses for the children from a potato sack. Then, after the Yankees from up North bought one of the places, I worked a boat for seventeen years, for about four dollars a day, and raised my eight head of children."

He closed his eyes, and opened them. He was tired from the tale, living it and telling it. "Ain't no use in asking no more," he said. Finally, the story dropped off in the present.

"You see where Social Security has me today, got me laying down and getting checks. I thank the Lord that I'm living. I don't look to get rich, but I can live until I die. We're living a millionaire's life compared to where we come from. This here is heaven. It's a glorious, glorious, glorious land compared to where we come from."

The waves of black migration rolled into most corners of America, and I followed some of them. From time to time I hit a case of mistaken identity, and arranged a meeting with a black family whom I thought came from the Ball places but, as it turned out, did not. The most interesting near miss of this kind took place in California.

Of the many families who got free from Comingtee, one took an unusual name, for which I will substitute the pseudonym Withers. After several phone calls to Withers households, I located a middle-aged Ms. Withers, who said that her family had come from Berkeley County and that one of her relatives had known the last slave in the family, a man called Scipio. She put me in touch with a cousin whom she thought would know more, and that man led me to his older brother, a minister, known as the family historian. The brother was about eighty, lived in California, and in his childhood had known Scipio.

As I pointed out early on, the Roman name Scipio appeared often among Ball slaves. In the third century B.C., the Roman general Publius Cornelius Scipio (later called Scipio the Elder) fought his way through several campaigns and was given rule over Sicily. In 204 B.C., Scipio sailed with his army for Africa to invade Carthage, and two years later routed his enemy, Hannibal, and won the honorific surname Africanus for having seized a piece of the continent. Scipio Africanus became head of the Roman Senate, then an ambassador to Rome's African colonies. In eighteenth-century Europe, the story of Scipio Africanus inspired a spate of history paintings—like "The Continence of Scipio" and "Scipio Granting Massinissa His Freedom" (or "Scipio Freeing the Slave"), both by Giambattista Tiepolo—after which time American planters picked up the name for black children. On an 1847 slave list from Comingtee plantation, I found one such Scipio (perhaps the one who, as Dorothy Dame Gibbs had told me, had been taught to mimic Latin).

I telephoned the Reverend Peter Withers, who lived in the vicinity of San Francisco, and told him of our possible affiliation. His voice showed no emotion. When I fell silent, he cleared his throat.

"They used to call him 'Uncle Scip,' " he said, with a chuckle. "He was my grandfather."

The voice was reassuring, and had a sonorous lyric. Mr. Withers's accent had the echo of several regions—part Carolinian, part Jamaican. I heard crisp *P*s, sliding *S*s, and the confident cadence of the pulpit. I asked whether the minister wouldn't mind telling me about Scipio in person.

When I met Peter Withers, he was standing on the lawn in front of the church he called home. His smile was vigorous and his handshake forceful, and he wore a white suit and white shoes. On the grass stood a lettered sign—MISSION WORD CHURCH, REV. PETER WITHERS, FOUNDER—next to which the minister seemed to glow in the light of San Francisco Bay. In the watery sun, my skin was colored by freckles and reddening patches, but Mr. Withers's skin was like an eggplant, pitch dark and shining, with purple highlights. Fifty years of the New Testament had made the minister stand straight as a rifle, and prevented him from aging. His eyes were as bright as matches, and he had handsome cheekbones and a head of salt-and-pepper hair cut close to the scalp.

Mr. Withers's church occupied a converted suburban ranch-style house in a residential neighborhood, and the sanctuary consisted of a large room that had been added on. At the front of the room stood a drum kit, a pulpit, and an organ, and twenty wooden pews filled out the remaining space. I brought out the papers that had led me to his door. We looked at a map of Berkeley County and the plantation district, photocopies of the Comingtee labor contract, and, finally, copies of the slave lists showing the name of Scipio. Mr. Withers remained silent, then raised his hand like a traffic cop.

"Scipio was definitely in slavery," he said. "He told me all about it. I'm sorry I didn't know the value of what he said at the time. Being young, I didn't consider it until later. But he died at the age of ninety, happy. If I remember correctly, it was in 1935 or 1936. When he died—this was unusual, this might sound strange to you—but there were almost as many Caucasian people at his funeral as blacks."

The minister spoke slowly, with a lilt and a smile. He admired his grandfather, and hoped I would do the same. Everything fit what I knew of Scipio: by the minister's account, his grandfather would have been born in 1846, about when Scipio appeared in the slave lists.

"In these documents," I said, "the name Scipio appears on a plantation called Comingtee, in the year 1847. Where was your grandfather in slavery?" I asked.

"All I know is that he was in Berkeley County, South Carolina."

Mr. Withers said that in the 1920s, his grandfather had seven children and owned ten acres of land. He lived with his second wife, Margaret, after his first wife, Alice, died. The sons, the minister's father among them, helped to support the old man in his last years.

"Scipio was tall, maybe six feet, and about my build," said Mr. Withers. "He was straight, and walked upright until the day he died." The minister himself had strong arms and a trim frame.

"My grandfather's facial expression was almost like Mr. Abraham Lincoln's face," he said. "He had naturally white hair. He was pleasant and relaxed. You could sit in his company all day long and never be tired of it."

I asked if he had a picture of his grandfather, and his face twisted when he admitted he had once had a photograph but had lost it.

"Did Scipio ever tell you stories about being in slavery?" I asked.

"What he said over and over was how he organized a prayer group among his friends, and how they were never beaten. He said that over and over," Mr. Withers answered. "What is interesting is that Scipio was a man of God. He told me never hate. God takes care of everything. Because of that fact, Scipio said, he wasn't tortured or anything. They didn't set dogs on him."

"Did he tell you stories about other people who had dogs put on them?"

"Oh yes, he did."

"Can you remember any of those stories?"

"Not so clear," said the minister. "But he said many of the—"

The minister stopped himself. His memory turned away from Scipio's harsh stories and drifted in the direction of euphemism.

"You know, there was quite a deal there," he went on from his new footing. "Many of the slaves and the slaveholders, they had a lot of conflict. But my grandfather said he never had any."

"Did he tell you about the conditions under which he lived?" I asked.

"He used the word 'flogging' to describe punishment meted out to some slaves," said the minister, relenting. "Another, older man I knew confirmed the same thing that Uncle Scip said. They used to call him 'Uncle Scip.'" The minister laughed, and his careful manner became serene. "And this man said he knew Uncle Scip way back in slavery, and that they never had any problems in terms of torture, or anything. This was his testimony to me, over and over."

It was a confusing record. Scipio had spoken about plantation violence, but had also said that at least some of his friends and family never felt the whip.

"You know, Uncle Scip told me this," Mr. Withers began, settling on a last memory. "He said, 'In slavery, the people who were really against us, and tried to torture and flog us, they were in more slavery than I was. They were slaves to their idea of punishing me, but I was a free man in my spirit.'

"A godly man has wisdom, just like the prophets of old," he went on. "When you are in a place like that, rebellion is not going to get the job done. To stay on the place, that's wisdom."

I asked about his grandfather's manner, the way he talked to people.

"When you would meet him, he would quote something from the Psalms, or from something else. One of his favorites was Psalm Thirty-seven, 'Fret not thyself because of evil doers, neither be thou envious against them.' You see, Scipio didn't believe, from what I could gather, in retaliation."

"You have to love your oppressor," I said. "You have to believe in the humanity of your oppressor."

"Definitely." Mr. Withers pursed his lips and lifted his voice. "'Bless them that curse you, do good to them that hate you!' You see, when I was young, I hated the system of segregation! But bitterness is no good for the mechanism of the body. You have to purge yourself of it."

"I want you to try to remember your hate," I answered.

"I've seen some injustices that were horrible," came the remark, after a long pause.

"For example?" I asked.

"I don't want to bring up memories that are detrimental." Mr. Withers withdrew again. "It's not there anymore. That system is gone, that lifestyle—it's been swept away. And when I found out about the Lord, it decimated my hate."

In 1946, at age thirty-one, Peter Withers was born again. He became a missionary, and began traveling as an evangelist in the Caribbean, starting in Jamaica in 1949. Flying between the United States and the islands, the Reverend Peter Withers developed a lifestyle he would keep. In 1958, with his wife—by then also a missionary—the minister moved from Jamaica to Haiti.

"There we really got involved," he said. "We have fifteen churches in Haiti. Each has a mission school, because the illiteracy rate is very high. We have three thousand children attending the schools, and sixty teachers. In the main mission compound, we have a medical clinic staffed with a Haitian doctor. We also have a nutrition center, which gives one hot meal a day to the children."

"Why are you a missionary?" I asked.

"Because people are in need. We have everything here in America —hospitals, churches, schools, comforts. There, they have nothing . . . nothing!"

In 1976, Mr. Withers began to evangelize in Africa.

"Kenya has forty-three different tribes," he said. "Each has its own culture, its own dialect. We've concentrated mostly with the Masai. The average Masai's house is a little hut, covered with refuse, built out of patches of wood." In Kenya, the minister said, he and his wife arranged for the translation of the New Testament into the Masai language, and his church financed a well to bring running water to a dry village.

"Now we are working on a building project, a combined mission and medical building, in which the Masai ladies can give birth to their babies. Because the paganistic way is horrible—it's being supervised by the witch doctors." Mr. Withers twisted his face on the phrase "witch doctors."

"In Haiti, did you deal with voodoo?" I asked.

"Voodoo is demonic," he came back. "You cannot suppress it successfully. You've got to deal with the root of it, which takes time. It cannot coexist with Christianity. What we believe is nonnegotiable."

We talked for a minute about voodoo, and traditional African religion, which Mr. Withers clearly wanted to exterminate. Suddenly the minister asked, "Mr. Ball, what do you think caused slavery?"

"I think greed cause slavery."

"That's your concept," he said skeptically. "But you see, the Christian culture was well planted in Africa when slavery came. Africa went astray from the teaching of God. Understand me?"

"Did Africans bring slavery on themselves?" I asked.

"Through disobedience and rebellion." The minister put his hand in the air. "They brought destruction, and it could happen to any one of us. Take the story of Israel. God loved Israel. But when the Israelites disobeyed God, He said, 'I'm going to punish you. I'm going to send you into slavery.' "

"Africans, and the Jews, were punished with slavery for disobeying the word of God?" I asked.

"That's exactly what I'm saying."

I told Mr. Withers that I did not accept his idea of black racial guilt and punishment, and I asked what he would say to black people who live with the legacy of the plantation.

"I would say to them, 'Let God straighten you out.' America has superabundance. Much of the American suffering could be alleviated." His bright eyes were unblinking, with a punitive gaze. "There are many lazy people in America. We have no excuse for them."

I got up to leave. As I reached the door of the church, Mr. Withers took me by the arm and gave me what seemed to be a painted-on smile. Outside, standing near the placard of the Mission Word Church, the Reverend Peter Withers waved good-bye.

Later I tried to sort out Mr. Withers's family. I looked again in the Ball slave lists, and saw the name Scipio in the year 1847. But this Scipio wasn't a child, as I had initially thought. In fact, he was fifty years old. Looking further, I found a note that the Scipio on Comingtee had died of "dropsy" on August 19, 1857, at age sixty. Peter Withers could not have known him, or been his grandson, and the Withers family had no ancestral connection to the Balls.

Every summer around the country, the progeny of ex–Ball slaves gathered at family reunions. I had spoken with a woman named Sarah Roper England, who said her people came from the Ball places, and wanted me to meet her relatives. The right occasion, she added, would be a big dinner that brought together two branches—some people named Roper, others called Roberson. ("Sometimes we spell it Robertson," she said.)

"My grandmother used to talk about 'Maussa Ball,' " said Sarah England. "It was never 'Mr. Ball,' always 'Maussa.' "

The reunion dinner was to be held at a new suburban hotel, whose cookie-cutter architecture, which rose in the midst of a big parking lot, resembled that of ten thousand other freeway inns. I arrived on the appointed day to a lobby in which a Formica counter sat on synthetic carpet and nondescript music tinkled from hidden speakers. In a conference room rented for the occasion stood two rows of tables set for dinner, and some thirty-five black people milling about. My acquaintance, Sarah England, in her late fifties, showed her warmest manner and took me to a corner, where we went over the family story.

"Our people came from Pawley's plantation," Mrs. England said, "and from Buck Hall." She brought out a booklet she had compiled for the reunion, with thirty pages of photographs, family trees, traditions, and an address list of relatives. On one page, Mrs. England had transcribed stories she learned from her grandmother. In the early 1800s, the booklet said, ancestors of the Ropers and Robersons lived at Brick House plantation on Edisto Island, down the coast from Charleston, where they were the property of planter J. W. Roper. After Roper lost his land, the text went on, "our ancestors went to work for the Ball family, on Buck Hall, next to Pawley's plantation. . . . When the Civil War ended, the Balls freed all slaves. The family continued to use slave master J. W. Roper's last name, instead of 'Ball.' " A roster at the back of the booklet listed 186 family members around the country, descendants of the last two or three slaves. The clan lived in Alabama, California, Connecticut, Delaware, Florida, Georgia, Maryland, New York, North Carolina, Pennsylvania, South Carolina, Tennessee, Virginia, and Washington, D.C.

Mrs. England's story was corroborated by paperwork, whose trail led to a daughter of Ann Simons Ball, or Captain Nancy. In 1815, thirty-nine-year-old Ann Ball had a daughter, Ann, who married the physician Elias Horry Deas. Ann Ball and Horry Deas bought Buck Hall, moved there in 1850, and the following year bought Pawley (or Pawley's), a 793-acre tract next door. In the National Archives in Washington, I found records that placed Mrs. England's family on Pawley and Buck Hall.

The story of the Roper-Roberson family included a singular fact: Mrs. England had oral tradition about the way the Balls dealt with their former slaves.

"The Balls were good to work for," she said, speaking carefully. "One good thing came out of the plantations. My grandmother said that when they were children working for the Balls, they were one of the families that made sure their slaves got an education. She said there was another family, the Cordes, who were slave masters, who were very mean. After freedom, the Cordes family would not let the former slaves get an education. But my grandmother could read and write, because the Balls encouraged their people to get educated."

The dinner party chattered around us as Mrs. England explained there were differences in the way slave-owning whites reacted to emancipation. She pointed to the written version of her family's story.

"The Ropers . . . and Robersons were able to attend school, and they took advantage of the opportunity," read the booklet. "After slavery, they continued to stay on the plantation and work for the Ball family, until Frank Roper was able to buy land, and build a small house."

Since I had found much evidence of cruelty and deprivation on the rice plantations, Mrs. England's tale came as a surprise. But a few months later I met another family, who came from the Balls' Pimlico and The Bluff plantations, who said much the same thing. In meetings with that family, one woman said that her grandmother had told her about the years after freedom, when the Balls at The Bluff encouraged their house servants, former slaves, to go to school. When they did attend, the woman said, sometimes Mr. and Mrs. Ball helped them with their lessons.

Elsewhere I stumbled on an affidavit that seemed to support something of what Mrs. England and the other family said. In 1903, at an Army pension hearing, a former Ball slave named Patty Moultrie testified that Isaac Ball had written letters for her in the years after the Civil War. At the time, Patty Moultrie's husband, Stepney Moultrie, was away from home in the Union army. While she and Stepney were separated, Isaac Ball, the Confederate veteran, helped them stay in touch. "When Stepney was in the Army," Patty Moultrie testified, "and after my young master, Mr. Isaac Ball, came home from the war, he [Isaac Ball] used to read me my letters from Stepney, and write to him for me."

Later, Sarah England went further, saying that her ancestors not only had been encouraged to get an education but had actually done better in general than other former slaves, because the Balls had helped them.

"Most everybody who worked for the Balls became more prosperous than other people," Mrs. England said. When I looked surprised, she pointed her finger in the air and said, "This is a fact." Another man at Mrs. England's reunion, her cousin, Kenneth Cook, echoed this report. Kenneth Cook was a friendly, stocky man in his thirties, who worked for the Metropolitan Area Transit Authority in Washington, D.C. "Everybody in the family did well right after freedom," he said. "Somebody had a shoe store, and a grocery. My uncle had his own business, and later someone had a dry cleaning store. In 1948, one of the family took flying lessons, to become a pilot. That was the unbelievable one, a black man trying to be a pilot during segregation."

I asked Mrs. England to tell me the names of other families who might have been helped by the Balls after freedom. Without hesitating, she said, "Besides the Ropers, there were the Chisolms, and the Evans families. They worked for the Balls, became literate, and later they owned a lot of property."

Some freedpeople took the family name. I met one black Ball family with branches in Delaware, Maryland, Pennsylvania, South Carolina, and Virginia. I could not link them to the white Balls with certainty, but their oral tradition placed ancestors on the South Carolina coast, near Charleston. They may well have been Ball slaves, but the documents to prove it never surfaced. Nevertheless, on a cool November afternoon, I met a member of the clan, Jacqueline Ball, a single mother living outside of Washington, D.C.

Jackie Ball was tall and thin, with straightened hair that fell just below her ears. Jackie came from a military family and worked in the Pentagon as a petty officer, second class, in the Navy. Her father and his two brothers had fought in World War II, and in addition to her own ten years of Navy service, she had two cousins recently retired from the Army, a man and a woman, each with the rank of major. Rounding things out, Jackie's daughter, LaShawn, was joining the Army Reserves. At the Pentagon, Jackie answered the phone with her rank—"YN2 Ball, may I help you?"

"I'm in a classified, vaulted area," she explained about her job, "with security clearance." Jackie wouldn't say much about the nature of her work. "It deals with warfare and bombing people," she said airily. "I help carry out the bomb plans. I'll tell you this, when the cleaning people come through at the end of the day, we have two trash bins, classified and not—and we make sure they empty the right trash bins."

"I met a man once who was a nuclear targeting expert," I said. "His job was to single out places to drop those bombs."

"I can imagine," Jackie replied. "They have protesters every Monday at the Pentagon. The police have a video camera, and they tape all of them. When they had the anniversary of Hiroshima, there were a lot more protesters, and it was really uncomfortable. They threw a substance on the building, symbolizing blood, and I was really shaken."

For a bombing analyst, Jackie had a manner that could not have been more sweet, and there was something tender about her speech. Jackie, fortyish, had been raised in Los Angeles by her mother. During childhood, her father, Joseph M. Ball, was completely absent.

"I did not know my father that well," Jackie said. "My parents met when my father was a student-teacher in Baltimore. My mother was a daughter of a Methodist minister. They married, and moved to South Carolina, his home. My mother didn't care for the South. In fact, she hated it. They broke up soon after I was born, then my mother moved with me to Los Angeles."

Jackie went to college at San Diego State University, married a fellow student, then had a daughter, LaShawn McGhee. The marriage didn't last, and Jackie moved with her daughter from California to Washington, D.C., where she raised LaShawn alone. I asked whether her father, who died in South Carolina, knew where his family had come from.

"Someone contacted my father in the 1980s, by mail," Jackie replied. "The letter was about the Ball plantations, and whoever wrote it wanted to tell him something, or maybe ask him something. And I heard from my stepmother that my father just threw the letter away."

"Why?"

"Apparently he didn't want to have anything to do with it," she said. "So he just got rid of it. I think whatever it was, he didn't want to remember." Jackie's father died before she could ask about the letter.

I spoke on the phone to Jackie's cousin, Denise, a retired major. She was excited and chatty, and wondered aloud when we would meet. "I'm so happy someone in the family is doing the history," she said. Denise talked about where her ancestors might have lived, and where the family ended up, then said something that told me Jackie had not given her a full briefing.

"I'm a nurse," she said, "and once I worked with a Dr. Ball, a white guy."

"I have kin in medicine," I answered.

"No, this guy was white," Denise said.

"Right," I said. "I'm white."

There was a pause on the phone.

"You are! Okay!" Denise shrieked. "Well! You just happen to be!"

I explained who I was, and asked whether Denise would still like to meet.

"Well, it's very interesting, and it's nice to know your history," she answered carefully. "We've all made improvements, and that's a part of history, that's what happened."

Jackie, Denise, and I met in a steak restaurant on a suburban strip. Denise was shorter than Jackie, with more flesh on her bones, and in her late forties. She had a blunt manner and seemed able to say whatever came to mind.

"Denise was shocked when you told her you were white," Jackie said. "Then we had a big laugh about it."

"Yeah, I'm not hung up," Denise said sarcastically.

I had sent the family a handwritten letter, and Denise brought it up.

"That was such a beautiful letter you wrote to us."

"Thank you," I said.

"I was going to act like a real field slave, and write you back on some lined paper with holes in it," Denise went on, straight-faced. "I was going to have the spelling and punctuation correct, but use block letters. My family talked me out of it."

We laughed a good laugh, rocking a bit in the vinyl booth. Denise said she was a retired officer who once supervised teams of nurses.

"You have so many in the service," I said, "you could start your own Ball division."

"We'll get you in the military with us," Jackie joked.

"They'll take you in a minute, make you an officer," Denise put in. "They're looking for an original, blue-blood white boy."

Jackie had the service records of her father, Joseph Ball, and one day we went over them. Born in 1910, Joseph Ball got a degree in education from Morris College, in Sumter, South Carolina, and when World War II began he was a school principal at a black public school, earning $16.50 a week. He enlisted in the Army in April 1942, was sent to Camp Claiborne, Louisiana, spent three months as a private, and was promoted to sergeant. In a photograph taken after the promotion, Joseph Ball appeared trim, with a pencil mustache, a smile, and a direct gaze. The Army medical put his height at five feet, eight inches, his weight at 154 pounds. In January 1943, Joseph Ball was sent to North Africa to the campaign against the German army there, where he worked as a sergeant, running the company supply room. In September 1944, Joseph Ball's battalion passed through southern France, as the Allies retook occupied areas; and at the end of the war, he was in Germany, in the Rhineland campaign of spring 1945. Returning to the United States that fall, he went back to his education career and spent the rest of his life as a principal in the South Carolina public schools. He died in 1985.

"I was an only child," Jackie said. "And believe it or not, I only met my father one time. I must have been about twenty-nine. It was so uncomfortable, though it's kind of funny now that I look back on it. I was working at the Library of Congress, in Washington, and I drove down to South Carolina and stayed the afternoon. I remember introducing myself. I was his daughter, but I introduced myself! He was friendly, and his wife, my stepmother, was there. But my father and I didn't talk about each other, or where I had been for thirty years. I remember that Ronald Reagan was the President, so we talked about him. We talked current events, and the price of clothing—everything but us. It was so awkward. When I went back a second time to see him, he had passed away."

Jackie's daughter, LaShawn McGhee, grew up with her mother in the Washington suburbs. She spent a couple of years in college in Ohio, left before finishing, and joined the Army Reserves. The week I met her family, LaShawn, still a teenager, was set to graduate from basic training on a huge military base.

Jackie and I arrived at a parade ground flanked by bleachers filled with hundreds of families, half of them black. Five hundred young soldiers in new green uniforms marched to the center of the field. On the day of the event, I showed Jackie some slave lists and letters from the Ball plantations. We looked at a deed of gift, with which one of the Ball masters offered a child to a relative as a present. As she pored over the documents, Jackie was silent, trembling.

"I was really shaken after you showed me the slave lists," Jackie admitted. "It was too emotional, I had to hold back the tears, but I told myself to try to feel what was written."

The columns of soldiers, separated into companies of a hundred each, marched to a brass band. From the faraway bleachers, the clusters of recruits looked like clouds floating across the grass.

"Try to remember," I told Jackie, who was quiet, "that those people, the slaves, had a community. They had pleasure, they had music, and they had love, in the midst of everything."

LaShawn was part of the Second Battalion, Thirty-ninth Infantry Regiment, the "Fighting Falcons." It was the same battalion that had fought in North Africa in 1943, when LaShawn's grandfather, Joseph Ball, served in World War II.

"What was it like to be given as a gift to somebody?" Jackie asked. "Not a pony as a gift, but a person?"

A stern male voice came over the public address system: "This is a landmark occasion that symbolizes a new beginning for each and every one of you, a fresh start in life. It makes no difference who you are, where you came from, your race, religion, or cultural background. You are each now members of a single team, the United States Army."

Jackie free-associated about the past. "How could you really love someone? Yes, they were in love, like you said, but at any moment, that love could be snatched away."

We found the graduate after the ceremony. LaShawn McGhee, a model of youth and vigor, stood about five feet, four inches, and held her body straight as a door. Her green jacket, pinched at the waist, showed the wave of her figure. She affected a tough pose, jutting out her jaw and swinging her shoulders when she walked. During the eight weeks of training, LaShawn had been made a leader of her platoon, and her voice was hoarse from yelling orders.

"Let me take a look at you," Jackie said, widening her eyes. "I don't recognize my daughter—or even her face. The haircut!"

"I lost a lot of weight," LaShawn said.

"What are these medals?" asked Jackie, fingering her daughter's chest.

"One's for marksmanship, and the other is for throwing grenades," said the recruit.

The most mysterious of all the black Ball families was a clan in New York. One day I received a letter from an elderly lady, a stranger who said that someone had given her a photograph of me. She asked that I protect her privacy, and to do so I will call her Evelyn Post. Mrs. Post said that in studying the photograph, she saw a resemblance to a long-lost member of her own family. The connection was distant—the man was the nephew of her dead stepfather—but her stepfather was called Luther Ball, and the man in question, his nephew, was named Edward Ball.

Mrs. Evelyn Post was about eighty, with skin the color of cardboard, white hair, a delicate frame, and precise diction. She lived in a town-house with a small backyard, and when we sat down, she served a slice of cake followed by coffee in good porcelain. Edward Ball was a mulatto, she explained. When Mrs. Post's mother was married a second time, in the 1920s, to a man named Luther Ball, Edward, Luther's nephew, had come into her life. Mrs. Post had a beautiful photograph of Edward Ball. The studio portrait showed a young man with light skin and wavy dark hair, wearing a high, starched white collar and wool jacket. He appeared to be in his early twenties when the picture was taken. Later I learned that he had been born in 1888.

"He lived up on the Hudson River, many years ago," Mrs. Post pointed out. "Then he moved with his wife to the Bronx. After that, my stepfather died, in 1945. I gradually lost touch with the family." Mrs. Post knew little about Edward Ball, except that she thought he came to New York from South Carolina. "I haven't been in touch with the Balls in thirty years," she said, "but I had his photograph, and I'm sure the picture is from Charleston, because that's where my mother came from." Edward Ball died in the 1960s, Mrs. Post said.

"My grandfather was white," she went on. "And Edward Ball, whom I knew when I was a young woman, was also very light. Mrs. Edith Ball, Edward Ball's wife, was quite a pretty woman. The two would visit my mother from time to time, after my stepfather Luther died. Later, as we drifted out of touch, I would write to them on behalf of my mother. Edward Ball's wife would write us back, but she never put their return address on the envelope. I think they were, they used to call it, 'gone on the other side.' I mean they passed for white. That's why some people never put the return addresses on their letters, because they didn't want to show a connection between themselves and black folks, where we were living. I was afraid to mention all this to you. Anyway, when I saw your picture, I said, 'My goodness, this is a relative of Mr. Ball.' Look at the ears! Now that I see you, I remember that he also had hands like yours."

I searched, but was never able to locate the family of the mulatto

Edward Ball, or find his connection to the Ball plantations, if there was one.

Eventually I retrieved Edward Ball's death certificate from the New York Department of Health. He died in November 1969, at eighty-one, on Riverdale Avenue in the Bronx. The coroner's statement described him as a retired postal clerk who had lived in New York City for sixty-four years. The death record listed the names of his parents, James Ball and Matilda Faison, but the coroner gave no indication of the dead man's color or ethnicity. It did state, however, that Edward Ball was buried not far from Manhattan.

"Sometimes, it just be's like that," Mrs. Post said.

17

THE PRESERVATION SOCIETY

The doorbell rang at the Branford-Horry mansion on Meeting Street, my temporary home in Charleston, and out on the sidewalk stood a distant cousin, John Gibbs. John, approaching sixty, has coarse hair and noticeably dark skin, the color of cardboard. Owing to the slight negritude of his appearance, he had acquired a nickname in childhood: Black John. The branch of the family that John came from once owned Hyde Park plantation, a tract that stayed in the hands of the Balls and their kin for 253 years. Black John was a grandson of Anne Simons Ball, one of the last heiresses, and his mother was Dorothy Dame Gibbs, venerable carrier of the family story. John had come to take me to dinner at his club, the South Carolina Society.

"The South Carolina Society is basically a bachelor party," said John, standing in the gray shade of the streetlights, beneath the overhanging piazza of the house.

Black John is a physician who smokes cigarettes. He had stopped drinking in middle life, but the combination of decades of liquor and tobacco had given his face good character. His head was square, his brow furrowed, and his cheeks had little rivers of lines, like streams through the mud of a marsh. The tobacco had given his voice a lot of depth; when he spoke, John rasped and boomed.

"Do you know who used to live next door to you?" he graveled. Next to the Branford-Horry House, on the same side of Meeting Street, was a smaller building made from stuccoed brick, the old carriage house and slave quarters for the mansion. It had since been converted into a townhouse, lined with marble and lit with chandeliers. "That was Judge Waring's place," said John. "I'll tell you the story sometime."

Our destination, the South Carolina Society's clubhouse, stood within sight of the carriage house, across the street and up about shouting distance, near the intersection of Meeting and Broad streets. In the distance, the building looked like a whitewashed mausoleum, the hard shine of its face, bright during day, gone flat with night. The South Carolina Society is one of the oldest institutions in Charleston, and John was pleased to have the chance to show it off. It is a men's club, founded in 1737, though the Ball family men joined a little late, beginning only in 1803. A brotherhood with strict rules of belonging, the Society can be counted on as one of the city's most unforgiving judges of blood. Members consist almost wholly of descendants of plantation owners— a coterie held together by repetition, in which each new generation of the clique tends to be sons of the old. The Society takes pride in its orthodoxy; this was a Tuesday, night of the monthly dinner, the same weeknight the club has been meeting since the 1700s.

"We have a rule that a speaker can be invited to address the dinner meeting only once every hundred years," said John, as we walked to the clubhouse. He smiled at the thought, a little joke that was true. The last dinner speaker, it turned out, lectured in 1937. "That's so they don't bore us," he said.

The Society is exclusive, but that is local habit. Most associations of interest to white people in Charleston have no black participation— not clubs, churches, or professional groups. Some clubs admit only men, with women in the permanent role of guests. The South Carolina Society is older and more efficient in the sifting out of color and sex, and sets the standard for the way others operate.

From the street, the clubhouse—known as South Carolina Hall— resembles a modified Roman temple. Built in 1804, the hall has two tiers of columns, like a set of teeth, the lower group rising to twenty-five feet and holding up a balcony that extends over the sidewalk like a tongue, so that pedestrians have to cross under it. A second array of columns goes from the balcony to the roof, and supports a large, triangular pediment. Fixed to the pediment, like a medallion on the forehead of the building, there appears a symbol or crest in a gold oval frame. The crest contains a wooden relief of a hand holding the stem of an indigo plant. Indigo is a bush that produces a blue dye once exported from the colonies; in the 1740s indigo rivaled rice as a money source for some landlords. The crop faded after the American Revolution, but the Society held on to its symbol and its motto, carved around the edges: *Posteritati*, "For posterity."

In a formal anteroom the size of a chapel, some forty men in jackets muttered and milled about. Right hands held drinks; left hands were jammed into pockets. A spartan do-it-yourself bar to the side had a bottle of bourbon, a bottle of scotch, a few softer drinks, and ice. The average age of the men was sixty, but in the middle sat a man in his forties, stage-managing the others. This was the president, or steward, of the Society, who belted out greetings to a stream of men coming through the door.

"How do you do, Budge? How do you do, René? How are you doing, John?"

The steward's chair resembled a wooden throne, with a tall back and coat of arms attached. Next to the throne was a less ornate seat reserved for the steward's deputy, the clerk (pronounced "clark" in imitation of colonial English). The clerk called out each member's full name as he entered the room. From the anteroom, a pair of tall wooden doors opened into a long ballroom, the more graceful of the two spaces, with twenty-foot ceilings and detailed woodwork. On the walls hung portraits of men in powdered wigs and gold-buttoned jackets, forebears of the membership.

The steward rapped a gavel.

"Gentlemen, please come to order!" he said. "We're going to close the doors."

The room fell to murmuring, and, herdlike, we sat down in a semicircle of chairs around the steward's throne. The clerk opened a ledger and began to read from the minutes of the last meeting.

"The regular meeting was called to order at 7:30 P.M.," he said. "Those present at the meeting . . ." The clerk's voice began languidly, but it soon turned into the voice of an auctioneer. With a barker's honk, he made a single word out of the last names of the membership.

"Those present at the meeting were RavenelBennettGibbsStevens-

LucasSimmonsPringleLowndesMaybankWalkerWilsonClementPorcher-
GaillardKingRiversFordBryan . . ." As the clerk read off the names,
there appeared in my mind's eye a map of the area near Charleston.
The names settled one at a time onto the large squares and rectangles
that marked the boundaries of the old plantations.

Many of the names were those of slave owners from the Cooper
River. Among the oldest white families there used to be a distinction
between families on the Ashley River, which winds from the west down
to Charleston harbor, and those on the Cooper River, which comes down
from the north. The geographical separation and difficulty of travel
meant that each river had its own white community—churches, horse
tracks, taverns—and people along those banks married one another
rather than going "outside" to the other river to find a partner. The
names read off by the clerk showed that the South Carolina Society
was heavily a Cooper River club, from the slave days down to the
present.

The minutes were approved, and the steward cracked his gavel to
open the evening agenda. Before dinner there were several pieces of
business and a vote on new members. The first agenda item concerned
the Society's portrait of George Washington. The painting had been on
loan to the local museum, which wished to extend the deal and make
it permanent.

"I suggest we draw up a renewable contract for the loan with a term
of five years," said one member, opening the debate. A wave of mut-
tering crossed the room. A man in a gray wool suit rose to say that it
was a rather nice picture, but in any case the walls of South Carolina
Hall had long ago been filled with portraits. There wasn't room for
another, so let the museum have it.

I remembered George Washington's mother, Mary Ball. The South
Carolina Balls did not appear to be linked to the clan of the Founding
Father. Too bad. It was a subject that dangled in the imagination, a
nugget of genealogical gold hanging just out of reach.

The tone of the discussion suddenly sharpened when an agitated
man stood up. "You give a painting, and you get back a piece of paper!"
he said. "Pieces of paper get lost!"

A white-haired gentleman rose, displeased, and said that he had
lent a painting of one of his favorite ancestors to the same museum.
"And when I went to get it back from them, they treated me like I was

trying to steal a horse!" The red in his old cheeks glowed as he sat down, spent.

The subject of Washington's portrait seemed too upsetting, and the steward tabled the issue.

The next item seemed safer. A woman had given the Society a beautiful chandelier, and one member made a motion to send her a letter of thanks. The motion was seconded and passed. Another member moved to have the chandelier cleaned. Passed. The steward clapped his gavel.

The South Carolina Society takes more than passing interest in the purity of blood. Blood is its reason for being, which made the nickname of my host, Black John, seem all the more strange. Once, John and I talked about his skin color. By his manner, I gathered he'd been talking about it his whole life. John laughed at the suggestion that there might have been some mingling on the slave street, then he told a story.

When he was a child, the other children did not let him forget the sepia color of his skin, until one year he went through a frightening incident. As a boy of about eight or nine, John said, he had a black friend. One day he and the friend were riding around Charleston in a trolley, sitting in the back of the streetcar, with black people on either side. Suddenly, a police officer jumped on the trolley, grabbed John and the other boy, and threw them into a patrol car. The policeman took the children down to the station, where John's parents and the parents of the black child were notified. All four parents rushed to the depot. By the time they arrived, the boys had set the police straight, and the officer admitted a foolish mistake. The policeman explained sheepishly that he thought the black child had kidnapped John, because the two boys had been riding together in the colored section of the trolley.

"Did I tell you the story of Judge Waring?" said Black John one day after the Society dinner we attended. "Judge Waties Waring, who lived on Meeting Street in that carriage house, next door to where you live." John's eyes were conspiring.

The story of the hated and loved Judge Waring is known to everyone in Charleston.

In 1880, a son, Julius Waties Waring, was born to an old Charleston family. In harmony with his bloodline, Waring attended the local college, studied law, and became an attorney. He moved with his family into the converted carriage house next door to my borrowed home and across the street from South Carolina Hall. Waring was named assistant U.S. attorney for South Carolina, then attorney for the City of Charleston; in 1942 he was appointed to a federal judgeship, the capstone of his career.

At that time something in Waring turned. The new judge, in his early sixties, began to use his position to chip away at the society that had made his own path smooth. In February 1944, a case came to Waring's bench that involved black teachers suing for equal pay with whites. To everyone's surprise, Waring favored wage parity. In 1947, a peonage suit came along in which some black sharecroppers had managed to sue their employer—and Waring ruled for the sharecroppers. Next came the case of a black veteran of World War II who had been beaten and permanently blinded by a white policeman. Waring favored the veteran. When it seemed he could go no further, Judge Waring took the case of *Elmore* v. *Rice*.

Since the end of Reconstruction, which followed the Civil War, all elected officials in South Carolina had been white, a situation partly secured by the "white primary." The white primary took place before proper elections, and by law, only whites could vote in it. Primary voters chose candidates for the Democratic Party, the monopoly party in state politics, and after the candidates were tapped, they were shoed-in to power in the main election. In 1944, the U.S. Supreme Court ruled that a similar primary in Texas was unconstitutional, but South Carolina refused to abandon the practice. In July 1947, in *Elmore* v. *Rice*, Judge Waring abolished the state's white primary, allowing black people to vote for the first time since the 1880s.

A little earlier, Judge Waring had divorced his wife of thirty-two years and married a twice-divorced woman from a Northern state. With the voting rights case on his left shoulder and his Yankee wife on the right, Judge Waring found himself shunned by his white friends.

Three years later, the most important case of Waring's career came along, a school desegregation suit, *Briggs* v. *Elliott*. In 1950, Waring headed a three-judge panel in the South Carolina case. Two judges upheld the doctrine that allowed separate but equal facilities for colored and white citizens, and that had stood since the Supreme Court case of *Plessy* v. *Ferguson* in 1896, but Waring dissented. Then, his house was attacked.

"I was a teenager when one of those civil rights cases of his came down," said Black John. "My friends and I were out to have a good time. We got a bunch of rocks in our pockets and went over to his house, and we stoned the building. There was also a cross burned on the grass in front of the house, a small one. I can't say who burned the cross, but we stoned the house, and I know one of my rocks hit the front door." John laughed hoarsely. His eyes were wet and wistful. "Judge Waring told the newspaper someone shot at his house! We were just hellions looking for fun. All we did was break some of his windows."

On appeal, *Briggs* v. *Elliott* was linked to another desegregation suit, *Brown* v. *Board of Education of Topeka.* In May 1954, ruling on the combined cases, the Supreme Court mandated desegregation nationwide.

"Finally the good judge moved to New York," said John. "I think he died there."

Black John was honest, and he knew which among the stories might be important.

The South Carolina Society began as a social club for French Huguenot men—Protestants who had come to America to get free of the Catholic Church. They met from time to time in a tavern and, as they drank, took up collections to support French immigrants poorer than themselves. English-speaking men gradually joined in and within a few years, by greater numbers, took over the meetings.

The Society developed into a dinner club with a charitable sideline. When they came to town from their plantations, the men sat at card tables, drank Madeira, and debated politics. Between rounds they collected money to support the education of poor white boys in Charleston. The Society built its clubhouse, South Carolina Hall, at the beginning of the 1800s, and with the showy new building, the Ball men began to join. The hall initially housed a school for poor boys on the first floor and meeting rooms on the second. In its first year of operation, the boys' school enrolled seventy-two pupils, while the Tuesday dinners were held upstairs. John Ball, owner of Kensington and Hyde Park plantations, became a member in July 1803. He was followed by his brother Elias Ball, of Limerick plantation, in December 1804. Two sons of John Ball joined in 1810, when they were in their midtwenties. Other Ball cousins and in-laws came in throughout the 1800s. By the time of the Civil

War, most of the male Cooper River slave owners ate at South Carolina Hall when they were in town.

Little changed after the Civil War. Control of the economy slipped from the hands of the planters, but the South Carolina Society remained a monument to former times. My grandfather, Nathaniel Ball, joined, as did some in my father's generation.

"I joined because my father belonged," said John. "He was treasurer, and it was so important to him."

The Society, John seemed to say, had become a wispy remnant of the slave days. It was a bit like a man who continues to stand on the curb after a parade, hoping it might turn around and come by a second time.

"The present order of business is the election of new members," bellowed the steward. "The next person to be considered is Jeremiah Bennett, who was proposed by his father, Theodore Bennett. Jeremiah Bennett was endorsed for membership on April 28, 1973."

Black John leaned on my shoulder. "There is a waiting list for membership of twenty-five years, sometimes thirty," he whispered. "More or less. Fathers usually sponsor their sons for membership when they're children, so they get in before they hit forty. We have a limit on the number of people in the Society. I don't know, it's maybe two hundred. So the only way you are going to get in is if someone dies. Fortunately, three people died in the past month."

The father of the applicant had apparently been deceased for some time, so an uncle stood to speak on the man's behalf.

"Jeremiah Bennett. As far as I know, he's a delightful person," said the uncle. "He graduated from the University of South Carolina, having gone to Aiken Prep. He stopped for a year in college and worked with the Chicago Board of Trade, and was a licensed broker up there for a while. He lost more money than he made, but he did the right thing and came back to South Carolina. He's working for a mortgage brokerage firm. His father was a member of this Society for twenty-some-odd years. His brother is a member. That should do it."

The steward spoke from his throne. "Does anyone have anything else to say about Mr. Bennett?" Silence. "Then membership will proceed to a vote. Is the ballot box prepared?"

The steward turned to the clerk, who nodded at a wooden box on a table in front of him. The ballot box, made from dark wood, measured the size of a bread box. On the side facing the room there appeared two small drawers, and on top was a little hole, with a wooden funnel fixed into it.

The clerk cleared his throat and again read off the names of the members. As each name was called, a man stood to approach the clerk.

The first voter pulled open the bottom drawer of the box, whose tray contained black and white balls the size of marbles. He withdrew a marble, brought it to the top of the box, and dropped it through the funnel into the hole, where it made a little sound—*pock*—as it fell.

"One black ball is all it takes to veto membership," said Black John under his breath.

"When was the last time somebody dropped a black ball?" I asked.

"No one has been blackballed for about thirty-five years," John replied. "The last one was a guy called DeCosta, or maybe it was Goldblum. He was sponsored for membership, but he was Jewish. But we've changed, and we've got Jews now. There are maybe two. Token."

The voting continued a few minutes, and at the end, the steward removed the upper drawer and made a show of inspecting its contents, all white balls. "Mr. Bennett," he said, looking around the room, "has been admitted."

The evening at South Carolina Hall continued through its paces. Nominees were announced, discussed, and admitted to the membership. A little flourish of applause followed each vote. At the end of the last ballot, Black John leaned into my shoulder.

"Wait," he said. "There was a more recent blackball. The mayor of Charleston used to be a member. But he was at some meeting or another, and he began to talk about school integration. He was apparently for it, and everyone listened politely. Later, the mayor put up his son for membership. He was blackballed."

It was a mild evening, a Thursday, the kind of soft Southern twilight when the winter, never severe, could be forgotten altogether. A concert was scheduled at the Dock Street Theatre, an old hall made of brown stone on a block with two churches. The Society for the Preservation of Spirituals, a venerable Charleston troupe, was giving one of its annual recitals. The group had been performing the same songs in the same style each spring for several dozen years, and tonight's event was certain to have a much-handled quality. About forty men and women, among them Pinckney Ball—to give him a name consanguine with his real one—could be counted on to sing the old songs.

Pinckney Ball, in his seventies, made a lingering impression, partly because of his clothes, which made it always possible to recognize him on the street, even from a distance. His uniform consisted of a tweed jacket (seersucker in the summer), bow tie (often striped red-and-blue silk), khaki trousers, and white canvas sneakers. As a younger man, Pinckney may have used leather footwear, but at some point he traded his oxfords and loafers for tennis shoes. Pinckney was a first cousin of my father, most of whose generation was now dead, though as one of the youngest Pinckney showed no sign of slowing down. A retired scientist, he lived in restless dotage with his wife, Ann Louise, a lovable wit.

The Ball family has been part of the Society for the Preservation of Spirituals from its beginnings, in the 1920s, when my grandparents were two of the founders. Cousin Pinckney has sung for some fifty years. Three things make the choir singular: the bloodline of its members, the repertoire, and the style of song. The singers are all descendants of families who once owned slaves. Second, the members perform only the songs of the slaves—spirituals. Last, choir members sing in an imitation of Gullah, the black dialect from the plantations. The dialect the Spirituals Society uses, with much care in pronunciation, is so strong that it cannot be understood by some audiences.

The space of the Dock Street Theatre forms an exact cube, with about four hundred seats at orchestra level and fifteen boxes at balcony height. Behind the raised wooden stage that Thursday hung a painted backdrop that showed a swamp, the old vista of a plantation. The members of the Spirituals Society appeared from the wings dressed in their usual costume, formal clothes from the antebellum period. Pinckney and the rest of the men wore waist-cut jackets with tails, ruffled shirts, and long ribbon ties. The suit, which Abraham Lincoln might have worn, flattered Pinckney's tall, angular frame. The women had their hair pinned up, and each wore a pastel gown that seemed to have been made from an acre of satin. The shimmering dresses had giant hoop skirts with flounces, and many came off the shoulder in a design that exposed the pale white of the women's necks and bosoms. With skirts that trailed the floor, the pink, yellow, or green gowns gave the women's entrance the appearance of so many bells floating onstage. The women curtsied and settled onto little stools in front of the men, arranging their dresses around their legs like slipcovers. Here were the masters and mistresses, brought back from the dead.

Pinckney stood in the back row, among others his own height. He was bald, with a corona of white hair around the ears, white eyebrows, and a large jaw, which gave out a frequent laugh. Pinckney moved broadly for emphasis, bending from time to time at the waist, and his loud reedy voice made an unforgettable sound. It was a voice that could not settle on one note but wavered between two, dancing up and down between octaves.

A white-haired gentleman, the evening's master of ceremonies, stepped to the front and cleared his throat. "The Society was founded with a threefold purpose," he began in a voice both soft and commanding. "It was meant to preserve the spirituals, to teach them to the rising generation, and to provide a social club with pleasure for its members." A bit older than most members, the choir leader leaned on an ebony cane with a rather beautiful handle made from the small antler of a deer. "We have been performing almost from the beginning, when our parents and grandparents first got together. In 1935, President Roosevelt invited the group to sing in the White House. We went, and we've been talking about it ever since."

Titters rolled around the theater, where there appeared to be nearly a full house, all faces around the room white, save two.

Spirituals were sung without instruments, in a call-and-response cadence, with one line called out by a leader, the verse hailed back by the others. When the singing started, Pinckney and the line of tall men leaped slightly and began to sway. Coattails flapped as the men stamped out the first rhythms. In front of the men, the petticoats rustled as the women sat upright, clapped daintily, and cleared a few notes from their throats.

When the singers opened their mouths to call out the first lines of slave dialect, the rolling melody of a beautiful, sad song came overhead, the old spiritual, "In My Time of Dying," whose lines tripped off the tongues of the masters and their ladies.

> *Een muh time ob dyin'*
> *Don' wan' nobody tuh moan.*
> *All I wan' fuh yuh to do*
> *Is tuh close my dyin' eyes.*
>
> *Well, well, well*
> *So I kin die easy,*
> *Well, well, well*
> *Lawd, lemme die easy,*
> *Well, well, well*
> *Wan' tuh die easy,*
> *Jedus gwine mek up my dyin' bed.*

When the song dropped down, a good burst of applause rattled around the room. The next spiritual came up, "I Know I've Been Changed," and the choir leaned into it, this time dancing harder, and shouting.

> *I know I bin chainge*
> *I know I bin chainge*
> *Angul een de hebun dun changed muh name.*
>
> *Oh two white horses side by side,*
> *Angul een de hebun dun changed muh name*
> *One ob dese horse King Jedus ride,*
> *Angul een de hebun dun changed muh name.*
>
> *I know I bin chainge*
> *I know I bin chainge*
> *Angul een de hebun dun changed muh name.*

Ten songs later, the concert ended. As the choir took its bows, my eyes drifted over the heads of the singers up to the proscenium and toward the ceiling, where there was hung a peculiar coat of arms, evidently an emblem of the theater. The painted symbol depicted a lion and a unicorn, and around the edges there appeared an inscription, *Honi soit qui mal y pense*—"Shamed be he who thinks evil of it."

Some months later, the Society for the Preservation of Spirituals was preparing for another performance, and I went to the rehearsal. Pinckney Ball and his wife, Ann Louise, had offered the invitation. "Come on with us," Ann Louise had said with a wry smile. "This is your heritage."

From around Charleston, the members of the Spirituals Society made their way to a large house overlooking the harbor. It was a delicate night, and a soft wind pulled over the waters of the port. The air had a downy texture that breathed through the crevices of the rambling wooden house and into the rooms.

Pinckney wore a dark sports jacket, silk bow tie, white shirt, tan pants, and bright, clean sneakers. It was a friendly, cluttered event, and Pinckney introduced me around. Most of the members were married couples in their middle and upper years, though a handful were younger, down to about age thirty-five. Every face was fortified by an old name from the plantation days—Grimball, Horlbeck, Hutson, Smythe, Townsend, Waring. To prepare for rehearsal, we poured large drafts of bourbon, scotch, or vodka over small quantities of ice, talked half an hour, then repeated the process. Finally we retired to a large, high-ceilinged drawing room with sofas and chairs and bookshelves.

Each spiritual was led by a different singer. Everyone in the room knew the songs from memory, but the leader stood and sang out the first line, after which the rest came in with the end of the verse. A man in a jacket rose from his chair and let go with one of the old standards.

> *Well uh look'd een de grabe,*
> *An' de grabe so watry,*
> *I got to lay een dat watry grabe.*
> *Uh look'd in the grabe*
> *I got to lay down in de watry grabe.*

The song ended, we sipped our drinks, and another singer stood up. His song was a spiritual about the end of slavery called "How Long,

Watchman?" And in a moment, the heirs to the plantation families sang out the old question the slaves used to cry out to each other.

> *My Lawd I dun jes like yuh said,*
> *How long watchman, how long?*
> *De rich man lib an' de po' man dead.*
> *How long watchman, how long?*
>
> *How long?*
> *How long?*
> *How long watchman, how long?*

We went through the repertoire. We sang songs about death. We sang songs about disappointment. We sang songs of relief, songs about laying down burdens, and songs about wandering. We did not sing any songs of love. The spirituals were the songs of sorrow, and there were no songs from the plantations about love.

During a break, a balding man in a tweed jacket stood up, a bit irritated.

"Look here, ya'll, in 'Uh Look Down Duh Road,' we have a problem," he said. "I'm singing, 'Uh look in de grabe, an duh grabe so watry, uh got to *lay* in dat watry grave.' Not *lie* in duh grabe, but *lay*."

The room nodded and murmured, and another man stood up.

"In my song, it's not 'way beyond the moon,' " he put in. "Listen, it's 'way beyan' de moon.' " He sat down.

A woman in middle age, wearing pants, said, "All right, how about this? It's not 'hold the light.' It's 'hole 'he light.' "

The message seemed clear: the Gullah stood in danger of being whitened, and its blackness had to be protected with vigilance.

The last song of the rehearsal went up, "Leave You in the Hand," and Pinckney came over and put his arm around my shoulder. We started out slowly, singing together.

"I'm a gonna lebe yuh een duh han'!" Pinckney sang in his reedy voice. "I'm a gonna lebe yuh een duh han' ob duh kine sabior!"

I sang along with Pinckney. "I'm a gonna lebe yuh een duh han' ob duh kine sabior!"

"Come on!" Pinckney shouted. "Open your mouth and sing! Louder!"

The refrain came around, and Pinckney grabbed my hand. We danced together, shouting out the old song. "I'm a gonna lebe yuh een duh han' ob duh kine sabior!"

My father's father, Nathaniel Ingraham Ball, spent his childhood on The Bluff, the former rice plantation turned into a sharecrop farm by his father, Isaac the Confederate. Grandfather Nat grew up among the "colored folk," listening to their work songs and religious music from a distance. I imagine Grandfather Nat heard more spirituals during his childhood than anything else—white folk music, hymns, the classical repertoire. But before he was grown, he heard no more, because the rice business collapsed and the planters and their families moved to Charleston to start again.

Grandfather Nat married Susan Porter, whose family, in addition to its clergymen, were former rice planters with roots in nearby Georgetown. The two lived in Charleston among friends of a similar background, whites raised on plantations, nostalgic for their childhood and the vanished world of the landlords. In 1922, a group of these adults who had lost a similar youth began to get together to drink, remember, and sing black spirituals. They wrote down the verses they could recall in a way that caught some of the Gullah dialect. The drinking club formed itself into the Society for the Preservation of Spirituals and was swiftly invited by a church, St. Philip's, to sing at an annual fund-raiser. The choir's first performance took place at a venerable old house; the admission charge was twenty-five cents. My grandparents became perennial members of the Spirituals Society, until Grandfather Nat died in 1962.

When the choir went public, in the 1920s, another group sprang up, the Plantation Melody Singers, ten white women with a similar love of black music. Among the women were two sisters, Mary Ball and Lydia C. Ball, cousins of Grandfather Nat. Both unmarried, both in their fifties, Lydia and Mary had been raised on Limerick plantation and decided to use their acquaintance with black people on the river to collect their repertoire. Each rice farm was a settlement or village in its own right, whose musical heritage differed slightly from that of the others, so Lydia and Mary went from one field to another, asking the colored folk to sing their different songs. At Quenby plantation, the sisters heard and wrote down the Ball slaves' version of "Mary and Martha." From Middleburg, next to Quenby, came "Roll Jordan, Roll" and "Shout Jubilee." From Limerick, which the Balls owned for 130 years, came versions of "Christ Comin'" and "Nobody Knows the Trouble I've Seen." After writing down what they heard, the sisters typed up a songbook. In 1925, the Plantation Melody Singers performed ten concerts for white audiences. They kept singing until the mid-1930s, when they disbanded.

Lydia and Mary's group and the Society for the Preservation of Spirituals did the same thing, more or less, with one conspicuous difference. For its concerts, the Spirituals Society dressed in tuxedos and gowns, whereas the Melody Singers dressed themselves, as best as they were able, as slaves. A photograph taken about 1925 shows Lydia Ball wearing the clothing of a black cook. She has a bandanna tied around her head and is wearing a long calico skirt, an apron frock, and a long necklace of beads. She looks a bit uncomfortable, as though she hasn't quite got it right.

Credible or not, the imitation of slaves by the women's choir made a hit with white audiences. After one concert at a church, Lydia's singers were written up in the *Charleston News and Courier* by a reviewer who praised the realism of the charade:

> The entertainment given recently at the Holy Communion Parish hall by the "Plantation Melody Singers" was of exceptional merit. . . . The manner in which the entertainment was conducted was admirable. The dialect, attire, attitudes, expressions, and the actions of the singers were typical of that rapidly disappearing, respectful, superstitious, indolent, but ever faithful and good-natured race, the "old fashioned" plantation negroes. . . . The president of this unique group is Miss Lydia C. Ball.

Drinking hour resumed after rehearsal, and we broke into clumps of conversation. The president of the Spirituals Society was a tall, slender man his late forties, a banker at a local savings and loan.

"Obviously, we're an anachronism," he said good-naturedly. "A lot of people don't really feel it's politically correct for us to sing the spirituals, and we've gotten criticism."

"The spirituals are the gift of the plantation to music," I said.

"There was a woman who came to a performance recently," the banker went on, "bought a ticket and sat down. We came out onto the stage, and she saw that we were white. We have a pamphlet about the group that we hand out, with no picture, and she must have gotten one of those. Suddenly the woman got up, walked out of the theater, and demanded her money back. We weren't what she expected."

The banker laughed an understanding laugh.

"Almost all of us were raised by blacks," said an older man in a tweed jacket. "We have a lot in common with the blacks. We're actually more the same than different. We come from the same Protestant background, for instance. The ideals we have are the same ideals." He was eager in his argument, and looked into my eyes for encouragement.

A gentle lady in her seventies, wearing a print dress and a barrette in her white hair, came over, cocked her head back, and spoke with a delicate diction.

"I'm a member of this group because of your grandfather," she said. Her eyes were wide and full of remembrance. "I was six years old, and the Society was giving a concert, I think at the Dock Street Theatre. The decorations on the stage were imitation pine trees, because we always had pine trees as stage decor. I climbed up in one of them, and sat there, perched and looking down at the stage. Suddenly, my pine tree fell over, and I landed on your grandfather's lap. And he picked me up and pushed me to the front of the stage. From that night, I've been singing."

"We are trying to find more young people to join," said a young woman dressed in yellow. "The membership is too old. Would you like to join? You qualify!"

"I joined," said Pinckney, leaning on my shoulder, "because in the Episcopal church, you couldn't sing out. My God, nobody made enough noise! Here you can sing out, because hell, nobody's going to stop you! It's kind of fun to be an Episcopalian and still get to holler!"

The woman in yellow pressed forward and said, "It may be hypocritical for us to sing the songs, dressed like we are onstage, but it's fun. How did you like it?"

"It's too bad there are no more slaves," I said, smiling, "so we could compare styles. I think the slaves couldn't have done it better themselves."

18

~>—<+>—O—<+>—<~

A RECKONING

I wrote an item for a weekly black newspaper in Charleston, the *Chronicle*, in which I explained that I was a member of a clan who had once owned plantations near the city. In a few days I received a letter from a woman about her family. "My grandmother's mother was enslaved on Limerick plantation," she wrote. "So was her father, whose name was Philip Lucas. He fought in the Civil War. . . . We would like to see and talk to you. My mother is named for Marie Ball, of Logan Street." The closing of the letter read "Hopefully."

The family lived in a boxy building on a corner, an old grocery converted into a house. The woman who had written, Luzena King, greeted me at the door and led the way down a hall past a staircase. "We feel like we run a hotel," she said, looking at the banister, "because there are five generations living here." I had come to see Mrs. King's mother, Emily Marie Frayer, who was in her nineties and was said to have a good memory.

We passed through a sliding double door and entered a very large room: the former store. There were sofas and chairs, cabinets and bookshelves lined with memorabilia. Here and there were hung family pictures, including a framed chart showing the family's lines of descent.

At the end of the room stood a long, narrow dining table, and at its head, alone, sat an aged woman.

Emily Marie Frayer was small and stooped, held both of her hands on the grip of a cane, wore a simple frock and sweater, and a kerchief around her head. Lines were deeply etched on her cheeks, like grooves, but parts of her brow were still smooth. Her eyes were moist in the way age wets the vision.

"We have a lot to talk about," she said, a nice understatement.

I took my place at the dining table, facing the elderly lady. Mrs. Frayer's children, grandchildren, and great-grandchildren settled into corners and onto couches, turning toward us at a little distance. Among the group was a soft-spoken woman, Sonya Fordham, one of Mrs. Frayer's granddaughters. Sonya introduced her teenage daughter, Chiemeka, whom she instructed to bring me coffee. Mrs. Frayer began speaking, and the room fell silent.

"I was born on Hyde Park, in 1901, January 30th." Her voice was resonant, and she lifted up her chin slightly, as though to propel the words.

Hyde Park was bought in March 1740 by John Coming Ball, and sold 253 years later by the Gibbs family, who had intermarried with the Balls. Mrs. Frayer told me she lived there during the last seasons when rice was still a cash crop.

"When I was a child, they used to plant rice in Hyde Park," she said. "I used to sit in the door, and I would see them have the rice stacked way up on the cart, and the people would be up there drivin'. I used to be so frightened, think the man was going to fall off. I watched them all day, watching people haul that rice down to the barnyard. There was a big barnyard, and they stack rice in that yard, right off the river. The yard run right to the river, and from there, they carry the rice away by boat."

Mrs. Frayer spoke in rhythmic stops and starts, each parcel of her sentences measured out.

"Limerick is where my parents came from," she said, pronouncing the name "Lim-brick."

"My father's grandfather was a man called Isaac Ball," I told her.

"Yeah, I heard a lot about him," she answered.

"He's known in the family as Isaac the Confederate, because he fought in the Civil War," I said.

Mrs. Frayer let out a cackle, and fixed her mouth in a crooked smile. "That's it, all right."

"Isaac was the son of a man called William James Ball," I said, "who owned Limerick."

"William Ball? Oh, yes."

"That means that your grandparents were enslaved by William James Ball."

I said this to make sure, but Emily Frayer did not need me as an informant. Later she told me that her grandfather, Philip, was born on Limerick in slavery, and that his parents, Philip Sr. and Flora, had been born there as well. Then she told what happened to Philip Sr.

"My grandfather's father was sold from Limerick, and went to Stoney Landing," said Mrs. Frayer, naming a place about fifteen miles west of Limerick. The name of the tract to which Philip was sold, she added later, was Kid Field. "He had a family there, and left his family in Limerick. So he had two families. And when he died, he left two sets of children."

The room was quiet, and to fill the silence I repeated the story about Philip Sr. in a gentler form.

"So, on Limerick, your great-grandfather left a family," I said, "went to Stoney Landing, and started another family."

"You see, he didn't 'left,' " Mrs. Frayer corrected me. "They sold him. They sold him from Limerick. They been selling you just like you sell a chicken. If a man come and want you, and they say, 'He's a good hand,' then they sell him. That's the way they been doin'. That was an awful time."

Oral tradition among the Balls (I had heard many times) had it that plantation masters, if so inclined, sold only entire families; but only a handful of invoices from slave sales survived. Most records of slave deals, if they had been preserved at all, seem to have disappeared from the family archives before they were deposited in public libraries.

"He used a boat to visit his two families from one family to the other," Mrs. Frayer explained. "One time come home, he used a boat from there, and one time he go back, he used a boat to go back." Later, one of Mrs. Frayer's kin told me some of the names in this other branch of the family, distant cousins descended from Kid Field.

"He came under the cover of night?" I said.

"That's it," said Mrs. Frayer, nodding. "That's what they all do, and they bury the dead in the night. And my grandmother says, you could hear the people screaming in the night, big fire light, big torch light, buryin' their dead."

"Enslaved people buried their dead at night?" I asked, leaning in.

"They had to, because they got to work in the day," Mrs. Frayer came back. "They ain't got time for buryin' no dead in the day. If you dead, you wait till night for bury."

She peered at me with an ironic smile. I had spoken to many people, but few people knew as much as Emily Frayer about life on the plantation. Many of her stories, she said, came from her grandmother, Ellen Lucas, who was eighteen when she was freed.

"We were just little children sittin' around the fire when my grandmother tell us that. That was an awful time. I'm glad I wasn't there then." She chuckled.

This was the first I heard that black people had to bury after sundown. But a memoir written by one of the Ball women corroborated what Mrs. Frayer said. The memoir that Mary Gibbs Ball wrote in 1923, at eighty-six, detailed her life as a young bride on Limerick; among her memories was a description of the burial of Fortune, the blacksmith. "I remember Daddy Fortune's funeral was at midnight," she wrote. "It was a very solemn sight to see the funeral procession with lightwood torches, marching to the graveyard, chanting their requiem at that silent hour."

Mrs. Frayer laughed bitterly, then caught herself. "No, man, slavery time is no time, no joke at all."

"I talk to my relatives," I said, "and, one after another, they say that the Balls were gentle masters."

Emily Frayer's kin, seated around the room, erupted in laughter. When the hilarity died down, Mrs. Frayer took in a breath and began to speak slowly, like a teacher. "You see, they had a overseer, and this overseer, he do all the lickin'. So my grand-aunt, Rachel—my grandmother's sister—she fight the driver."

"If a master wanted to beat one of his slaves, he would call the overseer and tell him so?" I asked.

"No, the overseer would call him and tell him something was wrong," Mrs. Frayer clarified. "The overseer does everything—look over the people, see them do the work on time, and when it's time to lick, he do all the lickin'. That's how come when he start to whip my grandaunt, she hit him back."

Later I looked at the Limerick account books and found Rachel, born in 1840. She was perhaps in her teens when this happened.

"The overseer was so mad, the maussa step in," Mrs. Frayer went on. "She called him 'maussa.' The maussa said, 'No you cannot lick her, I'll lick Rachel myself.' "

"And did the master lick Rachel?" I asked.

"Yes, he lick 'em."

"What was the name of that master?"

"The maussa was a Ball," Mrs. Frayer finished.

"The maussa" was William Ball. By personally beating Rachel, William Ball may have believed he was protecting her from the more sadistic hands of his overseer.

Mrs. Frayer chuckled, and there was murmuring around the room. Her family had plenty of inside stories about what happened and how it all worked.

Emily Frayer was born Emily Marie Bryant in 1901, in a cabin on a bluff overlooking the rice fields at Hyde Park plantation. Hyde Park was owned at the time by John Coming Ball, a fifty-two-year-old sharecropping landlord (known as "Coming Ball" to distinguish him from others of the same name in the family tree). Coming Ball had a twenty-year-old daughter, Marie, whose name was added to that of the black child by her parents, with the approval of Mr. Ball. When Emily Marie was about five, her family moved out of the cabin and, shortly after that, to Charleston. In the city, Emily lived with one of her aunts, who occupied the servants' quarters behind a fine house on Ladson Street. This new home was not far from White Point Gardens, the pleasant little park overlooking Charleston harbor (the same park in which Isaac the Confederate would walk most days about this time). The park was restricted to whites only, but the little girl found a certain bench on the edge where she could sit undisturbed, with her back to the trees, facing the buildings. Her skin was dark, Mrs. Frayer said, and before sending her out to the park, her mother would always tie a brown ribbon in her hair. According to custom, brown or blue, but no other colors, were acceptable shades for dark-skinned Negroes.

Emily Bryant went to a primary school for black children, called

Shaw, then to what was known as the Charleston Colored Industrial School (later renamed J. E. Burke High School), graduating in 1918. At the time, black students were allowed four years of elementary education, followed by three years of vocational education at Charleston Colored, with all classes run by whites, until the ban on black teachers was lifted in 1920. Soon Emily Bryant met her future husband, Eugene Frayer. They married in 1921, and had their first son, Eugene Jr. In 1924 Emily's husband persuaded her that better times could be found up North, and the young family, with two children by now, moved to New York. They stayed in the Bronx with relatives who had already come up from South Carolina, then found their own rooms elsewhere. In New York, Eugene Frayer got work as a longshoreman, and Emily Frayer had her third child, Helen. But one night, when Mrs. Frayer was alone with the girl, Helen fell badly ill and died before she could be taken to the hospital. Emily Frayer persuaded her husband to move back to the South, and the couple came home to Charleston.

Throughout the 1920s and 1930s, Mrs. Frayer worked as a cook for white families in Charleston. She changed jobs often, she said, because she did not care for the condescending treatment she received from the white women, and talked back to her employers. Mrs. Frayer remembered one typical lady of the house who measured out each serving of unprepared food to make sure there were no leftovers that her cook might wish to take home.

During World War II she started a small catering business. Charleston had become a center of operations for the military, and the Navy Yard on the Cooper River hired hundreds of black men to new jobs. Black workers, however, were not allowed to eat at the restaurants and canteens of the base, so the men turned to food vendors for their lunch. Each morning Mrs. Frayer and several other women cooked great quantities of beans, collard greens, ham, fried chicken, and cornbread, which they brought by bus to the gates of the military base and set up on outdoor tables. The business thrived for years, and with the profits Mrs. Frayer and her family, who now included three adult children, bought a house in Charleston.

The children married, started their own families, moved out. Mrs. Frayer's husband died in 1991. By then she was long retired, and living with the family of her daughter, Luzena King, in Charleston.

...

"I heard you say she stole the hams from the house," said Mrs. King, referring to her grandmother, Emily Frayer's mother. Turning to the room, she added, "Her mother told me that they would steal the hams from the big house at Limerick, and they would cook them at night, and have a good time—because the next day, they had to go to work."

"They had a big breakfast, I heard," said someone else in the room, "but they did not have any lunch. They had to work all day long, and in late evening they had their supper, because if a slave was fed, that slave would fall asleep."

"I was looking in some records from Limerick," I said, adding my part, "and there was the occasion, twice a year, when the master would hand out cloth to the slaves."

"Yeah, they sure is," said Mrs. Frayer, holding her cane with two hands. "They sure used to distribute the cloth, twice a year. When they gettin' married, they got cloth, too."

"Tell him about Uncle Francis, when he was bad," a voice coaxed. "What did they do with Uncle Francis when he drank so much?"

"Uncle Francis." Mrs. Frayer cleared the memory, thinking back on her great-uncle. "He was a drunkard, and he was a stable man. He went to see about the horses, and he was so drunk, he couldn't mind 'em. So the maussa just put him in this dark hole—there was a little hole— and he lock 'em up."

Every plantation had a jail, where the owner would lock up troublesome workers, usually on Saturday, the big night off.

"And my grandmother, Elsie, would go see Uncle Francis where the door was shut. He would say, 'Elsie, go home. You're going to be punished for this.' And all she could do was look through the hole in the door, and cry."

The elderly lady laughed, tickled at the predicament of the drunk Francis. Then a silence settled in the room, and through a window I heard the whoosh of a passing car. From behind me, very softly, came the voice of one of Mrs. Frayer's grandchildren. "Tell him about waiting for Sherman."

To the white South, General William Tecumseh Sherman was the most feared and hated of the Yankees. To Emily Frayer's family, the small, ruthless general was a hero, their liberator.

"Tell him about waiting for Sherman," said the voice again. Mrs. Frayer lowered her eyes, then looked up and leveled her gaze. Suddenly it was February 1865, on the lawn at Limerick, in the last hour of slavery.

"My grandmother," she began, "she said she was standing in the door." The Limerick papers showed that some of Mrs. Frayer's family had been house servants, and thus "the door" was that of the Ball house.

"They knew freedom was coming," said someone in the room.

"She was standing in the door, and the Yankees come through, and take her hat off. My grandmother said she had a skullcap on, and he took it off her head, and throw 'em up. The Yankee said, 'You're free as a bird in the air!' She said she drop on her knee, and said, 'Thank God!' And 'Thank you, Maussa!' to the Yankee."

There were giggles around the room, and a sigh of relief. Mrs. Frayer laughed at the memory.

"I declare we little children done cry from all we hear!" Emily Frayer stared ahead. "My grandmother said, 'They tell 'em to find everybody who been hiding, and tell 'em, you're free!' "

The Ball family version of "waiting for Sherman" was nearly the same as Mrs. Frayer's, only reversed as in a mirror.

"We felt hopeless [and] looked forward with dread," Mary Ball wrote in her memoir, recalling the defeat of the Confederacy. "When Sherman came marching through Georgia . . . burning houses and waging war on helpless women and children, we felt weak."

When the Federal soldiers reached Limerick, a cavalryman in a blue uniform rode up to the mansion at the head of his company, dismounted, and let himself in. Mary Ball remembered the first words out of his mouth.

"I want all the colored people to come up to the house! I want to tell them they're free."

Mary described how the black village had gathered—field hands, cooks, boatmen, hostlers, nurses, carpenters, mothers, leatherworkers, children, old people—and the Yankee had stood in front.

"I don't remember if the whole plantation were there," Mary Ball wrote, "but a good many came, and he said, 'You are free! Free as a bird, you don't have to work any more.' Women dropped a curtsey and said, 'Tenke Maussa.'"

According to plantation papers, Philip Lucas, Emily Frayer's grandfather, was born on Limerick on December 11, 1843, the fourth child of Philip and Flora, a couple in their early thirties. The younger Philip was twenty-one when the Yankees arrived. After the surrender, the Union army sent out recruiters to enlist black soldiers to help with the occupation of South Carolina. Philip signed on as a private in the U.S. Colored Infantry, 128th Regiment, Company D.

In the course of things, Philip took a surname, Coaxum. But according to Mrs. Frayer, too many other freed blacks nearby were adopting the same name, so Philip decided to choose another. There was a well-known white woman in Charleston lore named Eliza Lucas Pinckney, who, as an unmarried woman in the mid-1700s, ran her family's rice and indigo plantation, Wappoo, not far from Limerick. Eliza Lucas, according to the story, was said to have taught some of her slaves to read. Paying homage to her memory, and to this rare act, Philip added the name Lucas to his own.

Eighteen months after emancipation, on September 20, 1866, Philip Lucas walked into the Freedmen's Bank on Broad Street, in downtown Charleston. The bank had been established as a place where black soldiers and other freedpeople could deposit their new wages. When Lucas stepped forward, a clerk turned to a fresh page in a ledger and wrote the words "Depositor #277" on an account application that would eventually be filed, with thousands of others, at the National Archives in Washington, D.C. To open a savings account, Lucas had to respond to a series of questions. He told the clerk that he was born in St. John's Parish, north of Charleston, where his parents, Philip and Flora, still lived; that he was single, and a soldier; and that the name of his last owner was William Ball. The bank clerk wrote the information down, and Lucas signed with an *X* next to his name. Three years later, during another visit Lucas made to the bank, a different clerk wrote a note in the same ledger: "Aug 9/'69, says he is now married, wife name Ellen."

Ellen Lucas, whom Philip had known since childhood, was the daughter of Benjamin Irving and Myrtilla, both slaves at Limerick.

Philip Lucas got out of the Army, and, with his new wife, worked as a sharecropper. According to Emily Frayer, the Ball family refused to sell the couple any land, because that would give them no reason to work for Mr. Ball. So, using savings from his Army pay, and with sacks of rice earned from sharecropping, Philip Lucas bought a field a couple of miles from Limerick from a white family who was willing to sell. Philip and Ellen Lucas eventually had eleven children, five of whom survived to adulthood. One of their daughters became the mother of Emily Frayer.

Philip and Ellen Lucas, coincidentally, each had four brothers and a sister freed from Limerick at the same time they were. Most of these siblings married and had families, and as the years passed, their children and further progeny stayed in touch. Adding up their living kin, Emily Frayer and her immediate family could name perhaps two hundred people who lived in more than ten states. It was a large number, but only a small piece of the legacy. Based on normal rates of increase, by the year 2000, descendants of the two sets of Lucas siblings from Limerick would number more than twelve hundred throughout the United States.

The Lucas clan came from an "old family" on the Cooper River with a reputation for rebellion. From plantation papers, I learned that Emily Frayer's great-great-great-great-grandfather was Tom White, whose arrest and interrogation in connection with an alleged conspiracy to overthrow white rule I've described.

Brought to Comingtee from Angola in 1731, Tom acquired the name Tom White, probably to distinguish him from another field hand in Red Cap's ledgers, Tom Black. Whether the skin of Tom White was lighter than that of Tom Black is impossible to say, however. In any case, when he was about twenty, Tom White found a partner named Julatta.

The fragmentary evidence that survives from the life of Julatta suggests that she worked around the clock to make things a bit easier for her family. One year Julatta raised some corn or rice, which she sold to Elias Ball for nine shillings. An entry in Elias's account book shows that Julatta used the money to buy extra fabric for clothing.

Tom's subversiveness, demonstrated by his role in the alleged up-rising plot in 1748, seems to have become a trait in the family. Between 1740 and 1750, Tom and Julatta had five children, one of whom—the firstborn, Tom Jr.—grew up and took after his father. Tom Jr. became a regular runaway. Born in 1742, "above the dikes," according to his owner—perhaps in a hut away from the main plantation settlement—Tom Jr. worked until his midtwenties as a field hand at Comingtee and Kensington. But in February 1768, Elias Ball Jr. (Second Elias) placed a notice in the Charleston newspaper advertising that Tom Jr. had fled. The advertisement was the one that described Tom, twenty-seven, as having a missing toe, and was signed, "Elias Ball, Hyde Park," naming the plantation next to Kensington where Second Elias was evidently living for the season.

Young Tom had a sister, Bessie, who in 1780 was a thirty-year-old field hand and mother of three children, ages two to ten. Her middle child had been "born at ye dam at ye pounding mill," suggesting that Bessie, like her runaway brother, lived away from the middle of the plantation, near the work buildings. That spring, with the country caught up in the Revolutionary War, the British Army managed to occupy much of the land around Kensington. When the royal soldiers moved in, doz-ens of Ball slaves, among them Bessie, decided to take their chances with the enemy. On May 10, according to a Ball notebook, Bessie "& her children, Roebuck, January, & Betty" ran off. The previous day another family had escaped; but that night Bessie took flight alone, carrying her two-year-old in her arms (or on her back). Her two boys, presumably, ran alongside, grasping at their mother's skirts.

Bessie's freedom didn't last, and a short time later the slave lists show that Bessie and her children were back in the rice fields. Her owner had made a note that another escapee, Charlotte, had been "brought home"; and Tom's sister may have also been captured on her way to British lines. Bessie's life had only this brief moment of liberty. A few years after the end of the Revolution, the account book shows, she died giving birth to a son.

By the third generation, the family likely had a reputation as the plantation zealots. But Bessie's children seem to have lost the will openly to defy the Balls. Bessie's daughter Betty, the two-year-old car-ried off by her mother, grew up at Kensington and married a man named Joe Bailey, a house servant. As the wife of Joe Bailey, a butler or valet,

Betty would have spent most of her days inside the big house, among her masters during their most vulnerable hours. With this arrangement, the Balls may have forgiven, or forgotten, the legacy she carried.

In the early 1800s, Kensington was the property of John Ball, the sharp businessman who lived high and grew fat by his midthirties. After five children, John had buried one wife, Jane, and, in 1806, started a second family with his new bride, Martha Caroline (Buzzard Wing). The new Mrs. Ball reorganized the staff of house servants, getting rid of some and bringing in new faces. In the shake-up, Betty and Joe Bailey were sent away from Kensington, to Limerick plantation, to work for John Ball's brother, Third Elias.

At Limerick, on January 9, 1810, Betty and Joe Bailey had their first child, Flora. When Third Elias died, Betty's family then came under the ownership of Isaac Ball. A few years later, Betty had a son, then another daughter. Fifteen years passed; in 1825, when Isaac died, the family of Betty and Joe Bailey was split up. Betty's two-year-old daughter, Lucretia, along with an eight-year-old son, were deeded to Jane Ball, who was only two years old but nonetheless the owner of Quenby plantation. In time, Lucretia and her brother were moved away from their kin to work for Jane Ball at Quenby.

This development left the aging Betty and Joe Bailey alone at Limerick with their daughter Flora, who grew up working in the main house as a servant to the widowed mistress there, Eliza Ball, and her three children. In the 1830s, Flora, in the fourth generation in the family, began a relationship with another hand at Limerick, Philip, and thus became mother of the child who would be known to his descendants as Philip Lucas, veteran of the Civil War.

In his own way Philip Lucas carried on the legacy of Tom the Angolan. For a black man to join the Union Army at the moment of freedom was a plain act of defiance. It meant that Philip wanted to do his part to end white rule.

"I was a history major," Sonya Fordham began. "And I learned to analyze things. But still, we black people were not supposed to ask the question 'What about us?'"

Sonya Fordham, a granddaughter of Emily Frayer, lived in a little wooden cottage in Charleston, with two rooms upstairs, two down, and a tiny porch. Sonya was in her late forties, wore glasses, and had a pleasing, broad face. She had a mild manner, and a light laugh that carried a touch of sadness. Whereas her grandmother was small but outspoken, Sonya Fordham, tall and strong, had a soft voice.

"When I was a child," said Sonya, "I didn't know any white children. There were none in the neighborhood, none in the school. In fact, I didn't meet any white people until I went to graduate school. The only white person I knew was my doctor."

I saw Sonya Fordham for dinner from time to time, and she often dressed for these occasions. One night she wore a black suit with high heels and a jacket with leopard-skin cuffs and lapels. Sonya was a divorced mother. In 1980, while living in Washington, D.C., she had married a Nigerian, Sylvester Egwu, and moved to Nigeria. Four years later, when the marriage broke up, she moved back to Charleston with her daughter, Chiemeka. The girl was a teenager when we met, and in high school—poised and tall, with a lovely smile.

Chiemeka had been chosen as a beauty queen in a local parade, and Sonya showed me a photograph of her daughter riding in a convertible, holding a bouquet of flowers, surrounded by young men. While raising Chiemeka alone, Sonya had enrolled in the law school at Georgia State University. In 1989, Hurricane Hugo nearly destroyed the house where her grandmother lived. Sonya left law school, not to return, and went to work to help pay for repairs.

At one dinner Sonya told me about her youth. "I was a shy student," she said, "a bookworm, with just a few friends." Sonya explained that she had come through the public education system in Charleston, graduating from high school in 1964, after which she enrolled at South Carolina State College on a scholarship from the City of Charleston. South Carolina State, a conservative, historically black school in the town of Orangeburg, founded in 1896 and based on the doctrine of separate but equal education. The "white" institution, the University of South Carolina, in Columbia, was better funded but did not welcome black students.

"My brother went there, to USC," Sonya remembered, "and had a lot of problems. They kicked in the door of his room."

The early 1960s, high years of black assertion, brought the Civil Rights Act of 1964 and the Voting Rights Act of 1965, but the racial caste system remained. Most black students at South Carolina State,

Sonya said, were cautious and uninterested in "the movement." In her own family, protest was off-limits, because her mother worked as a teacher in the public schools and black teachers had been known to lose their jobs if they or someone in their family got too involved in politics.

"In 1965," I said, "the neighborhood of Watts burned in Los Angeles. Did you hear anything about that?"

Sonya pursed her lips, a little embarrassed. "We were very sheltered," she said. "We didn't know anything. For instance, I knew nothing about Malcolm X when he was alive. Can you believe that?"

At college, however, some course offerings opened Sonya's eyes, and she learned for the first time about the literature of white superiority.

"I remember that one teacher in the history department at State, a white man, came from Syracuse, New York," said Sonya. "Ruben Weston was his name. He made us study Rudyard Kipling and the idea of the 'white man's burden,' as an example of what had been written. It opened a door in my mind." Sonya Fordham spoke gently, with a light smile punctuating her story. She showed no rancor.

In October 1966, the Black Panther Party formed in Oakland, California. The following summer Detroit, as well as Newark, New Jersey, burned in riots in black neighborhoods.

"I was quiet," said Sonya, "but in 1967, I joined the movement. I became one of the student leaders." In South Carolina black protest was rare, and Sonya was one of only a handful of activists on campus.

"During the 1950s," she said, "the presidents of South Carolina State were very light-skinned, and pro-white. They were whiter than you. The NAACP was not even allowed on State's campus. We decided we had had enough of this. In the fall of 1967, a group of eight of us came together and formed something we called the Black Awareness Coordinating Committee. We wanted to get rid of the president, B. C. Turner, and bring in another one. We started by going to the president's yard and lying down on the grass, which was posted 'Don't step on the grass.' Stepping on the grass was enough to get you kicked out of school at that time. Then we called for a school boycott."

Sonya told her story shyly, with a light smile. It seemed a long time ago, and she gave the impression that she did not know what it had amounted to.

"Somehow we got rid of Turner," she continued, "and a new president came into the office, the first in the school's history who was actually dark-skinned. We kept agitating, and got our first black history class. It wasn't perfect, because it was being taught by a white gay man! But still, it was there. We next got interested in community development. We explored Orangeburg, which we had not done, and started going to the black businesses instead of patronizing the white, which we had been doing. We wanted to begin to develop black consciousness. The Vietnam War was going on, and we knew black guys were getting killed. So we made a picture of Uncle Sam that said, 'Uncle Sam wants you, Nigger.' We picketed Dow Chemical when they came to campus to recruit—they made the napalm that was dropped in Vietnam. We found documentation that proved the inequities of funding for black colleges in South Carolina, as compared to white, and we publicized that. It was wanting to be knowledgeable about your community, and about yourself! We put out a newsletter. But after all that, we were still really on the margins. Most people wouldn't pick up the newsletter. I grew an Afro, and all of a sudden I became an outcast on campus."

"How many women on campus had an Afro?" I asked.

"First there were two, then the other woman left school, and that left me."

I tried to picture Sonya, who now had processed hair, with an Afro, but couldn't.

"In the midst of all this, an activist, Cleve Sellers, came down from Howard University, in Washington. He was originally from South Carolina. He was a member of SNCC." Sonya pronounced SNCC, the acronym for the Student Nonviolent Coordinating Committee, as "Snick," its old nickname.

"At the end of 1967, when Cleve was there, the idea of integrating a local bowling alley came up. I wasn't much for it, because by then we were starting to think that black people should not be about integration but about developing our communities. But some of the group wanted to integrate, so we did some planning. We went home for Christmas, then came back. In January 1968, we met with the administration, talked about the bowling alley, talked about more classes in black history. There was a lot going on. Martin Luther King had just mentioned the need for people to get more involved with Vietnam, and so we were researching it. We were in a meeting, our own group, waiting for Cleve to come around with a film about Vietnam, when someone ran in and said, 'Cleve has been arrested at the bowling alley!' He had been arrested for trying get in the front door. Then somebody said, 'Let's go down there.'

"It was a Monday night. When we got to the bowling alley, there were about a thousand students who showed up. Most of them were not in the mood to fight, but we were. I had rocks in my pocket." Sonya's story slowed down, and the details became more vivid. She seemed to remember events of February 1968 with an hourly precision.

"A fire truck pulled up next to us. Next thing I knew, I heard a gunshot. I don't know who shot, but it was probably the police shooting over our heads. We scattered, and ran back to campus. We threw our rocks through some store windows on the way back."

"Did you break them?" I asked.

Sonya nodded. "That was just rage."

Her smiling stopped, and her pleasant manner fled, replaced by a reporter's flat gaze.

"The next night, Tuesday, there was some shooting on the campus," she said.

"Who was shooting?"

"We heard it was white people, but I didn't see it. They were shooting at some students, but nobody was hit." Sonya nodded her head in a way that meant this incident required no explanation. "A lot of the white people in Orangeburg really didn't like us.

"The administration canceled classes, but we stayed on campus. The next night, Wednesday, I was walking on the campus, alone, and all of a sudden there was a shot. I fell to the ground, and saw a car racing through the campus. There were some black guys who chased the car down, and caught it. They dragged the white guys out of the car, and beat them up."

Sonya then remembered another night when she came near face-to-face fighting. "Another time, I was on the road in North Carolina, in a car full of black kids, at night, and the car broke down. A car full of white men pulled up behind us and just sat there, for five minutes— the longest five minutes I can remember. We could not figure out why they did not attack us. Then they slowly drove off."

"The mood was reckless on campus by this time," I said.

"We knew something was going to happen," Sonya answered. "By Thursday the National Guard came in, hundreds of them. They were white, they had on green uniforms, and carried rifles. Some of the students were out on the lawn on a knoll in front of the campus, facing the National Guard, just watching them. I tried to get the students to leave, because as a black person, you do not stand in front of a white person with a gun. That's just crazy. But a lot of them stayed.

"Anyway, we had some meetings." Sonya looked down, and tried to decide whether she would tell me her next thought. "We decided we were going to blow up something, a building off campus."

"Did anyone know how to blow something up?" I asked.

"I didn't." She laughed.

"Did anyone take concrete steps to prepare a bomb?"

"All I can say is, there was never a bomb that blew up," Sonya went on. "Nothing happened." Sonya's comrades in the movement either decided against planting a bomb in an empty building or did not have time to do so.

"Later we found out that somebody at some of our meetings was an informant," she continued.

"Is it possible that the National Guard knew something from this informant?"

Sonya nodded, chagrined. "That night, people were still on the knoll, and the National Guard was there. Around six-thirty, I went back to the dorm. About an hour later, the National Guard opened fire. There were about a hundred people on the knoll at the time. It lasted about ten seconds. I wasn't there. From the dorm we heard the shooting, and someone came in and told us what had happened. We got real quiet, and sat in the hall of our dorm, just facing each other, away from the windows. We just knew we were all going to get killed! We were afraid, and crying."

The shooting, on February 8, 1968, became known as the Orangeburg Massacre.

"What were the students doing on the knoll when the National Guard started firing?" I asked.

Sonya was leaning forward. "Just standing there!" she broke out. "There were forty-eight people hit. Three people were killed. None of these people were in the movement.

"An hour later I went over to the infirmary, but they wouldn't let me in. One guy who was killed, Smitty, his death was the most suspicious, because he was hit in the leg with a bullet. Photographs of Smitty, after he was shot, show that he was sitting up, conscious. Then they put him in the van and took him to the hospital. He was said to have died on the way, but we think he was killed in custody. We always thought that Smitty probably resisted arrest, and they just beat him to death."

"Was there an investigation?" I asked, then looked down at the table, a little embarrassed at my naive question.

"Nothing was investigated." Sonya shook her head bitterly. "Next morning, black leaders came from around the state. We were made to get off the campus, and as we left, we saw the tanks coming into town. That was power. Tanks!"

Sonya laughed, and rested her brow on her palm. In my mind's eye I saw the tanks wandering through the pleasant Carolina town.

"Three weeks later, SNCC came to me and said, 'Go back to the school.' We were demoralized. But we got telegrams from around the country about what had happened, and letters of support. So I got on the phone in a phone booth, and made long-distance calls to people who had written us, collect calls, and asked them to send us money. They were strangers, and they were white people. To my amazement, a lot of them sent money.

"We used the money to rent buses to go to Columbia, to invade the state legislature. We got to the capitol, and into the senate chambers, and into the balcony. We wanted the governor and legislature to admit that they had murdered our fellow students. We started reading our grievances, but we were arrested, and they carried us to jail. It was the first time I'd ever been in jail. After we got out on bond, we decided to go back again, and this time to make it bigger.

"The second time we went to Columbia," she said, "I had never seen so many white police officers, and I haven't seen so many since. Imagine one thousand highway patrolmen, and they're all six foot five, with big billy clubs, and rifles, standing shoulder to shoulder, around the State House. There were cops on top of the buildings! Our own group had nine or twelve busloads, and there were black students from around the South. Some of them had guns, because we didn't know what was going to happen. The students from State had arrived, but they got frightened. The president of the college came out, and told the students to leave. Then the police started to move. We backed down, and a lot of the buses turned around, and we gave the city back to the police."

"Did you go back again?" I asked.

"We lost," answered Sonya sadly, then let out a giggle to cover it. "If you try to reach out too far, either you will destroy yourself or you will be destroyed. People will kill. The movement never got its momentum. Our grievances were never addressed. In April, Dr. King died, but there wasn't a lot of commotion on our campus, because we had been through so much already. That was more or less the end."

A sarcastic edge entered Sonya's voice.

"I never wanted to sing 'We shall overcome, someday.' I always wanted to say 'We shall overcome—*today.*' Today is the day we become first-class citizens, not tomorrow."

Sonya laughed sadly, and looked down again, embarrassed. "The day before my graduation, my mother came up to Orangeburg from Charleston. And that night she made me straighten my hair. That was very important to her, that I look like the other students."

I told Sonya about Tom White, the Angolan accused of plotting a slave uprising. She was silent for a while. Then she said, "Sometimes, in the movement, I felt like I was speaking in tongues. I would give a speech, and it was as though someone was speaking through me, like I was possessed. Maybe in a family, the dead are able to communicate through the living."

"In my family's lore," I said to Emily Frayer, sitting in her living room, "the story is maintained that the slave owners did not sleep with the slaves. Is there anything that would lead you to believe that women on the Ball plantations were forced to sleep with their masters?"

Mrs. Frayer's family, seated around the room, let go a group sigh. Half a minute passed, and the elderly lady began slowly to speak.

"Yes, I heard them say that," she said. "I heard them say that a long time ago, they had children by the slaves. I don't know if it's the master, but I think it was the master's children."

Mrs. Frayer had gotten it from her grandparents that the young sons of the big house, boys in their teens and twenties, had sex with black women when they could.

"Yes, it was common all right," said Mrs. Frayer. "Now and then you hear somebody say something. I remember one lady—her name was Abby—who had a son. This was in Hyde Park, so I know him. That boy, he was a Ball."

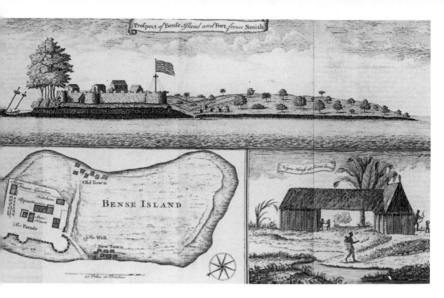

PRISCILLA AND THE MARTIN FAMILY

In 1756 in Sierra Leone, a ten-year-old girl was captured and held at Bunce Island (then called Bense Island), an English fortress and slave prison in the Sierra Leone River.

JUST imported in the *Hare*, Capt. *Caleb Godfrey*, directly from *Sierra-Leon*, a Cargo of Likely and Healthy SLAVES, To be sold upon easy Terms, on *Taesday* the 29th Instant *June*, by AUSTIN & LAURENS.

A ship called the Hare loaded about 170 people (including the ten-year-old girl) at Bunce Island and sailed for ⌐rleston, where it arrived in June 1756 with some 110 captives still alive under deck. They were advertised for sale by the slave import firm Austin & Laurens in the June 17 issue of the South Carolina Gazette.

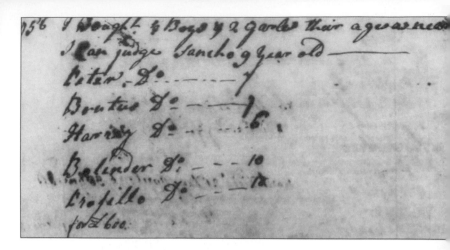

On June 30 Second Elias Ball bought the ten-year-old girl, whom he named Priscilla, and five other children from Sierra Leone. He wrote in his ledger: "I bought 4 boys & 2 girls—their ages as near as I can judge Sancho=9 years old, Peter=7, Brutus=7, Harry=6, Belinda=10, Priscilla=10, for £600."

Peter Henry Martin (1855–1933), center, a great-great-grandson of Priscilla, with his wife, Anna Cruz Martin, and their seven children, in a photography studio in Charleston about 1898. Freed at age ten from Limerick plantation, P. Henry Martin kept up a long association with the Ball family, to the extent of sending sentimental letters to his former owners about his childhood in slavery ("As long as there are Balls, I will have mistresses and masters," he wrote in 1933, at age seventy-seven).

*...he first son of P. Henry Martin and
...ruz, P. H. Martin Jr. (1886–1957),
...ne a roofer for a black-run contractor
...arleston, the H. A. DeCosta Company.*

*Thomas P. Martin, grandson of P. Henry Martin,
seventh-generation descendant of Priscilla, and retired assistant school principal, in Charleston, 1994.*

*Thomas P. Martin and the author on a visit to Limerick plantation,
home of Mr. Martin's grandfather, P. Henry Martin, before the Civil War.*

BALL FAMILIES

father often spoke about The Bluff plantation, the 1,100-acre sharecrop farm twenty-five miles from Charleston where grandparents, Isaac and Mary Louisa Ball, raised their family before giving up farming in 1894. In the early 1900s The Bluff was a country retreat for the Ball kin, including Isaac and Mary Louisa's ten adult children and thirty-six grandchildren.

father, Theodore Porter Ball ("Porter")—his hand is on the fender—and some of his cousins at The Bluff, about 1922. The Charleston Ball families visited the plantation on weekends, arriving in muddied cars, sending the boys to fish for dinner and the girls to play around the house or, as here, to remain watchful in doorways.

My grandfather, Nathaniel I. Ball (1881–1[...] center, was raised at The Bluff plantation. [...] he was thirteen, his parents quit as sharecro[...] landlords and moved the family to Charlest[...] ending the Ball clan's 196-year involvemen[...] rice cultivation. Grandfather Nat became a construction contractor and, with his wife, Susan Magdalene Porter, parented one dau[...] Magdalene, and two sons, Nat Jr., right, ar[...] Theodore Porter left, knickered according to [...] fashion about 1929.

In Charleston, to marry someone "from off" means to leave the city for a spouse, which my father did at age forty-two, after fifteen years as an Episcopal clergyman, when he married my mother, Janet Rowley, thirty-six, in her hometown of New Orleans in 1956.

The christening of my brother, Theodore Porter Ball Jr., in the arms of Grandmother Ball, by my father, right, flanked with many South Carolina kin, in our backyard in Savannah, Georgia, 1957; my mother handled the camera.

birth my parents hired Rebecca, whose ...me does not appear on the back of ...otograph and has disappeared from ...memory. A year later Rebecca, having ...er service, was "let go" and vanished ...ur world.

My brother, Theodore Jr., left, and me at the Lincoln Memorial in Washington, D.C., 1964, having briefly admired the feet and fingers of the statue of Abraham Lincoln.

Joseph Ball (1910–85), of Marion, South Carolina, ninety miles from the Ball lands, was a school principal when he enlisted in the Army in April 1942, four months after the bombing of Pearl Harbor. Contrary to wide legend, few freed slaves from the Cooper River plantations adopted the family names of their former owners. Joseph Ball may have been an exception, descended from a Ball family slave; but no evidence has survived that might prove the connection.

Jacqueline Ball, right, a Navy officer at the Pentagon and daughter of Joseph Ball, at the graduation ceremony of her daughter, LaShawn McGhee, from Army boot camp, in 1995.

THE HARLESTON COUSINS

Edwin A. Harleston (1882–1931), distant kin of the Ball family, was a grandson of rice planter William Harleston and Kate Wilson, his slave. In the early 1900s, Kate Wilson's eight children by William Harleston, and her children's children, made up a large, light-skinned, and elite African-American family in Charleston whose fortunes were made secure by their prosperous business, the Harleston Funeral Home.

DR. W.E.B. DU BOIS & S GHT SEEING PARTY
CHARLESTON, S.C. MARCH, 1917

Edwin Harleston, far left, attended Atlanta University, where he befriended one of his professors, W. E. B. Du Bois, cent 1916, Harleston became founding president of the Charleston chapter of the National Association for the Advanceme of Colored People; his work brought W. E. B. Du Bois, editor of the NAACP magazine The Crisis, on periodic visits to Charleston and to the Harleston family home.

An artist whose desire to paint outstripped his pleasure in undertaking, Edwin Harleston—who studied at the school of the Boston Museum of Fine Arts as well as the Art Institute of Chicago—defied race custom and probability to become one of a small number of black American painters in the early 1900s with a serious career.

"Girl in Blue," oil on canvas, by Edwin A. Harleston, 1920s.

A charcoal drawing that Edwin Harleston made of his niece, Gussie Louise Harleston, about 1922. The subject of this picture later changed her name to Edwina (to honor her uncle), had a career in journalism, and retired in Atlanta.

Ray M. Fleming, whose grandmother, Katherine Harleston, was a sister of the painter Edwin, at the start of his career as a music producer, in New York, about 1965.

RAY FLEMING
World Records

1 . . .

. . . and Alison Gentry, grandchildren of Edwina Harleston and sixth-generation descendants of Kate Wilson and William Harleston, in Atlanta, 1989.

BRIGHT MA'S FAMILY

In 1865, a twenty-five-year-old field hand named Katie (who would later be known as "Bright Ma" to her descendants) was freed from the Balls' Buck Hall plantation, after which she took the surname Heyward and, with her husband Zachariah, built her own house. No photograph of Katie Heyward has survived, but Wesley T. Simmons, Katie's son-in-law, a cotton farmer and fisherman, sits in front of the Heyward family house in Cordesville, South Carolina, about 1910.

Katie Simmons (later Roper), born 1912, a granddaughter of Bright Ma, about 1935 in a photography studio, wearing a fur that she bought on a trip to New York.

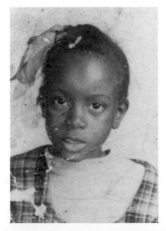

Charlotte Roper (later Dunn), daughter of Katie Roper and great-granddaughter of Bright Ma, photographed at school, 1954.

Delores Roper (later Singletary), sister of Charlotte, at the Roper family grocery store, James Island, South Carolina, about 1974.

Some of the Heyward-Roper family of South Carolina in 1996. Left to right: Delores Singletary, Rosalyn DeSaussure, Michael Singletary, Charlotte Dunn, Katie Roper, Rosalie Frasier.

RUN away from the subf... ber, two young NEGI fellows, one this country bo named TOM, a middling tall low, has one of his toes cut o the other is a fellow of the G ney country, something fhor than *Tom*, of a black complexi named JEMMY ; it is thou that they may be gone towa the Congarees ; a reward of ten pounds for *Tom*, : five pounds for *Jemmy*, on delivery of them, or eit of them, to the warden of the work-houfe, or to ELIAS BALL, of Hyde-park

In 1768 an American-born slave named Tom was advertised by Second Elias Ball as having escaped the plant There is no evidence of Tom's eventual fate (he may have either died or fled for good), but the descendants of Tom Bessie would include Philip Lucas, freed at twenty-one from Limerick, another Ball family tract.

Sonya Fordham, a granddaughter of Emily Frayer, and her husband, Sylvester Egwu, a Nigerian, at a 1981 cer Charleston commemorating their wedding, which had earlier taken place in Washington, D.C.

Emily Frayer (with cane), sixth-generation descendant of the runaway Tom's sister, Bessie, and granddaughter Philip Lucas. In 1994, I joined Mrs. Frayer on a visit to the ruined master's house at Comingtee plantation, with (right to left) her grandson George Fordham, granddaughter Sonya Fordham, daughter Luzena King, and friend Carutha Williams—all descended from people enslaved on Ball family lands.

Chiemeka Egwu, sixteen-year-old daughter of Sonya Fordham and ninth-generation descendant of the family of the runaway Tom, was elected Miss Junior R.O.T.C. by young recruits in the Reserve Officers' Training Corps, in Charleston, 1996.

"You knew a man on Hyde Park—" I began.

"No, I knew a lady used to live on Hyde Park," Mrs. Frayer corrected. "Abby. She had a son. This boy, he didn't go to school there, because when he was a little boy, they sent him to an orphanage, in Moncks Corner. They called him Sonny. That's his little raisin' name. His real name was Moses. And he was raised up in this orphanage, so he could get his schoolin'."

"Who was his father?" I asked.

"He was a Ball, but I didn't know which one." Mrs. Frayer added that Moses was about the same age as she. "I don't know who was his father. I asked him one time. I said, 'Look here, what name you carry?' He said, 'You know, I carry Dent here, but when I go away, I carry my own name. My name is Moses Dent here, but when I go off, I'm Moses Ball.'"

One of Mrs. Frayer's kin added, "He went to Boston."

"Yes, he went to Boston when he was quite a boy," Mrs. Frayer nodded. "He used to visit home, but after his mother died, he didn't come back. I don't think he's alive, and I don't know if he has children or not."

"If I went to Boston," I said, "and looked for black folks called Ball, I might find Moses Ball's family."

"I hope you will," answered Mrs. Frayer, "and if you do, tell them hello for me."

Before blood tests, before genetic matching, the identity of a father rested on the report of the mother. Mrs. Frayer had gotten the story from Abby, the child's mother, and, a lifetime later, repeated the tale. On other subjects, Mrs. Frayer's hearsay had been very precise. Her tale of the end of slavery at Limerick plantation was, word for word, nearly the same as the description written down by Mary Ball.

In probate law, when courts seek to establish family relations, three forms of evidence are admitted: documentary records, "real" evidence, and hearsay. Documentary evidence includes accounts produced by governing authorities—wills, marriage certificates, and death records. Real evidence includes artifacts that corroborate the structure of a family, such as photographs, heirlooms, or inscriptions on tombstones. Hearsay evidence consists of what others reported before any controversy around heredity arose. The standard of proof for blood relations among the long-dead does not rest on one or another type of evidence but on the preponderance.

For Moses Dent Ball, real evidence did not exist. If he moved out of state as a young man, no artifacts relevant to his parents could reasonably be found. As for documentary evidence, paper records of his birth did not exist either. South Carolina did not require the registration of births until 1905, after Moses was born; before that year, many children went unrecorded.

Other records related to the life of Moses Dent Ball did survive, however. According to the federal census of 1880, three black families named Dent were living in the vicinity of the Balls' Hyde Park plantation. In one of the households lived Abby Dent, fifteen years old. To judge from court papers, the Ball family also had dealings with Abby's family. In 1881, Abby's father, Marcus Dent, a sixty-one-year-old farm worker, died, after which the probate judge in the county appointed Abby's mother, Amy Dent, executor of her husband's small estate. Among the signatures of witnesses in the matter were three men, all members of the Ball family. What's more, from the Ball plantation books, it appeared that Marcus Dent, Abby's father, had been a slave on Hyde Park. A boy called Marcus was born there in May 1822, to parents named Peter and Beda. Abby's father, according to the probate file, was a man of the same name and age, living on the same piece of land.

In 1910, in the federal census, Moses Ball, age ten, lived in the town of Moncks Corner, west of Hyde Park, with several other children and a guardian. This would have been the orphanage where the mulatto child of Abby Dent and the unknown Mr. Ball was sent to school.

Mrs. Frayer said that Moses Ball had moved to Massachusetts as a young man. Moses is not listed in the 1920 South Carolina census, and the Massachusetts census for the same year shows a Moses Ball, age nineteen, living in the village of Watertown, outside Boston. The census enumerator wrote that this Moses Ball gave his birthplace as South Carolina.

I went to Massachusetts.

Watertown is an old industrial district five miles from central Boston and a mile west of Cambridge. Its main road, Arsenal Street, is named for a military depot that opened in the 1820s. During the Civil War, the Watertown Arsenal made cannons and ammunition for Union troops. After 1900 Watertown became a transit point for cattle sent by rail from Chicago, and experienced an economic boom. A slaughterhouse was put up in the neighboring town of Brighton, and packinghouses opened to process the beef. Another boom came during World War I, when weapons production was increased, and the number of employees at the Arsenal rose to sixteen hundred. About the same time, the town got a rubber plant, operated by the Hood Company. In 1919, that plant employed eighty-seven hundred people, who made galoshes.

I arrived in Watertown on a sunny Saturday to find the moldering aftermath of this former prosperity. The brick factories from the early 1900s stood shuttered or decaying, and the wood-frame houses lining the streets, the old workers' districts, looked run-down. The arsenal itself, a piecemeal compound of brick buildings, was locked up. A painted sign near the front gate faintly promised ARMY RESEARCH CENTER.

The 1920 census recorded Moses Ball's address as 42 Arsenal Street. He rented a room that year from a black laundress named Frannie Lucas, and worked in one of the packinghouses. In the Watertown library, I found a residential directory from the period which confirmed that a man named Moses Ball had boarded with Frannie Lucas. According to the census, Arsenal Street, in Moses's time, was a neighborhood of white immigrants. North of Moses's house on Arsenal Street lived several nurses and machinists, from Wales and Scotland. South along the same street lived a couple of painters and roofers, as well as a seamstress or two, born, among other places, in Ireland and Sweden. The only people of color on the street were Moses Ball and Frannie Lucas. It occurred to me that Moses, if he had a white father, might have been fair-skinned. Although the census called him black, he might have moved easily among whites.

I went to his old address, 42 Arsenal, at the corner of Taylor Street. The house was gone, replaced by a tire dealer. Across the street stood a furniture store and another tire shop.

In Boston, at the Registry of Vital Records and Statistics, I found the record of Moses Ball's marriage—on May 11, 1921, to twenty-eight-year-old Carrie Redmond, from Holyoke, Massachusetts. On the mar-

riage license, Carrie Redmond gave her occupation as "beauty cultur-
ist," and added that she had been born in Montclair, New Jersey.
Moses Ball gave his job as "steelworker." By then he had probably
gotten work at the arsenal, whose open-hearth foundry was still in
operation.

When the marriage clerk asked Moses Ball about his parents, he
gave his mother's name as Abby—the Abby Dent of Hyde Park. As for
his father, Moses stated that he lived in Charleston and was named
James Ball. The name of his father might have been a sensitive subject
at home in South Carolina, but in Boston, a thousand miles away, Moses
Ball had little reason to lie or invent a name. There was a James Austin
Ball in the South Carolina clan. At the time of Moses's birth, he was
twenty-five, and unmarried. His father, Isaac Ball, and his uncle, Elias,
ran sharecrop plantations on the Cooper River. The evidence that this
was Moses's father is slim and circumstantial, yet plausible.

After two or three years, Moses and Carrie Ball disappeared from
public records. By 1923 they were no longer listed in residential direc-
tories for Watertown or Boston. In the Massachusetts birth records, I
found numerous children named Ball, all described as white, but no
black children recorded as born to a Moses or Carrie Ball. I then looked
through death records and newspaper obituaries for a fifty-year period
but found no mention of the couple.

Emily Frayer remembered seeing Moses Ball about 1940, at a funeral in Charleston, when he was still living in Massachusetts. The
couple did not move back to South Carolina, she said. Moses and Carrie
Ball may have simply left Boston. But when I told one of Mrs. Frayer's
family members that Moses Ball had vanished, she speculated that he
had "crossed over," that is, begun to pass for white. It is possible, of
course, that both Moses and Carrie Ball were light-skinned. If they did
pass, this would explain why they disappear from official records that
might identify them as "colored."

It occurred to me that Moses Ball, like many husbands, died before
his wife, and that she may well have returned to her birthplace in New
Jersey. In Social Security records, I found a Carrie Ball, age eighty-
four, who died in New Jersey, a few miles from the town where Moses's
wife was born. Her birthdate showed her to be the right age to have
been married to Moses Ball of Hyde Park. I retrieved her death certificate from the New Jersey State Department of Health. It reported that

Carrie Ball was a former production worker in a pencil factory, retired, with no children, and white.

On a crisp morning in early February, I set off with some of the descendants of Philip and Ellen Lucas for Hyde Park plantation. Emily Frayer was born there in 1901 in a cabin which her great-aunt, Rachel, occupied as a tenant. Rachel later moved off Hyde Park, and after that none of the Lucas clan lived there. Hyde Park had recently been sold by relatives of the Balls, making it the last plantation to go out of the family. Mrs. Frayer said she had not been home to Hyde Park in more than eighty years, and wanted to see it one last time before she died.

Outside the entrance gate stood a church. In the cemetery was the grave of Philip Lucas, Mrs. Frayer's grandfather, beneath a tombstone with the outline of two upheld swords chiseled on its face. Because Philip Lucas had been a Union soldier at the end of the Civil War, his family had requested the swords, so as not to forget.

We drove along a long dusty lane until we came to the main house, a two-story cottage with a porch. It stood on a bluff with a splendid vista, facing down a rolling lawn toward the Cooper River. The porch hung out from the front like a great wooden chair. From the house, you could see the old rice fields, or what was left of them, and beyond that, making a narrow yet sluggish path through the marshes, the river.

The earliest house at Hyde Park burned down around the time of the American Revolution. A few years later, since none of the Balls wanted to live there, the family put up a small "marooning cottage," which the Ball ladies could use to maroon—that is, to get away from home to socialize—and men might use while hunting. Built in 1799, the wooden cottage rested on brick pilings and had a sloping tin roof. Fifty yards beyond the house stood a narrow cabin, shaped like a railroad car, with two doors and a pair of windows. It was dilapidated beyond repair and sat in a hollow surrounded by brush.

Along with Emily Frayer had come her daughter, two of her grandchildren, and a family friend. We walked toward the two houses, Mrs. Frayer leading with her cane. She was tiny and stooped, but she navigated as though walking through her own living room.

"The road used to run past the barnyard," she said, "then over a little bridge on a creek, down toward the river and the fields."

Mrs. Frayer hardly looked at the main house. I offered to take her inside, and she waved me off. She looked down at the ground, then up across the lawn, at the narrow cabin in the distance. I asked how she came to be born here.

"You see, my grand-aunt come back to live here, because her home burned down," she answered. "And she asked Mas' Coming to come back, if she could get a place to stay. And he tell her, 'Yeah, come on back.' " "Mas' Coming" was Coming Ball, and the great-aunt was Rachel Lucas, the Limerick field hand who had fought the overseer, only to be personally whipped by William Ball.

We moved with slow purpose across the brow of the hill.

"I've had the chance to think a lot about what the Ball family did," I told Emily Frayer. "There is nothing I can do to give back for the pain that my family caused your family."

"No, nothing," she said. "So don't think nothing of that, because that is past and gone. This is a new day, and we must try to live up to the new day. And we see the light. Sometime it's short, and sometime it's long. But thank God, we got this far."

"I don't know if I can speak for the Ball family," I went on. "I have many relatives, and some of them would not like for me to speak on their behalf. But I'm sorry for what my family did to your family."

"Oh, man," said Mrs. Frayer. "You been on God's mantelpiece that time. That's out of your jurisdiction altogether."

"It's out of my jurisdiction, because it wasn't in my lifetime that people were in slavery."

"That's what I said, you was on the mantelpiece," Mrs. Frayer replied. "It wasn't in this time at all. So you must don't feel bad."

"Forgiveness has to be asked," I told her.

"Yes, we forgive," she answered. "It didn't hurt me, now, but the people before me, and they all gone."

"We're not responsible for what our ancestors did or did not do," I said, "but we're accountable for it."

"That's right, we are not responsible," answered Mrs. Frayer. "He's a merciful God, and he pardon all of us for what we done. He pardon you for what you think, and what you don't think—for what you know, and what you don't know.

"There's a lot to be thankful for. Because you didn't have to wait until now to come," she said. "You could have come a long time ago, but you come in due time. You. When you come, you come in due time. You can explain yourself, and you can think. But a lot gone. They didn't even think about that."

"I came at the right time?"

"You come at the right time. You'll mend many fences. You just keep up the work, boy. Keep 'em up, because there's a lot to be done."

"The fences are still down," I said.

"Oh boy, isn't it though? A lot of building to be done yet," she answered. "But you have a beginning. And if you don't see me no more, just remember me in your prayer."

At the edge of the cleared ground stood the old cabin, which sagged in the middle, and was surrounded by weeds.

"I want to look for something," said Mrs. Frayer. "See if it can come to me. Oh, there the house back there!" We made our way to the cabin, and Mrs. Frayer pointed with her cane.

"Yeah, I was born down in this house here."

"You were born in that house?"

"Yeah, the house was high then off the ground, 'cause you had two or three steps coming down. I used to sit in the door. There used to be a mulberry tree right behind the house. It wasn't but one chimney, and that chimney answered to the two sides of the house—one family on this side window, one family on that side. But the house seemed like it was bigger than that."

"Of course it looked bigger," I said. "You were five years old."

"I wasn't even five!"

Sometime after her family moved out, the cabin was made into a chicken house. The big fireplace was as Mrs. Frayer remembered it, but now there was a dirt floor and the smell of animals, with empty chicken coops and filth piled in a corner. There was a rustle in the pine trees, and Mrs. Frayer began to cry.

"I didn't think I would see it," she wept. "I won't have to wonder now, anymore."

"I'm glad you allowed me to bring you here," I said. As the old woman cried, I wept with her.

"I'm thankin' you to bring me, 'cause I had wanted to come a long time." We stood together and wept, looking at the sagging cabin.

I asked Emily Frayer why she was crying.

"You weep sometime 'cause you're happy, and you weep sometimes when you mourn," she answered. "So take your choice."

A sound of birds came down from the pines.

"Time bring on changes," Mrs. Frayer said in a moment. "Time really bring on changes. You live, you see the changes."

Next to the house was a little bridge over a creek. "I used to play on this little bridge," she said. I gestured to the bridge, and we made a step to walk across.

"Yes," said Mrs. Frayer, "but only God knows what's on the other end."

EPILOGUE

>———o———<

BUNCE ISLAND

The black slave dealers who once sold people along the coast of Africa and I had a common past. I came from a family of slave buyers; in Congo, Ghana, Senegal, and Sierra Leone lived the heirs of slave sellers. I went to West Africa to try to find some of them. Throughout the American South, it's possible for a stranger to arrive with a question—Who used to own the plantations around here?—and expect a straight reply. The answer to the riddle of which American families held slaves would be local knowledge. In some African countries, the mirror question—Which families used to sell people to the whites?—might also bring forth a list of names.

The moldering house in Charleston in which I had been living had finally sold, and I packed my few belongings to move out. One morning before leaving, I took a walk on the beach at Sullivan's Island, the little sandbar at the entrance to Charleston harbor where the slave transports had first touched land. A gray stripe of sand runs the length of the two-mile island next to the surf, a white one closer to the dunes. Although the island was once the most important landing place for black people brought to America, there was no museum, no monument, not even a handmade sign.

The deportation business on the West African coast was run from a

chain of fortresses, or factories, that were built by Europeans and operated by white factors with teams of black assistants. One of the busiest
forts, Elmina, stood on the coast of what would become Ghana; others
hugged the shore of Gambia (James Fort), Senegal (Gorée), Ivory Coast
(Assini), and Benin (Ouidah). The main factory in Sierra Leone occupied
an oval rock called Bunce Island. Bunce Island mirrors Sullivan's Island, as exports turn into imports, and the nation of Sierra Leone echoes
South Carolina, being the same size as the American state and sitting
on the great bulge in northwest Africa like a twin, only flipped over, its
west shore facing the Atlantic. The terrain of Sierra Leone also resembles that of parts of the American Southeast, a coastal swamp and plain
reaching twenty to forty miles inland, then a dry, rolling interior. Bunce
Island stayed in business, with interruptions, from the mid-1600s until
the early 1800s, during which time many thousands of people were
shipped from behind its prison walls to Charleston.

There were three reasons to go to Sierra Leone rather than elsewhere. First, the Ball family in-law Henry Laurens had handled the
ships from Bunce Island and sold some of his human cargo from Sierra
Leone to the Balls. Second, I had spoken about it to Thomas Martin
and his family in Charleston, descendants of one of the Bunce Island
captives, the ten-year-old girl shipped out in 1756 whose buyer, Elias
Ball Jr., had named Priscilla. The island would have been the last place
where the girl touched land before setting foot in America. The third
reason came down from the American Revolution, when the nineteen-
year-old carpenter named Boston escaped from his owners, Ann Ball
and her husband Richard Waring, of Tranquil Hill. In 1792, Boston
King (as he became known) and twelve hundred other escaped slaves
boarded ships bound for Sierra Leone, where they helped establish a
new colony of black Americans at Freetown. The descendants of the
runaway Boston King might still be in the country.

I arrived at night outside Freetown, to a lighted airport in the dark pool
of a forest. Sierra Leone is poor, and the government has run paved
roads and electricity only to limited districts. Freetown sits on a peninsula that juts into the Atlantic, and faces north onto a big harbor
formed by the wide estuary of the Sierra Leone River. The only mountains of the coast stand on the peninsula, and the metropolis starts at

the water and rises up the incline of hills behind it. In the mid-1400s, Portuguese sailors called the land Serra Lyoa, which means lion mountain, because of the appearance of the forested range; eventually the name devolved into Sierra Leone. When English interlopers pushed the Portuguese aside, the area became a place of British trade, then a Crown colony for 150 years, until independence in 1961. Afterward came a pair of civilian governments, some coups, and military rule. There was an internal war in progress when I went, with random fighting between the army and rebels in the bush, which made it dangerous to leave the capital. Refugees in Freetown had swollen the city's usual population of half a million, and the shantytowns of the poor overflowed with people from inland cities.

White travelers to Freetown can feel like the old colonial intruders, because attention flows to foreigners who have a little money and an agenda. Children in the street, begging, call out to any white person, "Hey, Master," before asking for money. In restaurants, waiters nod and say, "Yes, boss," and people point at the "whiteman" who has come around and wants something.

It was March, the tail end of the six-month dry season, and heat and dust suffocated the capital. Semi-asphalt roads released dry clay from beneath their decay, and a red powder covered the cars and smeared the buildings. Freetown was built in waves, with each successive layer of new buildings all since dilapidated. The traditional thatched huts had been shouldered out of the way by Victorian houses put up at the end of the 1800s, a handful of which survived in sagging, unpainted chintz. Colonial offices came in the 1900s, their columned pride now embarrassed by neglect. A few Modernist rectangles appeared in the 1950s—banks, schools, businesses—their white facades since gone blotchy, their air-conditioning broken. A last building wave had come with the invention of the cinderblock, which raised thousands of gray boxes around town, half of them never finished. Everywhere, filling in the gaps, were shanties pieced together from wood boxes, with mud for their floors and tin roofs held down by pots and pans.

The first descendant of slave sellers I encountered was a native of Freetown named Peter Karefa-Smart. Peter, as he allowed most people to call him, was in his early fifties and lived in a pleasant white house behind a high fence on a rocky hill. He worked as an official in the Ministry of Culture and Tourism but was on temporary leave from his job. He wore a white shirt and dark trousers, and had skin the color of stained oak, a high brow, a wide face, precise diction, and a gap between his two front teeth. In a plain office with fluorescent lights and a shelf of books, I asked Peter the meaning of Bunce Island.

"Bunce Island is a place that a lot of Sierra Leonians would like to forget about," he began, "a place where a lot of African Americans, as they are called now, were shipped out of Sierra Leone. It is an icon in our history."

Peter was plumper than most of his countrymen, who could not afford to put on weight. He was introspective, chose his sentences carefully, and spoke with an endearing gentleness. His own surname, Karefa-Smart, gave him a family connection to Bunce Island that was well known in the country.

"There is a famous Smart—named Gumbu Smart," Peter said. Peter's manner was understated, even rueful. He had few hand gestures, but gently tilted his head from left to right while working through a thought. "Historically, they say he was born in a northern province, the Bombali district, and lived from 1750 to 1820. He was captured when he was a young boy. The story goes that he had killed a brother of his, and he ran away from his village, where he was then caught by slave bounty hunters. He was sold to the factors at Bunce Island, and he was fortunate not to have been sent across the ocean."

Gumbu Smart, founder of Peter's family, was something of a national legend. The white factors who put him to work on Bunce Island thought him clever and thus named him Smart, keeping him around rather than loading him onto one of the ships that came for human cargo. Smart became accustomed to the business, and as a young man was made foreman of the African workers on the island, known as *grumettas*. Grumettas (probably from the Old French *gromet*, and Spanish *grumete*, meaning servant or cabin boy) served as carriers, guards, masons, carpenters, and seamstresses; they numbered about 140 men and women during Smart's years. Successful as a boss, Smart grew further in power when he was made a slave buyer by the whites.

"Smart was sent out with goods to purchase slaves," said Peter, telling the tale as he had heard it since childhood. "And because he realized what he was doing, he bought a lot of his countrymen, the Loko people, and he kept them and he built up a formidable force. He got enough power to control an area of the country around the town of Rokon."

As a purchasing agent for the English, Smart made regular trips up the nearby Rokel River and returned with captives in chains and ropes. He bought extra people from his own tribe and, instead of enslaving them, settled them in the village of Rokon. Leaning on their gratitude, perhaps, Smart formed the Loko captives into his personal following. Finally, rebelling against his own white masters, Smart fortified the settlement at Rokon, cut off trade coming down the Rokel, and began to charge fees to other traders who wanted to pass upriver to buy people.

"He got the name Gumbu later on," Peter added, "when he was initiated into the preeminent secret society of the Mendes—'Gumbu,' meaning fire."

"Your ancestor was a slave dealer," I said.

"He was a factor for the English, a middleman," answered Peter, wary.

"He bought people and delivered them," I pressed.

"Not all," Peter protested. "He took care of his own tribe. You should realize the situation then, with tribes fighting each other, and he himself already sold into slavery."

"Gumbu Smart was a victim who became a tyrant," I suggested. "He was captured as a child, a victim. And he grew up to be a slave trader, a tyrant."

"That's the language we throw around today," Peter came back, irritated. "That's just intellectualizing it. If you grow up inside of it, how do you know? Slavery was practiced in all societies . . ." His voice dwindled.

Peter knew the gray areas of behavior, and although he was no apologist for the slave business, he understood why his family sold people to America. I asked how his kin talked among themselves about Gumbu Smart.

"There is a myth about him," he answered. "Our family feels just a bit lucky. I'm proud when I see his name, and I have no reason not to be proud of it."

"But he was engaged in an evil business," I repeated.

"That is for us to say now," Peter resisted a second time. "Nobody is innocent. Nobody can point the finger and say, 'You are the guilty party.' We can only sit back and say, 'It happened.' Human beings have nasty parts, and we have our good parts. There is a nastiness in you that emerges now and again. It's part and parcel of what I believe to be my heritage. I'm not guilty about it, not sad about it. I just accept it. If we listen to the Bible, the sins of the fathers are visited on the seventh generation, and that's a lot of baggage to take around with you. But I'm not caught up in that kind of thinking."

"There was greed here," I said.

Peter's sadness seemed to deepen slightly, but he never became angry, and his eyes remained focused.

"Wherever commerce is, greed is there," he said quietly. "But what were people sold for? Things of fascination for us—copper pans, beads, rum. If you go through the list, today we couldn't understand it. To get drunk! These were new experiences. These were new sensations for them—I hope."

When the end of the legal slave business came in 1808, the British sent a fleet to Freetown to enforce the ban. Peter's ancestors lost some of their power when Gumbu Smart's son, also called Gumbu, fell out with a local ruler and was killed. But other Smart kin formed alliances with ruling families in the network of chiefdoms, and one, Samuel Smart, became governor of Sierra Leone under British rule. The Smart family stayed in politics off and on throughout the 1900s; Peter's uncle nearly won the presidency in a 1996 election. I asked Peter whether the success of Gumbu Smart's slave business gave his descendants advantages that were passed down through the generations.

"To be honest with you, I've never sat down and considered the effect of Gumbu Smart's participation in the slave trade on my own reality," Peter said, surprised at the question. "But history is in all of us—so, yes."

I asked how many people had passed through Gumbu Smart's operation. "That is the bane of the African societies," Peter replied, frowning. "We are not a people of the book. We don't, as a people, document things. I know you could find people who would know the villages where people came from, but in order to be accurate about the figures, no. Our society has its bards, whose profession it is to know the history. We bring them out, and they tell us what happened."

The conversation turned to the involvement of England, which had launched the human trade, then to America. Peter talked about his youth, when he listened to black American music and followed news about the civil rights movement. His eyes gleamed sentimentally, his expression lightened, and he seemed to emerge briefly from his ambivalence.

"Today, I can look to America and feel proud that some of my kith and kin went there," he summed up, a rising in his voice. "It was painful, traumatic, but they went with the spirit of our people. They survived. If they had failed as a people, that pride wouldn't be ours." Peter looked straight ahead, his face an island of contentment. "When I was a student, black Americans were the ones we Africans aspired to be! They conquered their own environment, and we admired them! They are people to be proud of in the world. It's been said, 'They were the weak ones, the ones who were caught.' But maybe we are the weak ones, the ones who stayed behind, and they are the strong ones."

Peter's conscience appeared to waver again, and he became quiet. He had no desire to question his family or his country, but he was not afraid to admit some complicity.

"People who defend it, the slave business, say, 'If there were no buyers, there would be no sellers,'" Peter said, wincing slightly. "But you could turn it around and say, if there were no sellers, there would have been no buyers."

Although I had pieced together the story of Boston King's life, his African descendants proved impossible to find. Records show that soon after he arrived in Sierra Leone in 1792 with his wife, Violet, Boston King moved ten miles across the harbor from Freetown to a coast known as Bullom Shore, where he taught in a school set up for the native Temne tribe. His wife died and he eventually got remarried to a woman whose name has not survived. King became an evangelist for the Methodist Church, and kept up a correspondence with sponsors of the Sierra Leone colony in London. In 1796, in his midthirties, King traveled to England, studied Methodism for about two years, then returned to Freetown, where he was appointed schoolmaster in an outlying settlement called Granville. About 1800, King and his second wife evidently moved to the Sherbro country, an area around an estuary one hundred miles south of Freetown, where King died about 1802; his wife died soon after. Twenty-five years later, in 1827, a census of the original settlers of Freetown listed the remaining family of Boston King as consisting of a single daughter, who lived in Sherbro. Sherbro society was nonliterate, and so if the woman stayed and had children, no records of the family would have survived. I hoped to go to Sherbro to ask oral historians about the King family but was warned away because the area had seen fighting in the recent war.

Bunce Island lies abandoned in the Sierra Leone River. I visited the uninhabited rock in the company of Joseph Opala, an American anthropologist. Opala, white, in his forties, was raised in Oklahoma, joined the Peace Corps out of college, moved to West Africa, and settled in Sierra Leone. He had a head of short, dark hair, an easy smile, and a gray-and-black beard. His manner was smooth from years of explaining local history to visitors, and when he spoke, he gestured with the easy hand movements of a teacher, a few signals in front of his face, an occasional framing motion in the air. Opala had spent years researching Bunce Island, and he was fond of telling the story of the island's disastrous past in a calm, almost soothing way.

There were no regular visits to the ruined slave prison, so Opala hired a boat to take us there. It was a dry, hot day; wearing a brown short-sleeved shirt and white trousers, Opala looked out over the water with characteristic composure. Arriving, we set foot on a small, rocky jetty the length of a train car. It was the place where the slave galleys moored, and the last bit of land where captives stepped before they descended into the hold of the ship. During its long years in business, Bunce Island was kept clear, but now it stood overgrown with thicket and palms. The government makes no effort to promote tours, but it does pay a part-time caretaker, who showed up suddenly in a canoe holding a ledger—the visitors book.

A path led up a hill from the jetty to the northwest tip of the island, where the stone ruins of the fortress stood overlooking the water. The compound, a gray labyrinth of walls without a roof, covered about a square acre. Tangles of vines had grown into the bastions, splitting them open and making them lean this way or that. Trees grew up out of parapets in one or two places. Despite the heavy foliage, there was a strange absence of animal life—no birds or rustling in the bush—and a loud silence.

"This was what was called Bunce Island House," Joe Opala said, gesturing at the two-story shell. "The upper story was where the chief agent, or the big man, lived. The ground floor was where they had storerooms and office space. There was a heavy wooden door, and up above were windows and a tower. An armed man stood above and monitored the movement below."

Joe's voice was reassuring, as though he was describing movements of the weather. He gazed through an empty arch that led into a small room floored with grass.

"The arched door was the entrance into the office area, and it was really quite fancy. It had a false fireplace. Of course, they didn't need a fireplace in Africa, where it was hot year-round, but it was for a fancy effect. This is where you would have found them at their accounting tables with their ledger books, conducting business, no doubt over a couple of glasses of port or brandy."

A sapling came up from the ground in the little room, flanked by the remains of handsome stuccoed walls. I later learned that during the waiting period between ships, one of the amenities that kept the whites amused was a two-hole golf course, laid out on the island in the mid-1700s, east of the mansion.

The story of Bunce Island began in the seventeenth century, when English traders arrived at the Sierra Leone coast to buy ivory, as well as camwood, a tree used to make red dye. In 1663, King Charles II chartered a company called the Royal Adventurers of England Trading into Africa, with instructions to imitate the Dutch and Portuguese, that is, to buy people in addition to timber. The company put up two forts, but when one of them was seized by a Dutch admiral, the English moved to what was then known as Bence (or Bense) Island, probably after a squire named Bence, who had links to the London firm. The spelling of the place would later change to "Bance," still later, to "Bunce."

English tenants of Bunce Island paid rent and tribute to the so-called paramount chiefs, rulers of local clans in the Temne tribe, and bought people from them using manufactured goods as currency. At the death of a chief, uncertainty reigned while new arrangements were fixed with his successor. In 1672, the Royal Adventurers became the Royal

African Company, which operated Bunce Island for fifty-six years, until 1728, when the fort was attacked by French ships and burned. The island stood abandoned until 1748, when the slave franchise was sold to the London firm of Grant, Oswald & Co.

Grant, Oswald & Co.—named for partners Richard Oswald and Alexander Grant—sent a new white crew from England to revive the dormant business and set about repairing the dilapidated fortress and holding pens. Whereas previously captives were kept tied in huts, Grant, Oswald & Co. had a fifteen-foot stone wall built around an area about 150 feet square, so that people could be held in larger numbers outdoors. In 1751 the British firm sent to the fortress one hundred shackles, one hundred pairs of handcuffs, one thousand forelocks (another restraint), and some chain, along with goods the whites could use to pay local chiefs.

It was about this time that the Ball family became involved with the slave trade. The firm of Austin & Laurens, whose principals, George Austin and Henry Laurens, were married to, respectively, Ann Ball and Eleanor Ball, handled ships that originated in England, sailed to West Africa, and brought black captives to Charleston. In June 1756, Austin & Laurens received its first ship from Bunce Island, sent by Grant, Oswald & Co. It was from this galley, the *Hare*, that Elias Ball Jr., owner of Kensington plantation, bought six children who had spent an unknown period in the slave yard on Bunce Island before being deported.

Traffic picked up after the *Hare*, until it averaged several shipments a year sent from Sierra Leone to Charleston, where each cargo was sold by the Ball in-laws. One ledger that survives shows that in a single twelve months in 1759–60, four ships left Bunce Island bound for Charleston—the *Marlborough*, the *Nestor*, the *True Blue*, and the *Two Brothers*—carrying 928 people between them. Grant, Oswald & Co. stayed in business until the death of Richard Oswald in 1784, after which Henry Laurens seems to have stopped dealings with the company, which was taken over by two of Oswald's nephews.

Joe Opala stood in the counting room of the collapsed fort, motionless, with a peaceful expression, making small gestures as he spoke.

"The currency the whites used to buy people fell into several categories, the most important of which was cloth, in the volume traded," he said softly. "In addition to cloth, there were firearms and ammunition, metal goods, such as axes and swords, and many different types of liquor. The last items were trinkets, like glass beads, gun flints, and clay tobacco pipes, which were bonuses or dashes." A "dash" was a tip thrown in at the end of the deal.

The business would not have succeeded without companies like Austin & Laurens, but from the local perspective slavery allowed a few rich Africans to buy cloth for themselves, using other people as a form of money. The unit of pricing was known as a bar, which was initially a measured piece of iron and later, after inflation, an imaginary unit. A length of cloth was said to be worth so many bars, and a gun another number. Prices rose steadily over time so that in the century from 1690 to 1790 the quantity of goods a slave would buy for a chief increased fivefold.

"At a particular period, a slave might be fifty bars," said Joe. "When the Africans came to sell the slaves, they wanted, of course, fifty bars for the slave, but not in just one item. They would want so many bars of cloth, and so many bars of firearms, and so many bars of liquor. It was the assortment they were after. A slave-trading operation that didn't have the proper assortment of goods wouldn't do much business."

In the busy years, some fifty whites lived on the island, along with a black workforce of up to several hundred, depending on the volume of deportations. Some workers were slaves themselves; others were paid employees whose obedience could be guaranteed by the threat of being shipped to America. The black slave suppliers came down in boats with their captives from the Rokel River, a tributary to the Sierra Leone River (and center of operations for Gumbu Smart), as well as from nearby Port Loko Creek, which empties into the estuary five miles upstream from Bunce Island.

It takes about ten minutes to walk the length of the island, three minutes to walk across the middle. On the western ramparts of the ruin, overlooking the water, there was a high clearing of grass known as the parade. Here, the barrels of six cannons lay like bodies on the ground, their wooden mounts having disintegrated, their business end still aimed at the approach from the sea. One of the guns bore the date 1796, and others carried the royal cipher of King George III. Behind the guns, the remnants of the fortress had two distinct halves—the two-story mansion containing the bedrooms, offices, and storage space of the whites and, next to the house (where normally there might be a garden), the slave yard. The open-air yard, once filled with bodies, was placed so that it might be watched from a second-floor parlor. As Joe led the way into the rectangular yard, empty but for grass, the heat was fierce and the air full of bugs. Three sides of the pen had high stone walls, the fourth side being a wall of the mansion. Next to the main yard stood another, smaller pen, possibly used to keep the sexes separate.

"The big yard alone would hold between two and three hundred people," said Joe, his voice an undertone, "so probably altogether five hundred people could be held during the dry season, which was the peak season of trading. Inside the yard they were chained together in circles, and there were several circles. When they fed them, they would put a trough of rice in the middle of the circle. It would be impossible for anyone to get over the wall, because he was tied down or chained down to a lot of other people. I've found no evidence of anyone escaping. The management of the prisoners was so well handled, it was virtually impossible for anyone to get away."

The yard in operation would have been crowded with people milling around a shadeless patch, the place smelling of feces and sweat. The captives—snatched from their families, some of them having witnessed the murder of their parents or children—were likely to have been in shock, terrified of what was to happen to them.

"The slaves brought here would have been from three hundred miles up the coast, three hundred down," Joe said. "They would have spoken dozens of languages, and the handlers would have had to use translators. If a slave trader was wise, he told as many people as he could what would happen to them, that they were going to become workers in America, and reassured them as best he could, because when they weren't reassured, they would sometimes lose all hope and become catatonic. That was so common that the slave traders had a name for it—they called it 'the lethargy.' People would lose contact with reality and stop eating; they wouldn't see anything in front of them, and gradually they would just die. It was abject hopelessness. People thought they would be killed, or even eaten, and they would give up hope—or they would just lose their minds."

The main pen was entered by two doorways, a guarded entrance for new captives and a security entrance. The security door had a system of double gates; a courier brought barrels of food and water from outside the yard into a small antechamber, where he was locked inside and then let into the slave yard through a second door. The doorway was very narrow, so that if prisoners rushed the entrance, only one person could get out at a time, and those at the head of the attack would be trapped.

Joe nodded and smiled lightly, coming to the end of his tour. His eyes brightened as he remembered one more detail that he knew would be interesting.

"In the early days, when the Royal African Company ran the fort, they branded the slaves when they purchased them," Joe said, touching his shoulder. "Before they were taken into the yard, they were branded on one shoulder with the letters R-A-C-E, for Royal African Company of England. Then, when they were about to be put aboard ship and taken back through that door again, they were branded a second time on the other shoulder, with the letters S-L, to let the buyers on the American side know they came from Sierra Leone."

If there was a center of supply for Bunce Island, it was the town of Port Loko, forty-five miles inland from Freetown. Histories of Sierra Leone named this one place, as did local people, both in the streets and in the universities. The skinny stream known as Port Loko Creek empties into the Sierra Leone River near Bunce Island, and twenty miles toward the headwaters of the creek lies Port Loko.

The ruling families, or chiefs, played a significant role in the slave trade, although they did not monopolize it. The chiefdom system still survives. With a weak national government, and many of the old families still in power, Sierra Leone depends on local dynasties to carry out regional administration. I applied through a government ministry to speak to the ruling family in Port Loko, seat of the Maforki chiefdom, a five-sided district of three hundred square miles. A deputy minister wrote the office of the Maforki chief, Alikali Modu III, asking that he receive me and detailing the agenda.

"In view of the fact that all matters relating to Local Authorities fall under the domain or within the purview of [the] Ministry," the letter began, "I am therefore obliged to request your kind assistance on this matter, by furnishing Paramount Chief Modu III with the desire of Mr. Edward Ball . . . to visit Port Loko . . . and hold discussions with him and his authorities . . . focusing on the Maforki Chiefdom's involvement in the Slave Trade. . . . Your usual co-operation and kind understanding on this matter, would be immensely appreciated."

As I awaited a reply, I visited another descendant of slave sellers, Doris Lenga-Kroma, a dignified woman in her fifties. Mrs. Lenga-Kroma lived in a pleasant hilltop neighborhood of Freetown where many of the city's well-off class could be found. When we met, in the evening after dinner, Mrs. Lenga-Kroma wore a purple robe that reached from her shoulders to her ankles, hoop earrings, and a crucifix. She was thin, with a triangular face, owlish glasses, and dark, mahogany skin. Doris Lenga-Kroma was born Doris Caulker, of the powerful Caulker family, hereditary chiefs in the district of Shenge, a day's trip from the capital in the Sherbro country, the province down the shore. Her compound name, Lenga-Kroma, was that of her husband, a retired professor. Mrs. Lenga-Kroma taught in the Theology Department of Fourah Bay College, the city's main university, and was a pastor in the United Methodist Church. In the living room of her simple modern house, I asked Mrs. Lenga-Kroma how long her family had ruled in Shenge.

"For years, since the seventeenth century," she answered. "History has it that my father's family came from Plymouth, England. They were agents for the British trade on the coast, and the first man, Thomas Corker, was sent to the Shenge area by the Royal African Company. We are told that he got married to one of the ruling women, of the Ya Kumba house of Shenge, and their children became the Caulkers."

Mrs. Lenga-Kroma sat absolutely still, commanding the room with her emphatic delivery. She was the daughter of a chief, and her upbringing gave her a formidable presence. Since the lifetime of those distant ancestors, the Englishman and the African princess, the spelling of the family name had changed, from Corker to Caulker. I asked what the main business of Thomas Corker had been in Sierra Leone.

"Trade of timber," came the answer.

"The main business of the Royal African Company was slaves," I said.

"Yes." Mrs. Lenga-Kroma relented. "There were intertribal wars, and people were taken as slaves and kept. When these boats came, they would take them. They would sell them to the white man, whoever came.

There is still a pen where the slaves were kept until the ships came, and there were transactions. This was told to me by my father and from history, because I was not yet born."

The arrival of Thomas Corker had strengthened a regional dynasty. Corker had been sent to the Shenge coast in 1684 as a broker for the Royal African Company. He had two sons with a woman whom the whites called the Duchess of Sherbro, a member of the Ya Kumba house, which rules the area between the peninsula near Bunce Island and the Sherbro estuary farther down. Corker later went to Gambia, then returned to England, where he died in 1700. In Sierra Leone, his sons, Stephen and Robin, took the claim to rule from their mother's family, paired it with their father's name, and kept up trade with England. Before long, the Caulker chiefdom extended offshore to encompass the Plantain and Banana Islands, long strings of land in the path of the European ships. The Caulker domain split once with internal feuds, then again, but continued as a knot of separate fiefs, which fought one another while continuing to sell people to the English. On the mainland, Doris Lenga-Kroma's branch of the family held on to its chiefdom for more than two hundred years, until the death of her father, Alphonso Theodore Caulker, after which the title passed to another family.

The daughter of the last chief, Doris Caulker had become a Christian, and was ordained a Methodist elder in 1994, after some years as a deacon. In midlife, Mrs. Lenga-Kroma had adopted ten children, orphans and refugees from the country's internal war and, when we met, was raising them with her husband.

"Were the Caulkers slave traders?" I asked.

"Yes," she said. There was a pause. "Well, being chiefs, they would have been go-betweens, so it could be that they bought these people, then they would deal with the white man. I remember asking my father, and he just said, 'Well, this was part of the system.' Personally, I have a thought that, although I am not responsible for being born in the family where I am born, seeing the evils, I am sort of ashamed to know that my grandparents and ancestors took part in such an act. But then, I think again that in their own time, they might not have thought it to be anything evil."

"How could they not have thought it was evil?" I asked.

"I don't know, or else they wouldn't have done it!" The question irritated Mrs. Lenga-Kroma, and caused her momentarily to lose her composure. "You can only stop doing something if you know it is bad!"

Had her family benefited from the slave traffic?

"I really don't know!" she said. A furrowed brow indicated struggle with the subject. "By the time my father became chief, there was no longer this sort of slave trade. It was my great-grandfather and my grandfather, and they must have benefited in one way or the other. The way they benefited most was from the slaves working in their farms, and producing, having people to work for them, or fish for them. Whatever was got was meant for the chief and his wife, and the children, and the guests who would come."

"The slave business was run by the British," I said, "but Africans sold the captives. Do Africans bear a shared responsibility for the damage caused?"

"I doubt it" was the answer, finite. "If I don't expect you to have diamonds, then I won't try to buy diamonds from you. But if I come and say, 'Hey, I want diamonds,' I am encouraging you to go get diamonds. The British came, and they needed people. If they did not continue to come for slaves, those Africans who were poor would not have sold their brothers. I am not making excuses for them, but that's how it happened."

The conscience of Mrs. Lenga-Kroma seemed divided between cool denial (the Caulker family as victims of powerful whites) and her feeling of being "ashamed," as she said, of her family's legacy.

"I will not go back in time to scold them. I will not," she persisted, a hand in the air. "I will just assume that many of them did not really know this was evil. They did it and they accepted it as part of life. You and I come along years later, and we say that this was bad. This is present opinion and reflection. I can but live in this generation. I can look at it now and say it was evil, but I don't know what I would have done if I were in my great-grandfather's position."

"What would you say to black Americans whose ancestors were sold away by the Caulker family?" I asked.

"I don't know them!" she said. "They are no longer the same people who were sold!" A moment passed, and more gently she added, "What I know is that today they would be my brothers and sisters. This race problem continues in America because of the white idea of wanting to still dominate and rule. After all, you were this! I mean, they did it, your ancestors. The whites, the majority, tried to refuse that these were human beings, like them. I wish it were possible to get from their brains what they were thinking, even though they are dead."

In a moment Mrs. Lenga-Kroma's ten adopted children, ages five to eighteen, came out and introduced themselves. Many of them were mild-mannered, and all seemed quickly at ease. After a few words they fell silent and listened as their adoptive mother held forth.

"We should try to forget, and live today. Reflect on what has happened—it was bad. But what can I do now to amend?" said Mrs. Lenga-Kroma, surrounded by the sea of youth. "We must live our lives! I can't continue to bear the guilt about what my great-grandparents have done. I'll think about it and say, 'Oh, how could people have dreamed such a thing?' I'm born in such a family. I'm not responsible for being born there, but I'm there. What a shame! But what can I do now? What you do with the present is what really matters."

The word came that the ruling family in Port Loko would receive me. Almost certainly their forebears had sold many people who ended up on Ball plantations.

Centuries ago, Portuguese traders had sailed up a creek among the Loko tribe, made deals to trade, and put a bartering post at a place they called Os Alagoas; the village became known as Port Logo, or Port Loko. The Loko people were eventually driven out by the more numerous Temne tribe, but the name stayed. After the Portuguese left and the English took up residence on the coast, whites never came inland, leaving it to blacks to bring them people.

On a fiercely hot morning, I headed inland from the capital and soon came to a roadblock manned by soldiers with machine guns. There had been attacks on nearby villages, and settlements along the way showed damage from mortars and arson. After a few words the green-uniformed men waved the car through. The road turned from pavement to clay, and the car raised clouds of red powder. A bit farther came more questions and guns, then just forest and bush.

After two hours on jolting roads, I came to Port Loko, a dusty town on some low hills, with mud huts on the outskirts, dignified old buildings in the middle, and a pale, beautiful mosque. Port Loko Creek flowed through the center of town, the stream where the captives were once forced into small boats before being drifted downriver to Bunce Island. On one of the hills stood the villa of the chief, Alikali Modu III. The chief's residence was a squarish one-story compound of modern construction, painted green, with a portico. Several windows had been shattered by the bullets of rebels, who had lately swept through, killing some townspeople but sparing the ruling family.

Alikali Modu III presented himself at the door. The title Alikali comes from the Arabic *El Kadi*, meaning "the judge." Chief Modu was a handsome man in his eighties, wearing a long smock and trousers of the purest white, starched smooth, the smock with a beautiful pattern of eyelet holes. His decorous presence was enhanced by gold rings, a gold necklace, and a brocaded black-and-gold fez, with a gold tassel hanging like a length of hair. The chief appeared thin, a bit feeble, and spoke in a hoarse, tentative voice. Although he moved gracefully, his eyes held a timid air, as though he had passed the height of his power, and knew it.

Madame Haja Fatu Modu, the wife of the chief, led me out of the unrelenting sun into the cool of the receiving room. She was in her sixties, solid, with a beautiful smile, and wore a blue turban with gold embroidery. Her muslin robe had pale sleeves and a green pattern that flowed from her shoulders to her legs. The receiving room resembled a large den, with the notable exception of one or two animal-skin rugs. There were simple wood-frame sofas and chairs dating from the 1950s, knickknacks on kidney-shaped tables, and dozens of framed photographs on the wall, many showing Chief Modu in ceremonial pomp.

The chief's retinue entered, a train of five men, polished and elegant in defiance of the dust and heat. With their courtly manners and soft confidence, the men betrayed generations of comfort and service. Among the entourage was a thin, poised man in a white shirt and white trousers, perhaps forty-five, introduced as Pakerur Kamara, the ceremonial head of the clan, whose role was to lead official observances. A more stout, buoyant man, wearing a long white shirt and blue skullcap, gave his name as Maligie Omar Kanu. Maligie Kanu, about fifty, had an easy laugh and a compelling baritone voice. It later emerged that the ceremonial head came from the chief's family, the Kamaras, while Kanu came from another family allied with the Kamara clan.

Like most ruling houses in Sierra Leone, the chief's had converted to Islam centuries ago. Chief Modu spoke careful English, as did his wife and some in his retinue, the elite having been educated in schools built by the British. Others in the room spoke Temne, the local tongue; the main conversation settled into English, with some translation.

The chief took his customary chair, and small talk was passed around—the roads, the heat. At the end of the pleasantries I asked the chief, "What do you know about the slave traffic?"

"Well, very little," he answered in his thin voice. "What I know, we have a wharf here where they used to take the slaves to Freetown. Let me ask the speaker here. I would prefer that, because I stammer too much."

The elderly chief did have noticeably halting speech, but it was not immediately clear whether he was a stammering prince or whether the subject merely made him nervous. Chief Modu turned to a heavyset man wearing a blue smock. This was the ritual speaker, responsible for expressing the chief's desires, a man different from the ceremonial head. The speaker, with heavy eyelids and an imperious air, recited a brief narrative about the human traffic that hid more than it revealed, then deferred again to Modu.

"The speaker knows much about this," repeated Chief Modu. "I was in school then."

Alikali Modu slouched in his chair and held his fingers laced above his chest, gesturing now and then with a wave of the hand. The chief had indeed been a student at the end of the slave trade. Although Parliament's effort to abolish the Atlantic traffic in 1808 had largely succeeded, the sale of humans continued within Sierra Leone for well over a century. When Chief Modu was a boy in the 1920s his family still owned many people, up until 1926, when the British colonial office ordered emancipation.

"There are books on the slave trade," said the chief, with a deflective wave.

"I think your family and your chiefdom participated in the slave trade," I said.

"Yes, they did," came the answer. Suddenly Modu called over a messenger and told him to go retrieve someone in the village; the messenger disappeared.

"Would the Maforki chiefdom be as strong as it is today without the contribution of the slaves?" I asked.

"No."

To ease the tension, I asked Chief Modu when he had assumed power.

"In 1949," he said, relaxing.

"There was a coronation," said Madame Modu, next to her husband, smiling. "We also married in 1949."

Chief Modu pointed to a corner, where cascades of photographs hung on the wall. One framed picture showed him as a young man wearing the insignia of rule, a white turban finished with a jewel. Another showed King George VI, and a third showed King George's daughter and successor, Queen Elizabeth II. Madame Modu explained that after the death of George VI, she and the chief had attended the coronation of the twenty-six-year-old queen in 1953.

"Do you remember it?" I asked.

"We remember everything," said Madame Modu, her eyes traveling back.

One photograph showed Chief Modu, a bit older, in the streets of Port Loko shaking the hand of Queen Elizabeth, with Elizabeth's husband, Prince Philip, Duke of Edinburgh, looking on. The royal couple had come to visit them in 1961, Madame Modu said, at the moment of Sierra Leone's independence from Britain.

"The queen came here to Port Loko to spend the day, and we fed her," she said, flashing her searchlight of a smile.

"How does one behave in front of the queen?" I asked.

"You behave properly," came the answer, and a laugh.

The recollection of the English royals brought light to the chief's eyes, and a smirk. He rose from his chair and called to an attendant, and soon held in his hands a heavy sword in a sculpted gold scabbard. The gold was dusty and tarnished, but its beauty shone through.

"This was presented to my father by King George V," said Modu, handing over the relic, which weighed several pounds. From a shelf, the chief pulled down a green volume, *The Secret Book of Maforki*. The "book" turned out to be a solid block of wood, painted to resemble a leatherbound text. "If you can open it, all those things you have been asking me will be answered," said Modu teasingly. I pretended to struggle with the book, then said that the dynasty's secrets seemed safe.

The unusual attention paid by the British royal family to Chief Modu seemed to grow out of the town's role as a trade center. Port Loko stood on the Futa Jalon Highway, an ancient caravan route that leads down from the savannah five hundred miles north, into Senegal, through Guinea, and into Sierra Leone. Beef, gold, and cloth traveled this way, and, when slaving began, people. Traffic passed through the Futa Jalon, a region of expert traders who practiced a strident form of Islam. In this area lived the Fula, black Muslims who in the 1700s became accomplished at raiding villages for slaves. The Futa Jalon banned the capture and sale of Muslims but preyed on people who had not converted to Islam. When caravans from the Futa Jalon reached Port Loko, the people in the cargoes were taken over by the local chief and unloaded into boats bound for the Atlantic coast. After the demise of the human export market, but during the next century of English rule, the British colonial government became dependent on Port Loko's continued access to the caravans, especially for beef. Because the Alikali of the Maforki chiefdom controlled a pivot point in the route, he required special handling, and gifts.

The chat about the House of Windsor ended, and an old man entered the room, stooped over a black cane, moving with dignity. He was perhaps eighty-five, and gave his name as Alhaji Said Deen Kanu; it was made clear that he was the griot, or historian, of the Kamara house. Deen Kanu had white eyebrows and a brief white beard at the point of his chin; he wore a white robe, a fez embroidered with gold, and a red scarf.

"He can explain to you what he knows of the slave trade," said Madame Modu. The room fell silent.

Deen Kanu had intelligent eyes, focused straight ahead. Speaking through an interpreter, in Temne, he began by saying that the slave business was finished and that therefore it should not be spoken about. He turned to Chief Modu, asked permission to describe what he knew, and the chief assented with a wave. Hand on cane, the historian launched a monologue that began with the 1500s and the arrival of a few Portuguese sailors on the African coast. He named the first trading posts where white dealmakers set up business, and the first places where slaves were held for export. The griot moved from event to event, identifying the trade routes and the villages drawn into the human traffic, painting a wide canvas. He mentioned a gun battle, some centuries old, which led to the opening of another supply source.

"Were there people from the Maforki chiefdom who were sold and sent to America?" I asked at length.

"Yes," said the historian, "there were some who were bought from here."

In addition to relying on people trapped in raids, who were usually of a different tribe from that of the raiders, slave making became a part of the justice system of each village. Women accused of adultery could be punished by being sold to the whites, as could those accused of theft. If a person owed money and couldn't pay, she or he could also be sold. Tribes winnowed out their own ranks in this way, as well as the ranks of their enemies.

"Why did the chiefs allow people to be sold from here?" I asked.

There was a chuckle from Chief Modu, but it was not clear whether it came from nervousness or amusement.

"It was a business which everybody was doing," said Deen Kanu. "One can't say why a businessman does business." Smiles around the room.

"If the chief of Maforki wanted to protect his people," I said, "why would he allow them to be sold?" This time laughter rolled from one end of the room to the other. "Is that a stupid question?" I asked.

"Yes," giggled Madame Modu. Then, embarrassed, "No, no. It's not a stupid question." A nervous pause.

"I've never asked myself this question," said Chief Modu from his chair, stuttering.

"It's not an obvious question," said Madame Modu.

There were looks exchanged, and the moments passed until finally Deen Kanu said flatly, "They wanted money."

"They wanted money," Madame Modu echoed.

And with this rather small, grotesque admission, the feeling in the room changed completely. The prevailing mood of nervous denial seemed broken, and a sense of relief swept into the air. Maligie Omar Kanu, the fiftyish man with the blue skullcap and baritone voice, suddenly began to speak. A nephew of the griot, Maligie Kanu had been silent as his uncle recited ancient events.

"There are two families," said Kanu, "the Kamaras and the Kanus. We are more or less responsible for the slave trade." Maligie Kanu, barrel-chested, his right arm hitched on the back of the sofa where he sat, wore a curious smile. His gaze was unblinking, and his voice like a horn.

"The paramount chiefs knew that by getting a lot of slaves, they would become very powerful," he went on. "Slavery was encouraged by the chiefs, with their warriors. If you are powerful, you can conquer people, then you have slaves. If you went to any town, it was to conquer the town, and take some captives. These people become slaves. You could sell them, or you could use them to farm for you."

Kanu's easy talk compared well with his uncle's list of events, and Chief Modu's ceremonial silence. He had a disarming expression, as though a threat had been brandished, and it had fallen to him to make peace.

"People were not born slaves," I clarified. "They were captured and made slaves."

"Exactly," said Maligie Kanu.

"Did some of them did die?"

"Yes," Kanu answered, "because some were beaten, because they didn't want to go off and be slaves." After beginning calmly, Kanu now spoke with emphasis, his mouth in a strange smile, his eyes alight.

"If you owned a lot of people, or captured many, that was sign of status," I said.

"Yes," Kanu nodded. The chief and his entourage kept quiet, pleased to surrender the story to a single teller. According to histories, Port Loko had been the scene of political struggles in the eighteenth and nineteenth centuries. Eventually the feuding families struck a deal that rotated control of the chiefdom among three clans, with power passing to new blood after the death of each chief. After the current chief, Alikali Modu III, authority would go to another clan, some of whose family members sat in the room.

"You are the elite of the chiefdom," I said.

"Mmmnnn," said Kanu.

"What do the elite today think about the old slave business?" I asked.

"The slave trade," Kanu replied, "was not actually good for us at all."

"In America," I went on, "there are millions of black people who think it was a terrible thing."

"It was dreadful thing," said Kanu.

"It was a terrible thing," Madame Modu echoed from across the room.

"The things the British gave to your families in exchange for slaves," I said, "weren't unusual."

"Not special, no," said Kanu.

"Rum, guns—"

"Tobacco," Kanu added. "In that time, only people who were wealthy smoked tobacco. And to have a gun, only rich people had guns."

"Was it worth it?" I asked.

"It wasn't," said Kanu.

"What would you say to black Americans who point out that Africans sold their brothers and sisters?"

There was a burst of nervous laughter, then a pause, before eyes returned to Kanu.

"Well, this is a question," the baritone mused. His eyes looked down, searching for the thought, then up. "We say that it was a long mistake," he answered, "a long mistake by our ancestors."

"A two-hundred-and-fifty-year mistake," I measured.

"It was evil, actually, to sell your brother," Kanu said.

"When someone does evil in your society, how does he or she compensate for it?"

Kanu looked to Chief Modu. "I think this question should be answered by the paramount chief," he said, with a nervous laugh. Modu said nothing.

"You pray for forgiveness to the Almighty," said Kanu at last. "When we sit together, we sometimes pray for those things that our ancestors have done, two, three hundred years ago."

"You pray for the slave traders?"

"Yes. We pray that these people will be forgiven by the Almighty, for they have done evil things in the past," he said with a resigned expression.

"I think our families have a shared responsibility," I said.

"I'm glad we can say that," Kanu answered, smiling again.

"In part, it's my family's responsibility—"

"Yes," Madame Modu put in.

"And in part it's the responsibility of the Africans who sold their own people."

"Of the Africans, true," said Kanu, to the sound of murmuring around the room. "When you discover this collective responsibility," Kanu went on, "this evil act which had been committed both by the Africans and by the Americans, by your ancestors, what are you to do now to remedy it? We know slavery has been abolished, but the evil has already been committed. Can we organize something?"

"I would take part in an act of some kind," I said. "But I come as an individual, not as a representative of the American government."

"I know." Kanu smiled.

The moment was right and would not be repeated. I asked Chief Modu and his entourage if any of them would be willing to go to the dock on the creek where people were sent off and, on behalf of their families, take part in a ceremony of commemoration. The chief stared straight ahead, his lips moving, but without a sound. I waited for him to dismiss the matter, then Madame Modu straightened in her chair.

"The chief would have to be represented by someone else," she said, "because his health is poor, and he can't go." Chief Modu nodded and said that he was weak.

"But led by Deen," said Maligie Kanu, gesturing to his uncle, "and myself, and Pakerur, the ceremonial head," naming the man responsible for ritual, "we'd be willing to go down."

There was a much discussion in Temne, then Madame Modu spoke up again.

"If my husband wants me to go, I will go," she said. "I will represent him."

Suddenly we all stood.

Most West Africans believe that the dead watch over the living and can affect those still on earth, for better or worse. A common ceremony permits the living to speak with the ancestors and ask for blessing, or for forgiveness. The event begins with the pouring on the ground of a libation, usually rum, followed by prayer and speaking aloud with the dead. Then a kola nut, a kernel the size of an egg, is broken in two, and the halves are rolled on the ground. The way the pieces land tells whether or not the appeal has been heard. If both halves fall with the inside flesh of the nut facing up, the supplication is answered. Muslims have adapted this ancient ritual, which predates Islam, and use it to communicate with the Almighty.

A trail of curious townspeople followed our procession to the banks of Port Loko Creek. The streets of Port Loko slope down a hill, past a market and some old Victorian buildings, to a clearing by the water where a wall of warehouses lines the stream. The creek was beautiful, its far bank carpeted with trees and bushes. A plain, dusty dock about twenty feet square jutted into the stream, the wharf where people were loaded. It was all but certain that many Ball family slaves, put on the market by the Kamaras and the Kanus, had crossed here. The chief's delegation stepped onto the dock—the elderly Deen Kanu, his nephew Maligie Kanu, Madame Modu, and the leader of ceremony, Pakerur Kamara, the thin man in the white suit.

"This is the place where they shipped them to Bunce Island, and from there to America," Maligie Kanu said. "The boats would come from downstream."

Kanu pointed at a wooden boat about twenty feet long, painted blue, anchored in the creek. It was something like the ones used to carry people off, he said.

"For much of the country, this was the only route to the coast," said Madame Modu, squinting in the sun. "Each boat held ten to twenty people."

"They were tied," Kanu added.

A crowd looked on from the shore. The creek flowed around a bend, but the boat traffic was still. I wondered aloud how many people had been sent off from here.

"Thousands," said Madame Modu.

Pakerur Kamara crouched on the ground, wrinkling his white suit; he then took a cup of dark rum from a small bottle and poured four splashes on the dock. He spoke in Temne about what had happened on the dock, then threw the halves of the kola nut. The two pieces landed on the ground, facing up. He prayed and threw the kola nut a second time; again the halves came up right.

"That's very good," Maligie Kanu said, with a chuckle.

My turn came, so I crouched, poured a splash of rum, and offered words of commemoration.

I threw the kola nuts, which rolled and landed in the face-up position. A murmur ran around the dock at this third success.

"That's very good," said Maligie Kanu, smiling. "It means our prayers were accepted."

Maligie Kanu laughed, and so did the chief's wife. Madame Modu nodded, and made a smile that glowed like a flare.

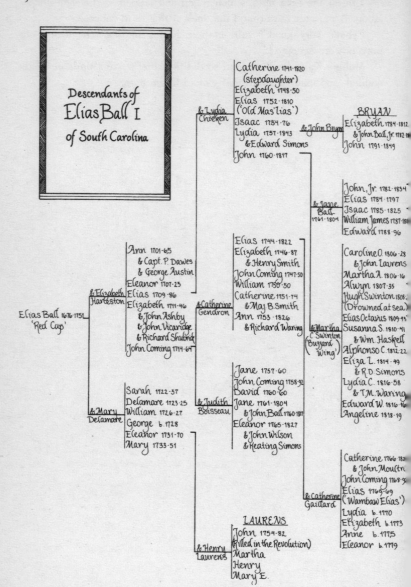

Descendants of
Elias Ball I
of South Carolina

Elias Ball 1676-1751
'Red Cap'

& Elizabeth Harleston

& Mary Delamare

& Lydia Chicken

Catherine 1741-1820 (stepdaughter)
Elizabeth 1748-50
Elias 1752-1810 ('Old Mas'Lias')
Isaac 1754-76
Lydia 1757-1843 & Edward Simons
John 1760-1817

& John Bryan

BRYAN
Elizabeth 1784-1812 & John Ball, Jr. 1782-18
John 1791-1849

& Jane Ball 1761-1804

John, Jr. 1782-1834
Elias 1784-1797
Isaac 1785-1825
William James 1787-18
Edward 1788-96

Ann 1701-65
& Capt. P. Dawes
& George Austin
Eleanor 1707-23
Elias 1709-86
Elizabeth 1711-46
& John Ashby
& John Vicaridge
& Richard Shubrick
John Coming 1714-64

& Catherine Gendron

Elias 1744-1822
Elizabeth 1746-87 & Henry Smith
John Coming 1747-50
William 1750-50
Catherine 1751-74 & May B. Smith
Ann 1753-1826 & Richard Waring

& Martha C. Swinton ('Buzzard Wing')

Caroline O. 1806-28 & John Lawrens
Martha A. 1806-16
Alwyn 1807-35
Hugh Swinton 1808- (Drowned at sea)
Elias Octarius 1809-45
Susanna S. 1810-41 & Wm. Haskell
Alphonso C. 1812-22
Eliza L. 1814-49 & R.D. Simons
Lydia C. 1816-58 & T.M. Waring
Edward W. 1816-16
Angeline 1818-19

Sarah 1722-37
Delamare 1723-25
William 1726-27
George b. 1728
Eleanor 1731-70
Mary 1733-51

& Judith Boisseau

Jane 1757-60
John Coming 1758-92
David 1760-60
Jane 1761-1804 & John Ball 1760-181
Eleanor 1765-1827 & John Wilson & Keating Simons

& Catherine Gaillard

Catherine 1766-182 & John Moultri
John Coming 1768-9
Elias 1769-69 ('Wambaw Elias')
Lydia b. 1770
Elizabeth b. 1773
Anne b. 1775
Eleanor b. 1779

& Henry Laurens

LAURENS
John 1754-82 (Killed in the Revolution)
Martha
Henry
Mary E.

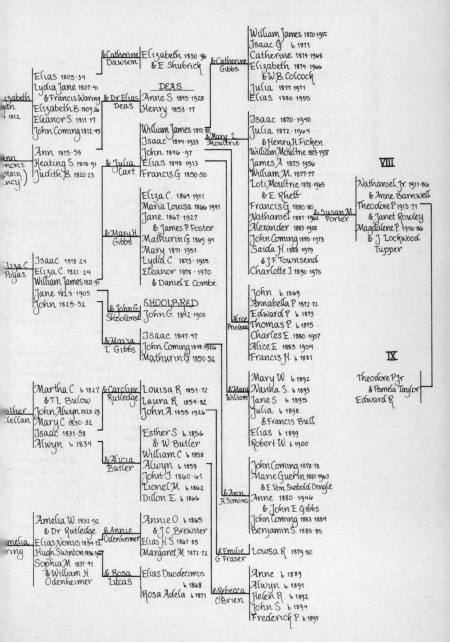

V | VI | VII | VIII | IX

VII (top):
William James 1870-1955
Isaac G. b. 1871
Catherine 1874-1968
Elizabeth 1874-1966 & W.B. Colcock
Julia 1877-1971
Elias 1880-1955
& Catherine Gibbs

VI:
& Catherine Dawson | Elizabeth 1830-96 & E. Shubrick

DEAS
& Dr Elias Deas | Anne S. 1845-1928 | Henry 1853-77

V:
Elias 1805-34
Lydia Jane 1807-41 & Francis Waring
Elizabeth B. 1809-26
Eleanor S. 1811-17
John Coming 1812-45
...zabeth jan ..1812

VI:
William James 1842-80 & Mary ? Moultrie
Isaac 1844-1933
John 1846-97
Elias 1848-1913
Francis G. 1850-50

VII:
Isaac 1870-1940
Julia 1872-1964 & Henry H. Ficken
William Moultrie 1873-1937
James A 1875-1956
William M. 1877-77
Loti Moultrie 1878-1965 & E. Rhett
Francis G. 1880-80
Nathaniel 1881-1962 & Susan M. Porter
Alexander 1883-1958
John Coming 1885-1973
Saida H. 1888-1979 & J.F. Townsend
Charlotte J. 1890-1975

VIII:
Nathaniel, Jr. 1911-86 & Anne Barnwell
Theodore P. 1913-71 & Janet Rowley
Magdalene P. 1916-86 & J. Lockwood Tupper

V:
Ann 1815-59
Keating S. 1818-91 & Julia Cart
Judith B. 1820-23
ann mons ..tain ncy')

VI:
& Mary H Gibbs
Eliza C. 1864-1951
Maria Louisa 1866-1941
Jane 1867-1927 & James P Foster
Mathurin G. 1869-94
Mary 1871-1951
Lydia C 1873-1935
Eleanor 1878-1970 & Daniel E Combe

SHOOLBRED
& John G. Shoolbred | John G. 1842-1900

VII:
John b.1869
Annabella P. 1872-72
Edward P. b 1873
Thomas P. b.1875
Charles E. 1880-1957
Alice E. 1883-1904
Francis H. b 1881
& Alice Prioleau

V:
Isaac 1818-24
Eliza C. 1821-24
William James 1821-91
Jane 1823-1905
John 1825-52
liza C Poyas

VI:
& Maria L Gibbs
Isaac 1847-47
John Coming 1848-1926
Mathurin G. 1850-52

VII:
Mary W. b.1892
Nantha S. b 1893 & Mary Wilson
Jane S. b 1895
Julia b 1898 & Francis Bull
Elias b 1899
Robert W. b 1900

IX:
Theodore P. Jr & Pamela Taylor
Edward R.

V:
Martha C. b.1827 & T.L. Bulow
John Alwyn 1828-29
Mary C. 1830-32
Isaac 1831-58
Alwyn b 1834
sther lellan

VI:
& Caroline Rutledge
Louisa R 1851-72
Laura R 1854-82
John A 1855-1926

Esther S. b.1856 & W Butler
William C b 1858
Alwyn b 1859
John J. 1860-61
Lionel M. b 1862
Dillon E. b 1866
& Alicia Butler

VII:
John Coming 1878-78
Marie Guerin 1881-1963 & E. Von Siebold Dingle
Anne 1880-1946 & John E Gibbs
John Coming 1883-1884
Benjamin S. 1885-85
& Ann H Simons

V:
Amelia W. 1832-92 & Dr Rutledge
Elias Nonus 1834-26
Hugh Swinton 1836-1900
Sophia M. 1837-91 & William H. Odenheimer
melia ring

VI:
& Annie Odenheimer
Annie O b.1865 & J C Brewster
Elias H.S 1867-85
Margaret M 1872-72

& Rosa Lucas
Elias Duodecimus b.1868
Rosa Adela b 1871

VII:
Louisa R 1879-80 & Emilie G Fraser

Anne b 1889
Alwyn b 1891
Helen R. b 1892
John S. b 1894
Frederick P. b 1895
& Rebecca O'Brien

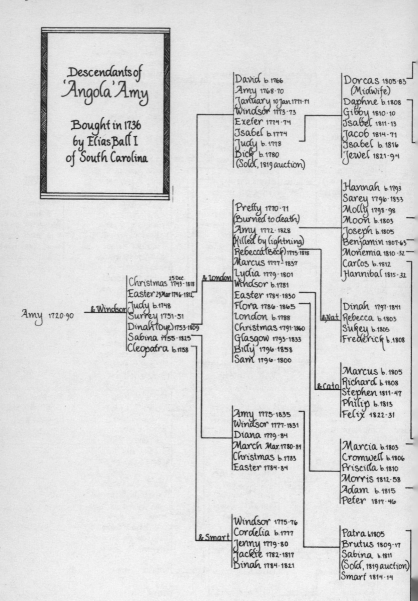

Descendants of
'Angola' Amy

Bought in 1736
by Elias Ball I
of South Carolina

David b.1766
Amy 1768-70
January 10 Jan 1771-71
Windsor 1773-73
Exeter 1774-74
Isabel b.1774
Judy b.1778
Dick b.1780
(Sold, 1819 auction)

Dorcas 1805-83
(Midwife)
Daphne b.1808
Gibby 1810-10
Isabel 1811-13
Jacob 1814-71
Isabel b.1816
Jewel 1821-94

Pretty 1770-71
(Burned to death)
Amy 1772-1828
(Killed by lightning)
Rebecca (Beck) 1775-1818
Marcus 1777-1837
Lydia 1779-1801
Windsor b.1781
Easter 1784-1830
Flora 1786-1865
London b.1788
Christmas 1791-1860
Glasgow 1793-1833
Billy 1796-1858
Sam 1796-1800

Hannah b.1793
Sarey 1796-1833
Molly 1798-98
Moon b.1803
Joseph b.1805
Benjamin 1807-63
Moriemia 1810-32
Carlos b.1812
Hannibal 1815-32

Amy 1720-90

& Windsor

Christmas 1743-1818 25 Dec
Easter 29 Mar 1746-1812
Judy b.1748
Surrey 1751-51
Dinah (Dye) 1753-1809
Sabina 1755-1825
Cleopatra b.1758

& London

Dinah 1797-1841
Rebecca b.1803
Sukey b.1805
Frederick b.1808

& Nat

Marcus b.1805
Richard b.1808
Stephen 1811-47
Philip b.1813
Felix 1822-31

& Cato

Amy 1775-1835
Windsor 1777-1831
Diana 1779-84
March Mar.1780-84
Christmas b.1783
Easter 1784-84

Marcia b.1803
Cromwell b.1806
Priscilla b.1810
Morris 1812-58
Adam b.1815
Peter 1817-46

& Smart

Windsor 1775-76
Cordelia b.1777
Jenny 1779-80
Jackie 1782-1817
Dinah 1784-1821

Patra b.1805
Brutus 1809-17
Sabina b.1811
(Sold, 1819 auction)
Smart 1814-14

V

PINCKNEY
Handy 1823-26
Gibby 1826-83
Nelson 1828-30
William 1830-31
Celia 1833-88
Daniel b.1840
Mary Ann b.1852
Judy b.1845

Billy b.1825
Patty b.1827
Sylvia 1830-51
Rachel 1832-33
Isaac b.1834

Christmas b.25 Dec 1835
Samuel b.1837
Joseph b.1839
Gabriel b.1843
Billy b.1846
Sander b.1850
Abraham b.1845
Flora b.1845
Emma b.1850
Vipper b.1852
William b.1850

Binah 1848-49
Monemia b.1850
Dinah b.1856
Hannah b.1863

Marcus 1821-9?
Mary b.1826
George b.1828
Job b.1830

WIGFALL
Mary b.1850
George 1856-56
Carlos b.1843
Ezekiel b.1845

Tiller b.1835
Giley b.1837
Abraham 1843-65
Pompey b.1846

ASH
Dinah b.1846
Phyllis b.1846
Ezekiel 1849-94
Sylvia b.1854
Nellie b.1855

Patty 1822-22
Drummer 1823-24
Mauney 1825-25
Sander b.1826

(margin left: surrey nckney, Maria, elta, nnah ubbs, anmy fall, ompey, annah)

VI

GREEN
Dorcas (Penny) 1854-1912   & Stephen
Binah b.1857   Green

PINCKNEY
Fanny 1864-65
Sarah 1866-66
Samuel 1867-86
Pompey b.1869
Gibby b.1870   & Judith
Percy b.1870
Dorcas b.1872
Lucy b.1876
Daniel 1876-88
Robert Rhodes b.1878
William 1881-96
Wat Surrey b.1884

JOHNSON
Bella 1861-62
Tom 1863-64
Thomas b.1865
Claus b.1867   & Claus
Easter b.1869   Johnson
Ben b.1876
Nancy b.1871
Susannah b.1874
William b.1879

TRENT
Josephine b.1877

SIMMONS
Cuffie b.1847
Patras b.1849
Devonshire b.1850   & Elsie
Sukey b.1851
Mary b.1853

WHITE
Gibby b.1855
Brawley 1858-1901   & Peter
Rebecca 1861-69
Jewel b.1865

Sarah b.1852   & Philip
Dinah b.1854
Abraham 1856-56

Heffy b.1853   & Carlos
Sukey b.1859
Nathan 1861-61
Binah b.1863

SINGLETON
Hannah b.1867
Judith b.1868   & Hannibal
Tara b.1869   Singleton
Windsor b.1869
Adam b.1872

VII

BLAKE
Celia (Diane) 1875-1912
Sylvia b.1877
Judy b.1879
George b.1881   & Thomas
Ezekiel 1884-85   Gadsden
Lavenia b.1886
Serena b.1887
Sarah b.1889

BROWN
Hannah b.1875
Stephen b.1878
Bella 1883-83
Christina b.1884
Jerry b.1887
Maria b.1891

VIII

GADSDEN
Belle ca. 1900-25
Sing ca. 1903-10
Vinnie ca. 1907-
Georgianna 1910-97
  & R. Richardson
Daniel 1912-72
B-Boy 1915-22

IX

RICHARDSON
Celia Ann b.1925
Rias b.1940
nephew

X

Barbara Jean b.1958
& Leroy Brown

XI

James Marcill b.1978
Steven b.1983
Shanice b.1988

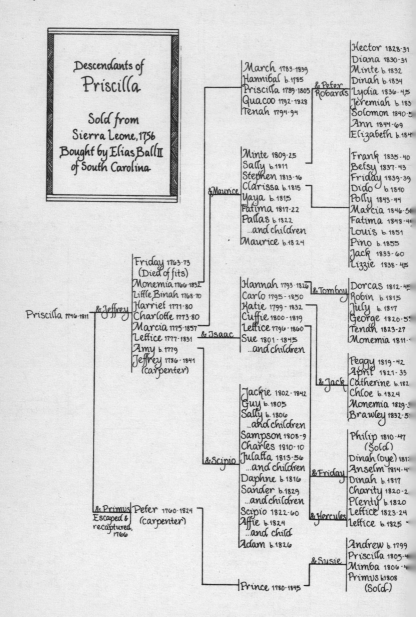

Generation I   II   III   IV

Descendants of Priscilla

Sold from Sierra Leone, 1756
Bought by Elias Ball II
of South Carolina

Priscilla 1746-1811 & Jeffrey

& Primus
(Escaped & recaptured 1766)

Generation II

- Friday 1763-73 (Died of fits)
- Monemia 1766-1832
- Little Binah 1768-70
- Harriet 1771-80
- Charlotte 1773-80
- Marcia 1775-1857
- Lettice 1777-1831
- Amy b.1779
- Jeffrey 1786-1841 (carpenter)
- Peter 1760-1824 (carpenter)

Generation III

March 1783-1839 & Maurice
Hannibal b.1785
Priscilla 1789-1805 & Peter Robards
Quaco 1792-1828
Tenah 1794-94

Minte 1809-25
Sally b.1811
Stephen 1813-16
Clarissa b.1815
Yaya b.1815
Fatima 1817-22
Pallas b.1822
...and children
Maurice b.1824

Hannah 1793-1826 & Tomboy
Carlo 1795-1850
Katie 1799-1832
Cuffie 1800-1819
Lettice 1796-1860
Sue 1801-1845
...and children

& Isaac

& Scipio
Jackie 1802-1842 & Jack
Guy b.1805
Sally b.1806
...and children
Sampson 1808-9
Charles 1810-10
Julatta 1813-56 & Friday
...and children
Daphne b.1816
Sander b.1829
...and children
Scipio 1822-60 & Hercules
Affie b.1824
...and child
Adam b.1826

Prince 1780-1845 & Susie

Generation IV

Hector 1828-31
Diana 1830-31
Minte b.1832
Dinah b.1834
Lydia 1836-45
Jeremiah b.183_
Solomon 1840-5_
Ann 1844-69
Elizabeth b.184_

Frank 1835-40
Betsy 1837-43
Friddy 1839-39
Dido b.1840
Polly 1843-44
Marcia 1846-5_
Fatima 1848-4_
Louis b.1851
Pino b.1855
Jack 1833-60
Lizzie 1838-45

Dorcas 1812-45
Robin b.1815
July b.1817
George 1820-5_
Tenah 1823-27
Monemia 1811-_

Peggy 1819-42
April 1821-33
Catherine b.182_
Chloe b.1824
Monemia 1829-3_
Brawley 1832-5_

Philip 1810-47 (Sold)
Dinah (dye) 181_
Anselm 1814-4_
Dinah b.1817
Charity 1820-2_
Plenty b.1820
Lettice 1823-24
Lettice b.1825

Andrew b.1799
Priscilla 1805-4_
Mimba 1806-1_
Primus b.1808 (Sold)

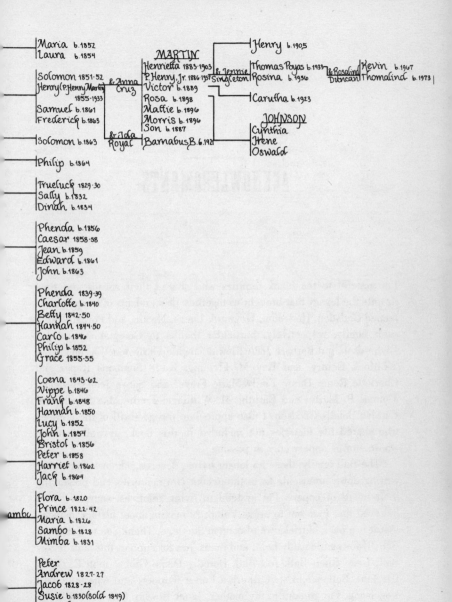

V   VI   VII   VIII

Maria b. 1852
Laura b. 1854

MARTIN

Henry b. 1905

Henrietta 1885-1903

Solomon 1851-52   & Anna   Thomas Poyas b. 1933   & Rosalind   Kevin b. 1967
Henry (P.Henry Martin)   Cruz   P. Henry, Jr. 1886 & Jennie Singleton   Duncan   Thomalind b. 1973
  1855-1933   Rosina b. 1956
Samuel b. 1861   Victor b. 1889
Frederick b. 1863   Rosa b. 1898
                                         Mattie b. 1896   Carutha b. 1923
Solomon b. 1863   & Ida   Morris b. 1896
                          Royal   Son b. 1887   JOHNSON
                                         Barnabus B. b. 1921   Cynthia
Philip b. 1864   Irene
                                                                   Oswald

Trueluck 1829-30
Sally b. 1832
Dinah b. 1834

Phenda b. 1856
Caesar 1858-58
Jean b. 1859
Edward b. 1861
John b. 1863

Phenda 1839-39
Charlotte b. 1840
Betty 1842-50
Hannah 1844-50
Carlo b. 1846
Philip b. 1852
Grace 1855-55

Coena 1843-62
Nippe b. 1846
Frank b. 1848
Hannah b. 1850
Lucy b. 1852
John b. 1854
Bristol b. 1856
Peter b. 1858
Harriet b. 1862
Jack b. 1864

Flora b. 1820
Prince 1822-42
amba   Maria b. 1826
Sambo b. 1828
Mimba b. 1831

Peter
Andrew 1827-27
Jacob 1828-28
Susie b. 1830 (sold 1849)
Hannah b. 1832
Toby b. 1834

＞•＊＞－❍－＜＊•＜

ACKNOWLEDGMENTS

I'm grateful to the black families who shared their stories and trust despite the legacy that brought us together: descendants of former slaves named Gadsden, Harleston, Hcyward, Lucas, Martin, and Poyas. Within each family, respectively, particular thanks to Georgianna Gadsden Richardson and Barbara Jean Brown; Edwina Harleston Whitlock, Mae Whitlock Gentry, and Ray M. Fleming; Katie Simmons Roper and Charlotte Roper Dunn; Emily Marie Frayer and Sonya Jean Fordham; Thomas P. Martin and Carutha M. Williams; Fredie Mae Smalls and Carolyn Smalls Goodson. I also appreciate the goodwill of the families who shared life histories not included in this book, as well as those whose stories appear only in passing.

The Ball family, those no longer living, deserve acknowledgment for writing down minuscule facts throughout two centuries and preserving their hoard of papers. I'm grateful to living relatives, some of whom believed that I set out to prove Voltaire's maxim about history, namely, that it is a pack of tricks we play upon the dead. Thank you to Nathaniel Ball III for gentlemanly help, and thank you for support to Frank Jervey Ball, Isaac Rhett Ball, Jeff Ball, Dorothy Dame Gibbs, John E. Gibbs III, Jane Ball Gilchrist, Catherine Porter Tupper, and Charlotte Ball Vogelsang. I'm grateful to my mother, Janet Rowley Ball, for being the independent woman she is; and to my late father, Theodore Porter Ball, for the memorable power of his conscience.

For initial support, thanks to Sharon Green and David Isay of National Public Radio, which helped to launch this project; and, for early encouragement, to members of the Afro-American Historical and Genealogical Society. I'm grateful to Lucy D. Rosenfeld for constructing provisional genealogies of families in slavery to the Balls, and to Lucinda Rosenfeld for her help and support. Researcher Cherisse R. Jones assisted in the first stage of work, and W. Marvin Dulaney of the Avery Research Center for African American History and Culture in Charleston gave key help when I asked. I appreciate those people, white and black, who contributed photographs to the book, as well as artwork from private collections. Rich-Steele Pro Labs of Charleston did careful reproductions of many borrowed and fragile images. Thanks to Ruth Holmes Whitehead of the Nova Scotia Museum for help in telling the stories of escaped slaves. At the archives that hold the Ball family papers, I'm grateful to the librarians and staff, especially Stephen Hoffius and Alex Moore; and the institutions that preserve these manuscripts themselves deserve recognition. Thanks to Jane Gilchrist for sharing her private collection of papers and photographs. Near the end of my travels, in Sierra Leone, Joseph Opala gave important help and guidance. I'm grateful to archaeologist Leland G. Ferguson of the University of South Carolina for his research on the Cooper River plantations; and to Tim Belshaw of Columbia, South Carolina, who made the maps.

I give affectionate thanks to Elizabeth Guckenberger for her sense of humor and devotion, and to Josephine Humphreys, for many encouragements. Jessica B. Cohen, a gifted investigator, contributed greatly, helping to bring the project from a middle wilderness to conclusion. Jessica Cohen also filled out and constructed two principal genealogies, those of Angola Amy and Priscilla, and executed the artwork that illustrates them. The book would not have been as rich or full of human detail without her help.

Last, and also first, I'm grateful to Jonathan Galassi and Roger Straus of Farrar, Straus and Giroux. Without their patient, detached, unquestioning support, I would not have so easily found my way.

SOURCES

The statement of events in this book grew from both manuscript sources and oral history. I tried to keep the textual strands of remembrance separate from spoken recollection, so that assertions might be tied to one or the other. When quoting documents, I preserved original spellings with the exception of proper names, some of which I updated. Transcripts of interviews have been selected from a larger group and edited. At times I made an effort to convey white or black dialect, but not fastidiously, since even when politely asked, print fails to communicate sound.

The records kept by the Ball family in the period 1700 to 1900 provided material for the spine of the narrative. Most of those papers have been microfilmed, and they are housed as follows:

Ball Family Papers, 1645–1920, South Carolina Historical Society, Charleston.

Ball Family Papers, 1696–1896, South Caroliniana Library, University of South Carolina, Columbia.

John Ball and Keating Simons Ball Books, 1779–1911, and William J. Ball books, 1804–90, Southern Historical Collection, University of North Carolina, Chapel Hill.

John Ball Sr. and John Ball Jr. Papers, 1773–1892, Special Col-
    lections Library, Duke University, Durham, North Carolina.

This is the right place to make a plea to the families of former slave
owners as well as any other collectors who continue to keep records
from the plantation period. Because the lives of slaves were chronicled
by their owners, not by government scribes, such private letters and
papers contain the family histories of millions. They should be donated
to public hands—archives, historical societies, museums, universities.

The writings of many historians have helped me to fix chronology
and interpret events, but with a three-hundred-year narrative span, a
list of titles would be mainly esoteric. I have cited some writers in the
notes, and other authorities (if still living) may recognize themselves in
my text. I am grateful to the deceased for their scholarship and to the
living for sympathy with the principle of conservation of space. Among
those historians still writing, for their work pertinent to South Carolina,
I looked frequently to Alpha Bah, Ira Berlin, Peter A. Coclanis, David
B. Davis, Leland G. Ferguson, Eric Foner, William W. Freehling, Christopher Fyfe, Eugene D. Genovese, Jack P. Greene, Graham R. Hodges,
Norrece T. Jones, Winthrop D. Jordan, Charles W. Joyner, Daniel C.
Littlefield, Philip D. Morgan, Bernard E. Powers Jr., Theodore Rosen-
garten, Margaret Washington, Robert M. Weir, and Peter H. Wood.

The most novel aspect of the documentary research was that on families
in slavery. To build a family history, I began with oral tradition from
the keepers of memory in a given family—corroborated by birth, marriage, and death records housed in county collections, as well as census
returns, wills, and probate documents at state archives. I confirmed a
lineage back to the years immediately after the Civil War. To link a
family in freedom to a family in slavery, I turned often to papers at the
National Archives and Records Administration, in Washington, D.C.,
including the following: (1) records of the Bureau of Refugees, Freedmen and Abandoned Lands (the Freedmen's Bureau), especially labor
(sharecrop) contracts for the years 1866–70, which contain an early use
of surnames by black Americans and connect individuals to plantations,
(2) registers of depositors in the Freedman's Savings and Trust Company
(banking records of recently freed blacks that sometimes refer to former

masters), and (3) military service records and pension claims for black veterans of the Civil War, who signed up with the Union once they were freed, which contain biographical information and (sometimes) references to birthplaces and plantations. The link to a plantation was confirmed by slave lists in the Ball files. Family trees for people in slavery were constructed from these same lists, which recorded births, deaths, and household arrangements. In state archives, wills and estate inventories, tax records, and deeds from slave sales sometimes filled gaps. Biographical facts about individual slaves came from correspondence kept by whites, and sometimes from oral history within black families. I identified the name and place of origin of two African women who founded families in America, and met some of their descendants, thanks only to the unusual completeness of records kept by slave owners named Ball.

>─⊷•⊶─◁

NOTES

1: PLANTATION MEMORIES

Page 7. **close to four thousand black people**: Estimate based on slave lists in: Ball Family Papers, 1645–1920, South Carolina Historical Society, Charleston; Ball Family Papers, 1696–1896, South Caroliniana Library, University of South Carolina, Columbia; John Ball and Keating Simons Ball Books, 1779–1911, William J. Ball Books, 1804–90, microfilm 1820-B, Southern Historical Collection, University of North Carolina, Chapel Hill; and John Ball Sr. and John Ball Jr. Papers, 1773–1892, Special Collections Library, Duke University, Durham, North Carolina. Ball papers in all collections are hereafter cited BP, and archives by abbreviation: South Carolina Historical Society = SCHS; South Caroliniana Library, University of South Carolina = USC; Southern Historical Collection, University of North Carolina = UNC; and Special Collections Library, Duke University = Duke.

Page 17. **thirty-four slaves**: *Heads of Families at the First Census of the United States Taken in the Year 1790—South Carolina* (Washington, D.C.: U.S. Government Printing Office, 1908), 40.

Page 18. **"Ball Family Papers"**: See note 1 and Sources.

Page 20. **at least 842 people were freed**: In 1865, The Blessing, Cedar Hill, Cherry Hill, Halidon Hill, and Limerick were owned by William James Ball (1821–91); Comingtee belonged to his cousin, Keating Simons Ball (1818–91). Hyde Park was the property of Maria Louisa Gibbs Ball, widow of John Ball (1825–52), and Quenby was owned by Jane Ball Shoolbred (1823–1905). Pawley and Buck Hall belonged to Elias Horry Deas, widower of Ann Ball Deas (1815–59); Dean Hall belonged Elias Nonus Ball (1834–72); Kensington and St. James belonged to the Ball family between 1747 and 1846; and Pimlico was Ball property from 1802 until 1844. Number of slaves on the plantations in 1865: Plantation book, 1804–90, BP-UNC; Record Book of Comingtee plantation, 1850–59, BP-Duke; and South Carolina Census, 1860, Slave Schedules,

Charleston District, which list Ball family slave owners and the number of people they owned.

Page 20. **at least seventy-five thousand living descendants**: I'm grateful to Allen Hutcheson of Charleston for this calculation.

Given 850 freed slaves, 1865, Berkeley County, SC:

1865 U.S. black population = approximately 4,000,000

1995 U.S. black population = 33,117,000

$$D_{n+1} = D_n(f) - ID_n(f)$$

D = number of descendants of Ball slaves

———

n = generation

$(n = 0 - 5)$

130 years 1865–1995

25 years for a generation (mean age of mother at births)

1865–1995 is 5.2 generations

———

f = average number of successful births

$(f = 3)$ derived as an average for African Americans based on whole population increase (ignoring the effects of black immigration to the United States)

Using 25-year generations, the population increases 8 times in five generations, meaning:

a replacement of 150 percent in each generation

3 children per couple (or $r = 1.62$)

———

I = rate of "inbreeding," i.e., marriage and partnering with other descendants of Ball slaves

$(I = 0.25)$

Each instance of inbreeding removes f descendants

I = number of instances per generation

  = ½ of people per generation who in-marry (expressed as a percentage)

An assumption based on relative stability of villages of freed slaves, 1865–1900: approximately half of the people in each generation, for the first three generations, marry or partner with other descendants.

———

$(D_0 = 400)$

Of 850, D_0 is the number still liable to have the full complement of children.

$D_0 = 400$

$D_1 = 400(3) - 0.25 \times 400(3) = 900$

$D_2 = 2,025$

$D_3 = 6,075$

$D_4 = 13,669$

$D_5 = 30,755$

$D_6 = 69,198$

In 1995, 69,168 descendants; in the year 2000, at least 75,000. In effect, some of generations 4, 5, and 6 would be alive in the year 2000. After 1920, the incidence of inmarriage decreases, due to migration of blacks to the North; a reasonable assumption is that inmarriage would decline sharply with the dissolution of earlier rural communities. If this single variable is decreased by one-half (from $I = 0.25$ to $I = 0.125$), the number of descendants increases by 33 percent (to 35,881 in generation 5, and 94,188 in generation 6), to approximately 100,000 in the year 2000.

Page 21. **his will filled four pages**: Will of Elias Ball, 31 Aug 1750, BP-SCHS.

2: MASTERS FROM ENGLAND

Page 22. **Elias Ball . . . was born**: Nan S. Ball, *Ball Family of Stoke-in-Teignhead, Devon, England*, pamphlet (Charleston, S.C.: 1944).

Page 23. **John Ball, the "mad priest of Kent"**: R. B. Dobson, ed., *The Peasants' Revolt of 1381* (New York: St. Martin's, 1970), 369–77; Rodney Hilton, *Bond Men Made Free: Medieval Peasant Movements and the English Rising of 1381* (New York: Viking, 1973), 213–22.

Page 26. **Uncle John . . . sailor**: Langdon Cheves, ed., *The Shaftesbury Papers and Other Records Relating to Carolina Prior to the Year 1676* (Charleston: South Carolina Historical Society, 1897), 231 n.

Page 29. **"a deep Chestnut Colour"**: Thomas Ashe, "Carolina, or a Description of the Present State of that Country . . . 1682," in *Narratives of Early Carolina, 1650–1708*, Alexander S. Salley Jr., ed. (New York: Barnes & Noble, 1911), 156.

Page 29. **women practiced abortion**: Robert Ferguson, "The Present State of Carolina with Advice to the Settlers" (1682), and J. F. D. Smyth, "A Tour of the United States of America . . . with a Description of the Indian Nations" (1784), quoted in Gene Waddell, *Indians of the South Carolina Lowcountry 1562–1751* (Columbia: University of South Carolina, 1980), 8–9.

Page 30. **Fundamental Constitutions**: A copy of the Fundamental Constitutions: *Abstracts of Grants and Commissions of Lords Proprietors, 1692–1718, 1733–1736, 1775–1820*, part 2, 41–46, South Carolina Department of Archives and History, Columbia, S.C. (hereafter, SCDAH).

Page 30. **a kidnap-and-sale system**: John Wesley, A.M., *Thoughts on Slavery*, pamphlet (London, 1774), 4–10.

Page 31. **"does thereby put himself into a State of War"**: John Locke, *Two Treatises on Government* (London: J. Whiston, 1772), Second Treatise, chap. 3, section 17.

Page 32. **first Carolina slave raid**: Murder: Gov. Joseph West to Anthony Lord Ashley, 3 Sep 1671, in Cheves, ed., *Shaftesbury Papers*, 336; "Warr": Grand Council Journal, 27 Sep 1671, *Journal of the Grand Council of South Carolina, 25 August 1671–24 June 1680*, A. S. Salley, ed. (Columbia, S.C.: Historical Commission of South Carolina, 1907); "transport the said Indians": Grand Council Journal, 2 Oct 1671; wall around village: Anthony Lord Ashley to John Yeamans, 18 Sep 1671, *Shaftesbury Papers*, 343.

Page 34. **An inventory of the contents of the dwelling**: Inventory of goods belonging to Mr. John Harleston, 1631, and Elizabeth Harleston to David Edwards, power of attorney, 1 Aug 1659, BP-SCHS.

Page 34. **John Coming . . . returned with . . . indentured servants**: John Coming, warrant, 22 Nov 1672, in *Warrants for Land in South Carolina 1672–1711*, A. S. Salley, ed. (Columbia, S.C.: University of South Carolina, 1973).

Page 35. **"one and twenty lashes upon his naked back"**: Grand Council Journal, 4 Jun 1672.

Page 35. **a name, Charlestown**: Grand Council Journal, 1 Jun 1680, a hearing "before the Grand Council at Kiawah sometimes called Charlestowne."

Page 35. **John Coming . . . turned in some warrants for land**: Henry A. M.

Smith, *Rivers and Regions of Early South Carolina* (Charleston: South Carolina Historical Society, 1988), 27–31; "Granted to Cap¹ John Coming one Town lott N° 49 by Governor Joseph West 1680 March the fifth," Lands granted to Elias Ball the first, BP-SCHS.

Page 35. **Coming's T**: Between 1672 and his death in 1695, John Coming was given five land grants: 17 Oct 1672, 375 acres on Oyster Point; 27 Nov 1672, 810 acres; 30 Nov 1678, 740 acres [Coming's T]; 10 Nov 1680, "one towne lott"; 30 Apr 1681, 210 acres (Salley, *Warrants for Land*). A 1682 map ("A New Map of the Country of Carolina," by Joel Gascoyne) shows a promontory where Goose Creek meets the Cooper River, labeled "Commins" (Coming's) land. This tract, perhaps the 810 acres taken up in November 1672, seems to have been sold before Coming's death. Another 150–200 acres was ceded back to the colony in 1672 to endow the Anglican church.

Page 36. **"live oak, hickory, pine"**: Plat of Strawberry plantation, 17 Oct 1680, BP-SCHS.

Page 36. **the Natives made room**: Waddell, *Indians*; George D. Terry, " 'Champaign Country': A Social History of an Eighteenth Century Lowcountry Parish in South Carolina, St. Johns Berkeley County" (Ph.D. dissertation, University of South Carolina, 1981), 36.

Page 36. **a simple wooden cottage**: Anne Simons Deas, *Recollections of the Ball Family of South Carolina and the Comingtee Plantation* (Charleston, 1909), reprint (Charleston: South Carolina Historical Society, 1978), 12.

Page 37. **Africans and Natives built . . . shelters**: Leland Ferguson, *Uncommon Ground: Archaeology and Early African America, 1650–1800* (Washington, D.C.: Smithsonian Institution, 1992), chap. 3.

Page 38. **a four-year-old [child]**: Grand Council Journal, 23 Oct 1671.

Page 38. **John Coming died**: Cheves, *Shaftesbury Papers*, 231 n; Will of John Coming, 20 Aug 1694, Charleston County Wills, Works Progress Administration transcripts, Charleston County Library, Charleston (hereafter, Charleston Wills).

Page 38. **"All Negroes, Mollatoes, and Indians"**: M. Eugene Sirmans, "The Legal Status of the Slave in South Carolina, 1670–1740," *Journal of Southern History* 28, no. 4 (Nov 1962).

Page 38. **"my sad state of widowhood"**: A copy of Mrs. Affra Coming's letter to her sister Ann Harleston Bulkeley, 1696, BP-SCHS.

Page 39. **the option fell to Elias**: Nan S. Ball, *Ball Family of Stoke-in-Teignhead*.

Page 39. **Affra . . . etymology**: Isaac Taylor, M.A., *Words and Places, or Etymological Illustrations of History Ethnology and Geography* (London, 1909), 56, 368; Genesis 25:4, Micah 1:10.

Page 40. **"I Give unto yᵉ sᵈ John Harleston & Elias Ball all my Negroes"**: Will of Affra Coming, 28 Dec 1698, Charleston Wills.

Page 40. **Elias Ball sailed into the harbor**: No precise record of Elias Ball's arrival in South Carolina survives, but two pieces of evidence make summer or fall of 1698 nearly certain. A letter written by Affra Coming to her sister Elizabeth Harleston in March 1698 shows that neither the Harleston nor the Ball heir has yet come to Charleston (quoted in Deas, *Recollections of the Ball Family*, 29–30), while Elias Ball's mention in the 28 Dec 1698 will of Affra Coming suggests that he has since arrived. The will gives a bequest to John Harleston "of Dublin in yʳ Kingdom of Ireland" as well as "to Elias Ball," whose whereabouts are not stated, presumably because he is already in the colony.

Page 41. **3,800 free whites and 3,000 slaves**: Peter H. Wood, *Black Majority:*

Negroes in Colonial South Carolina from 1670 through the Stono Rebellion (New York: Knopf, 1974), 26 n, 144.

Page 42. **the "most noted plantations"**: Terry, " 'Champaign Country,' " 66; John Oldmixon, "The History of the British Empire in America, 1708," *Narratives of Early Carolina*, Salley, ed., 366.

Page 42. **"I sent my fouor Cheldren to Mr. Faur"**: Memorandum, 23 Jan 1721, Account and Blanket Book, 1720–78, BP-SCHS.

3: THE WELL OF TRADITION

Page 43. **a distant cousin, Elias Ball Bull**: Author's conversations with Elias Ball Bull, Charleston.

Page 44. **Bull . . . tried to fight the uprising**: Edward McCrady, *History of South Carolina Under the Royal Government, 1719–1776* (New York: MacMillan, 1899), 794–95.

Page 44. **Elias Ball . . . commission his portrait**: Elias Ball, oil on canvas, ca. 1740s, by Jeremiah Theus, private collection; a copy of the painting is in the collection of the Gibbes Museum of Art, Charleston.

Page 50. **Dorothy Dame Gibbs . . . Ball family lore**: Author's conversation with Dorothy Dame Gibbs, Charleston.

Page 56. **Work House . . . floggings for a fee**: Thomas G. Finklea to John Ball, 26 Oct 1827, 8 Mar 1832, and 11 Oct 1833, BP-SCHS; "[18 Nov 1819] Work house fees for confinement of Joe . . . $65.25," "Oct 14, 1828 paid W. E. Gordon, work house fees for Town, $8.87," in Pimlico plantation book, 1810–30, BP-Duke; Charles R. Simpson to Isaac Ball, 15 Mar 1814, BP-SCL.

Page 56. **receipts for slave purchases**: Bill of sale, "mulatto fellow Sam," John Ball to Banks & Lockwood, merchant, 27 Jan 1803, Misc. records, vol. 3X, p. 525; bill of sale, "man named George," Martha C. Ball to Herman Bourhaus, 13 Feb 1821, Misc. records, vol. 4V, 83; bills of sale, "girl named Mary," Elias O. Ball to Thomas Waring, n.d. Dec 1839, and "girl named Nancy," Elias O. Ball to Mrs. E. Belin, 17 Dec 1839, Misc. records, vol. 5W, 90–91; bill of sale, "Lewis and Daniel," James Poyas, exor., est. Isaac Ball to Wm. W. Smith, 10 Jan 1845, vol. 6A, 335, all at SCDAH.

4: BRIGHT MA

Page 70. **a slave named Tenah . . . Mende**: Tenah: List of Negroes at Limerick, 25 Mar 1806, BP-SCHS; provenance of names: Professor Alpha Bah, Department of History, College of Charleston, S.C., and Prof. Akintola Wyse, Fourah Bay College, Freetown, Sierra Leone; villages: A. P. Kup, *Sierra Leone: A Concise History* (New York: St. Martin's Press, 1975), 35, 38 (map).

Page 71. **"I . . . give to my said nephew"**: Will of Elias Ball, 6 Dec 1809, Charleston Wills; plantation record book, 1803–34, BP-UNC.

Page 72. **his specialty . . . pigeons**: Thomas G. Finklea to John Ball, 19 Oct and 15 Nov 1833, BP-SCHS.

Page 72. **another child, Binah**: Plantation record book, 1818–33, BP-UNC.

Page 72. **Tenah and Adonis . . . felt the whip**: Thomas G. Finklea to John Ball, 26 Oct 1827, BP-SCHS.

Page 73. **"the torturing lash"**: *American Slavery As It Is: Testimony of a Thousand Witnesses* (American Anti-Slavery Society, 1839), reprint (New York: Arno Press, 1968), 52–54.

Page 73. **the plantation infirmary**: Ann Ball to John Ball, 27 Nov 1823, Thomas G. Finklea to John Ball, 2 Aug 1833, BP-SCHS.

Page 73. **most of his belongings . . . were auctioned**: Will of John Ball, 26 Jun 1834, Charleston Wills; List of Negroes belonging to Mrs. Ann Ball purchased from the estate of John Ball (1834), BP-SCHS.

Page 75. **the lawsuit . . . divided the slaves**: Keating S. Ball, bond, 1843, and E. R. Laurens, report, Charleston Library Society (hereafter, CLS); Mortgage, Elias Horry Deas and Keating S. Ball . . . Lydia Jane Waring, 1 Mar 1841, Misc. records, vol. 5S, 123, SCDAH.

Page 75. **their village . . . split in two**: Plantation Record book, 1849–71, BP-UNC; Comingtee plantation Blanket Book, 1841–61, Charleston Museum, Charleston (the notation EHD, for Elias Horry Deas, appears next to the names of people selected to move to Buck Hall).

Page 75. **Buck Hall, a 635-acre plantation**: Berkeley County, South Carolina, Register of Mesne Conveyance, A11-41 (hereafter, RMC).

Page 76. **"He could not get along with" the black people**: Misc. note, Anne S. Deas, private collection, Charleston.

Page 76. **Federal soldiers . . . headed for the slave street**: Statement of possession of Buck Hall and Washington plantations, F. M. Montell, Commander of the *Potomaska*, 9 Mar 1865, Elias H. Deas to Anne S. Deas, 5 May 1865, E. H. Deas papers, SCL.

Page 77. **Katie Roper**: Author's conversations with Heyward-Roper family, South Carolina.

Page 78. **Katie . . . became . . . Mrs. Heyward**: Moncks Corner, South Carolina, labor contracts, Jan–May 1866, vol. 237, entry 3286, record group 105, Bureau of Refugees, Freedmen and Abandoned Lands, National Archives, Washington, D.C. (hereafter, Freedmen's Bureau, National Archives).

Page 86. **Heyward clan . . . numbered more than 150**: Heyward Family Reunion, booklet, Jul 1995, private collection.

5: A FAMILY BUSINESS

Page 89. **the "pest house"**: An Act for the . . . Defence of this Province, 12 Jul 1707, in Nicholas Trott, "The Laws of the Province of South Carolina" (1719), part II, no. 5, p. 23, SCDAH.

Page 89. **forty percent of . . . Africans . . . came through Charleston**: Elaine Nichols, "Sullivan's Island Pest Houses: Beginning an Archaeological Investigation," conference paper, Archaeology and the Black Experience, University of Mississippi, Oxford, 17–20 May 1989; Wood, *Black Majority*, xiv.

Page 90. **"what for Filth, putrid Air, and 'putrid Dysenteries' "**: Alexander Garden, quoted in Edmund Berkeley and Dorothy Smith Berkeley, *Dr. Alexander Garden of Charles Town* (Chapel Hill: University of North Carolina, 1969), 124; corpses: *South Carolina Gazette*, 8 Jun 1769. (Eighteenth- and nineteenth-century South Carolina newspapers are collected at the Charleston Library Society, Charleston, and in various collections.)

Page 90. **"15 negro men [and] 15 Indian women"**: Early agriculture: John Norris, "Profitable Advice for Rich and Poor . . . a Description, or True Relation of South Carolina" (1712), in *Selling a New World: Two Colonial South Carolina Promotional Pamphlets*, Jack Greene, ed. (Columbia, S.C.: University of South Carolina, 1989); John Lawson, *A New Voyage to Carolina* (1709), reprint (Readex Microprint Corporation,

1966); Lewis Cecil Gray, *History of Agriculture in the Southern United States to 1860* (New York: Peter Smith, 1941), I:153–60; Account and Blanket Book, 1720–78, BP-SCHS.

Page 92. **Anabaptists . . . refused to buy slaves**: Terry, " 'Champaign Country,' " 48–52, 88; J. Russell Cross, *Historic Ramblin's Through Berkeley* (Columbia, S.C.: R. L. Bryan, 1985), 130–32.

Page 92. **uprising of Native slaves**: A. S. Salley, ed., *Commissions and Instructions from the Lords Proprietors of Carolina Public Officials to Public Officials of South Carolina, 1685–1715* (Columbia, S.C.: Historical Commission of South Carolina, 1916), 144.

Page 93. **the Balls expanded operations**: Lands granted to Elias Ball the first, and Memorial of several tracts of land belonging to Elias Ball of St. Johns Parish in Berkly County, BP-SCHS.

Page 93. **between £20 and £30 per adult**: People sold in Virginia, 1699–1708, cost of indentured servants in late 1600s; Gray, *History of Agriculture*, I:368–70.

Page 93. **Native workers . . . purchased with animal skins**: Minutes, 17 Apr 1712, 4 May 1714, A. S. Salley, ed., *Journal of the Commissioners of the Indian Trade of South Carolina September 20, 1710–April 12, 1715* (Columbia, S.C.: Historical Commission of South Carolina, 1926).

Page 94. **Elias's neighborhood . . . the domestic slave trade**: Strawberry Ferry: An additional act for the making of high ways, and for appointing a ferry over ye Western Branch of Cooper River, 17 Feb 1705, BP-SCHS; slave raid: Verner W. Crane, *The Southern Frontier, 1670–1732* (Durham, N.C.: Duke University, 1928), 147.

Page 94. **"He had frequently commanded scouting parties after Indians"**: A short history of the family of the Balls since my grandfather settled in South Carolina, wrote by John Ball (1786), BP-SCL.

Page 94. **children who lived past infancy**: Ball family genealogy, in Deas, *Recollections of the Ball Family*, 184–85.

Page 94. **John Harleston . . . moved to the opposite end of Comingtee**: John Ball, Chronicles of Comingtee (1892), BP-Duke.

Page 95. **fifteen Native nations formed an alliance**: Appeals to colonial government: Minutes, Commissioners of the Indian Trade, Salley, ed., throughout; Yamasee War: Crane, *Southern Frontier*, 166–184; George Chicken, "1715 . . . Journal of the March into the Cherokee Mountains in the Yemassee War," *Year Book of the City of Charleston, 1894* (Charleston), 342–52; John Barnwell, Map showing the route . . . from North Carolina in 1715 to aid South Carolina during the Yamasee War, SCHS; Captain Elias Ball: Officer's commission, Gov. Charles Craven to Capt. Ball, 4 Apr 1715, private collection; "Military Men . . . bent upon Revenge": Gideon Johnston, Charleston, to Secretary of the Society for the Propagation of the Gospel, London, 19 Dec 1715, quoted in Crane, *Southern Frontier*, 179; "not to buy . . . slaves above the age of 14 years": 10 Jul 1716, Commissioners of the Indian Trade.

Page 96. **Elias acquired still more land**: Land records, 1680–1842 & n.d., and Memorial of several tracts of land belonging to Elias Ball, BP-SCHS; names of tracts deduced from Will of Elias Ball, 31 Aug 1750, BP-SCHS.

Page 97. **Elizabeth "was taken with a Malignant Fever"**: John Harleston (South Carolina) to Ann Bulkeley (Dublin), Feb 1721, quoted in Deas, *Recollections of the Ball Family*, 35–36.

Page 97. **Elias bought a new account book**: Account and Blanket Book, 1720–78, BP-SCHS.

Page 97. **"Bella had of me 3 yards of negero cloth"**: Bella: memoranda, 10 Nov 1720 (cloth), n.d. Nov 1749 (blankets), 20 Oct 1753 (shoes), Account and Blanket Book, 1720–78; first . . . purchase of people: slave lists for 1721, Account and Blanket Book, 1720–78, BP-SCHS.

Page 98. **slow . . . slave traffic**: Wood, *Black Majority*, 151.

Page 98. **Fatima**: Biography: memoranda, "1721—Bought . . . Fatima," "Born 1725—Pino (Fatima's girl)," "Giley, Fatima's son was born [23 Apr 1742]" (disappears after birth, perhaps dead), Account and Blanket Book, 1720–78, BP-SCHS.

Page 99. **the market, one Saturday each month**: An act for settling a fair and market in Childsberry Town in St. Johns Parish in Berkly County (1723), BP-SCHS.

Page 100. **"Taken with the runaway Negroes . . . a jacket and britches"**: 4 Sep 1731, Account and Blanket Book, 1720–78, BP-SCHS.

Page 100. **law concerning the treatment of runaway slaves**: "Acts for the Better Ordering of Slaves," Thomas Cooper, ed., *The Statutes at Large of South Carolina* (Columbia, S.C.: 1837), Act #314, 7 Jun 1712.

Page 100. **Elias hired a music teacher**: Memoranda, 1722/3, 1731, 1735, Account and Blanket Book, 1720–78, BP-SCHS.

Page 101. **4,328 acres and forty-three slaves**: Property in 1727: Terry, " 'Champaign Country,' " 331–35; overseers and new house: May 1721, Sep 1722, ca. 1736, Account and Blanket Book, 1720–78, BP-SCHS.

Page 103. **The first rice fields**: Gray, *History of Agriculture*, I:278–286.

Page 105. **"the name that stands out . . . is 'Dolly' "**: Deas, *Recollections of the Ball Family*, 169; "Molattoe Wench": Will of Elias Ball, 31 Aug 1750, BP-SCHS; death of Dolly: "Old Dolly died ye 5 Dec 1774, age 62," Account and Blanket Book, 1720–78, BP-SCHS.

Page 106. **evidence of white-black sex**: Legislation against: Wood, *Black Majority*, 99; La Salle case: Grand Council Journal, 6 May 1692.

Page 106. **Dolly was born in 1712**: Biography of Dolly: memoranda, 13 May 1727 and 28 Jan 1728 (doctor), n.d. 1745 (shoes), April 1735 (Cupid), Account and Blanket Book, 1720–78, BP-SCHS.

Page 107. **Dolly gave birth to . . . [a] child . . . Edward**: Birth: 16 Sep 1740, Account and Blanket Book, 1720–78, BP-SCHS; sister: Catherine Johnston, receipt for legacy, 5 Feb 1821, papers of Edward Tanner, in BP-Duke; as executor of sister's estate: "Citation to Edward Tanner to administer on estate of Free Kate . . . 5 Sep 1768," Abstracts from Records of the Court of Ordinary, *South Carolina Historical and Genealogical Magazine* (hereafter, *SCHM*) vol. 27 (1926).

Page 108. **"frequent less with their black Lovers the open Lots"**: *South Carolina Gazette*, 18 Mar 1732; "Africain Ladies": 24 Jul 1736.

6: WRITTEN IN THE BLOOD

Page 111. **Carolyn Goodson's family**: Author's conversations with Smalls and Goodson families, Pennsylvania.

Page 118. **Frederick Poyas . . . mulatto**: Census of the United States, 1880, Charleston County, South Carolina, Parish of St. Thomas & St. Denis, enumeration district 97, p. 44; birth lists, Cedar Hill, cloth list for 1850, Limerick cloth list, 1851, in Plantation Book, 1804–90, BP-UNC.

Page 121. **James Poyas . . . inherited money from Isaac Ball**: Will of Isaac Ball, 15 Nov 1825, Charleston Wills; Mathurin G. Gibbs to Isaac Ball 11 Feb 1825,

16 Feb 1825, and Conveyance, Cedar Hill plantation, James Poyas to William James Ball, 1 Jan 1850, BP-SCL; William J. Ball and James Poyas, 4 Feb 1850, Charleston County RMC, E-12, 343; Henry A. M. Smith, *The Baronies of South Carolina* (Charleston: South Carolina Historical Society, 1931), 172.

Page 131. **the trial of his accused killer**: *State of South Carolina* v. *Tony Lewis McNeil II* (1996), case #E-291072, Ninth Judicial Circuit, Charleston County.

7: THE MAKING OF A DYNASTY

Page 134. **Angola Amy**: "Bought—1736 . . . Amey," later "Angola Amey," Account and Blanket Book, 1720–78, BP-SCHS; Wood, *Black Majority*, Appendix C.

Page 135. **Amy and Windsor worked . . . until . . . 1790**: Amy and Windsor and their progeny: A list of Negroes the property of Elias Ball made the 12th day of May 1784; death dates: [List of] Superannuated Negroes as Incumbrance, in Appraisement and division of the Negroes late the property of Elias Ball (1787), BP-SCHS; Cheryll Ann Cody, "There Was No 'Absalom' on the Ball Plantations: Slave-Naming Practices in the South Carolina Low Country, 1720–1865," *American Historical Review* 92 (Jun 1987). Amy's relationship with Windsor is hypothesized from this evidence: (1) on two lists of slaves, made years apart, Amy and Windsor share a house; and (2) in context of the slave practice of naming children after grandparents, four of Angola Amy's grandchildren would carry the name Windsor. Amy's family tree: research by Lucy D. Rosenfeld and Jessica B. Cohen; tree constructed by Jessica B. Cohen.

Page 135. **slave dealers [in] "Angola"**: Daniel C. Littlefield, *Rice and Slaves: Ethnicity and the Slave Trade in Colonial South Carolina* (Chicago: University of Illinois, 1991), 41–44; John K. Thornton, "African Dimensions of the Stono Rebellion," *American Historical Review*, 96:4 (Oct 1991), 1101–13; Joseph Miller, *Way of Death: Merchant Capitalism and the Angolan Slave Trade, 1730–1830* (Madison: University of Wisconsin, 1988).

Page 137. **pay . . . for . . . extra work**: Memoranda, Jan 1728, Jan 1736, and 1740, Account and Blanket Book, 1720–78, BP-SCHS.

Page 138. **"task system"**: Philip D. Morgan, "Work and Culture: The Task System and the World of Lowcountry Blacks, 1700 to 1880," *William and Mary Quarterly*, 39:4 (1982), 563–99.

Page 139. **Hannah . . . grew . . . tobacco**: Account and Blanket Book, 1720–78, BP-SCHS.

Page 139. **[Elias] would move to . . . Charleston**: Conveyance, Elias Ball Sr. to Elias Ball Jr., 1000 acres, Aug 1733, BP-SCL; memoranda, May 1738 and "5 February [1739]—My father went down to live being of a Tuesday," Account and Blanket Book, 1720–78, BP-SCHS.

Page 140. **The rebellion started on a Sunday**: John K. Thornton, "African Dimensions of the Stono Rebellion"; Wood, *Black Majority*, 314–26.

Page 140. **Elias . . . in the fort**: Deas, *Recollections of the Ball Family*, 47.

Page 141. **Negro Act of 1740**: Joseph Brevard, *An Alphabetical Digest of the Public Statute Law of South-Carolina* (Charleston, 1814), II:228–44.

Page 141. **Charleston had grown**: Peter A. Coclanis, *The Shadow of a Dream: Economic Life and Death in the South Carolina Low Country, 1670–1920* (New York: Oxford University Press, 1989), Introduction.

Page 142. **Elias's townhouse . . . overlooking the wharfs**: Plat, 17 Oct 1750

. . . Showing dispute between Charles Pinckney and Jonathan Scott, by surveyor Thomas Blythe, SCHS.

Page 142. **Dolly . . . lived with the old man**: Memoranda, "[22 Jun 1742] Dolly went too town by water with Mrs. Dogett," "[23 Dec 1742] Sanders Doleys son was born," Account and Blanket Book, 1720–78, BP-SCHS.

Page 142. **Elias sold two men**: Misc. records, 20 Nov 1741, vol. EE, 102–108, SCDAH.

Page 142. **a painter named Jeremiah Theus**: Margaret S. Middleton, *Jeremiah Theus: Colonial Artist of Charles Town* (Columbia, S.C.: University of South Carolina, 1953).

Page 144. **[John Coming] called his new stake Hyde Park**: Smith, *Baronies of South Carolina*, 33. Smith confuses Hyde Park with Kensington plantation, purchased in 1747 by Elias Ball II.

Page 145. **a builder named Amos**: Memoranda, 20 Oct 1741, 4 Aug 1743, 8 Oct 1743, Mar 1745, Account and Blanket Book, 1720–78, BP-SCHS.

Page 146. **Second Elias . . . felt . . . isolated**: Deas, *Recollections of the Ball Family*, 66–69; Alexander Murfee to Elias Ball, 5 Aug 1763, and memoranda, 25 Mar 1740, 22 Jan 1741, Account and Blanket Book 1720–78, BP-SCHS.

Page 146. **Second Elias . . . Kensington**: Richard Gough to Elias Ball, 27 Feb 1747, Charleston deeds, vol. 2F, 51–55, SCDAH.

Page 147. **Lydia Chicken brought [slaves]**: "Ratclif and Amey," Jenny Buller, Account and Blanket Book, 1720–78, BP-SCHS.

Page 148. **"name of 'Jenny Buller' "**: Deas, *Recollections of the Ball Family*, 163–64.

Page 148. **1748 . . . slave . . . conspiracy**: Report: South Carolina Council Journal, #17 (20 Dec 1748–16 Dec 1749), SCDAH; Akinfield: Smith, *Baronies of South Carolina*, 174; Cornelia: memorandum, Jun–Aug 1738, "Cornelah, from Feb . . . to August . . . 22 weeks at £30," Account and Blanket Book, 1720–78, BP-SCHS; Thom Paine: memorandum, 14 Aug 1739, "[to Mrs. Elizabeth Harleston] a bottel of rum lent you sent by Tompane," Account and Blanket Book, 1720–78; Tom White: 1777 list of male slaves and where born, "Tomwhit — Angola — [age] 55," May 1751 slave list (Tom White, Carolina, Pompey, and Violet), Account and Blanket Book, 1720–78; Carolina: "Runaway from my plantation . . . Carolina," *South Carolina Gazette*, 4 May 1752.

Page 153. **The wedding took place at Comingtee**: Cross, *Historic Ramblin's Through Berkeley*, 53.

Page 154. **largest slave trader in the British colonies**: Richard Waterhouse, *South Carolina's Colonial Elite: A Study in the Social Structure and Political Culture of a Southern Colony, 1670–1760* (Ph.D. dissertation, Johns Hopkins University, 1973), 160–65.

Page 154. **"I, Elias Ball of Charles Town"**: Will of Elias Ball, 31 Aug 1750, BP-SCHS.

Page 154. **Elias died**: No record of the death or burial of Elias Ball survives, but the last week of September 1751 is most likely. In a posthumous inventory of Elias Ball's property, begun October 4, 1751, there is a slave child named Surrey, listed as a son of Angola Amy. According to slave lists in Elias's Account and Blanket Book, 1720–78, Surrey was born September 25, 1751, and died soon after. Because the infant appears in the inventory, Elias died after September 25 and before October 4.

Page 154. **a posthumous inventory**: Inventory of Elias Ball, 8 Nov 1751, Charleston inventories, vol. R(1), 119–25, SCDAH.

8: SAWMILL

Page 157. **Georgianna Gadsden Richardson**: Author's conversations with Gadsden-Richardson family, South Carolina.

Page 158. **Comingtee, the first Ball plantation . . . [and] one of the last**: Will of Affra Coming, 28 Dec 1698, Charleston Wills; Irving, John B. Irving, *Day on Cooper River*, Louisa Cheves Stoney, ed. (Columbia, S.C.: R. L. Bryan, 1969), 80, 125; conveyances of Comingtee: Ann Deas to Alwyn Ball Jr., 1 Jan 1901; Union Corp. to Comingtee Corp., 1 Apr 1918; Comingtee Corp. to Joseph Frelinghuysen, 19 May 1927; Leigh Banana Case Company to WestVaco, 28 Jun 1949, Berkeley County RMC, books C-4, 793; C-19, 537; A-55, 195; and C-46, 58.

Page 162. **Maum Mary Ann [and family]**: Deas, *Recollections of the Ball Family*, 166; eulogy: Keating Simons Ball Plantation Journal, 1850–59, 1866, BP-Duke; Mary Ann Royal and Surrey Pinckney, memoranda, 6 Feb 1862 and 31 March 1866, Plantation Record Book, 1849–90, BP-SCL; Celia Pinckney birthdate: Plantation Record Book, 1803–34, BP-UNC.

Page 163. **Daniel . . . was whipped**: Thomas G. Finklea to John Ball, 11 Oct 1833, BP-SCHS.

Page 171. **"The negro cemetery . . . a grove of tall white-oaks"**: Deas, *Recollections of the Ball Family*, 15, 151.

Page 173. **a couple on Comingtee, Binah and Brawley**: Ibid., 166–68.

Page 175. **the great-great-great-great-great-granddaughter of Angola Amy**: Angola Amy: "Slaves born and bought, 1721–36," and later birth lists, Account and Blanket Book, 1720–78, BP-SCHS; Plantation Record Books, 1779–1817 and 1803–34, BP-UNC; Will of Elias Ball [III], 6 Dec 1809, Charleston Wills; Plantation Record Book, 1849–90, BP-SCL; Keating Simons Ball Plantation Journal, 1850–59, 1866, BP-Duke; Comingtee labor contract: Moncks Corner, South Carolina, labor contracts, Jan–May 1866, vol. 237, entry 3286, Freedmen's Bureau, National Archives; Probate records, Charleston and Berkeley counties.

9: BLOODLINES

Page 176. **a tiny hereditary cadre**: Will of John Coming Ball, 28 Mar 1764, Charleston Wills; Terry, " 'Champaign Country,' " 114, 331–35, Appendix II.

Page 177. **the new young patriarch**: Will of Elias Ball, 30 Aug 1750, Memorial of several tracts of land belonging to Elias Ball, BP-SCHS.

Page 177. **thoroughbred racing**: Irving, *Day on Cooper River*, 53, 81; Foaling register, 1745–77, BP-SCHS.

Page 178. **birthplace of . . . male slaves**: List of Males at Comingtee, 27 Jul 1777, in Account and Blanket Book 1720–78, BP-SCHS.

Page 178. **"Slaves from the River Gambia are preferr'd"**: Henry Laurens to Richard Oswald, 17 May 1756, Laurens to Smith and Clifton, 17 Jul 1755, in George C. Rogers Jr. et al., eds., *The Papers of Henry Laurens* (Columbia, S.C.: University of South Carolina, 1968 ff.), II:186 and I:295 (hereafter, *Papers of Henry Laurens*); J. F. Ade Ajayi and Michael Crowder, eds., *The Historical Atlas of Africa* (Cambridge: Cambridge University Press, 1985), plates 35 and 72.

Page 178. **the "Species" of slaves**: Henry Laurens to Law, Satterthwaite and Jones, 14 Dec 1755, Laurens to John Knight, 28 May 1756, and Laurens to Smith and Baillies, 1 Mar 1764, in *Papers of Henry Laurens*, II:38, II:204, IV:193.

Page 179. **Mandinka . . . Coromantees . . . Popo**: Littlefield, *Rice and Slaves*,

10, 13; Henry Laurens, Charleston, to Richard Oswald and Co., London, 17 May 1756, Henry Laurens, Charleston, to Smith and Clifton, St. Christopher's, 17 Jul 1755, *Papers of Henry Laurens*, II:186, I:295.

Page 180. **Laurens [had an] interest in botany**: Irving, *Day on Cooper River*, 83.

Page 181. **price of rice . . . doubled**: Coclanis, *Shadow of a Dream*, 106.

Page 181. **Second Elias . . . bought Limerick**: Smith, *Baronies of South Carolina*, 30–32; Elias Ball, bought of Daniel Huger, 3 Apr 1764, BP-SCL.

Page 181. **an English carver named Thomas Elfe**: "Thomas Elfe Account Book, 1768–1775," SCHM, vol. 36 (1935), 133; vol. 37 (1936), 25.

Page 182. **the Balls commissioned paintings**: Middleton, *Jeremiah Theus*, 103, 113, 166, 171, and throughout.

Page 182. **a clothier named Jacob Tobias**: Receipt, Jacob Tobias to Nelly Ball, 10 Dec 1784, BP-SCHS.

Page 182. **peacock of the family . . . John Ball**: Catherine Simons to John Ball, 10 Jan 1775, 24 Jan 1775, 6 Mar 1775; Diana: Account and Blanket Book, 1720–78; Memo Book of John Ball, 1774–80, BP-SCHS.

Page 184. **Death came often**: Account and Blanket Book, 1720–78, BP-SCHS, 23 Feb 1771, and throughout; Cheryll Ann Cody, *Slave Demography and Family Formation: A Community Study of the Ball Family Plantations, 1720–1896* (Ph.D. dissertation, University of Minnesota, 1982), 211, 232.

Page 184. **murder . . . ménage**: Henry Laurens to Elias Ball, 2 May 1766, *Papers of Henry Laurens*, V:123.

Page 185. **many slaves . . . tried to escape**: *South Carolina Gazette*, 4 May 1752, 20 Oct 1766, 22 Feb 1768; Carolina, Patra, and Truman: 15 Apr 1742 and 20 Oct 1753, Account and Blanket Book, 1720–78, BP-SCHS.

Page 186. **More people tried to escape in South Carolina**: Billy G. Smith and Richard Wojtowicz, *Blacks Who Stole Themselves: Advertisements for Runaways in the Pennsylvania Gazette, 1728–1790* (Philadelphia: University of Pennsylvania, 1989), 13.

Page 186. **Tom . . . from a rebellious family**: Birth: 18 Jan 1741, Account and Blanket Book, 1720–78, BP-SCHS.

Page 187. **"Two Toes . . . cut off"**: *South Carolina Gazette*, 23 Aug 1740.

Page 187. **The slave child named Edward . . . presented a problem**: Elias Ball to Richard Shubrick, deed of gift for the child Ned, 19 Nov 1741, Misc. records, volume EE, 102–3, SCDAH; Smith, *Baronies of South Carolina*, 154; "Doley & her Children went to St. James to Live," 19 Feb 1748, and throughout, Account and Blanket Book, 1720–78, BP-SCHS.

Page 189. **Edward Tanner . . . hostler**: Foaling register, 1745–77, BP-SCHS.

Page 189. **free people of color**: Coclanis, *Shadow of a Dream*, 64; Terry, " 'Champaign Country,' " 116; David Duncan Wallace, *South Carolina: A Short History, 1520–1948* (Chapel Hill: University of North Carolina, 1951), 247.

Page 189. **Kate died**: "Abstracts from records of the Court of Ordinary," SCHM, vol. 27 (1926), 92–93.

Page 190. **"Dolly died ye 5 Dec 1774"**: Account and Blanket Book, 1720–78, BP-SCHS.

Page 190. **9.5 million people were carried from Africa**: A credible study of the human traffic appears in Philip D. Curtin, *The Atlantic Slave Trade: A Census* (Madison: University of Wisconsin, 1969), with sections relevant to the United States, chap. 3, "The Colonies of the North Europeans," and chap. 5, "The English Slave Trade of the Eighteenth Century."

Page 190. **Ball in-laws became the largest slave dealers**: W. Robert Higgins,

"Charles Town Merchants and Factors Dealing in the External Negro Trade, 1735–1775," SCHM, vol. 65 (1964), 205–17.

Page 191. **Laurens wrote the Balls**: Henry Laurens to John Ball, 3 May 1756, Letterbook, 12 May 1755–25 Apr 1757, Henry Laurens papers (unpublished), SCHS; Henry Laurens to Smith and Clifton, 26 May 1755, *Papers of Henry Laurens*, I:255.

Page 192. **Brewton & Smith**: Waterhouse, *South Carolina's Colonial Elite*, 163.

Page 192. **"refuse Negroes"**: Henry Laurens to Ross and Mill, 11 Mar 1769, *Papers of Henry Laurens*, VI: 407.

Page 192. **"the *Hare* . . . from Sierra Leon"**: *South Carolina Gazette*, 17 Jun 1756.

Page 192. **Limba, Kono, Mende . . . among others**: Kup, *Sierra Leone*, 38 and throughout.

Page 193. **Henry Laurens . . . wrote several letters to friends**: Henry Laurens to John Knight, 28 May 1756; Henry Laurens, Charleston, to Richard Oswald, London, 29 Jun 1756; Henry Laurens to Samuel & William Vernon, 5 Jul 1756; Henry Laurens to John Knight, 5 Jul 1756; Henry Laurens to Robert & John Thompson & Co., 24 Jul 1756; Henry Laurens to Augustus & John Boyd & Co., 30 Jul 1756; Henry Laurens, Charleston, to Richard Oswald & Co., London, 14 Aug 1756; Henry Laurens Papers, II:204–05, 232–33, 238–39, 239–43, 269–70, 272–73, 283–85.

Page 193. **Second Elias picked out six [children]**: Account of Sale, Charges & Net Proceed of 63 new Negro slaves receiv'd per the sloop Hare . . . (17 Jul 1756), *Papers of Henry Laurens*, II:256–258; "[1756] 1 bought 4 boys and 2 girls," "[13 Sep 1769] Bought 13 Gambias . . . 11 boys and 2 girls," Account and Blanket Book, 1720–78, BP-SCHS.

10: "YOURS, OBEDIENTLY"

Page 197. **Thomas Martin . . . retired teacher**: Author's conversations with Martin family, South Carolina.

Page 200. **life of P. Henry Martin**: Plantation Book, 1804–90, BP-UNC; P. Henry Martin to Isaac Ball, 20 Feb 1926, P. Henry Martin to Mary H. Ball, 2 Oct 1932, P. Henry Martin to Mrs. Henry H. Ficken (Julia Ball), 27 Mar 1933, private collection; conversations with Martin family.

Page 201. **a rudimentary education**: F. W. Liedtke to Lieut. C. E. Campbell, 1 May 1868, Moncks Corner, South Carolina, Letters and circulars, Aug 1866–Jan 1868, entry 3279, Miscellaneous reports, 1866–68, entry 3280, teacher's monthly school report for Nazareth Church School, Lists and Registers, 1866–68, entry 3287, record group 105, Freedmen's Bureau, National Archives.

Page 210. **remains of Limerick**: Smith, *Baronies of South Carolina*, 30–32; William B. Lees, *Limerick: Old and in the Way: Archaeological Investigations at Limerick Plantation*, Anthropological Studies 5, Papers of the Institute of Archaeology and Anthropology (Columbia, S.C.: University of South Carolina, 1980), 31–32, and throughout.

Page 212. **[Martin family] descendants of Priscilla**: The *South Carolina Gazette* for 17 June 1756 reads, "Just imported in the *Hare*, Capt. Caleb Godfrey, directly from Sierra Leon, a Cargo of Likely and Healthy Slaves, To be sold upon easy Terms, on Tuesday the 29th Instant June, by Austin & Laurens." In an account book of Henry Laurens, Charleston slave trader, there is a note, "Account of Sale, Charges & Net Proceed of 63 new Negro slaves receiv'd per the sloop Hare. . . ." (*Papers of Henry Laurens*, II:256–58). For the sale, which took place 29–30 June 1756, Laurens lists his customers, including Elias Ball [Jr.], Laurens's brother-in-law, who bought three boys and two girls on June 30th, paying £460 in cash. Elias Ball seems to have bought another boy separately, at £140. In a ledger kept by Elias Ball Jr. (1709–86), who owned Comingtee plantation, there is a note: "I bought 4 boys and 2 girls their ages near as I can judge Sancho = 9 year old, Peter = 7, Brutus = 7, Harry = 6, Belinder = 10, Prosillo [Priscilla] = 10, for £600," Account and Blanket Book, 1720–78, BP-SCHS. The subsequent records of births and deaths are good enough that it is possible to reconstruct much of the family of Priscilla's descendants (Account and Blanket Book, 1720–78, Slave Registers and Blanket Book, 1804–21, Slave Lists, 1804–10, Limerick plantation, all in BP-SCHS; Plantation Record Book, 1804–90 and Birth Lists, 1735–1817, in John and Keating S. Ball Books, 1779–1911, BP-UNC). According to these records, Priscilla had nine children, probably by a man named Jeffrey: Friday, Monemia, Little Binah, Harriet, Charlotte, Marcia, Lettice, Amy, and Jeffrey. Jeffrey and Priscilla's children had forty children between them. One of them, Priscilla's granddaughter Sally, had a daughter named Dinah (b. 1834). On October 6, 1855, Dinah became the mother of Henry, who was freed in 1865, and took the name Peter Henry Martin.

11: A HOUSE DIVIDED

Page 216. **The Ball holdings . . . five hundred black people**: An Inventory of the estate of John Coming Ball, 12 Jan 1765 (Charleston inventories, vol. W, 198–202, SCDAH) names 249 people as the property of one planter. Other villages at Comingtee: Account and Blanket Book, 1720–78, BP-SCHS; Hyde Park, Kensington, Limerick: Smith, *Baronies of South Carolina,* 32–33; Old Goose Creek: Irving, *Day on Cooper River,* 100; and Tranquil Hill: Henry A. M. Smith, *Cities and Towns of Early South Carolina* (Charleston: South Carolina Historical Society, 1988), 22.

Page 216. **South Carolina was the bulwark of plantation slavery**: Coclanis, *Shadow of a Dream,* 64.

Page 217. **the rebellion became linked . . . with a threat to slavery**: Events of 1775–76: Benjamin Quarles, *The Negro in the American Revolution* (Chapel Hill: University of North Carolina, 1961); Robert A. Olwell, " 'Domestick Enemies': Slavery and Political Independence in South Carolina, May 1775–March 1776," *Journal of Southern History,* LV:1 (February 1989), throughout.

Page 218. **Third Elias decided . . . to join a militia**: *South Carolina Provincial Troops, Named in Papers of the First Council of Safety in the Revolutionary Party of South Carolina, June–November 1775,* compiled by A. S. Salley (Baltimore: Genealogical Publishing, 1977); Elias Ball to John Ball, 27 Aug 1775, BP-SCHS.

Page 219. **a plan to defend the colony in the event of British attack**: Robert W. Gibbes, ed., "Report of the Committee for Forming a Plan of Defence for the Colony," in *Documentary History of the American Revolution: Consisting of Letters and Papers Relating to the Contest for Liberty, Chiefly in South Carolina, From Originals in the Possession of the Editor, and Other Sources, 1774–1776* (three volumes, 1855), reprint, three volumes in one (New York: Arno Press, 1971), I:205.

Page 220. **"our Governor [Campbell] who is now found out to be an old Traitor"**: John Ball to Isaac Ball, 19 Sep 1775, BP-SCHS.

Page 220. **"We are making all warlike preparations"**: Elias Ball to John Ball, 18 Nov 1775, BP-SCHS.

Page 220. **"[Y]ou are hereby ordered . . . to Sullivan's Island"**: Olwell, " 'Domestick Enemies,' " 45; *Papers of Henry Laurens,* X:546.

Page 221. **the battle of Fort Sullivan:** Robert M. Weir, *Colonial South Carolina: A History* (Millwood, N.Y.: KTO Press, 1983), 328–30.

Page 221. **"[The King] has waged cruel war":** Carl Becker, *The Declaration of Independence* (New York: Knopf, 1969), 180–81.

Page 223. **"advantages . . . in raising a Regiment of White Men":** John Laurens to Henry Laurens, 2 Feb 1778, *The Army Correspondence of Colonel John Laurens in the Years 1777–8, now first printed from original letters addressed to his father Henry Laurens, President of Congress, with a memoir by Wm. Gilmore Simms* (New York, 1867), 114; John Laurens to George Washington, 19 May 1782, quoted in Quarles, *The Negro in the American Revolution*, 67; Henry Laurens to John Laurens, 6 Feb 1778, "Correspondence between Hon. Henry Laurens and his son, John, 1777–1780," SCHM, vol. 6 (Apr 1905), 47–52.

Page 224. **Boston King . . . born in 1760:** "Memoirs of the Life of Boston King, a Black Preacher, Written by Himself, during his Residence at Kingswood School [England]," *The Methodist Magazine* (London) 21 (1798), 105–10, 157–61, 209–13, 261–65.

Page 224. **Ann Ball in the big house, Boston became a Ball slave:** Will of Richard Waring, 8 Jun 1780, Charleston Wills; Waring family, misc. file, SCHS; Legaré Walker, *Dorchester County: A History of Its Genesis . . . and other matters of a historical nature* (ms., 1941/1979), SCHS, 23; Elizabeth Ann Poyas, *The Olden Time of Carolina* (Charleston, 1855), 79–80.

Page 225. **Tranquil Hill . . . in the Revolution:** Smith, *Cities and Towns of Early South Carolina*, 22; Weir, *Colonial South Carolina*, 334–35.

Page 226. **a watercolor . . . depicting Tranquil Hill:** "Tranquil Hill," watercolor on paper, artist unknown [ca. 1800], Gibbes Museum of Art/Carolina Art Association, Charleston.

Page 226. **British authorities called for an occupation force:** Gregory Palmer, *Biographical Sketches of Loyalists of the American Revolution* (London: Meckler Publishing, 1984), 38; Murtie June Clark, *Loyalists in the Southern Campaign of the Revolutionary War* (Baltimore: Genealogical Publishing, 1981), I:183

Page 227. **Wambaw plantation, on the Santee River:** Lease and release, John Coming Ball to Henry Laurens, 11 May 1756, Indenture and release, Henry Laurens to Elias Ball, 25 May 1769, Charleston deeds, vol. 2Y, 513–30 and vol. 3N, 171–79, SCDAH.

Page 227. **two relatives stayed with the rebel underdogs:** Sara Sullivan Ervin, *South Carolinians in the Revolution* (Baltimore: Genealogical Publishing Company, 1965), 90; Orderly book for the regiment of Light Dragoons, Commanded by Col. D. Horry, 1779, BP-SCHS.

Page 227–28. **"a blue cloth coatee, faced and cuffed with scarlet cloth":** Extract from Capt. F. Marion's Orderly Book, 1775, and Regimental Orders, Col. Marion, 23 Jun 1777, Gibbes, ed., *Documentary History of the American Revolution*, I:104, II:59–60.

Page 228. **two hundred barrels of rice . . . eaten up by troops:** Account Book, 1780–84, BP-Duke.

Page 228. **"I am in a very dirty condition":** John Ball to Elias Ball, 28 May 1779, BP-SCL.

Page 228. **London, a thirty-six-year-old Gambian:** List of males at Comingtee, 1777, in Account and Blanket Book, 1720–78, BP-SCHS; John Ball to Elias Ball, 4 Jun 1779, BP-SCL.

Page 230. **fifty-one people . . . fled from Kensington:** Fifty-one people: A fair list of the Negroes that is gone from Kensington [1780], and misc. note, 1 Jun 1780, in Account Book, 1780–84, BP-Duke; ages: A list of male slaves from sixteen to sixty at Kensington with each Negroes age to the best of our Knowledge, 8 Mar 1780, BP-UNC; newspaper: *Royal Gazette*, 21 Mar 1781; petition: Terry, " 'Champaign Country,' " 352; 12,000: Ralph Izard to Mrs. Izard, 7 Oct 1782, quoted in Quarles, *The Negro in the American Revolution*, 158.

Page 231. **the visits he made followed a careful etiquette**: Edward McCrady, *The History of South Carolina in the Revolution, 1780–1783* (New York, 1902), reprint (New York: Russell & Russell, 1969), Appendix B, 746–47; Irving, *Day on Cooper River*, 40 ff., 170.

Page 233. **The dead from both sides were buried**: McCrady, *Revolution*, 331–40; Marion: quoted in Ferguson, *Uncommon Ground*, 77.

Page 235. **the company tried to corral the unarmed blacks**: Cross, *Historic Ramblin's Through Berkeley*, 257; Robert Stansbury Lambert, *South Carolina Loyalists in the American Revolution* (Columbia: University of South Carolina, 1987), 243.

Page 235. **"[R]ice and corn [were] supplyd my Negroes contrary to my positive order"**: Elias Ball, aboard ship for St. Augustine, to Elias Ball, Charleston, 5 Jun 1784, BP-SCL.

Page 236. **fifty-two former Wambaw workers, consisting of nine families, were . . . sold**: Account of sale of estate of Elias Ball of Wambaw (22 Jun 1782), 20 May 1786, BP-SCHS.

Page 236. **As fugitive blacks . . . their destiny would not be sweet**: Quarles, *The Negro in the American Revolution*, 177.

Page 237. **Wambaw Elias was given £12,700 sterling**: Palmer, *Biographical Sketches of Loyalists*, 38; Memorial [claim] of Col. Elias Ball, late of the Province of South Carolina, 20 Mar 1784, private collection; Decisions of Loyalist Claims Commission for South Carolina, 1784–88, AO 12/68; Claim of Elias Ball Sr., AO 12/50, Public Record Office, London.

Page 238. **An American-born painter . . . Benjamin West**: "American Commissioners of the Preliminary Peace Negotiations with Great Britain," by Benjamin West, oil on canvas (1783), Henry Francis du Pont Winterthur Museum, Winterthur, Delaware.

Page 238. **"we are in general lookd on as black sheep"**: Militia Officers at Present Refugees in Charleston, SC, 4 Jun 1782, in Clark, *Loyalists in the Southern Campaign*, I:419; Lambert, *South Carolina Loyalists*, 292; Elias Ball, Limerick, to Elias Ball, Bristol, England, 15 May 1784, BP-SCHS.

Page 239. **123 workers belonging to the brothers**: List of Negroes the property of Elias Ball made the 12th day of May 1784, BP-SCHS.

Page 239. **"[I am] plagued almost out of my life with the negroes"**: Quoted in Deas, *Recollections of the Ball Family*, 116–17.

Page 239. **a list of the runaways**: Boston King, Frank Symons, Polly Shubrick: Inspection Roll of Negroes Book No. 1, New York City, 23 Apr–13 Sep 1783, Miscellaneous Papers of the Continental Congress, 1774–89, National Archives, Washington, D.C.; Graham Russell Hodges, ed., *The Black Loyalist Directory* (New York: Garland, 1996) compiles all of the so-called Inspection Rolls; Frank Symons's owners: Indenture, John Bryan and Lydia Simons of Charleston, and Benjamin Simons and John Ball, 25 Jan 1783, BP-SCHS; Polly Shubrick's owners: Smith, *Baronies of South Carolina*, 153.

Page 240. **The fate of . . . New York fugitives**. Quarles, *The Negro in the American Revolution*, 173, 179–81.

Page 241. **Boston King . . . arrived on the western shore of Africa**: Names of Settlers Located on the 1st Nova Scotian Allotment (1792), Sierra Leone National Archives, Freetown, Sierra Leone.

12: THE WIDTH OF THE REALM

Page 242. **Leviticus . . . the old Mosaic law**: Leviticus 18.

Page 243. **an uncontrolled swelling in one hand**: Jane Ball to John Ball Jr., 24 Feb 1800, John Ball to John Ball Jr., 29 Dec 1799, 18 Mar 1800, BP-SCHS.

Page 243. **"I was too fat before"**: John Ball to John Ball Jr., 5 Aug 1801, BP-SCHS.

Page 243–44. **he had a companion in a slave woman named Nancy**: Will of Elias Ball [III], 6 Dec 1809, Charleston Wills; memorandum by Isaac Ball, "Limerick, April 1822, paid Free Nancy $100 agreeably to my uncle's will," Plantation book, 1804–90, BP-UNC.

Page 244. **to lend it out at interest or to "buy Young Slaves"**: Will of Elias Ball II (1772), BP-SCHS.

Page 244. **"A Short History of the Family of the Balls"**: "A short history of the family of the Balls since my grandfather settled in South Carolina, wrote by John Ball for the satisfaction of the posterity of the Balls, wrote in August 1786," BP-SCL, printed in Deas, *Recollections of the Ball Family*, 174–82.

Page 244. **John and Third Elias divided "their people"**: Division of the Negroes belonging to Mrs. Judith Ball's Estate, An Inventory and Appraisement of the Estate of Mrs. Judith Ball, deceased, 31 Mar 1783, A list of Negroes the property of Elias Ball made the 12th day of May 1784, and Appraisement and Division of the Negroes late the property of Elias Ball, 22 Jan 1787, BP-SCHS.

Page 245. **In 1790, the first census**: 1790 population: U.S. Bureau of the Census, *Statistical Abstract of the United States*, 115th ed. (Washington, D.C.: 1995); slave and slave-owning population: Jessie Carney Smith and Carrell Peterson Horton, eds., *Historical Statistics of Black America* (New York: International Thomson Publishing, 1995), "Population: Slave and Free, 1790–1860" and "Slaveholding and Non-slave-holding Families: by State, 1790–1850."

Page 246. **"strive to make the bitter portion of slavery . . . comfortable"**: John Ball to John Ball Jr., 6 Oct 1801, BP-SCHS.

Page 246. **trained doctors brought . . . cures**: Jane Ball to Isaac Ball, 18 and 24 May 1802, BP-SCL; John Ball to John Ball Jr., 14 Oct 1801, BP-SCHS; Account book of John Ball, 1796–1817, throughout, and Bill for services, Alexander Garden to John Ball, 6 May 1806, BP-Duke.

Page 246. **John Coming Ball . . . opened an account with a physician**: Samuel McCormick in a/c with John Coming Ball, 23 Apr 1785, BP-SCHS.

Page 247. **the Ball slaves had alternative medicines**: James Simons to Frenau & Williams, 6 Sep 1803, BP-SCHS; John Ball Jr., Estate Account Book of John Ball Sr., Pimlico plantation, 1810–29, BP-Duke.

Page 248. **small clay pots . . . to prepare medicines**: Ferguson, *Uncommon Ground*, Appendices 1–3.

Page 248. **"I am to pay Robin . . . for curing Hagar of the venereal disease"**: Memoranda, 21 Dec 1795, 5 Jan 1799, 26 Jan 1818, Account Book of John Ball, 1788–1818, BP-SCHS.

Page 249. **tidal rice farming**: Technique: Gray, *History of Agriculture*, I:280–81; drawing: reproduced in Kup, *Sierra Leone*, 34.

Page 250. **"I strongly recommended it to you"**: Joseph Purcell, A plan exhib-
iting the shape and form of a body of land called Limerick (1786), SCL; John Hardwick,
A plan of Limerick, a plantation belonging to Elias Ball, Esquire (1797), SCDAH; Elias
Ball, England, to Elias Ball, South Carolina, 25 Jun 1787, BP-SCL.

Page 250. **six million cubic feet of earth**: Rice banks: Ferguson, *Uncommon
Ground*, xxiv; exports: Edward A. Pearson, *From Stono to Vesey: Slavery, Resistance,
and Ideology in South Carolina, 1739–1822* (Ph.D. dissertation, University of Wisconsin, Madison, 1992), 293.

Page 250. **"the enormous sum of . . . £1365"**: Clothing: Invoice of Sundry
Merchandize . . . by order of Col. Elias Ball, Bristol, and addressed to Mr. Elias Ball
Jr. (South Carolina), 2 Jul 1787, BP-SCL; purchase of workers: Pocket account book,
1795–1808, BP-SCL.

Page 251. **build new housing**: Floor: Directions for making a tar floor by E. Ball
& J. Ball, 20 Jul 1794, BP-SCHS; whitewash: Composition for white wash to be put
on outbuildings [ca. 1794], BP-SCL, and Deas, *Recollections of the Ball Family*,
150; houses: *South Carolina Gazette*, 11 Jun 1792, CLS; carpenters: memoranda,
1786–90, in Account book of John Ball, Back River plantation, 1786–1803, private
collection.

Page 251. **The Balls took back their lifestyle as rice barons**: Tax Return of
Elias Ball for the year 1790, BP-SCHS; Heads of Families at the First Census of the
United States Taken in the Year 1790, South Carolina (Washington, D.C.: U.S. Gov-
ernment Printing Office, 1908), 31.

Page 252. **"I hope those French dogs will be thoroughly humbled"**: Elias
Ball, Bristol, to Elias Ball, South Carolina, 19 Jan 1793, BP-SCL.

Page 253. **"tied up and sorely whipped"**: Patrol Command, 26 May 1792,
BP-SCHS; R. Matthews to John Ball, 13 May 1817, BP-Duke.

Page 253. **A modest school had been incorporated in Charleston**: George C.
Rogers Jr., *Charleston in the Age of the Pinckneys* (Columbia, S.C.: University of South
Carolina, 1980), 98.

Page 254. **a trip up the East Coast**: Adonis, valet: Henry Laurens Jr. to John Ball,
31 Jul 1786, BP-SCHS; chronicle of trip: Account Book, 1796–1817, BP-UNC.

Page 256. **"We met the President riding on horseback"**: Isaac Ball to John
Ball, 18 Oct 1806, BP-SCL.

Page 256. **Letters of recommendation . . . [and] good money**: Dr. Purcell and
George Buist letter, Charleston, 15 Sep 1798, John Ball to John Ball Jr., 30 Sep 1798,
BP-SCHS.

Page 257. **John Jr. [in] Massachusetts**: "My education . . . neglected," A short
history of the family of the Balls, BP-SCL; "rank and fortune," John Ball to John Ball
Jr., 9 May 1802; "you might have enter'd higher," 17 Jun 1799; "respectable young
gentlemen," 15 Aug 1799; "the infamy of the family," 12 Aug 1798; "the fair sex of
the north," Jane Ball to John Ball Jr., 28 Aug 1799, all BP-SCHS.

Page 258. **William James Ball [in] Edinburgh, Scotland**: Brothel: William James
Ball, Edinburgh, to John Ball Jr., South Carolina, 26 Jul 1806, 7 Jan 1807; "You ought
now to get a plaything": William James Ball, Edinburgh, to John Ball Jr., South Carolina,
25 Jan 1805, BP-SCL.

Page 259. **liberal education had had no deranging effect**: "your family . . .
made beggars," John Ball to John Ball Jr., 29 Sep 1799; homecoming: John Ball to John
Ball Jr., 24 Jun and 1 Jul 1802, BP-SCHS.

Page 259. **used the money to expand operations**: Limerick mill: Receipt, Jonathan Lucas to Elias Ball, 10 Feb 1795, and Jonathan Lucas Jr., receipt for repairing

and furnishing material for a mill at Limerick, 23 & 28 Jan 1801, BP-SCL; Pimlico and Kecklico: Ann Shreve Norris, *Pimlico Plantation: Now and Long Ago* (Mt. Pleasant, S.C., 1994), 28; Midway: John Ball to John Ball Jr., 19 Mar 1799, BP-SCHS; Belle Isle and Marshlands: Thomas Slater to John Ball, sales offer for Cat Island plantation, 13 Jan 1810, W. H. Gibbes to John Ball, 16 Jul 1810, BP-Duke.

Page 260. **Africans flooded onto the Ball lands**: Resumption of slave trade: George C. Rogers Jr. and C. James Taylor, *A South Carolina Chronology, 1497–1992* (Columbia, S.C.: University of South Carolina, 1994), 70; "new Negroes": memoranda, Jan 1804 and Oct 1805, in Plantation record book, 1779–1817, BP-UNC; Misc. memorandum, 11 May 1804, BP-Duke.

Page 261. **tax return . . . five hundred people**: Elias Ball, tax return for the year 1805, private collection.

Page 261. **One person . . . known as Jew**: List of Negroes at Limerick, 25 Mar 1806, BP-SCHS.

Page 262. **a pair of child slaves**: Jane Ball's illness: Jane Ball to John Ball Jr., 16 Jul 1800, John Ball to John Ball Jr., 19 Aug 1801, 7 Sep 1801, 21 Sep 1801, BP-SCHS; gift of four children: "two twins for my daughters," List of Negroes at Pimlico, 6 Feb 1810, and Deed of gift, John Ball to Caroline Olivia Ball and Martha Angeline Ball, 17 Oct 1806, BP-Duke; shoes: Copy of order for plate by Mr. Thos. Naylor, 5 Jun 1806, BP-SCHS.

Page 262. **Parliament tried to outlaw the international trade**: Sierra Leone: Christopher Fyfe, ed., *"Our Children Free and Happy": Letters from Black Settlers in Africa in the 1790s* (Edinburgh: Edinburgh University, 1991), 19; "prime windward coast slaves": *Charleston Courier*, 4 Jan 1808, CLS.

Page 263. **"Mr. Ball's character"**: *Charleston Times*, 8 Jan 1810.

Page 263. **one of the grandest residences in the city**: Charleston County RMC, B8-346, A8-411; Isaac Ball in a/c Thos. Elfe Jr., 21 Mar 1811, Isaac Ball in a/c Robert Roulain, 10 Dec 1811, BP-SCL; misc. file, Isaac Ball house, SCHS.

Page 263. **"I have got a sore leg"**: John Ball, Charleston, to Thos. Slater, London, 8 Oct 1816, BP-Duke.

Page 264. **The auction house of William Payne & Son handled the business**: Inventory of Estate of John Ball, 14 Nov 1817–1 Jan 1818, Charleston District Ordinary Inventory Books, SCDAH; Sales on a/c of the Estate of John Ball, deceased . . . 8th & 9th February 1819, BP-Duke.

Page 265. **"The nigger-trader got me"**: H. M. Henry, *The Police Control of the Slave in South Carolina* (Emory, Va., 1914), 56.

Page 265. **a conspiracy to overthrow white rule**: "An Account of the Late Intended Insurrection among a portion of the blacks of this city," pamphlet (Charleston: Corporation of Charleston, 1822); Court Proceedings and Testimony Regarding the Vesey Rebellion, Governor's Message to the General Assembly (1822), SCDAH.

Page 268. **"saving us & our city from fire & murder"**: Religious diary of Eliza Ball, entry for 28 Sep 1822, private collection.

Page 268. **"insurrection and murdering of the Whites"**: John Moultrie to Isaac Ball, 17 Mar 1823, BP-SCL.

Page 269. **he was sentenced to death**: Biography of Paris: Plantation record book, 1803–34, BP-UNC; Court Proceedings and Testimony Regarding the Vesey Rebellion, Petition of Kennedy, et al., re: Paris Ball, 24 Jul 1822, SCDAH; contemporary newspaper sources.

Page 270. **Paris . . . aboard a cargo vessel in the harbor**: *Carolina Gazette*, 26 Oct 1822.

13: A PAINTER'S LEGACY

Page 272. **Edwina Harleston Whitlock**: Author's conversations with Harleston-Whitlock and Fleming families, Georgia and California.

Page 276. **"Uncle John and Uncle William Harleston, two old bachelors"**: Mary Louisa Ball, "The Bluff," three-page typescript, ca. 1910, private collection.

Page 276. **Kate [at Elwood plantation]**: Elwood purchase: Charleston County RMC, 19–77; Caroline Ball Laurens to John Ball Jr. 13 Feb 1828, BP-Duke; eighty-two workers: Schedule and appraisement of the plantations Mepshew, Pimlico & Kecklico, also of the negro slaves . . . 20 Jul 1830, BP-Duke; Elwood resold: Charleston County RMC, S10–248.

Page 277. **of the . . . free black people in Charleston, women outnumbered men**: Michael P. Johnson and James L. Roark, eds., *No Chariot Let Down: Charleston's Free People of Color on the Eve of the Civil War* (New York: Norton, 1984), Introduction; Bernard E. Powers Jr., *Black Charlestonians: A Social History, 1822–1885* (Fayetteville: Univ. of Arkansas, 1994), 41.

Page 277. **"William Harleston of the Hut plantation an able assistant"**: Plantation record book, 1849–71, BP-UNC.

Page 282. **The story of Edwin Harleston, painter**: Edwina Harleston Whitlock, "Edwin A. Harleston," in *Edwin A. Harleston: Painter of an Era, 1882–1931*, exhibition catalogue (Detroit: Your Heritage House, 1983), 9–29.

14: THE CURSE OF BUZZARD WING

Page 295. **a reputation . . . for frivolous spending**: Copy of order for plate by Mr. Thos. Naylor, 5 Jun 1806, BP-SCHS; Mrs. [Martha C.] Ball in a/c with Ann Savage, 1812–16, BP-Duke; Bill of sale [for George, tailor], 30 Feb 1821, Misc. records, vol. 4V, p. 83, SCDAH.

Page 296. **Money was not a problem**: Account of six per cent and other stock of the estate of John Ball, 1820–21, Schedule of bonds due the estate of John Ball, 1 Apr 1826, Tax for 1824, John Ball's negroes, BP-Duke; Tax return of Isaac Ball's property, 1824, BP-SCHS.

Page 297. **to raise the young ones in proper style**: Lawsuit: John Ball Jr. and Isaac Ball, executors of John Ball, deceased . . . 9 Jul 1819, Misc. records, vol. 4R, 244–48, SCDAH; Taveau marriage: Caroline Ball to John Ball, 30 Mar 1821, BP-SCHS; Taveau: "Guide to the manuscript collections in the Duke University Library," *Historical Papers of the Trinity College Historical Society*, series 27–28 (Durham, N.C.: Duke University Press, 1947), 223–28; lawsuits: "Taveau v. John Ball, esq., 4 Jan 1826," in John Ball Jr., Estate Account Book of John Ball Sr., 1826–32, and Case of Augustus Taveau & wife vs. the Executors of John Ball, 19 Mar 1828, BP-Duke.

Page 297. **the renting out of single workers, or whole families**: Ball addresses: *Negrin's Directory for the Year 1807* (Charleston, 1807); *An Almanac for the Year of Our Lord 1822* (Charleston); *Guide to the Residences and Places of Business . . . City of Charleston* (1829); renting out: John Ball Jr., Estate Account Book of John Ball Sr., 1826–32, BP-Duke.

Page 297. **"Spanish flies," an aphrodisiac**: Inventory, 18 Mar 1819, articles of household and kitchen furniture received by Martha Caroline Ball of John & Isaac Ball, executors to the estate of John Ball Sr., deceased; Spanish fly: William Burgoyne in a/c Estate of John Ball, Feb–Nov 1827, Bills and Receipts, John Ball Jr., 1823–24, BP-Duke.

Page 298. **Alwyn Ball, Hugh Swinton Ball, and Elias Octavus Ball**: Their education: Isaac Ball to Elias O. Ball, 19 Sep 1823, BP-SCHS; Hugh Swinton Ball to Isaac Ball, 1 Jan 1823, BP-SCL; John Ball Jr. to Capt. Alden Partridge, 20 Jul 1823; Misc. note, 9 Jan 1824; John Ball Jr., Charleston, to Thomas Crowder, Liverpool, 23 Oct 1824 and 27 Mar 1825; James Balfour and Thos. Crowder, Liverpool, to John Ball Jr., Charleston, 5–7 August 1824; John Ball, Charleston, to Alwyn Ball, Liverpool, 23 Oct 1824; Thomas Crowder, Liverpool, to John Ball Jr., Charleston, 1 and 9 Feb 1825; memorandum, Estimate of costs of Hugh S. Ball and Elias O. Ball, education in England (1824–25), all BP-Duke.

Page 300. **the decline of the rice barons**: Santee Canal: F. A. Porcher, "The History of the Santee Canal," pamphlet (Charleston: South Carolina Historical Society, 1875); Virginia slave exports: Hugh Brogan, *The Penguin History of the United States of America* (New York: Penguin, 1985), 303.

Page 302. **Caroline's daughters . . . lived . . . to spend**: Receipt, 23 Jun 1825, Peter Fayotte to John Ball, Esq., Account for Miss Catherine Ball and Account for Miss Lucilla Ball, Jul–Dec 1827, George Granniss, Richard McKensie to estate of John Ball, 10 Jan 1829, Receipt, James Peters to Lucilla Ball, Dec 1830–Jun 1831, BP-Duke.

Page 302. **the three Ball brothers**: Swinton in Charleston: Isaac Ball, Charleston, to Elias O. Ball, Liverpool, 1 Dec 1824, BP-SCHS; buying spree: Hugh S. Ball to John Ball Jr., 16 and 30 Nov 1824, 17 and 18 Dec 1824, BP-Duke; Elias O.: E. L. Roche in a/c Elias O. Ball, Jan. 1827–May 1828 (clothes), Elias O. Ball to John Ball Jr. 2 Jun 1827 (valet), BP-Duke; marriages: Elias O. Ball to John Ball Jr., 9 Oct 1825, Hugh S. Ball to John Ball Jr., 30 Aug 1826, 16 and 24 March 1827, BP-Duke; Alwyn's nine slaves: Bill of sale, James Doughty, M.D., to Alwyn Ball, 25 Jan 1827, in Misc. records, vol. 5G, p. 10, SCDAH.

Page 304. **"taking down the little whip"**: Captain Nancy: Irving, *Day on Cooper River*, 127; Midway slaves: Ann Ball to John Ball, 4 Apr 1823, BP-SCHS; advice to sell, and auction: J. E. Holmes to Ann Ball, 30 Jan 1835, List of Negroes belonging to Mrs. Ann Ball purchased from the estate of John Ball (1834), BP-SCHS; whipping of Betty: Ann Ball to John Ball, 26 Nov 1823, BP-SCHS.

Page 304–5. **the Ball family . . . customers of the Work House**: Services: Charles R. Simpson to Isaac Ball, 15 Mar 1814, BP-SCL; "Work house fees . . . $65.25 [18 Nov 1819]," and "Oct 14, 1828 paid W. E. Gordon, work house fees for Town, $8.87," in Pimlico plantation book, 1810–30, BP-Duke.

Page 305. **Karl Bernhard, Duke of Saxe-Weimar**: Bernhard, Duke of Saxe-Weimar Eisenach, *Travels through North America during the Years 1825 and 1826* (Philadelphia, 1828), II:8–10, quoted in Willie Lee Rose, ed., *A Documentary History of Slavery in North America* (New York: Oxford, 1976), and Rogers, *Charleston in the Age of the Pinckneys*, 146–48.

Page 306. **the Missouri Compromise**: Chronology of events and quotes from political debate, 1820–35: William W. Freehling, *Prelude to Civil War: The Nullification Controversy in South Carolina, 1816–1836* (New York: Harper and Row, 1965), part II.

Page 307. **"I wish that some . . . would learn to play on the Hoeboy"**: Elias Ball to Isaac Ball, 23 Jul 1823, BP-SCL.

Page 307. **"the Negroes . . . are much happier . . . in their present situation"**: John Moultrie, Liverpool, to Isaac Ball, South Carolina, 10 Oct 1823, BP-SCL.

Page 308. **Isaac Ball . . . dictated his last wishes**: Will of Isaac Ball, 15 Nov 1825, Charleston Wills.

Page 309. **John Jr. . . . went into politics**: *Charleston Mercury*, 5 and 15 Oct 1830, 29 Jun 1831, CLS.

Page 310. **Morris's gunshot wound**: Thomas G. Finklea to John Ball, 26 Jul and 16 Aug 1833, BP-SCHS.

Page 311. **"equality [is] but another name for barbarism"**: pamphlets quoted in Freehling, *Prelude to Civil War*, 81–82.

Page 312. **One poem . . . "Limerick; or Country Life in South-Carolina"**: Catharine Gendron Poyas, *"The Huguenot Daughters" and Other Poems* (Charleston: John Russell, 1849), 66–91.

Page 313. **Occasionally Swinton would sell . . . workers**: Bills of sale, 1 Jan 1834, 2 & 6 Mar 1837, Misc. records, vol. 50, p. 417, and vol. 5T, pp. 131, 142, SCDAH.

Page 314. **"the negro slaves [be] sold . . . in lots"**: "Anna dislikes the sea": Hugh Swinton Ball to John Ball Jr., 26 Jul 1830, BP-Duke; shipwreck: Elias Ball, Ball family history, compiled ca. 1950, BP-SCHS, and Deas, *Recollections of the Ball Family*, 140–41; trial: Irving, *Day on Cooper River*, 164, and Helen Tunnicliff Catterall, *Judicial Cases Concerning American Slavery and the Negro* (Washington, D.C.: Carnegie Institute, 1929), II:395.

Page 315. **"I did not mean . . . a college education was useless"**: William James Ball to Eliza Ball, 22 Apr 1840, BP-SCHS.

Page 315. **William and Julia Ball . . . controlled three plantations**: Halidon Hill: memorandum by William James Ball, 1842, Plantation book, 1804–90; 450 people: Plantation book, 1804–90, BP-UNC; Cedar Hill: Conveyance, James Poyas to William James Ball, 1 Jan 1850, BP-SCL.

Page 316. **"I was given to Stepney by my master"**: Affidavits of William Gaillard and Patty Moultrie (1903), Civil War pension file of Stepney Moultrie (128th U.S. Colored Troops, Company D), cert. no. 559536, Records of the Veterans Administration, National Archives, Washington.

Page 317. **the "committee on manures"**: Account book, Strawberry Agricultural Society, 1847–59, private collection.

Page 318. **two Ball field hands . . . killed their work-gang leader**: Trial and death sentences: *Charleston Courier*, 7 Jun 1844; family of Pino, Amelia, Sambo: Plantation book, 1804–90, BP-UNC; sale of Amelia: Bond of Daniel Cook for purchase of Amelia, banished from State of South Carolina by Court of Freeholders, 12 Feb 1847, private collection.

Page 318. **a private tutor and violin lessons**: Mat. F. Davis to Eliza Ball, 10 Nov 1855, Eliza Ball to William J. Ball, 13 Nov 1855, William James Ball Jr. to Eliza Ball, 16 Feb 1862, BP-SCL.

Page 319. **"I went to see the Campbell Minstrels"**: Isaac Ball to Julia Cart Ball, 1 Oct 1853, private collection.

Page 319. **the strong rice economy**: Cherry Hill: Agreement for purchase of Cherry Hill plantation, and Karwan's Tract, William J. Ball and Duncan N. Ingraham, 27 Dec 1856, and James Simons to W. J. Ball, 31 Mar 1857, BP-SCL; bushels: Rice crop, 1858, BP-SCL; deaths: Slave mortality and wartime provisions notebook, 1857–64, BP-SCL.

Page 320. **William brought . . . gifts for . . . Limerick field hands**: Diary and memo book, 1853–63, BP-SCL.

Page 320. **The Blessing, a 631-acre tract**: Smith, *Baronies of South Carolina*, 172.

Page 320. **his mind was on . . . his slaves**: Diary and memo book, 1853–63, BP-SCL.

15: THE SIEGE

Page 322. **"we looked forward to our Southern Confederacy"**: Memoir of Mary Gibbs Ball (1923), 168-page ms., private collection.

Page 323. **3,950,000 . . . in slavery**: U.S. Bureau of the Census, *Statistical Abstract of the United States*, 115th ed.; Smith and Horton, eds., *Historical Statistics of Black America*. "Population: Slave and Free, 1790–1860," "Slaveholding and Non-slaveholding Families."

Page 324. **South Carolina broke off in December**: These sources have been useful in narrating events of the Civil War: Mark Boatner, *The Civil War Dictionary* (New York: David McKay, 1959); Patricia L. Faust, ed., *Historical Times Illustrated Encyclopedia of the Civil War* (New York: Harper & Row, 1986); John Johnson, *The Defense of Charleston Harbor* (Charleston: Walker, Evans & Cogswell, 1890); E. B. Long with Barbara Long, *The Civil War Day by Day: An Almanac* (New York: Doubleday, 1971); Stewart Sifakis, *Compendium of the Confederate Armies: South Carolina and Georgia* (New York, 1995); Jon L. Wakelyn, *Biographical Dictionary of the Confederacy* (Westport, Conn.: Greenwood Press, 1977); *The War of the Rebellion: A Compilation of the Official Records of the Union and Confederate Armies*, series I, vol. XIV (Washington, D.C.: U.S. Government Printing Office, 1885).

Page 324. **"Slavery is in the course of ultimate extinction"**: *Declaration of the Immediate Causes Which Induce and Justify the Secession of South Carolina From the Federal Union; and the Ordinance of Secession* (Charleston: Evans & Cogswell, 1860), Special Collections, College of Charleston.

Page 325. **"Georgia has seceded"**: Eliza Ball to William James Ball, 21 Jan 1861, BP-SCL.

Page 325. **Elias Nonus Ball**: Confederate States Service Records, National Archives, Washington, D.C.; Elias N. Ball to Robert Barnwell Rhett, 22 Feb 1861, Elias N. Ball to W. Porcher Miles, 30 Mar 1861, Elias N. Ball to LeRoy P. Walker, 30 Mar 1861, in Confederate papers relating to citizens or business firms, M346, National Archives.

Page 326. **"[T]he Ladies generally are very warlike"**: Eliza Ball to Julia Obear, 7 Mar 1861, private collection.

Page 327. **"Greeting for Victory"**: *Charleston Courier*, 17 Apr 1861.

Page 328. **harvests . . . declined sharply**: Diary and memo book, 1853–63, BP-SCL.

Page 328. **Southern blacks were Christians**: On the changing spiritual life of the black population in South Carolina, see Margaret Washington Creel, *"A Peculiar People": Slave Religion and Community-Culture Among the Gullahs* (New York: New York University, 1988).

Page 328. **"Ostler John"**: Plantation record book, 1804–90, BP-UNC.

Page 329. **"fine orchestra playing" [and] "Virginia don't deserve it"**: Eliza Ball to Julia Obear, 29 May 1861, private collection.

Page 331. **twenty-five men . . . to dig trenches**: "Men who went to work on fortifications, Christ Church parish, Dec 1861," Diary and memo book, 1853–63, BP-SCL.

Page 331. **"We have given up long ago Tea & Coffee"**: Jane Ball Shoolbred to Julia Obear, 7 May 1862, private collection; "This paper": Jane Ball Shoolbred to Julia Obear, 14 Mar 1864; "the Ball ladies made . . . shirts": Confederate papers relating to citizens or business firms, M346, National Archives.

Page 332. **Balls seemed not to worry**: Catherine Theus to Julia Obear, 20 Feb

1862, private collection; Eliza Ball to William Ball, 17 Jan and 4 Feb 1862, BP-SCL.

Page 332. **"the men are volunteering"**: William Ball Jr. to Eliza Ball, 16 Feb 1862, "this state particularly they would wish to crush": Eliza Ball to William James Ball, 20 and 28 Feb 1862, BP-SCL.

Page 334. **Shanks Evans . . . Secessionville**: *The War of the Rebellion: A Compilation of the Official Records of the Union and Confederate Armies*, series I, vol. XIV, 18–19, 42–47; John Johnson, *The Defense of Charleston Harbor*, 25.

Page 334. **"the whole seaboard will be taken"**: Eliza Ball to Julia Obear, 7 May 1862, private collection; "Negroes . . . will be very insolent": Jane Ball Shoolbred to Julia Obear, 7 May 1862, private collection; a house in Columbia: Indenture, Eliza Ball to Edmund Davis, 4 Jun 1862, BP-SCL.

Page 336. **"so pleased with your wife"**: Eliza Ball to William James Ball, 19 Jan 1863, BP-SCL.

Page 336. **"I saw Cupid yesterday"**: William Ball Jr. to William Ball Sr., 30 Aug and 26 Nov 1863, private collection.

Page 336. **"death in a more preferable place"**: Eliza Ball to William Ball, 17 Feb 1863, BP-SCL.

Page 337. **Nat . . . companion and servant**: William Ball Jr. to William Ball Sr., 26 Nov and 28 Dec 1863, private collection.

Page 337. **"brisk engagement"**: Eliza Ball to William James Ball, 15 Jul 1863, BP-SCL; "John's Island, 1863," entry in diary of D. E. Huger Smith, private collection.

Page 338. **"Don't . . . give up entirely"**: Eliza Ball to William James Ball, 23 Jul 1863, BP-SCL; "the most despondent man": Eliza Ball to William James Ball, 3 Aug 1863, BP-SCL; "fragments of Yankees": Jane Ball Shoolbred to Mary Gibbs Ball, 4 Aug 1863, BP-SCL; "braver or cooler Boys": Eliza Ball to William James Ball, 7 Aug 1863, BP-SCL.

Page 339–40. **"I can't conceive how we escaped"**: William Ball Jr. to William Ball Sr., 30 Aug 1863, private collection.

Page 341. **"I fully expect it to be in ruins"**: Jane Ball Shoolbred to William James Ball, 24 Aug 1863, BP-SCL.

Page 341. **Isaac B. Gibbs**: Johnson Hagood, *Memoirs of the War of Secession* (Columbia, S.C.: The State Co., 1910); "The Pure Hearted," eulogy, *Charleston Courier*, 8 Dec 1864; Memoir of Mary Gibbs Ball.

Page 342. **"darkest day that the Confederacy has yet seen"**: William Ball Jr. to William Ball Sr., 25 Dec 1864, private collection; "outrages of the enemy": William Ball Jr. to William Ball Sr., 18 Jan 1865, private collection.

Page 343. **"Some could not sing, but wept"**: Memoir of Mary Gibbs Ball.

Page 343. **The last day of slavery came at Limerick**: "Greasy Yankees": Isaac Ball to William James Ball, 16 Jun 1867, private collection; Lamentations: Mary Ball's memoir states that Federal troops arrived at Limerick on a Sunday, when her husband was reading from the Book of Lamentations. Charleston fell February 17, 1865. According to a contemporary Episcopal calendar, verses from Lamentations were read on Quinquagesima Sunday, fifty days before Easter. In 1865, Easter fell on April 16, Quinquagesima on February 26. The personal prayer book of one of the women present at Limerick, Jane Ball Shoolbred (*The Church Service*, New York, 1854), calls for the reading of Lamentations 1.

Page 344. **The crowd came from the cabins**: Sylvia, seamstress: Eliza Ball to William James Ball, 21 Jan 1861, BP-SCHS; "Daddy Ben": Memoir of Mary Gibbs Ball.

Page 348. **Isaac began a diary**: "Campaign of 1865," Diary of Isaac Ball, 7 Feb–12 May 1865, private collection.

Page 350. **"the companies were skeleton companies"**: Captain Charles In-glesby, *Historical Sketch of the First Regiment of South Carolina Artillery* (pamphlet, Charleston: Walker, Evans & Cogswell, 1894).

16: AFTERMATH

Page 352. **black Americans began to use surnames**: Benjamin Quarles, *The Negro in the Civil War* (Boston: Little Brown, 1953; New York: Da Capo, 1989), 287.

Page 352. **black families on Ball lands**: One of the first written uses of surnames by former slaves appears in sharecrop contracts drawn up after the Civil War. The list of names adopted by former Ball slaves is compiled from contracts written at Ball plantations in the period 1865–68, which are preserved at the National Archives: Charleston, South Carolina, labor contracts, Jun 1865–Mar 1868, entry 3130; Moncks Corner, South Carolina, labor contracts, Jan–May 1866, vol. 237, entry 3286; Moncks Corner Register of contracts, vol. 238, Jan 1867–Apr 1868, entry 3285; Berkeley district labor contracts, Jan 1866–May 1868, entry 3120, all in record group 105, Records of the Bureau of Refugees, Freedmen and Abandoned Lands (Freedmen's Bureau), National Archives, Washington.

Page 353. **William Ball . . . sold four plantations**: Smith, *Baronies of South Carolina*, 172.

Page 353. **"The Yankees . . . gave it to the Negroes"**: Memoir of Mary Gibbs Ball (1923).

Page 354. **29 [people] put their names on [the] contract at Limerick**: Limerick labor contract, 2 Mar 1866, in Moncks Corner, South Carolina, labor contracts, Jan–May 1866, vol. 237, entry 3286, Freedmen's Bureau, National Archives.

Page 354. **demolished about 1920**: Artillery shell: Francis G. Cart to William J. Ball, 1 Jun 1865, private collection; appraisal: International Insurance Co., New York, policy issued to Eliza Ball, for dwelling at N.E. corner of Vernon and East Bay Streets, Charleston, 30 Jul 1866, BP-SCHS; house in decline: Memorandum for my executors in the event of my death, 29 Jun 1877, by James McElvey, Statement of rents collected and disbursed by T. Grange Simons . . . for Estate of Mrs. Eliza Ball, 24 Apr 1878, a/c sales of house and lot at N.E. corner of East Bay and Vernon Streets . . . 12 Mar 1879, Statement of rents collected and disbursed by T. Grange Simons . . . 27 Mar 1879, BP-SCHS.

Page 354. **"I have been effectually cured of all desire for drink"**: Alwyn Ball to William J. Ball, 20 Feb 1872, BP-SCHS.

Page 355. **A tax return . . . appraised the property**: Tax return, William J. Ball, 24 Feb 1876, BP-SCHS; sale of land: Berkeley County RMC, A7-407.

Page 355. **"now-a-days can't compare to those of the good old days"**: William J. Ball to Mary Ball, 12 Jan 1891, BP-SCHS.

Page 355. **The last of William's land**: Lawsuit: *State of South Carolina, County of Berkeley, Fanny R. Heyward, et al., executrixes of W. B. Smith* v. *Mathurin G. Ball, executor of William J. Ball, and Mary H. Ball et al.*, 7 Sep 1893, private collection; sale of Limerick: Berkeley County RMC, A10-346; sale of The Bluff: Berkeley RMC, A52-243.

Page 356. **black population of Charleston rose by two-thirds**: Powers, *Black Charlestonians*, 100.

Page 365. **Scipio . . . died . . . on August 19, 1857**: Comingtee plantation record book, 1849–90, BP-SCL.

Page 365. **Sarah Roper England**: Author's conversations with Roper-Roberson family.

Page 366. **Pawley . . . a 793-acre tract**: Pawley: Charleston RMC, H11-347, N12, 309–11, X15, 129–131; Roper-Roberson family: Pawley's labor contract, 6 Mar 1866, Moncks Corner, South Carolina, labor contracts, Jan–May 1866, vol. 237, entry 3286, Freedmen's Bureau, National Archives.

Page 367. **"[Isaac Ball] used to . . . write to him for me"**: Affidavit of Patty Moultrie (1903), Civil War pension file of Stepney Moultrie (128th U.S. Colored Troops, Company D), cert. no. 559536, Records of the Veterans Administration, National Archives, Washington.

Page 368. **Jacqueline Ball**: Author's conversations with Ball family of Virginia and South Carolina.

Page 370. **Joseph Ball**: Separation qualification for Army personnel, Joseph M. Ball (1945), private collection.

Page 374. **Edward Ball was buried**: Death certificate of Edward Ball, 2 Nov 1969, Department of Health, City of New York, cert. #56-69-211842.

17: THE PRESERVATION SOCIETY

Page 379. **[Judge] Julius Waties Waring**: William D. Smyth, "Segregation in Charleston in the 1950s," SCHM, vol. 92 (1991), 99–123.

Page 381. **The South Carolina Society began**: "Rules of the Incorporated South Carolina Society," pamphlet (1795), Special Collections, College of Charleston Library; "Rules of the South Carolina Society," pamphlet (1827), CLS.

Page 389. **Society for the Preservation of Spirituals**: Misc. file, "Society for the Preservation of Spirituals," SCHS.

Page 389. **Plantation Melody Singers**: Plantation Melody Singers, notebooks, private collection.

18: A RECKONING

Page 392. **Emily Marie Frayer**: Author's conversations with Lucas-Frayer family, South Carolina.

Page 395. **"Daddy Fortune's funeral was at midnight"**: Memoir of Mary Gibbs Ball (1923), private collection.

Page 397. **four years of elementary education . . . three years of vocational**: Edmund L. Drago, *Initiative, Paternalism, & Race Relations: Charleston's Avery Normal Institute* (Athens: University of Georgia, 1990), 124–25, and throughout.

Page 400. **"[Philip Lucas] . . . wife name Ellen"**: "Registers of Signatures of Depositors in Branches of the Freedman's Savings and Trust Company 1865–1874, Charleston, S.C.," Record Group 105, Microcopy No. 816, roll 21, Freedmen's Bureau, National Archives.

Page 401. **The Lucas clan came from an "old family" on the Cooper River**: Biographies of Tom, Julatta, and their descendants, 1731–1865: Account and Blanket Book, 1720–78, BP-SCHS; Plantation Record Book, 1804–90, BP-UNC; Slave Registers and Blanket Book, 1804–21, BP-SCHS; Birth and Blanket Lists for Comingtee, Kensington, Hyde Park and Midway, in John and Keating S. Ball Books, 1735–1817, BP-UNC; Will of Isaac Ball, 15 Nov 1825, Charleston Wills; conversations with Sonya Fordham; Census of the United States, 1870, Charleston County, and 1900, Berkeley County, South Carolina.

Page 401. **Julatta raised . . . corn or rice**: Memorandum, 28 Jan 1735, Account and Blanket Book, 1720–78, BP-SCHS.

Page 402. **Tom . . . alleged uprising plot in 1748**: Tom White: Account and Blanket Book, 1720–78, misc. slave lists, and 1777 list of male slaves and where born, "Tomwhit — Angola — [age] 55"; conspiracy: South Carolina Council Journal, #17 (20 Dec 1748–16 Dec 1749), SCDAH.

Page 402. **notice in the Charleston newspaper**: *South Carolina Gazette*, 22 Feb 1768.

Page 402. **Bessie took flight**: "A fair list of the Negroes that is gone from Kensington [1780]," and misc. note 1 Jun 1780, in Account Book, 1780–84, BP-Duke.

Page 402. **Betty . . . married a man named Joe Bailey**: Will of Isaac Ball, 15 Nov 1825, Charleston Wills; Slave Registers and Blanket Book, 1804–21, BP-SCHS.

Page 411. **three forms of evidence**: Milton Rubincam, ed., *Genealogical Research Methods and Sources* (Washington, D.C.: American Society of Genealogists, 1960), 38–44.

Page 412. **Other records [for Moses Ball] . . . did survive**: Census of the United States, 1880, Berkeley County, South Carolina, enumeration district 88, p. 35; Ball family witnesses, F. E. Gibbs, John Shoolbred, and Keating Ball: Petition in matter est. Marcus Dent, 28 Feb 1887, filed 25 June 1888, and Est. of Marcus Dent Administration Bond, 10 Jul 1888, Berkeley County, South Carolina; Marcus Dent at Hyde Park: Plantation book, 1804–90, BP-UNC; Moses Ball in Massachusetts: *Directory of Watertown, MA*, 1921 (Boston: W.A. Greenough); Watertown residence: Census of the United States, 1920, Massachusetts, vol. 83, enumeration district 510; marriage license: Registry of Vital Records and Statistics, State Department of Public Health, Commonwealth of Massachusetts.

Page 415. **"marooning cottage" . . . in 1799**: Jane Ball to John Ball Jr., 30 Nov 1798; Jane Ball to John Ball Jr., 2 Apr 1799, BP-SCHS.

EPILOGUE: BUNCE ISLAND

Page 421. **the name . . . Sierra Leone**: Vignettes of Sierra Leone history and culture: Christopher Fyfe, *A History of Sierra Leone* (London: Oxford, 1962).

Page 421. **Peter Karefa-Smart**: Conversation with the author, Freetown, Sierra Leone.

Page 422. **Gumbu Smart**: Fyfe, *History of the Sierra Leone*, 65–66, 173, 185.

Page 425. **Boston King moved ten miles**: I'm grateful to Prof. Christopher Fyfe, of London, for these citations. Boston King's letters: Christopher Fyfe, *Our Children Free and Happy* (Edinburgh: Edinburgh Univ., 1991); King as missionary and teacher: Zachary Macaulay's Journal, Huntington Library, San Marino, California, and Minutes of Governor's Council, CO/272, Public Record Office, London (PRO); death of: List of Nova Scotians, WO 1/352, PRO; daughter of: Report of the Commission of Enquiry, 1827, CO 267/91, PRO.

Page 428. **Grant, Oswald & Co**: David Hancock, *Citizens of the World: London Merchants and the Integration of the British Atlantic Community, 1735–1785* (New York: Cambridge Univ., 1995), chap. 6.

Page 428. **928 people**: Annual Register of the Number of Slaves exported from the Gold Coast of Africa from Jan 1755 to Dec 1768 . . . produced in 1771, T 70/1263, PRO.

Page 432. **Doris Lenga-Kroma**: Conversation with the author, Freetown, Sierra Leone.

Page 433. **the Caulker chiefdom**: Fyfe, 10, 81.

Page 436. **Alikali Modu III [and] . . . retinue**: Conversation with the author, Port Loko, Sierra Leone.

PICTURE CREDITS

Maps: Plantations on the Cooper River, South Carolina, belonging to the Ball family, page 2–3; map by Tim Belshaw

Limerick, Kensington, Hyde Park & Quenby Plantations, page 5; map by Tim Belshaw

Elias Ball (1676–1751), oil on canvas, by Jeremiah Theus (Private collection)

"A plan of Charles Town from a Survery of Edwd Crisp, Esq in 1704" (Courtesy of Charleston Library Society, Charleston, S.C.)

Comingtee plantation, main house, nineteenth-century photograph (Private collection)

Water reserve, Comingtee plantation, nineteenth-century photograph (Courtesy of the Charleston Museum, Charleston, S.C.)

"Charles Town, the Metropolis," 1739, watercolor, by Bishop Roberts (Colonial Williamsburg Foundation)

Escaped slave ad concerning Elias Ball, *South Carolina Gazette*, 18 Mar 1751 (Courtesy of Charleston Library Society)

Elias Ball II (1709–86), oil on canvas, by Jeremiah Theus (Collection of the Museum of Early Southern Decorative Arts)

Kensington plantation, main house, nineteenth-century photograph (Private collection)

Ruined slave cabin, Kensington plantation (Photograph by Richard Stoney)

Escaped slave advertisement placed by Elias Ball II, *South Carolina Gazette*, 20 Oct 1766 (Courtesy of Charleston Library Society)

Headstone of "Old Peter" (Photograph by E. Ball)

Henry Laurens (1724–1792), oil on canvas, by John Singleton Copley, 1782 (National Portrait Gallery, Smithsonian Institution)

Ann Ball Austin (Mrs. George Austin, 1701–65), oil on canvas, by Jeremiah Theus (Private collection)

Advertisement for slave auction, by Austin & Laurens, *South Carolina Gazette*, 11 May 1752 (Courtesy of Charleston Library Society)

"American Commissioners of the Preliminary Peace Negotiations with Great Britain," oil on canvas, 1783, by Benjamin West (Courtesy of the Winterthur Museum)

"Tranquil Hill, seat of Mrs. Ann Waring, near Dorchester," watercolor on paper (Gibbes Museum of Art/Carolina Art Association)

"View of the Colony of Sierra Leone Previous to the Transports being discharged/March 16, 1792," watercolor, by J. Beckett (Private collection, Canada; photograph: History Collection, Nova Scotia Museum, Halifax, Canada)

John Ball (1760–1817), oil on canvas (Private collection)

Martha Swinton Ball (Mrs. John Ball, 1786–1847), miniature (Gibbes Museum of Art/Carolina Art Association)

Work house, Charleston, engraving, *Harper's New Monthly Magazine*, July 1865 (Collections of the Library of Congress)

John Ball, Jr. (1782–1834), miniature, by Charles Fraser (Courtesy of the Frick Art Reference Library)

Ann Simons Ball (Mrs. John Ball, Jr., 1776–1840), oil on canvas, by Samuel F. B. Morse (Collection of the Museum of Early Southern Decorative Arts)

Announcement of death sentence for "Paris . . . the slave of Mrs. Ball," *Charleston Courier*, 19 Jul 1822 (Courtesy of Charleston Library Society, Charleston, S.C.)

Isaac Ball (1785–1825), oil on canvas (Private collection)

Eliza Poyas Ball (Mrs. Isaac Ball, 1794–1867), miniature (Private collection)

Limerick plantation, main house, nineteenth-century photograph (Courtesy of the Charleston Museum, Charleston, S.C.)

Isaac Ball house, Charleston, photograph about 1915 (Courtesy of Charleston Library Society, Charleston, S.C.)

James Poyas (1806–50), daguerreotype (Private collection)

Frederick Poyas (1841–ca. 1900), right, Caroline Poyas, left, and son, George Poyas, charcoal drawing, about 1885 (Private collection)

Florence Poyas (Mrs. Joseph Wilson, 1872–1952), about 1895 (Private collection)

Postal Smalls and Fredie Mae Smalls, fiftieth wedding anniversary, 1990 (Private collection)

Leon Smalls, Philadelphia, 1990 (Private collection)

Carolyn Smalls and James Goodson, Philadelphia, 1972 (Private collection)

Michael Goodson, Philadelphia, 1978 (Private collection)

Carolyn Smalls Goodson and E. Ball (Photograph by William Struhs)

Jane Ball Shoolbred (Mrs. John G. Shoolbred, 1823–1905), oil on canvas, by James and Robert Bogle (Gibbes Museum of Art/Carolina Art Association)

Watercolor view of Quenby plantation, 1844, by J. P. Hall (Private collection)

Quenby plantation, main house, nineteenth-century photograph (Private collection)

Nat Watson ("Daddy Nat," 1845–1922), left, Binah Watson, standing, and family, Quenby plantation, nineteenth-century photograph (Private collection)

Binah Watson, Quenby plantation, nineteenth-century photograph (Private collection)
Nat Watson carrying tray, about 1910 (Private collection)
Middleburg plantation, main house, nineteenth-century photograph (Courtesy of the Charleston Museum, Charleston, S.C.)
"Maum Sue," Middleburg plantation, nineteenth-century photograph (Private collection)
Middleburg plantation, rice mill, nineteenth-century photograph (Courtesy of the Charleston Museum, Charleston, S.C.)
Middleburg plantation slave jail, with Louise J. DuBose, reporter for *The State* of Columbia, South Carolina, and Edward von Siebold Dingle, about 1962 (Photograph by C. R. Banks)
Elias Ball III (1752–1810), oil on canvas, by Jeremiah Theus (Private collection)
Pino ———'s house, Cedar Hill plantation, nineteenth-century photograph (Private collection)
Fortune Ford, Comingtee plantation, nineteenth-century photograph (Courtesy of the Charleston Museum)
Worker cutting rice, Comingtee plantation, nineteenth-century photograph (Courtesy of the Charleston Museum)
Black woman in doorway, Comingtee plantation, nineteenth-century photograph (Courtesy of the Charleston Museum)
Barn with two-horse rig and driver, Comingtee plantation, nineteenth-century photograph (Private collection)
Girls drawing water from crane well, Comingtee plantation, nineteenth-century photograph (Private collection)
Water carrier, Quenby plantation, nineteenth-century photograph (Private collection)
Hannah ———, Comingtee plantation, nineteenth-century photograph (Private collection)
"The City of Charleston," aerial view, engraving, 1850 (Courtesy of the South Carolina Historical Society)
William James Ball (1821–91), daguerreotype (Courtesy of the South Carolina Historical Society)
Julia Cart Ball (Mrs. William J. Ball, 1824–58), daguerreotype (Private collection)
"Federals Shelling the City of Charleston," engraving, *Illustrated London News*, 5 Dec 1863 (South Caroliniana Library, University of South Carolina)
Isaac Ball (1844–1933) (Private collection)
Nat Watson ("Daddy Nat," 1845–1922), with children, Quenby plantation, nineteenth-century photograph (Private collection)
"The Fifty-fifth Massachusetts Colored Regiment Singing John Brown's March in the Streets of Charleston, February 21, 1865," engraving, *Harper's Weekly*, 18 Mar 1865 (Collections of the Library of Congress)
Isaac Ball (1844–1933) and Mary Louisa Moultrie Ball (1846–1926) (Private collection)
Limerick plantation, main house, rig and driver, nineteenth-century photograph (Private collection)
Black family in cabin doorway, nineteenth-century photograph (Private collection)
Black family, Quenby plantation, nineteenth-century photograph (Private collection)
Robert and Nannie Nelson, Quenby plantation, nineteenth-century photograph (Private collection)
Sarah ———, fishing at Quenby plantation, nineteenth-century photograph (Private collection)

Church of the Holy Innocents, Cordesville, South Carolina, nineteenth-century photograph (Private collection)

Strawberry ferry, Cooper River, South Carolina, about 1900 (South Caroliniana Library, University of South Carolina)

Ball ladies at the beach, about 1910 (Private collection)

"Maum Agnes," seated, and family, Brickyard plantation, early-twentieth century (Private collection)

Lydia Child Ball (1873–1935) (Private collection)

"De Stadt Van Loango," engraving, seventeenth century, by Olfert Dapper (By permission of the Houghton Library, Harvard University)

Mary Ann Royal ("Maum Mary," 1786–1866) (Private collection)

Slave street at Comingtee plantation, nineteenth-century photograph (Private collection)

Georgianna G. Richardson (1910–97), Robert Richardson, nieces and nephews, Charleston, about 1968 (Private collection)

Richardson-Brown family, South Carolina, 1997 (Photograph by William Struhs)

"Prospect of Bense [Bunce] Island and Fort," engraving, 1745, *A General Collection of Voyages and Travels* (Harvard College Library)

Advertisement for slave auction, by Austin & Laurens, *South Carolina Gazette*, 17 Jun 1756 (Courtesy of Charleston Library Society)

"[30 June] 1756: I bought 4 boys and 2 girls their ages as near as I can judge . . . ," Ball family papers (Courtesy of the South Carolina Historical Society)

Peter Henry Martin (1855–1933), Anna Cruz Martin, and children, about 1898 (Private collection)

Peter Henry Martin, Jr. (1886–1957) (Private collection)

Thomas P. Martin and E. Ball, Limerick plantation (Photograph by D. Gorton)

Bluff plantation, main house, nineteenth-century photograph (Courtesy of the Charleston Museum)

Young Ball cousins at the Bluff plantation, 1922 (Private collection)

Theodore P. Ball (1913–71), left, Nathaniel I. Ball (1881–1962), Nathaniel I. Ball, Jr. (1911–86), Charleston (Private collection)

Theodore P. Ball and Janet Rowley Ball, 1956, New Orleans (Private collection)

Christening of Theodore P. Ball, Jr., Savannah, Georgia, 1957 (Private collection)

Rebecca ———— and E. Ball, 1958 (Private collection)

Theodore Ball, Jr., and E.B. at the Lincoln Memorial, Washington, 1964 (Private collection)

Joseph Ball (1910–85), 1940s (Private collection)

Lashawn McGhee, left, and her mother, Jacqueline Ball, 1995 (Private collection)

Edwin A. Harleston (Private collection)

W.E.B. Du Bois and sightseeing party (Courtesy of Avery Research Center for African American History and Culture, Charleston, S.C.)

Edwin A. Harleston, at his easel (Private collection)

"Girl in blue," oil on canvas, by Edwin A. Harleston (Private collection)

Gussie Louise Harleston, charcoal drawing, about 1922, by Edwin A. Harleston (Private collection)

Ray M. Fleming, World Records, about 1965, songwriter for World Records (Private collection)

Sylvia Gentry, Georgia, about 1989 (Private collection)

Alison Gentry, Georgia, about 1989 (Private collection)

Wesley T. Simmons, Cordesville, South Carolina, early-twentieth century photograph (Private collection)

Katie Simmons (Mrs. Ned Roper), about 1935, Charleston (Private collection)

Charlotte Roper (Mrs. Gralin Dunn), 1954 (Private collection)

Delores Roper and Roper family grocery, South Carolina, about 1974 (Private collection)

Heyward-Roper family of South Carolina (Private collection)

Escaped slave advertisement placed by Elias Ball II, *South Carolina Gazette*, 22 Feb 1768 (Courtesy of Charleston Library Society)

Emily Frayer (with cane) and companions, ruins of the main house, Comingtee plantation, 1994 (Private collection)

Sonya J. Fordham and Sylvester Egwu, wedding commemoration ceremony, 1981 (Private collection)

Chiemeka Egwu as Miss Junior R.O.T.C., 1996 (Private collection)

INDEX